LABOUR ECONOMICS, 2ND EDITION

In the nine years since the appearance of the first edition of Stephen Smith's book, labour economics has become a more firmly entrenched subject on the curriculum. Previously regarded as a subsection within industrial economics, there are now very few universities that do not devote a course to it in its own right. The focus of topics covered within it has also altered – the notion of human capital has now become much more central and microeconomic considerations are now as widely studied as macroeconomic phenomena.

The 2nd edition will address these changes and give greater centrality to micro-economics to reflect current course teaching. The book adopts an international focus and covers important themes such as:

- labour demand and supply
- wage determination and unions
- personnel economics
- unemployment and globalisation.

With features such as case studies, end of chapter questions, further reading sections, this new edition will prove popular with all students of labour economics.

Stephen Smith is at the London Metropolitan University, UK.

LABOUR ECONOMICS, 2ND EDITION

STEPHEN SMITH

Routledge
Taylor & Francis Group

LONDON AND NEW YORK

First edition published 1994
by Routledge
11 New Fetter Lane, London EC4P 4EE

Simultaneously published in the USA and Canada
by Routledge
29 West 35th Street, New York, NY 10001

Second edition first published 2003

Routledge is an imprint of the Taylor & Francis Group

© 1994, 2003 Stephen Smith

Typeset in 10^1/$_2$/13pt Goudy by Graphicraft Limited, Hong Kong
Printed and bound in Great Britain by TJ International Ltd, Padstow, Cornwall

British Library Cataloguing in Publication Data
A catalogue record for this book is available from the British Library

Library of Congress Cataloging in Publication Data
A catalog record for this book has been requested

ISBN 0-415-25985-1 (Hbk)
ISBN 0-415-25986-X (Pbk)

Contents

List of tables

Acknowledgements

I wish to thank Rob Langham at Routledge for asking me to write this second edition; thanks also to Terry Clague for seeing it through to completion.

Many thanks to all those who kindly read, used, reviewed and above all bought the first edition! This includes the many cohorts of students taking the E0303 module in Labour Market Economics at the old University of North London, especially those who said, 'The book was more interesting than I thought it would be' and 'You write exactly how you speak in lectures!' Praise indeed. A big thank you to my colleagues in the Economics Department, including John Sedgwick, John Curran, Photis Lysandrou, Tony Mananyi, Craig Duckworth, Gugliemo Volpe, Brian MacAulay and Bob Morgan for their kindness and willingness to take on a lot of extra teaching and administration during 2001/2002.

Once again I have drawn heavily on the support of Angela Bradding and our sons Adam and Ashley. I have also benefited from the close friendship of so many people, including Dr Iain Williamson, Nigel and Bev, Dr Mike O'Donnell, Tony and Julie, Dr Robert Wimperoy and Ronan and Ivan. Heartfelt thanks also go to the staff of the hostpitals at La Spezia and Rapallo, Italy. Particularly I would like to thank Drs Paolo Pantaleo and Alessandro Bellisario at Villa Azzurra, Rappallo, who put me back in working order during August and September of 2001.

Finally I owe a large debt of gratitude to the late Norman Stang, who was largely responsible for getting me started on an economics teaching career.

The publishers would like to thank Edward Elgar, Blackwell Publishing and Oxford University Press for permission to reproduce material within the book. We would also like to thank the staff at Felix Rosentiels Widow and Son Limited and Sefton MBC Leisure Services Department, Atkinson Art Gallery for permission to reproduce the wonderful *Street Scene, Southport* by L.S. Lowry on the front cover.

Every effort has been made to contact copyright holders for their permission to reprint material in this book. The publishers would be grateful to hear from any copyright holder who is not here acknowledged and will undertake to rectify any errors or omissions in future editions of this book.

Stephen Smith

Introduction

Labour economics is now a well-established, distinct area of specialisation within the discipline of economics. The purpose of this book is to provide students encountering labour economics for the first time, yet possessing a knowledge of intermediate undergraduate economics, with a grounding in the specialism. This should enable the student to participate in the discussion of labour market issues from a more informed perspective and will provide them with the confidence to tackle 'state of the art' journal articles and research papers in the area. It covers the significant topic areas of labour economics with a combination of pure theory, economic statistics, summaries of important empirical studies and discussions of labour market issues and policies.

The emphasis is very much upon providing an accessible survey of the content of labour economics. We will identify how the market forces of labour supply and labour demand interact. We will demonstrate how that interaction determines wages. The book introduces personnel economics as an application of labour economics concepts. We need to examine the quality of labour and how this may affect the growth performance of economies. When we consider trade unions as a labour market institution, we will concentrate on their links with output, inflation, productivity and unemployment. Job search and vacancies will be analysed in relation to unemployment. Finally we will be concerned with an aspect of industrial decline, deindustrialisation, as we examine how international trade and globalisation have affected labour markets. Thus, whilst essential theories are explained, the main thrust of the book is to apply such theories to examine issues relevant to the understanding of unemployment.

Explaining the phenomenon of persistent, mass unemployment remains as important a challenge to economists in the 2000s as it did in the 1930s when Keynes (1936) was incorporating an explanation of unemployment into his 'General Theory'. Unemployment lies at the core of labour economics and, as such, is a coherent theme which runs throughout this book. We are therefore engaged in an analysis of why the labour market does not appear to clear at anything like a full employment equilibrium.

The use of the term 'labour market' should not be taken to indicate that we believe there to be a single, integrated auction house for human factor services. Quite the contrary, labour markets can be delineated and subdivided according to numerous criteria, of which geography and occupation are only the most obvious. The labour market is an important theoretical construct of which we will make full use throughout this book. Yet bear in mind that actual markets for human factor services are decentralised, fragmented, imperfect markets whose actors are heterogeneous, burdened by limited information, and subject to significant transactions costs.

In order to conduct an analysis of the labour market we need to abstract from the complexity of labour market outcomes the crucial elements of the behaviour of economic agents. In seeking to understand labour market activity, the labour economist theorises as a means of simplifying the complex web of interactions that occupies this aspect of human action. The most pervasive theory of the labour market is the neoclassical theory of labour supply and labour demand interacting to determine an optimal combination of wages and employment. This theory represents a good starting point for a textbook on labour economics because it is consistent with the microeconomic analysis found in the traditional theory of the firm and the analysis of consumer behaviour. It also provides a foundation upon which we can build empirical aspects of labour markets. It is a background against which we can examine theoretical extensions such as job search, screening and human capital. And it can be used to inform our discussion of unemployment, the impact of trades unions and the role of Government labour market policies.

Although our analysis is rooted within the neoclassical framework, this does not mean that more recent developments such as principal–agent relationships, efficiency wages and the insider–outsider distinction will be ignored. Such developments which challenge the standard neoclassical approach will be incorporated where appropriate throughout the book. Thus, for example, the chapter on discrimination will examine segmented labour markets. Our treatment of unemployment will include the distinction between insiders who are in work and outsiders, those without jobs. The chapter on trade unions will cover principal–agent relationships within the bargaining process. Students will also recognise the use of Coase's notion of transactions costs in our treatment of labour demand. This approach to these new concepts in a labour market context is guided by the desire to integrate them into our attempt to understand the labour market, rather than to isolate them as an awkward postscript to our neoclassically based modelling.

The book will also endeavour to reflect, in small measure, contributions to labour market analysis from nonneoclassical schools of thought within economics. It will do so by combining in an eclectic fashion elements of different schools of thought. For example, the chapter on globalisation contains the essentially post-Keynesian, deindustrialisation thesis as a labour demand topic. Perspectives on unemployment as diverse as Keynesian and New Classical economics will be represented. The importance of institutional factors on labour market outcomes will also be emphasised; the power of trade unions; the legislative framework with regard to discrimination; and the arrangements for welfare payments to the unemployed.

STRUCTURE OF THE BOOK

Although this book has been written with students specialising in labour economics in mind, we have deliberately kept the level of technical complexity down to a minimum. Consequently it can be read by those interested in human resource management, especially Chapters 3–8. Chapter 10 will be of interest to all concerned with understanding the problem of unemployment. Each chapter contains a short summary which highlights the main features of the topic area, along with some suggested questions for discussion, designed to gauge the reader's understanding of the subject and a couple of important readings on the topic.

The first two chapters establish the basic model of the labour market with the forces of labour supply and labour demand interacting to determine real wages and employment. Our theoretical treatment in both chapters is supplemented with relevant statistics on labour supply, labour demand and productivity with applications geared towards explaining the phenomenon of unemployment. In Chapter 1, the supply-side view of unemployment is related to an understanding of the theory of labour supply. In the case of labour demand (Chapter 2), we examine the productivity performance of the UK given the links between productivity and unemployment. Chapter 3 brings labour supply and demand together to determine wages. We are concerned to explain trends in wage inequality and discuss the merits of minimum wage legislation.

A distinguishing feature of this edition is the explicit treatment that personnel economics receives in Chapter 4. Personnel economics deserves to be examined in its own right because of the growing interest in issues such as providing incentives at work, the role of non-monetary fringe benefits and debates about the pay of chief executive officers. Chapter 4 also introduces the important concept of internal labour markets.

Chapter 5 contains the influential economic explanation of how labour productivity can be enhanced by investing in human capital acquisition. New growth theories emphasise the importance of human capital's contribution to the growth and development of economies. Education is an important process by which the quality of labour can be improved, with differences in educational attainment explaining significant and enduring wage differentials between workers. We also examine the provision of work-related training. The chapter looks at whether growing wage differentials between the skilled (more highly educated and trained) workers and their unskilled colleagues, plus higher unemployment rates for unskilled workers, might be due to technological change and specifically how the introduction of computers has favoured skilled workers.

The fact that wage differentials between groups of workers remain after accounting for differences in human capital investment provides the spur for the economic analysis of labour market discrimination to be found in Chapter 6. Beginning with sex discrimination, neoclassical and alternative segmented market theories of discrimination are set in the context of persistent wage and employment differences between males and females. We attempt to assess the impact of equal opportunities legislation and consider the likely effect of moves towards policies based upon the principle of comparable worth. We also look at a model of racial discrimination and examine the labour market experiences of immigrant workers.

Chapter 7 deals with trade unions as a potentially powerful labour market institution. We look at aspects of union power, examining the theoretical as well as the empirical evidence about the impact of organised labour on output, productivity, inflation and unemployment. There appears to be a strong case supporting adverse union effects on unemployment, although the magnitude of those effects is contentious. It seems likely that the impact of trade unions will depend upon the bargaining environment in which they operate. We discover that trade unions are a force for greater equality in labour market outcomes.

The influential concept of labour market flexibility is set out in Chapter 8. Various aspects of flexibility are covered and progress towards greater flexibility, particularly in UK labour markets, is examined. We also find out that labour market flexibility could well be a crucial ingredient for the success of European Monetary Union which introduced the Euro as a fully operational currency in January 2001.

Job search theory provides a microeconomic, supply-side explanation for unemployment. Chapter 9 highlights the importance of the welfare benefit regime influencing the job search activity of the unemployed. However, it may well be that the most important aspect of benefits, in an unemployment context, is their duration rather than their generosity or the lack of it. The role of vacancies in the labour market is often overlooked; thus while the path unemployment has taken over time may be well known, knowledge of the changes in available jobs is likely to be scant. In Chapter 9 vacancies form an integral part of our analysis of unemployment. We are able to establish that the relationship between vacancies and unemployment has deteriorated markedly since the 1960s in the European Union (EU) countries, yet much less so in the USA. A feature of the rise in EU unemployment since the 1960s has been a dramatic decline in the rate at which people leave the unemployment register. This could be linked to job search by the unemployed. Certainly in the UK the link between unemployment and vacancies improved markedly during the 1990s.

Chapter 10 draws together a number of the observations we were able to make about unemployment in the earlier chapters. Descriptive statistics provide a picture of the unemployment problem against which to sketch out the main theoretical approaches to unemployment: the Classical; Keynesian; Monetarist; and New Classical schools of thought. However, through the concept of hysteresis, the self-generating property of unemployment, particularly with regard to the long-term unemployed, leads us to Layard *et al.*'s (1991) eclectic theory, which examines unemployment under conditions of imperfect product markets, unionised workforces and differing welfare benefit regimes. The empirical performance of this model is impressive and it points to the importance of increasing the centralisation of wage bargaining, reducing the duration of benefits coupled with quality education and training, employment subsidies and even public sector work placements as policies to combat unemployment. We attempt to assess the effectiveness of such policies in reducing the waste and misery caused by persistent mass unemployment.

Chapter 11 examines the impact of the growth of international trade and increasing integration of the world economy (globalisation) on labour markets. We focus on the deindustrialisation thesis because of the light it may shed on the rapid rise in unemployment, particularly during the recessions of the early 1980s and early 1990s, which was common to all the advanced industrialised economies. We conclude that although unskilled workers in basic manufacturing may have been vulnerable to globalisation, this has not been the main cause of their declining relative wages and increasing unemployment.

1

Labour supply

INTRODUCTION

Currently labour supply is one of the most active research areas in labour economics. According to Blundell and MaCurdy (1999) 'research on labour supply during the past decade has been at the forefront of developments in empirical microeconomics' (p. 1560). The surveys by Killingsworth (1983), Pencavel (1986) and Heckman (1993) bear witness to this activity at both the theoretical and empirical levels. It is not our intention either to replicate or to replace such near-exhaustive treatments. Instead this chapter will outline the dominant neoclassical theory of labour supply before extending the analysis to examine the effects of varying wage rates, incorporate income taxation, and introduce non-work welfare benefits. We shall distinguish between male and female labour supply both in theory and empirically. The more dynamic lifecycle modelling of labour supply will also be considered. There are important topical policy aspects of labour supply that need to be addressed, ranging across: concern over demographic changes; discussion about the role of women in the paid labour market; and consideration of the impacts of the tax and welfare benefit regimes. Our analysis of labour supply will touch upon all of these policy issues. It will also lay the foundation for the subsequent treatment of the other areas of labour economics, in particular, job search (Chapter 9), education, training and employee signalling (Chapter 5) and the supply-side view of unemployment (Chapter 10). An understanding of labour supply will also enter into an assessment of movements in labour productivity through an examination of labour supply responses to varying wage rates, a link that will be made explicit in Chapter 3.

INDIVIDUAL LABOUR SUPPLY

The supply of labour can be analysed at two levels: the microeconomic level, concerned with individual and household labour supply, and the macroeconomic or aggregate economy level. The following account of the economic analysis of labour supply begins with a microeconomic theory based upon the neoclassical solution to the consumers' allocation problem.

The analysis constructs a simple model of an individual's labour supply decision. Basically it involves a choice between work and leisure, subject to a budget or income constraint. We are not concerned with any particular individual, instead we are dealing with an 'idealised' microeconomic individual who seeks rationally to maximise his/her utility.

Utility is the benefit or satisfaction an individual presumably derives from the activity of consuming goods/services. Work is assumed to confer a certain amount of disutility. Wages help to offset that negative aspect and enable the individual to generate income, which can be used to consume goods and services in future time periods. Without resorting to excessive detail, the main results of the microeconomic analysis of labour supply can be simply reproduced. On the basis of the simplifying assumption that individuals are free to determine the hours they wish to work, Figure 1.1 shows the relationship between work and pay. Obviously in choosing how much labour to supply (hours worked, H), the individual is simultaneously determining leisure time (L). Hence labour supply and the demand for leisure are being decided jointly, with the opportunity cost of leisure being the wage earnings forgone by not working. Leisure is assumed to be a normal good, which features in the rational

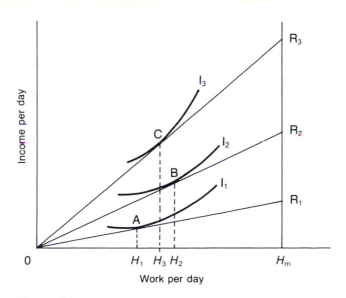

Figure 1.1

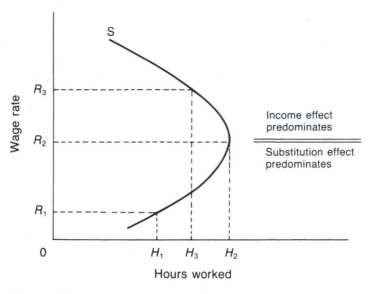

Figure 1.2

individual's utility function. H_m is an imposed maximum duration of the working day.[1] Wages bring utility through the consumption of goods, services and leisure. Work brings disutility.[2]

The curves I_1, I_2 and I_3 form part of the individual's indifference mapping. Each indifference curve joins together combinations of income and hours of work, which yield the same level of utility to the individual. The higher the indifference curve, the greater the level of utility.

The rays emanating from the origin O, R_1, R_2 and R_3 have slopes which represent different wage rates (OR$_1$ wage rate = £OA/OH$_1$ per hour). The parallels between this analysis and the microeconomic indifference analysis of consumption are obvious.

According to Pencavel (1986), 'the neoclassical theory of labour supply is a straightforward extension of the consumers' allocation problem' (p. 6). We are in the familiar territory of constrained maximisation. If we plot the individual labour supply curve passing through the points of tangency A, B and C, we derive the labour supply function illustrated in Figure 1.2.

The individual labour supply curve (S) is backward bending, a feature which leaves open the question about whether greater remuneration results in increased work effort. As the wage rate rises from R_1 to R_2, the individual offers to work longer hours, i.e., he/she substitutes extra hours of work for leisure, hence the term 'substitution effect'. Yet the individual's income is also increasing, which increases the demand for goods including leisure, hence the term 'income effect'. The substitution effect tends towards more work whilst the income effect tends towards more leisure. Both are occurring simultaneously throughout the length of the whole supply curve. Which one is the predominant effect determines the shape of the curve at any particular wage rate. Empirically, if the labour supply function were known, the income and substitution effects could be calculated. Take the case where hours of work H are related to the real wage w and real non-labour income b,

$$H = f(w,b).$$

Considering an increase in wage rates, the Slutsky equation can be used to identify substitution and income effects influencing labour supply,

$$\frac{\partial H}{\partial W} = \left(\frac{\partial H}{\partial W}\right)_s + H\frac{\partial H}{\partial b}.$$

The substitution effect (the first term on the right-hand side) should be positive as a rise in wages increases the opportunity cost of leisure, thereby reducing the demand for leisure and increasing labour supply H. The income effect (the second term on the right-hand side) of a wage increase should be negative because as wage rates rise, income rises with no extra work effort – it is as if b had risen thereby tending to reduce H. The total wage effect $\partial H/\partial w$) clearly depends upon the balance of these substitution and income effects. Empirically the magnitude of both income and substitution effects tends to be quite small (Welch 1997), reflecting the fact that labour supply is not very responsive to changes in wages.

The backward bending labour supply function is an important outcome of microeconomic theorising. Yet the neoclassical model of labour supply can be elaborated upon to consider a number of different aspects of labour market activity.

WELFARE BENEFITS AND LABOUR SUPPLY

The analysis can be adapted to examine the impact of non-labour income b. Non-labour income may either arise from existing wealth holdings or more importantly from the perspective of labour economics, come from the receipt of unemployment labour supply, and benefits. Introducing non-labour income into the analysis modifies labour supply outcomes in a significant manner. Consider the situation presented in Figure 1.3. At a low wage rate R_o, H_o hours per day of labour will be supplied. Yet when we introduce non-labour income of b, point A becomes crucial so we continue our analysis from there.

In the case of Figure 1.4 the decision about whether to participate in the labour market and supply labour services depends upon the relationship between the wage rate (R) and the income (b) derived from state benefits. The corner solution defines the critical point.

At the market wage rate R_1, the amount of labour supplied becomes indeterminate as the individual is indifferent between not working (0) and working H_1 hours. At any wage rate below R_1 labour supply falls to zero. At any wage rate above R_1 a positive amount of labour is supplied in excess of H_1. The absolute value of the slope of $R_1 - b$ at its point of tangency with the indifference curve I_1 (point A) is the individual's reservation wage. For any market wage equal to, or lower than the reservation wage

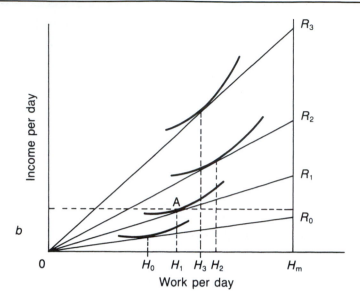

Figure 1.3

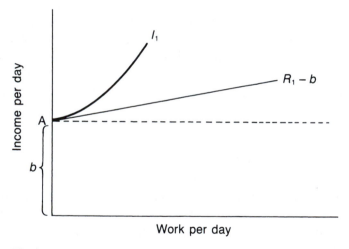

Figure 1.4

the individual would not work. Positive hours of labour are only supplied when the market wage rate exceeds the reservation wage. The important outcomes from this microeconomic analysis should not be overlooked. Firstly, it suggests that the labour supply function is going to be discontinuous taking the generic characteristics of Figure 1.5. Labour is only supplied once the hurdle of the reservation wage (W_R) has been overcome. Then, because there are fixed costs involved in working which have to be recovered, like the money and time spent commuting, a certain minimum amount of labour needs to be supplied (h_{min}).

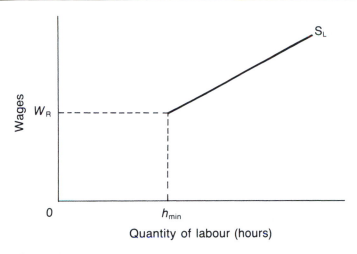

Figure 1.5

The analysis also provides an important intellectual justification for the disincentive effects of state benefits, because it clearly demonstrates that such non-work income reduces the willingness of rational utility maximising individuals to supply labour services at 'low' wages. Indeed if state benefits were to increase relative to real wages so would the individuals' reservation wage, thereby reducing the likelihood of labour being supplied. This is an element of the supply-side view of unemployment to which we shall return in Chapter 9. The crucial point to bear in mind is that standard neoclassical microeconomic analysis predicts that benefits will have an adverse effect on labour supply.

INCOME TAX AND LABOUR SUPPLY

The analysis can also be adapted to examine the impact of taxation on labour supply, particularly focusing on the issues of where to begin taxing income, i.e., determining how large the 'tax free' exemption should be, and the effect of changing the rate of income tax. Consider the example of the imposition of an income tax illustrated in Figure 1.6, where R_2 is the existing wage rate, t is the income tax rate and f^0 the initial tax-free allowance.

Imposing income tax reduces the slope of the wage rate ray from $0R_2$ to $0(R_2 - t)$, which is non-linear (kinked) due to the existence of the tax-free allowance, f^0. This change in after-tax disposable income (take home pay) produces both income and substitution effects. The income effect would suggest that because our representative worker will now have less disposable income from H_2 hours of work, he/she should increase labour supply. The substitution effect acts through the effective reduction in the price of leisure, brought about by a tax on working, which would tend towards a reduction in labour supply. Thus introducing (or increasing) income tax generates an

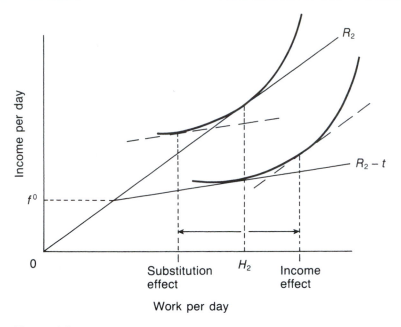

Figure 1.6

income effect which tends towards an increase in labour supply and a substitution effect which reduces labour supply. If these two effects are exactly balanced, as in Figure 1.6, then imposing a tax on earned income will leave labour supply unchanged at H_2.

Increasing income will reduce labour supply if the substitution effect is greater than the income effect. Raising income tax rates will increase labour supply if the substitution effect is outweighed by the income effect. Thus the net effect of income tax on labour supply remains in theory profoundly indeterminate.

Whether a greater 'tax free' allowance would lead to more labour being supplied is also open to doubt. An increase in tax allowances should induce an income effect tending towards working less as workers who are now better off, consume more leisure. However, more labour may be supplied ($H_2 t f^1$) if increasing tax-free allowances from f^0 to f^1 in the circumstances shown in Figure 1.7 results in a corner solution on a higher indifference curve.

A reduction in income tax is considered in Figure 1.8. As before, $0R_2$ is the before-tax wage rate and f^0 is the tax-free allowance with t^0 as our initial rate of income tax. A reduction in the rate of tax is illustrated by the increase in the slope of the post-tax wage rate function from $0(R_2 - t^0)$ to $0(R_2 - t^1)$. Thus a reduction in the rate of income tax from t^0 to t^1 provokes an income effect which would lessen labour supply and a substitution effect which would induce an increase in the number of hours worked.

Once again the exact impact of a reduction in direct taxation depends upon the balance of income and substitution effects. Direct income taxation can be shown to

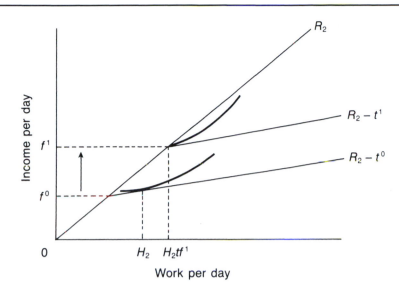

Figure 1.7

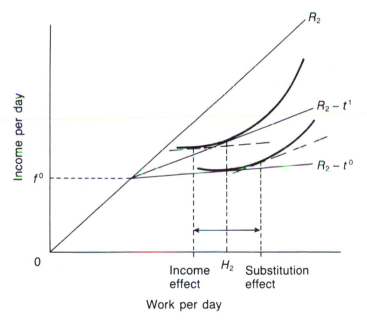

Figure 1.8

represent a disincentive to work, with any subsequent reduction in tax rates increasing labour supply. Yet, as our analysis has been at pains to point out, this holds true only if one makes specific statements about the comparative magnitude of the income and substitution effects accompanying changes in direct taxation.

TAX AND BENEFIT POLICY AND LABOUR SUPPLY

It can be shown using fairly elementary microeconomic analysis that the willingness of the labour force to work is influenced by the extent of non-work income available and the nature of the income tax regime. An obvious labour supply policy prescription for a Government which wished to increase the supply of labour available to the economy under conditions where it believed the substitution effects of direct taxation to be dominant, would be to

• reduce non-work income, possibly by eroding the real value of unemployment benefits,
• increase the real value of tax-free allowances, and
• reduce the rate of income tax.

For the student of UK Government economic policy this prescription will have a certain resonance. The general thrust of UK labour market policies since 1979 has been to increase the attractiveness of income from work (through income tax rate cuts) and reduce the generosity of the benefit system by linking benefit payment increases to inflation rather than to the more rapidly increasing average earnings. Anderton and Mayhew (1994) provide evidence of the fact that UK unemployment benefits became markedly less generous compared to average earnings in the early 1980s. In the 1970s unemployment benefit per unemployed person as a proportion of earnings per employee (the replacement ratio) averaged 29 per cent. Between 1980–1985 this had fallen to 23 per cent. By 1995 in the UK the replacement ratio had fallen to 17 per cent and unemployment benefits were less generous than those in most advanced industrialised economies as the data in Table 1.1 demonstrates.

In Japan, Switzerland and the USA unemployment benefits were less generous than those in the UK and all three countries had lower unemployment rates in 1995 than the UK. However, countries with much more generous unemployment benefit schemes also enjoyed lower unemployment rates in 1995 than the UK, namely Austria, Denmark, Germany, Netherlands, Norway, New Zealand and Portugal. In Sweden in 1995 unemployment benefits were less generous than in the UK but the unemployment rate was higher. During the 1970s, a period when unemployment rates were on a markedly rising trend, unemployment benefits in the UK were not any more generous than they had been in the second half of the 1960s. Thus although the theoretical link between the generosity of benefits and the willingness of the unemployed to supply labour appears to be a strong and straightforward one the real world picture is much less clear. Indeed a number of empirical studies (Layard *et al.* 1991) find that the most significant aspect of the benefit system is not its generosity (or the lack of it) but the duration of benefit entitlement, a point we will return to in Chapter 10.

The impact of UK Government's cutting the higher rate of income tax from 83 per cent in 1979 to 40 per cent by 2002, reducing the standard rate from 33 per cent in 1979 to 22 per cent in 2002 and having a starting rate of 10 per cent on the first

Table 1.1 Unemployment schemes replacement ratios (%) and unemployment rates (%), 1995

	Replacement ratio	Unemployment rate
Australia	26.9	8.6
Austria	48.9	3.9
Belgium	38.9	9.9
Canada	17.9	9.5
Denmark	71.5	7.1
Finland	64.1	16.6
France	23.0	11.7
Germany	39.4	8.2
Ireland	24.0	12.4
Italy	74.0	11.9
Japan	3.0	3.1
Netherlands	52.5	6.9
Norway	17.2	5.0
New Zealand	24.0	6.3
Portugal	61.6	7.3
Spain	37.1	22.9
Sweden	14.4	9.2
Switzerland	10.7	3.3
UK	16.9	8.8
USA	6.4	5.6

Source: OECD

£1,880 of income in the tax year 2001–2002 is indeterminate. Empirical studies of the impact of income tax on labour supply also point to no clear conclusion (Killingsworth 1983, Pencavel 1986). Studies of UK income tax cuts tend to find that any work incentive effects have been negligible (Brown 1988, Brown and Sandford 1991). However, Eissa (1995) did find that substantial income tax cuts in the USA in 1986 did bring about increased labour supply from women in already high earning households.

We shall now examine whether changing the unit of analysis from the individual to the household yields any further insights into labour supply.

HOUSEHOLD LABOUR SUPPLY

Treating labour supply decisions from the perspective of the household is an attempt to incorporate the fact that such decisions often result from the interdependence of individuals within family units. Throughout this book the reader will be presented with data which reflects significant differences in the labour market experiences of the population of working age when classified by gender, marital and dependent child status. The microeconomic analysis of household labour supply can be viewed as an attempt to explain such experiences in a manner consistent with the way in which other aspects of economic activity (e.g., production and consumption) are analysed.

We begin by assuming that the household is composed of two individuals of working age. Bowing to convention we shall label them male (M) and female (F). Once again these economic agents, M and F are deemed to display economic rationality as they seek to maximise their household utility U, which consists of a set of consumption goods and services X coupled with the leisure time of the male (L_M) and female (L_F),

$$U = f(X, L_M, L_F).$$

This neoclassical approach entails the household seeking to maximise a single joint utility function subject to a common income constraint. An alternative formulation stemming from Leuthold (1968) would suggest that each household member had an independent utility function but operates within a household income constraint, taking the hours worked by the other household member as given. For the present we will focus upon the neoclassical model reserving comparison with the Leuthold model until later.

In seeking to maximise their utility the neoclassical household is constrained by an income level required to purchase the consumption set X and, by implication, their leisure time,

$$W_M, H_M + W_F, H_F + b = P_x X$$

where W_M is the husband's wage rate, H_M is the husband's hours of work, W_F is the wife's wage rate, b is the non-work income, P_x is the price of goods and services and X is the consumption of goods and services.

Diagrammatically the income constraint can be represented by the line joining the points O, A, B and, C in Figure 1.9. Points B and C coincide with the male's (H_{mM}) and female's (H_{mF}) maximum hours of work respectively. The kink in the ABC line reflects the assumption that the male wage rate is greater than that of the female. At present this is an arbitrary feature of the model, yet it could be justified given that significant and enduring differentials do exist in the earnings of male and female workers, a fact which receives closer scrutiny in Chapter 6.

The fact that the kink occurs at a predetermined distance from the vertical axis implies that the male's work activity affects the female's work pattern but not vice versa. Thus the diagrams do convey a form of implicit sexism which does not exist in the initial algebraic statement of the model. For simplicity of exposition we will continue to use this type of diagram but be aware that the model contained in endnote 3 and the findings of Ashworth and Ulph (1981), which are reported later, question this one-way flow of influence upon partner's work patterns.[3] In order that we may determine who in the household works and for how long we need to superimpose a household indifference map onto Figure 1.9. At this stage of the analysis a number of options present themselves; we examine three possibilities in Figure 1.10.

As can be seen from the three variants presented in Figure 1.10, the optimal solution depends upon the nature/location of the household indifference map. The three indifference maps illustrated in Figure 1.10 represent different attitudes on the

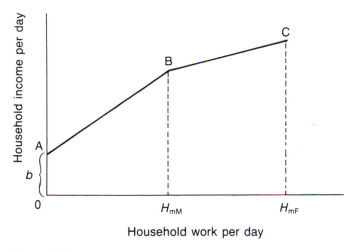

Figure 1.9

part of household members to income and leisure. Leisure in this context may be considered a misnomer in that it covers non-market home working, which includes the provision of meals, home-keeping and child rearing services.

In the first case (Figure 1.10 (a)) only the male works to the extent of H_1 hours. In the second set of circumstances (Figure 1.10 (b)) the male works up to his maximum of H_2 (which coincides with the point $B = H_{mM}$ in Figure 1.9) and the female works part-time to the extent of $H_3 - H_2$ hours. Only in the final example (Figure 1.10 (c)) are both male and female working full-time.

This analysis can be adapted to investigate a number of different scenarios. Taking the situation presented in Figure 1.10 (b), let us consider the effect of an increase in the male wage rate, relative to that of the female, on household labour supply.

The justification for highlighting this particular variant is the prevalence of female part-time employment in the UK labour market. The increase in the male wage rate is reflected in the upward shift of the income constraint from A B C to A B′ C′ in Figure 1.11. Applying the same indifference map that produced H_3 as an optimal solution in Figure 1.10 (b) the impact of an increase in male relative to female wage rates has been to reduce female labour supply by $H_3 - H_5$. Male labour supply remains unaffected at H_2, although overall household labour supply has been reduced.

Note that when dealing with the household there are two substitution effects operating. That of the 'own substitution effect' which influences the male labour supply response to a change in his own wage, and the 'cross substitution effect' on female labour supply coming about from the change in the male wage rate. If cross substitution effects for both male and female are zero then the only effect on F's labour supply of a rise in M's wage rate, is a pure income effect. This serves to greatly simplify the household model.

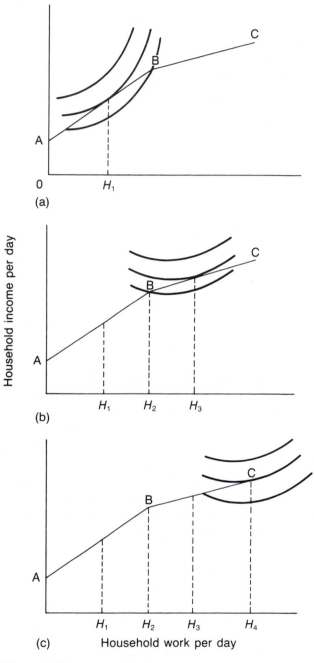

(a)

(b)

(c)

Household income per day

Household work per day

Figure 1.10

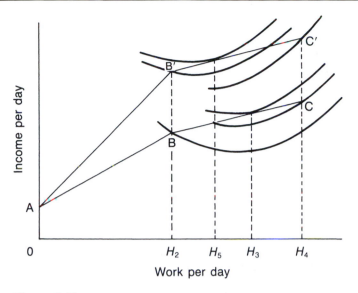

Figure 1.11

We can use this particular example to illustrate a more dramatic change which would occur if, instead of assuming that hours of working are completely flexible household members were faced with the stark choice of either working full-time or not at all. Under these more restrictive, possibly more realistic, terms of employment we note from Figure 1.11 that, at the old combination of wage rates (A B C), both male and female would have worked full-time. This is because, despite being sub-optimal, point C lies on a higher indifference curve than point B. Following the change in relative wage rates, the shift to A, B′, C′, the ranking is reversed. Now B′ lies on a higher indifference curve than does C′. Therefore the female gives up work and household labour supply falls from OH₄ to OH₂. The budget constraint is now discontinuous having been reduced in the female's case to only two points, B and C. This results initially in over-employment at C and then in underemployment at B′. Hence if male wage rates rise relative to female wage rates, *ceteris paribus*, this would tend to reduce the degree of female participation in the labour force. Conversely if female wage rates were to rise relative to those of men, possibly as a consequence of equal pay and opportunities policies then one would expect this to increase the probability of female labour force participation.[4] It is worth bearing these predictions in mind when we come to examine female labour market participation in the macro section of this chapter and when we discuss anti-discrimination policies in Chapter 6.

In their empirical study of labour supply Ashworth and Ulph (1981) compare the performance of a neoclassical household model with a model based upon Leutholds (1968) idea of there being independent utility functions for the male (husband) and the female (wife). Ashworth and Ulph incorporate into each household member's utility function a concern not only for their own leisure but also for that of their spouse as well. Data on eighty-eight households in 1971 where the wives worked more than 8 hours per week with no children under the age of 11 yielded the following main conclusions. Generally the Leuthold model produced long-run labour supply elasticities of larger absolute magnitudes than the single utility function neoclassical model, although not in the case of the husband's own price elasticity. For both models an increase in the wife's wage would tend to reduce the wife's hours worked.

Interestingly they found that while an increase in work by the wife induced the husband to work less hard, 'an increase in work by the husband led the wife to work substantially harder' (p. 130). Although the usual econometric caveats about the specification of the models and the adequacy of the data apply, Ashworth and Ulph appear to show that the Leuthold type model fits the data better than the standard neoclassical model.

There remains an extension of the microeconomic theory of household labour supply worthy of a brief explanation before we move on to view the macro labour supply picture. This is an example of an allocation of time model applied to the case of married women or women with dependent children. The household's time (T) can be divided up into leisure L, paid market work HP and domestic work in the home associated with child rearing HD. Thus:

$$T = HD + HP + L.$$

Assuming an unequal distribution of responsibilities within the household and that only the wife's time is divided up between paid work (HP) and domestic activities (HD) then the value of that domestic work can be defined as the shadow wage of her market work. If wage rates decline as the willingness to work falls, a reasonable supposition given that pay rates for part-time work are generally lower than for full-time work, then the shadow wage for the married woman falls as she increases the amount of domestic activity undertaken.[5] Figure 1.12 shows just such a relationship between shadow wages and household domestic activity. The market wage MW reflects the opportunity cost of staying at home and engaging in domestic activities. From the household perspective domestic activity that the wife undertakes is only worthwhile when the value of that activity exceeds its opportunity cost, i.e., when SW > MW. Thus the wife's time is allocated to work in the home to the extent of hd hours, up to the point where SW = MW. Obviously were market wages for women to increase to MW_1 then the amount of time allocated to domestic activity would tend to fall to hd_1, thereby increasing the labour supply available for paid market work.

Similarly the household's evaluation of the necessity of domestic activity might change. The existence of young children especially those under 5 (the age at which school attendance is compulsory) would increase the value of domestic activities which now includes child rearing. This would shift the shadow wage function to the right to SW_1, thereby increasing the time spent by the woman in the home to hd_2. Such a time allocation model suggests that the labour force participation of household members is dependent upon a number of factors: the wage; the evaluation of domestic activity; the division of labour within the household; the existence of children and their ages. If on average women's wage rates are below those attainable by men and if

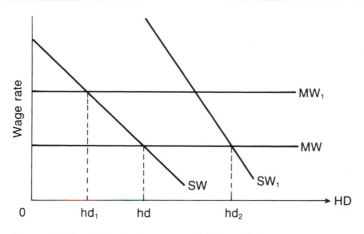

Figure 1.12   SW, shadow wage; MW, market wage

there exists an unequal division of labour within the household, such that women bear the responsibility for the majority of domestic work, then the model would yield lower labour force participation for women than for men.[6] Yet it would also predict lower participation rates for married women as compared with single women. And it would suggest a higher participation rate for childless women than mothers. Given that child rearing responsibilities vary with the age of the child one would expect older married mothers to offer more labour services than younger married mothers. In general wage changes do generate responsive reactions, especially in terms of labour force participation from married women (Pencavel 1998).

This completes our examination of the theory of labour supply at the microeconomic level. Not only have the general characteristics of the individual and household labour supply functions been determined, we have also been able to suggest the general impact that benefits and taxation will have on the supply of labour. Furthermore we have provided an example of the sorts of policy prescription that fall out of this type of neoclassical microeconomic analysis of the labour market. Through an allocation of time model we were able to begin to raise the issue of the equality of opportunity as a significant feature of labour market outcomes and their analysis. Let us now examine labour supply at the aggregate level.

AGGREGATE LABOUR SUPPLY

When dealing with labour supply at the total economy level, economics views the supply of labour as the aggregation of all individual supply decisions. Yet even if virtually every individual labour supply function were backward bending there is no reason why all utility functions would be identical. Hence at each wage rate there could be a mixture of labour supply decisions, which lie on the positive and negative ranges of individual labour supply curves. The aggregate labour supply function would have a positive slope, illustrated in Figure 1.13, if real wage increases enticed enough

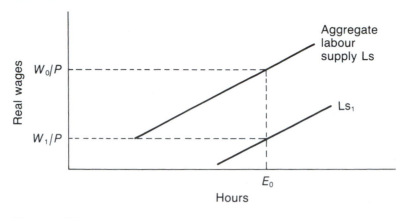

Figure 1.13

new entrants into the labour force to offset any reductions in supply from workers moving along the negative region of their labour supply functions. Thus we are suggesting a conventional positively sloped function to represent the relationship between real wages and the quantity of labour supplied in aggregate.

The positioning of a labour supply curve (L_s) reflects the expectations of labour suppliers. From an initial situation where employment of E_0 results from a real wage of W_0/P, suppose that unemployment increases because of an unanticipated adverse shock to labour demand. The recently unemployed will attempt to find work at a wage of W_0/P. Yet because unemployment persists this initial expectation clearly has not been fulfilled. Consistent with neoclassical job search theory (set out in Chapter 9) the unemployed adjust their expectations and the reservation wage is lowered, to W_1/P for example. In effect the labour supply curve has shifted downward from L_s to L_{s1} to reflect the changed state of labour suppliers' expectations. Although we have not explicitly modelled expectations, whose formation receives a more detailed treatment in the context of unemployment (Chapter 10), with regard to labour supply, the position of the labour supply function implies a given state of expectations. Let us now examine some important features of labour supply at the aggregate level.

MACRO LABOUR SUPPLY TRENDS

The most important trends in aggregate labour supply in the UK have centred upon the increase in female labour force participation during the twentieth century. This will be examined in some detail, but first we make a number of general observations about aggregate labour supply.

The most obvious influences on total labour supply are the size of the population and its age structure. The importance of this latter factor reflects the distinction between the total population and the population of working age, consisting of males aged 16–64 and females aged 16–59. (See the Appendix to this chapter for definitions of various labour market statistical categories.) Up to age 16 there is only a very

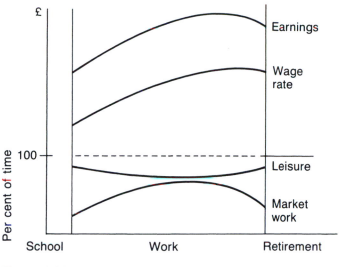

Figure 1.14

limited opportunity to engage in economic activity. Compulsory schooling is a cultur-ally determined and legally enforced constraint on the size of the labour force. At 16 the individual makes his/her first major economic decision – to remain at school or join the labour force. Economics views this decision, as we shall see when we come to investigate human capital theory, as a rational economic calculation. The individual is supposed to trade off the opportunity cost of further education in terms of current earnings forgone in the expectation of higher earnings in the future. Higher earnings after further education 16+ are a return for supplying labour of a higher quality.

Figure 1.14 presents a number of stylised facts about earnings and labour supply over the life cycle of a worker. Earnings decline before retirement not because of any change in wage rates but because of a fall in hours worked. Consequently the time devoted to leisure rises long before retirement. Typically the peak in hours worked precedes the peak in earnings. Figure 1.15 shows male full-time earnings peak in the 40–49 age range whereas female weekly earnings peak in the 30–39 range. Note that male pay exceeds female earnings in each category, with female non-manual weekly pay being almost identical to male manual pay in each age group. The marked differ-ences in lifecycle male and female earnings' patterns illustrated in Figure 1.15 will be examined in detail in Chapter 6.

Within gender groups non-manual workers earn more than their manual counter-parts, a fact we shall analyse in Chapter 5, but for present purposes we need only consider whether differences in the earnings of males and females reflect significant variations in their labour supply. To do this we need to look at the participation of males and females of working age in the labour force.

The statistical measure of labour supply activity within the population is the labour force participation ratio (LFPR). Quite simply the LFPR measures the proportion of the population in the labour force, whether employed or not. If we take the labour

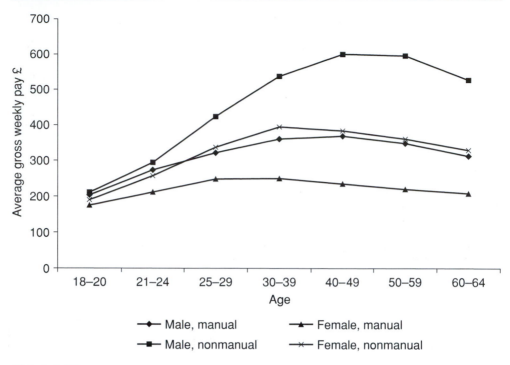

Figure 1.15

Source: Constructed from the New Earnings Survey, 2000, tables A16, A17

force participation of men in 1990 from Table 1.2 the figure of 75.5 per cent was obtained as follows:

$$\text{LFPR Males} = \frac{\text{Male labour force}}{\text{Male population}} = 0.755$$

$$0.755 \times 100 = 75.5\%.$$

One can make the calculation for very specific groups of workers provided the statistical authorities collect and publish the relevant data. For example UK Labour Force Survey data reveals that in 1975 the LFPR for women aged 25–9 was 60.8 per cent, by 1998 this figure had risen to 75.4 per cent.

Thus we are able to access aggregate statistical indications of the willingness to supply labour of various categories of the population. This informs our discussion of the differing levels of economic activity for different demographic groups whether classified by age, sex or race. It is instructive to look at the male and female participation rates in Table 1.2 and how they have developed over time.

Note how relatively stable the total participation rate has remained at around 60–62 per cent for much of this century. Yet within this stable total a number of important changes are discernible.

Table 1.2 Relative participation rates (all ages), Great Britain (%), 1921–98

	Males	All females	Married females	Total
1921	87.1	32.3	8.7	58.1
1931	90.5	34.2	10.0	60.7
1951	87.6	34.7	21.7	59.6
1961	86.0	37.4	29.7	60.5
1971	82.5	43.0	42.3	61.3
1975	78.7	45.7	47.9	61.5
1980	77.0	47.7	49.3	61.8
1985	75.8	49.6	51.0	62.2
1990	75.5	53.2	58.0	64.0
1991	74.8	53.1	59.0	63.6
1995	72.2	53.1	n.a.	62.4
1998	71.3	53.8	n.a.	62.3

Sources: Pre-1985, Dept of Employment, *Employment Gazette*, various years; 1985–1991, ONS, *Labour Force Survey, Historical Supp.*, 4/1993; 1995–1998, ONS 1999, *Annual Abstract of Statistics*

CASE STUDY – PAY AND LABOUR SUPPLY IN THE PUBLIC SECTOR IN BRITAIN

The theoretical link between wages and labour supply has been set out in this chapter. In an interesting empirical study Stephen Nickell and Glenda Quintini, (2002) 'The Consequences of the Decline in Public Sector Pay in Britain: A Little Bit of Evidence', *Economic Journal*, 112 (477): F107–F118, examine how changes in the relative pay of public sector workers in Britain have impacted on the quality of various groups of public sector employees. The aim of the study is to investigate whether falls in the wages of public sector jobs, compared to the pay available elsewhere in the labour market, have not only lead to a decline in the quantity of labour being supplied to the public sector, but also a fall in the quality of that labour supply.

> it is becoming increasingly difficult to recruit certain types of public sector workers, . . . shortages of teachers and nurses are currently receiving a great deal of press attention. One of the reasons for this is the significant decline in the relative pay of most occupational groups in the public sector . . . which began in the late 1970s.

In order to gauge the magnitude of changes in the relative pay of public sector workers in Britain, Nickell and Quintini (2002) use New Earnings Survey data from 1975 to 1999 to look at where in the distribution of wages public sector occupational groups are. They split the sample into public sector workers in their thirties (31–40) and older employees (41–50). Their findings are summarised in Table A.

Table A   Mean percentile position of public sector occupations in the overall pay structure

Women	Age	1975–79	1995–99	% point change
General administration	30s	55.1	47.7	−7.1
	40s	57.5	49.7	−7.8
Police and customs	30s	82.6	83.9	+1.3
	40s	82.0	84.0	+2.0
Nurses	30s	64.1	55.9	−8.2
	40s	66.4	58.9	−7.5
Social workers	30s	64.0	64.1	+0.1
	40s	65.8	71.1	+5.3
Teachers	30s	86.8	74.4	−12.4
	40s	91.4	80.0	−11.4
Manual workers	30s	54.1	38.6	−15.5
	40s	54.5	41.2	−13.3

Source: Adapted from Nickell and Quintini 2002, table 3, p. F110

To help you understand the data in Table A the figure of 80.0 for women teachers in their 40s during 1995–9 means that female teachers were ranked, on average, in the 80th percentile position of the population of all women workers aged 41–50 in the late 1990s.

> For women, we see that . . . police, customs and excise, social workers have done relatively well in the last twenty-five years, having more than held their own in the female earnings distribution. This is in contrast to the other groups. . . . Civil servants, local authority workers [General Administration workers at the central/federal and local/state government levels respectively] and nurses have seen a gradual relative decline of between 7 and 8 percentage points whereas teachers and manual workers have seen more substantial relative falls of 11 percentage points or more. All these declines have continued up to the last available year, 1999.
>
> *For men*, (Table B) we again see some stark contrasts. The police/customs and excise group has done relatively well whereas teachers of all kinds have lost out dramatically. Doctors, by contrast have kept reasonably in step.

In addition to the changes in the pay position of each occupational group in the public sector, we also report the percentage of workers in each occupation who are in the older age group. This shows that the rise in the number of women entering the police force has reduced the percentage of older female police, customs and excise employees from 52% in 1975–79 to 24% in 1995–99. By contrast, the men in the teaching professions have been ageing rapidly for some time as the number of younger men entering declines. During 1975–9

Table B Mean percentile position of public sector occupations in the overall pay structure

Men	Age	1975–79	1995–99	% point change
General administration	30s	56.4	49.9	−6.5
	40s	61.4	53.6	−7.8
Police and customs	30s	63.1	72.4	+9.3
	40s	70.8	73.7	+2.9
Doctors	30s	84.6	87.9	+3.3
	40s	92.5	89.6	−2.9
University lecturers	30s	82.0	68.7	−13.3
	40s	83.8	78.4	−5.5
Teachers	30s	71.6	64.2	−7.4
	40s	79.0	67.6	−11.4
Manual workers	30s	40.2	38.2	−2.0
	40s	42.1	35.6	−6.5

Source: Adapted from Nickell and Quintini 2002, table 4, p. F111

around 45 per cent of male university lecturers and teachers were in their 40s, by 1995–9 this had risen to 60 per cent of male lecturers and 65% of male teachers.

Overall, then, we can see some substantial shifts in the relative pay of different public sector groups and it should come as no surprise that we now face well publicised shortages in those areas of the public sector which have suffered large relative declines in remuneration.

To investigate the quality element of labour supply Nickell and Quintini (2002) compare changes in the relative position of those workers entering six public sector occupational groups (3 female, 3 male) aged 21 in 1979 and 1991. These workers were a subset of subjects in large cohort studies that included taking both general tests and specific maths tests. By comparing those test scores between the different cohorts entering public sector jobs (see Table C) Nickell and Quintini (2002) are able to draw some conclusions about changes in the quality of public sector employees over time.

Although there are some changes in the general and maths test scores between the different cohorts in the three female public sector occupational groups only the slight increase in the general test score of female General Administrators is of any significance.

Overall, however, the results for women yield no clear pattern. . . . By contrast, the results for men are quite decisive.

There was a small yet statistically insignificant increase in the test scores of male police officers who, you will remember, witnessed increases in relative pay. There

Table C Average (mean) test score rankings by public sector occupation

	Test	21 in 1979	21 in 1991	change
Female				
General administration	General	61.8	63.3	+1.5*
	Maths	60.6	59.8	−0.8
Nurses	General	55.5	53.6	−1.9
	Maths	52.7	51.2	−1.5
Teachers	General	74.2	75.7	+1.5
	Maths	72.8	70.2	−2.6
Male				
General administration	General	75.2	66.6	−8.6*
	Maths	72.8	63.4	−9.4*
Police	General	58.4	59.0	+0.6
	Maths	55.4	55.7	+0.3
Teachers	General	76.6	65.9	−10.7*
	Maths	76.1	63.5	−12.6*

Source: Adapted from Nickell and Quintini 2002, table 5, p. F114
Note: * Change is statistically significant at the 10 per cent level.

were, however, substantial and significant reductions in the test scores (both general and maths) of male administrators and teachers across the cohorts. These falling test scores positions accompanied the substantial reductions in relative pay for these two occupational groups.

> So, broadly speaking for men this . . . evidence on test scores is consistent with the . . . prediction . . . that relative quality would follow relative pay.

The difference in the co-movements of relative pay and relative quality, between men and women in the public sector, might be due to the fact that, although private sector pay has risen relative to public sector pay, for both men and women, this has been offset, to some extent, by increases in female labour force participation that has drawn able women into work in the public sector despite falling relative pay levels.

This case study serves to point out that shortages of public sector professionals like teachers and nurses might well be connected with the substantial falls in the relative pay of these occupations within the British labour force. After all, simple labour supply theory suggests that lower wages (in relation to wages in the private sector in this case) will lower labour supply. Furthermore, while shifts in female labour force participation may have undermined the statistical significance of declines in test score rankings across cohorts of women workers, there are clear links between not only the quantity of labour supply and relative pay of men in public sector occupations but the quality of that labour supplied as well.

Table 1.3 Male participation rates (%), (workers aged less than 64)

	USA	UK
1890/91	73.9	65.4
1910/11	58.1	56.8

Source: Adapted from Pencavel 1986, tables 1.1 and 1.2, p. 8

Firstly, note the secular decline in UK male participation from the 1930s peak, which was particularly rapid during the 1960s and 1970s. Male labour force participation rates have declined by more than 19 percentage points between 1931 and the late 1990s. However, it is interesting to note that this long-run labour supply trend decline in male participation rates is not confined to the UK labour force. USA census data shows a similar trend profile of high LFPRs declining markedly during the 1960s and 1970s.

	1920	1930	1940	1950	1960	1970	1980	1990	1995
Male labour force participation (%)	84.6	82.1	82.5	86.8	84.0	80.6	77.9	76.8	75.0

Although the existence of welfare payments, including old age pensions and the changes in taxation which accompanied their expansion, may have had some impact, especially amongst older males, it is evident that the labour supply trend decline was well underway before the great expansion of welfare benefits following the end of the First World War (1914–18). This is clear from the statistics on the labour supply of older males contained in Table 1.3.

By 1995 the LFPR for American males aged 65 and over was 16.8 per cent. The decline in male labour force participation contrasts markedly with the general increase in female labour force participation. The increase in the willingness of married women to seek market work is even more spectacular, particularly during the 1960s, but this trend continued throughout the 1970s and the 1980s as well. After a period of stagnation during the early 1990s female labour force participation rates begin to rise again during the late 1990s. Yet despite these important changes, which are reflected in the obvious convergence of male and female economic activity rates in Figure 1.16, there still remains a significant difference between male and female labour force participation. Although the total rate of economic activity in the UK remained in the 74–80 per cent range throughout the 1971–98 period, male economic activity rates were on a downward trend and female rates were clearly rising. Over the period (1971–98) the proportion of males deemed economically inactive (i.e., students, housekeepers, retired early, those permanently unable to work) has risen from 9 per cent to 16 per cent. The proportion of females deemed inactive has fallen sharply from 46 per cent to 28 per cent.

The most marked increase in female labour force participation has occurred amongst women with dependent children. Data from the Labour Force Survey contained in Table 1.4 shows that economic activity rates for females with no dependent children

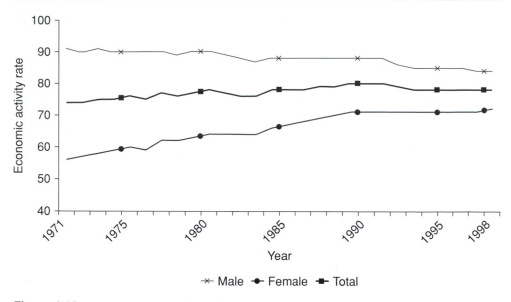

Figure 1.16

Source: Office of National Statistics (ONS), Social Trends Dataset, 2000

Table 1.4   Female economic activity (%), 1987–2000

	No of dependent children	Dependent child < 18	Dependent child 0–4
1987	76.1	59.3	42.4
1988	76.3	61.1	45.3
1989	77.2	62.3	47.4
1990	77.5	63.0	48.1
1991	76.8	63.1	48.6
1992	75.7	63.4	48.4
1993	75.2	64.5	51.2
1994	75.5	64.1	50.7
1995	74.8	65.1	51.9
1996	75.1	65.8	53.6
1997	75.1	66.5	55.0
1998	75.1	66.9	55.0
1999	75.0	68.2	57.2
2000	75.3	68.8	58.2

Source: ONS, *Labour Force Survey* 2000

are higher than those with children younger than 18 years of age. However, the main growth in female labour force participation since 1987 has come from women with children, especially from those with young children up to 4 years old.

In order to begin to understand the trends in female labour supply it might be useful to list the general influences on aggregate labour force participation. Leslie (1982) suggests six factors which determine the decision to participate in the labour force or not. These are:

1) Economic circumstances.
2) Personal characteristics, e.g., age, sex, race.
3) Government legislation, e.g., the raising of the school leaving age to 16 in 1972.
4) Arbitrary convention. Including statistical conventions concerning what is to be counted as economic activity. Housework in the home is by convention inactivity, because it does not involve a market transaction. The definition of unemployment will influence calculations of the size of the labour force.
5) General health/morbidity of the population.
6) Custom and Social Convention, a whole plethora of influences which vary enormously. One might wish to cite the growth of the women's movement in the 1960s and 1970s as a factor influencing labour supply.

It has been implicitly assumed that labour supply decisions can be and are readily reversible, such that a married woman working full-time would give up work completely in response to an increase in her husband's wage rate (see p. 19). Yet it is worth considering the enduring nature of labour market decisions usually referred to as 'persistence'. Persistence is a feature not only of unemployment, whereby experience of unemployment reduces one's chance of regaining employment, but also of labour force participation. Take for example Leslie's first category. If the economy is booming, with real wages and job opportunities increasing, this might induce an increase in labour supply. Persistence would suggest that these additional workers would remain as labour force participants after the boom had ended thus increasing unemployment during slumps over time. As Clark and Summers (1988) state, 'previous employment experience has an important effect on subsequent labour supply. This implies that labour supply decisions are not very responsive to transitory changes in employment opportunities' (p. 227). Thus persistence could be incorporated into an account of the marked increase in female labour force participation, particularly that of married women during this century. Table 1.2 shows that in Britain the labour force participation ratio for married women more than doubled between 1931 (10.0 per cent) and 1951 (21.7 per cent). The implication is that changes in wages and employment opportunities connected with the Second World War (1939–45) persisted in raising the threshold of female labour force participation in an irreversible manner. Table 1.5 presents detailed USA data which lends support to this view of events.

Accompanying this increase in participation was a change in social attitudes to women working but it appears as though this followed, rather than preceded, the experience of women in the workplace during wartime. Therefore persistence had effects on labour supply decisions after the Second World War in a manner that permanently increased married female participation.

Table 1.6 compares recent participation rates in some industrialised economies. Such a comparison at a single point in time will incorporate different macroeconomic conditions but it may be that legislative and varying social influences are also being

Table 1.5 USA female labour force participation
(Great Britain comparison from Table 1.2)

	Labour force participation rate (%), married women
1920 (1921)	9.0 (8.7)
1930 (1931)	11.7 (10.0)
1940	15.6
1944	23.9
1947	20.0
1950 (1951)	23.0 (21.7)
1960	31.9
1970	40.5
1980	49.8
1995	61.0

Sources: Clark and Summers 1988, table 11.1, p. 208; US
Department of Labour Bureau of Labour Statistics

Table 1.6 Comparative labour force (15–64) economic activity rates (%), 1999

	Male	Female	Total
Australia	82.7	64.5	73.6
Canada	82.0	69.8	75.9
Japan	85.3	59.5	72.5
USA	84.0	70.7	77.2
Austria	80.5	62.7	71.6
Belgium	73.0	56.0	64.6
Denmark	85.0	76.1	80.6
Finland	78.9	73.9	76.4
France	75.5	62.2	68.8
Germany	79.3	62.9	71.2
Greece	76.9	49.7	62.9
Ireland	78.3	54.4	66.4
Italy	73.7	45.6	59.6
Luxembourg	75.7	50.2	63.1
Netherlands	82.6	64.4	73.6
Portugal	79.1	63.0	70.9
Spain	76.2	48.5	62.1
Sweden	79.5	74.8	77.2
UK	84.1	68.4	76.3

Sources: ILO 2000; Eurostat 2000

picked up. High male participation rates are found throughout these countries. In all cases male participation rates were greater than female rates in 1999. The smallest differential between male and female rates occurs in Sweden (4.7 percentage points) whereas the greatest difference amongst this sample is in Italy (28.1 percentage points). Notice that the highest overall activity rate is due to Denmark's high male rate combined with the highest female participation. The data from these nations records a rather large variation in female participation rates, a range of 30.5 percentage points compared to a male range of 12.3. The UK had a high rate of male economic activity

Table 1.7   Great Britain civilian labour force (millions)

	Males	Females	Total
1971	15.6	9.3	24.9
1976	15.6	10.1	25.7
1981	15.6	10.6	26.5
1985	15.7	11.1	26.9
1990	16.0	12.2	28.2
1991	15.9	12.1	28.1
1995	15.7	12.0	27.7
1996	15.8	12.1	27.9
1997	15.8	12.2	28.0
1998	15.8	12.3	28.1
2000	15.9	12.4	28.3

Sources: ONS, Labour Force Survey, 1993; Regional
Trends Dataset, 2001

(84.1 per cent), which is only bettered by those of Japan and Denmark, yet it had a female activity rate (68.4 per cent) that is only sixth highest below those of the apparently egalitarian Scandinavian countries (Denmark, Finland and Sweden) and North America (Canada and the USA).

Returning to a closer examination of the domestic labour force, contained in Table 1.7, between 1971 and 2000 the civilian labour force of Great Britain increased by 3.4 million persons from 24.9 to 28.3 million. Virtually this entire increase was accounted for by a 3.1 million increase in the number of women in the labour force. The entire net increase in the British labour force during the 1990s was accounted for by greater female participation. However, the fact that the numbers in the labour force declined between 1990 and 1995 before continuing to grow demonstrates the impact of the decline in the number of new entrants, a wholly demographic influence on labour supply. Figure 1.17 charts the decline in school leavers between 1980 and the year 2000, which, in demographic terms, was spectacular. What this development meant was that greater reliance was placed upon the role of female participation in determining the overall supply of labour available to the UK economy in the 1990s.

Our knowledge of the theory of labour supply suggests that in order to exact more labour services out of the working population wages would have to rise. The analysis of wage movements in the 1990s contained in Chapter 3 confirms that wages did indeed rise in real terms in the UK. We would also expect employers to look towards alternative sources of labour supply, namely re-entrants to the labour market, mature workers aged over 50 and recruitment from the unemployed. Steps that might aid labour market re-entry, particularly of women, would include resorting to part-time work coupled with an interest in accommodating working mothers. However, progress on flexible employment and maternity conditions coupled with improved childcare provision is still largely confined to the banking and public sectors. Employers do have a number of alternatives to young people when it comes to adapting their approach to recruitment. Foremost amongst these alternative sources of labour supply are women re-entrants and ethnic minority adults.

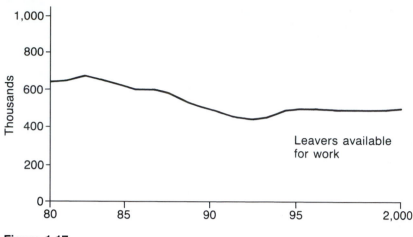

Figure 1.17

Source: Department of Employment

When we come to examine ethic group data on labour force participation, interesting and significant divergences appear. As the data in Table 1.8 shows levels of economic activity, i.e., labour force participation, were fairly even for males across the white, black Caribbean and Indian ethnic origin groups. This is not to overlook the fact that substantial differences exist between the ethnic group males when it comes to the experience of unemployment (see Chapter 10).

Generally rates of economic activity for females are lower than for their male counterparts. The rates range from the 77 per cent for black other females down to 18 per cent for Bangladeshi women. The striking differences in the level of labour force participation between women of different ethnic origins are primarily due to the different proportions classified as housewives, which are low for white and black

Table 1.8 Great Britain participation rates (%) by ethnic origin, 1998–9

	Males 16–64	*Females 16–59*
White	85	74
Black Caribbean	81	72
Black African	77	59
Black Other	80	77
Indian	80	62
Pakistani	71	30
Bangladeshi	68	18
Chinese	62	62
Others	75	60
All groups	85	73

Source: *Social Trends Dataset*, 2000.
Note: Others include those of mixed origin.

Table 1.9 Average actual hours worked per
week (full-time employees), 1998

	Male	Female
Austria	40.2	39.8
Belgium	39.1	37.5
Denmark	39.3	37.7
Finland	40.1	38.2
France	40.3	38.7
Germany	40.5	39.3
Greece	41.7	39.3
Italy	39.7	36.3
Luxembourg	40.3	37.4
Netherlands	39.2	38.5
Portugal	42.1	39.6
Spain	41.2	39.6
Sweden	40.2	40.0
UK	45.7	40.7
USA	41.9	35.3

Source: Social Trends Dataset, 2000

women but much higher for Pakistani and Bangladeshi women. The term housewife is an accurate one because the category 'looking after the home' has no recorded entries for economically inactive males at this level of aggregation. The discrepancies between the ethnic origin groups when it comes to females classified as looking after the home are most likely due to factors associated with Leslie's custom and social convention category. Note also the high level of economically active black Caribbean and black other women, there are high proportions of female students from these ethnic groups.

Our microeconomic analysis was conducted in terms of hours of labour supplied, reminding us that numbers in the labour force and participation rates do not tell us the full story. Table 1.9 provides an international comparison of weekly hours worked. The hours of male full-time workers are higher in each case than those of female workers. Both males and females in the UK work longer hours than their international counterparts in this sample of countries.

However, this data conceals the prevalence of female part-time working in the UK. OECD data in Table 1.10 shows that while the proportions of male workers who worked part-time in the UK and the USA were almost identical (8.5 per cent and 8.1 per cent respectively), more than 40 per cent of female workers in the UK were working part-time, which was more than twice the proportion of American females who worked part-time. In the UK part-time work is disproportionately common, with almost 1 in 4 (23 per cent) of all employees working less than 30 hours per week in 1999. In the Czech Republic only 1 in 30 workers (3.4 per cent) work less than 30 hours per week. Internationally, but particularly in the Netherlands, Australia and the UK, part-time working is a female phenomenon.

More than 40 per cent of all females employed in Australia work part-time, second only to the Netherlands (55.4 per cent) in this sample of countries. Australia also

Table 1.10　Part-time working (percentage of employment), 1999

	Percentage of total part-time	Percentage of male part-time	Percentage of female part-time
Australia	26.1	14.3	41.4
Austria	12.3	2.8	24.4
Belgium	19.9	7.3	36.6
Canada	18.5	10.3	28.0
Czech Republic	3.4	1.7	5.6
Denmark	15.3	8.9	22.7
Finland	9.9	6.6	13.5
France	14.7	5.8	24.7
Germany	17.1	4.8	33.1
Greece (1998)	9.0	5.3	15.4
Ireland	18.3	7.9	31.9
Italy	11.8	5.3	23.2
Japan	24.1	13.4	39.7
Netherlands	30.4	11.9	55.4
New Zealand	23.0	11.3	37.2
Portugal	9.3	5.0	14.6
Spain	7.9	2.9	16.8
Sweden	14.5	7.3	22.3
UK	23.0	8.5	40.6
USA	13.3	8.1	19.0

Source: OECD, *Employment Outlook*, 2000

has the highest rate of male part-time employment. The dominance of part-time work for females feeds through lower wage rates and shorter average hours to be reflected as a component of the discrepancy between male and female earnings. In Chapter 6 we will attempt to assess this factor when dealing with discrimination in labour markets.

These types of aggregate labour force data have important applications in labour economics especially when dealing with the topics of unemployment, human capital and discrimination. Let us for the time being just focus on the most general of these applications, the topic of unemployment.

LABOUR SUPPLY AND UNEMPLOYMENT

The unemployed are an important component of the labour force. For a given level of unemployment, what proportion is voluntary or supply related? This is a problem with enormous implications for economics not only at the empirical and theoretical levels but also at the policy prescription stage. Theoretically we can separate explanations of unemployment into 'supply-side' and 'demand-side' categories. If unemployment is caused by supply based factors, such as the ratio of state benefits received when out of work to wages received when employed (the replacement ratio), then the appropriate policy response is not for Government to try and stimulate economic activity in general, but to reduce the real value of unemployment benefit.

The theory underlying the notion of state benefit induced unemployment is, as we discovered in the first part of this chapter, essentially a simple one. Benefits have an adverse effect on labour supply decisions. For example a worker earns X per week. In the absence of benefit the cost of leisure $= X$ per week – taxes, work expenses, etc. Now if benefit $= B$ per week, the cost of leisure is reduced to $= X - B$. B/X is the replacement ratio. Hence,

Unemployment $= f(B/X, \text{DSQL})$

where DSQL are the 'costs' incurred by a worker in avoiding being disqualified for unemployment benefit (i.e., cost of proving that search fails to find suitable work, initial period of no benefit, cost of finding a job at the end of the benefit period). The theory postulates that the greater the replacement ratio (B/X), the greater the level of unemployment. The greater the degree of disqualification (DSQL), the lower the level of unemployment.

A generous and accessible benefit system makes effective withdrawal from the labour force more attractive at the margin between job search and employment. It makes effective withdrawal from the labour force more attractive at the margin between job search and complete leisure. The tendency would be for people to search longer before accepting employment, hence reducing the amount of work the labour force would be willing to do at any real wage rate.[7] Those on the margin of labour force participation, such as married women, might be induced, by the prospect of benefits, to enter the labour force and work temporarily in order to qualify for unemployment benefits. In these ways a benefit regime that is benign, generous or lasts indefinitely might encourage unemployment to rise in a manner which may well persist over time.

Wasmer (1999) models the interesting scenario where an increase in the supply of inexperienced young workers and increased female labour force participation can bring about a fall in the wage of unskilled workers and an increase in unemployment and its persistence. This may well have been the situation in France between 1970 and 1977. This initial shock is followed by more investment in human capital (see Chapter 5) as young workers and female workers undertake education and on-the-job training, which increases the supply of skilled workers. In contrast Kim (1999) found that in the USA increasing female labour supply did not simply bring about reductions in real wages for unskilled male workers and growing wage inequality in the USA labour market (see Chapter 3). The main causes of the deteriorating labour market position of unskilled men have been shifts in labour demand, (see the employment trends in Chapter 2 and skill biased technological change in Chapter 5), not increases in female labour supply.

Our purpose here is not to exhaustively discuss the merits of a supply-side view of unemployment, only to show that the analysis of labour supply is of crucial importance as a foundation to other more applied aspects of labour economics, like unemployment in the context of a welfare benefit system that can influence labour supply decisions.

LABOUR SUPPLY – SUMMARY

Microeconomic analysis of labour supply yielded:

- the importance of substitution and income effects in relation to wage rates and hours of work
- the backward bending individual labour supply curve
- state benefits will reduce labour supply if they are generous relative to post-tax wage rates
- the impact of income tax changes on labour supply depends crucially upon the balance of the substitution and income effects
- increasing income tax acts as a disincentive to work only if the substitution effect is dominant; reductions in income tax, common to the UK and USA during the 1980s and 1990s, will only increase labour supply if the substitution effect prevails
- household models can be used to analyse the division of labour within the home and assess the labour supply response to narrowing sex-based earnings differentials

At the macroeconomic level our analysis highlighted:

- a significant increase in female labour force participation, especially among married women, during the twentieth century, coupled with a gradual but general decline in male participation rates
- the persistence of labour supply decisions which are not readily reversed
- that since 1971 virtually the entire 3.4 million increase in the British labour force came about because of increased female labour supply (plus 3.1 million), much of it part-time

Finally we pointed out the link between the hypothesised disincentive effects of benefits and taxation on the willingness to work, and the New Classical/supply-side view of unemployment.

LABOUR SUPPLY – QUESTIONS FOR DISCUSSION

1) Analyse the increase in female labour force participation since 1971 using a household model of labour supply.
2) What aggregate level considerations might lie behind the increase in female labour force participation during the twentieth century?
3) Demonstrate the importance of substitution effects in determining adverse and favourable labour supply responses to increasing and decreasing income tax rates.
4) Assess the likely labour supply response to Government policies which will reduce the marginal rate of income tax, particularly the base rate, and reduce the real value of welfare benefits.

5) If tax-free allowances are not increased to take account of inflation, what would tend to happen to labour supply?

6) What does the data on male and female working contained in Tables 1.7 and 1.8 appear to indicate about gender-based and international differences in labour supply? Do we need to understand more about labour demand conditions to provide a more complete answer?

SELECTED READINGS

Blundell, R. and MaCurdy, T. (1999) 'Labour Supply: A Review of Alternative Approaches', in O. Ashenfelter and D. Card (eds) *Handbook of Labour Economics, Volume 3*, Amsterdam: Elsevier Science.

Heckman, J. (1993) 'What Has Been Learned About Labour Supply in the Last Twenty Years', *American Economic Review*, 83: 116–21.

APPENDIX – GLOSSARY OF TERMS

Economically active People in employment, including the armed forces, unemployed people who are identified by censuses and surveys as seeking work in a reference week, people participating in the government's employment and training schemes and full-time students who are working or seeking work and not prevented from starting work by the need to complete their education.

Economically inactive People who are not economically active, e.g., full-time students who neither have, nor are seeking, paid work and those who are keeping house, have retired early or are permanently unable to work.

Total labour force The economically active.

Civilian labour force The total labour force less the armed forces.

Employees in employment A count of civilian jobs, both main and secondary, which are as an employee paid by an employer who runs a PAYE tax scheme.

Self-employed persons Those who in their main employment work on their own account, whether or not they have any employees.

Employed labour force Employees in employment, HM Forces and the self-employed.

Working population The employed labour force and people claiming benefit at Unemployment Benefit Offices who on the day of the monthly count were unemployed and able and willing to do any suitable work.

Population of working age Males aged 16–64 years and females aged 16–59 years.

Economic activity rate The percentage of the home population aged 16 or over who are in the civilian labour force.

Data on Great Britain excludes Northern Ireland whereas figures referring to the United Kingdom include Northern Ireland.

2

Labour demand and productivity

INTRODUCTION

Essentially the demand for labour is a derived demand because no firm demands labour for its own sake. Labour is one of the factors of production which firms combine and organise in order to generate output. Consumers demand goods and services which producers seek to supply profitably. Hence they demand labour to help produce goods and services to meet the requirements of consumers. To illustrate the derived nature of labour demand consider the case where a firm expects demand for its products to increase due to greater personal disposable incomes arising from tax cuts. In such circumstances if the extra supply to meet the rising demand is commensurate with the firm's business plans, then one may reasonably expect that the demand for labour will increase. Yet whatever the objective of the firm (profit maximisation, growth, market share, etc.) the decision to employ workers will entail a comparison of the costs and benefits to the firm of doing so. Employing labour gives rise to costs – primarily wages but other costs also exist, national insurance, basic training, etc. The benefit to the firm is mainly the revenue generated by sales of goods/services produced by labour. If the net benefit (total benefit less total cost) is not sufficient then the firm will not employ additional labour or it may lay some workers off. However, it is not necessarily the case that all fluctuations in product demand will result in changes in employment. The firm's labour demand response to variations in product demand will depend upon the significance and duration of such variations. If a firm is faced with short-run or minor changes in demand for its products then it can counter those fluctuations by adjusting its stocks of unsold goods. Substantial and longer-term changes in demand will induce changes in employment. Productivity is a key ingredient for labour demand so we will analyse the productivity performance of the UK.

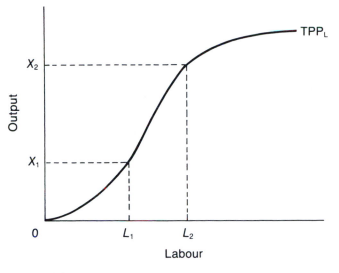

Figure 2.1

MICROECONOMIC ANALYSIS OF LABOUR DEMAND

In order to construct the simple neoclassical model of labour demand we reiterate a familiar proposition about the performance of labour in the production process. The generic characteristic of the returns, in the form of output, to the human factor of production incorporates the notion of diminishing returns. No matter what the nature of the production function, as units of labour are added to the production process, when those of land and capital are held constant, eventually the rate of increase of total product in physical terms begins to decrease. This is illustrated in Figure 2.1.

Take the example of a profit maximising firm with a fixed amount of machinery available for a set number of hours per day. As labour is increasingly employed on this fixed capital stock, output grows. Initially up to L_1 increasing returns to the factor might exist. But eventually diminishing returns will set in, especially beyond L, as the machinery approaches full capacity utilisation. From the total physical productivity of labour (TPP_L) one can calculate functions for both the average and marginal physical productivity of labour (APP_L and MPP_L respectively).

$$APP_L = \frac{TPP_L}{L}$$

$$MPP_L = \frac{\delta TPP_L}{\delta L}.$$

These will have the general forms shown in Figure 2.2 derived from a total physical product (TPP) function exhibiting diminishing returns.

Obviously a firm is not primarily concerned with the physical productivity of labour as such but with the revenues that such labour can generate. Therefore we simply turn

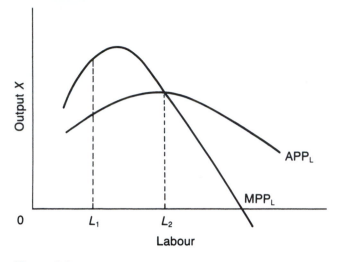

Figure 2.2

marginal physical product into marginal revenue product by multiplying MPP_L by MR_X (the marginal revenue from selling output X). Since in perfect competition $MR_X = P_X$, we can multiply MPP_L by the price P_X of output to obtain the MRP_L. If we assume a constant price for labour, i.e., wage W, then we can draw a total factor outlay (TFO) function as a straight line emanating from the origin. The firm is therefore assumed to be a price taker in both the product and factor markets. Thus Figure 2.1 is transformed into the situation shown in Figure 2.3.

Profits are maximised where the vertical distance between the total revenue product of labour (TRP_L) and the firm's total outlay on labour (TFO_L) is greatest, i.e., at L_0. As the parallel line shows, this is also the point at which the slopes of the revenue

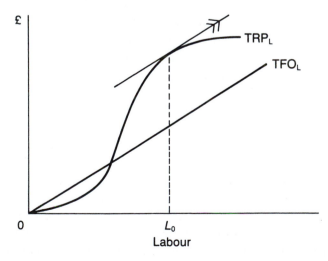

Figure 2.3

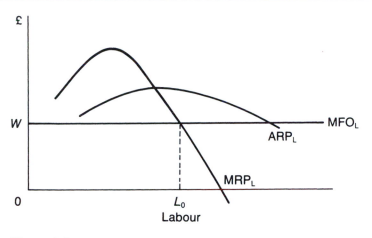

Figure 2.4

and outlay functions are equal. The significance of this latter observation is clearly shown in Figure 2.4. Its similarity with Figure 2.2 is evident except that we are now dealing with revenue functions derived from the TRP_L in Figure 2.3. As wage rates were fixed the marginal factor outlay for labour is a constant. Profit maximising employment (L_0) is achieved where MFO_L equals MRP_L, i.e., where the marginal cost of employing labour equals the marginal revenue to be gained from employing labour. In other words where the costs and benefits of a single extra unit of labour are exactly equal, which is the level of employment at which maximum profits from the production and sale of goods/services (X) are to be achieved.

We are now in a position to identify the individual firm's demand for labour function. The short-run demand curve for labour for a profit maximising firm operating under conditions of perfect competition is simply the MRP_L function. However, not the whole of the marginal revenue product of labour (MRP_L) function constitutes the firm's demand for labour. The microeconomic labour demand function is limited to the negatively sloped range between points a and b in Figure 2.5. Point a coincides with the maximum wage W_2 the firm would be prepared to pay under these price and productivity conditions, because at any higher wage rate employment costs would exceed the average revenue generated by the employment of labour. Point b limits the firm's effective labour demand as it is assumed that workers are unlikely to turn up for negative wages. At point c the monetary surplus indicated by the difference between average revenue productivity (ARP) and average wages W_1 could be used by the firm to meet fixed costs.

From this analysis we can deduce a number of important conclusions. Firstly, the inter-relationship between pay, productivity and employment is established, to which we shall return in more detail later in this chapter. We can also establish that the demand curve for labour in the whole industry will not be the sum of all the individual firm demand curves in that industry. Why? Because whilst it may be permissible to assume that for a single firm prices are constant even as output expands, for the entire

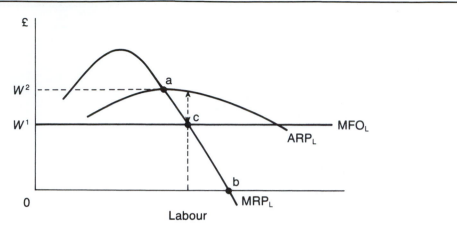

Figure 2.5

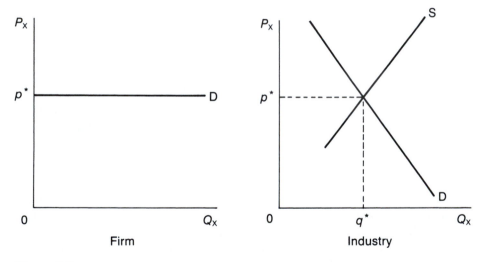

Figure 2.6

industry this is not the case. If as in Figure 2.6 industry output expands beyond q^* the market price will fall below p^* (as long as the demand curve D does not shift, because of changes in tastes, income, etc.) The result of this, as Figure 2.7 shows, is that as output and employment increase, the price of output falls. Thus when wage rates fall from W_1 to W_2 the summed MRP curve shifts down and employment increases from L_1 to L_2.

Strictly speaking the outcome of the above analysis, that wages are related to the marginal productivity of labour, flows from the assumption not of profit maximisation but of cost minimisation. This is illustrated in Figure 2.8. The isoquant Q_x joins points of equal output. The isocost function kl joins equal cost combinations of capital K and labour L. Cost minimisation for a given level of output Q_x is achieved at point A where the isoquant curve is tangential to the isocost line. The slope of kl is equal to

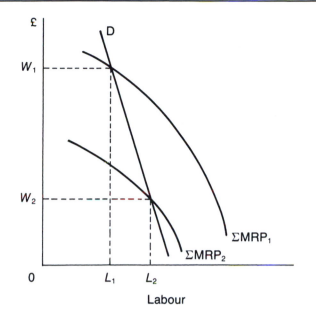

Figure 2.7

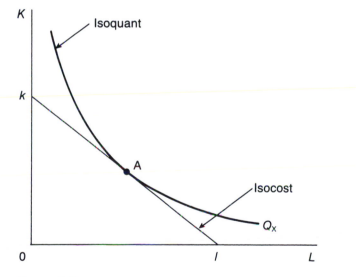

Figure 2.8

the ratio of factor prices W/R (where W is the cost of labour and R is the cost of capital),

$$Q_x = f(K,L)$$

$$W = \lambda \frac{\delta Q_x}{\delta L}$$

$$R = \lambda \frac{\delta Q_x}{\delta K}$$

where λ is the marginal cost.

At point A, since the slopes of the isoquant and the isocost curves are equal the proportionality between wages and marginal products is determined,

$$\lambda = \frac{R}{\delta Q_x/dK} = \frac{W}{\delta Q_x/dL}$$

In the long run when all factor inputs can be varied the position of the demand for labour function will be influenced by the degree of substitutability between labour and capital. This, theoretically, will be determined by the extent to which the ratio in which capital and labour are used in production changes when the ratio of their prices change. Generally the greater the degree of substitutability between labour and capital the more sensitive the demand for labour will be in the long run to changes in real wage rates, i.e., the more elastic the demand curve will be. This is the first of the four Marshall–Hicks 'laws of derived demand'. The other three state that the demand for labour will be more elastic if:

- the elasticity of demand for the final product increases;
- the share of wages in total cost of production rises; and
- the elasticities of supply of other factors of production increase.

EMPIRICAL ASPECTS OF LABOUR DEMAND

The empirical status of the downward sloping demand curve for labour was the subject of some doubt as a number of studies failed to yield the expected negative relationship between real wages and employment. However, Symons and Layard (1984) report strong support for the neoclassical demand for labour function, with a model, which includes the effect of raw material prices. In their variable lag version of the model, tested on quarterly data from five countries covering the 1955–80 period, the negative relationship between real wages and employment is evident. The elasticities of labour demand with respect to wages and raw material prices calculated by Symons and Layard are given in Table 2.1.

Table 2.1 Labour demand, elasticity estimates

	Real wages	*Material prices*
Germany	−1.8	−2.1
France	−0.3	−0.1
Japan	−2.4	−2.6
Canada	−2.6	−1.8
USA	−0.6	−3.4

Source: Adapted from Symons and Layard 1984, table 5

While too much should not be read into the cross country differences in these elasticity estimates because of inadequacies and inconsistencies arising from the data, these results do lend support for the neoclassical proposition that labour demand and real wages are negatively related. The authors conclude that 'the level of employment is determined by and large by real factor prices' (p. 797). Layard and Nickell (1985a) estimate that in the UK the elasticity of labour demand with respect to the wage rate was −0.33 after one year, rising to −0.9 in the longer run. Hamermesh (1993) provides estimates of overall labour demand elasticity of −0.93 in British manufacturing plants and in the range −1.0 to −1.4 in British coal mines before 1980.

Hamermesh (1986) surveys a vast literature regarding empirical estimates of labour demand elasticity. He examines studies which hold output constant along with both fixed capital prices and where the price of capital is specified. In the case of homogeneous labour, demand appears to be inelastic, 'in developed economies in the late twentieth century, the aggregate long run, constant-output, labour demand elasticity lies roughly in the range 0.15–0.50' (p. 453).

Studies which recognise the differences between labour suppliers generally yield lower demand elasticities for non-production workers than their 'blue-collar' counterparts. This is consistent with the view that there is greater substitutability between production workers and physical capital than between 'white-collar' workers and capital. As Hamermesh (1986) explains, 'the own-price demand elasticity declines the more education is embodied in the group of workers' (p. 462). Such a finding is consistent with neoclassical human capital theory (see Chapter 5). Haskel[1] discovered that the demand for unskilled labour (−0.365 in 1990) in UK manufacturing is more elastic than that for skilled labour (−0.267 in 1990) and that these elasticities had increased during the 1980s, especially that of unskilled workers (see Figure 11.2). Demand elasticities tend to be lower for adult men than for other categories of workers, which indicates that adult men are in a stronger labour market position than other groups of workers. This might reflect an expression of employers' preferences for certain categories of workers, an issue to which we shall return in Chapter 6.

However, as we noted earlier, demand for labour depends not only on the price of labour (wages and fixed employment costs) but is derived from the demand for goods and services. Labour demand does not respond instantly nor need it respond fully to changes in demand for final products. Sims' (1974) study of US manufacturing, referred to in Nickell (1986), discovered that labour demand takes in excess of one year to fully respond to a shift in final product sales. The reasons for such a tardy response are clear. Adjusting labour demand is not a costless exercise. A firm faced with the doubling of its sales illustrated in Figure 2.9 will incur hiring costs associated with the recruitment and training of new labour.[2]

Another consideration is that labour supply is unlikely to be perfectly elastic thereby restricting the increase in employment. A further consideration is the firm's expectation of future sales. The firm in Figure 2.9 must assess whether the shift in sales is likely to be a temporary or a permanent phenomenon. These types of consideration mean that demanding labour is a dynamic process.

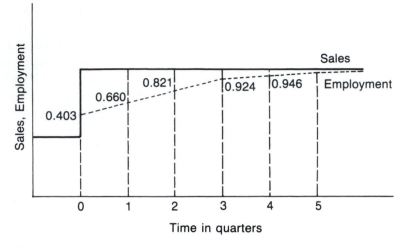

Figure 2.9
Source: Nickell 1986, figure 9.1, p. 474

DYNAMIC LABOUR DEMAND

Nickell (1986) indicates the possible scale of labour adjustment costs facing the firm. Hiring costs including both recruitment and training may amount to approximately one week's pay for unskilled workers. Average hiring costs are more than five times as large for skilled workers and some twelve times as great for professional and managerial staff. Such estimates underline the debilitating effect of high labour turnover. Unless workers quit voluntarily, the cost to the firm of firing or making labour redundant under current UK employment protection legislation averages out at a minimum of five weeks' pay. In many cases unions and departing executives negotiate somewhat better terms. Such considerations lead Nickell to conclude that, 'the costs of both hiring and firing are not trivial and . . . vary dramatically between unskilled and skilled workers' (p. 476). The impact of adjustment costs on labour demand is to moderate changes in employment across the cycle of booms and slumps in economic activity.[3] On the basis that no employees voluntarily leave the firm and that hiring and firing costs are assumed to be linear but asymmetric, i.e., that hiring is more expensive person for person than firing, then labour demand would generate the type of employment changes shown in Figure 2.10.[4]

Adjustment costs produce the familiar phenomena of labour hoarding during a slump and the increased use of overtime during a boom. The asymmetry between hiring and firing costs in the above example produces lower levels of employment in each successive cycle of the same amplitude. Thus high and low plateau employment during the first boom and slump (E_b^1 and E_s^1 respectively) are not matched in the second cycle (E_b^2 and E_s^2). Employers' expectations of future business prospects produce, in this model, periods of rapid employment change coupled with periods when labour demand is static. Firms, in trying to follow a completely optimal strategy,

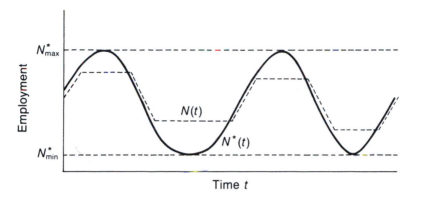

Figure 2.10 ——, equilibrium employment (no adjustment costs); ------, actual employment (linear adjustment costs)

Source: Adapted from Nickell 1986, figure 9.10, p. 494

generate a pattern of labour demand, which ensures that employment does not fluctuate as greatly as product demand.

Given that there are periods when labour demand in terms of the actual number of workers employed is constant, unless there are changes in firms' inventories (stocks of unsold goods), which we shall assume there are not, then employers must adjust the hours worked in order to respond to changes in product demand. The most obvious example of adjusting the hours worked by labour is the increasing/decreasing availability of 'overtime'. Increasing overtime enables the firm to delay the hiring of new workers without sacrificing any output. Reducing overtime allows firms to lower output without incurring firing costs. In the presence of a fixed stock of machinery labour adjustments both in terms of the number of employees and the hours worked have implications for the number of machines in use and their degree of capacity utilisation. Following Nickell (1978) we can comment on the utilisation of labour and capital across the business cycle based upon the outcome obtained in Figure 2.10. Let us examine one complete cycle, illustrated in Figure 2.11, in more detail.

Under the assumed conditions of no voluntary quits, a fixed price for output, single shift working with a fixed capital stock and no inventories, we can comment on features of the various phases of the cycle.[5] Initially up until the point in time t_0 output demand exceeds labour demand. All the machinery is being fully utilised (the number of machines in use is M_{max}) and the workforce E_b is employed for the maximum number of hours h^*. This maximum number of hours includes overtime and is conditioned by the increasing marginal cost of hours worked. Depicted in Figure 2.12, h^* represents the maximum number of hours for which it is profitable to operate the machinery in a single shift.

In other words h^* marks the point at which overtime payments become prohibitive. If output prices were allowed to vary then h^* would alter. If prices increased then the profitable maximum number of hours worked would increase, but with constant output prices h^* also remains stationary. Yet even with employment at its peak level

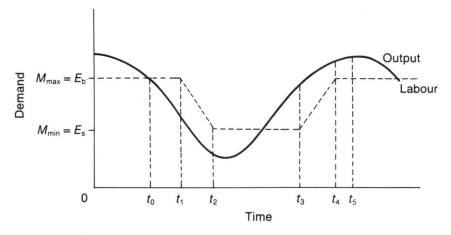

Figure 2.11

Source: Adapted from Nickell 1978, figures 2 and 4

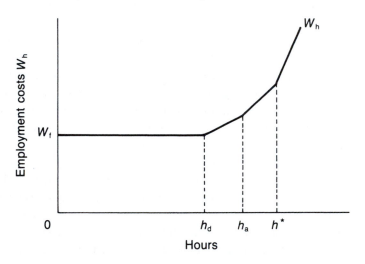

Figure 2.12

E_b, working to its maximum h^*, total output generated by $E_b h^*$ remains less than the demand for output until t_0. Hence the initial phase is a period of excess demand. During the period $t_0 - t_1$ all the machines are still in use but this time the output produced is sufficient to meet demand. Employment is still at E_b but the fall in output demand throughout the $t_0 - t_1$ period is being accommodated by a decline in the number of hours being worked from h^* at t_0 towards h_d at t_1. At point t_1 when the number of hours worked reaches h_d the firm begins to fire labour. The rate at which the firm lays off workers is determined by output demand. The process of shedding labour continues until t_2 when the workforce is kept constant at E_s and the number of machines in use is at its lowest, M_{min}. The worst of the recession impacts on the number of hours worked which could fall to anywhere between h_d and zero in Figure 2.12 with workers still receiving their fixed or basic wage W_f. This is the phenomenon of labour hoarding, where workers receive a wage related to the hours they are officially employed although they are only productively employed for a fraction of that time. As the cycle turns up the increasing demand for output is met by an increase in the hours being worked through h_d. When hours worked reach h_a at time t_3 then the firm begins to take on new workers. Hiring during $t_3 - t_4$ is being determined by demand for the final product and continues until all the machines are again in operation at M_{max}. During the period $t_4 - t_5$ all the machines are in use with the number of hours worked by the labour force increasing in response to the demand for output up to its maximum of h^*. Beyond t_5 the product market is again encountering excess demand that in an open economy would be satisfied by increasing imports whilst domestic employment does not rise beyond E_b.

It is evident from this description of the relationship between output, hours worked and employment that labour demand follows a lagged pro-cyclical pattern. But so must labour productivity, especially if it is measured as output per employee. Thus as output and hours worked fall during the downturn then so does labour productivity. Conversely as output rises due to an increase in hours worked rather than any corresponding increase in employment, productivity gains will be recorded. Such an effect would be compounded if the productivity of hours worked increased as working hours increased. Intuitively it is easy to imagine that as working hours increase the impact of set up time, mandatory breaks and clearing up would diminish on average. It might also be the case that greater capacity utilisation might yield the benefit of increasing capital productivity. An empirical study of twenty-eight UK manufacturing industries during the 1950s and 1960s conducted by Leslie and Wise (1980) suggested that if employment and capital were held constant each 10 per cent increase in hours worked would result in a 16.1 per cent increase in output. Although certain caveats regarding the interpretation of such econometric findings are necessary, especially considering the difference we have already noted between hours worked and hours paid for, combined with errors which may arise from standardising production functions across different industries, they do strongly suggest that differences in the productivity of hours worked are significant. This implies that unless firms can continually vary wages, the relationship between wages W and the marginal revenue productivity MRP of workers will not be a constant one. Indeed it is unlikely that W will equal MRP. Productivity will oscillate around the wage across the business cycle. During a slump conspicuous labour hoarding means that $W > $ MRP. During the upswing it is likely that, in spite of higher wage rates for overtime working, on balance $W < $ MRP.

AGGREGATE LABOUR DEMAND

In their influential study of unemployment Layard and Nickell (1985a) model aggregate labour demand N as follows. They begin by assuming that UK employers are imperfectly competitive firms who set prices P on a cost plus basis.[6] The capital stock K and the technical progress A it incorporates is taken as given within a single time period t. Obviously wages and product demand must feature in the model. Real wages W/P are couched in terms of the real cost per worker in units of gross domestic product (GDP), where P is the GDP deflator or price of value added in the production process. Product demand enters via the aggregate demand variable Q which measures deviations of total demand in the economy from a fluctuating full employment (of both labour and capital) level of aggregate demand. Using logs and incorporating time lags to capture non-linear aspects of employment Layard and Nickell's (1985a, equation 21, p. 66) labour demand function takes the following form.

$$\log N_t = a_0 + a_1 \log N_{t-1} + a_2 \log N_{t-2} + a_3 \log (W/P)t + a_4 Q \\ + a_5 \log A_t + (1 - a_1 - a_2) \log K_t$$

Econometric results from this multiple regression suggest a number of important features of labour demand. Firstly, the negative relationship between labour demand N and real wages W/P is established. The estimated value for the a_3 coefficient is -0.325, which clearly indicates that as real wages rise labour demand will fall. The long run responsiveness of labour demand to wage changes is calculated at -0.90, a finding that is consistent with a view about the greater elasticity of labour demand over longer time periods. Although we do not examine the impact of trade unions until Chapter 7, this parameter does indicate that if unions can raise workers' real product wages over time then employment might well be reduced. The study also finds a direct positive relationship between its aggregate demand variable Q and labour demand. Q has three component elements, which are as follows:

1) the change in the Government's fiscal stance relative to national income, $AD + AD_{-1}$, where AD is adjusted deficit/GDP;
2) a ratio measure of world prices against domestic prices for manufactured goods, $\log(P^*/P)$;
3) a measure of the movement of world trade from its longer-term trend performance (WT).

The estimated coefficients for all three components of aggregate demand were positive, clearly indicating that labour demand is susceptible to demand-side shocks caused by either benign or unfavourable shifts in Government deficit spending, international price competitiveness or world trade.

As an illustration of how the demand for labour fluctuates over time examine the data for employment presented in Table 2.2. Obviously employment does not exactly equate with labour demand but we may treat it as a rough proxy for showing the manner in which both the level and composition of the demand for labour changes across the economy over time. The period which the data in Table 2.2 covers includes two significant demand-side shocks, the 1979–83 recession when total employment fell by 9.5 per cent and the 1989–93 recession which saw employment fall by 4.6 per cent, as well as a sustained attempt led by Government to improve the supply-side of the labour market. More than 1.7 million fewer people were employed in manufacturing industries by 1983 than in 1979, an indication of the severity of the early 1980s recession. Almost 1.3 million manufacturing jobs were lost during the early 1990s

Table 2.2 UK employees in employment (thousands, seasonally adjusted)

	1979	1983	1986	1989	1993	1996	1999
Manufacturing	7,253	5,525	5,227	5,187	3,906	4,106	3,984
Other production*	1,960	1,692	1,534	1,548	1,162	1,110	1,308
Agriculture, forestry, fisheries	380	350	329	299	326	277	317
Service sector#	13,580	13,501	14,297	15,627	16,219	17,213	18,304
Industry total	22,173	20,067	21,387	22,661	21,613	22,706	23,913
Plus the self-employed	1,906	2,221	2,633	3,253	3,400	3,355	3,255

Sources: ONS, *Annual Abstract of Statistics*, 1992, 1999
Notes:
* Energy, water and construction
# Includes transport, communication, wholesale and retail trade

recession (1989–93). The boom during the remainder of the 1990s appears to have stabilised manufacturing employment at just below the 4 million mark, although the strength of sterling (£) on foreign exchange markets in 2000/2001 did lead to manufacturing job losses. Almost two-thirds of a million jobs were lost in the other production category, which includes energy and construction, during the 1980s and 1990s. The long-term trend decline in employment in the agricultural sector continued unabated during the 1980s but seems to have stabilised during the 1990s. Employment in the service sector grew by 1.85 million between 1979 and 1989 of which an impressive 1.13 million were employed in the late 1980s (1986 onwards) 'Lawson boom'. By 1999 more than 76 per cent of all UK employees worked in the service sector.

There has been a sharp increase in the number of self-employed in the UK during the 1980s but in spite of an increase during the early 1990s recession self-employment had fallen back to around 3.25 million by 1999. This rate of self-employment, which stood at almost 12 per cent of the employed population in 1999, is somewhat low compared to the USA (16 per cent) and Italy (26 per cent). Self-employment is a predominantly male phenomenon and is largely concentrated in the service sector and construction industry.[7]

Comparing the structure of labour demand internationally one finds a similar dominance of the service sector amongst the sample of industrialised economies in Table 2.3. Agriculture accounts for a very small share of employment in Germany, the UK and the US, it plays a larger role in France although this is declining over time, and a much more substantial role in the smaller economies of Ireland and Portugal. Manufacturing employment is clustered between 11 per cent and 15 per cent of the working age population in this sample. In Ireland and Portugal much of this manufacturing employment is as a result of inward investment by multinational corporations. The UK and the USA share the highest proportions in the five service categories in Table 2.3 from wholesale and retail trade through to public administration, education, health and social work. The dominance of the service sector employment in the UK is confirmed by data in Table 2.4.

Table 2.3 Sectoral distribution (%) of the working population, 1997

	France	Germany	Ireland	Italy	Portugal	UK	USA
Agriculture, forestry, Fishing	2.8	1.8	6.3	3.3	9.0	1.3	1.9
Mining/quarrying	0.1	0.4	0.3	0.2	0.2	0.3	0.4
Manufacturing	11.3	14.7	11.1	11.5	14.1	13.3	11.9
Other production and construction	4.6	6.3	5.2	4.5	6.6	5.5	5.4
Wholesale/retail trade	8.1	8.8	8.2	8.6	9.7	11.0	12.4
Transport and communication	3.8	3.3	2.7	2.8	2.6	4.6	4.1
Financial services	1.9	2.2	2.1	1.7	1.8	3.1	3.4
Business services real estate	5.2	4.3	3.6	2.8	3.3	7.0	7.7
Public Admin., education health, social services	16.4	14.5	11.8	10.8	12.2	17.3	17.5
Other services	6.0	5.3	6.6	5.0	8.0	7.5	9.4
Total employment	60.1	61.8	57.8	51.3	67.5	70.8	74.0

Source: *Employment in Europe*, 1999

Table 2.4 Civilian employment in the UK, occupational distribution (%), 1961–99

	1961	1981	1991	1999
Professionals/managerial	11.4	26.9	24.0	27.2
Clerical	13.0	16.5	8.8	10.2
Sales workers	9.7	5.9	15.9	15.1
Service workers	10.5	15.0	16.6	18.7
Agricultural	4.3	1.5	2.2	1.5
Production workers	49.6	33.4	31.9	27.1
Not classified	1.6	0.9	0.7	0.2
Total (millions)	23.44	24.26	26.40	27.44

Source: ILO, *Yearbook of Labour Statistics*, various years

The decline in the proportion of production workers was continual during 1961–99. By the end of the period a slightly larger share of employment was accounted for by the professional and management category than that of production workers. The rise in the proportion of service workers is quite clear. Employment in retailing boomed in the 1980s attaining a 15 per cent share with over 4 million sales workers.

It is interesting to compare the occupational distribution of employment in the UK with the situation elsewhere. Table 2.5 compares the UK with the USA and Ireland. Ireland has a much larger share of employment accounted for by agriculture than either the UK or the USA. In the USA in 1999 over one-third of employees were professionals/managers compared to just over one-quarter in the UK and Ireland. Only in Ireland do production workers make up a bigger share of employment than the first occupational category in Table 2.5.

Table 2.5   Occupational distribution of civilian employment (%), 1999

	UK	Ireland	USA
Professionals/managerial	27.2	26.5	33.6
Clerical	10.2	6.5	13.8
Sales workers	15.1	13.5	12.1
Service workers	18.7	14.1	13.4
Agricultural	1.5	7.7	2.6
Production workers	27.1	31.9	24.5
Not classified	0.2	0.0	0.0
Total (millions)	27.4	1.6	133.5

Source: ILO, *Yearbook of Labour Statistics*, 2000

Changes in the structure of employment have been incorporated into wider explanations of the growth and development of economies. Of particular relevance given the rapid and substantial reduction in the manufacturing sector employment and production worker occupation experienced in the UK during the early 1980s and again in the early 1990s is the deindustrialisation thesis. We shall discuss the process of deindustrialisation coupled with the impact of international trade and globalisation on labour markets in Chapter 11.

CASE STUDY – REGULATION AND LABOUR DEMAND

There is an extensive literature discussing the relationship between labour market regulation and unemployment (see Chapters 8 and 10 for more details). A key link between regulation and unemployment is the effect of that regulation on employers' willingness to take on workers, namely how labour market regulation will impact on labour demand. The following extract from the UK newspaper *The Guardian* (18/02/2002) illustrates the fears of the employers' organisation – the Confederation of British Industry – about proposals to extend the regulation of temporary workers (temps) supplied by private sector employment agencies in the EU.

Business Concern Over Plans for Temp Workers' Rights
The Confederation of British Industry (CBI) today expressed alarm at EU proposals to extend equal pay and employment rights to agency workers.

   The CBI director general, Digby Jones, has written to Romano Prodi, president of the European commission, arguing that current EU draft proposals are 'likely to be very damaging to the UK labour market'. Mr Jones was responding to EU proposals that would give temps rights to the same pay, holidays, health insurance, share schemes and pensions as long-term workers doing similar jobs.

More than 1 million people are employed as temps in Britain, which has the biggest agency workforce in the EU. Many secretaries, teachers, nurses, engineers and catering staff work as temps. The draft EU directive . . . takes in workers employed by agencies, who are not covered by earlier legislation on fixed term employees.

'It's depressing that Europe decides it's going to try and bring everyone down to some sort of low common denominator . . . It's socialism coming straight out of Brussels,' Mr Jones said. Instead of the EU proposals, the CBI favours plans for a non-discrimination clause based on a comparison with another agency worker from the same agency. This would ensure, the CBI argues, that there was no discrimination of workers working for the same employer.

Pointing out that agency work is often a route into employment for young people and the long-term unemployed, the CBI says that 40 per cent of new agency workers are in long-term employment within one year of starting their first assignment. 'By efficiently matching labour supply to demand', the CBI says 'agency work plays an invaluable role in helping companies cover absences, fill skill gaps and meet temporary upturns in demand'. In his letter to Mr Prodi, Mr Jones writes that the consequence of the draft directive is that agency workers would require equal treatment with companies' permanent employees. 'This is not the case at present in the UK, and is impractical here. Employers would respond by reducing their use of agency workers, to the disadvantage of all concerned,' he argues.

If Britain tries to water down the directive, it could find itself the odd man out in the EU. Some member states, including Spain, France and Italy, already have stringent legislation restricting the use of agency labour. Germany and the Netherlands are more flexible, but agencies in these countries have to reach agreements at a national level with trade unions. The Trade Union Congress (TUC) favours 'robust' legislation and opposes a watering down of the directive that would render it meaningless.

The CBI are clearly linking the EU proposals with heavily regulated socialism and contrasting this with the valuable and efficient job done by employment agencies.

Note that the CBI wants employment agencies to regulate themselves by ensuring the internal consistency of their own employment practices.

The CBI are suggesting that a negative relationship exists between labour market regulation and labour demand. The case study makes it clear that in resisting the proposed increase in regulation, the CBI will find very little support coming from other countries in the EU nor will it get the support of organised labour (the TUC) in the UK.

PRODUCTIVITY

Having established the strong theoretical relationship between labour demand, productivity and real wages we are now able to analyse the productivity performance of the UK. The UK's record on labour productivity both relatively (over time) and comparatively (across countries) is set out in Table 2.6. The data looks at output per worker, therefore it provides some measure of every employee's changing contribution to general economic growth. Obviously the contributions of capital investment, technical progress, knowledge and skill acquisition are also being captured in an unattributable manner in this data.

Generally the period from 1950 to 1973 saw more rapid productivity growth. The 1970s witnessed a productivity growth slowdown after 1973 associated with the problems of coming to terms with higher fuel prices. Although the UK shortens the productivity growth lead of both France and Germany during the 1973–2000 period, the data clearly shows that output per worker was growing more slowly in the UK than in France or Germany throughout 1950–2000. Productivity growth that is faster in the UK than in the USA helps to close the large productivity gap with the USA. The rapid slowdown in German productivity growth is associated with the unification of East and West Germany in 1990. Although the data in Table 2.6 mainly refers to West Germany, the impact of unification is revealed by the following examination of German productivity growth.

| 1981–1990 | 1.86% |
| 1991–2000 | −0.05% |

Annual average productivity growth slowed during the decade after unification compared to the previous ten-year period. This is primarily due to a −14.08 per cent performance in 1991, the first full year following unification.

Figure 2.13 splits the total economy UK labour productivity into the two main sectors, manufacturing and services. Now we can clearly see from this figure that from about the end of 1981 until 1995 labour productivity in the manufacturing sector has grown more rapidly that that of the service sector. The total economy labour productivity line is a weighted average of the two sectors. During 1995–8 manufacturing labour productivity appears to have stalled, total economy productivity only grew

Table 2.6 Labour productivity growth (output per worker, percentage, per annum)

	1950–1973	1973–2000
UK	2.99	2.14
France	4.62	2.63 (1999)
Germany	5.18	2.36
USA	2.34	1.06

Sources: O'Mahony 1999; NIER 2001

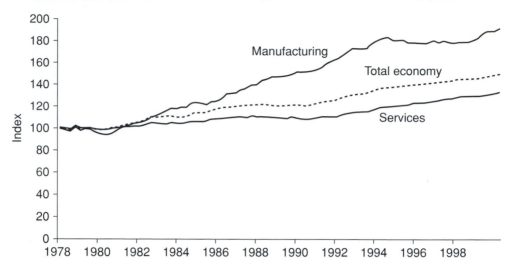

Figure 2.13   UK productivity index by sector (1978 Q3 to 2000 Q2)

Source: ONS
Notes: Productivity is measured as output per worker, 1978 Q3 = 100.

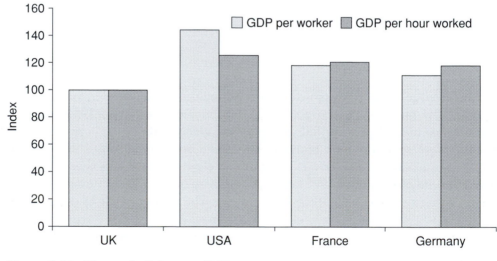

Figure 2.14   The productivity gap, 1999

Source: OECD
Note: UK = 100.

because of increasing labour efficiency in the service sector. UK manufacturing labour productivity growth resumed in 1999 and the first half of 2000. Although the UK's comparative labour productivity growth appears to have improved in more recent years there still exists a substantial gap between the productivity levels of the UK and its major comparator countries. Figure 2.14 shows UK labour productivity levels that

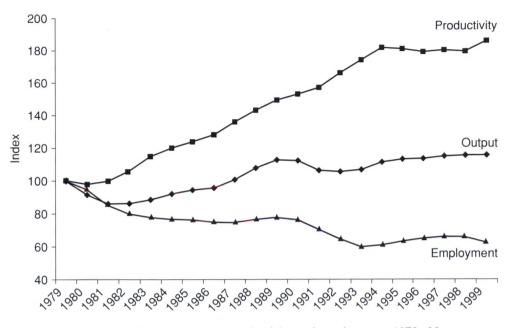

Figure 2.15 UK manufacturing output, productivity and employment, 1979–99

Source: ONS, Monthly Digest of Statistics, December 1982–2000

were lower in 1999 than in Germany, France and the USA in ascending order, whether measured by output per worker or output per hour worked.

From this comparison we can tell that USA workers are some 45 per cent more productive than UK workers but that they work longer hours than British workers. It is worth contemplating the role productivity has played in the recovery of UK manufacturing output during the 1980s and 1990s. From 1979 manufacturing output falls and it is not until 1987 that the 1979 level of output is re-established. Figure 2.15 demonstrates that the revival of manufacturing output during the 1980s was facilitated by productivity gains rather than by any recovery in manufacturing employment. After 1990 manufacturing output falls with the 1990 level of output being regained in 1994, thereafter manufacturing output grows very slowly. The rise in manufacturing output between 1995 and 1998 is being driven by slight employment growth as productivity remains virtually unchanged during that period.

Figure 2.15 should not be taken to mean that productivity growth displaces employment in a static manner. Indeed the effect should be the reverse based upon the following reasoning within a dynamic framework. Productivity growth should reduce average costs which, if passed on as price reductions should increase demand which in turn should encourage the firm to expand thereby increasing employment. Even if consumers do not receive the full benefit of greater production efficiency in the form of lower prices the firm will benefit from the increased profitability of its activity, which should induce a tendency towards greater investment and thus increasing

Table 2.7   Labour Productivity (as % of West Germany), 1997

Austria	90.9
Belgium	97.6
Finland	81.4
France	95.3
Germany	92.9
(West)	100.0
(East)	60.4
Ireland	69.5
Italy	85.3
Netherlands	85.4
Portugal	34.5
Spain	62.0
UK	71.7

Source: OECD 1998, *Quarterly National Accounts, Main Economic Indicators*

employment. In both cases as long as productivity gains are not completely translated into pay increases (for either managers or workers) they provide an incentive for employment to expand. In an open economy differential productivity performance will play an important role in determining international competitiveness. Indeed the Ricardian trade theory of 'comparative advantage' is based upon such differential productivity being reflected in differing relative prices across countries thereby accounting for patterns of international specialisation and trade. This will be especially important in a free trade environment; given that the UK is in a free trade area, the EU, it would be interesting to look at labour productivity in the EU in more detail. Data on labour productivity in most EU countries is contained in Table 2.7.

Among the EU countries in Table 2.7 West Germany had the highest labour productivity level in 1997. There were substantial productivity differences within the EU; there was an almost 30 percentage point productivity gap between the UK and West Germany. We can also see that the poor productivity performance of the former East Germany pulls down the united Germany's overall productivity yet this still remains more than 20 percentage points above that of the UK. Given the wide disparity of labour productivity levels between parts of the free trading EU, labour cost levels should reflect that disparity. Labour costs will mainly consist of wages but will also include employment taxes that firms have to pay, such as National Insurance in the UK. Indeed when we come to examine the labour cost levels of the same set of countries we find that lower labour costs than those of West Germany more than compensate for lower productivity in Austria, Italy and the UK. Figure 2.16 plots the productivity levels from Table 2.7 with comparative labour cost levels.

Countries above the 45° line in Figure 2.16, including former East Germany, have higher unit labour costs than West Germany which means than they will be at a labour cost competitive disadvantage: Whereas countries below the diagonal line will enjoy a competitive advantage, in the form of lower unit labour costs, over West Germany.

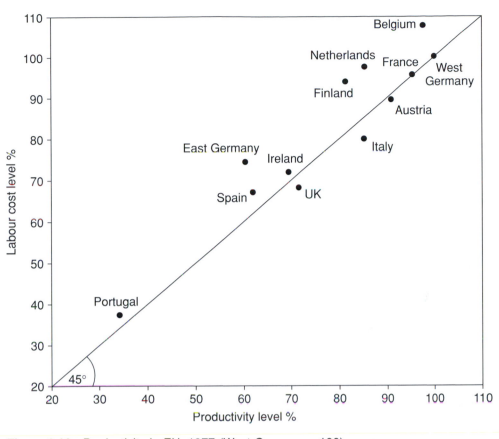

Figure 2.16 Productivity in EU, 1977 (West Germany = 100)

Source: Siebert 1998, figure 2, p. 7
Note: Countries above 45° line have higher unit labour costs than West Germany.

Productivity levels will vary from sector to sector and from industry to industry. The following extract from Milner (2001) in the *Guardian* (29/6/01) newspaper reveals that the two most productive car plants in 2000 were in the UK.

> Nissan's Sunderland factory is Europe's most efficient car manufacturer . . . The Sunderland plant again came top in a productivity analysis, leaving its nearest rival, the Toyota plant in Burnaston, Derbyshire, far behind. Productivity last year was 101 cars per employee, close to its own European record of 105 set in 1998 and well ahead of Burnaston's 86, according to World Market Research Centre's annual report on automotive productivity. Sunderland has a young, well-motivated, flexible, workforce using very lean Japanese manufacturing methods . . . The Japanese have always had a lead in designing cars which are easier to build . . . Ford and General Motors plants in Germany took third and fourth slots in the analysis, while Renault's plant in Slovenia made its debut . . . at number 10, with 73 cars per employee. Overall, Renault plants took six of the

top 15 places. The worst performing plant in the survey was Volkswagen's German factory at Emden, which makes the Passat model, with productivity of 27 cars per employee – less than half the European average of 58.3 cars. The report again sees a British plant competing with the top global performers . . . A record of 165 cars per employee was set by Daewoo's plant, Changwon, in South Korea in 1998 . . . what this year's index also shows is that intense competition is accelerating the adoption of new working practices to boost quality and efficiency.

The fact that UK car plants exhibit leading levels of productivity in the late 1990s and early 2000s is an aspect of a marked turnaround in the productivity experience of the UK since 1980. In his influential study Muellbauer (1986) identifies five hypotheses, which have been advanced to account for the increase in labour productivity (output per employee) experienced by UK manufacturing (including car production) since the end of 1980. These are as follows.

1) The 'industrial relations hypothesis' in which rising unemployment and the changes in trade union legislation, especially during the first half of the 1980s shifted the balance of power in the workplace in the employers' favour, leaving employees less able to resist productivity enhancing changes in working practices and the introduction of new technology. While this gives an indirect influence to unemployment, there is a logical problem inherent in relying on rising unemployment to secure productivity gains, since it cannot explain simultaneous long-run productivity and employment gains. In the extreme, unemployment has to continue rising for productivity to rise continuously, which could lead to the absurd result that employment would have to tend towards zero. With regard to unions this hypothesis presumes that their activities are unambiguously detrimental to productivity, a view about which there are mixed opinions and contradictory empirical findings (see Chapter 7 for a discussion of the relationship between trade union power and productivity).

2) The 'microchip hypothesis' proposes that technological advances have opened up the possibility of faster productivity growth which should endure. In manufacturing the use of computers to operate machine tools and to assist in the design stage would be examples of microchip technology aiding a more productive workforce. For this explanation to hold it is not enough to assert that new technology is 'better' than that which it replaces. One must demonstrate that the technological advances being made use of in the 1980s represent a greater improvement on 1970s technology than did the 1970s advances on the technology of the 1960s. Or, failing that, one must show that new technologies were being introduced at a faster rate in the 1980s than hitherto.

3) The 'shedding of the below-average hypothesis' also known as the 'batting average' hypothesis, suggests that in the main it has been the less productive workers who have been made redundant during the early 1980s recession, thereby improving the average quality of the remaining workforce. The same fate is said to have befallen less effective managements and the less efficient components of the cap-

ital stock. In order for this to have been the case one must be able to identify a movement within manufacturing away from below-average firms towards above-average ones. Even if one could detect such a redistribution of manufacturing it would only represent a one-off boost for measured productivity. Blackaby and Hunt (1989) find that the dominant effect on labour productivity growth was not a redistribution of manufacturing activity but a growth of productivity within sub-sectors of manufacturing activity. The acceleration in the growth in labour productivity during the 1980s is overwhelmingly due to improvements within sectors rather than any 'batting average' effects arising as a consequence of a redistribution of manufacturing employment. As they conclude, 'the hypothesis that the manufacturing productivity 'miracle' was . . . a re-allocation of resources away from low- to high-productivity sectors is rejected' (p. 129). However, Disney *et al.* (2000) estimate that about 50 per cent of the productivity growth in British manufacturing between 1980 and 1992 came about due to low productivity plants closing and new high productivity plants entering an industry – the rest was due to existing plants steadily improving productivity.

4) The 'capital scrapping and utilisation hypothesis' suggests that the growth in output per head is a consequence of a reduction in the rate at which equipment has been scrapped and its more intensive use after 1981. This follows a period in the previous decade (1973–9) when capital scrapping rose and when plant and machinery were used less intensively, phenomena associated with the rise in energy costs and recession during the mid-1970s.

5) the 'labour utilisation hypothesis' applies the point made in Chapter 2 that in a dynamic model of labour demand changes in employment will lag behind and will not fully reflect variations in product demand. The argument being that because of adjustment costs, particularly in this context firing costs, the shedding of labour initially lagged behind the collapse in manufacturing output during 1979–80. This is implied by the fall in output per head discernible during 1979 and 1980 in Figure 2.15, which is a symptom of labour hoarding. Then as output stabilises and employment continues to decline as labour demand 'catches up' with product demand one notices a short term increase in labour productivity.

Muellbauer's own empirical study favours the 'capital scrapping and utilisation' hypothesis as an explanation of UK manufacturing productivity performance. He accounts for the fall in productivity during the 1970s, particularly from the beginning of 1973, as the result of

a combination of capital scrapping not recorded in the official figures, lower utilisation of capital not captured by the labour utilisation measure and possibly the switch to older vintages of capital.

(1986, p. xiv)

This suggests that during the 1973–80 period UK manufacturers were scrapping plant and machinery at a faster rate than was supposed at the time. In the extreme,

Muellbauer indicates that actual capital retirement may have exceeded the official figures by four times between 1973 and 1979 and by a massive five-fold in 1979–80. If so then a great deal of inefficient and unprofitable capital equipment had been disposed of before the 1980–1 'shake out' in manufacturing output and employment. After the 'shake out' as capital utilisation rises and scrapping falls below the officially recorded rate, measured total factor productivity growth accelerates. Another consequence of such an explanation of events is that the growth in capital stock during the 1980s is faster than the official data suggests, in order to compensate for the greater scrapping of the 1970s. Thus during the 1980s labour has more capital to work with than the official data implies because it assumes retirements of machines which may have already been scrapped.

The spur for the hypothesised surge in capital scrapping and fall in capital utilisation in the 1970s is the rise in intermediate input prices, including the OPEC-inspired energy price shocks, plus the severe recession of the mid-1970s. The fact that energy price increases were not confined to the UKs but were felt throughout the industrialised world can be used to imply that a similar phenomenon was at work in other countries. Berndt and Wood (1986) clearly demonstrate that capital utilisation in the USA fell following the oil price shocks, thereby providing some corroborating evidence for Muellbauer's explanation.

Oulton (1990) presents a different explanation, which is couched in terms of a variant of the 'industrial relations' hypothesis. This emphasises the shock effect of the early 1980s labour 'shake out' and the severe recession on workers and management. The notion that the recession shocked workers and managers into changing their attitudes in a manner that was more conducive to productivity growth, is explored empirically for the period 1971–86 using a sample of 93 manufacturing industries. The shock variable is taken to be the reduction in employment experienced by the sample industries during 1979–81. The impact of this shock is defined as the change in productivity (net output per employee, in constant prices) in the post-shock period compared with that in the pre-shock period.

Having reassured us that the post-shock rise in productivity was not just a simple cyclical reaction to a fall in employment during a recession, Oulton identifies the following causal factors: the 1980–1 employment shock itself; the price of intermediate inputs, including oil price effects; trade unions; plant size; but not investment and capital scrapping. As Oulton observes his finding concerning the insignificance of investment and capital scrapping should not be interpreted as meaning

> that investment and scrapping, the factors emphasised by the vintage capital model, are unimportant, only that they have not varied sufficiently over time or between industries to explain the variation in productivity growth.
>
> (1990, p. 81)

The status of the employment shock variable is somewhat ambiguous, given that it does not add markedly to the explanatory power of this model as measured by R^2 rising from 0.62 to 0.63 when it is included. The shock variable's significance is sensitive to the presence of the model's relative wage variables, becoming insignificant when they are included.[8] The role of rising intermediate input prices was found to be significant in reducing productivity. However, they do not tell the whole story of the 1970s productivity slowdown because of the small magnitude of the coefficients for the intermediate input variables. To illustrate this point, Oulton calculates that even if intermediate inputs accounted for half of total production costs, a doubling of such input prices would lead only to a 1.4 per cent fall in productivity after a lag of one year. Having ruled out investment and capital scrapping and having then denied intermediate input prices or the employment shock dominant roles in the productivity story this leaves trade union power and plant size, the proxy variables for industrial relations, as important causal factors. Taking trade union activity first, this is approached in this particular study by looking at the proportion of male manual workers covered by collectively bargained agreements. This is likely to only partially reflect trade union power because one would expect trade unions to have a significant effect on relative wages, for well-founded theoretical and empirical reasons which are explained in Chapter 7. Even so, Oulton is able to report that during the whole 1972–86 period, 'unionisation has reduced productivity growth' (1990: 84). To place the importance of unionisation in perspective, the productivity growth rates during the first half of the 1980s are, on average about 1.5 percentage points higher because of the decline in the adverse effect of trade unions in that period compared to the 1970s.

The plant size variables are trying to capture industrial relations effects based upon the assumption that industrial relations tend to be worse in large plants where the workforce may be represented by a larger number of unions. Oulton finds that productivity growth improves most in large plants after 1982. He also reports a not unrelated finding that productivity improves most during the 1980s in the most heavily unionised firms. Whilst these findings are consistent with the industrial relations hypothesis, they do contradict other studies which place less emphasis on the impact of trade unions on the 1970s productivity slowdown. Bean and Symons (1989) report that unionised industries experience the fastest growth in total factor productivity not only during 1980–6 but between 1973 and 1979 as well. According to Gregg et al. (1991) there appear to have been two differential productivity bursts favouring unionised firms during the 1980s, one in 1981–4 and the other in 1988–9. One might wish to question the credit Oulton allocates to the Thatcher Government's trade union reforms, given that the peak year for manufacturing labour productivity growth was 1983, that is before the 1984 showdown strike with the coal miners and the Acts (1984, 1988) which imposed pre-strike ballots and outlawed union action to enforce closed shop arrangements on employers and workers. As Brown and Wadhwani (1990) state, 'it is implausible that employers were stimulated to manage their labour better as a result of the altered legal circumstances of trade unions' (p. 33).

Yet even if Oulton is right to ascribe significant credit for improved productivity during the 1980s to the Thatcher Governments trade union reforms, the crucial question to be answered is how can such gains from a supply-side programme, designed to obtain increased output from existing inputs, be improved upon? After all productivity

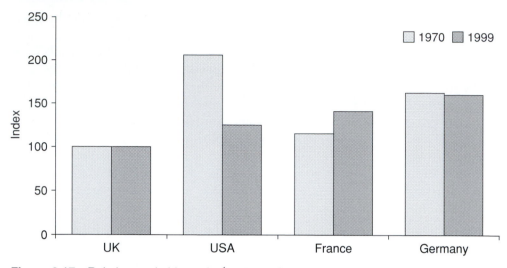

Figure 2.17   Relative capital intensity,[1] 1970 and 1999
Source: NIESR (O'Mahony 2000)
Note: 1 Measured as capital per hour worked, UK = 100.

growth has not accelerated because of any profound increase in capital per head in the UK. As Figure 2.17 shows, the amount of capital each worker in the UK has is much lower than in the USA, France or Germany.

Although there has been some narrowing of the capital intensity gap between the USA and the UK between 1970 and 1999, the gap has widened with France and remained virtually unchanged with Germany. In 1999 the USA had 25 per cent more capital per worker than the UK, France 40 per cent, and Germany some 60 per cent more. Business investment in the UK was low during the early 1980s accounting for less than 10 per cent of GDP during 1979–83, according to OECD data, only reaching 11 per cent by 1987. Rapid year on year investment growth was recorded in 1988 and 1989 taking the business investment share to over 12 per cent of GDP. The early 1990s recession saw investment tail off to around 11 per cent of GDP in 1993 and 1994. However, an investment boom after 1995 took the investment share up to 15 per cent by 1999. This compared to the nearly 14 per cent share of USA GDP, 13 per cent for Germany and 12 per cent for France. Research and development (R and D) activity should be the precursor of technical progress in the production process. Haskel and Kay (1990) report that between 1978 and 1983 R and D expenditure in the UK was roughly constant, rising modestly by around 10 per cent between 1983 and 1985. This would appear to rule out any substantial contribution by R and D activity to the 1980s productivity miracle. In the past, the UK has devoted slightly less of a share of economic activity to R and D than its major competitors. However, the data in Table 2.8 characterises the 1990s as a decade of declining R and D spending as a share of GDP in the UK.

This is not to say that there is no connection between such activity and productivity. Intuitively one would expect R and D to precede productivity gains, yet the

Table 2.8 Research and development (R and D) expenditure (% GDP), 1985–99

	1985	1990	1995	1999
UK	2.2	2.2	2.0	1.8
USA	2.9	2.8	2.6	2.9
France	2.3	2.4	2.3	2.2
Germany	2.7	2.8	2.3	2.3
Japan	2.6	2.9	2.8	2.9

Source: OECD

causation may flow in the opposite direction, with R and D spending increasing only after productivity and profitability rises. Yet both in terms of scale and timing R and D activity did not make a significant contribution to faster productivity growth during the 1980s and 1990s.

One should not ignore product market effects on labour productivity, independent of the changing level of demand. It may well be that the market power of firms influences productivity. Nickell *et al.* (1991) report interesting comparisons in the productivity performance of UK companies when categorised by their market share and their financial position. With regard to market structure they find that firms with high (i.e., above the sample median) market shares record faster rates of labour productivity growth than those with low market shares.

When it comes to financial considerations they find that, 'companies with higher borrowing ratios (a higher proportion of debt relative to equity) exhibit both higher levels of productivity and higher rates of productivity growth' (p. 22). Such a finding is consistent with the view that firms which borrow to expand experience improvements in productivity as they do so. Or it could be that the existence of significant debt imposes a greater sense of discipline upon the firm towards increasing effort and reducing slack in its activities. This 'discipline of debt' aspect of productivity becomes more important during periods of either rising real interest rates, or of sustained high real interest rates, such as mid-1988 to 1992 in the UK. Under such circumstances the relationship between efficiency and financial viability is brought into much sharper focus.

Nickell and van Reenen (2000) conclude their investigation into productivity in the UK by stating that

> over the period from 1970, Britain has improved its relative productivity per-
> formance, but there remains a significant market sector productivity gap . . . Much
> of the gap between Britain and Continental Europe is down to lower levels of
> capital intensity and skill. However, between Britain and the USA there re-
> mains a significant gap even if these are taken into account. These gaps cover all
> sectors and reflect . . . an inability to absorb best-practice technology and methods
> into wide swathes of the market sector.
>
> (p. 32)

Table 2.9 UK and USA productivity growth (%), 1996–2000, (GDP per person employed)

	UK	USA
1996	1.57	2.17
1997	1.64	2.03
1998	0.95	2.84
1999	1.51	2.67
2000	2.50	3.50

Source: NIER 2001

An interesting aspect of recent USA productivity performance has been the possibility of there being a new economy based upon information and communications technology (ICT). Certainly US investment in ICT equipment grew by almost 40 per cent between 1996 and 1999. Over the same period we can see from the data in Table 2.9 that USA productivity growth accelerated at a faster pace than in the UK. This may reflect the benefits of rapid productivity growth in the ICT sector itself due to technological progress and strong demand for ICT equipment. The rapid dissemination of ICT in the USA economy may have allowed more rapid adaptation of production and management processes, which have boosted labour productivity throughout the economy by the adoption of best-practice techniques. It may be that the severe slowdown of the ICT sector, and the more general recession of the USA economy in 2001, question the long-term link between ICT growth and more general productivity growth.

The productivity story is a complex and multifaceted one in which no single explanation for differential productivity performance dominates the discussion. We need to strive to understand productivity because of its importance for labour demand and employment and more general economic performance.

LABOUR DEMAND AND PRODUCTIVITY – SUMMARY

Our microeconomic analysis of the demand for labour stressed

- the importance of diminishing marginal returns to labour in the short-run production function
- the relationship between labour productivity and the firms demand for labour
- the inverse relationship between real wages and labour demand
- that in labour market equilibrium, wages equal marginal revenue productivity
- that taking hiring and firing costs into account enhanced our understanding of dynamic labour demand across the business cycle

At the aggregate level

- the labour market was placed into a general equilibrium context and
- we examined Layard and Nickell's (1985a) econometric labour demand function

These gave us some feel for the factors that might influence the level and nature of labour demand in an economy over time. For the UK we particularly noted

- a substantial and rapid decline in manufacturing employment between 1979 and 1983 and again between 1989 and 1993, and
- this will be linked to a later analysis (Chapter 11) of deindustrialisation in mature economies

Recognising the importance of productivity with regard to labour demand, we assessed the UK's productivity performance

- UK productivity growth during the 1980s was undoubtedly more rapid than during the 1970s
- the UK productivity growth performance improved compared to other OECD countries in the 1980s
- manufacturing labour productivity growth was significantly faster than service sector growth
- manufacturing labour productivity growth was faster in the 1980s than the 1990s

Analysing the causes of an improved productivity performance we found

- that Muellbauer (1986) identifies factors associated with capital measurement and utilisation
- Oulton (1990) argues in favour of an explanation based on changed industrial relations brought about by the severity of the early 1980s recession and restrictive trade union legislation
- Nickell *et al.* (1991) point out that productivity performance is not divorced from market structure, unionisation and firms' financial circumstances
- that productivity gaps with other countries persist and may be related to differences in capital investment, R and D investment and skill (see Chapter 5)
- US productivity may have been driven by best-practice linked to information and communications technology

After examining the various arguments concerning productivity performance, we concluded that no single explanation appears to guarantee accelerated productivity growth enduring.

LABOUR DEMAND AND PRODUCTIVITY – QUESTIONS FOR DISCUSSION

1) Explain the theoretical link between labour productivity and labour demand.
2) What is the general relationship between real wages and labour demand? How well established is this relationship empirically?
3) In what ways does the incorporation of adjustment costs enhance our understanding of how labour demand fluctuates during business cycles?
4) What do Tables 2.2, 2.3 and 2.4 tell us about the level and nature of labour demand in the UK during the 1980s and 1990s?
5) Why with faster productivity growth during the 1980s is UK labour less productive than that of the USA, France, and Germany?
6) Explain how the UK can be labour-cost competitive with the likes of Belgium and France even though it has lower levels of labour productivity?
7) Explain the arguments for and against an explanation of UK labour productivity growth based on the 'industrial relations hypothesis'.
8) What is capital intensity and how will it affect productivity?
9) It what ways does Research and Development (R and D) spending enter into a discussion of comparative productivity performance?

SELECTED READINGS

Baily, M. and Solow, R. (2001) 'International Productivity Comparisons Built From the Firm Level', *Journal of Economic Perspectives*, 15 (3): 151–72.
Hamermesh, D. (1986) 'The Demand for Labour in the Long Run', in O. Ashenfelter and R. Layard (eds) *Handbook of Labour Economics*, Volume 1, Amsterdam: North Holland.
Hamermesh, D. (1993) *Labour Demand*, Princeton: Princeton University Press.

3

Wage determination and inequality

INTRODUCTION

Bringing together the insights of the previous two chapters we are now in a position to understand how the labour market forces of supply and demand determine the price of labour, the wage. We will also examine the process of labour market adjustment to changes in supply and demand. We will explain what compensating wage differentials are. We will also examine the phenomenon of wage inequality, how it has developed over time and how the situation in the UK compares to other countries. Finally we will assess the significance of minimum wage legislation on the labour market.

THE SIMPLE LABOUR MARKET

By now the neoclassical economists view of the labour market should be clear. The demand for labour is roughly equivalent to its marginal productivity. With labour demand responding to changes in wages and to shifts in demand for firms' products tempered by the existence of non-trivial adjustment costs, supply is determined by the disutility of work relative to the utility of the wages offered. Labour demand is a function of pre-tax real wages whereas labour supply responds to post-income tax real wages. Between them these forces of supply and demand, illustrated in Figure 3.1, establish the market-clearing wage W^*. In such an equilibrium there is no involuntary unemployment because everyone who wants a job at W^* has one.

From this equilibrium position changes can be incorporated to demonstrate the smooth functioning of the labour market. Consider the example contained in Figure 3.2, where improved labour productivity or an increase in demand for goods would increase the demand for labour from D to D_1 in Figure 3.2 (a). Wages would rise to

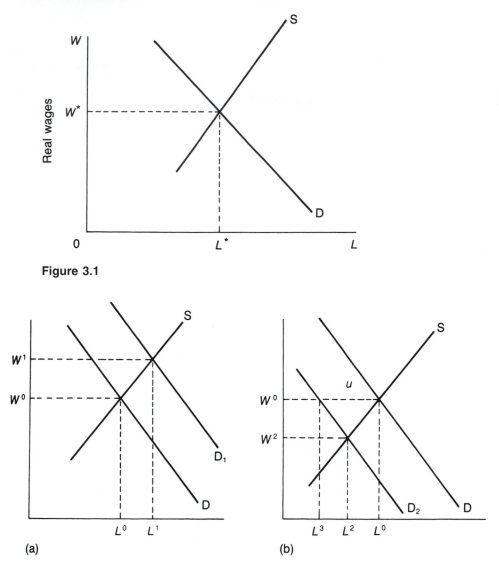

Figure 3.1

(a)

(b)

Figure 3.2

W^1. Workers would increase the hours they were prepared to supply or economically inactive persons would enter the labour market to expand labour supply until employment reached L^1.

Conversely if productivity or the demand for final output fell (Figure 3.2 (b)) then employers might wish to respond by reducing wages. At lower wage rates W^2, workers would contract the number of hours they were prepared to work as, at the margin, the disutility of some work exceeded the utility of income. Others would withdraw from the labour force altogether. Hence supply would contract as real wage rates fell until employment reached L^2.

In this labour market scenario nobody is involuntarily unemployed. Market imperfections like the existence of trade unions could be shown graphically to distort the operation of the market. Take the case of Figure 3.2(b) again. If union power was used to hold wage rates in real terms at W^0 when the market conditions and employers wished to reduce them to W^2, the result would be unemployment U of a scale $L^0 - L^3$. Note that employment, because of union resistance, is at L^3, lower than in a properly functioning labour market, which would settle upon L^2. Such unemployment, known as classical unemployment, is regarded as voluntary and occurs because real wages are too high, a situation that would not exist in a smoothly functioning labour market.

THE LABOUR MARKET AND THE PRODUCT MARKET

The crucial assumption behind the notion of a smoothly functioning labour market is that both wages and prices are flexible in their response to changing market conditions. But are they? Begg (1982) makes the point that

> Keynes regarded it as self-evident that the transaction costs of negotiating wage changes outweigh the transaction costs of changing prices. It is this asymmetry in real transactions costs which generate asymmetric wage and price behaviour.
>
> (p. 154)

This asymmetry could lead to a situation where the goods market traded away from its equilibrium with involuntary unemployment arising in the labour market. Such an outcome is in marked contrast to the Walrasian notion of General Equilibrium where an economy was thought to be able to experience simultaneous market clearing in all product and factor markets. This interplay between product markets and the particular factor market that we are interested in, that of labour, is demonstrated in Figure 3.3. The diagrammatic schema, abstracted from Sinclair (1987), may at first glance appear a little daunting. However, the strength of this form of explanation is that we can readily compare the general equilibrium position with the Keynesian scenario to which Begg (1982) referred.

Beginning with the product market in the top right hand quadrant of Figure 3.3 we have the conventionally sloped market forces of consumers' demand and producers' supply determining an equilibrium combination of price p_0 and quantity q_0 of the product. The production function in the bottom right hand quadrant provides the means to generate that product supply in the short run. Capital K is assumed fixed and the function incorporates diminishing marginal returns to the increasing use of the variable factor labour L. Under these production conditions an L_0 amount of labour is needed to produce a q_0 quantity of the product.

Figure 3.3 underlines the derived nature of labour demand D_L which is to be found in the bottom left hand quadrant. Labour demand is conventionally sloped to reflect the by now familiar inverse relationship between real wages W/P and employers' willingness to take on workers. We assume a fixed supply of labour L_s mainly for reasons of simplicity but it also reflects, in an extreme form, the short-run inelasticity of labour

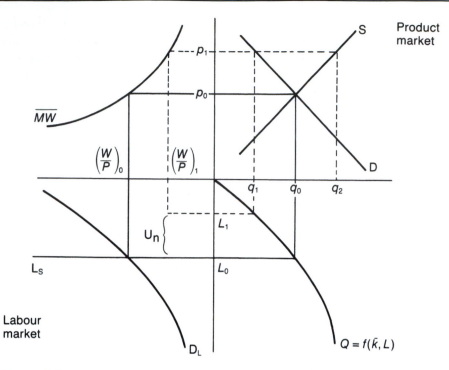

Figure 3.3

supply. The intersection of labour demand and supply determines equilibrium employment L_0 at a market clearing real wage $(W/P)_0$. The sequence is completed by an
endogenously generated money wage function in the top left hand quadrant which
shows the inverse relationship that must exist between real wages and price levels.

Initially a situation of general equilibrium exists where both the product and the
labour markets experience market clearing. This is denoted by the bold unbroken line
linking all four quadrants by passing through p_0, q_0, L_0 and $(W/P)_0$ in Figure 3.3.

Let us now examine the impact of an exogenous increase in non-labour production
costs under conditions of full cost pricing. This could be analogous to the OPEC
inspired increases in oil prices in 1973 and 1979. Firms, consistent with their pricing
practice, will pass on the average production cost rises by increasing product prices
from p_0 to p_1. Whilst these higher prices might induce firms to consider supplying
more, i.e., q_2, the crucial product market effect of higher prices is to reduce effective
demand to q_1. This level of output requires an employed workforce of only L_1, a
reduction in labour demand to L_1 generates measured unemployment U_n of $L_0 - L_1$.
Such an outcome is obtained because, while prices are flexible, money wages are
assumed to be inflexible in the short run due to the higher transactions cost associated
with negotiating wage changes. Thus real wages fall to $(W/P)_1$ and we end up with
both product and labour markets trading away from equilibrium. The product market
experiences excess effective supply, and Keynesian unemployment, a consequence of
deficient demand, is evident in the labour market.

Aggregate labour demand is dependent upon both the product demand and wages. The influence of wages and product demand on employers' demand for labour is theoretically well founded and therefore both variables feature prominently in empirical studies of labour demand.

COMPENSATING WAGE DIFFERENTIALS

A basic element of the analysis of wages in labour economics is the notion that wages must reflect the nature of the job. Jobs, which have different characteristics, must have different wages to account for those differences in the nature of jobs. Yet workers must be aware of different job characteristics for compensating wage differentials to operate. For example, workers need to be aware that one job is more dangerous than another in order to require a higher wage for the more dangerous job. It may be that one job requires more education than another and offers higher wages to entice more educated workers and to compensate them for the time, effort and expense of undergoing more education. We shall deal with these differences in more detail in Chapter 5 when we look at human capital. Compensating wage differentials incorporates the workers' assessment of non-wage aspects of a job, such as safety, working environment and job security as determinants of labour supply. Figure 3.4 illustrates the situation in two sections of a perfectly competitive labour market.

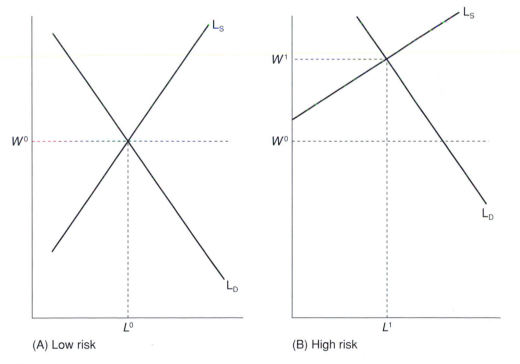

(A) Low risk (B) High risk

Figure 3.4

In the low risk sector (industry or occupation) the forces of supply and demand for low risk jobs determines an equilibrium wage W^0. However, this cannot be the wage rate prevailing across the labour market, otherwise nobody would do the high-risk jobs. Equilibrium in the high-risk sector is only achieved at the higher wage of W^1. This wage will not tend down towards W^0 by labour suppliers moving out of sector A into sector B because the existing wage differential $W^1 - W^0$ is not great enough to compensate any of the L^0 workers in sector A for the disutility of a higher risk job. Thus the wage differential will persist.

We have not specified what sort of risk distinguishes sector A from B in Figure 3.4. It could be danger, but it could be the probability of job loss. Sector B might also suffer from fewer fringe benefits such as sick leave, paid holidays, pension scheme and health insurance. It may be that sector B jobs are of a lower status than sector A jobs, jobs in the sewage and refuse collection industries might fall into this category. Sector B jobs might be in a harsh or out of the way location such as on a North Sea oilrig. Lower starting salaries in sector A might be compensating for better promotion and wage advancement prospects in the future. Sector B workers may have less control over the pace at which they work, the flexibility of their hours of work and less influence on what they do. We can examine the link between the risk of any of the above factors with the size of the compensating wage differential by referring to Figure 3.5.

All the elements of Figure 3.5 are in per worker terms. Given that there is a risk of an accident at work, workers will seek higher wages to compensate for this. As we can see in Figure 3.5, the wage function shows that workers require increasing wages as the risk of an accident grows. The firm could eliminate the risk of an accident entirely at the origin, but the costs per worker of the safety measures necessary to ensure an accident risk free zone are deemed to be too high. However, beyond the origin the risk of accidents grows and to compensate for this the firm has to offer workers wages above the risk free level W^0. This actually reduces the average cost of labour incorporating safety measures up to R^1, which corresponds to the minimum point M on the average cost curve. If the firm were to operate with any higher risk of accident such as at R^2 then the declining safety costs per worker are more than offset by the increased compensating wage differential $(W^2 - W^0)$ for R^2.

Note that it is the workers' demand for a wage premium that deters accidents in the workplace. If this were not the case then Figure 3.5 would be transformed into Figure 3.6. Without workers being aware of the risks involved or without the freedom to leave dangerous employment then the accident rate would rise above R_1 to its maximum at R_3.

At R^1 the firm can avoid the charge of negligence by spending as much on per worker safety $(C - R^1)$ as the workers own estimate of the damage of accidents, the compensating wage differential $W^1 - W^0$. At any point to the left of R^1 in Figure 3.5 the firm would be spending more on accident avoidance than the estimated damage caused by those accidents. At a point like R^2 the firm is being negligent as the estimated damage (wage differential) is much greater than the per worker cost of the safety measures being provided.

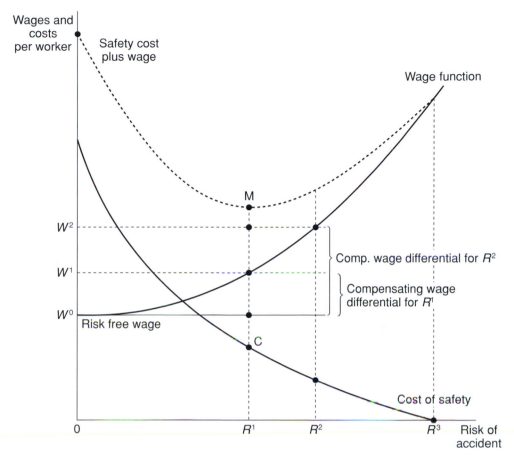

Figure 3.5

Government imposed health and safety standards might well oblige firms to have lower accident rates than the market determined R^1 in Figure 3.5. In such circumstances the average safety costs will be higher and the compensating differential lower than it would otherwise be. This may have adverse effects particularly on small firms.

Making firms liable for accidents sustained by their workers will reduce the compensating differential. The more generous the accident payouts the greater the effect on compensating wage differentials.

Another prediction to fall out of the analysis of compensating wage differentials is that poor people cannot afford to be too choosy about their attitude to risk and that they would be more willing to work for lower differentials than rich people. According to Polachek and Siebert (1993) 'the poor take the dangerous jobs, while the rich take the safe jobs' (p. 182). The role of trade unions in negotiating for better safety at work will help to alleviate the problem of poor people being more willing to accept riskier employment. Trade unions also bargain to try and increase compensating differentials; this collective voice may mean higher differentials for unionised workers.

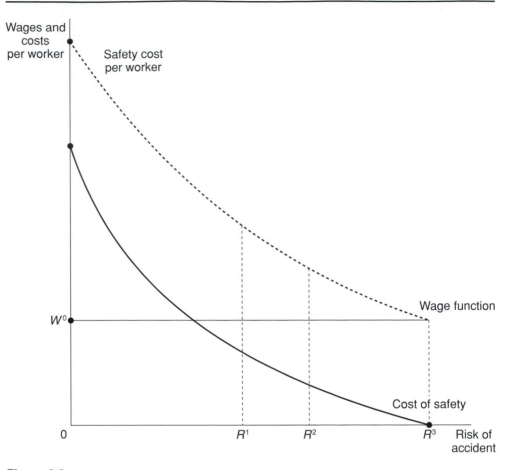

Figure 3.6

Empirical research on compensating wage differentials is largely supportive of the theoretical insights. Viscusi has estimated an earnings premium associated with injury and death of around 5 per cent. Viscusi (1993) showed that in US manufacturing there is an implied value of a worker's life in the range $3–$7 million. Viscusi and O'Connor (1984) showed that workers in the US chemical industry responded to information and warnings about risks by demanding a wage premium and by quitting. Abowd and Ashenfelter (1981) found compensating wage differentials in the region of 14 per cent for workers subject to substantial unemployment risk. Hamermesh and Wolfe (1990) found that virtually all the compensating differential was due to longer spells of unemployment rather than the increased probability of job loss. Li (1986) suggests that workers with little in the way of educational qualifications will be less risk averse. Allowing for the fact that the less educated and poorer workers tend to do the riskier jobs leads Garen (1988) to a substantially higher value of life for a worker at $9.2 million. Thus a policy to raise human capital investment would probably increase compensating differentials and cut accidents. Duncan and Stafford (1980) found that compensating wage differentials for poor working conditions formed part of unionised workers' higher pay than non-unionised workers. McNabb (1989) found that British workers working in poor conditions received wages some 3–4 per cent higher, providing some confirmation that the labour market does compensate workers for poor working conditions.

WAGE INEQUALITY

A concern with wage inequality is driven by a need to investigate the wage distribution as an important source of economic inequality. There are other aspects of economic inequality, namely: wealth, property, power, life expectancy, access to health services and education. However, we will concentrate on income because it helps determine a person's standard of living and it is associated with other elements of economic inequality. The basic assumption of the economic analysis of human well-being is that,

$$\uparrow \text{INCOME} \longrightarrow \uparrow \text{CONSUMPTION} \longrightarrow \uparrow \text{ECONOMIC WELFARE}$$

This is in spite of the problems of defining human welfare, differences and changes in prices of goods and services, varied consumption patterns and dealing with zero or negative income.

Income distribution data can be presented using the Lorenz curve. Figure 3.7 contains a Lorenz curve for the distribution of income in the UK in the tax year 1993/1994. Absolute income equality is represented by the diagonal line in Figure 3.7, with 10 per cent of the population earning 10 per cent of income, 20 per cent earning 20 per cent and so on. However, the actual income distribution in the UK was far from equal, with the income before-tax Lorenz curve being far from the diagonal, although the tax system did a little to reduce the inequality of the income distribution. From Figure 3.7 we can tell that the top 10 per cent of earners (0.9 on the x axis) accounted for almost 30 per cent of total income (0.7 on the y axis).[1]

A common measure of inequality is the Gini coefficient, which in Figure 3.7 is the area between the diagonal and the Lorenz curve as a proportion of the whole area of the triangle under the diagonal. For Figure 3.7 the Gini coefficient is

0.3860 before tax and
0.3427 after tax.

For the UK, the tax and benefit systems do contribute to reducing income inequality. Figure 3.8 shows that taxes and benefits in 1999 increased the income shares of the bottom three quintiles (20 per cent groups) or 60 per cent of households while reducing the income shares of the top 40 per cent of households. The greater the value of the Gini coefficient the greater the inequality, absolute income equality (the diagonal line) would have a Gini of zero. Gini coefficient data from the UK contained in Figure 3.9 shows that from the late 1970s there has been a marked rise in the

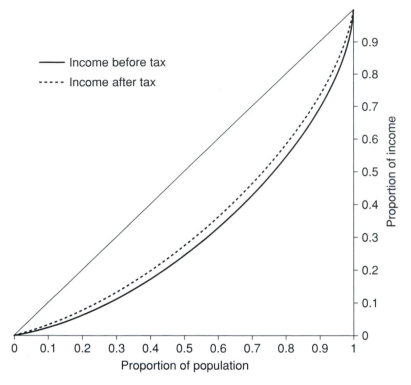

Figure 3.7   Lorenz curve of income, UK, 1993/4

Source: Champernowne and Cowell 1998, figure 2.3, p. 30

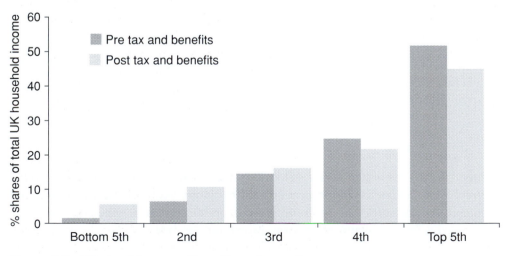

Figure 3.8   Effects of taxes and benefits on inequality

Source: Guardian 26/4/01

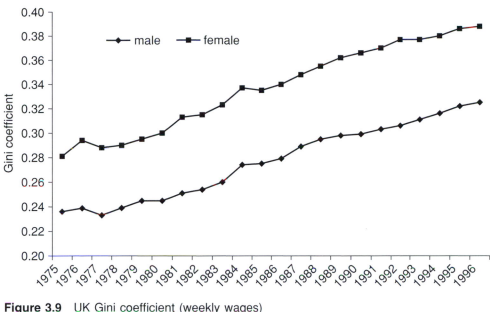

Figure 3.9 UK Gini coefficient (weekly wages)

Source: ONS, New Earnings Survey, various years

inequality of weekly wages for both male and female workers. Weekly wage inequality among female workers in the UK is greater than between male workers.

The UK is not alone in having an unequal distribution of income. Table 3.1 compares the Gini coefficients of the UK against other developed economies and a lesser developed country, Mexico. Among the sample of European countries in Table 3.1 the level of income inequality is quite high in the UK, being exceeded only by Greece, Ireland and Italy. There is a similar level of inequality in Australia, less inequality in Canada and Japan, yet greater inequality in the USA. Inequality tends to be greater in developing countries so in this respect Mexico is not exceptional. Although the level of inequality in the USA is greater than in the UK, the increases in the Gini coefficient illustrated in Figure 3.9 have been rapid enough to allow the UK to have the dubious achievement of closing the inequality gap between the USA and the UK as Figure 3.10 clearly shows.

In a wider comparative study of income inequality in 21 OECD countries, Forster (2000) finds no general long-term trend in the distribution of disposable household income since the mid-1970s. However, amongst his sample of countries, the UK records the fastest rate of growth in inequality of more than 12 per cent from the mid-1970s to the mid-1990s. From the mid-1980s to the mid-1990s there were significant increases in the Gini coefficient for nine of the countries namely, Belgium, Finland, Italy, Japan, Netherlands, Norway, Sweden, Turkey and the UK. There were no unambiguous decreases in inequality in any of the countries. Generally it has been

Table 3.1 Gini coefficients, mid-1990s

Austria	0.238
Belgium	0.272
Denmark	0.217
Finland	0.228
France	0.278
Germany	0.282
Greece	0.336
Ireland	0.324
Italy	0.345
Netherlands	0.255
Norway	0.256
Sweden	0.230
Switzerland	0.269
UK	0.312
Australia	0.305
Canada	0.285
Japan	0.265
USA	0.344
Mexico	0.526

Source: OECD (1998)

Figure 3.10 Income inequality in the UK and the USA, 1947–92

Source: Atkinson 1997, figure 2, p. 300

the increased inequality in gross earnings that has been behind greater inequality. This appears to be due to both increased wage inequality and employment polarisation. In the UK between 1985 and 1995 working age population shares changed as follows:

households with
 no worker   +0.6%
 one worker   −2.5%
 two (plus)workers +1.8%.

The relative income of single parents and workless households has suffered. People in multi-adult households, especially those with no children, with two or more earners have gained.

Hollowing out of the income distribution where both low and high earners gain at the expense of middle income groups was not a widespread phenomenon and did not occur except in Belgium, France and to a minor extent in the USA, as Figure 3.11 shows. In each of these three countries the bottom 20 per cent and the top 20 per cent in the income distribution have gained whilst the middle three quintiles have recorded declines in disposable income shares. Figure 3.12 shows that in Australia and Denmark the bottom 40 per cent of earners gained whereas the remaining 60 per cent saw reduced shares of disposable income. In the UK, however, it was the top quintile, which recorded an increased share whereas those in the lowest 20 per cent witnessed the largest fall in share.

Of the 20 countries analysed, 11 suffered falling shares for the bottom 20 per cent in the income distribution (including Germany, Italy, Japan, Netherlands and Sweden), while 14 saw rising shares for the top 20 per cent. Having established that income inequality exists and in some countries it is getting worse, we need to ask ourselves whether we need to worry about inequality. Concern about wage-based inequality is centred around notions of justice of what Champernowne and Cowell (1998) refer to as 'stark contrasts in economic conditions between different groups of people, that are not due to the fault or merit of the people themselves' (p. 7). We need to distinguish inequality of outcome, which may be justified in the context of human capital (higher wages being a reward for skill acquisition), risk taking (including compensating wage differentials) and responsibility bearing, from inequality of opportunity, which is more difficult to justify regarding the denial of access on the grounds of gender, race or class, which forms the subject matter of our analysis of labour market discrimination in Chapter 6. For mainstream economics the market for factors of production determines their rewards in line with efficiency. If we concentrate on two factors of production, skilled labour (SK) and unskilled labour (UL), then we can suggest how the proportions of total income flowing to each will be determined. Figure 3.13 represents an ideal market economy equilibrium, where not only employment of SK and UL is determined but also the wage rate paid to each.

Starting from a position of identical wage rates for both skilled and unskilled workers of W^0, suppose there is a new technology that favours skilled workers enabling

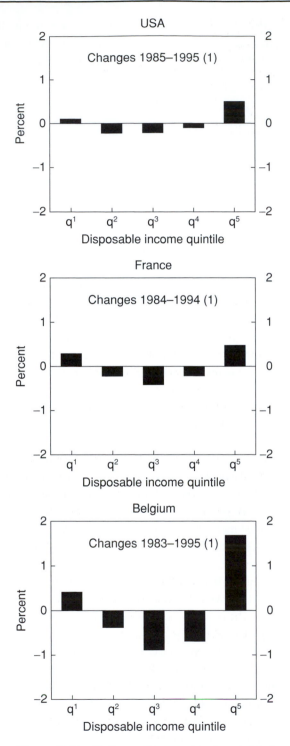

Figure 3.11   Gains and losses by disposable income quintiles, entire population (Belgium, France and USA), mid-1980s to mid-1990s

Source: Forster 2000, figure 2.2, pp. 119–22

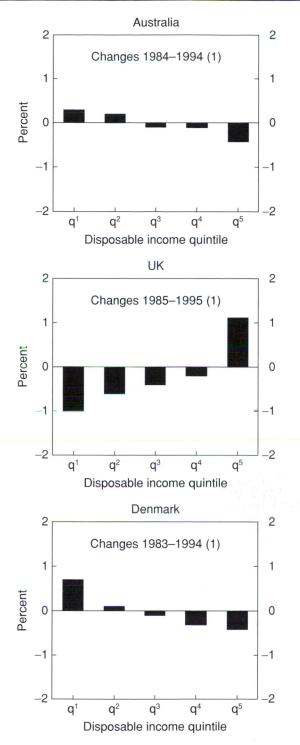

Figure 3.12 Gains and losses by disposable income quintiles, entire population (Australia, Denmark and UK), mid-1980s to mid-1990s

Source: As Figure 3.11

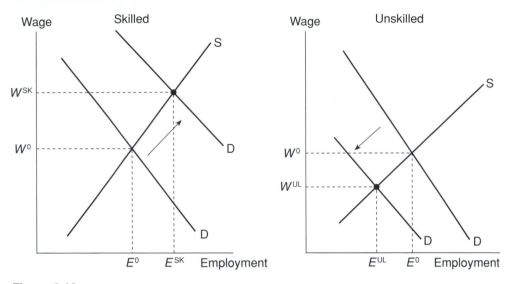

Figure 3.13

firms to replace unskilled workers with skilled labour. This brings about the shifts in labour demand such that unskilled employment and wages fall, whereas those for skilled workers rise, suggesting an increase in income inequality in favour of skilled workers. The key to this analysis is the elasticity of substitution of skilled workers for unskilled labour and the marginal productivity of skilled and unskilled workers. We shall return to this scenario when we examine the notion of skill biased technological change and especially the impact of computers on the labour market in Chapter 5.

If wage inequality reflects differences in skill, productivity and compensating differentials do we need to be concerned about it? Leaving aside the possibility of discrimination within the labour market, which we tackle in Chapter 6, there are legitimate economic concerns surrounding income inequality. The relationship between income inequality and macroeconomic growth is conventionally approached in terms of a trade-off between greater equality and lower efficiency. In this context any redistribution of income in favour of the lower paid would be viewed as detrimental to growth as it would lower the incentives for productive factors. However, developments in growth theory, particularly endogenous growth theory (Benabou, 1996), sees the unequal distribution of income harming economic growth by denying access to education and capital markets to the low paid. A number of empirical studies of developing countries (Rodrik 1994, World Bank 1993) point out that among other advantages successful countries have more equitable income distributions than less successful nations. Different preferences about societal income distribution can be reflected using different measurements of average income. Consider the examples contained in Figure 3.14.

If we are entirely indifferent to changes in income distribution then we can just accept the actual changes in mean real incomes, the bold lines in Figure 3.14. Yet if we are concerned about inequality then this can be reflected by what Atkinson (1997) terms the 'distributionally adjusted real mean income', the broken lines. Average

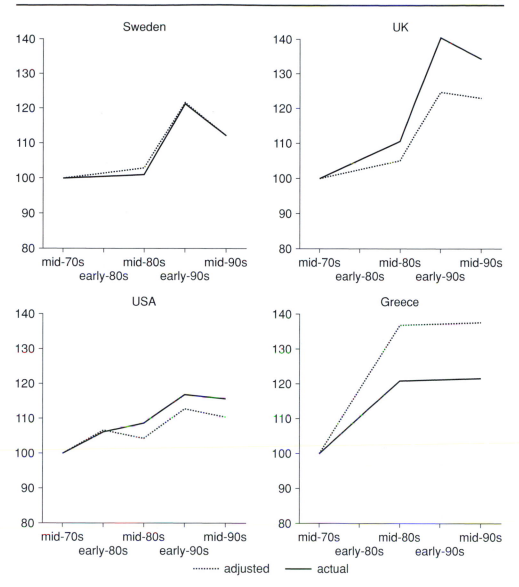

Figure 3.14 Trends in actual and 'inequality adjusted' real mean incomes

Source: Forster 2000, figure 2.1, pp. 117–18

income rises from the mid-1970s to the mid-1990s look less impressive in the UK and the USA because of growing inequality over time. In Sweden both measures are almost identical reflecting little change in income distribution whereas income rises in Greece seem more impressive because of growing income equality. Although we have concentrated on wage inequality across countries there exist significant differences in the earnings between different regions of the same country. Figure 3.15 shows that not only are there substantial gaps in average earnings between workers in London, the South East of England and the rest of the UK (the nine regions), but that these gaps have widened between 1982 and 1997. The main reasons for this are that returns

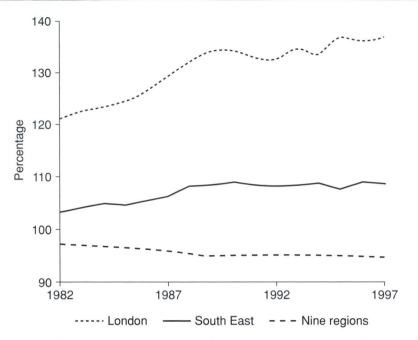

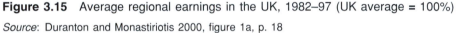

Figure 3.15   Average regional earnings in the UK, 1982–97 (UK average = 100%)

Source: Duranton and Monastiriotis 2000, figure 1a, p. 18

to education have risen at a time when according to Duranton and Monastiriotis (2000) 'the cross-region distribution of education is increasingly uneven' (p. 17). Over the period there were strong gains in the rate of return to education for workers in London combined with a faster increase in the level of educational attainment of the London workforce than elsewhere in the UK. A policy prescription concerned to achieve greater equality of earnings within a country should focus on education at the regional level.

CASE STUDY – THE SUPPLY OF SKILLED LABOUR AND THE SKILLED WAGE PREMIUM

We looked at the possibility that technological change could have favoured the employment of skilled labour in Figure 3.13. We will explore the notion of such skill-biased technological change in more detail in Chapter 5. We will also discover in Chapter 5 that the supply of skilled labour has increased markedly over time. What Michael Kiley (1999), 'The Supply of Skilled Labour and Skill-Biased Technological Progress', *Economic Journal*, 109 (458): 708–24, seeks to explain in the following extract is how in the face of increases in the supply of skilled labour in the USA the wage gap between skilled and unskilled labour increased. To start with the story is a little more straightforward as the supply of college (university) educated graduates increases between 1967 and 1974 (see

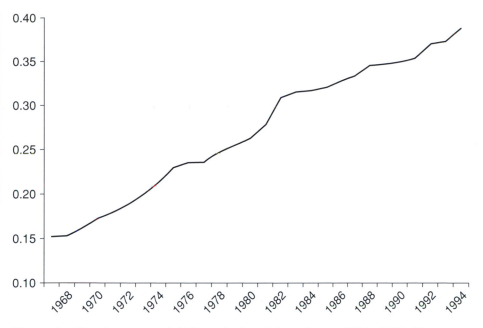

Figure A Relative supply of College (university) graduates, USA, 1967–94

Source: Kiley (1999)

Figure A) the wage differential between college graduates and other workers falls
(Figure B).

The 1980s witnessed a large increase in the wages of skilled labour relative
to unskilled labour, resulting in levels of wage inequality between high and
low skilled workers in the United States higher than at any time in the last
30 years . . .

Similar dynamics occurred in other countries (Japan, Sweden and the
UK.) . . . The experience in the United Kingdom is very similar to that of
the United States, with relative earnings for college educated workers
reaching levels above those of the early 1970s by the end of the 1980s.

The simple economic explanation for . . . these developments offered in
the applied labour literature relies on a basic supply and demand model; the
increased supply of more skilled workers depresses wages, but . . . could . . .
endogenous technology bias overturn the depressing effect of increases in
skilled labour supply on skilled labour's relative wage – at least in the long run?

Yes, . . . investment in applied R and D is directed towards either skill-
biased technology . . . or unskilled-biased technology . . . The attractiveness
of investing in skill-biased technology depends on the supply of the factor
that complements that technology; specifically, a larger number of skilled
workers raises the incentives to invest in technology that skilled labour
uses. . . . In the language of the labour economics literature, an increase in
the supply of skilled labour brings about an increase in the demand for

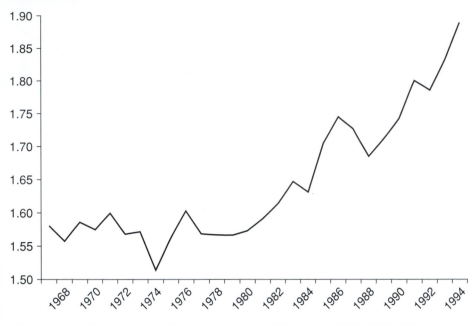

Figure B   College graduate/High school wage differential, USA, 1967–94

Source: As Figure A

skilled labour. This effect actually generates higher relative wages (in the long run) for skilled labour in response to an increase in skilled labour's share of the workforce . . .

. . . the relative supply of skilled labour rose dramatically in the United States during the 1970s, at least in part exogenously due to government support for higher education . . . Initially, the relative wages of skilled workers fell in response to the surge in supply, but in the 1980s the relative wages of skilled labour rose . . . In the model of this paper, the fall and rise of the skill premium both result from the endogenous adjustment of the economy towards the new, more skill-intensive technology mix that is appropriate for the more skilled workforce.

The supply of skilled labour rose rapidly in the 1970s as UK governments expanded higher education by creating Polytechnics. The expansion of higher education was accelerated during the 1980s and the former Polytechnics became new Universities in the early 1990s. The fact that skilled wage premium in the UK increased implies that skill-biased demand shifts outstripped the increased supply of university graduates. Although the model in Kiley (1999) is an abstract one it does generate qualitative predictions that fit the experience of the USA and the UK since the late 1960s. It is an interesting addition to the literature on skill-biased technological change because it tries to explain why such technology is developed as the availability of skilled labour increases.

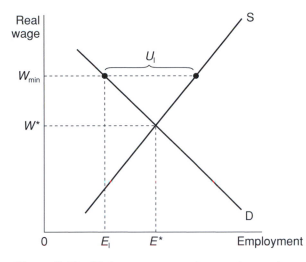

Figure 3.16   Minimum wage and unemployment

Source: Smith 1998, figure 8.11, p. 144

MINIMUM WAGE

The theoretical prediction that minimum wages reduce employment is a simple and general one arising from a presumption that the minimum wage is set above the market clearing level that would be determined in a competitive labour market. At its most basic a competitive labour market such as that being represented by Figure 3.16, will generate an equilibrium wage W* and employment E* combination at which there is no unemployment. When the minimum wage (W_{min}) is imposed, employment falls from E* to E_1 and a measured amount of unemployment emerges U_1.

Until April 1999 the UK never had a legally enforceable minimum wage. In that respect it used to stand out from other European countries. France, the Netherlands, Luxembourg, Spain and Portugal have national minimum wages set by the government. The Scandinavian countries along with Belgium and Greece have a national minimum wage set by collective bargaining. Denmark, Germany and Italy have different, negotiated minimum wages for different sectors of the economy covering virtually all workers in those sectors. In Japan minimum wages are negotiated at the regional level whereas in the USA and Canada there are both national and regional minimums.

Prior to the introduction of a national minimum wage, the UK provided wage protection for around 12 per cent of the workforce through Wages Councils, which had been established in 1909, composed of employer and employee representatives (Gregory and Sandoval 1994). In 1986 Wages Councils, which recommended minimum wages for young workers (under 21) were abolished, with all Wages Councils removed by the end of 1993. These Councils had no statutory power and it is doubtful that they ever had any disincentive effect on employment. In a study of the Agricultural Wages Boards for England, Wales, Scotland and Northern Ireland, Dickens *et al.*

(1994b) found that they did raise wages and increase income equality for agricultural workers. However, the study concludes that there is 'no evidence that minimum wages have significantly lowered employment in any country', indeed they might have even preserved agricultural employment (p. 20). For the USA, Kennan (1995) demonstrates that the 17 increases in the US federal minimum wage between 1939 and 1991 have averaged 12 per cent. Yet even with the per hour federal minimum wage rising from

$3.35 – $3.80 on April 1 1990,

and then from

$3.80 – $4.25 on April 1 1991,

the gap between the minimum wage in real terms and average hourly earnings is greater than in any previous period except perhaps the late 1980s (Kennan (1995) figure 2, p. 1955). A further two 45 cents increases took the federal minimum wage up to $5.15 by September 1st 1997. Overall the correlation between minimum wages and employment in the USA is low, insignificant and sensitive to the sample period.

On 1 April 1992 the state of New Jersey increased its minimum wage to $5.05 per hour, while Pennsylvania kept to the federal minimum of $4.25. Contrary to the standard prediction, fast-food restaurant employment actually increased in New Jersey and fell in Pennsylvania. Card (1992) examined what happened when in July 1988 the minimum wage in California rose from $3.35 to $4.25 per hour. The employment rate for California teenagers rose relative to states with no increase in minimum wages between 1987 and 1989. Card and Krueger (1995) conclude their re-analysis of US studies by stating that 'the bulk of the empirical evidence on the employment effects of the minimum wage ... suggest that increases in the minimum wage have had, if anything, a small, positive effect on employment, rather than an adverse effect' (p. 236). Keil *et al.* (2001) dispute this by producing results that show that rises in the US minimum wage during 1977–95 tended to reduce total employment. They calculate total employment elasticity to the minimum wage to be −0.11 in the short term, with a greater responsiveness of −0.19 in the long term.

For the UK, Dicken *et al.*'s (1994a) study of the impact of Wages Councils finds that 'counter to the conventional economic model, increases in Wages Council minimum rates of pay were associated with improved employment in the 1978 to 1990 time period' (p. 25). Machin and Manning (1996) report that since the Wages Councils were abolished wages appear to have fallen yet there have been no employment gains (p. 672).

How can we rationalise these findings with the conventional position set out in Figure 3.16? We can do so if we remember that Figure 3.16 shows a perfectly competitive labour market. In practice firms in the same industry offer workers different wages for what is essentially the same job. Low pay firms may well find themselves facing

Table 3.2   Comparative minimum wage levels, 1997 (hourly wage)

	Year started	USA $ (PPP)	Percentage of the median earnings of full-time workers
Australia	1907	6.65	54
Belgium	1975	6.40	50
Canada	1918	5.33	40
France	1950	5.56	57
Japan	1959	3.38	31
Netherlands	1968	6.00	49
Spain	1963	2.94	32
USA	1938	5.15	38
UK	1999	5.44	44

Source: Metcalf 1999b, table 4, p. 21

tight labour supply constraints compared to better paying firms. It may well take an increase in the minimum wage to force the low pay firms to offer higher wages and thereby attract an increase in labour supply and employment.[2] If we adopt this approach then there are no simple and general predictions about the impact of minimum wages on employment in theory, and experience should teach economists to keep an open mind about the implementation of minimum wages.

It is interesting to compare the level of the UK's first national minimum wage, which the Labour Government introduced in 1999, with minimum wages in some other OECD countries. The data in Table 3.2 compares the level of the minimum wage across countries both in absolute terms and in relation to average earnings. Experience from the USA suggests that a minimum wage, which is not particularly generous (38 per cent of average earnings), with no automatic increases does not adversely affect employment. Even after the 1997 increases, the federal minimum wage is worth less in purchasing power (in terms of the goods and services that it can buy) than it was in 1961. Figure 3.17 contrasts the nominal with the real value of the US federal minimum wage over the period 1960–2001. Note that whilst the nominal value of the minimum wage has risen from $1.00 per hour to $5.15 over that period, the effect of consumer price inflation has been to reduce its real (constant 1999 $) value from $5.18 to $4.85.

The US minimum wage does not appear to have had any impact on reducing income inequality, which has increased steadily since the late 1960s (Atkinson 1997). By contrast the French minimum wage (the SMIC) is increased automatically in line with inflation and the rise in manual workers earnings, making it much more generous than the US minimum wage at 57 per cent of French average earnings. This appears to have played a part in holding virtually constant income inequality in France across the 1980s (Atkinson 1997). However, there may have been adverse employment effects for young workers in France (Bazan and Martin 1991). Using US data for the

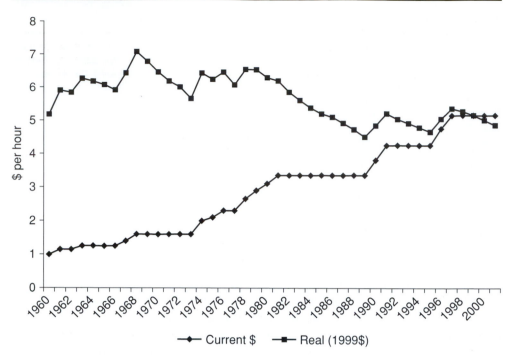

Figure 3.17   USA minimum wage, 1960–2001

Source: Compiled by author from data in Economic Policy Institute, *The State of Working America, 2000–01*, www.epinet.org

period 1977–95, Keil *et al.* (2001) find that changes in the minimum wage have an elasticity on youth employment of −0.37 in the short term and −0.69 in the long term. This is in line with Burkhauser *et al.*'s (2000) conclusion that US 'increases in the minimum wage during the 1990s led to modest but statistically significant declines in teenage employment' (p. 676). They estimate the elasticity of teenage employment to minimum wage changes to be in the range −0.2 to −0.6. More generally the OECD (1998) Employment Outlook concluded, 'a rise in the minimum wage has a negative effect on teenage employment' (p. 47). Brown (1999) concluded that 'evidence suggests that the short-term effect of the minimum wage on teenage employment is small . . . centred on an elasticity of −0.10' (p. 2154). The UK appears to have drawn upon this international experience by setting the initial minimum wage at 44 per cent of average earnings, making it markedly less generous than other European minimums, with the exception of Spain. It also contained a lower minimum wage rate for younger workers aged 18–20 years old of £3.20 per hour compared to the adult (21 years plus) rate of £3.60 per hour in 1999.

Whether minimum wages are an effective means of combating poverty is debateable. Burkhauser *et al.* (1996) estimated that only around 20 per cent of the earnings increases brought about by the 1990–1 rises in the US minimum wage went to poor

Table 3.3 Low pay, 1997

	Percentage earning less than £3.50/hour		Percentage earning less than £3.50/hour
Female	16	Private	14
Male	7	Public	5
Manual	18	Non-union	17
Non-manual	7	Unionised	4
Age 18–20	41	Hospitality	40
Age 21+	10	Retail/wholesale	19
White	11	Health/social	13
Non-white	13	Manufacturing	7
Part-time	25	< 25 workers	20
Full-time	7	25+ workers	7
Lone parent	19		
Not lone parent	11	All	11

Source: Metcalf 1999a, table 1, p. F50

families. Addison and Blackburn (1999) concluded that while increases in US minimum wages did reduce poverty in the 1990s, especially for high-school dropouts, this was not the case during the 1980s.

To give an indication of what type of workers would be affected by the UK national minimum wage, the data in Table 3.3 shows the incidence of low pay, defined as less than £3.50 per hour, in 1997. In terms of personal characteristics, low pay was more common among female workers and manual workers. It was more of a feature of young workers. There was not too great a difference in the incidence of low pay between white and ethnic minority workers. One quarter of part-timers were on low pay and low pay was more of a problem for single parents. Low pay was more common in private sector and non-unionised establishments. The greatest incidence of low pay was to be found in the hospitality, retail and wholesale trade sectors. It was not a particular feature of large firms whereas one in five workers in small establishments were low paid. Although there is no automatic mechanism for changes in the UK minimum wage, the Government has increased it to £4.10 for adults and £3.50 for younger workers from October 2001.

According to Metcalf (1999b), the minimum wage was expected to benefit mainly 'females, part-timers, youths, non-whites, those with short tenure, single parents and those with no other worker in the household' (p. 8). Given the fact that there do not appear to have been substantial adverse employment effects arising from the introduction of the minimum wage in the UK, and following the Conservative party dropping its opposition to the national minimum wage it looks set to become a permanent feature of the UK labour market. It should help those households at the bottom of the income distribution and so contribute to the growth of income equality. But its impact on poverty will be limited by the fact that the majority of poor families tend to be workless households.

WAGE DETERMINATION AND INEQUALITY – SUMMARY

In this chapter we have examined wage determination in the context of an interaction of the labour market forces of supply and demand. We also looked at how the labour market and the product market interacted at the aggregate level to determine wage and employment levels. If wages are less flexible than prices we saw how an external shock to the economy could lead to labour market disequilibrium, namely unemployment.

Returning to the microeconomics of wage determination we added the notion that wages might be unequal even in equilibrium due to compensating differentials. Higher wage rates may be needed to compensate workers for

- higher risk of injury or death
- higher risk of unemployment

In theory there is an optimal balance between risk and compensating differentials. For this optimum to be achieved workers needed accurate information to be able to assess risk associated with jobs with different characteristics. There may be a role for Government regulation of job risks. Two key predictions of the analysis of compensating wage differentials were that

- poor workers will crowd into high risk jobs
- poor workers will work for lower compensating differentials, than richer workers

The insights of compensating wage differentials were largely borne out by empirical studies.

We then examined the distribution of wages throughout the economy. We found evidence of large, persistent and in the case of the UK growing income inequality. In general income inequality

- was greater between women workers than amongst male employees
- was greater in developing countries like Mexico than in developed economies like the USA
- was greater in the UK than in Scandinavian countries and most of the rest of Europe, Canada and Japan
- was about the same in the UK as in Australia and Ireland
- was lower in the UK than in Greece, Italy and the USA

Increased income inequality appears to be the result of

- the growing inequality of pre-tax earnings
- employment polarisation

The groups that have suffered most from growing inequality are

- workless households
- households with children
- especially single parents

Concern over income distribution from a strictly economic perspective is driven by new growth theory and empirical studies of the better growth performance of more equitable nations.

Growing regional earnings inequality in the UK focused upon education as a key determinant of wages.

The minimum wage is a way of determining the wages of low paid workers and compressing the income distribution. In theory minimum wages can be shown to lead to a reduction in employment. However, this is contested by the findings of some empirical studies. In establishing a national minimum wage for the very first time in 1999 the UK Government appears to have recognised the potential threat of

- generous minimum wages
- high minimum rates for young workers

The main beneficiaries of minimum wages are:

- women workers
- part-time workers (mainly women)
- single parent workers (mainly women)
- ethnic minority workers
- young workers
- workers on short-term contracts
- households with only one worker

Although the direct impact on poverty may be limited, minimum wages look as though they are here to stay.

QUESTIONS FOR DISCUSSION

1) With regard to compensating wage differentials should the provision of safety at work be left entirely to the discretion of firms?
2) Is there any role for organised labour (trade unions) to play in the determination of compensating differentials?
3) Consider the following hypothetical Lorenz curves. Which country, A or B, has the greatest income inequality?

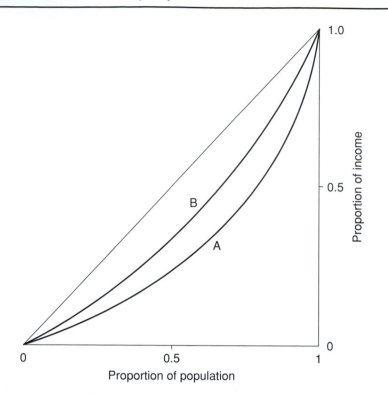

4) If for the countries in Question 3 the Gini coefficients were 0.278 and 0.305, which belongs to which country? From Table 3.1, which are the two countries being depicted in Questions 3 and 4?
5) As economists, should we be concerned about income distribution?
6) Do minimum wages cost jobs or not?

SUGGESTED READING

Champernowne, D. and Cowell, F. (1998) *Economic Inequality and Income Distribution*, Cambridge: Cambridge University Press.

Katz, L. and Autor, D. (1999) 'Changes in the Wage Structure and Earnings Inequality', in O. Ashenfelter and D. Card (eds) *Handbook of Labour Economics*, Volume 3, Amsterdam: Elsevier Science.

Metcalf, D. (1999a) 'The Low Pay Commission and the National Minimum Wage', *Economic Journal*, 109: F46–F66.

4

Personnel economics

INTRODUCTION

Lazear (1999) defines personnel economics as 'the application of labour economics principles to business issues' (p. 199). In recent years there has been a growth in the study of microeconomic aspects of the employment relationship between firms and their workers. This can be thought of in terms of principals and agents. We will analyse employment contracts, the provision of incentives for workers, examining fringe benefits, worker effort including shirking, and looking at promotion within the firm. In this chapter we will examine all these aspects of the employment relationship, which are among the insights stemming from the treatment of a firm's employees as an internal labour market.

PRINCIPALS AND AGENTS

The employment relationship is different from other business contracts, such as an agreement to purchase a commodity. The most obvious and most important difference is that a labour market contract involves a human being, the worker, agreeing to be told what to do by another human being, the manager. The principal (the firm) employs the agent (the worker) to perform tasks on its behalf and may even devolve some decision-making authority to the agent. However, in many employment environments there is scope for workers to engage in what is termed opportunistic behaviour. For example workers can increase their utility from leisure by shirking at work, taking unofficial breaks or by making less effort than they agreed to during work time. When agents pursue their own objectives which conflict with the interests of the principal we have the principal–agent problem, where the principal has to try to make the agent's interests coincide with its own. Firms have a profit incentive in reducing shirking by providing worker incentives in the form of pay and promotion. It will monitor the worker's performance to prevent shirking and establish rules of conduct and budgetary restraints on the agent. The agent may well invest in the employment relationship by undergoing training specific to the firm (see Chapter 5 for an analysis of specific training) and by being seen to cooperate with the principal.

Furthermore the employment relationship tends to be a long-term one, with job tenure lasting years as opposed to the almost instantaneous product market transactions.

From the outset the employment relationship between principals and agents is characterised by uncertainty. There is less than perfect information on both the employers' and the workers' side. Employers, for example, are less than fully informed about a job applicant's true potential productivity in the vacancy the firm is seeking to fill. The workers may have more accurate yet private information about their own likely productivity that it is not in their own best interest to divulge to the firm; this is an example of asymmetric information. Similarly the worker may not be fully aware of how his/her skills and experience match the firm's needs. In such circumstances the signalling and screening hypothesis is a useful analytical tool. We shall examine worker signalling and employer screening in more detail in Chapter 9, yet for the time being let us consider that both workers and firms may use the worker's credentials, especially educational qualifications, to gauge productivity potential. For example, it takes certain ability and a set of skills to obtain a university degree. If these abilities conform with the skills and abilities an employer requires then both workers and firms can use education as a proxy for productivity. However, it may be that education is a poor indicator of productivity especially if we allow for individual differences between graduates. We shall confirm in Chapter 5 that graduates earn more than non-graduates, but from the firm's perspective will the greater cost of graduate employees be justified by their greater productivity?

A possible solution to the problems of incomplete and asymmetric information is to structure the employment contract to take account of information shortcomings.

CONTRACTS

A traditional form of employment contract where a worker's output can be readily measured is to include piece-rate pay. This form of contract seeks to overcome principal–agent problems by linking a worker's pay directly to individual worker productivity. Knowing that a job is a piecework contract will tend to attract more productive workers. Less productive workers will be put off applying for piecework jobs and will go for salaried jobs which pay workers for their time input not their output. Workers who are inclined to shirk will not go for piece-rate jobs, knowing that their lack of effort will be reflected in their pay packet. Piece-rate wage rates are likely to be higher than time rates for the same job because piece rates generate extra effort from the worker and lead to more variable income for which a compensating differential must be paid. Piece-rate employment contracts are more a feature of production jobs particularly in large firms using less capital-intensive processes performed by blue-collar workers.

Most firms make the employment of new workers conditional upon the successful completion of a probationary period of up to a year, before they get a permanent contract or tenure. The intention of such a contingent contract is to deter unsuitable applicants and to rectify any mistakes in the hiring process. During the probationary period wage rates are lower than they are for workers on permanent contracts. Appropriately skilled workers will pass the probationary period whereas less skilled workers will be exposed during probation. However, if the chances of unskilled workers being exposed at the end of the probation period are low, then the probationary wage rate needs to be lowered relative to the unskilled wage elsewhere, in order to deter unskilled workers. However, the post-probation wage needs to be sufficiently high to attract skilled workers. The fact that labour market contracts tend to be of long duration makes probation schemes viable. A probationary scheme is more effective the greater the probability that the unskilled are detected and the narrower the gap between wages for the unskilled and the skilled. The fact that the gap between skilled and unskilled wages has widened over time (see Chapter 3) in the UK means that either wage rates for probationary workers will have had to fall or that scrutiny of probationary performance will have had to improve to retain the effectiveness of probationary contract schemes. Obviously firms that do not operate a probationary system will have more unskilled applicants. Such firms can adapt to this situation by offering lower wages than a firm with a probationary scheme. The existence of long-term employment contracts fixing salaries for at least a year, longer in the case of automatic incremental increases upon a salary scale, may embody wage rigidity. The significance of wage rigidity will be explained in the context of unemployment in Chapter 10, but it may distort the relationship between changes in product demand and labour demand.

IMPLICIT CONTRACT THEORY

Given the brief and non-technical exposition of implicit contract theory that follows, the interested reader is directed to Manning (1990) for a more comprehensive treatment of this topic. For our purposes the interesting aspect of implicit contract theory is the light it may shed on wage rigidity. What factors might prevent firms cutting the real (and possibly the money) wages of their workforce? Given that workers are more risk-averse than their employers they seek some form of insurance against wage fluctuations. There is a human capital element to this proposition, as workers cannot readily diversify their assets in the form of human capital, whereas owners of other forms of capital can, through the stock market, more easily diversify their assets and thus spread the risk. The benefit to firms of an implicit contract, which offers workers some wage security, is in a lower average wage bill than one determined by a competitive labour market. This allows them to offer the workforce a long-term wage contract that insulates workers wages from the vagaries of product and labour market fluctuations for the duration of that contract. Whilst employers might be tempted to renege on a wage contract during a period of excess product and/or labour supply, it faces adjustment costs in terms of workforce resistance and a loss of credibility in future negotiations. The implication is that they will wait until the end of an existing contract, in order to negotiate a lower real wage. Employment is greater under implicit contracts than it would be in competitive labour market conditions at any output price facing the firm. Firms can make minor adjustments to employment without breaking any implicit contract by natural wastage through not filling vacancies created by workers who quit or retire. But firms for whom implicit contracts are important tend to have lower labour turnover, and quit rates fall during a recession. If workers are risk averse, are they only risk averse about wages? During recessions firms make workers redundant and workers do not respond by reducing wages or offering job-sharing arrangements. Rebitzer (1989) questions whether implicit contracts actually exist for the majority of employees, given that large amounts of firm-specific training and large stable employers are needed to justify such contracts. What, he asks, accounts for the failure of wages to clear labour markets with low skill, poor job security and small firm characteristics, where the incentive for implicit contracts is weak? Fallon and Verry (1988) point out that as quit rates increase during a boom, the time when firms expect to benefit most from an implicit contract, this weakens their incentive for them. Nickell (1990) has questioned why, under an implicit contract, workers appear to prefer stable wages rather than stable employment.

Whilst implicit contract theory is not going to provide a convincing explanation of wage rigidity and unemployment persistence it does focus attention on the employment relationship.

INTERNAL LABOUR MARKETS

When an employer fills a vacancy by hiring a new worker, it is participating in the external labour market. The fact that labour contracts are long-term and that many job holders have long tenure helps account for the phenomenon of internal labour markets. Doeringer and Piore (1971) developed the concept of a labour market internal to the firm (see Chapter 6). The firm can, through training, develop skills in the existing workforce if they are scarce in the local external labour market. If a firm is faced with fairly stable product demand it can attract and retain good quality staff by paying high wages and invest in training its workers. Raff and Summers (1987) suggest that by paying above market clearing wages, Ford was able to reduce labour turnover and absence leading to more effort, greater productivity and profits. Ford increased worker tenure with the company and created internal labour markets. Kramarz and Roux (1999) find that for French firms low turnover is associated with higher productivity. Such firms could fill low-level jobs from the external labour market and look to fill higher-level jobs using promotion within the internal labour market. Furthermore, the firm could seek to reduce labour turnover by setting up schemes to increase worker tenure, such as seniority wage structures, and protection from redundancy by seniority. In general the longer a worker's tenure with a firm the greater the pay and the lower the risk of being laid off. Although most firms will have some form of internal labour market they tend to be more highly developed in large firms. A distinctive feature of internal labour markets is that wages are not set by the usual market forces, of supply and demand, but by administrative rules established either by the employer alone or through negotiation with trade unions. There are points of contact with external labour markets when for instance a higher level vacancy is filled by an external applicant, although the wage may well be above an external market clearing rate. Such aspects of internal labour markets mean that firm specific factors will dominate external labour market influences on wages, making wages unresponsive or rigid to external labour market conditions. Thurow (1976) developed a job competition model that is applicable to firms with high training costs and internal labour markets. If firms raise the standard for job applicants when the supply of labour increases for example during a recession, then this affects workers who are forced to change jobs, meaning in effect they must take lower paying jobs than they had. Workers who do not have to change jobs are left unaffected by this alteration of hiring standards. Similarly longer tenured workers, who may be active in training newer workers on the job, do not have their own jobs threatened by their trainees. In fact if the firm adopts a redundancy rule such as last in first out more senior employees have more job security. Thus it may be that the benefits of an internal labour market are only conferred on certain categories of workers rather than the entire workforce. Kramarz and Roux (1999) found that high turnover rates for workers employed on short-term contracts in France actually increased profitability. Furthermore firms may use the promise of greater employment security in order to negotiate greater flexibility from the workers.

Firms need to persuade workers to take a long-term stake in the success of the firm. The investment put into the employment relationship by both firm and workers, which has resulted in internal labour markets, is protected by lengthy and clearly specified dismissal procedures.

Because of internal labour markets firms need to design personnel policies that recognise the long-term nature of the employment relationship. Such policies concentrate on human resource management (HRM). It may be that the decline in trade union power, set out in Chapter 7, has increased the scope for HRM policies. The growing importance of flexible production methods, which make varying demands on the workforce and emphasise total quality management, has only increased the profile of HRM. HRM involves specifying the nature of the job and the personal characteristics required of the job holder. The wage for a job needs to be established both in relation to the external market and to the wages of related jobs within the firm. Recruitment can be from the external and internal labour markets. The advantage of the internal market is that it consists of applicants who the firm should know quite well. Using the internal market for promotion acts as a positive incentive for the existing workforce. However, there is a negative aspect of internal promotion in that it may undermine morale and cause conflict especially for those who have been passed over for promotion. Selection of a candidate can be based on a number of different devices: an application form; references; firm administered test results; and almost always a selection interview. Once a worker has been hired there are important orientation functions that are needed to familiarise the worker with the firm, its history, its organisation, its performance and its philosophy usually reflected in a mission statement. Training is crucial; it may be informal in nature such as showing the workings of the company filing system, or it may be formal sessions to enable workers to adapt to new technology. Training should not be confined to new or recently promoted employees.

Motivation is a key HRM topic. If McGregor (1960) is to be believed, the assumption for theory X is:

> Most workers avoid responsibility and are fundamentally lazy.

These employees need close supervision and need to be threatened with sanctions. The other set of assumptions for theory Y are:

> Workers motivated by a need for self-esteem and achievement are hard working and willingly accept responsibility. For these people threats do not motivate.

Traditional mass production would be characterised by theory X, whereas more modern flexible production methods are more suited to theory Y. Traditional mass production used dedicated capital machinery with labour performing a small set of specialised tasks that were easy to learn. The organisation of mass production was called 'Fordism' after the well-known car manufacturing company that pioneered mass car production. Although Fordism represented an efficient form of production it did suffer by having dedicated capital and a narrow range of specialised labour skills when confronted by changing business conditions in which employment stability was almost impossible to achieve. It was a good method of production to generate new jobs when the industry was growing. It was also good at taking on new workers, especially the young, because the skills were quickly learned. As the skills were transferable to other firms, turnover could be quite high. However, mass production operated in an environment of little trust between workers and management and a climate of conflict in industrial relations, sometimes referred to as 'Taylorism'.

The development of more flexible electronically controlled machine tools, brought about by microprocessor technology, meant that workers needed to have a more varied set of skills. In the mass production system the economies of scale lay with the production process, yet with more flexibility in the production process the emphasis shifted to research and development and marketing.

Piore and Sabel (1984) suggested that firms needed to move away from mass production to engage in 'flexible specialisation'. This is characterised by

- reorganising production, aided by computer technology
- firms specialising in an aspect of an industry

- limited entry to an industry
- competition promoting innovation
- industry wide wages and working conditions preventing cost cutting competition.

For flexible specialisation to work there has to be trust between managements and workers based on a degree of employment security. Workers' power will be weakened by management's enhanced ability to achieve flexibility in the workplace but wages and working conditions should improve in the long term as flexible specialised firms succeed. There is some doubt about whether flexible specialisation will deliver high wages and better working conditions in the long term. Amin (1991) pointed out that in small firms in Italy it was long hours and poor wages that delivered flexibility not the improved knowledge of workers.

Atkinson's (1984) notion of the 'flexible firm' was a departure from Taylorist notions of increasing productivity through tight management control reducing jobs to routine tasks. The rules that maintained this form of organisation would be removed creating a 'core' of high skilled employees, who would participate in decision-making, and a 'periphery' of low-wage workers with little job security. Flexibility would come from the firm being able to use core workers around the organisation and from task to task. It also would come from being able to vary the size of the peripheral workforce using short-term contracts, part-time workers, contracting work out, home-working, franchising, and using employment agency temporary workers. The distinction between core and peripheral workers is not a clear one. In many industries temporary contract and part-time workers are performing core functions. In a downturn core workers along with peripheral workers will often be made redundant.

More flexible production was linked to lean production developed by the Toyota car company in Japan. Just in time delivery systems got rid of expensive stocks of input materials and final product. Lean production did away with much of the costly supervision and management control of workers. According to Marsden (1995) lean production is a 'method of management, and a way of tackling organisational and technical problems directly, as they emerge' (p. 25). Lean production means fewer

- semi-skilled production workers
- supervisory jobs
- professional skills.

But it would lead to more

- long-term employment
- multi-skilling
- company specific skills
- devolution of decision-making.

And it would strengthen internal labour markets.

In more modern flexible production, the use of small, self-directed work teams may increase workers motivation, as it is easier to identify with the work team rather than the larger more anonymous firm. Social pressure within the team may bring about greater effort. Team working is also important at the top management level. West *et al.* (1999) demonstrate that in a sample of 42 UK manufacturing companies team performance is directly linked to productivity and profitability, with the average educational level of the team being an important predictor of team performance. Work teams are compatible with the ideas of total quality management (TQM). TQM is a more extensive concept than lean production and has been applied to services and the public sector as well as manufacturing. TQM defines quality in terms of the customer's needs and feedback from the customer. Senior management are tasked with incorporating quality. Workers are to suggest improvements to practice and process to enhance quality. TQM places great importance on exposing staff to customers. For TQM to succeed workers also need training in interpersonal skills including communication. Pay policies need to enhance problem solving and cooperation not competition amongst workers. For TQM to work effectively firms need to abandon old managerial practices where managers make decisions and workers do what they are told. It needs trust and long-term commitment on both sides, things that will be undermined by job insecurity. However, employment security needs to be offset by flexibility of the workforce (see Chapter 8) if it is not to harm competitiveness. The recognition that certain firm specific skills might gain the firm some competitive advantage lies behind the notion of organisational competencies. The term organisational competencies, is just a complicated way of saying something that the organisation does well. The interpersonal and team working skills that might help the firm do something well can be developed within the firm by its training programmes.

Polachek and Siebert (1993) estimated that about half the British workforce and 40 per cent of the US workforce, were in internal labour markets. The recent growth of more flexible forms of employment such as part-time work, fixed term contracts and self-employment might suggest that internal labour markets are now less prevalent than once they were. Polivka (1996) estimates that around 5 per cent of the US workforce, in 1995, was employed in insecure jobs.

CASE STUDY – INTERNAL LABOUR MARKETS IN AN INSURANCE CORPORATION

The nature of internal labour markets (ILMs) has changed often as a result of deliberate policy decisions taken by firms. Many firms try to restrict the internal mobility of labour by insisting on minimum job tenure (residency) periods and managerial approval for internal job applicants. Rado Korotov and Emily Hsu (2002) 'A Road-Map for Creating Efficient Corporate Internal Labour Markets', *Career Development International*, 7 (1): 37–46, provides some guidance for firms seeking to set up ILMs that operate more like proper markets for the benefit of both employees and firms. They also give a couple of case studies one of which, the US based The Chubb Group of Insurance Companies (Chubb), we reproduce here.

Since 1990, large corporations have been gradually liberating their . . . ILMs. The traditional . . . system, in which the employee's career path was determined by managerial discretion, has been replaced by . . . systems in which employees are free to post-[apply] for and move to new vacant positions. The filling of vacancy positions is based on market principles rather than on control and command principles. Employees are free to undertake any opportunities that fit their career goals, and managers have incentives to choose the best available candidate.

The transition to ILM . . . is triggered both by external and internal factors. First, the war for talent waged on corporations by external recruiters, head-hunters and aggressive HR [human resource] departments of competing firms has created unprecedented opportunities for employees to manage their careers. To stay competitive, companies have had to respond to the external pressures and demonstrate to employees that they could realise their opportunities inside rather than outside of the company. Second, corporate restructuring initiatives reorganised corporate units as individual profit centres with their own internal customers. This process, in fact, created internal markets, which increased the organisational efficiency and produced significant cost savings. If internal markets worked so well in the internal procurement process, why not apply the same model to the internal allocation of labour?

. . .

In 1997 Chubb, a publicly traded insurance company with approximately 15,000 employees worldwide, eliminated its residency policy and its requirement for managerial approval of employees' applications for internal positions. . . .

The corporate culture at Chubb is one of trust and support. Employees are encouraged to communicate career goals and position [job] dissatisfaction openly with their supervisors. Accordingly, supervisors are encouraged to help employees willing to leave their departments to find more suitable positions, thus preventing employees from migrating to another company. . . .

Chubb's culture reflects the support by all for honouring informal agreements. Managers and employees understand the highly specialised skills required for certain positions are learned over time on the job and/or through specialised training. For example, raters are highly specialised, highly trained employees, who need to stay in their positions for at least 18 months in order to realise any return on human capital investment. This understanding has led to an informal agreement between hiring managers and employees that employees should remain in position for the period necessary to realise a return on investment . . . To 'enforce' this . . . those who do not follow the informal agreements develop a reputation . . . , thereby adversely affecting their future employment opportunities within the organisation . . .

Managers, upon losing an employee to another position, are often hard-pressed to find a suitable replacement. At Chubb, to . . . eliminate managers' frustrations at trying to fill a highly specialised position, a new structural element has been added to the corporation, the 'farm'. The 'farm' is . . . the company's internal temp agency whose employees are used by managers to fill vacated positions . . . The 'farm' is organised as a cost centre to prevent disruptions in the work output required for Chubb's daily operations. Because the 'farm' absorbs the departmental cost of gaps in filling vacancies, it eliminates the incentives for managers to obstruct employee mobility and the operations of ILM in general, as well as to engage in hand-over conflicts with other managers.

. . . In addition to always being available to provide guidance and support, one of the key roles HR plays at Chubb is the development and maintenance of the career Web site . . . The site communicates and educates its employees about its policies, changes to policies, and open positions.

. . .

Open ILMs can benefit employees, managers and companies. . . . They help bring about lower employee turnover, better fitted [matched] employees to positions, improved employee return on investment and, in the end, a more competitive firm.

The importance of informal contracts and corporate culture are highlighted by this case study. ILMs appear to work best in large organisations which have built up a high level of trust between workers and managers. Chubb is large enough to have its own pool of temporary workers in the 'farm'. The provision of information and channels of communication seem to be important aspects of a successful ILM.

Note how these more market-orientated ILMs are restricted to talented workers who are being fought over both by external competitors like other firms, employment agencies and head-hunters as well as being sought by other managers in the same firm. The system at Chubb is arranged to fit around the special circumstances of key skilled workers in whom a great deal of training has been invested. The main conclusion seems to be that ILMs have evolved to try and retain highly skilled workers within the corporation against a background of tight labour markets.

PROMOTION

Promotion can be used as a performance enhancing incentive. Along with promotion comes an increase in pay, so in a way promotion is a form of performance related pay. However, the effectiveness of promotion as an incentive to greater effort on the part of workers depends on the likelihood of being promoted. For the UK Marsden *et al.* (2000) refer to the very slow pace of promotion in the civil service '20 years for a newly promoted Senior Executive Officer to reach the next grade up' (p. 2). In such circumstances promotion is an exceptionally weak incentive.

Lazear and Rosen (1981) in their tournament theory developed the idea that there is competition for promotion. In a situation where most promotion is internal, workers get promoted because their performance at their current level is better compared to their peers. The higher the difference between the current level salary and the promotion salaries the greater the effort exerted by workers to get the higher-level job. According to Lazear (1998) 'this is the key point of tournament theory. The larger the raise associated with a given promotion, the greater the incentive to be promoted' (p. 226). Firms can use substantial pay differentials between different levels of the firm's hierarchy to act as incentives to greater effort, productivity and profit. Obviously the more that promotion depends on things other than effort (luck, discrimination or favouritism) the more worker effort declines.

Bearing these considerations in mind we can compare the two salary structures represented in Figure 4.1. The salary structure in Figure 4.1(a) shows wage rises of equal size between the four levels of the firm's hierarchy. Figure 4.1(b) has a salary

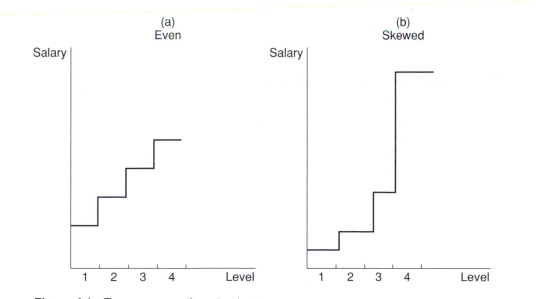

Figure 4.1 Two compensation structures

Source: Lazear 1998, figure 9.2, p. 239

structure of a greater range with the rises getting bigger with each promotion through the hierarchy. Figure 4.1(b) is the more common structure and provides the stronger incentives for promotion. Even getting promoted from level 1 to level 2 is worthwhile, because although the magnitude of the pay rise is not very great it does allow the promoted worker to begin to compete for the bigger prize of being promoted to level 3.

There is some empirical evidence to support the tournament model; for example, Drago and Garvey (1998) found that when Australian firms offered larger pay rises on promotion then effort did increase and absenteeism was reduced.

There are a number of problems with using promotion as an incentive. Once individuals have been promoted, they might ease up and rest on their laurels. How do you motivate the chief executive officer (CEO) of a firm when there is no further promotion to be had? Promotion may cease to act as an incentive for those workers who have been repeatedly passed over for promotion. Then there is the problem of providing opportunities for promotion. Without growth in the organisational structure promotion becomes a matter of waiting to fill 'dead men's shoes'. Then there is the problem of promotion based on the best performance at the current level, which does not ensure the best performance in the higher-level job. A failure to accurately match workers to jobs will lower efficiency.

McConnell and Brue (1995) doubt the relevance of the tournament theory for the pay of the upper echelons of business. If high CEO pay were determined by a tournament, then those competing for the top job might take opportunities to sabotage rivals' performance in a way that would not be optimal for the firm. CEO pay might be set by supply and demand for a scare resource, namely good senior executives. However, given the way in which CEO pay is administered at the corporate board level in the USA and the UK, it is more likely that the CEO's importance and worth might be overrated. There is a weak link between CEO pay and share price but a much stronger link between CEO pay and firm size. McConnell and Brue (1995) report that in the USA between 1980 and 1991,

factory worker pay rose	+57 per cent
corporate profits up	+73 per cent
CEO pay multiplied	+294 per cent.

In the UK in 2001 there was concern over the growth of senior executive pay in poorly performing companies such as BT, Marconi, Marks and Spencers and Railtrack. Yet as we can see from the data in Table 4.1, this did not prevent British CEOs from being the second most highly paid in a sample of seven OECD countries and British manufacturing workers the most lowly paid.

British CEOs were paid the most of the European countries in the sample, with German CEOs being paid the least. German manufacturing workers were the most highly paid of the European countries. We have compared manufacturing workers' productivity in Chapter 2, but how are we to assess whether British CEOs are about 71 per cent more productive than their German counterparts?

Table 4.1 CEO and manufacturing workers' pay
(£, average annual earnings)

	CEO	Worker
USA	992,974	31,603
Britain	509,019	20,475
Australia	457,139	21,010
Japan	385,645	36,779
France	382,128	24,574
Sweden	311,400	23,034
Germany	298,223	26,124

Source: Towers Perrin 2000

Murphy (1999) found that:

- CEO pay levels are higher and less sensitive to actual performance in larger firms;
- CEOs received lower levels of pay that were insensitive to performance in Government regulated utility firms;
- CEO pay levels were higher and more sensitive to performance in the USA than elsewhere.

Overall, CEO pay levels and performance sensitivity in the USA increased in the 1990s driven mainly by senior managers' stock (company share ownership) options.

FRINGE BENEFITS

Fringe benefits are a significant share of a worker's total compensation package, which has grown over time. According to the US Bureau of Labour Statistics fringe benefits accounted for 28 per cent of total compensation in private industry in 1992, up from 3 per cent in 1929. Fringe benefits include:

- Retirement pensions, even though all workers may be covered by a basic age-related state pension, the vast majority of firms operate an occupational pension scheme for their employees to which the firm contributes. In spite of the onus for pension provision shifting towards the individual in a number of countries, including the UK, company pension schemes remain a substantial and widespread fringe benefit.
- Paid holidays and sick pay are valuable fringe benefits, as is maternity and other parental leave.
- Private health insurance is a valuable benefit particularly in the USA where health insurance premiums have risen quite rapidly. In addition workers will be protected by sickness and accident insurance.
- Supplemental pay for overtime, holiday working, shift-work and bonuses are also benefits.
- Other benefits include redundancy payments and discounts on company products and the use of company cars.

Many of these fringe benefits have become embodied in law so that the firm is obliged to provide them. Benefits such as pension rights and holiday entitlement increase along with length of service and may therefore encourage longer tenure. Longer tenure leads to lower labour turnover thereby reducing hiring and training costs for the firm.

Fringe benefits usually have tax advantages over direct wage payments for both the firm and the individual worker. For the firm certain social and employment taxes may be levied on the size of the total payroll, whereas fringe benefits are exempt from such taxes. For the worker pension schemes mean deferring tax from current income which will almost certainly be taxed at a higher rate than the retirement income which the pension provides. Insurance benefits are unlikely to attract income taxes, although the benefit of a company car in the UK has been eroded by a series of tax increases on their use. When it comes to health insurance and pensions fringe benefits help compensate for myopia in an individual's consumption decisions. High marginal tax rates, for both firms and workers, encourage the use of fringe benefits. As workers have become better off in real terms this has increased their demand for fringe benefits.

Economies of scale such as cheaper group insurance have reduced the unit cost of fringe benefits. Trade unions have been important advocates of greater fringe benefits. These two factors mean that fringe benefits are more prevalent in large, unionised firms. In theory the right combination of wages and fringe benefits can be determined. Consider the scenario set out in Figure 4.2.

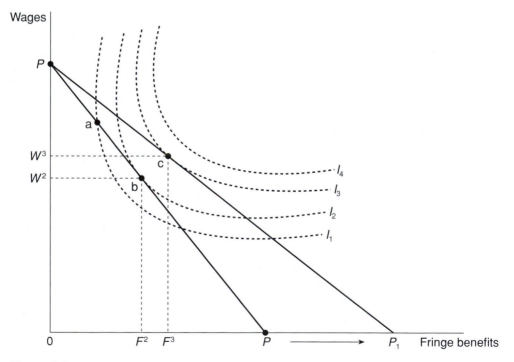

Figure 4.2

An optimum combination of wages and fringe benefits arises from the meeting of the workers' attitude to wages and non-wage benefits in total compensation with the firm's interests represented by the isoprofit line P–P in Figure 4.2. Starting with the isoprofit function P–P the highest attainable indifference curve is I_2 at point b. This gives a combination of wage W^2 and fringe benefits F^2 that the worker most prefers subject to the firms profit constraint. Point a is affordable but the worker values more fringe benefits and is willing to give up some wages in order to get them. Now if the cost to the firm of fringe benefits falls, the move from P–P to P–P_1, then the worker can increase his/her utility at point c with a combination of both more fringe benefits and higher wages. The cost of fringe benefits might fall due to better tax advantages of economies of scale and greater efficiency in the provision of fringe benefits. Note that at point c the cost of the total compensation package is no greater than it was at point b, nor have the firm's profits been affected.

Pension schemes are a form of deferred compensation because the workers usually have to wait until they reach retirement age at 60 or 65 in order to benefit. This form of fringe benefit requires a long-term relationship. During such a lengthy relationship a worker may be paid less than their marginal productivity at the start of their employment and end up being paid more than their productivity towards the end of their employment. Having a mandatory retirement age ensures that older workers, who are being paid in excess of their productivity, do not stay too long. Over the working lifetime of an employee the firm does not want to pay more in wages and fringe benefits than the value of that worker's output. In the absence of a compulsory retirement age a pension scheme needs to be arranged so that the maximum value of the pension coincides with the point at which total compensation and total value of output equate. Indeed, most pension schemes provide some incentives for early retirement. A characteristic of deferred compensation like pensions is that wages will rise faster than productivity as employment tenure increases.

PERFORMANCE RELATED PAY

Input based pay rewards workers for the amount of time and effort spent on a work activity. In contrast output based pay rewards workers according to the product of their work effort. We have already mentioned an output based pay system, piece work; this along with other performance related pay schemes is meant to encourage good workers to stay and inefficient workers to leave as well as encouraging greater effort at work.

To illustrate the screening aspect of performance related pay consider Figure 4.3, which contrasts two firms in the car retail industry but with different wage schemes. The European car company pays its sales staff a flat £600 per week irrespective of the number of cars they sell. However, over at the American car company showroom, sales staff are paid a basic £100 per week, and then a commission of £100 per car for every car that they sell. A salesperson capable of selling 5 cars per week will be indifferent about working for either company. However, a salesperson who can only

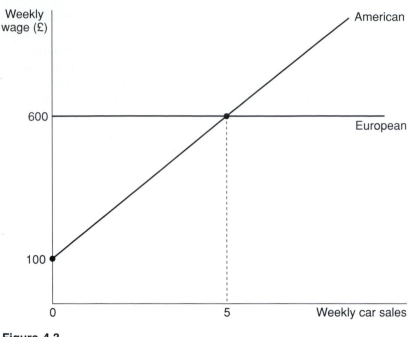

Figure 4.3

manage to sell 4 or fewer cars will prefer to work at the European car showroom. More effective sales staff, who can sell more than five cars per week, would be better off working for the American car firm.

Lazear (1996) contains an example of how effective performance related pay can be in a US car window glass replacement company. After moving from an hourly pay system to pay based on the number of glass installations, productivity rose by 36 per cent and average pay per worker increased by 9 per cent. Evidently both the workers and especially the firm benefited from the switch to performance related pay.

Using British data Booth and Frank (1999) discovered that performance related pay was associated with higher earnings, especially in non-unionised firms. For male workers performance related pay resulted in a 9.3 per cent boost in earnings and for women it gave a 5.6 per cent hike in earnings. These rises appeared to come in response to a productivity gain in the region of 20 per cent. The number of UK employees in profit sharing schemes including performance related pay rose rapidly from 232,000 in 1990 to 2,438,000 in 1995.

Providing incentives to groups of workers to encourage team working and greater effort might be achieved through share (stock) ownership and profit sharing schemes. Profit sharing among all employees of a company may provide an incentive to greater effort and help workers understand and identify with the firm's objectives. Workers and management are able to share a common goal, increasing the firm's profits. Share ownership also focuses on profits but encourages workers to think of themselves as owners and capitalists.

In spite of the incentives contained in large group performance related schemes like profit sharing there are some risks. Firstly, there is the problem of free-riders who will reap the same reward from profit sharing without additional work effort. Ordinarily the monetary value of an individual profit share or allocation of company shares (stock) is quite small and will not provide a powerful incentive to boost productivity. For individual CEOs profit sharing and share (stock) options are a substantial part of their compensation package.

Performance related pay is not limited to work environments, such as the above examples, where individual output is easy to measure. Fernie and Metcalf (1999) assert that performance related pay schemes are better than time based pay in precisely those circumstances where the worker is difficult to monitor and has a fair degree of control over their own work.

However, Marsden et al. (2000) found that when performance related pay was introduced into public services in Britain the impact was mixed. They found that performance related pay did indeed serve to motivate some employees, especially those who received above average performance related payments, yet the majority of workers (teachers, health service professionals, tax officials) felt that it had deteriorated relations in the workplace and had undermined cooperation at work. A particular problem with performance related pay is that the evaluation of performance rests upon an individual worker's line manager. This is a subjective assessment of achievement usually made against a set of individual objectives. Hence the issue of the fairness of appraisal, – do the workers trust the fairness of managers who control performance evaluation? Marsden et al. (2000) report that

> it was widely thought that performance pay was a device to cut the pay bill; over 60 per cent thought management applied a quota to good appraisals; around 55 per cent of employees thought they would not be awarded performance pay even if their work was good enough; and over 40 per cent thought line managers used performance pay to reward their favourites.
>
> (p. 3)

Clearly there was a great deal of suspicion about performance related pay in the public sector.

EFFICIENCY WAGES

When monitoring workers is costly and individual output is difficult to quantify efficiency wages may be used to deter shirking. Efficiency wages are wages paid by firms that are above the market clearing level, but that they find profit maximising. (See Weiss (1991) for an introduction to efficiency wage models.) Employers use high wages to assist in the recruitment, retention and motivation of their workforces. Firms need to ensure that the effort exerted by the workforce will lead to profit maximisation. Worker effort is influenced by wages in the firm relative to elsewhere. Where individual effort is difficult to monitor, especially in large firms, enhanced wages can serve to motivate the workforce. Higher wages may help prevent shirking by increasing the cost to the workers of losing their jobs should they be discovered shirking. According to Canziani (1997) workers who are fired are stigmatised and have to endure longer spells of unemployment before finding another job than workers who lose their jobs because a temporary employment contract ends and is not renewed. In the cases of Italy and Spain in the 1990s, temporary employment contract workers have 'respectively a 10 and 30 per cent lower probability than fired workers of remaining unemployed for more than 3 months' (p. 25).

Firms incur genuine costs associated with labour turnover and absenteeism, so they may use wages to try and dissuade their workers from leaving and encourage better attendance. Quits incur recruitment and training costs that firms would wish to minimise. The incentive for so doing increases as the firm specific human capital of the workforce rises.

Firms may also wish to influence the flow of applicants for any vacancy through the offered wage. Essentially the higher the offered wage, the better the average quality of applicant, enabling firms to impose and maintain stricter hiring standards. Recruitment costs should be lowered as workers approach the firm rather than the employer having to undertake extensive searches of the labour market. For non-unionised firms the high rates of pay implied by the efficiency wage argument might undermine the need for a union. In unionised firms efficiency wages may well reduce the losses arising from industrial disputes and stoppages. Furthermore, the reputation of the company and the sense of well being of the workforce may be enhanced by a high wage policy.

Such efficiency wage considerations result in wage differences between firms for identical workers. Thus wages in large, capital intensive firms tend to be higher in general than those paid by small firms. A clear implication of the efficiency wage argument is that wage rises increase productivity, thereby shifting the labour demand curve to the right.

In general wages do appear to be linked to productivity. Hellerstein *et al.* (1999) using data from US manufacturing plants found that wage differences did tend to reflect marginal productivity differences between workers irrespective of marital status or ethnic origin. However, this was not the case for female manufacturing workers who appeared to be paid less than their marginal productivity. We return to such evidence of discrimination in Chapter 6.

The efficiency wage argument is criticised by Polachek and Siebert (1993, pp. 261–5) on the grounds that the dismissal threat, which underlies it, does not have much credibility in large firms, which give workers better job tenure. It also ignores life-cycle earnings effects, which are dealt with by human capital theory. A firm would also need to consider whether shirking might be better countered by using deferred payment (like pensions) or performance related pay at less cost than efficiency wages.

Testing efficiency wage models has proved difficult but Manning and Thomas (1997) have used UK data to investigate the shirking model. While their results are not conclusive, 'overall [they] do not suggest that the shirking model is of great importance in the labour market' (p. 22). This does not mean that worker motivation is not a problem, only that firms tend not to pay higher wages to deal with shirking.

Yet the important point about wages based on efficiency considerations is that they do not clear the labour market but produce queues of applicants for jobs.

PERSONNEL ECONOMICS – SUMMARY

In this chapter we examined the new economics of personnel, which is centred upon the microeconomics of the employment relationship. Interesting aspects of this relationship revolved around the problems between principals (firms) and agents (workers). We found that employment contracts may recognise these problems by incorporating

- piecework pay
- probation periods

The notion that there may be implicit contracts between workers and firms helped explain certain features of the long-term nature of the employment relationship such as

- employment stability
- wage stability over the business cycle
- wage rigidity

The concept of an internal labour market helped to explain

- high wage policies
- internal promotion
- the link between wages and tenure
- human resource management practices

We saw that promotion could be used as an incentive to greater effort at work. However, the success of promotion as an incentive depended on

- the probability of promotion
- the pay hierarchy

We saw that promotion could be analysed in terms of competition for a higher-level job in the tournament model. Although there was some doubt about how applicable it was to CEOs.

An important component of the total compensation package a worker receives from the firm was found to be fringe benefits, namely

- pensions
- holiday, sick and parental pay
- health insurance

- overtime and shift pay
- redundancy pay
- company discounts

Fringe benefits conferred tax advantages on both workers and firms. In theory it was possible to determine the optimum combination of wages and fringe benefits in relation to the firm's desire for profits.

Performance related pay schemes could separate workers according to their productivity and induce more effort from the workforce. This was held to be effective in some cases but aroused suspicion among British public sector workers.

Finally we looked at the idea of efficiency wages. Firms appear to follow a high-wage–low-turnover policy because they find it profit maximising. However, the efficiency wages that are paid are above those that would clear a competitive labour market.

PERSONNEL ECONOMICS – QUESTIONS FOR DISCUSSION

1) What is the purpose of a probation period for newly hired workers?
2) Explain how implicit contracts might smooth employment and wage changes over a business cycle.
3) What is an internal labour market and how does it operate?
4) If the Government reduced the attractiveness of fringe benefits by taxing them more highly what would happen to the outcome of Figure 4.2?
5) Why might a firm not wish to see a worker stay on until they are 75 years old?
6) What advantages and what drawbacks can you suggest that a performance related pay scheme for university lecturers might contain?
7) Are there any advantages for the firm paying wages above the market clearing level?

SUGGESTED READING

Lazear, E. (1998) *Personnel Economics For Managers*, New York: J. Wiley and Sons.
Lazear, E. (1999) 'Personnel Economics: Past Lessons and Future Directions', *Journal of Labour Economics*, 17 (2): 199–236.

5

Human capital

INTRODUCTION

Economics identifies two important categories of expenditure: consumption, which yields immediate benefit in the form of utility; and investment expenditure which increases productive capacity and future incomes. Investment is conventionally regarded in terms of physical capital, such as plant and machinery, yet the notion that educating and training labour increases productive capacity in a manner analogous to physical capital investment goes back at least as far as Adam Smith (1776). In the *Wealth of Nations* he writes, 'a man educated at the expense of much labour and time . . . may be compared to one of those expensive machines'. However, the systematic analysis of education and training as a form of human capital investment began in earnest in the early 1960s with the pioneering work of Schultz (1961), Mincer (1962) and Becker (1964). As a consequence of this activity, the concept of human capital as an investment raising future income was developed and empirically tested. Since then human capital has played an important role in the neoclassical analysis of labour markets, especially with regard to wage determination, and has come to dominate the economic analysis of education. This should not be interpreted as meaning that economics does not acknowledge the consumption benefits of education, yet it does mean that important insights have been gained by viewing education as one of the routes by which human capital may be acquired. Human capital theory has also exerted a powerful influence on economic growth theory, the analysis of health care and of migration patterns.

Our treatment of human capital will concentrate on investigating the relationship between education and earnings. This chapter will set out an analysis of vocational training. We will discuss the possibility that some individuals are over educated. We will also look into the impact of computers on the labour market and examine whether recent technological change has favoured more educated workers. Finally we will examine the role of human capital in a general economic growth model and apply this to industrialised and developing countries.

THE BASIC MODEL

In developing a simple human capital model we will confine ourselves initially to the case where additional non-compulsory education (schooling) increases the productivity of labour in a perfectly competitive market. This last condition ensures that the rewards to labour are strictly dependent upon its productivity, such that wages equal marginal revenue productivity (W = MRP, see Chapter 2). Thus any wage differentials are based upon differences in productivity, which are the result of differences in human capital due to individual differences in the amount of an otherwise homogeneous education undertaken. By allowing only human capital to differ between individuals we are assuming them to be homogeneous with respect to age, sex, race, ability, experience and wealth. The simplicity of this line of reasoning will shortly be undermined but its strength is that it allows us to make a clear statement of the human capital model. Consider the example of a wealth maximising individual, in this case a representative female worker in the UK educated to 'A' level (usually taken at age 18), deciding whether to undertake an extra period of full-time education at university in order to obtain a first degree. The problem is effectively a comparison of the costs and benefits associated with that extra three years spent being educated. The costs include the direct cost of tuition fees and books and the indirect cost of earnings forgone. The indirect cost consists of the wages that could have been earned as an 'A' level worker instead of being an undergraduate student for three years and this represents the main cost component.

In 2000 the median gross annual earnings of a full-time employee in the UK with 'A' level qualifications was £16,640 (see Table 5.6 for earnings by qualification). This provides us with an over-estimate of the indirect cost of a year's full-time university education because it makes no allowance for income tax and national insurance contributions which would have been deducted from salary, but it shows that the individual's investment in terms of costs incurred by non-compulsory education is not insignificant.

Given that non-compulsory education incurs costs, both direct and indirect, which are not inconsequential, what is the benefit of additional education? The answer is that investment in education raises the productive capacity of the individual, which in turn yields higher potential earnings post-education. Thus the stream of higher earnings over one's working life is the return on the initial investment (costs incurred) in the acquisition of human capital. The earnings differential between graduate workers and workers with 'A' levels, maintained over the course of a working life, represents the benefit of acquiring a university education.

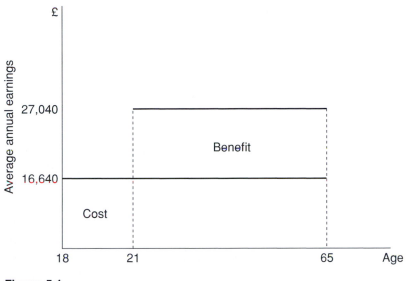

Figure 5.1

In our example of workers in an imaginary tax free Britain of 2000, let us simplify the analysis still further by assuming that their average earnings hold throughout their working life until they are 65. Figure 5.1 contains the essence of the cost–benefit comparison being made between 'A' level and graduate workers. Having already remained at school for two years voluntarily in order to obtain 'A' levels (the compulsory school leaving age in the UK is 16), a person could have entered the labour force in the expectation of earning on average £16,640 per year.

Those who choose to enter university and study for a degree full-time over three years incur the indirect cost of earnings foregone at a rate of £16,640 per year. This is obviously lessened by any state grants or scholarships, which subsidise students through higher education, but for the present we will ignore these features of the education system. Currently there are no examination fees for the individual to pay but a charge of £1,000 per year for tuition is levied on students whose parents are above a certain income threshold. On the assumption that if the student is charged tuition fees and that any book purchases (including I hope this one) are funded out of vacation work, we can confidently ignore the direct costs of this investment. The benefit is composed of the addition to earnings the qualification brings over the working life of the graduate employee.

A rational individual fully informed of the relevant costs and benefits is in a position to calculate the return from an investment in education in a manner analogous to that in which a firm would compute the return on physical capital investment. Hence the same investment appraisal techniques of Net Present Value and Internal Rate of Return that are used for physical capital investment can be applied to human capital. In the case of an optional period E of education the relevant comparison in net present value terms is between

$$\sum_{t=1}^{T-E} W_E - W_{E-1}/(1 + i)^t \quad \text{and} \quad W_{E-1} + C_E$$

This represents the present value of higher expected earnings, where $W_E > W_{E-1}$ due to the extra period of education over one's working life $(T - E)$. In a perfect capital market the rate of interest (i) would be the correct rate to take account of an individual's time preference and the opportunity cost of this investment as opposed to any other. The total cost of the investment is represented by the direct costs C_E and the loss of earnings W_{E-1} during the period of additional education. The extra education is worthwhile from an investment appraisal perspective if the present value of higher future earnings exceeds the cost of acquiring that additional education.

$$\sum_{t=1}^{T-E} W_E - W_{E-1}/(1 + i)^t > W_{E-1} + C_E \tag{5.1}$$

Another way of appraising an extra period of education as an investment is to calculate its internal rate of return r, which can then be compared with a market rate of interest i. The key to this approach is to find a value for r which will equate the costs and benefits accruing to additional education.

$$\sum_{t=1}^{T-E} W_E - W_{E-1}/(1 + r)^t = W_{E-1} + C_E \tag{5.2}$$

The extra education is worthwhile if the value of r contained in Equation (5.2) is greater than the rate of interest $(r > i)$. In order that we may discover what essentially determines the rate of return r let us strip Equation (5.2) down to its simplest form. Taking the view that for the individual the direct costs of education are insignificant where the state pays tuition fees, or are covered by vacation work where it does not, we can confidently abandon C_E. By further assuming that one's working life $(T - E)$ is sufficiently long, at 44 years for a 21-year-old in the UK, to be approximated as being infinite, then we can rewrite Equation (5.2) as

$$W_E - W_{E-1}/r = W_{E-1}$$

This can be transformed by multiplying both sides by r, and then dividing both sides by W_{E-1} to produce

$$W_E - W_{E-1}/W_{E-1} = r.$$

Therefore the essential determinant of the rate of return to an extra period E of education is higher post-education earnings generated as a proportion of pre-education earnings. In other words the rate of return measures benefit as a proportion of opportunity cost.

Applying this basic rate of return formula to the example of British workers' average earnings in 2000, the rate of return for the private individual investing in a degree amounts to

$$27,040 - 16,640/(16,640 \times 3) \times 100 = 20.8\%.$$

Although this numerical example is absurdly simple it does serve to show what the more sophisticated and more accurate empirical estimates of rates of return to education are essentially trying to convey from within a human capital framework. Incorporating a state subsidy will obviously reduce the private individual cost of university education by lowering the earnings forgone component, thereby increasing the rate of return. Charging students university (college) tuition fees, as has long been the case in the USA and which will remain the case in the UK, will reduce the individual's rate of return. For example if we incorporate tuition fees of £1,000 per year and £1,000 living expenses that are not covered by the student's part-time work, then the 20.8 per cent return falls to 18.6 per cent

$$27,040 - 16,640/(16,640 \times 3) + 6,000 \times 100 = 18.6\%.$$

The justification for setting fixed costs at £6,000 is that the 10th Barclays Bank Student Survey published in July 2001 had students averaging debts of £5,961 upon graduating.

The crucial comparison is between the estimated rate of return ($r = 18.6\%$) and the market rate of interest i. In order to maximise the present value of future earnings, the fully informed rational individual should invest in human capital acquisition up to the point where the rate of return on an increment of education equals the market rate of interest, that being where $r = i$.

We can represent diagrammatically the relationship between the internal rate of return r, the rate of interest i and human capital proxied by years in education. Figure 5.2 shows an internal rate of return schedule IRR, which slopes downwards to reflect the fact that as one's level of educational attainment increases the rate of return falls. This is because as one strives to become ever more educated the cost in terms of earnings foregone rises year by year (qualification by qualification) thereby depressing

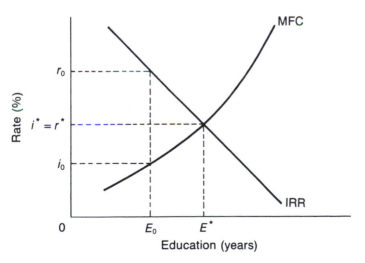

Figure 5.2

Table 5.1 UK unemployment rates (%), 2000

	Male	Female	All
Degree and above A Level	2.5	2.2	2.4
A Level/equivalent	4.5	4.5	4.5
GCSE A–C/equivalent	7.5	5.4	6.3
Other	8.6	6.6	7.7
No qualification	13.7	8.2	11.1

Source: ONS, Labour Force Survey, Spring 2000

the rate of return to education r. The interest rate i is linked to the financing cost of education. The marginal financing cost (MFC) schedule increases to reflect the view that in the early stages of one's education one may have access to low cost sources of finance, such as family savings. Thereafter one has to resort to lending institutions, which demand increasing rates of interest to compensate for increased risk assessed in the light of rising personal indebtedness. Thus MFC is associated with a set of interest rates.[1] At a level of educational attainment E_0 the rate of return r_0 exceeds the rate of interest i_0. There is an incentive to invest in more education up to the level of E^* where $r^* = i^*$. The intersection of the IRR and MFC schedules in Figure 5.2 denotes the optimal amount of human capital investment by the individual yielding a private rate of return r^*. Note that any educational attainment beyond E^* represents over-education where the rate of return to that education is below the market rate of interest.

The human capital model appears to justify income differentials between individuals on the basis of differential productivity due to different levels of human capital (in this case education) acquisition. Decisions about whether to undertake human capital investment are based upon a comparison of the costs and benefits to the private individual of doing so. These are compared by using the internal rate of return appraisal technique, which yields a set of private rates of return. However, human capital costs and benefits are expectations incorporating a view about the probability/likelihood of current and future employment. Graduate unemployment lowers the expected benefit, thereby depressing the rate of return to a degree. Unemployment amongst school leavers reduces the opportunity cost of further study, thereby increasing the anticipated rate of return to a degree course. Data on UK unemployment rates according to educational qualification, contained in Table 5.1, suggests that men with no qualifications are five times more likely to be unemployed than male graduates. For women the ratio is nearly four times. From a human capital perspective an additional benefit of greater educational attainment, over and above the earnings differential, is the greater probability of getting and keeping a job.

Once unemployment considerations have been incorporated, the IRR schedule represented in Figure 5.2 is in effect the private individual's demand curve for post-compulsory education within a human capital context. Whether a human capital project is worthwhile depends on the relation between its rate of return r to the individual and the market rate of interest i.

AGE, ABILITY, WEALTH AND SMOKING

In a number of important respects the basic human capital model presented in the previous section needs to be elaborated upon. This is especially so with regard to the age of potential human capital investors, their innate ability and their existing wealth holdings. In effect we are engaged in the process of relaxing the assumption of the homogeneity of individual human capital investors.

Consideration of the age of the potential human capital investor yields a number of intuitively appealing statements. The first of these being that the earlier the human capital investment is made the greater the return is likely to be. This is so because it provides a longer period during which the flow of enhanced discounted earnings can offset the cost of the investment. A student graduating in the UK at age 21 will anticipate a working life of 44 years in the graduate labour market. A mature student leaving university at 41 after completing a first degree will be likely to experience the benefits of an enhanced salary for only 24 years. Graduating at 61 one contributes to the supply of graduate labour for 4 years. The point being that the longer the period of time during which the benefits of a human capital investment can accrue the greater the likelihood that $r > i$. Hence within a human capital framework there is an incentive to invest heavily when one is young.

Such an incentive is strengthened by a second age-related factor. The age earnings profile presented in Chapter 1, suggests that there is a positive correlation between age and earnings. The most striking feature of the profile shown in Figure 1.15 is its curvature. This could be interpreted as a positive return to employment experience, yet within a human capital model the path of the age earnings profile could be affected by post-school/post-university investments or on-the-job training, which decline with age. The fact that earnings increase with age, for whatever reasons, means that the cost of human capital investment measured as earnings forgone for full-time or an imputed cost of leisure forgone for part-time investment, increases with age. This will act (*ceteris paribus*) as a disincentive to invest in human capital acquisition as the individual ages by depressing the rate of return.

What is being suggested is that internal rates of return to the same human capital acquisition are age-related. Thus our initial presentation, which culminated in Figure 5.2, should be amended to take account of the age of the investor. Figure 5.3 does just that on the assumption that both young and old face the same capital market conditions, that is a single MFC schedule.[2] The effect of taking age into account is that the amount of human capital investment undertaken and its rate of return generally declines with age.[3] Human capital deteriorates, which might account for the typical curve of an age earnings profile as human capital increases earnings but at a decreasing rate. Human capital deterioration is a problem for the unemployed, particularly those who are out of work for a long period of time (see Chapter 10). Groot (1998) has estimated rates of skill depreciation of between 11 per cent and 17 per cent per year.

Relaxing the homogeneity assumption with regard to the ability of individuals affects the basic analysis in one important respect. Irrespective of an individual's human

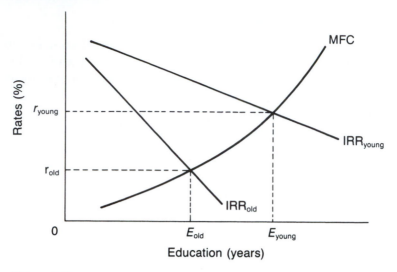

Figure 5.3

capital endowments, differential ability will be translated into differential productivity in the workplace. In this context ability is defined solely in relation to the demands of the employment task and can therefore include abilities such as physical strength and dexterity as well as intellectual abilities. What is being suggested is that two individuals, one of low ability A_L and the other of high ability A_H, with identical human capital acquisitions, will perform at different levels of efficiency in the same employment. The more able individual will have the higher productivity and will command a higher wage than the less able worker. If we are justified in making this link between ability and productivity, then the implication is that through the mechanism of higher earnings more able individuals will have a higher rate of return to a given level of human capital acquisition than the less able. Such an outcome would be reinforced if the high ability individuals were able to acquire a given level of human capital attainment at less cost.[4] To pick up on our earlier numerical example, a worker of high ability who passed his/her degree with two years of full-time study instead of three, will obviously reduce the indirect cost of that human capital investment from £49,920 to £33,280 (using 2000 average earnings). It may be that high ability individuals might be more efficient at converting education into human capital. The likely impact of ability related productivity and cost factors, illustrated in Figure 5.4, is that the rate of return for the more able will exceed that of the less able at all levels of human capital acquisition. The straightforward prediction being that more able individuals will invest so as to acquire more human capital than the less able.[5]

In practice it is quite clear that ability influences not only the amount of education but also the rate of return to a given amount of education. Figure 5.5 shows the effects of education on earnings in Ireland, Great Britain and Northern Ireland depending on the ability distribution. Ability, in the case of Figure 5.5, is measured by the scores obtained in quantitative and literacy tests. Clearly the higher up the ability distribution

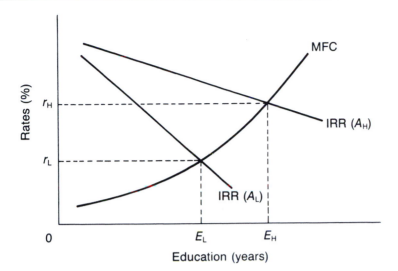

Figure 5.4

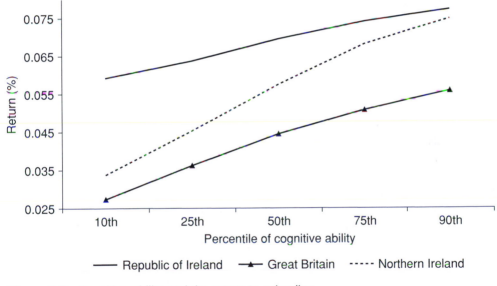

Figure 5.5 Cognitive ability and the return to schooling

Source: Harmon and Walker 2001, figure 3.1, p. 49

we go the greater the rate of return to education in all three countries. Great Britain seems sensitive to different levels of ability impacting on earnings. Underlying this benign view of human capital are some very attractive efficiency properties. We are in effect suggesting that the labour market and the education system combine to enable individuals to make choices that ensure that the most able are the most highly educated and occupy jobs where their marginal revenue productivity and therefore

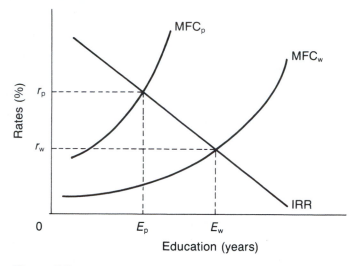

Figure 5.6

their earnings are greatest. The model also possesses attractive equity properties, because earnings differentials are due to different human capital investments based upon the different abilities among individuals.

The benign view of human capital theory begins to be undermined once we consider the impact of differential personal/family wealth on the analysis. Differential wealth effects mean that at any given level of education, the wealthy individuals, or at least those with access to greater existing family wealth, can take advantage of the lower financing costs that this provides.

In Figure 5.6 with individuals having the same abilities and facing the same set of rates of return IRR, the wealthy are faced with lower marginal financing costs MFC_w than their poorer counterparts MFC_p. Hence MFC_w lies below and to the right of MFC_p at all levels of education. The outcome is that wealth differences in the family background of individuals result in more human capital investment by the rich $(E_w > E_p)$ at lower rates of return than accrue to those from poorer families $(r_w < r_p)$. Therefore in a simple human capital framework with imperfect capital markets, those from wealthy families invest more in human capital acquisition than those from poorer families, thereby gaining access to higher paid employment and perpetuating differences in wealth endowments across generations.

There is also the possibility that individuals' preferences for current income versus future income vary. If this is the case then individuals will have different rates at which they discount future earnings. Lower discount rate individuals will choose more education. Differences in discount rate may well be reflecting ability and family wealth. According to Harmon and Walker (2001) childhood smoking can be used to distinguish between low and high discount rate individuals. The rationale is that if a young person is willing to risk long-term health problems due to the known risks of smoking then they must value short-term enjoyment from smoking over the long-term damage.

Table 5.2 Estimated return to education – grouped by smoking, Great Britain, 1978–96

		Smoker at 16	Non-smoker at 16	Difference	Estimated return
Male	log wage	2.36	2.51	0.16	0.16/0.97
	Ed years	12.11	13.08	0.97	= 0.164
Female	log wage	2.01	2.18	0.17	0.17/0.90
	Ed years	12.52	13.42	0.90	= 0.188

Source: Harmon and Walker 2001, table 4.2, p. 52

If so then they must have a high discount rate. Using data on smoking when young contained in the British General Household Survey for the period 1978–96 they calculate an estimated rate of return to education for non-smokers over smokers of 16 per cent for men and almost 19 per cent for women. This is, as we can see from the estimated returns in Table 5.2, due to the fact that non-smokers have both a wage advantage and a longer education advantage over smokers.

Having considered the ways in which incorporating age, ability, a differential access to wealth and even teenage smoking tend to amend the analysis we now move on to look at the empirical aspects of human capital theory.

EMPIRICAL ASPECTS

Human capital theory has attracted a great deal of empirical interest which is reflected in the surveys by Psacharopoulos (1981, 1985 and 1994), Siebert (1985), Willis (1986), Harmon et al. (2001) and Harmon and Walker (2001). This interest has centred upon estimating the rates of return to various types of human capital acquisition. The most commonly adopted approach has been to model the determination of earnings incorporating variables suggested by human capital theory. Mincer's (1974) human capital earnings function is a good example of such an approach:

$$\log y = \beta_0 + \beta_1 S + \beta_2 X - \beta_3 X^2 + u$$

where y is earnings;[6] S is schooling, or what we have termed education; X is experience; β_1 is the rate of return to schooling/education; β_2 is a coefficient reflecting a positive return to experience; β_3 is a negative coefficient of the quadratic experience term X^2 which produces an age earnings profile that is concave from below; and u is a residual error term. Mincer (1974) obtains a value of 0.107 for his β_1 coefficient using data from the 1960 census in the USA. Psacharopoulos and Layard (1979) using data from the 1972 census in England and Wales obtain a β_1 value of 0.097. These findings appear to suggest remarkably similar average rates of return to a year of schooling in the USA and the UK of about 10 per cent (10.7 per cent in the USA in 1959, 9.7 per cent in the UK in 1972).

The general picture is one of declining average rates of return to schooling in the USA between 1900 and 1940. Rates of return to higher education in the USA appear

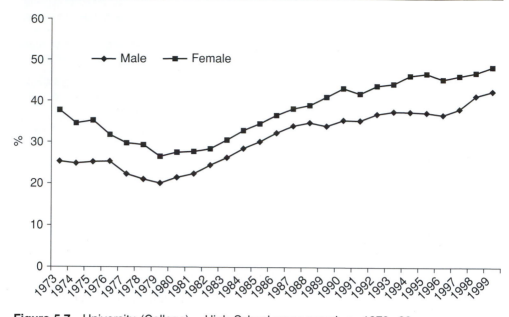

Figure 5.7   University (College) – High School wage premium, 1973–99

Source: Author's calculations from Economic Policy Institute (2001) *The State of Working America, 2000–01*, www.epinet.org

to be roughly constant between 1939 (10.7 per cent) and 1969 (10.9 per cent). However, the 1970s saw a marked reduction in the return to higher education. Pscharopoulos (1981) estimated that by 1975 the private rate of return to USA university education had fallen to 5.3 per cent.

Freeman (1977) suggested that the decline in returns was partly due to increases in US college tuition fees during the 1970s. Moreover, there was a rapid acceleration in the growth of the US labour force during in the 1970s, a demographic consequence of the early 1960s 'baby boom', accompanied by a marked increase in the educational attainment of the US labour force during the 1970s. However, it is clear from Figure 5.7 that the wage premium for university graduates was falling during the 1970s. However, by the early 1980s rates of return to US higher education were rising, as was the university graduate worker–high school graduate worker wage differential.

In Figure 5.8, data from the British Family Expenditure Survey for the period 1978–99 shows the real wage related to the age at which workers left full-time education. For both men and women wages rise until the age of 18 years then dip until age 21. This dip is between the normal age at which British students will finish A levels, which are the usual university entrance qualifications, and the completion of a first (Bachelors) degree at university. Thereafter wages continue to rise until leaving full-time education at age 24 years, which allows for the completion of a masters degree.

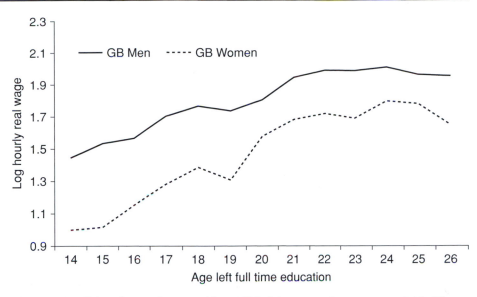

Figure 5.8 Education and wages (Great Britain) men and women aged 14–26, 1978–99

Source: Harmon and Walker 2001, figure 2.1, p. 19

Although there is a positive return to experience it is not a substantial one. Incorporating age as a quadratic X^2, Harmon and Walker (2001) estimate the rate of return to education in the UK, as 8 per cent for men and 11 per cent for women. Using other measures of experience, namely actual age minus education leaving age (potential experience), and actual experience (number of years worked since leaving education) had less effect on the impact of education producing returns of around 9.5 per cent for men and 12 per cent for women. So although experience is statistically significant in multiple regressions its effects on rates of return to education are not substantial. Exactly the same can be said of other variables including union membership, plant size, part-time working, marital status and number of children (Harmon and Walker (2001) tables 2.4 and 2.5, p. 27).

Blundell *et al.* (2000) examined the effect of higher education on British workers' wages over those for workers who had at least one A level but had not gone to university. The results are shown in Table 5.3. Even after accounting for factors

Table 5.3 Effect of higher education on hourly wage rates (%)

Qualification	Men	Women
Non-degree	13.6	21.8
First degree	12.2	33.7
Higher degree	8.4	31.9

Source: Blundell *et al.* 2000, table 3, p. F90

including family background, ability, school type and employer type, there are substantial wage premiums for those who have some form of higher education qualification. The benefit for male workers declines the further up the higher education qualifications ladder we go. This is not the case for female workers; their higher education wage premium peaks at the first degree level. The effect on women's hourly wage rate is greater than for men's at all levels of higher education attainment. However, once higher education has been embarked upon the individual must see it through. The effect of failing a higher education course was especially detrimental to the earnings of men, minus 12.9 per cent. For women failing higher education there was a small, statistically insignificant penalty of minus 1.6 per cent.

Psacharopoulos (1985) provides evidence of the international variation of private individuals' rate of return to higher education in the late 1970s, when returns in the USA appeared to hover around 5.3 per cent. In Japan the rate was 8.3 per cent, in Germany it was 10.5 per cent, in Australia, which had a similar state grant system to the UK at that time, the return was 21.1 per cent, and in the UK it is estimated to have been 23.0 per cent. The enormous range of these estimated returns arises primarily from the funding arrangements for higher education. In the late 1970s UK higher education catered for a very small proportion of school leavers. Those who went on to higher education had their tuition fees paid by the state and received a maintenance grant which did not have to be repaid, and which was available, subject to a sliding scale of parental contributions, to all bar those from the wealthiest backgrounds. State subsidies did not exist to the same extent in the USA, so more of the direct cost of higher education was borne by the individual than was the case in the UK. With the freezing of maintenance grants in 1990 and the introduction of a repayable student loan and tuition fees during a time of rapid expansion in student admissions to higher education, one would have expected private rates of return in the UK to have declined in the 1990s unless there had been an expansionary shift in the demand for graduates. We shall examine the relative shifts in the supply and demand for graduates when we consider skills biased technological change later in this chapter. Looking at the comparative rates of return to education for 1995 contained in Table 5.4 we can see that the UK in the form of Great Britain and Northern Ireland had high returns, which were only approached by those in the Republic of Ireland.

In this sample of countries female rates of return tend to be higher than male rates, the only exceptions being the Netherlands, Spain, Northern Ireland and New Zealand. Rates of return in the Scandinavian countries and the Netherlands are low. Rates in some former communist countries of Eastern Europe (Hungary, Poland, Slovakia and Slovenia) are quite high, whereas those in Russia itself and the Czech Republic are more modest. Although rates in the UK are high by international standards in 1995, they have fallen since the late 1970s. By 1995 rates of return in Australia are nowhere near as high as those in the UK. Although the extent varies, state involvement in education is a universal phenomenon. This in itself is a strong indication that there may be important social aspects of the education process. From a labour economics

Table 5.4 International returns to education (%), 1995

	Male	Female
Austria	3.6	6.2
Czech Republic	2.9	4.5
Germany (West)	3.5	4.4
Germany (East)	2.7	4.5
Hungary	7.0	7.2
Italy	4.0	5.7
Ireland	10.2	11.6
Netherlands	3.3	1.8
Norway	2.3	2.7
Poland	7.4	10.3
Russia	4.2	5.6
Slovakia	5.0	6.4
Slovenia	8.9	11.2
Spain	5.2	4.7
Sweden	3.7	4.2
Switzerland	4.3	5.2
Great Britain	13.0	14.7
Northern Ireland	17.7	16.8
Australia	5.1	5.7
Canada	3.7	5.0
New Zealand	4.2	3.8
Japan	7.5	9.2
USA	7.8	9.8

Source: International Social Survey Programme

perspective there are externalities, which ensure that the effects of education are not confined to the individual human capital investor. There are social costs and benefits associated with education as a knowledge industry. If there are social benefits to education over and above the private benefits to the individual then there is an economic rationale for state involvement in the provision of education. Consider the situation illustrated in Figure 5.9.

There is a given amount of education E^p that would be provided if we only considered the private costs and benefits. However, if we take account of the social benefits as well then this would lead to more education E^s and a state subsidy at this higher level of provision.

Among the social benefits are: more rapid economic growth; promoting social tolerance and cohesion; enabling participatory democracy; facilitating social mobility; and greater tax revenues from better educated higher earners. It may also be that the better educated are able to raise the productivity of the less well educated by training them on the job or by improving production practices. These benefits may then be set against a group of social costs including: direct cost of education provision at compulsory and higher levels; cost of subsidising students; and possible discontent from raising expectations. Having identified groups of social costs and benefits it is possible

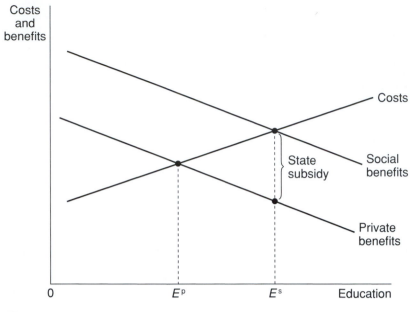

Figure 5.9

Table 5.5 Private and social rates of return to education

	Primary	Secondary	Higher
Private returns (%)			
Sub-Saharan Africa	41	27	28
Non-OECD Europe/Middle East/North Africa	17	16	22
Asia	39	19	20
Latin America/Caribbean	26	17	20
OECD countries	22	12	12
World	29	18	20
Social returns (%)			
Sub-Saharan Africa	24	18	11
Non-OECD Europe/Middle East/North Africa	16	11	11
Asia	20	13	12
Latin America/Caribbean	18	13	12
OECD countries	14	10	9
World	18	13	11

Source: Adapted from Psacharopoulos 1994

to calculate the social rate of return to education. Because of the enormous direct cost of education (e.g., buildings, books and staff) estimates of the social rate of return are significantly lower than those of private returns. This holds true for all levels of education across a wide range of countries as the data in Table 5.5 shows.

The picture that emerges from such comparisons is that rates of return tend to be greater the less developed the economy and that returns tend to decline with increasing levels of education. To confirm that rates of return decline as the level of education increases the average (of private and social) rates of return (percentages) to full-time study in England and Wales for 1987 were

9.0	A level
12.5	Bachelor degree
3.0	Masters degree
2.5	Doctorate

Harmon and Walker (2001) cite studies estimating social rates of return to UK male graduates by degree subject of

zero for humanities and biological science
11% plus for medicine, science, computing, business studies and social studies

Social rates of return average around 10 per cent for OECD countries. Acemoglu and Angrist (1999) suggest that for the USA the social rate of return may be close to the level of the private return.

Underlying all these empirical estimates of the rate of return to education is a positive relationship between earnings and the level of educational attainment. Human capital theory suggests that it is meaningful to view this relationship as a consequence of productivity enhancing investment. Table 5.6 presents raw evidence in favour of such a positive correlation between levels of education and earnings in the UK.

Human capital theory seeks to explain the earnings differentials as justified by differential productivity resulting from different human capital investment. Focusing on education, Willis (1986) suggests 'the observed positive correlation between school-ing and earnings provides support for . . . the hypothesis that education is an invest-ment which receives a pecuniary return in the labour market' (p. 535). Thus it would appear as though human capital theory has strong theoretical and empirical support. It suggests that education enhances labour productivity, which in turn justifies observed earnings differentials between workers. Yet bear in mind that this posits a very benign view of the education process, ensuring that the most productive indi-viduals occupy the most demanding jobs attracting the highest salaries. It is now time to question that view of education and the status of human capital theory.

Table 5.6 Usual gross weekly earnings of all UK employees, 2000 (£)

No qualifications	200
GCSE grade A–C	240
A Level	320
Sub-degree Higher	390
Degree level	520

Source: ONS, *Labour Force Survey*, Spring 2000

SCREENING, SIGNALLING, AGENCY THEORY AND OTHER CRITICISMS OF HUMAN CAPITAL THEORY

Within labour economics the screening/signalling hypothesis challenges the human capital interpretation of the function of education. Employers are held to screen potential employees using educational qualifications as a guide to potential productivity. The employer is faced with making a hiring decision under conditions of uncertainty about the productivity of applicants. Job seekers use their educational achievements to signal their productivity potential to employers.

Employer screening and worker signalling can be viewed as a means of sorting the most able people into the most demanding jobs. Or it can be seen as a way of ensuring that the already better off continue to get the best jobs, what Bowles and Gintis (1975) describe as 'legitimising the intergenerational transfer of inequality'. Whether education has a social benefit associated with an efficient sorting process depends upon educational success being related to certain productivity enhancing abilities. Yet education has strong connections with social stratification.

If employers are to use education as a screening device they must believe that it reflects certain abilities. Bear in mind that it is only one of a number of screening devices they have at their disposal. Employers may use interviews, questionnaires, simulation exercises, medical reports, references, employment history and post-appointment screening during a probationary period. The advantage of using particularly post-school educational attainment is that the costs are incurred by the state and the individual, plus the firm is able to take advantage of the screening already undertaken at higher education entry level. This evolves from Arrow's (1973) view of higher education acting as a filter in a model based upon the extreme assumption that education is the only information an employer has about an individual. The screening/signalling hypothesis need not go that far and it can endow the employer with the ability to learn from experience to form a connection between education data and subsequent productivity performance. Universities set entrance standards. Students then undergo courses of specific length and emerge as graduates of a certain standard. If universities set high entrance standards they run the risk of wasting abilities by refusing students who are competent to read for a degree. Lower entrance standards avoid this risk but may run the risk of seemingly devaluing the qualification as a screening/signalling device. The use of higher education as a screening and signalling device rests upon the universities identifying and enhancing pre-existing abilities. Take the example of a firm interested in the expected quality of graduate applicants. Let us suppose that there are two types of university, one employing high entrance criteria the other setting lower entrance standards. If employers adopt a simple rule, based on either prejudice or experience, which equates higher entrance criteria with higher potential productivity of the graduate, then the situation shown in Figure 5.10 would evolve.

For employers to use higher education to screen for high quality applicants the standard three year degree needs to be coupled with high entrance qualifications. A lower entry barrier would need courses of longer duration, a degree followed by a masters programme for example, to convince employers that they produce high quality gradu-

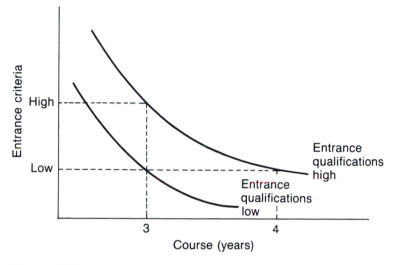

Figure 5.10

ates. Yet this analysis of education as a screening/signalling device implies that employer's expectations are based upon identifiable differences in quality. An alternative view, 'credentialism' is where employment is rationed according to educational qualifications which are required by employers but which are not necessary for the job. This is a form of discrimination with employers having a definite taste for educated workers. The weakness of 'credentialism' is that the economic rents (or profit) from those occupations that restrict entry must rely on more than education as a barrier. They need to invoke class, family background, accent, school history and so forth. Layard and Psacharopoulos (1974) also point out that credentialist practices are confined to uncompetitive, non-profit-maximising organisations such as the upper echelons of the civil service.

Another aspect to credentialism focuses on the fact that the credential is more important than the years of education (schooling). If so then there might be a wage premium over and above the return to education for completing a particular year of education, the final year of secondary (high) school at 18 or the final year of university (college) at 21. Remember the dip we noticed in Figure 5.6 between the ages of 18 and 21? However, it seems that although we might take the dip as an indication of credentialism, the link between credentials and years of education is sufficiently strong that a straight line is a reasonable approximation (see Harmon and Walker (2001) figure 2.8, p. 32), meaning that we can confidently ignore credentialism.

In his signalling model Spence (1974) suggests that firms faced with a hiring decision may pay more for better educated workers even if education has no effect on productivity. This is because information about potential productivity is imperfect. However, it should be the case that more able workers can obtain an educational signal (i.e., a qualification) more easily and cheaply than their less able counterparts. Yet the screening/signalling hypothesis constructs a world within which as Joll *et al.*

(1983) describe 'the function of education is then merely to provide the qualification . . . , educational establishments . . . will come to acquire a reputation among both workers and firms as good signallers' (p. 90). It also raises doubts about the efficiency of educational investment being determined through a market. There is clearly a massive amount of overinvestment in education if it does nothing to increase labour productivity in general. In denying any fundamental positive relationship between education and actual productivity the screening/signalling hypothesis is clearly at odds with human capital theory (see Weiss 1995).

However, the screening/signalling hypothesis suffers from what is, in my opinion, a critical inconsistency. It relies upon uncertainty but it allows for employers to use past hiring experience to generate expectations concerning productivity relative to the signal. Spence assumed that such past experience is relevant data for present and future decisions. For this to be so other things such as the nature of the job must remain constant over time. This increases the certainty of historical fact with conditional probabilities getting closer to one. Indeed in equilibrium, conditional expectations are self-confirming and if Riley (1974, 1976) is correct to assert that the signalling equilibrium is Pareto-dominant, then there is no incentive to move from it. In such circumstances employers have a certain prediction of an applicant's future productivity. The screening/signalling model is not dealing with uncertainty at all; employers possess all the knowledge they require to offer a wage schedule which will tell workers all they need to know in order to provide the firm with the workforce it knows that it needs. Additionally Woodhall (1987) makes the point that in a number of important respects the screening/signalling hypothesis does not fit the observed facts,

> the fact that age earnings profiles by level of education diverge, rather than converge over time, demonstrates that employers continue to pay educated workers more, throughout their working lives, when they have direct evidence about their productivity.

> (p. 217)

Harmon and Walker (2001) estimate the extent of signalling by comparing the education and earnings relationship of the self-employed with that of employees. The idea being, that the self-employed have no need for education as a signalling device because they are aware of their own productivity. The results of their comparison, using British Household Panel Survey Data, contained in Table 5.7 indicate a very minor role for signalling. Therefore the screening/signalling hypothesis, whilst

Table 5.7 Returns to education, percentage of the employed and self-employed

	Employees	*Self-employed*	*Signalling*
Men	6.4	5.1	1.3
Women	10.3	7.6	2.6

Source: Harmon and Walker 2001, table 3.1, p. 42

indicating that there are credentialist aspects to education, does not threaten to fundamentally undermine human capital theory. As Freeman (1986) observes 'screening/ signalling effects are undoubtedly part of the world, but no empirical study has found them to be a major factor in the demand for education' (p. 362).

Agency theory offers a new perspective on earnings, which differs from the emphasis that human capital theory and neoclassical labour market theory place on productivity. Agency theory deals with the principal–agent problem that we covered in Chapter 4, linking earnings with employers' need to provide incentives for workers in circumstances where the self-interest of workers need not and probably is not consistent with the objectives of the firm. Thus the firm, the 'principal', devises schedules of reward and punishment to encourage behaviour consistent with the firm's objectives on the part of the worker, the 'agent'. If this takes the form of withholding performance related payments this implies that initial wage payments are below the worker's marginal revenue productivity, followed by an excess terminal payment to ensure that $W = MRP$ over the period as a whole.

If agency theory is right then life cycle earnings profiles have little to do with the pattern of productivity over time; they are explained by contracts framed by the 'principals' to offer incentives to the 'agents'. Thus productivity and pay are not as closely linked as human capital theory would have us believe. However, the weakness of agency theory is that whilst it sheds some light on institutional practices it does not represent a general theory of wage determination. Furthermore there is no unambiguous or particularly strong empirical support for the agency theory approach to wage determination. Among the other criticisms levelled at human capital theory are the following.

1) That it is a supply-side theory in which demand only influences earnings differentials in the short term, as opposed to the screening/signalling hypothesis which stressed the factors influencing the demand for educational qualifications.
2) There is no precise means of measuring human capital, we only know that it takes time and involves cost to acquire it. Human capital is being measured by its observable cost of production.
3) Individuals may be more varied than human capital theory allows, in that they may well have different productivities after they have successfully completed the same course at the same institution at the same time.
4) Human capital theory is accused of not taking the non-pecuniary aspects of various occupations into account.
5) By measuring education in terms of years it does not take account of the possible differences in education quality, although 'quality' may be a proxy for ability or institutional factors like social class and family background.

Yet none of these criticisms threaten the viability of human capital theory.[7] They are peripheral criticisms, which do not strike at the heart of what Blaug (1976) called the 'hard core of the human capital research programme' (p. 829). It is a progressive research programme in the sense that it has grown to encompass 'health, education, job search, information retrieval, migration, and in-service training . . . as investment consumption, whether undertaken by individuals on their own behalf or undertaken by society' (p. 829). Earnings functions of the Mincer type have proved themselves to be empirically robust. As Willis (1986) attests 'the initial insights of Becker and Mincer who first developed human capital theory have been repeatedly confirmed with data from around the world' (p. 598).

VOCATIONAL TRAINING

The data in Table 5.8 shows that the UK compares fairly well with Germany when it comes to educational attainment, yet both countries lag behind France in the proportion of the workforce with level 2 and 3 educational qualifications. There are important differences in the provision of vocational training, especially between the UK and Germany. In order to gauge the significance of these differences we need to examine the economics of training. Becker (1964) contained one of the first models to focus on training. This distinguished

- general training, which lead to the provision of general skills that increased worker productivity by the same amount in all firms
- specific training, which created specific skills that increased worker productivity only in the firm that provides that training.

In perfectly competitive labour markets, workers would pay for all the general training they underwent and would receive the total return to that training; whereas, specific training costs and benefits would be shared by the worker and the firm.

An obvious prediction of the Becker model is that firms should never pay for general training. However, they do; Bardeleben *et al.* (1995) estimated that the cost of general training in the German apprenticeship system in the range of 7,575 DM per apprentice per year, after adjusting for the apprentice's lower productivity and part-time working, to a gross cost of 35,692 DM in large firms of 500 workers or more. Other studies, e.g., Loewenstein and Spletzer (1999), find similar evidence of firm sponsored general training in the UK and the USA. Workers are partially paying for

Table 5.8 Education and training qualifications in the UK, France and Germany, 1998 (percentage of workforce)

	Level 2 GCSE Equivalent Level			Level 3 A Level Equivalent		
	UK	*Fra*	*Ger*	*UK*	*Fra*	*Ger*
Education						
Total workforce	27	31	25	20	25	22
Vocational						
Total workforce	27	41	58	17	12	52

Source: DFEE, *Skills For All*, 2000

general training by receiving a lower wage, a common feature of apprenticeship systems. However, the lower wage may not fully compensate firms for their share of general training costs, firm sponsored MBAs are a good example of when they fail to do so. Barron *et al.* (1997) reported that although wages were lower during training the reduction was not substantial. Lynch and Black (1998) from a survey of almost 3,000 USA establishments, both manufacturing and non-manufacturing, found the following.

- Most employers (81 per cent) offered some kind of formal training
- Training had increased since 1991 in the majority (57 per cent) of establishments
- Only 2 per cent recorded a decrease in training activity
- Training in 75 per cent of establishments appeared to be company specific, orientation for new workers, company health and safety, new methods/procedures, sales and customer service, managerial and supervisory training
- There was a lower incidence (50 per cent of establishments) of training for more portable skills like operating computers, teamwork, and repaying tuition fees
- Just over 25 per cent of establishments offered literacy, numeracy and basic educational training

In general the findings support the notion of firms being primarily interested in specific training although there is a large amount of general training going on. They also found that training increases

- the larger the establishment
- the greater the firm's investment in R and D
- the greater the investment in physical capital
- the greater the employment of educated workers
- the greater the use of new working practices (like TQM in Chapter 4)

It appears as though training complements rather than substitutes for physical capital investment. Human capital investment by the individual is augmented by firms' investment in training of more educated workers. This is certainly the case when we compare employer-provided training in France and Britain. Hocquet (1999) found that because French firms with more than 10 workers are obliged to spend 1.5 per cent of their wage bill on training, French firms tend to train more of the less well educated and less experienced workers than was the case in Britain, which has no training levy or obligation on firms. As a result training had a bigger impact on workers' wages in France (21 per cent) than in Britain (15 per cent). The French system appears to guard against increases in income inequality due to different probabilities of vocational training. As Hocquet concludes 'government intervention leads the market to train the less efficient workers in France, which is socially fair and equitable as it gives individuals a second chance' (p. 249).

Acemoglu and Pischke (1999) suggest that because general and specific skills are complementary, an increase in general skills can increase the value of specific skills to a firm. Stevens (1994) argues that skills are rarely completely general or entirely specific. Training programmes are therefore transferable, which will reduce the degree of competition in a market. Firms that do not train their workers can always expect a share of the return on training, which will always be partly general, by poaching workers from firms that do train. Stevens (1999) suggested that the fear of poaching might lead firms to over-invest in specific training, unless workers could be constrained from leaving by contracts or internal labour markets (see Chapter 4). Empirical studies of such training related market failures are in Booth and Snower (1996).

If labour markets are less than perfect and/or firms have some monopsony power, then general skills are rewarded as if they were partly specific, with workers not being paid their full marginal product. If the productivity minus wage gap is dependent on the worker's level of skill, then firms have an incentive to invest in general training. Market imperfections can include

- job search (see Chapter 9) and job matching (hiring and induction) transactions costs
- imperfect information about other firms, nature and extent of training, productivity, ability, effort and diligence (see Chapter 4)
- labour market institutions such as minimum wages (Chapter 3) and trade unions (Chapter 7).

The Becker model predicts that a minimum wage will reduce training activity by preventing workers financing general training via wage cuts. Neumark and Wascher (1998) report that minimum wages have had a large negative effect on the training of particularly young workers in California. Acemoglu and Pischke (1999) are critical of this study and can find 'no evidence of a reduction in training in response to minimum wages' (p. F131) in their research of the USA.

With regard to unions and training the situation is a mixed one. Barron *et al.* (1997) along with Lillard and Tan (1992) report negative impacts of unions on training in the USA. Yet Barron *et al.* (1997) reported a combination of insignificant union negative and positive impacts on formal training. Lynch (1992) found that unions had a positive impact on the training of young workers. Booth (1991) reported more training for unionised workers in the UK, and Green (1993) found a positive union impact on training in small plants but not in large plants.

In a comparison of training in the USA and Germany, Acemoglu and Pischke (1999) pointed to within-country time trends that showed increasing training of both highly and less qualified workers in Germany, but more training for the highly qualified and less training for the less qualified in the USA (see their table 4, p. F139). Of young workers in Germany, 71.5 per cent receive company-provided formal training, whilst only 10.2 per cent of US workers receive any formal training in the first seven years of their labour market experience. When it comes to job tenure, the typical German male worker has 1–2 jobs in their first ten years of labour market experience, whereas the US male worker has 6 jobs in ten years. Putting these facts together we can characterise Germany as a high training, low labour mobility market and the USA as a low training, high mobility labour market.

Training activity in the UK has risen over time. Labour Force Survey data reveals that the proportion of the workforce receiving training over the four weeks prior to the survey increased from

10.6% in 1986 to
14.3% in 1990 to
14.8% in 1996 to
15.1% in 2000.

In spite of these increases, McIntosh (1999) finds that the UK engages in markedly less training than is the case in Germany. Training in the UK is concentrated on those who already have a university degree meaning that 'as a result, the UK continues to have a much larger proportion of its working population at the unskilled level' (p. 17).

The comparative lack of vocational training in the UK reflects a lack of actual parity between academic qualifications and their vocational counterparts. Robinson (1997) found that workers with a certain level of academic qualification earned the same as those with vocational qualifications that were meant to be at a higher level than the academic qualification. Obviously the labour market in the UK values academic more than the notionally equivalent vocational qualification.

The organisation of vocational training in the UK has had a troubled history. Technical schools were established on a small scale and then allowed to decline. The traditional apprenticeship training was in decline from the late 1960s and was effectively killed off by a combination of recession, employer indifference and Government hostility in the 1980s. Concern over the comparative lack of intermediate vocational skills in the UK labour force lead to a change in Government attitude and the nationwide introduction of a series of Modern Apprenticeships in 1995. Whilst this is an employer based system that has increased the supply of vocational training places it is too early to fully assess its impact. However, Gospel (1997) pointed out that it was restricted to employed 16–19 year olds rather than the lower skilled unemployed and that there was a shortage of firms offering good quality apprentice places. Overall he believes that Modern Apprenticeships represent 'the last opportunity . . . to revive the employment based route to training' (p. 25). Sanderson (1999) warns that the record of training policy is a

plethora of unsatisfactory . . . schemes . . . [that] suggests a failure of employers themselves to get a grip on the system to help create something of a stable nature with solid standards . . . For a lack of this they are left to recurrently complain of skill shortages and unsatisfactory recruits.

(p. 106)

OVEREDUCATION

The proportion of 15-year-olds in England gaining 5 or more GCSEs (basic school leaving qualification) at grade A* to C, increased from

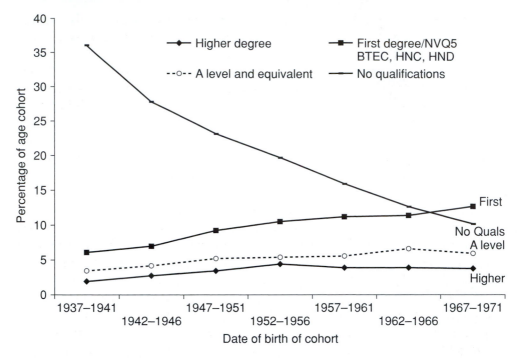

Figure 5.11   The supply of selected UK qualifications across cohorts (1997 Labour Force Survey)

Source: Green *et al.* 1999, chart 1, p. 38

35%   1989/1990 to
44%   1994/1995 to
48%   1998/1999.

The proportion of 16 and 17-year-olds who stayed on to undergo some form of education or training also rose from

66% in 1985 to
77% in 1990 to
83% in 1995 then fell to
82% in 1998.

The data in Figure 5.11 shows the rise in the stock of qualifications in the UK across various age cohorts. There has been a dramatic collapse in the proportion of younger workers with no qualifications. This has been accompanied by a marked rise in the proportion of younger workers with a first degree from university. This is set to increase further as about 30 per cent of the cohort enters university in the early 2000s. Against a background of the expansion of higher education and subsidies for university students the concept of overeducation has received increased attention in recent years. The key problem to address is whether some workers have over-invested in gaining educational qualifications that are not particularly productive either for the individual or the nation. Given the increase in the supply of educated workers, unless demand has kept pace then overeducation will emerge.

Before we examine the scale of overeducation we require a few definitions. Over-education occurs when individual workers are in jobs, either temporarily or perman-ently, that under-utilise their skills or education. Being overeducated will lower the rate of return to education. It cannot exist if labour markets are fully efficient and equate wages with marginal revenue productivity. Therefore overeducation requires some rigidity in the labour market, some labour market mismatch, or imperfect information, which could cause or arise from an excess stock of human capital or job search inefficiencies.

Under-education is the opposite situation where individuals are in jobs for which they have insufficient education. Under-education might come about if there is a shortage of adequately qualified workers, or if workers find themselves in a job whose required education rises over time. In the case of older workers they may be substituting exper-ience for a lack of education. Under-education will exaggerate the rate of return.

Qualifications inflation refers to the process whereby employers increase the required qualification level for a particular job. As we have already seen, signalling relies on the cost of acquiring education being lower for higher ability workers. If learning costs fall, for example, by allowing easier access to university education, then lower ability workers invest more in education which pushes up the average education level of young workers. If firms begin to find that a certain qualification no longer brings workers of the right ability, then they will upgrade their educational requirements.

Grade drift refers to the deterioration of educational standards. If the standards at GCSE level are falling enabling a greater proportion of an age cohort to pass the exam, then employers will seek workers with A levels. If there is dumbing down of undergraduate education then employers will seek workers with masters degrees.

When it comes to gauging the magnitude of overeducation the first point to note is that there has been no fall in rates of return to education, implying that while the supply of qualified workers has undoubtedly increased so has the demand for qualified workers. Indeed in the UK the wage mark-up for graduates over those with no quali-fications has risen from

> 1.93 in 1985 to
> 2.32 in 1995.

Along with this increasing wage inequality between education levels has come in-creased inequality within education levels. Green et al. (1999) refer to this as 'increasing heterogeneity within each educational group' (p. 8).

Such heterogeneity could be due to

- grade drift caused by greater variation in the quality of education,
- the decline in trade union power increasing the inequality of earnings,

- greater labour market mismatch – a rising proportion of overeducated workers getting lower wages than their better matched peers.

Groot (1996) found that between 13 per cent and 15 per cent of British male workers and between 8 per cent and 10 per cent of British female workers were overeducated. Mason (1996) reported that some 45 per cent of UK graduates were in non-mainstream graduate jobs. This accords with a finding from Green *et al.* (1999) that overeducation among graduates amounted to 30 per cent in 1986 rising to 32 per cent in 1997. This suggests that, contrary to human capital theory, overeducation is not a temporary phenomenon. Yet, could overeducation be a fairly permanent feature of the labour market but temporary for the individual? Data on 1980 graduates reported by Green *et al.* (1999, p. 14) shows that the majority of overeducated male graduates had not moved into graduate jobs within six years.

Evidence on under-education indicates that it is much less of a problem. Data from a 1998 Newcastle University Alumni Survey of 2,200 graduates resulted in 46 per cent claiming to be overeducated with only 10 per cent reporting to be under-educated. There was no evidence of qualification inflation. Battu *et al.* (1999) using a survey of 15,000 graduates, report that about 40 per cent say they are in jobs that do not require a degree.

Using data from the UK Skills Survey, Green *et al.* (1999) construct a model showing quite clearly that overeducation reduces earnings for both male and female workers and that under-education does the opposite. An explanation for this is that 'educational human capital cannot be characterised as a homogeneous stock' (p. 19). In other words, productivity and earnings will vary according to

- grade of qualification,
- place of study,
- subject studied.

It appears as though factors that increase the likelihood of overeducation are

- lower class of degree,
- a new university (former polytechnic) degree,
- being a social science, arts or languages graduate.

Thus the overeducated may suffer from having a lower quality degree or the wrong type of education. Dolton and Vignoles (2000) question whether the class of degree makes any difference to the lower earnings of the overeducated. Another important consideration is innate ability. The overeducated may actually hold jobs that are commensurate with lower ability. Green *et al.* (1999) try to test for ability using data from the UK National Child Development Study on maths and reading tests taken at age 16. Their main finding is that those 'individuals who scored more highly on the mathematics test . . . are significantly less likely to be overeducated later in life' (p. 20). The reading test results were insignificant. For the USA, Pryor and Schaffer (1999) report that university graduates in occupations where the average level

Table 5.9 Overskilling by field of study

	Percentage overskilled	Percentage not overskilled
Fine and Applied Arts	2.6	0.9
Humanities	6.3	2.2
Other	16.6	10.8
No specialisation	4.8	2.5
Commerce, Management, Business	15.2	19.9
Engineering, Applied Sciences	14.5	21.7
Health, Science, Technology	11.4	16.4

Source: Green *et al.* 1999, table 11, p. 37

of education is below a degree have lower functional literacy than well matched graduates. Green *et al.* (1999) found that private sector workers were more likely to be overeducated as were part-time workers. They also looked at some data from the 1995 International Adult Literacy Survey (IALS). The results (Green *et al.* (1999) table T3, p. 43) show

- increased qualification leads to increased earnings,
- increased literacy is associated with higher earnings,
- the greater the overskilling the greater the loss of earnings,
- the greater the underskilling the greater the effect on earnings.

Chevalier (2000) found that many workers who defined themselves as being overeducated for the job they were doing were not genuinely overeducated. These apparently overeducated workers were paid around 6 per cent less than well matched graduates but once ability was introduced the pay penalty disappeared. The genuinely overeducated did suffer a substantial pay penalty.

Looking at the subjects studied the IALS data for Britain revealed greater proportions of overskilling than not overskilled in the first four categories of degree in Table 5.9. Whereas the proportions for the not overskilled were greater in the final three subject fields.

There are four main conclusions that arise from the Green *et al.* (1999) study:

1) little evidence of qualification inflation,
2) overeducation exists as evidence of mismatch in the labour market,
3) overeducated workers earn less than similarly qualified workers who are well matched,
4) overeducated workers have lower numerical ability than well matched workers.

Such findings are consistent with skill biased technological change that we examine next, increasing the demand for skills including numeracy. When it comes to the supply of skills we need to consider the appropriateness of the skills – it is not just a question of more education but what type of education.

COMPUTERS AND SKILLS

The use of computers in the workplace has grown markedly over recent decades. But what impact have they had on labour markets? Figure 5.12 suggests the way in which computers may have influenced labour markets. We will examine the role of skill-biased technological change (SBTC) a little later but the thread of the argument in Figure 5.12 is to attribute the changing skill structure to the impact of computers. A number of studies including Haskel and Heden (1999) and Bresnahan (1999) have found that computerisation definitely increases the demand for skilled labour. There has been an upwards trend in skill supply and demand in a wide range of countries. Green *et al.* (2000) provides evidence of the increasing use of skills in Britain between 1986 and 1997. Using data from the Social Change in Economic Life Initiative (SCELI) research project covering six local labour markets: Aberdeen; Coventry; Kirkcaldy; Northampton; Rochdale and Swindon, they found increases in all the three measures of the skills used in jobs as the data in Table 5.10 shows.

The skills used in a job were measured by the qualifications the employer required of job applicants, the amount of training time needed for the job and how long it took

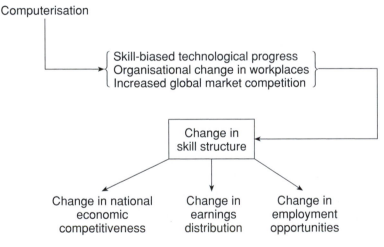

Figure 5.12

Table 5.10   Skills increases on three measures, 1986–97

		All	*Males*	*Females*
Required qualifications index	1986	1.81	2.09	1.43
	1997	2.04	2.17	1.89
Training time	1986	2.01	2.47	1.39
	1997	2.53	2.74	2.28
Learning time	1986	2.30	2.83	1.63
	1997	2.48	2.85	2.08

Source: Green *et al.* 2000, table 1, p. 16

Table 5.11 Proportion of jobs (%) using a degree and requiring a degree, 1986–97

	All	Male	Female	Degree required
1986	7.5	9.9	4.6	9.7
1997	10.6	11.2	10.2	14.1

Source: Green *et al.* 2000, table 2, p. 17

to learn what the job demanded. The rise in female workers' job skills rose rapidly for all three measures, such that the female–male difference in these broad skills was almost halved between 1986 and 1997. Weinberg (2000) estimated that the increased use of computers may explain over half (55 per cent) of the rising demand for women workers in the USA between 1975 and 1993 as the importance of physical strength in the workplace is de-emphasised.

However, do these skills trends show genuine skills upgrading or do they indicate aspects of grade drift, overeducation and credentialism? Although we have already covered these issues, it is interesting to see what Green *et al.* (2000) found. On grade drift Green *et al.* (2000) maintain that there is 'no systematic objective evidence to support claims of falling standards' (p. 5). Overeducation would mean that job holders had higher qualifications than the employer requires. There has been a marked increase in the Required Qualifications Index, up by 13 per cent between 1986 and 1997. Given that there has been an increase in rates of return to qualifications during this period there is no strong evidence of overeducation. When it comes to credentialism, not only have the 'required qualifications' increased but so have the other two skills measures, 'training time' up by 26 per cent and 'learning time' up by 8 per cent, with both showing female–male convergence. When Green *et al.* (2000) look at university degrees in more detail, they find that not only is a degree required to get a job but that it is also deemed 'fairly necessary' or 'essential' to do that job competently. This is called 'using a degree' and as Table 5.11 shows a larger proportion of jobs especially for female job holders have been using a degree.

This growth in the proportion of jobs using a degree and the female–male convergence is entirely consistent with the other measures of skill. Furthermore the proportion of jobs requiring a degree rose but the ratio of jobs requiring a degree to those using a degree remained constant at 1.3:1. Obviously, as Green *et al.* (2000) conclude, 'credentialism appears to be too small to prompt any major adjustment to the upskilling trend' (p. 7).

Increases in skill measures have taken place both across occupations and within occupations in almost equal measure. This skills upgrading has been accompanied by a rapid increase in the use of computers as the data in Table 5.12 confirms. Computer usage is not just acting as a time trend on skills. The level of correlation between computerisation and skills is very high. For instance the increased use of computers predicts increased skill usage equivalent to 99 per cent of the actual skill change during 1986–97. Greater computer usage in female jobs appears to explain 26 per cent

Table 5.12   Proportion (%) of jobs using computers

	All	Male	Female
1986	40.3	46.0	33.2
1992	53.3	55.4	50.8
1997	69.4	70.1	68.6

Source: Green *et al.* 2000, table A1, p. 25

Table 5.13   Estimated IT skills shortages (thousands) in the UK

	Demand	Supply	Shortage	Shortage (percentage)
1998	1,671	1,574	97	6
1999	1,761	1,606	155	9
2000	1,906	1,685	221	12
2001	2,047	1,782	265	13
2002	2,212	1,914	297	13
2003	2,349	2,019	330	14

Source: *Guardian* (23/3/2000)

of the narrowing skills gap with male jobs. While this does not 'prove' that computers caused rising skills, it does support the SBTC approach. It undermines the Robinson and Mannacorda (1997) view that much of the growth of skills has been credentialist, having used changes in occupational composition between 1984 and 1994 to demonstrate that the increase in the supply of skills has been more rapid than the rise in the demand for skills. Yet because computerisation has occurred across all occupations, all sectors and age groups the facts point to SBTC. Given that SBTC is a demand led change in skills, estimates of the shortfall in Information Technology (IT) skills reported in Table 5.13, also undermine supply-led explanations.

Haskel (1999) found that new physical capital (machinery) incorporating micro-electronic technology, might account for as much as half of the rise in the skilled–unskilled wage differential in the 1980s. Green *et al.*'s (2000) main conclusion is that Information Technology has had an important impact on the British labour market, a finding consistent with US studies such as Autor *et al.* (1998) and SBTC.

SKILL-BIASED TECHNOLOGICAL CHANGE

The idea behind SBTC is a straightforward one, that technological change in recent decades has favoured the employment of skilled labour. This is depicted in Figure 5.13 as a shift away from an equal employment of skilled workers S and the unskilled U to produce a given level of output, to employing workers in the ratio of 2 skilled to 1 unskilled.

Berman *et al.* (1997) investigate SBTC in manufacturing industries in ten OECD countries. Their main conclusion is that SBTC has resulted in the substitution

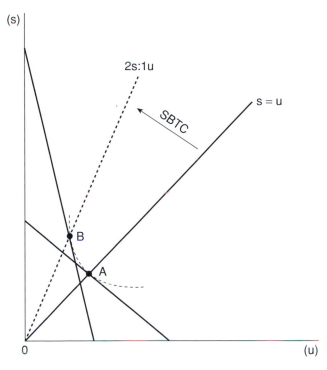

Figure 5.13 Skill-biased technological change

towards skilled workers in all ten countries during 1970–90. Figure 5.14 illustrates this by charting the growth in the employment shares of non-production workers in US and UK manufacturing.

Shifts in favour of skilled workers have taken place in spite of constant and in most cases increasing relative wages of skilled labour. In other words although the price of skilled labour has risen, firms still want more of it. The shift in favour of skilled labour has been widespread and remarkably uniform. Berman *et al.* (1997) found that the same industries that substituted in favour of skilled labour in the USA did so in all other countries. There were large increases in the relative demand for skilled labour within industries, some 40 per cent of this increase occurred in the machinery, computing, electrical machinery, printing and publishing industries. Consistent with our analysis of the impact of computers, technological change seems to have been largely associated with the development and assimilation of microprocessor techno-logy. Berman *et al.* (1997) estimate that as much as 70 per cent of the displacement of unskilled workers from manufacturing may be due to SBTC. They speculate that similar SBTC may also have impacted on the structure of employment and pay outside of manufacturing, especially in financial services. An obvious consequence of a SBTC shock is increased unemployment for unskilled workers (see Chapters 10 and 11). Figure 5.15 shows that in most countries in the sample, the skill-biased nature of employment growth means the skill upgrading of those in employment has

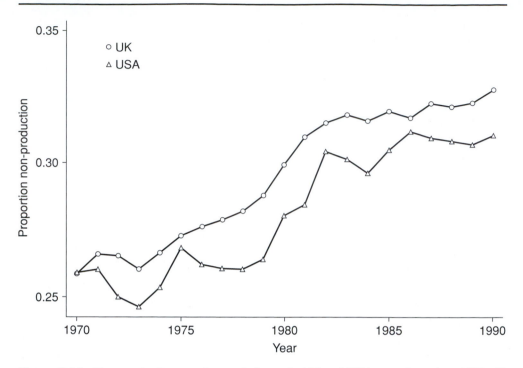

Figure 5.14   Non-production employment shares in UK and USA manufacturing, 1970–90

Source: Berman *et al.* 1997, figure 3, p. 43

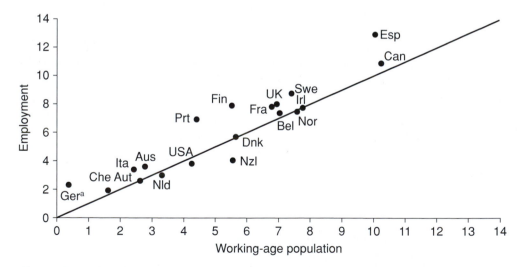

Figure 5.15   Changes of human capital in total working-age population and in employment, 1989–96[8]

Source: Bassanini *et al.* 2000, figure 5, p. 14
Notes: Share of individuals with higher educational levels in total, percentage point change (higher education levels refer to ISCED codes 5, 6 and 7).
[a] 1991–96.

Table 5.14 Employment growth (annual average percentage change) EU and USA, 1992–9

Group of occupations	Growth
Knowledge workers	3.3
Service workers	2.2
Management workers	1.6
Data workers	0.9
Goods-producing workers	−0.2

Source: Arnal *et al.* 2001, chart 3, p. 16

increased faster than the skill upgrading of the general population of working age, i.e., there are more countries above the bold diagonal line.

Haskel and Heden (1999) found that most of the skill upgrading of firms' workforces came about because of within-establishment changes. The higher demand for skilled workers might be evidence of a bias in favour of knowledge intensive employment. Certainly in the EU and the USA the employment growth of knowledge workers has been rapid between 1992 and 1999, as the data in Table 5.14 shows.

SBTC will bring about a wider spread of labour productivities. Given the German–USA differences in training and job mobility we referred to earlier in this chapter, in the face of SBTC the German training system encourages training of both the skilled and the unskilled, which need not have any impact on wage inequality between the two groups of workers. Yet in the USA, in the face of SBTC, the productivity of the unskilled falls, while that of the skilled rises, the incidence of training follows the same pattern resulting in widening wage inequality.

Acemoglu (1997) has suggested that if workers' skills and firms' technologies are complementary, then the increased supply of skills increases the demand of firms for technologies that will use those skills. Steedman (1999) reaffirms the importance of numeracy when concluding that

> those who do not continue beyond the lower secondary school level of education [those with no educational qualifications] are likely to have a poor grasp of arithmetic and be inadequately equipped with the skills needed for employment and lifelong learning in the labour markets of the future.
>
> (p. 17)

HUMAN CAPITAL AND GROWTH

The concept of human capital has come to play a crucial role in the new theories of economic growth, most closely associated with Romer (1986, 1990). Human capital theory linked the investment in its acquisition with productivity and earnings. The relationship being suggested was:

↑ EDUCATION ⟶ ↑ HUMAN CAPITAL ⟶ ↑ PRODUCTIVITY ⟶ ↑ WAGES

But what part, if any, does the creation, acquisition and application of knowledge and skill play in the determination of general economic activity and its growth? If human capital theory is right to propose such a link between knowledge and productivity, then the answer to our rhetorical question is that the knowledge embodied in the factor inputs of capital and labour plays a crucially important part in the growth path of general economic activity. To understand why this should be so let us return to simple growth theory, which traditionally adopts a production function approach, where output Q is determined by a combination of factor inputs, capital equipment K, labour L and raw materials RM, often referred to as land.

$$Q = f(K,L,RM)$$

Output can be increased either by increasing the amount of factor input or by increasing the effectiveness of those inputs, i.e., improving the productivity of their use. Total factor productivity can be defined as the difference between the growth of outputs minus the growth in inputs. If we let A stand for productivity or technical progress because they are both components of the growth accounting residual, which is that change in output which cannot be explained by changes in inputs we arrive at

$$\delta A/A = \delta Q/Q - (\delta K/K + \delta L/L + \delta RM/RM).$$

The $\delta A/A$ productivity/technical progress term is in fact a tremendously important element of the general economic growth story. The growth accounting work of Denison (1979) calculated that for the period 1948–73 some 40 per cent of the growth of national income in the USA was accounted for by changes in factor productivity. Bassanini et al. (2000) found that labour productivity growth 'accounts for at least half of GDP per capita growth in most OECD countries' (p. 7). The proportion rose in the 1990s compared to the 1980s in Australia, Denmark, Norway, Portugal and the USA where employment was either rising or was stable, and in Germany, Finland and Sweden where employment was falling. The contribution of increases in human capital to labour productivity is shown in Figure 5.16.

Increases in the average education levels helped to boost productivity in all countries except the Netherlands between 1985 and 1998. Skill upgrading seems to have had important growth effects in Portugal, the UK, France and Finland. The effect of increased human capital on productivity was fairly weak in Australia and the USA whose employment base was widened by favourable labour market conditions. The lowering of the average education level in Germany is a consequence of unification in 1990.

But where does this growth enhancing increase in productivity come from? Human capital theory provides some theoretically secure and empirically robust suspects. In relation to the USA Denison (1980) maintains that of a growth rate in potential national income of 3.8 per cent per annum between 1948 and 1973,

> 15 percent [of that growth] resulted from more capital . . . 15 percent is ascribed to changes in employment and working hours . . . 14 percent was due to increased

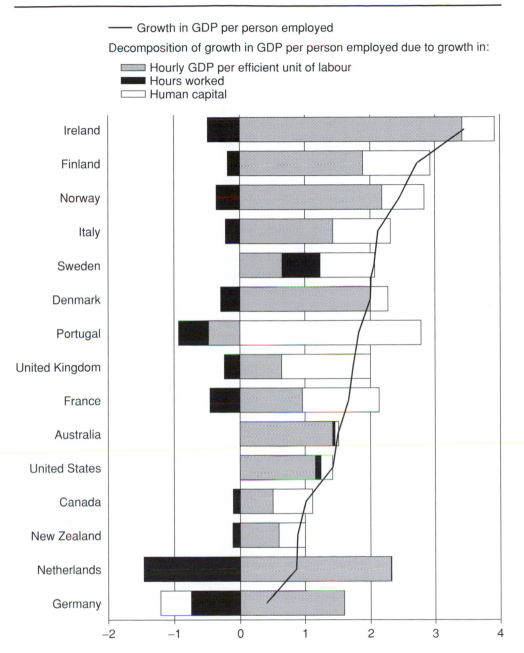

Figure 5.16   Effects on labour productivity of adjusting for hours and human capital (average annual rates of change), 1985–98

Source: Bassanini *et al.* 2000, figure 4, p. 13
Note: Based on the quantitative decomposition: growth in GDP per person employed = labour productivity adjusted for hours and human capital + growth in average hours worked + human capital adjustment.

capabilities of workers resulting from more education. 10 percent resulted from improved resource allocation . . . [and] 37 percent was contributed by advances in technological, managerial, and organisational knowledge . . .

(p. 220)

Griliches (1997) estimates that greater educational attainment in the USA appears to account for 0.5 percentage points of annual economic growth in the 1950s and 1960s and about half of that during the slowdown of the 1970s.

With regard to the UK, Bowden and Turner (1991) report that the variables they included to capture human capital effects exert the strongest influence when it comes to explaining productivity growth over the 1924–68 period. They conclude their empirical study by stating that the

results demonstrate that human capital factors dominate product market and labour relations factors in explaining differences in productivity between industrial groups in the twentieth century UK economy.

(p. 1431)

Gemmell (1996) found that for 21 OECD countries there was a positive relationship between higher education qualifications and subsequent economic growth. Topel (1999) shows that, based on cross-country regressions, the social rate of return to education could amount to 33 per cent. This implies a large impact on economic growth. Di Liberto and Symons (2001) found that Italian economic growth was boosted by the investment in primary education in the South, which eliminated illiteracy in that region.

The important point for growth theory to address is where the human capital-induced productivity/technological change is coming from. Is it endogenous, from within the economic system, or is it exogenously determined outside of the economy? Traditionally economists have relied on exogenous technological progress as the result of scientific breakthroughs increasing productivity. Solow's (1956) influential model treats A as an exogenously provided public good, freely available to the firm. The novelty of the new theories of economic growth propounded by Lucas (1988) and Romer (1986, 1990) is that knowledge, including human capital, which can enhance technological progress and productivity A is determined endogenously. Indeed knowledge is treated as a factor of production.

In Lucas (1988) output is regarded as a function of the stock of human capital. Growth of output needs increases in the stock of human capital. The term human capital is more accurately defined as knowledge, so growth could be fuelled by the better quality of education being more effective at producing knowledge. It is debateable whether the quality of education does improve over time in order to facilitate growth and there is no complete explanation of how the quality of education is to be continually improved.

Romer's (1990) model has four basic factor inputs: physical capital K; labour L; human capital; and the level of technology. The economy is modelled in terms

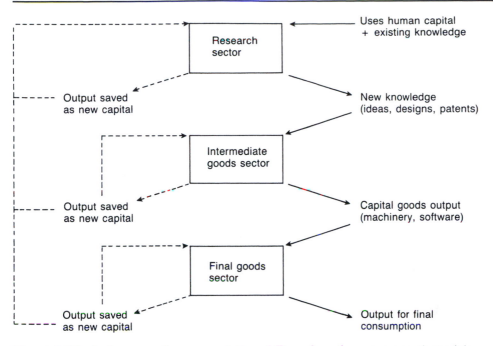

Figure 5.17 A diagrammatic representation of Romer's endogenous growth model:
Note: ——, investment, including research and development expenditure

of having three sectors which are related in the manner suggested by Figure 5.17. Human capital and the level of technology related to ideas are two aspects of knowledge as a factor of production. Human capital is taken to be the cumulative effect of formal education and on-the-job training. This is treated as a rival rather than a public good in the sense that it cannot be increased on a per capita basis without end. Human capital is inseparable from the individual human capital investor, each person has only a finite number of years within which to acquire knowledge and skills, and that human capital is lost when the person dies. On the other hand, the level of technology and ideas are non-rival in that their growth is unbounded. As Romer (1990) observes in relation to death 'any non-rival good that this person produces – a scientific law; a principle of . . . engineering; a mathematical result; software; a patent; a . . . drawing; or a blueprint – lives on after the person is gone' (p. 75). Thus Romer has separated the human capital component of knowledge, which is rival in form, from the non-rival technological component of knowledge.

An important element of this theory is that knowledge costs, and has to be at some point the consequence of intentional decision-making, and it has to be paid for by forgoing current consumption. For the economy as a whole human capital and knowledge in general is not an exogenous windfall gain. Human capital is a key input into the generation of new ideas and knowledge. The main conclusions of Romer's model are:

Table 5.15 Research and development (R&D) spending, 1996

	$ per capita	Gross (percentage of GPD)	Percentage financed by industry	Researchers per 10,000 of labour force
UK	362	1.94	47	50
Austria	325	1.52	49	34
Belgium	335	1.59	64	53
Czech Republic	135	1.07	60	25
Denmark	451	2.01	50	58
Finland	489	2.58	60	67
France	477	2.32	49	60
Germany	485	2.29	61	59
Greece	53	0.48	20	20
Hungary	61	0.66	39	26
Ireland	238	1.39	69	58
Italy	205	1.03	46	32
Netherlands	439	2.09	49	46
Norway	390	1.71	50	73
Poland	53	0.76	39	31
Portugal	76	0.58	19	24
Spain	129	0.87	46	32
Sweden	672	3.59	66	78
EU-15 average	355	1.84	53	49
Australia	355	1.68	47	66
Canada	352	1.64	49	54
Japan	658	2.83	73	92
Korea	379	2.79	78	47
New Zealand	164	0.97	34	35
USA	730	2.62	63	74

Source: OECD

1) the stock of human capital determines the rate of economic growth;
2) human capital devoted to research is crucially important.

Even a one-off increase in the stock of human capital above a certain threshold level can increase the growth rate indefinitely. Research and Development (R and D) spending could bring about an increase in the stock of human capital. With this in mind let us look more closely at some data on comparative levels of spending on research and development contained in Table 5.15.

We know from Chapter 2 that UK labour productivity growth exceeded that of the higher research spending in the USA during the 1970s and 1980s. R and D spending in the former communist East European countries is lower than the EU-15 average as is R and D activity in the Southern European countries. R and D activity is about the same in Australia and Canada as it is in the UK. R and D activity was greater in Korea than in the UK in 1996. Generally private sector R and D is believed to be more productive than Government R and D which tends to be concentrated in the military sector. The UK percentage of private industry financed R and D tends to be

Table 5.16 Index of labour productivity, USA = 100

	1913	1938	1948	1973	1988	1998
USA	100	100	100	100	100	100
France	42	47	36	66	83	103
Germany	50	55	30	66	82	90
Italy	43	47	33	65	78	100
UK	78	74	58	62	73	81
Japan	20	36	16	51	71	70

Sources: Feinstein 1990; OECD 2000

low by international standards of similarly developed countries. In terms of researchers per 10,000 of the labour force, the UK is at the EU-15 average but below its North European comparators, and well behind the USA and Japan.

Bayoumi *et al.* (1999) produce results implying that R and D can increase productivity as can trading with countries with large stocks of knowledge from R and D. However, it is worth bearing in mind that, as Table 5.16 shows, there is a significant labour productivity gap between the USA and other advanced industrialised countries. During the 1990s the European countries continued to close the productivity gap with the USA, Japan did not. What Table 5.16 appears to demonstrate is a certain degree of catching up by countries, especially France and Italy, that have achieved a certain capability threshold in terms of education, research and development, but that the UK has failed to take advantage of its pre-Second World War position. Furthermore, the slowdown in US productivity growth does not undermine human capital theory, in fact quite the reverse, it is explicable within a human capital framework. In their study of US labour productivity growth between 1950 and 1989, Rasmussen and Kim (1992) conclude

> [t]he decline during our sample period is not the result of a secular decline in labour productivity, *ceteris paribus*, but is caused by a persistent decline in an important determinant of output per worker, improvements in labour quality.
>
> (p. 289)

When it comes to the developing countries the role of human capital in growth is both clear and important. Contrasting the growth performance of the Phillipines at 1.8 per cent per annum, 1960–88, with that of South Korea of 6.2 per cent per annum, 1960–88, Lucas (1993) agrees that '[t]he main engine of growth is the accumulation of human capital – of knowledge – and the main source of differences in living standards among nations is differences in human capital' (p. 270).

What we hope to have indicated in this section is that productivity (the efficiency with which productive resources are used) is the key to economic growth. Improved productivity is driven by increased labour quality and better technology. Labour quality and new technology are two aspects of what Romer calls knowledge, i.e., human capital and ideas. A country with a large stock of human capital has a large growth potential. A country investing in its knowledge producing research sector, will aid economic growth thereby increasing the output likely to be available for both current consumption and for saving and reinvesting in the future growth of knowledge.

CASE STUDY – HUMAN CAPITAL AND ECONOMIC GROWTH IN CANADA

Human capital investment is an important part of the growth story of many countries. Serge Coulombe and Jean-Francois Tremblay (2001) 'Human Capital and Regional Convergence in Canada', *Journal of Economic Studies*, 28 (3): 154–80, examine the role that human capital investment has played in bringing income per person closer together in the various parts of Canada. Given that Canada is an open trading economy with capital able to flow freely between the various provinces, Coulombe and Tremblay (2001) are able to use a standard neoclassical growth model to assess the contribution of human capital to the growth performance of Canadian provinces.

> Our indices of human capital are based on census data that measure the percentage of the population who have at least achieved a given level of education. . . . this approach to evaluate human capital is widely used by labour economists . . . The data are available for the censuses of 1951, 1961 and 1971 and since, for every five years up to 1996. . . .

Figure A shows a clear pattern of convergence of the 10 provinces in terms of university education between 1951 and 1996. Provinces that were well below the Canadian average in 1951, like New Brunswick (NB), Prince Edward Island (PEI) and Newfoundland (NF), have moved much closer to the average (1) in terms of the proportion of the population who are university graduates by 1996. Provinces who had much higher initial stocks of graduates, Ontario (ONT) and British Columbia (BC), have moved much closer to the average by 1996.

> Provinces with higher per capita income, Ontario (ONT), British Columbia (BC) and Alberta (ALB), tend to have a better educated population. In general, provinces with lower per capita income, Newfoundland (NF), New Brunswick (NB), and Prince Edward Island (PEI), are below average in terms of educational achievement. Saskatchewan (SASK) and Manitoba (MAN), two provinces with per capita income close to the provinces' average, have educational achievements close to the average. Nova Scotia (NS) and Quebec (QUE) are, however, two notable exceptions regarding the university education indicator in that income was below average yet university education was above average. . . . Furthermore, the indicators

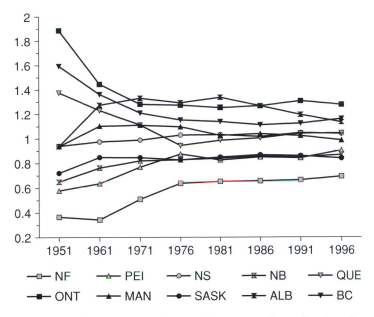

Figure A Convergence of the relative proportions of university students in the provinces of Canada, 1951–96

of human capital have grown faster since 1951 in the provinces that were originally less endowed with human capital. . . . Convergence speeds are . . . much faster for the 15 to 24 years group . . . and . . . are slightly faster for the females than for the males in the 15 to 24 years group. . . . If investment in human capital is the driving force of the convergence process, the slowness of the catch-up process could be attributed to the fact that an important portion of the total population does not have a clear incentive to invest in education. The opportunity cost of investing in education is usually higher for the population over 25 years of age and the expected return on the investment decreases when people get older.

Coulombe and Tremblay (2001) maintain that their model 'explains roughly 50 per cent of the convergence observed across Canadian provinces since 1951'. . . . The key ingredient is

the dynamic accumulation of human capital . . . Interestingly, this result corroborates the Barro and Sala-I-Martin (1995) and Barro (1997) findings that, at the cross-country level, investment in advanced education is one of the most important determinants of long-run growth. . . .

By itself, the human capital catch-up process . . . explains roughly 50 per cent of the relative growth of per capita income since 1951 across the Canadian provinces and more than 80 per cent of the relative income levels. . . .

Despite the relative scarcity of physical capital in the poorer regions, capital did not flow to these regions, because the availability of a well-educated population is a necessary requirement for the productivity of machines. . . . Since a subset only of the total population, the young, has a clear incentive to invest in education, the catch-up process of human capital is slowed down by the stock effect of the less-educated older people, who remain in the poorer provinces.

The catch-up by the poorer provinces has been assisted by

the rise of the welfare state and the creation of massive interregional redistribution programs, like . . . joint-financing of public spending in education . . . just after WWII, per capita income disparities across the Canadian provinces were much larger than those observed across the US border states. Economic development seems to have spread out more evenly just south of the Canadian border . . . [partly because of] the phenomenal public investment in secondary education in the Far West, the Great Plains, and parts of New England between 1910 and 1940.

The general message to come out of this case study is that education matters for economic growth even in rich countries like Canada.

HUMAN CAPITAL – SUMMARY

The concept of human capital was applied to education as an activity which raises the quality and productivity of the labour force. The basic human capital model examined:

- the costs of non-compulsory education, of which possible earnings forgone were identified as the main component
- the pecuniary benefit of such education being increased income levels over the span of human capital investors' working lives
- a standard investment appraisal technique with which one could assess education in terms of its rate of return both to the private individual and for society in general

The human capital model:

- justified earnings differentials on the basis of differential productivity resulting from differences in human capital investment
- could also be adapted to take account of differences in the age, ability, wealth and time preference (smoking) of investors
- generally predicted greater investment from the young, able, wealthy and non-smokers

Empirically the human capital model appears to demonstrate:

- the importance of education for developing countries
- greater private than social rates of return to all levels of education
- variable private rates of return to higher education among developed countries largely due to different university funding arrangements

The main alternative to human capital theory is the screening and signalling hypothesis which:

- stresses the uncertainty employers have about individuals' potential productivity
- emphasises credentialist aspects of education
- does not serve as part of a general theory of income determination or undermine human capital theory.

We found that overeducation was a significant feature of labour markets, which brought about a pay penalty for the overeducated worker. However, there was no evidence of qualifications inflation or grade drift.

Skills upgrading and increased wage inequality appear to have been driven by skill-biased technological change including the introduction of computers.

Human capital also features as an important contributor to general economic growth:

- this can be explained in the context of endogenous growth modelling such as Romer (1990)
- as a general policy prescription education as a form of human capital is worth investing in
- this was especially true for developing countries

HUMAN CAPITAL – QUESTIONS FOR DISCUSSION

1) Explain the link between educational attainment and earnings shown in Table 5.6 using human capital theory.
2) What other explanations for the relationship between education and earnings might labour economists advance?
3) Does it make sense for an individual to study full-time for a degree in the UK when the indirect cost could be as high as £50,000?
4) Giving your reasons, when you leave university would you rather be overeducated, well matched or under-educated?
5) How have computers affected labour markets?
6) What is skill-biased technological change and what impact has it had on labour markets?

7) Examine the evidence for a link between human capital investment and general economic growth.

8) What lessons for developing countries appear to arise from an understanding of human capital theory?

SUGGESTED READING

Belfield, C. (2000) *Economic Principles for Education: Theory and Evidence*, Cheltenham: Edward Elgar.

Card, D. (1999) 'Education and Earnings', in O. Ashenfelter and D. Card (eds) (1999) *Handbook of Labour Economics*, Volume 3, Amsterdam: Elsevier Science.

Krueger, A. (2000) *Education Matters: Selected Essays by Alan B. Krueger*, Cheltenham: Edward Elgar.

6

Labour market discrimination

INTRODUCTION

The economic analysis of discrimination focuses upon the possibility that significant wage and employment differences persist between groups within the labour force that are not justified by differential productivity and human capital investment. Do characteristics such as gender and race, which are economically irrelevant *per se*, significantly affect the labour market outcomes for individual labour suppliers? If so then the impact of gender and racial characteristics on earnings and employment outcomes can be regarded as labour market consequences of discrimination. In order to address the phenomenon of discrimination we need to examine economic theories of discrimination and the evidence provided by empirical studies of the topic. At the theoretical level there are two main schools of economic thought regarding discrimination. One is the neoclassical theory stemming from the work of Becker (1957) which is based on the notion that prejudice is expressed in discriminatory tastes on the part of employers, workers and consumers. The alternative is the segmented labour market approach, which can trace its heritage back to the theory of non-competing groups in the work of J.S. Mill (1885). The segmented labour market approach essentially maintains that the labour market is split into sectors including delineations according to sex and racial origin, and that there is very little interaction between those sectors. Examples of this approach are the 'job crowding' and the 'dual labour market' hypotheses.

In this chapter we set out the neoclassical and segmented market approaches and survey some of the empirical evidence in the light of statistical data indicating discrimination. As a special focus to our treatment of discrimination we will assess the effectiveness of equal pay and opportunities legislation and consider the case for 'comparable worth' policies. We are aware that our coverage of the economics of

discrimination concentrates on sex discrimination. Racial discrimination is not ignored, it is covered in a separate section later in the chapter. We regret that the issue
of the labour market experiences of disabled workers receives no systematic attention,
although many of the general conclusions can be applied to disabled labour suppliers.
For disabled workers discrimination takes the form of earnings and employment differentials over and above what appears to be justified by any legitimate productivity
differentials or additional costs incurred by firms providing special facilities specifically
for disabled recruits.

GENDER AND LABOUR MARKETS

Essentially this chapter attempts to provide a coherent analysis of the phenomenon of
significant differentials in the pay of men and women which persist over time and
which are international in their scope. Figure 6.1 presents the ratio of female to male
average earnings in the USA between 1955 and 1995. In the USA earnings differences
increased in the late 1950s, remained fairly constant during the 1960s and 1970s, yet
greater equality came about during the 1980s when the gender pay gap narrowed as
the real earnings of women workers began to rise and those of male workers, particularly the low skilled, declined. For the UK, as the data in Table 6.1 shows, the weekly
earnings of female workers rose rapidly from 54 per cent of male earnings in 1970 to

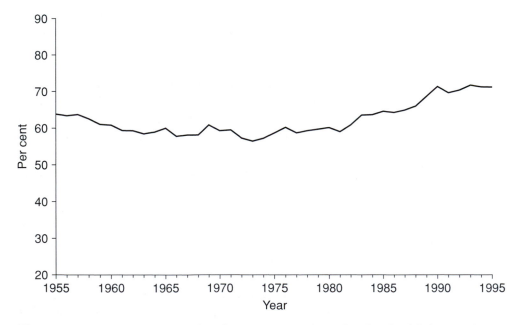

Figure 6.1   Median earnings of females as a percentage of males' for full-time workers,
1955–95

Source: Reynolds *et al.* 1998, figure 7.1, p. 169

Table 6.1 Gender pay gap (%), Great Britain, weekly earnings, 1970–99

Ratio of female to male pay

1970	54	1980	63	1990	68
1971	56	1981	65	1991	70
1972	56	1982	64	1992	71
1973	55	1983	66	1993	71
1974	56	1984	66	1994	72
1975	62	1985	66	1995	72
1976	64	1986	66	1996	72
1977	65	1987	66	1997	73
1978	63	1988	67	1998	72
1979	62	1989	68	1999	74

Source: ONS, *New Earnings Survey*
Note: Average gross hourly earnings, including overtime for full-time workers.

Table 6.2 University undergraduates (thousands), Great Britain, 1999

	Full-time	*Part-time*
Male	424.7	37.3
Female	462.1	52.4

Source: Higher Education Statistics Agency

62 per cent in 1975. The 1980s witnessed a somewhat less dramatic narrowing of the gender pay gap that continued during the 1990s.

One of the main reasons for increases in female workers' pay relative to male workers' earnings is that the educational attainments of women workers relative to their male colleagues have increased markedly over time. According to General Household Survey data, between the mid-1970s and the mid-1990s the UK moved from a position where women were less qualified than men to a situation where women aged 16–34 are more qualified than men. It is only among the older age groups (35–59) that men remain better qualified than women, but with much reduced differences in qualifications. In 1999 in their last year of compulsory schooling only 51 per cent of men gained passes at grade C or above in the GCSE (school leaving qualification usually taken at age 16) whereas 61 per cent of women managed to do so. In the same year there were also more female than male undergraduates at British universities, whether studying full or part-time (Table 6.2).

Comparing the UK to other EU countries Figure 6.2 shows that the UK is towards the bottom of a range of female:male earnings ratios in 1995. Measured using full-time workers' average gross hourly earnings, the UK gender pay gap was narrower than that in the Netherlands and Portugal, but was wider than those in Italy, France and Germany. In terms of gender pay equality the UK lagged behind the Scandinavian countries, especially Sweden.

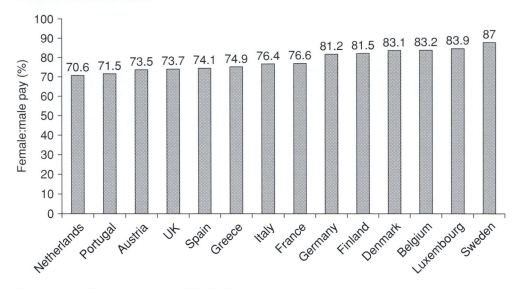

Figure 6.2   Gender pay gap, EU 1995
Source: Structure of Earnings Survey, 1995

Now that we have some basic data about possible sex discrimination in labour markets we can begin to analyse the phenomenon by setting out some theories of discrimination.

THE NEOCLASSICAL TASTE MODEL

The modern economic analysis of discrimination in the labour market is founded upon the seminal work of the American economist Gary Becker. Becker (1957) integrated the concept of discrimination with mainstream neoclassical microeconomic analysis, by suggesting that one group has a 'taste' for discriminating against another group and that this taste was a factor in their utility function. Becker identified a number of groups that could be ascribed a taste for discrimination: employers; workers; and consumers. However, most of the neoclassical analysis of discrimination has centred on the employer as an agent of discrimination. Accordingly we will set out the neoclassical employer taste model.

Employers have a taste for discrimination in the sense that their utility is adversely affected by employment of, and wages paid to the group being discriminated against, in this case females (F). Although the monetary cost of employing males and females is given by their wages, W_M and W_F respectively, the disutility experienced from hiring women affects the net cost such that

$$W_F = W_F(1 + d),$$

where d is what Becker termed the 'discrimination coefficient'. If an employer favours women workers d will assume a negative value. If the firm is completely indifferent between males and females, when it comes to hiring workers, $d = 0$. Yet if an employer

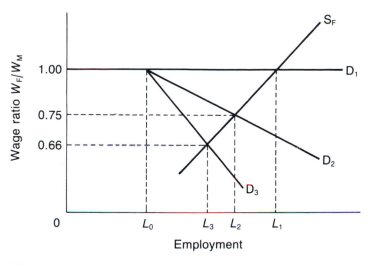

Figure 6.3

discriminates against women, *d* will acquire a positive value. The stronger the prejudice against women workers the greater the value of *d*. The implications of this employer taste model for women's labour market outcomes can be represented in Figure 6.3.[1] It shows a situation where a conventionally sloped female labour supply curve (S_F) encounters three different sets of demand conditions facing female workers. The first, D_1, represents a situation where the lack of any discrimination identifies a maximum potential employment level L_1, at wage rates which equal those of male workers, i.e., a wage ratio equal to unity. If a certain proportion of employers discriminate against women in their hiring practices, this gives the demand curve for female labour a kink at employment level L_0. Consider the case of D_2: non-discriminating firms' demand female labour up to L_0; Beyond L_0 prejudiced employers require a wage differential to compensate for a loss of utility arising from the hiring of female workers. Hence discrimination creates a gap between the market wages of men and women. The wage ratio $W_F/W_M < 1$, in our example women earn only three quarters of what a man would earn ($W_F/W_M = 0.75$). Note that actual female employment at L_2 is less than its potential maximum because of discrimination in the labour market. If the intensity of discrimination increases, illustrated by the steeper slope of the D_3 demand curve in Figure 6.3, this results in even lower levels of female employment at L_3 and a wider sex earnings gap as the ratio of female to male wages falls to 0.66.[2]

Even though a proportion of firms are prepared not to discriminate against employing women (L_0) they will pay the going market rate of two-thirds of a male worker's wage rate in the case of D_3. If it is the case that female wages relative to men's have increased over time and the earnings gap has narrowed, this implies a change in employer tastes. Such a change could be brought about by competition from less discriminating firms, or it could be due to a greater awareness of the worth of women workers acquired from information, direct experience, or enforced by equal pay and opportunities legislation. A movement from D_3 to D_2 is being suggested in the context of the employer taste model of discrimination for the 1970–2000 period.

A fundamental assumption underlying the theoretical work on economic discrimination is that male and female workers are equally productive. However, discrimination in this model results in women having to accept wage rates lower than those of men if both men and women are to be employed.

An important prediction which falls out of the employer taste model is that competitive labour and product markets would ensure that discrimination would only be a short-term phenomenon. More prejudiced employers will employ a higher proportion of male workers than their more egalitarian rivals. This means that they face higher wage bills than those firms that employ a greater proportion of equally productive female workers, because $W_M > W_F$. Take the following simple example of a competitive industry consisting of two types of firms facing market wage rates of £100 per week for men and £66 per week for women workers. Hence the wage ratio $W_F/W_M = 0.66$. If these two types of firms both need to employ 100 workers the weekly wage bill for each is

discriminator   100 men @ £100 = £10,000
egalitarian   100 women @ £66 = £6,600

In this trivial example the basic prediction of the employer taste model emerges, extremely prejudiced firms for which the existing wage differential is insufficient to overcome their disutility from employing women, will face a wage bill of £10,000 per week. For firms which are prepared to take full advantage of existing wage differentials, direct labour costs are only £6,600 per week. Egalitarian firms face lower unit labour costs and will make greater profits and/or be able to charge lower prices than their discriminating rivals. Higher profits attract other non-discriminating firms into the market and should entice existing firms to change their recruitment policies in favour of women workers. New entrants will increase output and depress prices and profits. Discriminating firms must either employ female workers or face making losses, declining market shares and eventually going out of business. New entrants and altered hiring policies increase the demand for female workers, a shift from D_3 to D_2 in Figure 6.3, this increases female employment and raises women's wage rates relative to those of men. The sex–earnings gap narrows as competitive forces drive the labour market towards the equality $W_F = W_M$. Discrimination can only exist in the long run if the competitive mechanism fails to operate effectively. Thus our attention is drawn towards considering the role of market imperfections.

If firms possess a degree of market power as in an oligopolistic market structure, then discrimination could be accommodated. Similarly if firms do not seek the objective of maximum profits, discrimination could be tolerated as a drain on profits. New non-discriminating firms could arise from the group being discriminated against, in this case women, but this is less likely the more capital intensive the industry and the greater the minimum efficient scale, in terms of optimum output as a proportion of total market demand. Women may also possess little capital because of past and present

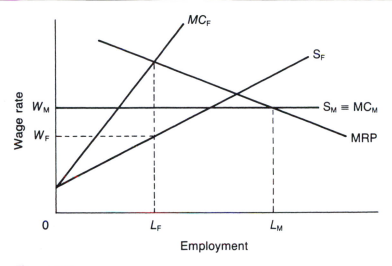

Figure 6.4

inequality of access to the capital markets, a further barrier to reducing labour market discrimination. Furthermore the erosion of discrimination via competition could be a lengthy and incomplete process because of the adjustment (hiring and firing) costs associated with replacing male with female workers to take advantage of the fact that $W_F < W_M$. Costs such as redundancy payments for displaced male workers, the recruitment and specific training of female workers are unlikely to be insignificant even without the protection given to existing workers by the law and trade unions. The prospects for reducing discrimination may well vary over the business cycle. Recession may result in a greater preference for female workers as cost cutting and keener product market conditions prevail in order to secure a share of a dwindling market. However, a boom may give firms more scope for recruiting workers previously discriminated against and thus changing the composition of their expanding labour force. Female labour suppliers may be more able to negotiate higher wages in tight labour market conditions. The exact impact of boom and recession cannot be settled by theory alone. We will have to review the empirical evidence on this matter.

Another aspect of sex discrimination is based upon what is perceived to be women's strategic weakness in the labour market, their comparative immobility. This can be formalised via Joan Robinson's (1933) theory of monopsony.[3] To illustrate this consider the case of a monopsonist facing a labour market in which women are less mobile than men because of family and social conventions. The greater mobility, both occupationally and geographically, of males compared to females is reflected in Figure 6.4, by the different elasticities (slopes) of their labour supply curves. In this example the labour supply curve for males (S_M) is perfectly elastic (horizontal).

If the profit maximising monopsonist firm is allowed to discriminate between males and females, it will set total employment, 0–LM, such that marginal revenue productivity equates to the male wage rate, $MRP = W_M$. For females the firm sets their marginal cost equal to their marginal revenue productivity, $MC_F = MRP$. The female wage rate (W_F) is set equal to the supply price of female workers at the equilibrium level of female employment L_F. Male employment amounts to $L_M - L_F$ and a wage differential of $W_M - W_F$ is observed in a profit maximising equilibrium.

Such imperfect market considerations may go some way to explain the persistent nature of discrimination in labour market outcomes but the question which must be asked of the employer taste model is, why would decades of even imperfect market interactions fail to erode wage and employment differentials? One might also question whether the employer taste model accurately reflects the fact that large scale oligopolistic firms, which dominate much of the activity in advanced industrialised economies, have divorced ownership from control and operate within a framework of equal opportunities legislation. One is therefore assigning discriminatory tastes to personnel department practices rather than to individual capitalists. Another criticism of the neoclassical model is that it does not concern itself with any explanation of where the taste for discrimination comes from. It is therefore primarily an analysis of the labour market effects of discrimination rather than an analysis of the causes of discrimination. As such it is open to the charge that the policy prescriptions which fall out of the employer taste model, encouraging competition and adjusting behaviour through equal pay and opportunity laws, address some of the symptoms but not the root cause of discrimination and therefore they will always prove inadequate. Thus the focus of attention should also cover pre-labour market entry discrimination as part of a wider explanation of the historical, sociological and psychological dimensions of prejudice, which is beyond the scope of this book.

Perhaps the main weakness of the neoclassical model is that it is addressing problems of wage discrimination, whereas employment discrimination may be the more significant labour market result of prejudice. If employers offer a structured hierarchy of jobs at different wage levels reflecting different productivity levels, discrimination against women will ensure that women are employed in the job structure below their potential. Thus if the wages of females depend upon their productivity and the discrimination they encounter,

$$W_F = MRP_F - DF$$

where DF is a discrimination factor, then at any level of the job structure, say at level i

$$W_F = W_i = MRP_i = MRP_F - DF.$$

Therefore in order to obtain and maintain employment at level i in the job structure, females need to exhibit a productivity equal to

$$MRP_F = MRP_i + DF.$$

In other words women must always work to a higher standard than their male colleagues at any given level of the job hierarchy and to a higher standard than the job actually requires. As a consequence of employer discrimination, equally productive men and women will occupy different jobs in the employment structure and receive different wage rates with the top jobs being dominated by males. This final criticism leads on to a more detailed examination of the segmented labour market approach to discrimination.

SEGMENTED LABOUR MARKETS

Segmented labour markets represent an alternative approach to that of neoclassical theory. In essence segmented labour market theories maintain that we should move away from the concept of the competitive labour market and view it as being split into a variety of constituent parts, which interact imperfectly with each other to only a very limited extent. Such an approach can be traced back to John Stuart Mill (1885), who rejected Adam Smith's competitive conception in favour of analysing the labour market in terms of non-competing groups; Variants of the segmented market approach include: the 'dual labour market' hypothesis which identifies primary and secondary sectors of employment; the 'job crowding' hypothesis which identifies predominantly male and mainly female occupations in the context of sex discrimination; and the 'insider–outsider theory' which splits the labour market into those in work or in unions, and the unemployed or non-unionised workers. We intend to deal with 'insider–outsider theory' in the context of unemployment (Chapter 10) and trade unions (Chapter 7), but the job crowding and dual labour market hypotheses are important contributions to the analysis of discrimination and therefore warrant our immediate attention.

Job crowding hypothesis

The job crowding hypothesis which is sometimes known as job segregation, has its roots in the pre-neoclassical analysis of discrimination. Fawcett (1918) and Edgeworth (1922) are early examples of an analysis that suggested women were over-represented in certain occupational categories and therefore depressed wages in those occupations. For Edgeworth

> [t]he pressure of male trade unions appears to be largely responsible for that crowding of women into a comparatively few occupations, which is universally recognised as a main factor in the depression of their wages. Such crowding is prima facie a flagrant violation of that free competition which results in maximum production and in . . . equal pay for equal work.
>
> (p. 439)

Although we would dispute the universal recognition accorded to crowding and question the prime cause of crowding, the quotation implies that any wage differential between male and female workers is due to the fact that men and women do essentially different jobs. In a compact summary of the economics of sex discrimination Pike (1984) suggests that discrimination 'could equally well result if females are excluded from jobs which they have the ability to do. If such jobs tend to be high wage jobs then this will

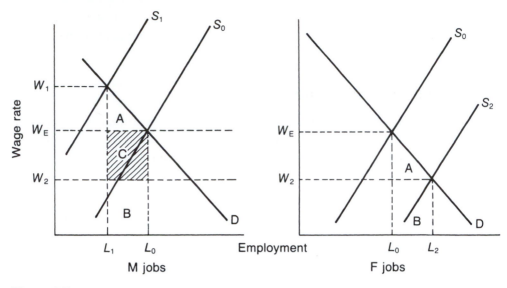

Figure 6.5

create wage differentials between males and females' (p. 3). Her analysis sees job segregation occurring as a result of women being faced with difficult access to certain jobs especially the professions. This does not need to take the form of reactionary trade unions or a crude veto on hiring women; the entry criteria may take the form of lengthy training or employment history which inadvertently excludes access to a disproportionate number of women. Women are thereby crowded into the remaining more easily accessible jobs. This process is shown using Figure 6.5.

In a perfect world both occupations are open to males and females, the labour market is a competitive one such that supply and demand conditions establish an identical equilibrium wage W_E in both jobs. If we now introduce a discriminatory access criterion in the M job market, labour supply is restricted to S_1 as the number of female entrants falls, although females do not need to be excluded entirely from working in the M job sector. Employment falls to L_1 and wage rates rise to W_1. Female workers crowd into the more easily accessible F jobs increasing labour supply to S_2, thus reducing wage rates to W_2. Under these circumstances wage discrimination in the sense that it was defined in the neoclassical taste model does not occur. In both M and F jobs workers are being paid according to their marginal revenue productivity, it is just that $MRP_M > MRP_F$. Neither do employers bear any profit reduction in this situation, hence there is no tendency for this form of discrimination to be competed away in the long run. Thus the apparent differential between male and female earnings associated with the divergence of $W_1 - W_2$ from W_E which has arisen will not be eroded.

The crucial question is now, does the existence of job crowding and earnings differentials prove discrimination? No simple or straightforward answer emerges from the economic analysis. Wage differentials might reflect different human capital investment. Job segregation and crowding might reflect female choices geared to combining child bearing and rearing responsibilities with less demanding, low mobility jobs. Once again we need to examine the empirical evidence to properly evaluate the significance of the job crowding hypothesis.

Dual labour market hypothesis

The dual labour market hypothesis is a popular and relatively recent formulation of a special case of a segmented labour market split into 'primary' and 'secondary' segments. Doeringer and Piore (1971) comprehensively defined the segments as follows:

> Jobs in the primary market possess several of the following characteristics: high wages, good working conditions, employment stability, chances of advancement, equity and due process in the administration of work rules. Jobs in the secondary market, in contrast, tend to have low wages and fringe benefits, poor working conditions, high labour turnover, little chance of advancement, and often arbitrary and capricious supervision.
>
> (p. 165)

There needs to be a barrier to prevent workers moving freely between the two segments of the labour market. Experience in the secondary market could be an adverse signal when seeking employment in the primary segment. Those displaced from the primary market may well prefer unemployment to jobs in the secondary market.

The dual labour market hypothesis would suggest that male–female age differentials reflect the fact that male workers are by and large, involved in the primary market, whereas female workers tend to dominate the secondary market. Such differentials will persist over time because of the limited and imperfect interactions between these two segments of the labour market. The dual labour market hypothesis lends itself to the concept of an internal labour market composed of those workers already employed by the firm. Doeringer and Piore (1971) see internal labour markets as 'a logical development in a competitive market in which three factors . . . may be present: 1) enterprise-specific skills, 2) on-the-job training, and 3) custom' (p. 39). This is an example of the concept of transactions costs applied to the labour market. As such the internal labour market need not be incompatible with competitive pressures on the firm to minimise costs. In the face of high labour turnover costs due to firm specific technology and a significant specific training component, firms and their workers insulate themselves from the external labour market. Yet internal labour markets may result in inefficiencies by impeding labour mobility and interfering with pay and employment decisions in a manner that may well be discriminatory. Custom and administrative rules determine employment and pay decisions in internal labour markets rather than the outcomes of competitive market processes. Such rules governing the internal appointment process, which trade unions help to negotiate and enforce, may entail the firm hiring at low levels and filling higher vacancies by internal promotion. Thus by such devices access to primary segment jobs is limited to existing members of an institution be it a firm, a trade union or a professional body.

SEGMENTED MARKETS APPROACH: A SUMMARY

Labour market segmentation of some form is an integral part of radical and Marxian perspectives on economics. It is also consistent with Mill's analysis couched in terms of non-competing groups, which we have referred to as exhibiting 'limited or imperfect interaction' between groups, within the labour market. Mill (1885) maintained that social, occupational and geographical barriers impeded the mobility of workers moving from one part of the labour market to another. These barriers may take the form of social class, gender, race, skill levels, education or a division between town and country. Mill identified unskilled manual workers in particular as occupying a low paid segment and unable to acquire the skills necessary to advance into the better paid segments. The critical feature of the segmented markets approach is not the identification of what delineates the groups within the markets, but the denial of equal access to all groups within those markets. Thus contrary to Mill's division along the lines of skill, the job crowding example from Pike (1984) outlines a scenario where secondary segment workers (females) are capable of performing primary jobs but that restricted access to such good jobs deny them the opportunity to do so. Darity and Williams (1985) apply a Marxist conception of competition to a labour market where workers can erect and maintain discriminatory barriers to entry, thereby creating and perpetuating wage differentials. The labour market, instead of reflecting differential ability and productivity, is an active generator of economic inequality.

Theories of labour market segmentation argue that the long-run equilibrium in the labour market will be characterised by the rationing of high wage primary sector jobs. Primary and secondary sector workers do not have to be equally able or productive, segmentation stresses that the difference in labour quality is less than the difference in pay between sectors. An important divergence between segmentation and neoclassical theory is that productivity is being seen as a feature of the job rather than an attribute of the individual worker. Neoclassical theory would see married females' confinement to the secondary sector as exogenous to an analysis of the labour market. Segmentation would see it as part of a wider attempt to explain their subordination within the family and society. Thus segmentation can be made consistent with radical or Marxist interpretations of wider social phenomena.

In determining which occupations are going to be in which labour market segment, the key element is identified as product market stability. Stable product demand encourages primary sector employment. Unstable product demand tends to encourage secondary sector job characteristics. Yet this is not a clear demarcation; it may be influenced by whether an industry is growing or declining, the technology and skill requirements of a job and whether the economy is booming or in recession. For other segmentation theorists such as Edwards (1979), the key factor is how the capitalist firm seeks to control and motivate its workforce. The argument being that the growth of larger and larger firms results in a breakdown of personalised discipline, hence firms resort to using job security and career prospects to encourage loyalty, which in turn leads to the creation of an internal labour market. Such internal labour markets need norms of conduct with respect to pay, training and promotion. Thus custom is seen as an important component in identifying and enforcing established practices in the conduct of employer–worker transactions. Therefore segmentation in labour markets arises from cross-sectional variation in the control mechanisms adopted by firms. Edwards (1979) identifies three forms of labour control mechanism:

- simple control using the close supervision of workers by managers
- technical control, which uses machinery to control the pace of production and worker effort, for example assembly line speed
- bureaucratic control, which aims at getting workers to internalise the firm's goals using high wages, loyalty bonuses and fair governance structures such as promotion and grievance procedures

According to Rebitzer (1993) in the USA

simple control is . . . found primarily in small enterprises where employees are doing simple, easy to monitor tasks. Technical control applies most strongly in large, mass production firms employing large numbers of semi-skilled workers. Bureaucratic control was developed originally by large, non-union employers as a means of managing their white-collar labour force.

(p. 1412)

Bulow and Summers (1986) construct a dual labour market model with a primary segment, where jobs are difficult to monitor so firms offer workers wages above the alternative market wage, and a secondary segment with no significant problems in monitoring worker effort so firms pay a market clearing wage. This is a job crowding model with a primary segment emerging from firms' adoption of higher wages as a worker incentive scheme. Firms can use the threat of dismissal and therefore the loss of the wage premium to encourage high levels of worker effort. Sex discrimination would result from restricting women's access to primary segment jobs. Employers could make hiring decisions from a queue of primary job seekers on the basis of 'statistical discrimination' by ascribing general characteristics to individual applicants. Because of imperfect information, employers cannot directly observe applicants' expected job tenure or preference for long hours of work; they may therefore use statistical evidence of women's shorter job tenure and shorter working hours and apply these to women in the job queue. If so then hiring decisions for primary segment jobs will favour men.

EMPIRICAL EVIDENCE OF DISCRIMINATION

There is something intuitively credible about the content of the segmented market approach to labour market analysis. Descriptive statistics contained in Grimshaw and Rubery (2001) show that in 1998 more than 60 per cent of female employment in the UK was concentrated in 10 out of 77 occupational categories. The data in Table 6.3 does bear out the fact that certain occupations do contain workforces that are

Table 6.3 Occupational female share and relative pay (%), UK 1998

	Female share	Occupational pay
Teaching professionals	60.7	148.9
Catering occupations	63.9	51.1
Other sales and services	67.4	50.0
Numerical clerks/Cashiers	71.3	83.8
Sales assistants/Check-out staff	73.9	52.9
Clerks	75.7	72.8
Health associate professionals	81.8	110.6
Childcare	83.6	59.0
Health and related occupations	86.8	62.3
Secretaries/Personal assistants	93.4	83.6

Source: Grimshaw and Rubery 2001, tables 2.1, 2.2, pp. 6–7
Note: Female Share is women workers in an occupation as a percentage of all workers in that occupation. Occupational Pay is the average pay of all workers in an occupation as a percentage of the pay of all occupations.

predominantly female. Furthermore in most of those predominantly female occupations pay is lower than the average for all occupations, which will contribute to a gender pay gap. However, the situation is not straightforward; we can see that two of the predominantly female occupations pay above average wages. In the 1990s more men entered sales occupations with lower pay compared to the all occupation average. In general the extent to which men and women do different jobs is declining over time. Blau (1998) documents a convergence of gender employment patterns in the USA during the 1970–95 period. The data in Table 6.3, which includes part-time workers, cannot tell us the extent to which female shares represent occupational choices.

Theoretically whether it is better to view labour market phenomena as the product of non-competing groups rather than the outcome of essentially competitive situations is a debatable point. A theoretical weakness of the job crowding hypothesis is that it is an incomplete model of discrimination. It does not address the issues of how occupations come to be segregated and why discrimination might persist or be eroded over time. Yet when we move on to the empirical status of the segmented market approach we are faced with a number of evident weaknesses.

Firstly, it is very difficult to formulate strong tests of the segmentation hypotheses. McNabb and Ryan (1990) mention some empirical problems, chief among which is that if schooling and work experience are included in econometric studies as indicators of labour quality, the difference between the primary and secondary segments would disappear. Furthermore, the dual labour market hypothesis, the one that strictly posits two segments, receives no empirical support. As McNabb and Ryan (1989) report

> the bimodality (duality) established in such [empirical] studies refers to product market attributes rather than to labour market outcomes . . . No one has established the existence of a bimodal duality in pay or turnover . . . for the simple reason that they do not exist.

(p. 169)

Studies of the dual labour market hypothesis such as Rosenberg (1980) for the USA and Mayhew and Rosewell (1979) for the UK, typically report high levels of upward mobility among male workers from secondary segment jobs, associated with the human capital attributes of higher levels of schooling and work experience. Such findings tend to weaken the segmentation case, although one might reasonably expect a lower rate of migration for females from secondary segment jobs.

The econometric investigation of discrimination is usually based upon the by now familiar human capital real earnings function we encountered in Chapter 5:

$$\log (W/P)_i = \alpha_1 + \alpha_2 I_i + \alpha_3 I_i^2 + \alpha_4 X_i + \varepsilon_i$$

where α_1 is the log of basic earnings with no extra human capital investment or other productivity enhancing characteristics such as work experience; I_i is human capital investment usually in terms of additional years of education and training, with I_i^2 picking up non-linearities in its effects; X_i is a vector of other variables such as work experience, which may be picked up as a measurable productivity characteristic; and ε_i is an error term. One can then examine sex discrimination by including a dummy variable Z, which will indicate the fact that one is dealing with male ($Z = 0$) or female ($Z = 1$) workers. Thus,

$$\log (W/P)_i = \alpha_1 Z + \alpha_2 I_i + \alpha_3 I_i^2 + \alpha_4 X_i + \varepsilon_i.$$

Although this method is straightforward, we need a way of controlling for any differential in the human capital or work experience of male and female workers, which will result in justifiable differences in their earnings. Thus as an estimator of discrimination this method is only valid if the coefficients of variables I and X are equal across the gender groups. A better method involves the specification of earnings functions for each group separately. The relevant equations now become

$$\text{Male } \log (W/P)_M = \alpha_{1M} + \alpha_2 I_M + \alpha_3 I_M^2 + \alpha_4 X_M + \varepsilon_M$$

$$\text{Female } \log (W/P)_F = \alpha_{1F} + \alpha_2 I_F + \alpha_3 I_F^2 + \alpha_4 M_F + \varepsilon_F.$$

Now we are in a position to produce a somewhat more reliable estimate of sex discrimination in the labour market. Let us simplify matters by initially assuming that male and female workers have the same human capital investment, so that their years of schooling, level of academic achievement and training are identical, i.e., $I_M + I_M^2 = I_F + I_F^2$. This leaves X defined as work experience as the only legitimate determinant of a real earnings gap. Consider Figure 6.6, which reflects a situation where men have more labour market work experience than women (i.e., $X_M > X_F$) and where male earnings are greater than those of female workers. The extent of discrimination can be estimated by putting average female work experience X_F into the male earnings function and predicting what males would have earned, then calculate the difference between this and actual female earnings. This gives us the difference a as an estimate of discrimination or the ratio a/b to arrive at a proportionate measure of the discrimination against women. Another estimate can be obtained by looking for the discrimination

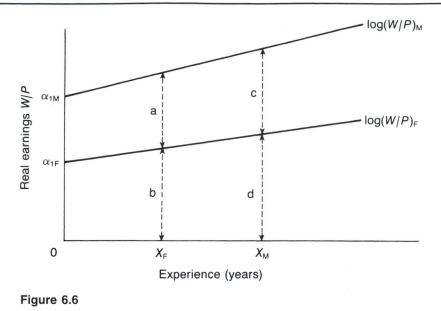

Figure 6.6

in favour of men. This is calculated by predicting what females would earn if they had the same work experience as men, X_M, and measuring the difference between this prediction and what males actually earned. This gives us the difference c, or the ratio $c/(c + d)$. Many studies, such as Greenhalgh (1980), estimate both measures of discrimination and present an average of both against female and in favour of male estimates. This approach to the empirical estimation of discrimination is known as the 'residual' approach because it tries to calculate what is left of the earnings differential after one has taken legitimate reasons, such as differences in human capital I and work experience X, into account.[4]

An example of a 'residual' estimation approach is Goldin's (1990) examination of sex discrimination in the US labour market. Her impressive study produces data for the ratio of female to male full-time earnings across a range of occupational groups. Table 6.4 serves to show that in the USA, the early twentieth century witnessed a marked reduction in the gender based earnings gap across all occupations, with the general ratio increasing from 0.46 to 0.56 between 1890 and 1930. Goldin attributes this improvement to 'increasing the returns to schooling, by expanding the labour market experience of women, and by decreasing the returns to physical strength' (p. 63). Advances in the education of women appear to have been responsible for a marked narrowing of the earnings differential in the professional and clerical sectors, accompanied by a substantial increase in female employment in these sectors. Goldin (1990) conducts an analysis of her findings to assess whether the increase in the overall female to male earnings ratio from 0.46 to 0.60 (1970) was due to changes in relative earnings within occupational categories or due to changes in the occupational structure itself. The outcome of this exercise is summarised in Table 6.5.

Table 6.4 USA ratio of female to male earnings (full-time working)*

	1890	1930	1970
Professional	0.26	0.39	0.71
Clerical	0.49	0.71	0.69
Sales	0.60	0.61	0.44
Manufacturing	0.54	0.58	0.56
Service	0.53	0.60	0.56
Agriculture	0.53	0.60	0.59
All occupations	0.46	0.56	0.60

Source: Adapted from Goldin 1990, table 3.2, p. 64
Note: * Not adjusted for hours worked; men generally work longer hours than women.

Table 6.5 Predicted ratios of female to male earnings

	1890	1930	1970
Actual ratios all occupations (from Table 6.4)	0.46	0.56	0.60
1890 Earnings constant occupational change	0.46	0.49	0.46
1930 Earnings constant occupational change	–	0.56	0.51

If, for the 1890–1930 period, earnings were held at their 1890 levels with only the occupational structure of male and female employment being permitted to vary, instead of the earnings ratio actually rising from 0.46 to 0.56 it would have risen to only 0.49. It appears as though occupational change during those 40 years accounts for a 0.03 rise in the ratio, whereas 0.07 is accounted for by better female earnings within occupations. More alarmingly, for the entire 1890–1970 period had there been no improvement in female earnings within occupations in the USA there would have been no reduction in the female to male earnings differential. The final row in Table 6.5 shows that had 1930 earnings remained constant up to 1970 shifts in the occupational structure would have led to a deterioration in the comparative earnings of females from 0.56 to 0.51 instead of the actual improvement to 0.60 observed during this period. Goldin therefore concludes that

> the increase in the relative earnings of females over the past century was due far more to changes in the ratio of female to male earnings within broad occupational groups than to changes in the distribution of these . . . groups between men and women.

> (p. 70)

A similar conclusion is reached by Begg *et al.* (2000) in an analysis of earnings and employment patterns in the UK for 1998. They observe that

Most men are industrial manual workers or belong to the professional and managerial occupations. Many women do secretarial or selling jobs. Yet the pattern of employment is not the major cause of the fact that women as a whole earn £7,500 a year less than men. If women had the employment pattern shown for men . . . but were paid the rates shown for women the overall earnings of women would hardly change . . . if women maintained their employment pattern but earned the pay rates shown for men, women as a whole would earn more than men.

(p. 205)

Thus Begg *et al.* would identify the primary cause of the observed female–male earnings differential as wage discrimination rather than being due to job crowding. Whilst there is no unanimity on this matter a number of other studies report similar findings. Sloane and Siebert (1980) find that female workers are not unduly concentrated in low paying occupations and that it is the difference in pay within occupations that is crucial. While Jones and Makepeace (1996) do find that women have to meet tougher criteria to gain promotion in a British financial institution, the impact of this discriminatory treatment is small compared to gender differences in work experience. Aldrich and Buchele (1986) conclude that US empirical studies generally view job segregation to be a significant but not the dominant source of earnings differentials. Dex and Shaw (1986) dispute this and claim that more disaggregated studies identify women's inferior position as being due primarily to occupational crowding. Goldin (1990) finds that even disaggregating her data to some 400 occupational categories does not significantly alter her conclusions.

Radical economists have, via some variant of segmented market theory, sought to show that contrary to the neoclassical taste model, those discriminating against either blacks or women have a powerful motive for doing so, and that the motive is financial gain. Examples of such radical based studies are Szymanski (1976,1978) and Riedesel (1979). They tend to suffer from a number of weaknesses to which the articles by Villemez (1978) and Beck (1980) refer. Chief amongst the criticisms of the radical perspective are that the use of family income leaves some important non-discriminatory sources of income unaccounted for, such as past wealth holdings. The use of median earnings differences does not take account of productivity differences, which may well exist between groups. More fundamentally one needs to be clear about what is being measured. Is it labour market discrimination as defined by Sloane (1985) as 'unequal treatment in terms and conditions of employment for groups of equally productive workers' (p. 79), or is it pre-entry discrimination as part of a wider picture of black or female subordination in advanced industrialised countries? The radical perspective appears to conflate these aspects of racial and gender group comparisons. We are inclined to concur with Dex and Sloane (1989) when they state that '[t]he work with the least flaws does suggest that the radical view is unsupported and Becker's prediction is upheld' (p. 87).

Dickens and Lang (1993) see inter-firm and inter-industry wage differentials as evidence of segmentation. They state that 'dual labour market theory . . . suggests

Table 6.6 Additional return to education
for men over women (%)

A Level	42.6
Non-degree H.E.	33.8
First degree	23.3
Higher degree	20.7

Source: Blundell *et al.* 2000, table 5, p. F95

many job characteristics are highly correlated' (p. 151). Yet so does human capital theory suggest a correlation between earnings and many of the factors they list such as productivity, education, job tenure and age. They find that 'only average education and profitability are consistently related to industry wages', which leads them to admit that 'dual market theory suggests that it is difficult to determine a priori who is in which sector' (p. 157).

In a study of the effects of higher education on British workers' wage rates, Blundell *et al.* (2000) find that the gender gap in hourly earnings, even after accounting for ability, family background, demographic and employer characteristics, is substantial. The data in Table 6.6 bears this out, but it also shows that the gender gap declines the further up the education qualifications ladder we go.

Desai *et al.* (1999) examine the components of the gender pay gap in the mid-1970s and the mid-1990s, a period in which the gap narrowed. They find (their table 10.10, p. 182) that all the gains in pay equality have been made by women in full-time employment, to the extent that it has more than offset the declining relative pay of female part-time workers. In terms of education and experience women working full-time have achieved near equality with men and these worker characteristics are now more equally rewarded than they once were. By the mid-1990s much of the remaining gender pay gap is accounted for by the unexplained residual (13 out of 24 percentage points), often interpreted as discrimination. Lissenburgh (2000) estimates a discrimination factor (DF) for British women of 9.5 per cent for full-time workers rising to 15.2 per cent for part-time workers.

For neoclassical economics discrimination is an irrational act in that it damages firms' profitability and prevents an optimum allocation of resources. An important prediction to fall out of the employer taste model is that increasing the degree of labour market activity and competition should erode discrimination. An associated prediction is that discrimination should be most marked and enduring in industries with greater concentrations of market power, be that monopoly or monopsony power. A study of the banking sector by Ashenfelter and Hannan (1986) strongly supports the notion that discrimination is greater where the product market is uncompetitive. Hodson and England's (1986) study questions this aspect of the Becker taste model prediction. They find that market concentration and profitability do not account for the female–male earnings differential. They stress that because women tend to work in industries with less unionisation and lower capital investment this reduces female earnings. However, unionisation and investment are not unrelated to market power.

The study displays a low level of explanatory power that may reflect in part the problems associated with measuring market structure and market power empirically. Shorey (1984) moves away from seeing the choice of neoclassical theory or segmented markets as a strict dichotomy of competitive versus institutional forces within the labour market. He presents an interesting model that incorporates elements of both approaches. Employers and workers have a taste for discrimination but there are two segments of the labour market. Firms also exercise a degree of monopsony power. His eclectic model suggests that even if the product market is competitive, discrimination may persist in the long run as firms use their monopsony power and workers use trade unions to express their taste for discrimination. The significance of this work is that maybe we should think in terms of degrees of segmentation combined with degrees of competitiveness rather than look to radical segmentation to usurp the neoclassical competitive conception of markets.

However, there is one issue about the topic of discrimination where there is agreement. As Tzannatos (1990) reminds us 'all economic theories of discrimination lead to the prediction that there are welfare losses associated with any kind of discrimination, irrespective of the particular assumptions of the model' (p. 191). Such welfare losses can be simply illustrated by referring back to the job crowding hypothesis example in Figure 6.5. Remember that moving from a position of equilibrium in both occupations, one becomes a higher wage, lower employment, male dominated job, the other a lower wage, higher employment, essentially female occupation. In welfare terms does the expansion of the female occupation compensate for the contraction of the male occupation under conditions of no change in unemployment? A quick re-examination of Figure 6.5 provides a ready answer. The gain from additional employment at lower wage rates W_2 in the female occupation equals the areas A + B. The loss from lower employment, albeit at higher wage rates W_1 in the male occupation is A + B + C. Therefore the shaded area C represents the welfare (deadweight) loss associated with discrimination in the labour market.

Having set out the basic economic theories of discrimination and assessed the findings from empirical studies of sex discrimination, which it is acknowledged causes general welfare losses, we now turn to examine the role and effectiveness of legislation as an anti-discrimination policy.

THE ECONOMICS OF COMPARABLE WORTH AND ANTI-SEX DISCRIMINATION LEGISLATION

The economic analysis of discrimination points to the importance of competition towards overcoming taste based discrimination. The provision of information is also needed to combat 'statistical discrimination', where employers make hiring decisions under conditions of uncertainty and screen applicants on the basis of the characteristics (real or inferred) of the group of which they are members. Yet if competitive forces within the product and labour markets are deemed not to be strong enough to erode discrimination, then a more interventionist anti-discrimination package

Table 6.7   Ratio of female to male wages (hourly wage rates)

	1960	1970	1980
Australia (weekly)	0.59	0.59	0.75
UK (manual workers)	0.61	0.61	0.79
USA	0.66	0.65	0.66
Sweden (manufacturing)	0.72	0.84	0.90

Source: Adapted from Mincer 1985, table 3, p. 6

including legislation is warranted. In trying to assess the impact of anti-discrimination laws on labour market outcomes over time, we have to explain the differences between the USA and the almost identical experiences of the UK and Australian gender earnings gap.

Sweden also needs to be considered as the economy displaying near equality in labour market outcomes for male and female workers. Data for these four countries contained in Table 6.7 provides us with the broad picture on sex discrimination between 1960 and 1980. The comparison between the USA on the one hand and the likes of Australia and the UK is an important one when assessing the efficacy of anti-discrimination law. The legislative landmarks for these three countries are as follows:

1963–4   USA; the Federal Equal Pay Act was passed in 1963; employment discrimination was outlawed by Title VII of the Civil Rights Act of 1964

1972   Australia; the Conciliation and Arbitration Commission moved from an equal pay principle to that of comparable worth

1970–5   UK; the Equal Pay Act was passed in 1970 and phased in until full enforcement in 1975; employment discrimination was outlawed by the 1975 Sex Discrimination Act which established an Equal Opportunities Commission

Given that the gender based earnings gap in Australia and the UK experienced a marked reduction during the 1970s, it is tempting to ascribe this to the equal pay and opportunities measures enacted and enforced by these countries during that decade. The problem with such an interpretation of events is that similar legislation enforced in the USA during the 1960s does not appear to have had any discernible impact on the labour market experiences of American women.

A possible explanation for this discrepancy is that by 1960 American women workers fared better than their Australian and British counterparts, they had a higher earnings ratio because of higher rates of labour force participation and they remained in the workforce longer thereby gaining more employment experience. Further increases in female labour force participation in the USA were believed to depress women's average earnings as less well educated and less experienced women joined and rejoined the workforce. This is consistent with the view that it is not until the

Table 6.8   UK ratio of female to male earnings (average gross hourly, full-time workers)

1970	0.63	1982	0.74	1989	0.76	1995	0.80
1975	0.72	1984	0.74	1990	0.77	1996	0.80
1977	0.76	1985	0.74	1991	0.78	1997	0.81
1979	0.73	1986	0.74	1992	0.79	1998	0.81
1980	0.74	1987	0.74	1993	0.79	1999	0.82
1981	0.75	1988	0.75	1994	0.80	2000	0.82

Source: ONS, *New Earnings Survey*

1980s that the growth of the importance of women working in the USA is reflected in a narrowing of the earnings differential. Goldin's (1990) data shows the overall female–male median annual earnings ratio remaining virtually constant at 0.60 between 1960 and 1980, yet during the 1980s there is a clear and enduring upward trend which leaves the ratio at 0.66 in 1987. This encourages Goldin to conclude that the

> continued expansion of female labour force participation, the increase in college education among women, and . . . the revival of feminism in the 1960s and 1970s together produced a vast change in the political strength of women that may yet alter the functioning of the labour market.
>
> (p. 210)

In the UK more detailed statistics of the earnings ratio, contained in Table 6.8, appear to show that the improvement in the 1970s was a one-off shift associated with the introduction of equal pay and opportunities legislation. Note that the gender gap for hourly pay is narrower than that for weekly earnings contained in Table 6.1 because even those women who work full-time do not work as many hours as men. A limited move to the principle of comparable worth in 1984 appears to have had no immediate impact on the general lot of women in the labour market. This resulted from a European Court ruling in January 1984 which gave UK women workers a new legal right to claim equal pay on the basis that their work was of 'equal value' when compared with that of a male worker, even though that work may not have been deemed as similar under the terms of the Equal Pay Act of 1970. If this move to the principle of comparable worth had so little impact on the overall position of women in the labour market during the 1980s, why did the original equal pay legislation appear to have had such a dramatic impact on the earnings gap in the early 1970s? A possible answer may rest in the nature of collective bargaining in the UK over this period. Before 1970 collective agreements between employers and trade unions treated female pay so as to maintain differentials with male pay. An example of an agreement that would maintain the status quo is an across-the-board pro rata increase in pay. Government incomes policies, by encouraging flat rate increases would also not have encouraged the reduction of gender based earnings differentials. By the time the Equal Pay Act was fully enforced in 1975, collective agreements affected the pay of 70 per cent of women workers. Such agreements were forced to accept the principle of equal pay. The importance of the positive role of union bargaining which had its greatest effect in the early 1970s within the new legislative framework, is reflected in a report by the Labour Research Department (1986), which states that 'through the bargaining machinery it is possible to negotiate for the benefit of all women workers, not just the individuals whose claims survive the hurdles of the tribunal system' (p. 31). However, the scope for future improvements via collective bargaining appears to be very restricted in view of the marked decline in trade union power in the UK since 1979 (see Chapter 7). Manning (1996) uses a monopsony model to explain why the UK Equal Pay Act did raise women's relative pay without harming the employment of women.

The Australian experience appears to tell a very similar story of a legislative/enforcement change having a major one-off impact upon labour market outcomes. In this case the adoption of the principle of comparable worth appears to have been the spur for an improvement in the ratio of female–male wages. This is good news for the advocates of stronger comparable worth policies, such as Sorensen (1990), but the limited nature of its impact on the Australian labour market in that it did not result in any progressive trend towards greater equality should be borne in mind. The 1990s saw a continual slow closing of the Australian gender pay gap.

Our examination of anti-discrimination policy strongly suggests that equal pay and comparable worth legislation are unlikely to reduce the female–male earnings differential in anything but a strictly limited, one-off manner. Remaining differences appear to be based largely upon the unequal burden women currently bear in the reproduction of the population.

WOMEN AND CHILDREN

Manning and Robinson (1998) found that earnings on leaving full-time education and subsequent earnings growth were very similar for men and women in the UK. They conclude that

> the bulk of the pay gap can be put down to the result of higher numbers of women having breaks in employment and the pay penalty associated with these breaks . . . it suggests that it is labour market interruptions that are the main cause of women's labour market disadvantage.
>
> (p. 15)

Labour market interruptions which impact on work experience, employment history and inevitably pay are more common amongst women. This is not unconnected with an unequal division of labour in the home, which results in women bearing a disproportionate burden of responsibility for home production, principally in the rearing of young children. In terms of policy to aid workers with child birth and rearing, the data in Table 6.9 shows that the UK has the lowest maternity provision in the EU, a fact

Table 6.9   Maternity entitlement in the EU, 1999

	Equivalent number of weeks on full pay
UK	8
Ireland	10
Sweden	11
Belgium	11
Spain	12
Portugal	13
France	13.5
Greece	14
Germany	14
Netherlands	16
Austria	16
Luxembourg	16
Italy	17
Denmark	22

Source: *Guardian*, 9/6/2001

Table 6.10   Unexplained differentials (%)

Married men:single men	10
Single men:single women	10
Single women:married women	12

Source: Greenhalgh 1980

that may encourage women to leave the labour force altogether once maternity pay has been exhausted.

It is well known amongst labour economists that marriage has an uneven impact upon the earnings of men and women. Greenhalgh (1980) reports residual UK earnings differentials, usually assigned to discrimination, according to marital status. These are reproduced in Table 6.10. Marriage appears to have the asymmetric effect of boosting men's earnings and depressing the earnings of women. Korenman and Neumark (1991) support the view that marriage enhances men's labour market productivity. They find that not only does a marriage premium in terms of higher hourly wage rates exist, but that it grows as the duration of marriage increases. Although as Goldin (1990) observes 'the role of marriage in enhancing the earnings of male workers is still only dimly understood' (p. 102), if it leads to labour market interruptions for women, marriage will depress the earnings of female workers. This will discriminate against women if employers use women's labour market interruptions and shorter work experience to pay women less than equivalent men. Discontinuous labour market participation does pose problems for women workers. In a longitudinal study Stewart and Greenhalgh (1984) found that two-thirds of women had one interruption in their labour force participation. Women with more frequent interruptions were less likely to

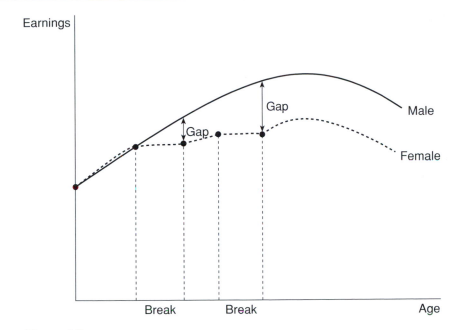

Figure 6.7

be in jobs with well defined career paths. Only about one-half of women returnees to the labour force retained their previous occupational status. This is evidence of downward occupational mobility of women across childbirth that corresponds to some important structural changes in the UK labour market, namely the growth of the service sector and the increase in part-time working. To illustrate the impact of employment breaks on the gender pay gap consider the simple scenario set out in Figure 6.7.

In Figure 6.7 men and women enter the full-time labour market with the same initial earnings and earnings growth as they accumulate work experience, to reflect identical ages and educational attainment. Assuming that only women have employment breaks, these cause a gender wage gap to emerge where there was no such gap before. The greater the number of employment breaks or the longer those breaks the greater the wage gap. Figure 6.7 has no downward mobility of earnings on returning from the break but if, as seems likely, women do experience downward mobility then the wage gap will increase. Downward mobility of earnings across an employment break might well reflect human capital depreciation – in other words use it or lose it. Knowledge and job skills depreciation may be particularly severe during periods of rapid technological change in the workplace. In the face of such depreciation a career break will have a permanent effect on earnings levels.

Waldfogel (1998) surveys a range of studies of the wage loss of women workers across childbirth. As differences in work experience in the Zabalza and Arrufat (1985) study accounted for 18 percentage points of the proportion of female–male earnings (0.80–0.62), if males and females had equality within the home then female earnings would be some 92 per cent of those of male workers (i.e., 74 + 18). This is remarkably close to the earnings differential in Sweden (90 per cent in 1980), which has what is probably the most egalitarian attitude and public policy towards the sexes in both the workplace and the home. Jones and Makepeace (1996) called for a policy of 'improved provisions for maternity leave which may increase the job attachment of women' (p. 408).

Yet in the UK and other countries the gender pay gap has narrowed over time even in the absence of more egalitarian policies. Women are delaying the average age at which they marry and are postponing starting a family. In the EU the average age at which women first give birth rose from 26.4 years in 1976 to 28.4 years in 1996. What is more, women are combining bringing up young children with work. The greatest gains in employment came from women with young children. The employment rate of women in the UK aged 28–34 rose from 52 per cent in 1979 to 69 per cent in 1999. By 2000 40 per cent of single women with children under 5 years old were economically active and 60 per cent of married/cohabiting mothers were either working or were unemployed.[5] Desai et al. (1999) point to the fact that mothers are returning to work more rapidly after childbirth thereby reducing the length of employment breaks.

Labour market inequality between the sexes is not a natural phenomenon. Obviously there is a natural element in allocating women the dominant role in the bearing of children, but employment interruptions associated with the rearing of children are a predominantly social phenomenon which are subject to change and which must be changed if the gender based earnings gap is to progressively decline. Furthermore, women tend to bear a disproportionate responsibility for looking after sick or elderly relatives in the home. The attendance demands of work are primarily a technological requirement and in part are socially determined, and as such are also liable to change. If we were to achieve a more even distribution of tasks within the home there would then be no legitimate reason for the labour market compensation of women not to be essentially equal to that of men.

As Tzannatos (1990) observes for the UK 'half of the nation's intelligence is in the heads of women and women still contribute less than a third to the country's recorded output' (p. 207).

A similar point is made by Esteve-Volart (2000) who examined the relationship between sex discrimination and economic growth. Using differences between female and male schooling as an indicator of discrimination, the data suggests that discrimination against women is worst in sub-Saharan Africa and the Middle East, yet even here sex discrimination is not total. Given that the study provides theoretical and empirical support for a U-shaped relationship between discrimination and economic growth, such as that illustrated in Figure 6.8, sex discrimination is clearly imposing an economic penalty on many countries. If only in the contexts of the welfare losses associated with discrimination, and economic growth models, this is a shameful waste.

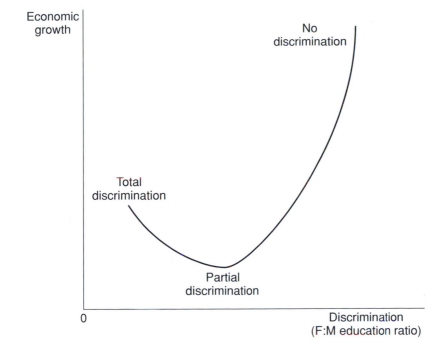

Figure 6.8

RACIAL DISCRIMINATION

It is interesting to note the general picture concerning the earnings differentials between ethnic groups within the labour market. Figure 6.9 presents data for the median wage income ratio for black and white workers in the USA. There was a sustained improvement in the earnings of black female workers relative to white female workers throughout the 1950s, the 1960s and the first part of the 1970s. The racial pay gap was narrowed to such an extent that from 1976–84 black female workers earned more than their white counterparts. The earnings ratio for black and white females in the early 1990s shows near equality but there still exists a substantial differential between female and male earnings in the US.

The progress of black male workers in closing the pay gap with white workers has been less dramatic. In 1950 black male workers earned 60 per cent of what white male workers earned, the same percentage is recorded for 1960 and 1965. The male pay gap does begin to narrow in a more consistent manner between 1965 and 1980, reflecting perhaps the beneficial impact of Title VII of the 1964 Civil Rights Act that made discrimination in employment illegal. The male pay gap widened in the recession of the early 1980s, which may reflect increasing concern over the quality of black schooling, the gap began to close thereafter with black male earnings reaching 70 per cent of white male earnings in 1990.

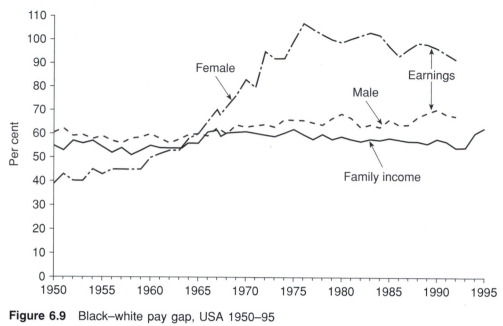

Figure 6.9   Black–white pay gap, USA 1950–95

Source: Reynolds *et al.* 1998, figure 7.3, p. 174
Note: Prior to 1967 data is not available for blacks only but for non-whites together.

McNabb and Psacharopoulos (1981) report that for the UK ethnic minority, workers earned some 20 per cent less than their white counterparts, yet they also identified some important differences across non-white racial groups.

Racial discrimination can be analysed by using the neoclassical taste model and the segmented market models we set out earlier in this chapter. Yet Becker (1957) also examined discrimination using an analogy with international trade based upon a variant of the Heckscher-Ohlin factor endowment model. In this whites are assumed to be capital rich whereas blacks are held to be comparatively labour rich. Thus it should be to the advantage of society for each group to trade its surplus factor. Hence whites 'export' capital and 'import' black labour. If white employers discriminate against black labour this in turn reduces white capital 'exports' and the return on white capital that could have been earned by combining it freely with black labour. Although white labour may benefit from such discrimination, it is globally irrational because it leads to a sub-optimal allocation of resources within society.

The welfare loss associated with discrimination in Becker's trade model analogy is presented in the Edgeworth box diagram in Figure 6.10. The broken lines are the isoquant maps of black (B) and white (W) society. The relative price lines XX and YY reflect the fact that capital is relatively expensive in black society, whereas it is labour that is relatively expensive in white society. Free trade between whites and blacks would result in an outcome along the contract curve CC, which consists of the points of tangency of the *B* and *W* isoquants.

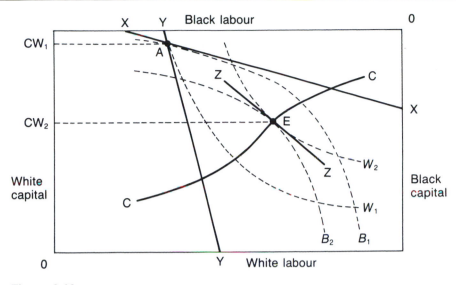

Figure 6.10

Source: Adapted from Sloane 1985, figure 3.1, p. 92

Joint output of black and white society is maximised at point E where B_2 and W_2 are tangential, leading to a ratio of factor prices illustrated by the price line ZZ. If white society discriminates against black society by refusing to export its capital CW_1 – CW_2 an outcome such as position A will occur, which lies on lower isoquants for both black and white society, i.e., B_1 and W_1. Remember any point laying off the contract curve, such as A, is inferior to a point on the CC curve, and is certainly inferior to the Pareto optimal point E. Segmentation theorists can point to aggregate gender differences in attributes like job tenure and hours worked being incorporated into statistical discrimination as a basis for restricting women's access to primary segment jobs. Yet the same mechanism cannot be said to operate in the case of race. According to Rebitzer (1993) there exists 'no empirical or theoretical reason to believe that turnover rates are higher (or desired hours lower) for blacks than for whites' (p. 1417).

The manner in which discrimination is measured, the unexplained residual approach, opens up the possibility that unexplained factors influence productivity and labour market outcomes. Chiswick (1984) found that some ethnic minorities in the USA, namely Chinese, Japanese and Jews, had been economically successful in spite of any discrimination that they had encountered. This lead him to ask whether 'the residual in the estimation technique [is] dominated by the missing factor (factors) rather than by discrimination?' (p. 1159). If so what could the powerful missing factor be? In a word, it could be 'culture', consisting of values, attitudes, skills, contacts and history. Woodbury and Bettinger (1991) attempt to test the culture explanation by contrasting white workers with American blacks and black workers of British West Indian decent in the USA. Using 1980 census data, Table 6.11 appears to show that if blacks had the same observable characteristics as whites (education, experience and

Table 6.11   Wages of white, black and West Indian Americans

	Average male wage $, 1979
White	14,988
West Indian	12,456
Black	9,604

	Gross wage ratio	Adjusted wage ratio
Black/White	0.64	0.78
WI/White	0.83	0.93
Black/WI	0.77	0.80

Source: Woodbury and Bettinger 1991

Table 6.12   Unexplained wage gap

Year of immigration	Immigrant group wage minus white workers' wage				
	1975–80	1970–74	1965–69	1960–64	1950–59
White English 2nd lang.	−26.6	−8.5	−1.0	+2.4	+4.1
White English only	+4.0	+1.8	+8.9	+3.8	+4.2
Black West Indian	−48.2	−27.3	−25.1	−25.9	−12.9
Black other	−72.7	−49.2	−36.2	−23.9	−40.4
Asians	−47.5	−20.7	−12.1	−8.1	−10.8
Hispanics	−44.8	−24.6	−18.7	−10.5	−7.5

Source: Woodbury and Bettinger 1991, table 6

so on) then the wage ratio would rise from 0.64 to 0.78. West Indian (WI) workers earn more than black American workers largely because of differences in observable characteristics, giving wage ratios in relation to white workers of 0.83 and 0.93, substantially higher than those of blacks to whites. However, even if black workers had the observable characteristics of West Indian workers, the black/WI wage ratio would only increase from 0.77 to 0.80. This appears to leave culture to explain a massive 22 percentage point difference (1.00 − 0.78) between white and black wages, yet only a 7 percentage point difference (1.00 − 0.93) in white and West Indian male wages.

The data in Table 6.12 provides estimates from Woodbury and Bettinger (1991) of how immigrant workers wages grow as they appear to become assimilated into the US labour market. In the case of white immigrant workers who have English as a second language, the implication is that as their English improves, as they make good an initial human capital deficit, so their relative and comparative earnings rise. From being paid 26.6 per cent less than native whites as recent immigrants, they end up being paid 4.1 per cent more than native whites. A similar process might well be at work in the case of the profile of immigrant Hispanic workers' earnings. Yet notice how the wage gaps are larger and more enduring for black immigrants than for Asian and Hispanic workers. This is in spite of the reasonable expectation that West Indian immigrants should have an initial English language advantage over Asian and Hispanic immigrants into the USA.

Borjas (1990) questions this type of data as evidence of assimilation by pointing out that it assumes that the immigrants who enter the USA are identical in each period of time and that the various categories of immigrants are homogeneous apart from their geographical origin. Borjas (1990) views immigration as the result of individuals assessing the net gain from working in one country rather than another. Immigrant flows into the USA are mainly of skilled labour from Western Europe and of unskilled labour from developing countries. Thus there are differences over and above language that impact on productivity and are reflected in the unexplained wage gaps between native workers and immigrants. Borjas (1990) rejects the suggestion that discrimination plays an important role in immigrant/native worker earnings differentials,

> several recent studies provide strong evidence that systematic discrimination against Hispanics or Asians (the two dominant groups in recent immigration waves) is not an important aspect of the American labour market.
>
> (p. 130)

Green (1999) found that male immigrants to Canada tend to be more highly skilled than native born men, probably due to the screening of immigrants where the more highly skilled and better educated score more immigration points. This difference has declined over successive cohorts of migrants. Immigrants are more occupationally mobile than native Canadians; immigration may help create a more flexible labour force.

For the UK, Bell (1997) found that education and work experience received prior to immigration was not highly valued in UK labour markets and contributed to lower wages for West Indian and Indian immigrants. However, assimilation effects reduce the magnitude of an initial entry wage disadvantage. For example, immigrants with 20 years of experience before migrating to the UK suffer an entry wage disadvantage of

> minus 34 per cent for West Indians
> minus 24 per cent for Indians.

By the end of their working lives these wage gaps would have fallen to

> minus 17 per cent for West Indians
> minus 19 per cent for Indians.

Clearly the group of immigrants that is most disadvantaged in the UK labour market are black workers from the Caribbean with substantial prior work experience. By contrast white immigrants from Europe or Old Commonwealth countries, like Canada and Australia, earn more than native whites on entry although this premium is rapidly eroded as white earnings converge.

Immigrants in many countries and especially to EU countries experience not only lower wages but also higher rates of unemployment than native workers. Figure 6.11 shows higher unemployment rates for immigrants in all the countries in this sample. However, the magnitude of the immigrant unemployment gap is much smaller in Australia, Canada and the USA.

Of the EU countries in this sample Italy has the narrowest gap between native and immigrant unemployment rates. Such unemployment gaps close in a similar way to

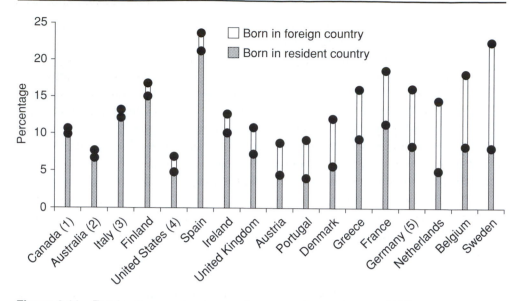

Figure 6.11   Foreign-born and native worker unemployment rates, 1995–98

Source: Coppel *et al.* 2001, figure 5, p. 13
Notes: 1 Data refers to 1996; 2 data refers to 1998; 3 Data refers to 1995–97; 4 Data refers to 1997; 5 Data refers to foreigners and nationals, instead of foreign-born and native.

which Borjas (1998) maintains that wage gaps close as assimilation progresses. There are three main sets of factors advanced to analyse the immigrant wage gap:

- assimilation effects (Chiswick, Bell)
- cohort effects, including culture and skill (Chiswick, Borjas, Bell)
- discrimination effects (Woodbury and Bettinger)

Radical economists have, via some variant of segmented market theory, sought to show that, contrary to the neoclassical taste model, those discriminating against ethnic minority workers have a powerful motive for doing so and that the motive is financial gain. Reich (1981) attempted to test and reject the neoclassical model of discrimination in favour of an explanation emphasising class conflict. Reich (1981) suggests that in a competitive economy the Becker model predicts a negative relationship between profits and the degree of discrimination measured by the ratio of black to white wages W_b/W_w. Reich (1981) interprets the Becker model as predicting that 'white capitalists lose and white labour gains from racial discrimination' (p. 111), which suggests a positive relationship between profits and W_b/W_w. If discrimination comes from a preference for white workers, an increase in prejudice will increase W_w, thereby decreasing W_b/W_w to the detriment of profits. Yet if discrimination comes from a dislike of black workers, stronger prejudice would lower W_b, which will also decrease W_b/W_w but would increase profits. Thus the hypothesised relationship between W_b/W_w and profit, which Reich (1981) uses to test neoclassical theory, is decidedly ambiguous. Reich (1981) also requires unobserved changes in employers' discriminatory attitudes to change observed profits and wages. But could firms with unchanged attitudes lower W_b as the ratio of black workers to white increases? Using cross section data for the USA, Reich (1981) tests his hypothesis about profits and W_b/W_w. This implies that if W_b/W_w varies across firms then so must employers tastes. In only 7 out of 43 regressions is the black to white population size included and in all 7 a negative relation between profits and W_b/W_w is reported. However, there are a number of criticisms of the measures used. Profits are measured by the percentage share of all white income received by the top 1 per cent of white families. But this will include rents, interest, wages and income from inherited wealth as well as the current profits from business that Reich needs. Instead of looking at the wages of whites and blacks he uses their incomes. Furthermore there is no adjustment made for any differences there might be between the education and work experience of black and white workers. Cain's (1986) overall assessment of Reich's study is to 'doubt that Becker's model was or can be well tested with such data' (p. 735).

CASE STUDY: DISABLED WORKERS

Having examined the phenomenon of labour market discrimination in the case of sex and race, we consider briefly whether there is any evidence that disabled workers face wage and employment discrimination. Michael Kidd, Peter Sloane and Ivan Ferko (2000) 'Disability and the Labour Market: An Analysis of British Males', *Journal of Health Economics*, 19: 961–81, attempt to gauge the extent of discrimination against disabled men using a sample drawn from the 1996 British Labour Force Survey. By limiting their study to males, Kidd *et al.* (2000) hope to avoid any complications arising from disability discrimination being combined with gender discrimination.

> the Discrimination Disability Act [passed in 1995 by the UK government with aspects relating to employment enforced at the end of 1996] . . . defines a disability as a physical or mental impairment which has a substantial and long-term (greater than 12 months) adverse effect on the ability to carry out day-to-day activities. . . .

Kidd *et al.* (2000) point out that '. . . there are few studies of discrimination against the disabled and virtually all of these are restricted to North America'. This is a bit surprising given that disability is not an especially uncommon phenomenon with

> around 14 per cent of the working age population in the UK had a long-term disability in the Autumn of 1997, compared to around 5 per cent who belong to a minority ethnic group. . . .
>
> Data from various sources . . . [for 1997 and 1998] . . . reveal that the employment participation rate of able-bodied working age males is around

twice that of the disabled group, i.e., 83 per cent vs. 40 per cent. Similarly, the unemployment rate is approximately three times higher for the disabled, i.e., 21.2 per cent vs. 7.6 per cent. Finally, . . . on average, disabled males earn substantially lower hourly wages than the able-bodied, of the order of 10 per cent less.

After dealing with problems surrounding the definition of disability and including differences in education, work experience, occupation, industry, regional location, marital status, race and dealing with selection bias, Kidd *et al.* (2000) make the following comparisons of the disabled with able-bodied men.

> The disabled are more likely to be absent from work due to sickness and length of absence is likely to be longer in their case. The able-bodied on average have higher educational qualifications than the disabled, but shorter labour market experience and slightly lower tenure with the current employer, reflecting the association of disability with age. The disabled are under-represented relative to the able-bodied in the high paying managerial and professional occupations and over-represented in manual occupations . . . They are also over-represented in manufacturing, but under-represented in Scotland in our sample. In line with expectations the disabled are more likely to be employed part-time than able-bodied men.
>
>   . . . For both able-bodied and the disabled, education increases the probability of being in employment compared to those without formal qualifications, as does being married or white.
>
>   . . . As an aside, a specification including the type of disability . . . suggests that the type of disability plays an important role in the probability of employment. Those with physiological disabilities affecting sight, hearing, breathing and heart problems are much more likely to be in employment than those with psychological or learning difficulties. . . .

Kidd *et al.*'s (2000) results indicate that 'the able-bodied have an actual participation rate of 84 per cent compared to a rate of 34 per cent for the disabled. . . . The total difference . . . is evenly split between the component reflecting able/disabled differences in personal characteristics and residual differences.'

Conventionally the unexplained residual is interpreted as discrimination. In this case we might hesitate before blaming labour market discrimination for a 25 percentage point difference in the employment participation rate between the able bodied and the disabled because it is very difficult to account for the precise impact of disability on productivity. However, we must bear in mind that personal characteristic variables, which should pick up productivity differences (education, experience and so on), are only accounting for half of a substantial employment participation gap.

When it comes to wages 'the disabled obtain a slightly greater return to education . . . and also obtain a greater return to working in the public sector'.

Overall the disabled earn 14.1 per cent less than the able-bodied. 'Decomposing this . . . wage gap once again leads to an even split between explained and unexplained components.'

Labour market discrimination against the disabled might account for up to a 7 percentage point wage gap with the able-bodied. Kidd *et al.* (2000) are fairly optimistic about the possibility of the wage gap being reduced by the 1995 Disability Act but they are less positive about the employment prospects of the disabled: '*even if legislation can lead towards wage convergence with the able-bodied, this will have little impact upon the participation rate*'.

Evidence from the USA suggests that Kidd *et al.* (2000) are right to be wary of the likely impact of anti-discrimination legislation on the employment of the disabled. Daron Acemoglu and Joshua Angrist (2001) 'Consequences of Employment Protection? The Case of the Americans with Disabilities Act', *Journal of Political Economy*, 109 (5): 915–57, conclude that falls in the employment of younger (21–39) men and women around 1993 were the result of the costs associated with conforming with the Americans with Disabilities Act, which came into effect in 1992. They see the costs of providing reasonable accommodation at work for the disabled to be at least as important as the cost of litigation connected with cases of wrongful employment termination (firing). Higher costs have reduced the employment of the disabled but have not reduced total employments.

DISCRIMINATION – SUMMARY

Concentrating on sex discrimination we established that significant and persistent differences exist between the labour market outcomes of male and female workers. These could be analysed using

- neoclassical theory – the Becker taste model
- segmented labour markets – the dual market and job crowding hypotheses

The neoclassical analysis suggests:

- that if competitive forces were strong enough, discrimination would be eroded
- that discrimination persists because of market (product and labour) imperfections
- that there may be a role for anti-discrimination legislation

From within the segmented markets approach:

- job crowding explained wage differentials by suggesting that men and women do essentially different jobs
- dual labour markets are split into primary, well paid predominantly male, and secondary, less well paid mainly female, segments

- empirically the segmented markets approach received little support
- Goldin (1990) shows that changes in US female earnings relative to male earnings came about because of improvements within occupations rather than between jobs or segments
- equal pay and opportunities legislation produced one-off upward shifts in the relative earnings of women
- around one-third of the sex based earnings gap is accounted for by direct discrimination
- the scope for further improvement via anti-discrimination and comparable worth legislation thus appears limited
- increases in the comparative education and experience of women workers in the UK along with more equitable rewards to those characteristics have contributed to narrowing the gender pay gap
- the relative pay of women working part-time has not improved

More labour market interruptions and shorter work experience are significant factors, which depress female earnings and career progression. This may reflect an unequal division of labour in the home and requires more active labour market and social policies.

When it came to racial discrimination we found substantial differences in the earnings of workers from different ethnic groups. Racial discrimination could be analysed using the same models we used for sex discrimination but we also considered Becker's trade analogy model.

Our review of studies of the labour market experiences of immigrant workers revealed the importance of their heterogeneity and culture. We discovered three main approaches focusing on

- assimilation
- cohorts
- discrimination

Radical approaches concentrating on some form of gain from racial discrimination were unable to unambiguously overturn the fundamental neoclassical conclusion that racial discrimination is globally irrational and results in economic welfare loss.

DISCRIMINATION – QUESTIONS FOR DISCUSSION

1) To what extent does the existence of product and labour market imperfections affect the neoclassical analysis of discrimination?
2) Explain how job crowding might lead to wage differentials between male and female workers.

3) What evidence is there for Goldin's (1990) assertion that the sex based earnings gap decreased because of changes '... within broad occupational groups rather than changes in the distribution of these ... groups between men and women'?

4) Try to assess the impact on the relative earnings of females of equal pay and opportunities legislation.

5) What effect does marriage appear to have on male and female earnings? What possible reasons do you think could account for such effects?

6) In terms of Figure 6.7, what policies might alleviate the wage gap effects of employment breaks?

7) Discuss whether racial discrimination is driven by economic gain.

8) What do studies of immigrant workers tell us about the nature of racial discrimination in labour markets?

SUGGESTED READING

Altonji, J. and Blank, R. (1999) 'Race and Gender in the Labour Market', in O. Ashenfelter and D. Card (eds) (1999) *Handbook of Labour Economics*, Volume 3, Amsterdam: Elsevier Science.

Blau, F. and Kahn, L. (2000) 'Gender Differences in Pay', *Journal of Economic Perspectives*, 14 (4): 75–99.

7

Trade unions and labour markets

INTRODUCTION

Trade unions are an important institutional influence at work within the labour market. Their influence will depend upon the power they are able to wield when bargaining with employers. This in turn will depend upon a number of factors related to union membership, the bargaining process, the threat of industrial action and the legislative framework within which they operate. In this chapter we will investigate aspects of trade union power and features of the bargaining process that have made the modelling of trade union behaviour somewhat problematic. In spite of the problems, the neoclassical approach to trade union impacts on labour markets consists of two models:

1) the efficient bargain model, in which unions negotiate about employment as well as wages;
2) the right-to-manage model, where the union negotiates about wages but the firm's management determine employment levels unilaterally.

As well as summarising these two models we will examine strike activity and the impact of unions on the efficiency of the firm, and try to evaluate the effect of trade union legislation. Our main concern is with the effect trade unions may have on the generation and persistence of unemployment. This will lead us to consider whether the nature of the bargaining framework affects the impact of union activity on the macro-economy and to introduce the insider–outsider theory of unemployment. Additionally we will discuss the link between unions and equality.

UNION POWER: THE STATISTICAL PICTURE

> There's power in a factory
> power in the land
> power in the hand of the worker,
> but it all amounts to nothing
> if together we don't stand
> there is power in a union.

Billy Bragg (1986) is reflecting favourably upon the enhanced power a union bestows upon workers. Given an asymmetry in the strength of the employer *vis-à-vis* an individual employee, one can view unions as a response by workers to try and redress the balance of power especially when it comes to determining pay and employment conditions.

In this section we present some quantitative indicators of possible union power in the UK both historically and comparatively. Table 7.1 contains figures on UK trade union membership since 1950. During the 1950s and 1960s the growth in union membership was fairly steady at approximately half a million members per decade. This accelerated sharply during the 1970s when an additional three million people (net) joined trade unions. Membership reached a peak of 13.29 million in 1979 before declining rapidly throughout the 1980s. In the six year period from the end of 1979 to the end of 1985, union membership fell by almost two and a half million. By the end of the decade membership numbers had returned to their pre-1970 level. Membership continued to fall during the 1990s, although 1999 recorded the first rise in union membership for 20 years.

The profile of union membership in the USA saw a rise from less than 4 million members in 1935 to 14 million in 1945, reaching a peak of 21 million in 1979, falling thereafter to stand at 15 million in 1995.

There has also been a marked decline in the number of trade unions in the UK. Table 7.2 shows that the fall in the number of unions reflects a long-term trend of amalgamation which has continued, almost uninterrupted since 1920. It would be

Table 7.1 Trade Union membership (millions)

1950	9.29	1980	12.95	1991	9.59
1955	9.74	1981	12.11	1992	9.05
1960	9.82	1982	11.59	1993	8.70
1965	10.18	1983	11.24	1994	8.28
1970	10.30	1984	10.99	1995	8.09
1974	11.76	1985	10.82	1996	7.99
1975	12.19	1986	10.54	1997	7.80
1976	12.38	1987	10.48	1998	7.71
1977	12.85	1988	10.38	1999	7.81
1978	13.11	1989	10.16		
1979	13.29	1990	9.95		

Source: ONS, *Annual Abstract of Statistics*, various years

Table 7.2   Number of Unions

1920	1384	1979	453	1991	275
1930	1121	1980	438	1992	268
1940	1004	1981	414	1993	254
1950	781	1983	394	1994	243
1960	654	1985	370	1995	238
1965	583	1987	330	1996	226
1970	555	1989	309	1997	234
1977	481	1990	287	1998	220

Source: ONS, *Annual Abstract of Statistics*, various years

wrong to view the decline in the number of unions as unambiguous evidence of a reduction in union power. Fewer unions may result in their being able to exercise more power. However, in spite of the amalgamations that have taken place, the union movement is still comparatively fragmented as we shall discover when we investigate the nature of the bargaining process later in this chapter and the effect of centralisation in the bargaining process, or the degree of corporatism, on unemployment in Chapter 10. The fall in the number of trade unionists on the other hand is a more reliable indicator of union strength, because not only have membership numbers declined during the 1980s and 1990s but so has union density.

Union density refers to the proportion of the employed labour force that is unionised and as such is a more potent indicator of union power than simple membership. Table 7.3 provides some data on union density over the 1970–99 period, which witnessed the spectacular rise and fall in membership, and compares this with the experience of other advanced industrialised countries.[1] In the case of the UK the rapid decline in union density requires some explanation. Firstly, it is not a cyclical phenomenon because union density has fallen during both recessions (1980–94 and 1990–94) as well as during booms (1985–90 and 1995–99). Changes in the structure of production away from largely male manufacturing, which is heavily unionised, towards more lightly unionised female service sector output. However, this process was already underway in the 1970s when union density was still rising. Certainly the legislative environment became a lot tougher for unions as they faced more restrictions after 1980 (see Chapter 8 for details). Machin (2000) confirms that unionised establishments did not suffer a higher rate of closure than non-union ones between 1984 and 1998. However, he did find that UK unions have been unable to organise in newer establishments. Whilst in 1984 68 per cent of workplaces with 25 or more workers that had existed for 10 years or more and 58 per cent of establishments less than 10 years old recognised trade unions by 1998 those proportions had fallen to 50 per cent and 27 per cent respectively. Among younger workers union density fell markedly between 1983 and 1998, as the data in Table 7.4 shows. Metcalf (2001) summarises the decline in density as due to the fact that 'in the 1980s unions lost the support of the state and managers, whereas in the 1990s they also lost the support of many employees' (p. 8).

Table 7.3 Union density, 1970 to 1999 (membership as percentage of all employees)

	1970	1975	1980	1985	1990	1995	1999
UK	48	51	53	43	38	32	29
Australia	50	54	52	51	41	35	n.a.
Canada	36	34	30	30	36	37	n.a.
Austria*	57	53	52	52	47	41	39
Denmark*	60	69	78	79	75	78	76
Finland	51	n.a.	70	n.a.	72	80	n.a.
France*	20	22	22	19	14	10	10
Germany*	37	39	39	37	36	29	26
Netherlands*	37	38	37	29	24	24	23
Ireland*	52	53	55	56	53	47	42
Italy*	33	42	43	40	39	39	38
Norway*	50	52	55	56	56	55	55
Japan	35	34	31	29	25	24	n.a.
Sweden*	74	79	88	88	84	88	88
USA	27	25	23	16	16	15	14

Sources: Brown and Wadhwani 1990, table 3, p. 37; Visser 1996; Boeri *et al*. 2001, table 2.1, p. 13
Note: The pre-1990 data and later figures for Canada are not compatible.
* 1998.

Table 7.4 Union density (%) by age, 1983 and 1998

Age	1983	1998
18–29	44	18
30–39	51	30
40+	57	33

Source: Adapted from Machin 2000 figure 1, p. 14

There is a great diversity in the degree to which workers in the countries in Table 7.3 are organised. Sweden has by far the highest union density, followed by Finland and Denmark. The UK used to have a quite highly unionised workforce, along with Norway and Ireland. However, more recent reductions in union membership has left the UK with substantially lower union density than Norway and Ireland. Levels and changes in union density in the UK and Australia are very similar. Next in terms of union density comes a group of countries including the Netherlands and Japan. Followed by France and the USA, which appear to have the lowest degrees of union organisation of their labour forces. In the case of the USA, union density among public sector workers held up over this period but was offset by the collapse in union density in the private sector.[2]

One would have thought that union density was the most obvious indicator of union power, referring as it does to the proportion of the workforce nominally under union control. Yet perhaps the power of a union to influence labour market outcomes

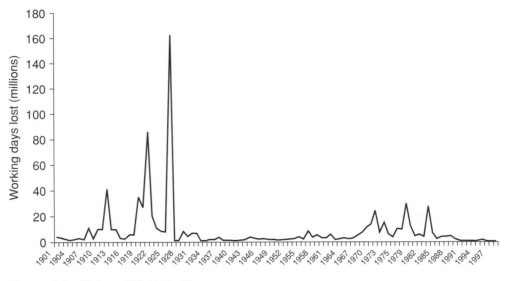

Figure 7.1   Strikes, UK 1901–99

Source: ONS, Social Trends Dataset 2000

depends upon its willingness to back up demands for better pay and working conditions with industrial action. Hence strikes, as the ultimate form of industrial action by organised labour, may be a good proxy indicator of union militancy and power. There is no consensus about the proper measure of strike activity, whether it should be related to the number of stoppages, workers involved, strike duration or the number of working days lost. When we come to examine the data in Figure 7.1 on working days lost as a result of strike activity, which is probably a better measure of industrial disruption, the 1970s stand out as a particularly bad period in the post-1945 industrial relations landscape. The period from the late 1960s through the 1970s does appear to have witnessed an upsurge in strike activity in the UK. Figure 7.1 reflects this as it charts the number of working days lost over almost a century. The impact of strike activity in terms of working days lost can clearly be seen to have declined since the largest number of working days lost in one year was recorded in 1926 during the General Strike. Working days lost due to strikes remained at historically low levels from 1927 through to 1970. Figure 7.2 examines the 1950–99 period in more detail.

Working days lost, which had began to increase in the late 1960s, rose to almost 24 million days in 1972, 29.5 million days in 1979 and just over 27 million days in 1984. The main losses were due to a miners' strike in 1972, an engineering workers' strike in 1979 and a long running miners' strike in 1984. According to Milner and Metcalf (1991), the coal industry accounted for almost one-third of all stoppages over the 1893–1989 period. After 1984 the number of working days lost to strike action falls and remains low. Indeed 1997 with 0.235 million working days lost and 1999

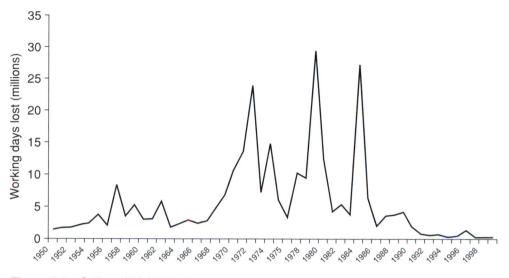

Figure 7.2 Strikes, UK 1950–99

Source: As Figure 7.1

with 0.242 are the years with the fewest days lost to industrial disputes in the UK since 1891. Annual average working days lost have fallen markedly from

12.90 million in the 1970s to
7.20 million in the 1980s to
0.66 million in the 1990s.

With the year 2000 recording 0.5 million days lost the recent experience of low impact strike activity in the UK appears well established.

In general strike activity in the UK during the 1990s was lower than in the rest of the EU. The data in Table 7.5 records working days lost per 1,000 employees, being lower than the EU average in every year except 1989 and 1996. Within the EU, Austria and Belgium are usually below the EU average in terms of working days lost to industrial disputes. So too is Denmark except for 1995 with 85 days and 1998 (1,317). Finland on the other hand usually has an above average experience of strike activity, for example 495 working days lost per thousand employees in 1995. Working days lost in France were below the EU average in every year except 1995 (108). Germany was consistently well below the EU average. In Greece strikes caused a large number of working days to be lost up to 1993, thereafter, industrial disruption declined with only 19 days lost per thousand employees in 1998. Industrial relations in Ireland produced a fairly volatile, yet usually above average, profile of working days lost ranging from 31 in 1998 to 266 in 1990. Working days lost figures for Italy in the 1990s were above the EU average in every year except 1998 (40). Data for the Netherlands reveal a very low number of working days lost (1998, 5 days lost per thousand employees) except for 1995 (115). Portugal's good record on industrial relations is reflected in days lost

Table 7.5 Labour disputes (working days lost per thousand employees), 1989–98

	1989	1990	1991	1992	1993	1994	1995	1996	1997	1998
UK	182	83	34	24	30	13	19	57	10	12
EU average	137	137	86	103	66	96	64	48	34	48
Australia	184	210	250	148	100	76	79	143	83	78
Canada	312	427	216	183	130	136	131	294	315	209
Japan	5	3	2	5	2	2	1	1	2	2
New Zealand	163	279	85	99	20	31	42	52	18	9
USA	153	55	43	37	36	45	51	42	38	42

Source: ONS, *Labour Market Trends* 2000, table 1, p. 148

figures that are consistently below the EU average, whereas neighbouring Spain experienced days lost per thousand employees that were consistently above the EU average for the 1990s. Days lost to labour disputes in Sweden are usually below average but are volatile ranging from 191 in 1990 down to 0 in 1998.

Days lost to industrial disputes are large in number in Australia and Canada, declined markedly in New Zealand as the 1990s progressed, were consistently modest in the USA after 1989 and are exceptionally low in Japan.

Year on year variation in data on the impact of labour disputes can be caused by a small number of disputes. There was a general strike in Greece in 1990, a 1995 public sector strike in France and a large strike in the Danish private sector in 1998. Davies (2000) makes the point that '60 per cent of working days lost in 1996 were as a result of one stoppage in the transport, storage and communication group' (p. 149). Generally in the EU, USA, Canada and more widely in the OECD, strike activity is greater in production and construction industries than in the service sector. Interestingly this was not the case for the UK and Ireland during the 1994–98 period. Overall the early part of the 1990s experienced more strike activity than the late 1990s. The following data confirms that average working days lost per thousand employees fell during the 1990s.

	1989–93	1994–8
UK	72	22
EU average	105	58
OECD average	86	52

The final aspect of trade union power that we are going to address is the wage mark-up. If unions are able to exert their influence on employers during wage negotiations, then this should be reflected in higher wages for union members than their non-union colleagues receive. Thus the differential between wages for unionised and non-unionised workers (the union mark-up) can be viewed as the result of the exercise of union power. The simple proposition being that the more powerful the union the greater the wage mark-up. Minford (1990) produces Figure 7.3 to show the magnitude and development of the union mark-up in the UK since the mid-1950s. For a

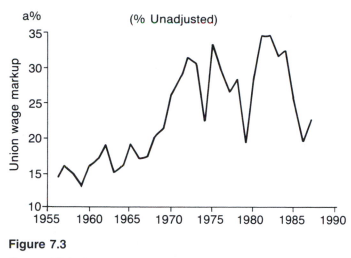

Figure 7.3

Source: Minford 1990, figure 4
Note: a unadjusted percentage.

number of reasons, including the fact that no adjustment is made for labour quality nor for the substantial differences between local and national collective bargains, these estimates undoubtedly exaggerate the wage differences attributable to union power. It may also be that high wages encourage union membership to some degree. Yet given these reservations, Figure 7.3 does appear to show that significant differences between the wages of unionised and non-unionised workers do exist in the UK labour market.

This mark-up increased during the 1970s but contrary to all the other indicators of trade union power, their ability to maintain wage differentials in favour of their members was not undermined during the 1980s. However, Forth and Millward (2000) found that by 1998 there was no general union wage mark-up in Britain, union wage effects were confined to sizeable mark-ups in work establishments (factories and offices) where unions had high coverage for their collective bargaining.

Other empirical studies have tended to support the notion that union wage bargaining does have a significant impact on the structure of wages in an economy. Estimates of the magnitude of that impact vary; Carline (1985) in a survey of UK based studies finds an average mark-up of around 20 per cent, while Lewis' (1986) survey of US studies reports mark-ups ranging from 10 per cent to 23 per cent for the 1970s. Blanchflower and Oswald (1990) present an interesting league table of estimated union mark-ups across countries. Although the US unions may appear to be weak in terms of union density (see Table 7.3 above) they are very effective at negotiating high wages for their members, as Table 7.6 shows. Freeman and Medoff (1984) estimated that the union wage mark-up in the USA was in the 15–30 per cent range in the 1970s and there is evidence that it has remained high in the face of declining union membership and a loss of political influence. Budd and Na (2000) estimate the union wage premium in the USA ranging from 12 per cent to 18 per

Table 7.6 Union mark-up (%)

USA	26
Australia	13
UK	8
Hungary	8
Germany	7
Austria	6
Switzerland	4

Source: Blanchflower and Oswald 1990

cent. For the UK Stewart (1990) finds a union mark-up of 8–10 per cent in firms with product market power, which disappears (0 per cent) when firms are in competitive product markets.

Having set out some descriptive statistics on a variety of aspects of trade union activity in the labour market, we now consider some of the attempts economists have made to analyse that activity.

MODELS OF UNION BEHAVIOUR

There are two main models of the influence of trade unions on wage and employment determination within labour markets. They are the 'efficient bargain' model and the 'right to manage' model. Some economics texts set out a 'union monopoly' model but it is best to regard this as a special case of the right to manage model, see Manning (1987) and Ulph and Ulph (1990).

The efficient bargain model

The best way to explain the efficient bargain model is to summarise the exposition contained in McDonald and Solow (1981). We begin by assuming that union attitudes to wages and employment can be represented by a utility function U,

$$U = U(W_u, L, W_a).$$

This takes the real wages unions can achieve W_u, the alternative wage available without unions W_a, and employment levels L, into account. Strictly speaking we are dealing with the expected utility function of the union,

$$U_u = L_u(U(W_u) - U(W_a)),$$

a point made by Laidler and Estrin (1989), with the indifference curves being derived from,

$$L_u - (U(W_u) - U(W_a)) = \text{constant}.$$

This gives us the unions indifference map shown in Figure 7.4, in which W_a acts as a floor below which firms cannot push union wages.

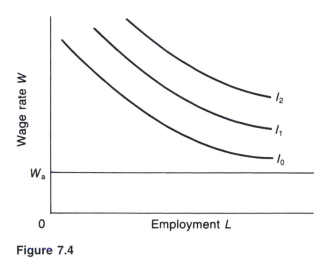

Figure 7.4

Unions prefer to be on the highest possible indifference curve, which in this case is I_2, given that $I_2 > I_1 > I_0$. The profit maximising firm also has a set of preferences that can be represented as a map of isoprofit curves in wage and employment space. The firm has a revenue function R which depends upon a production function f linking employment to output, $R = f(L)$. This function has the usual concavity characteristics and displays diminishing marginal revenue. The isoprofit curves π are derived from

$$R(L) - wL = \text{constant},$$

and are in effect the firm's indifference curves expressing preferences about combinations of real wages and employment levels. Firms will wish to be on their most preferred isoprofit curve, which in this case is π_2, given that of the three options in Figure 7.5 π_2 is the one associated with the highest level of profit. For the firm $\pi_2 > \pi_1 > \pi_0$.

From the isoprofit curve map we can identify the firm's demand curve for labour. Given any real wage rate such as W_1 the firm seeks out the greatest level of profit consistent with W_1, which is on the isoprofit curve π_1 in Figure 7.5. In effect the firm attempts to set the marginal revenue product of labour equal to the wage. The firm's demand for labour curve LD cuts through the peak points of the isoprofit curves. Thus each point on the labour demand curve is associated with a different isoprofit curve and therefore with a different level of profit. Putting the unions and the firm's preferences together enables us to show the most important characteristics of the efficient bargain model of wage and employment determination in unionised labour markets. All these components are brought together in Figure 7.6. If one takes a point on the labour demand curve such as A, this is an inefficient outcome within a bargaining framework where firms and unions negotiate over both employment and wages. Firms would prefer an outcome such as point B, which places them on a better isoprofit curve ($\pi_2 > \pi_1$) leaving union utility unaffected on indifference curve I_0. Unions

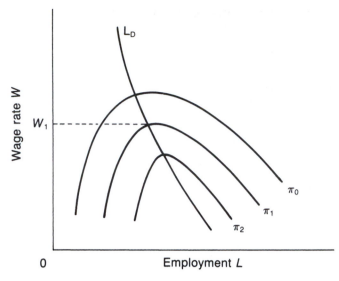

Figure 7.5

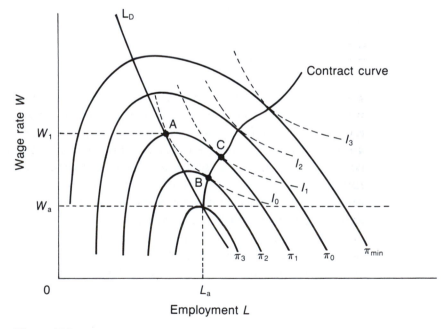

Figure 7.6

would prefer a point like C to A as this places them on a higher indifference curve $(I_1 > I_0)$ leaving firms' profit levels unaffected on isoprofit curve π_1.

Thus any point on the 'contract curve' between and including B and C is a Pareto welfare improvement on point A. The contract curve is formed by the points of tangency between the firm's isoprofit curves and the unions indifference curves within the wage and employment space. Efficient bargain outcomes are only to be found lying along the contract curve, which intersects the labour demand curve where wages are equal to W_a. This means that no bargains will be negotiated which result in the wage rate being less than W_a. However, it also means that apart from this point of intersection, everywhere along the contract curve entails wage rates exceeding the marginal revenue product from employing labour in excess of L_a. It appears as though the firm is being enticed to employ more workers than it would wish at any agreed wage rate other than W_a. In other words union activity is resulting in a tendency towards excessive employment. This is not an unbounded process, the firm will have a minimum profit constraint π_{min}, imposed either by shareholders or by capital market solvency criteria. Remember that the efficient bargain in this model is only efficient in the sense that it satisfies the specific preferences of the firm and the union; at the general societal level it results in a misallocation of resources by driving a wedge between wage rates and the marginal revenue productivity of labour.

The exact nature of the contract curve depends upon the particular specification of the firm's and the union's utility functions, i.e., the isoprofit and indifference curve maps. MaCurdy and Pencavel (1986) suggest that there are three possible forms the contract curve could take and these varieties are illustrated in Figure 7.7.

The first of these variants of the contract curve C_1 is the conventional type that emerged from our analysis of the efficient bargain model in Figure 7.6. Of the alternatives, C_2 implies that the union's sole concern is to maximise the union mark-up of $W_u - W_a$. Profit maximising firms on the other hand are trying to bargain towards a wage of W_a. Union activity under such circumstances seeks to gain a greater share of the firm's profits whilst leaving employment unaffected.[3] The downward sloping

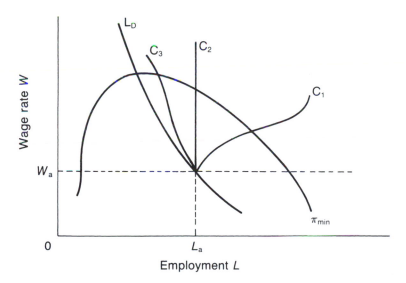

Figure 7.7

contract curve C_3 reflects the fact that the union is more interested in wage increases than in the employment of its members, a risk preference which it incorporates into its utility function. As to what form the contract curve might take within an efficient bargain framework is an empirical matter that cannot be pre-determined at the theoretical level. This is something we shall comment on when we come to evaluate models of union behaviour later in this chapter. In the meantime we examine the 'right to manage' model as an alternative to the efficient bargain.

The right to manage model

The fundamental proposition of the right to manage approach to trade union behaviour is that while the union has an influence on the wage rate the firm is free to set the level of employment which will maximise profits at any given wage rate. Given that we already know from Figure 7.5 that the labour demand curve cuts the isoprofit curves at their peaks, it follows that for any wage rate the firm will set an employment level consistent with its demand for labour function. In other words the outcomes in the wage and employment space of a right to manage model will lie along the labour demand curve. In the example portrayed in Figure 7.8 once the wage bargaining process is complete and an agreed union wage W_u has been decided, the profit maximising firm determines employment L_u as if it were reading it from the labour demand curve. The right to manage solution at point A when compared with two of the possible efficient bargain solutions B and C (refer back to Figure 7.6) results in higher wage and lower employment levels. However, it is a solution that is consistent with

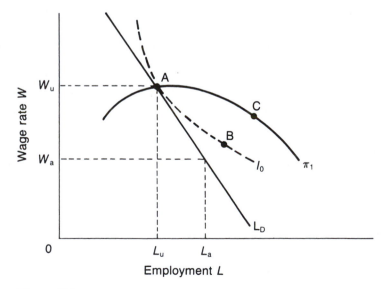

Figure 7.8

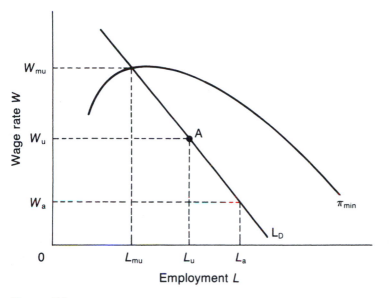

Figure 7.9

the firm's demand for labour, thus maintaining a close correspondence between union wages and the marginal revenue productivity of the unionised workforce.

The difference between a right to manage model and the traditional textbook union monopoly model is that whereas in the latter there is a strict demarcation between unions setting wages unilaterally and firms setting employment unilaterally, the right to manage model views the wage as an outcome of negotiation between the union and the firm – thereafter the firm goes ahead and sets employment unilaterally. The main impact of allowing firms to influence the agreed union wage through negotiation is to reduce wage rates for unionised workers to below the monopoly union level. Figure 7.9 makes this point by comparing the outcomes of a monopoly union case with a more general right to manage scenario. The monopoly union model allows the union to set wages unilaterally, constrained only by the firm's minimal profit condition ($\pi_{min} = V_L(w,L) = 0$) and the union's own attitude to the risk of job losses.[4] Thus an outcome such as W_{mu} is feasible. However, in a general right to manage model the outcome depends upon the power of the union (θ) in the wage negotiations. If the union is all powerful, W_{mu} is once again a likely outcome. If the union is totally ineffectual, W_a is the more likely result. For any less extreme balance of power between unions and firms, a wage rate such as W_u associated with point A is a likely outcome of the wage bargaining process.

Manning (1987) makes this comparison in algebraic form by suggesting that a typical union monopoly model would be

max U(w,L) subject to V_L(w,L) = 0

the marginal utility to the profit maximising firm of employing labour. Whereas a right to manage model needs to incorporate union power (θ) as a feature of wage bargaining and by implication the firm's bargaining power $(1 - \theta)$ as well,

$$\max \theta \log U(w,L) + (1 - \theta) \log V(w,L) \text{ subject to } V_L(w,L) = 0$$

Hence he is able to state that it 'should be apparent that the monopoly model is a special case of the right to manage model when $\theta = 1$' (p. 122). Just so, but what exactly constitutes union power θ is, as we have already noted, a more difficult problem. We now turn our attention to the empirical status of the efficient bargain and right to manage models of union behaviour.

THE EMPIRICAL STATUS OF TRADE UNION MODELS

Attempts to test the two main models of union behaviour have not resolved the problem of determining which is the most appropriate characterisation of trade union activity. Ulph and Ulph (1990) conclude their survey of empirical tests of the two models with the sobering statement that 'neither theory seems to be able to account satisfactorily for the data on negotiated wages and their associated employment levels' (p. 102). A good example of an empirical test of union models is MaCurdy and Pencavel's (1986) study of US print workers. This focuses on the monopoly union variant of the right to manage model and essentially attempts to ascertain whether observed wage and employment outcomes lie on the labour demand curve for that industry. If they do then this provides some support for the right to manage model. Whilst acknowledging that this is a quite demanding test of the model, they find that the right to manage model 'is not an appropriate description of this labour market' (p. 34). Unfortunately this empirical snub for the right to manage model does not warrant acceptance of the efficient bargain alternative. Brown and Ashenfelter (1986), in the very next article, attempt to test the efficient bargain model in both its vertical and non-vertical contract curve variants. They reject the vertical contract curve case, with support for the non-vertical form being weak and ambiguous. The problems surrounding the testing of these models are profound. To begin with one cannot observe union utility functions directly, union preferences need to be inferred from labour market outcomes. Brown and Ashenfelter (1986) make the valid point that by and large, unions do not appear to negotiate directly over employment levels. They seem to be more concerned with work practices that may include staffing levels and hours of work which will obviously have employment consequences, but they do not concern themselves with the numbers employed by the firm. McDonald and Solow (1981) suggest that negotiations about working practices are good proxies for direct negotiations over employment, yet Clark (1990) disagrees with this conjecture.

MaCurdy and Pencavel (1986) and Brown and Ashenfelter (1986) disagree about whether the non-union alternative wage W_a should be incorporated into empirical equations. Brown and Ashenfelter see W_a as an integral part of any efficient bargain model, which at a theoretical level is undoubtedly correct, whereas MaCurdy and

Pencavel take the view that the absence of W_a does not undermine their efficient bargain formulation. This dispute is an example of the sort of problem associated with the empirical testing of theories of trade union activity. Manning (1987) points out that because unions may bargain at different levels over different objectives, for example, a national wage and locally bargained working practices, empirical studies are likely to face serious identification problems. Furthermore the fact that the rules of the bargaining game change over time via changes in trade union legislation, is also likely to alter our perception of which model provides the most appropriate explanation of union impact on labour market outcomes. Mayhew and Turnbull (1989) make the point that because an outcome in the wage and employment space may not lie on a labour demand curve, one cannot assume that it rests on an efficient bargain contract curve. An associated point to remember is that firms always have a profit-enhancing incentive to reduce employment levels at any given real wage rate, back to the labour demand curve even if this means breaking an agreement with the union. Such a consideration emphasises the role of the transactions costs of altering employment levels (hiring and firing costs) and the ability of unions to enforce bargained solutions, both of which will vary over time subject to the legislative framework, the business cycle and product market competition. Where does this empirical ambiguity leave the economic modelling of trade union behaviour? Manning (1992) makes the startling but crucial point that the microeconomic models of trade union activity are not particularly robust. He demonstrates that if one breaks the assumption that the firm's revenue functions are the same after the agreement with the unions as they were before the agreement, then the conventional predictions of the two models can be undermined. For example, if unions adopt a negative efficient bargain contract curve, such as C_3 in Figure 7.7, Manning is able to generate higher employment in a right to manage model than in the efficient bargain set up.[5] Yet in spite of the empirical ambiguity and these theoretical doubts surrounding microeconomic models of trade union behaviour they generate the robust prediction that unions raise wages above the non-union alternative wage W_a. However, trade unions' ability to obtain higher wages may depend upon the institutional framework in which wage bargaining takes place. It is this aspect of union power in the labour market that is the focus of the next section.

THE BARGAINING FRAMEWORK

An important function of trade unions is to conduct negotiations on behalf of their members with employers. Metcalf (2001) provides information on the coverage of such collective bargaining in Britain in 1999. Of the 23.7 million employees in employment only some 7 million (30 per cent) were union members. Only 8.5 million (36 per cent) were covered by collective agreements. Of those 8.5 million, 3.1 million were not union members. Collective agreements negotiated by unions were benefiting 3.1 million 'free riders'. A further 1.6 million union members were employed on wages and conditions that lay outside of the scope of union negotiated collective agreements.

Table 7.7 Voice arrangements, Great Britain (percentage of workplaces), 1984–98

	1984	1990	1998
Representative voice only	29	18	14
Representative and direct voice	45	43	39
Direct voice only	11	20	30
No voice	16	19	17

Source: Metcalf 2001, table 5, p. 29
Note: Workplaces with 25 or more employees.

The majority (57 per cent) of British employees were neither union members nor were they covered by collective agreements. Whilst the coverage of collective bargaining has declined over time so has the extent to which firms look to unions to provide a channel of communication with the workforce ('representative voice'). More and more firms have opened up channels of communication between management and workers that do not rely on or pass through trade unions, the 'direct voice'. The data in Table 7.7 shows a clear move away from relying on unions to provide a 'representative voice' in the workplace, in favour of direct communication.

This does not just reflect a decline in firms' recognition of unions; it also picks up a shift away from relying on union voice in unionised workplaces. Bargaining between employers and workers, more often in the past through trade unions as workers' representative, requires information. Gospel *et al.* (2000) make the distinction that firms in the UK have traditionally been required by law to disclose information because of the needs of collective bargaining, whereas more recently the need for disclosure has stemmed partly from EU initiatives but also from the shift towards joint consultation between managers and their workers. Success at bargaining is important to the survival of trade unions. Charlwood (2001) suggests that workers' willingness to join a union depends upon three factors:

- dissatisfaction with the experience of work – that work does not meet workers' expectations in terms of satisfaction from work, the work environment and pay;
- the effectiveness of unions – dissatisfied workers will only join a union if they believe that it can do something to correct the causes of their dissatisfaction; and
- altruism in the form of attitudes to social solidarity that may be based on politics or ideology.

Charlwood (2001) found that workers' willingness to join a union did not appear to be increased by greater dissatisfaction with work, whereas greater satisfaction from work reduced workers' willingness to unionise. Geographically concentrated manual workers did appear to be more influenced by notions of social solidarity than those in more prosperous and more socially mixed areas. But such traditional demand for unions is in decline. The future of unions may rest on their ability to convince non-manual workers of their effectiveness. Unions in the UK have been helped by the

1999 Employment Relations Act that came into operation in June 2000 requiring any firm with more than 20 workers to recognise a union for the purposes of bargaining on pay, hours of work and holiday entitlement if the majority of the workforce wish to be unionised. This statutory recognition procedure gives unions the opportunity to demonstrate their effectiveness in previously non-union establishments.

During the 1990s the nature of collective pay bargaining in the UK became more straightforward. There was a shift towards many unions joining a single set of negotiations with the employer. According to Bryson (2001) in 1990 only 40 per cent of workplaces conducted such bargaining; by 1998 this had risen to 77 per cent.

European trade unions are not homogeneous entities varying only in terms of union density, strike activity and wage mark-up. There is a good deal of variety in terms of their structures, degree of union co-ordination and the level at which they bargain with employers. Only in Britain with the TUC (Trades Union Congress), in Ireland (ICTU) and in Austria with the OGB (Osterreichische Gewerkschaftsbund) are there single representative peak associations of trade unions. Germany has separate associations for white-collar workers, the DAG (Deutsche Angestellten-Gewerkschaft), civil servants, the DBB (Deutscher Beamtenbund) and managerial staff, the ULA (Union Leitender Angestellten). In Sweden the division is largely between white- and blue-collar workers. The socialist LO (Landsorganisationen i Sverige) is predominantly blue-collar, whereas the TCO (Tjanstemannens Centralorganisation) is a white-collar union association. In Italy with seven peak organisations there are three main union confederations, which are based upon and divided along political lines. There is the Communist and Socialist CGIL (Confederazione Generale Italiana del Lavoro), the Christian Democrat CISL (Confederazione Italiana dei Sindacati Lavoratori), and the Social Democrat UIL (Unione Italiana del Lavoro). In France there are five peak union associations vying for members, the Communist CGT (Confédération Générale du Travail), the non-communist CGT-FO (CGT-Force Ouvrière), the Socialist CFDT (Confédération Française Démocratique du Travail), the conservative Catholic CFTC (Confédération Française de Travailleurs Chrétiens), and the technical and managerial union association the CFE (Confédération Française d'Encadrement). The list of dominant union peak associations and the percentage of affilliated unions contained in Table 7.8 provides some indication of the degree of trade union fragmentation in Europe.

In terms of trade union organisational concentration Austria, Germany and Ireland are highly centralised, whereas France, Italy and Spain are very fragmented. In spite of having a single peak union association (the TUC) the UK has a fragmented union structure because of the large number of trade unions. In 1985 the TUC had 98 member unions whereas the German DGB contained only 17.

Beyond Europe, the Australian Council of Trade Unions (ACTU) and the American Federation of Labour–Congress of Industrial Organisations (AFC–CIO) are examples of single peak organisations of trade unions. Yet Australian union organisation combining both white- and blue-collar workers is more highly centralised than that of the USA. Peak organisation concentration appears to have increased in Australia,

Table 7.8 Union peak organisations

	Number of peak organisations 1998	Percentage of total membership 1991–6	Percentage of Unions not affiliated 1991–6
Austria (OGB)	1	100.0	0.0
Belgium (ACV/CSC)	3	53.6	n.a.
Denmark (LO)	4	69.5	5.6
France (CGT-FO)	5	29.9	21.8
Finland (SAK)	3	54.4	0.0
Germany (DGB)	3	83.3	9.8
Ireland (ICTU)	1	97.8	2.2
Italy (CGIL)	7	43.1	n.a.
Netherlands (NVV, FNV)	3	60.8	12.8
Norway (LO)	3	55.3	10.2
Portugal (CGTP-IN)	3	73.2	2.8
Spain (CCOO, UGT)	5	40.3	14.8
Sweden (LO)	4	56.4	0.7
UK (TUC)	1	84.0	16.0
Australia (ACTU)	1	100.0	0.0
Canada (CLC)	3	60.2	32.5
Japan (Sohyo, Rengo)	3	61.4	29.5
New Zealand (FOL,NZCTU)	2	80.7	15.2
USA (AFL–CIO)	1	81.2	18.8

Sources: Adapted from Visser 1990, tables 18–19, pp. 143–4, 7–8; Traxler *et al.* 2001, table II.1, p. 41

Japan and the Netherlands between 1970 and 1996 due to mergers, but decreased in Canada, Norway and Portugal as new confederations emerged. During the 1980s many unaffiliated unions rejoined the AFL–CIO in the USA. Unaffiliated union shares grew in Canada, France and the UK.

When it comes to negotiations between unions and employers, sectoral bargaining (i.e., where unions negotiate a wage bargain for an entire sector of the national economy) is commonplace in Denmark, the Netherlands, Norway and Sweden. Sectoral bargaining is conducted regionally in Germany, but is usually supervised at the national level. In the UK such sectoral agreements are virtually unknown, with pay rates and rises for the vast majority of workers being determined at company or even down at plant level. Sectoral bargaining in Italy has had a greater role than in the UK but is much less robust than in Germany. Italian sector bargains have been undermined by plant level militancy and by the political ambitions of the union confederations. There is very little collective bargaining in France with wages mainly being set by company level agreements. The growth of company unions (syndicats maison) in the 1980s reflects this bargaining framework and the decline in the influence of the peak associations.

For sectoral bargaining to succeed there needs to be a great deal of co-ordination not only on the part of unions, usually through their peak associations, but also on the part of employers. The degree to which unions and employers are co-ordinated in their approach to bargaining varies from the extremely uncoordinated US institutional set-up, to the very highly co-ordinated bargaining framework found in the Scandinavian countries. Layard *et al.* (1991) have catalogued the degree of bargaining co-ordination found in advanced industrialised economies as part of an analysis of unemployment. They find that Germany, France, Italy and the UK are not aligned with either of the extremes of co-ordination, but represent a range of bargaining institutions, from the fairly well co-ordinated German system to the exceedingly decentralised British set up, which combines a fairly high coverage for collectively bargained agreements with virtually no union or employer co-ordination.

In an influential study, Calmfors and Driffell (1988) argued that there exists a discernible relationship between the wage bargaining framework and unemployment across 17 advanced industrialised economies. Essentially they argue that very decentralised bargaining systems, such as that in the USA, appear to work well in terms of promoting wage moderation, limiting employment loss and thereby curtailing the growth of unemployment. Yet so do very highly centralised systems of wage bargaining, such as those in Norway and Sweden. The worst form of bargaining arrangement, from an unemployment perspective, is the mixture of high coverage of collective agreements coupled with a lack of union and employer co-ordination, that is the type of bargaining framework to be found especially in France, Italy and the UK. There is some dispute about the degree of coordination of wage bargaining in Japan. Although Japan has enterprise unions and a lack of formal coordination of employers through their associations, Sako (1997) points to the growth of union coordination and the importance of informal meetings of the main firms in each sector of the economy, 'there has also been a clear labour–management consensus that the export-dependent metal sector should remain the pattern setter' (p. 29). Hence wage bargaining in Japan is more coordinated than it appears and has delivered wage restraint.

Soskice (1990) illustrates the Calmfors and Driffell (1988) hypothesis using the diagram reproduced in Figure 7.10. The theoretical foundation for the results depicted in Figure 7.10 rests upon a simple set of propositions. In a very decentralised union bargaining environment, say plant level negotiations, the agreement will not have any discernible impact on general wage and price levels, therefore both unions and employers must be alert to the competitive pressures which restrain wage rises. At the highly centralised extreme, say sectoral national wage negotiations, the total economy effects of a wage bargain, including its overall employment consequences can be taken into account, thereby increasing the likelihood of wage moderation and lower unemployment consequences. In the mixed environment of high coverage of collective bargains and little union and employer co-ordination, unions seek higher real wages than they would at the highly centralised level, because they do not see the full employment picture. The mixed environment union will seek higher real wages than its very decentralised counterpart because the employment consequences of any real wage rise are lower at the company level than at the plant level, thus the perceived threat of job losses is lower for individual company level bargain union members. However, actual job losses are likely to be greater with intermediate (company) level

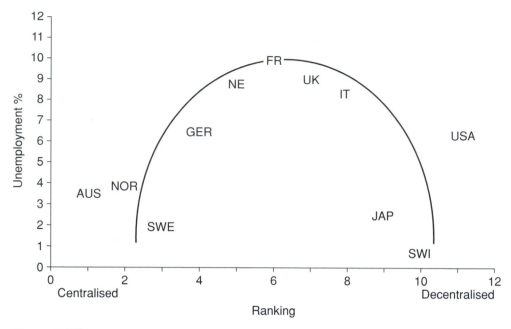

Figure 7.10[6]

Source: Soskice 1990, figure 3, p. 40

wage settlements as they are likely to exceed plant and sectoral settlements. Crouch (1993) argues that European countries with more centralised, co-ordinated systems of industrial relations, which he terms 'corporatist', record better economic performance than decentralised, uncoordinated 'non-corporatist' economies. Measuring economic performance using the Okun index, which sums inflation and unemployment rates to indicate a country's economic misery, Figure 7.11 shows that corporatist countries in Europe during the late 1980s experienced lower combined inflation and unemployment rates than those with non-corporatist industrial relations.

Using a model based upon rational choice theory, Crouch (1993) suggests that the Austrian (A) and German (D) systems of industrial relations, combining corporatism with weaker unions, may prove more stable than the Scandinavian system of corporatism which entails stronger union power. The combination of moderately powerful unions and a lack of bargaining co-ordination found in Italy (I), Ireland (EIR) and the United Kingdom (UK) Crouch (1993) deems to be 'an exceptionally unstable pattern and is unlikely to survive long without political intervention' (p. 289).

The German wage bargaining framework did display resilience to change in the 1980s but it came under increasing pressures, which partially undermined it, in the 1990s. Hassel (1999) reports that some firms began leaving employers' confederations and that trade union strength declined during the 1990s. The coverage of works councils and collective bargains began shrinking as German industrial relations became

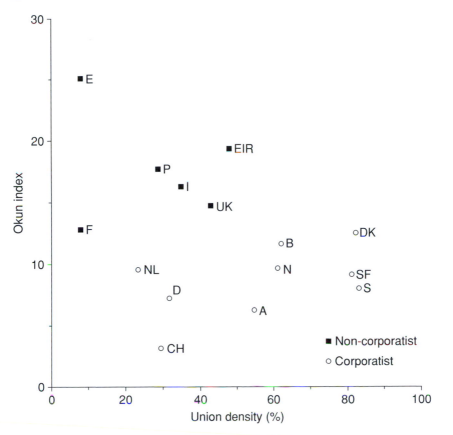

Figure 7.11[7]   Economic performance and union strength, 1986–90

Source: Crouch 1993, figure 7.2, p. 281

more decentralised. The proportion of decentralised company only bargains as a share of all agreements rose from 27 per cent in 1990 to 35 per cent in 1997.

Layard *et al*. (1991) report that when it comes to explaining changes in unemployment rates across 20 countries during the period 1983–8, the bargaining framework (collective bargaining coverage, union co-ordination and employer co-ordination) especially employer co-ordination, plays a significant role (see Layard *et al*., p. 55). The implication is that differences in the unemployment rates of different countries are partially due to differences in the wage bargaining institutions of different national labour markets.

THE ECONOMIC IMPACT OF UNION POWER

In this section we give concise summary analyses of the effects of trade union power on national output, productivity, profitability, wage inflation, strike activity, and perhaps most importantly, the part played by unions in generating unemployment.

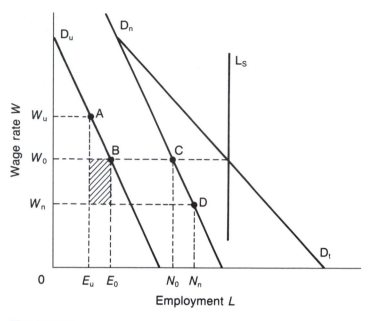

Figure 7.12

On output

The standard analysis of the impact of the power of unions to push up wages for their members on national income is usually based upon the monopoly union variant of the right to manage model. If unions alter the structure of wages, this will change the allocation of labour between unionised and unionised firms. Lower employment in the unionised sector will result in a reduction in the value of aggregate output, even if the overall level of employment throughout the economy remains unaffected. To understand this conventional prediction consider Figure 7.12 which is drawn from Rees (1963). This portrays an aggregate labour market split into a unionised sector (u) and a non-unionised sector (n). L_S is the total supply of labour which for simplicity is assumed to be fixed. D_t is the total demand for labour, which intersects labour supply to determine an initial market clearing wage W_0. However, the demand for labour has two components, D_u the demand for union labour and D_n the demand for non-unionised workers, with D_t being the horizontal sum of $D_u + D_n$. The equilibrium wage W_0 holds in both sectors of the economy generating employment levels for unionised workers of E_0 and for non-union workers of N_0. Now if we reflect the fact that unions use their bargaining power to raise wage rates to W_u, employment falls along the demand for unionised labour curve D_u to a level of E_u, illustrating the right to manage character of this analysis. Assuming these displaced workers $E_0 - E_u$ who are former union members, seek work in the non-unionised sector, they can only be accommodated by falling wages. Non-union employment increases from N_0 to N_n forcing the wage rate down to W_n. Where none existed before a wage differential has now emerged of $W_u - W_n$. There has also been a reallocation of labour away from the unionised sector towards the non-unionised part of the economy. This has resulted in a fall in the value of output from the unionised sector equivalent to the area A,B,E_0,E_u. The increase in the value of output from the rest of the economy is C,D,N_n,N_0. The difference between these two values (areas) is represented by the shaded area in the unionised sector which is a net loss in national output. In the case of Figure 7.12 where the sectoral demand functions have the same slope, the loss in the value of national output (the shaded area) is equal to the change in employment ($E_0 - E_u$), multiplied by half the difference in wages ($W_u - W_n$). Rees (1963) uses this approach to calculate that for the USA in 1957 the union impact on the wage and employment structure amounted to a loss of approximately 0.14 per cent of gross national product (GNP). This is based upon the upper bound of the union wage mark-up (the relative wage effect) estimated to range between 10 per cent and 15 per cent. The impact on GNP might well be greater than this for countries with greater union densities and/or higher union mark-ups. Output losses will be even greater if some of the displaced union workers become unemployed. Of the more recent studies of US output loss due to union relative wage effects, Johnson and Mieszkowski (1970) confirm an estimate of around 0.15 per cent of GNP, whereas DeFina (1983) places the estimated loss significantly lower as a proportion of total output. Mayhew and Turnbull (1989) show that such estimates are thrown into further doubt if one adopts an efficient bargain model of union behaviour.[8] Yet it may well be that non-wage effects of union power such as restrictive working practices, resistance to new technology, and overstaffing, impose additional burdens on an economy. If they do then this should be reflected in the adverse productivity performance of unionised labour.

On productivity and profits

We have just seen that efficiency losses resulting from the impact of union activity on the allocation of labour within the economy are estimated to be extremely small. The conventional wisdom amongst economists was that technical efficiency losses arising from union support for restrictive practices were likely to prove more damaging. Indeed Pencavel's (1977) study of the UK coal industry found that productivity fell as the workforce became more unionised. Pryke (1981) estimates the decline in labour productivity in the coal industry at −7 per cent between 1968 and 1978 when average labour productivity for manufacturing industry as a whole grew by +30 per cent. However, there is a large body of empirical evidence that contradicts the conventional impression that unions depress productivity (see Chapter 2 for more detail). Bowden and Turner (1991) in an analysis of labour productivity in the UK from 1924 to 1968 find little evidence of any significant negative relationship between unions and productivity. A number of studies of US industry such as Brown and Medoff (1978) find that labour productivity appears to be positively correlated with the degree of unionisation. This accords with the Freeman and Medoff (1984) view that unions act as an important informational link between workers and management. If workers quit this should pass a signal on to management, but the significance and clarity of that message may not be adequately understood. Unions may be able to amplify that message; if so then unionisation should reduce costly labour turnover and improve efficiency by passing on to management important information about the production process. This is consistent with the fact that firms might wish to protect job specific training in which they have invested by adopting a high wage, low turnover and better productivity policy with which organised labour co-operates. It is also possible that higher wages might directly stimulate union membership, thus reducing the relative wage differential attributable to trade union power. Brown and Wadhwani (1990) report that during the 1980–4 period, unionised companies in the UK were more likely to cut jobs and change the organisation of work than their non-unionised counterparts. Nickell *et al.* (1991) found that even after controlling for shock, financial and product market effects, total factor productivity growth in unionised firms was on average 2.9 percentage points per year faster than for non-unionised firms during 1980–4. Productivity growth was also faster in unionised firms by some 0.3 per cent per annum in the preceding 1975–9 period.

It appears as though no clear case has been made at either the theoretical or empirical level to support the conventional view that trade unions impair productivity growth.

When it comes to assessing the impact of unions on profits the situation is a lot more straightforward. In spite of the suggestion that unions may enhance productivity, the message from studies such as Voos and Mishel (1986) and Hirsch (1991) is that unions reduce the profitability of firms by around 15–20 per cent, although some studies find a greater effect and others less of an impact. Freeman and Medoff (1984) believe that unions have a greater impact on the profits of firms in more concentrated, less competitive industries. In effect unions are taking a share of the firm's monopoly profits. This appears reasonable as unions are stronger in less competitive industries in the private sector and of course in the public sector. Using US data, Freeman and Kleiner (1999) found that unions do indeed reduce the profitability of firms but they do not undermine the financial viability or long-term survival of those firms. If firms fear the effects of powerful unions they may cut initial investment plans. Denny and Nickell (1992) suggest that the net effect of unions on investment in UK manufacturing firms over the period 1973–85 may have been to have reduced investment by 16 per cent in competitive and by 3 per cent in non-competitive firms. However, Leahy and Montagna (2000) raise the possibility that, in the absence of distortions due to taxes and subsidies, large multinational firms might prefer centralised unions to decentralised ones when it comes to wage bargaining. Hence the presence of strong unions might attract inward investment.

On wage inflation and strikes

Rising labour costs may feed through to rising prices and thereby cause inflation if union power results in wage increases, which outpace any beneficial effect unions may have on enhancing productivity growth. For unions to be regarded as a cause of inflation one needs to adopt an essentially 'cost push' model of inflation where union power results in wage increases which through a mark-up pricing policy, e.g., full cost pricing, firms pass on to customers in the form of higher prices.

Yet in order to explain the acceleration of inflation, which was a widespread phenomenon dating back to at least 1967, and which was well underway before the first OPEC oil price shock of 1973, one needs to suggest increasing union power and/or an ever increasing readiness to use that power (militancy) under accommodating monetary conditions arising from a government commitment to full employment. Cost push inflation theories resulted in two models of the role of trade unions in the inflation process; the relative wage and the real wage models, both of which are surveyed in Carline (1985).

The relative wage model emphasises the importance of comparisons with workers doing similar jobs elsewhere and an awareness of differentials within the firm or industry affecting actual wage levels claimed and won by unions. This could be indicated by a national wage round and a desire by unions to maintain wage differentials through collective bargaining as significant influences on wages. However, Elliott (1976) failed to find any such wage round; instead he discovered a considerable diversity among negotiating groups in the size, timing and frequency of wage increases.

The real wage model suggests that unions may set a target growth of real wages and use their bargaining power to gain money wage rises to achieve that target. In order to be able to do this, unions will obviously have to estimate inflation over the future period of the wage bargain. A major problem with this approach is that if unions do have real wage growth targets they do not announce them and there is no way of determining the optimum growth path. It is not a sound theory of inflation in that it does not explain variations in the rate of inflation. Why does hyper-inflation not develop if unions who are disappointed by real wage growth put in and obtain ever higher wage settlements? Surely it is not because real wage targets just happen to equal productivity growth rates?

Both the real wage and the relative wage models regard unemployment even at high levels as an insufficient constraint on union wage bargaining. This is somewhat ironic given that cost push theories of inflation initially arose from the fear that post-1945 government policy commitment to full employment had removed the fear of unemployment. Both models propose that dissatisfaction with existing wages leads unions to exert pressure on firms to grant wage increases. A number of studies have looked for evidence of that pressure in the form of industrial action, namely strikes, the implicit assumption being that strikes would not take place without unions. Godfrey (1971) used the number of strikes as a measure of union militancy and found that they were an important determinant of the rate of change of wages and of inflation. Ward and Zis (1974) examined manufacturing industry in six West European countries, concluding that strikes did not appear to affect wage inflation in the UK or anywhere else with the possible exceptions of France and Italy. Zis (1977) re-examined Godfrey's work using annual rather than quarterly data and this time strikes were found to have a negative effect on wage inflation. In a study of UK strike activity during the 1980s, Metcalf et al. (1992) calculate that a strike boosts real pay rises by 0.3 per cent, a bonus that will need to last for 30 years for the average strike lasting eleven days, to prove worthwhile! Such empirical findings do not support the positive relationship between strike activity and inflation hypothesised by cost push theories. Yet if they are not primary causes of inflation why do strikes occur?

In order to analyse strike activity we need to refer to a model and the most widely used model is that developed by Hicks in 1932. This proposes an employers' concession curve (ECC) sloping upwards to reflect a greater willingness on the part of firms to concede a higher wage rise as the cost of a strike in term of lost sales and profit increase over time. Set against this is the workers' concession curve (WCC), which shows the increasing cost of a strike to the worker in terms of income and job security losses reflected in a greater willingness to accept a lower wage rise through time. If these functions are known to both parties at the outset of the wage negotiation then there is no rational reason for a strike to occur. Both parties could agree to settle at W^* immediately without incurring any strike costs at all. In the light of Metcalf et al.'s (1992) findings workers have little to gain on average from a strike. Yet as Mauro (1982) points out if neither side is particularly well informed of the other's true intentions, strikes can be viewed as a means of reconciling divergent expectations. This type of decision-making under conditions of uncertainty is illustrated in Figure 7.13. With WCC_0 and ECC_0 being the genuine attitudes towards a pay deal on the part of the union and firm respectively, the following game evolves. The union tries to convince employers that it is adopting WCC_1 as its bargaining position.

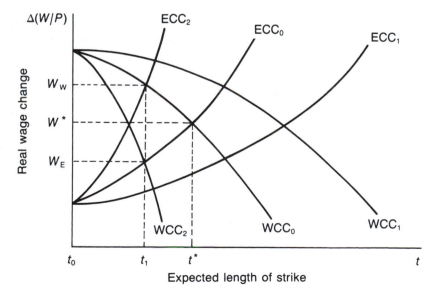

Figure 7.13

Employers know that this is an opening position and believe the unions true position to be WCC$_2$. Employers begin by claiming that they are limited to ECC$_1$. Workers disbelieve this and think ECC$_2$ is the real situation. Thus workers see W_W as the achievable outcome, whereas employers view W_E as the right settlement. The strike of t^* duration is the means by which these varying initial expectations are resolved.

Taking this view of strike activity as a consequence of both sides miscalculating the other's intentions yields some interesting insights at odds with the cost push view of inflation. Expectations themselves might diverge across the business cycle. For example at the peak of a boom in the cycle, workers may come to expect continued prosperity whereas an astute employer may have begun to see signs of decline. Changes in the rate of inflation itself will create greater uncertainty, increasing the likely divergence between the expectations of the negotiators. Hence, inflation could be a cause of strike activity rather than an effect. Indeed Davies (1979) reported a strong link between rising inflation and incomes policies on strike activity.

Other studies have concentrated on the link between union density with inflation. Hines (1964, 1971a) proposed that changes in union density are an indicator of union militancy, based on the notion that militant action will be accompanied by efforts to strengthen the union by increasing membership. The idea being that large membership and high density stiffens the negotiators' and the strikers' resolve and reduces the opportunity for firms to substitute non-union workers. These influences should result in higher wages; accordingly Hines found that changing union density had a greater effect on wages in the post-1945 period than at any time in the UK since 1893. Unemployment became insignificant in wage equations containing union density and the price level. Purdy and Zis (1974) re-estimated Hines' equations excluding the self-employed and the armed forces, they still found union density to be significant in explaining wage change, but much less important than suggested by Hines. For example, Hines (1971a) suggests that during the period 1949–69 a 1 per cent change in union density provokes an 8 per cent change in wages, Purdy and Zis estimate that a 1 per cent change in density brought about a 0.5 per cent movement in wages. During the period 1969–79 union density rose more than 20 per cent, in a period of increased strike activity and inflation. Yet this coincidence does not prove causation. Workers may join unions during periods of accelerating or high inflation as a defensive measure in order to protect real incomes and job security. There is empirical support for such a view stemming from Ashenfelter and Pencavel (1969) who modelled the percentage change in US union membership (ΔT) in terms of changes in the price level (ΔP), employment (ΔE), unemployment in the previous recession (U_n^p), and the extent of pro-union attitudes in the USA proxied by the proportion of Democrats in Congress (G). The basic argument is that workers seek the protection of unions when inflation threatens real wage growth.

$$\Delta T_t = \alpha_1 + \alpha_2 \Delta P_t + \alpha_3 \Delta E_t + \alpha_4 \Delta E_{t-1} + \alpha_5 \Delta E_{t-2} + \alpha_6 \Delta E_{t-3} + \alpha_7 (U_n^p)_t + \alpha_8 (T/E)_{t-1} + \alpha_9 G_t$$

where T/E is the union density.

Bain and Elsheikh (1976) adapted this basic model to test not only US data but to extend the study to UK, Australian and Swedish figures.[9] The results indicate that employment and price changes have positive effects on union membership. Carruth and Disney (1988) use a 'business cycle' model on union density in the UK which finds that, in the short run, membership fluctuates positively to changes in employment and price inflation and reacts negatively to wage inflation and unemployment. Fallon and Verry (1988) confirm this view when they state,

> the broad story does seem to fit the facts in the UK in which high rates of inflation in the 1970s could explain why union membership continued to rise in the face of generally slack labour market conditions. The fall-off in membership in the 1980s would then be explained by the much sharper fall in employment during this period and the lower rate of inflation.
>
> (p. 178)

If so, then why did we not see union density rise in the late 1980s as price inflation rose and unemployment fell? According to Disney (1990) the rapid rise in real wages during the 1980s ensured the continual demise of unionisation in the UK labour market.

The basic problem with union based cost push inflation models is that they are not complete theories of wage and price determination. They are, in fact, sociological explanations of the institutional behaviour of unions and firms which have less relevance in a period of high unemployment and falling union influence, in conditions where governments appeared unwilling to underwrite wage rises with monetary expansion.

On unemployment

In theory the unemployment consequences of labour unionisation can be easily demonstrated using a two sector general equilibrium framework. Figure 7.14 conveniently summarises the theoretical impact of unions on unemployment. The labour market is split into a unionised sector and a non-unionised sector, the demand curves for each being D_u and D_n respectively. Capital stocks for each sector are assumed fixed to reflect the short-run costs of adjusting capital inputs. If unions had no influence over wages, point E would represent the competitive equilibrium with wages in both sectors equal to W_E. Following the right to manage model let us now allow the union to obtain a wage bargain of W_u. Employers of union labour set a level of employment L_u consistent with this wage bargain and their own demand for labour D_u. Employment in the non-unionised sector could rise to $L_u - L_0$ but only if real wages for non-union labour are allowed to fall to W_n. But if the state provides welfare benefits to the unemployed of value b, such that the utility gained when out of work $U(b)$ equals that derived from working for a wage W_a, then $U(b) = U(W_f)$ is perfectly possible in spite of the fact that $W_f > b$, because of the disutility of work and the positive utility of leisure. Thus W_f becomes the 'reservation wage', the effective minimum wage below which labour will not work. Hence it becomes impossible for wages in the non-union

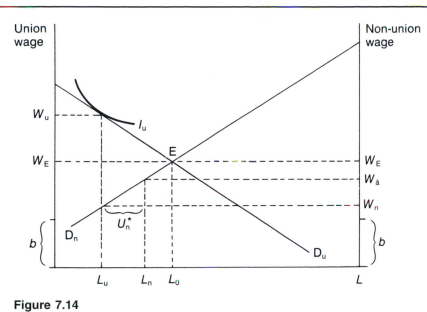

Figure 7.14

sector to fall below W_f and as a result unemployment of the magnitude $L_u - L_n$ is observed. This is an equilibrium level of unemployment and it is equivalent to a 'natural rate' of unemployment U_n^*, or to use its more precise label the NAIRU (non-accelerating inflation rate of unemployment). Note that the unemployment benefit system effectively acts as a floor for wages, which can have unemployment consequences even when this floor (W_f) is set below the competitive market clearing wage (W_E). As Sinclair (1987) remarks the 'message is simple and rather persuasive. Unemployment can arise as a consequence of the interaction of union behaviour and unemployment benefits' (p. 203).

Empirically the impact of trade union power on unemployment has been estimated by a number of studies. Probably the upper bound estimates for the UK are to be found in the work of Minford (1982, 1983). Using the Liverpool model he finds that the increase in union density between 1963 and 1979

> raised total real wages ... by 13 per cent compared with what they otherwise would have been. The effect on output would be to reduce it by 8.5 per cent ... The effect on unemployment, coming through the increased substitution of mechanisation for labour (about 650,000) and through the contraction of output (about 350,000), would be about 1 million.
>
> (1982, pp. 74–5)

In effect Minford is suggesting that union density accounts for about a 4 percentage point addition to unemployment rates in 1979. This may be because real benefits and unionisation are the only trended variables in Minford's (1983) wage equation, but another problem arises from using density as a measure of union power: density as such does not pick up the degree to which unions use their power to win higher wages for their members. Moreover, density in the UK, as elsewhere, began to fall after 1979 while unemployment continued to rise until 1986. More recent rises in unemployment between April 1990 and 1992 came at a time when density continued to decline. Layard and Nickell (1985a) using the union mark-up as a measure of trade union power in a right to manage model of bargaining, found that of the 10 percentage points rise in British male unemployment rates that occurred between 1967 and 1983 around 1.5 percentage points were directly attributable to union power. Bean (1992a) allocates a greater role to union militancy in the British unemployment story, with the result that of a 10.3 percentage points increase in unemployment rates between 1970 and 1986 some 2.9 points were due to union wage push. Yet when it came to the rapid reduction of unemployment during 1986–90, of the −6.7 point fall only −0.9 was seen as due to a wage push variable which combined the union mark-up and the unemployment benefit replacement ratio.

For the USA, Montgomery (1989) assessed the possible impact of unions on employment. The study found that a 10 per cent increase in union density was associated with a 0.2 per cent reduction in the likelihood of being employed and that a 10 per cent increase in the union wage mark-up reduced employment probability by 0.06 per cent. Quantitatively these effects are very small. Strong unions can increase unemployment unless they co-operate with employers over wage setting centrally. Layard and Nickell (1999) maintain that competition can reduce or even eliminate the negative aspects of union power.

Whilst empirical estimates of union induced unemployment vary quite markedly they do in general, support the view that unions, through their ability to push up wages do have an adverse effect on employment outcomes in the labour market. If so then what has been the effect of curbing union power through a policy of enacting restrictive trade union legislation during the 1980s? Brown and Wadhwani (1990) examine the economic effects of what has been an almost continual flow of legislation in the UK. The 1980 and 1982 Employment Acts reduced unions' ability to impose a 'closed shop' arrangement, reduced their ability to picket, and opened unions to civil liability fines for industrial action. The 1984 Trade Union Act imposed balloting criteria on union decision-making particularly with regard to industrial action. In 1986 the Wages Act reduced the role of wages councils in setting statutory minimum wages. The 1988 Employment Act made all action to enforce closed shops illegal and increased individual members' rights to resist union decisions. The Employment Bill of 1989 makes unions responsible for unofficial strikes, bans secondary action and the pre-entry closed shop. Following a 1992 White Paper all wages councils were abolished. This legislation has undoubtedly affected the ability of unions to act against employers as falling strike statistics appear to illustrate, but shows it has done nothing to reduce the union wage mark-up. To confirm this lack of impact, real wage growth accelerated from an average 1.5 per cent per annum during 1973–9, to 2.4 per cent per annum during 1979–86 in the face of the decline in trade unions and the rise in unemployment. Brown et al. (1997) maintain that the main impact of policy changes, aimed at giving firms more control over managing their workplaces, has been 'greater

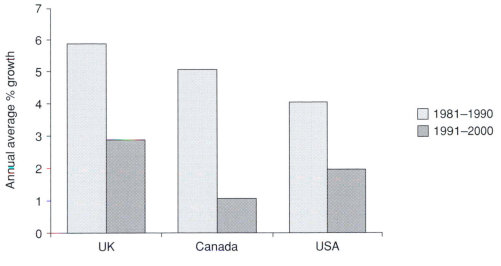

Figure 7.15 Unit labour costs, UK and North America, 1981–2000

Source: OECD, various years

dispersion in pay during the nineties, than in earlier decades' (p. 5), rather than changing the influences on pay settlements.

In spite of faster productivity growth, the UK record on unit labour cost growth compared to other industrialised countries has not been an impressive one since 1980. OECD data used to construct Figure 7.15 shows a more rapid rise of unit labour costs in the UK than in either Canada or the USA during both the 1980s and the 1990s. Remember that the faster rising unit labour costs for the UK means that UK firms are at an increasing labour cost disadvantage compared to US and Canadian firms. This has been brought about because the gap between wage rises and productivity growth has been greater in the UK than in the USA or Canada.

When it comes to comparing unit labour cost growth between the UK and some of its major EU competitors, the situation is slightly more complex, yet, as Figure 7.16 shows, it is no more flattering to the UK. Quite clearly the UK experiences faster unit labour cost growth than Germany in both the 1980s and the 1990s. Growth in unit labour costs in France and Ireland is almost as rapid as in the UK during the 1980s, thereafter labour cost growth slows markedly in France and Ireland. Italy experienced rapid rises in unit labour costs during the period 1980–91. From 1991 the rate of growth in Italian unit labour costs begins to slow to a slower rate of increase than the UK experienced during the 1990s.

We already know from Table 7.3 that UK trade union density falls from around 50 per cent in 1980 to about 30 per cent in 2000. We also know that union density is at a lower level and falling in the USA and France over the same period. Yet there is no straightforward correlation with comparative unit labour cost changes.[10] Brown and Wadhwani (1990) in an assessment of the economic effects of trade

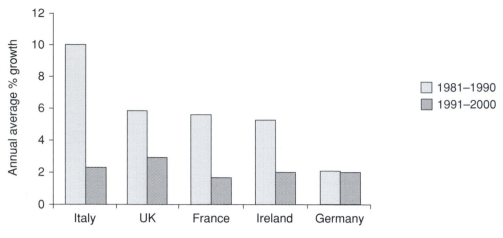

Figure 7.16   Unit labour costs in Europe, 1981–2000

Source: OECD, various years

union legislation during the 1980s suggest that it had little discernible influence. They conclude that

> the driving force behind changes . . . in the 1980s was not government policies aimed at increasing competition in the labour market and at weakening trade unions [but] increased product market competition, which has driven employers . . . to manage their own labour more effectively.
>
> (p. 31)

This completes our survey of the economic impact of trade union power. We now turn to 'insider–outsider theory' as a possible alternative explanation of how trade unions might influence labour market outcomes.

INSIDER–OUTSIDER THEORY

Probably the best reference to consult about insider–outsider theory is by its two pioneers Lindbeck and Snower (1988). They define insiders as existing employees whose position is protected by the existence of significant labour adjustment costs, such as hiring, training and firing costs. Outsiders, of whom the unemployed are the most important, can only exert an indirect influence on the wage and job security of insiders because they are prevented from direct competition by the barrier of labour turnover costs. Trade unions feature as representatives of insiders who can impose additional labour adjustment costs on firms through industrial action. Wages for in-siders will be bounded by an 'absolute profitability constraint' equal to marginal revenue productivity (MRP) plus the marginal hiring and firing costs. As workers MRP varies with the size of the existing workforce – a large workforce lowering MRP and a small workforce raising MRP (*ceteris paribus*) – the insider wage and level of employment depends upon the size of the incumbent workforce.

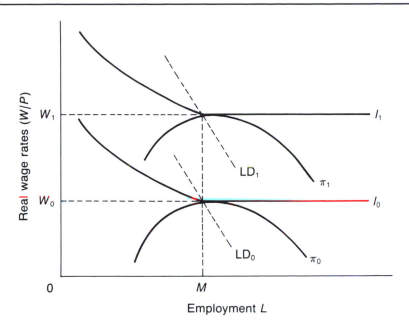

Figure 7.17

The insider–outsider framework suggests that wage rates are being determined on behalf of insiders by unions with no direct reference to the unemployed outsiders. Given that wages for insiders are to a significant extent insulated from external labour market conditions, the theory is a means of explaining real wage rigidity. Figure 7.17 characterises an insider–outsider bargaining situation. Once all existing insiders are employed M, then the union becomes indifferent about the employment consequences of the wage bargain, hence the horizontal part of the union indifference curves I. Employment and therefore potential union membership, is determined unilaterally by the employer. In the long run the union indifference curve kinks at M. Thus we have a form of right to manage model arising from insider–outsider theory, in which inefficient bargains are negotiated on the labour demand curve.

Unemployment can persist in such a model because if firms cut labour demand in response to an unanticipated downward shock to product demand, the wage bargain point shifts to the left. Any subsequent resurgence of labour demand, shown by the shift from LD_0 to LD_1 in Figure 7.17, will initially take the form of higher wages rather than a reduction in unemployment. Indeed any small increases in demand, that are foreseen, may be completely absorbed by rising wages (from W_0 to W_1) leaving employment (at M) unaffected.

If insider–outsider theory has any validity it does suggest a mechanism whereby union wage mark-ups could be relatively immune from rising unemployment and why unemployment might persist even when product demand recovers. In attempting to explain the persistence of unemployment, insider–outsider theory also provides some support for the 'hysteresis' view of unemployment, (hysteresis being perfect persistence) which we shall encounter in Chapter 10.

Yet how significant are insider–outsider dynamics? Alogoskoufis and Manning (1988) using a model in which insiders pursue a real wage target through union bargaining, produce results for sixteen OECD countries over the period 1952–85, which strongly suggest that persistence in the real wage targets set by unions rather than in the insider–outsider separation by labour turnover costs is the most important factor. They also find that persistence is greater in non-Scandinavian European Union countries than in the USA or Scandinavian countries, which report much lower unemployment persistence. This is a little perplexing because one would expect insider–outsider effects to be greatest in the heavily unionised Scandinavian economies. Nickell *et al.* (1992) in a study of data from more than 800 UK manufacturing companies over the period 1972–86 attempt to find indications of insider–outsider effects. Yet they report no marked differences between firms with large and small workforces or between unionised and non-unionised firms. In their wage equation they are not able to find any 'robust evidence of insider power in operation' (p. 20). Furthermore they report identical long-run impacts of unemployment on union and non-unionised firms. Perhaps in the light of this lack of empirical confirmation, the most important contribution of insider–outsider theory is to have suggested an economic reason why employed insiders and unemployed outsiders are treated differently in the labour market even under equilibrium conditions.

CASE STUDY – WORKING FOR THE UNION IN AUSTRALIA?

Having looked at aspects of trade union power and the economic impact of trade unions let us look at the nature of unionised compared to non-union workplaces in more detail. Stephen Deery, Janet Walsh and Angela Knox (2001) 'The Non-Union Workplace in Australia: Bleak House or Human Resource Innovator?', *International Journal of Human Resource Management*, 12 (4): 669–83, draw some interesting comparisons between unionised and non-union workplaces.

> The non-union workplace has become an increasingly important phenomenon in employment relations as trade union membership has retreated steadily over the last two decades. In Australia over a quarter of all workplaces with more than twenty employees have no union. . . . [*In Britain in 1998*] . . . almost a half of all workplaces with more than twenty-five employees had no union presence. . . . In the United States the non-union sector has been clearly dominant for most of the post-war period . . . The American human resource model that took shape in US firms in the 1960s emerged as an alternative to trade unionism . . .

The growth in the significance of non-union workplaces

> has stimulated academic interest . . . focused primarily on the question of whether these non-union workplaces have become human resource

Table A Characteristics of Australian non-union and union private sector workplaces, 1995

	Non-union	Union
Number of employees (average)	74.2	182.3
Share of female workers (%)	42.1	38.2
Part of larger organisation (%)	67.3	82.5
Owner at workplace (%)	48.0	22.0

Source: Adapted from Deery *et al.* 2001, table 1, p. 672

innovators or 'bleak houses'. . . . The bleak house model of employee relations refers to workplaces that lack systematic forms of consultation, communication and information sharing with employees as well as formalized procedures to resolve workplace grievances and disciplinary matters. . . . Has management used its greater freedom from trade union regulation in non-union workplaces to create more innovative and beneficial remuneration programmes for their staff or have they simply taken advantage of the lack of union presence to enforce stricter disciplinary regimes and impose less generous terms and conditions of employment on their workforce?

Using data from the 1995 Australian Workplace Industrial Relations Survey, Deery *et al.* (2001) analysed a sample of 1,053 private sector workplaces with twenty or more employees. The general characteristics of their sample are contained in Table A.

As we can see from the data in Table A, non-union workplaces tend to be smaller than unionised ones. They also have a slightly greater share of female employees in their total workforce. Non-union workplaces are less likely to be part of a larger organisation than unionised workplaces (although the majority of non-union workplaces are part of larger organisations) and the owner is much more likely to be on site at a non-union workplace.

Taking account of the fact that unionised workplaces tend to employ more people and are more likely to be part of a larger organisation, Deery *et al.* (2001) set out to establish statistically significant differences between non-union and union workplaces in terms of employee relations. Their main findings are summarised in Table B.

Non-union workplaces are significantly less likely to train their supervisors or first-line management in employee relations or to utilize formal written selection procedures for recruitment or promotion. Furthermore, they are less innovative in terms of their work practices and they have a significantly lower incidence of joint consultation with employees. Moreover, fewer non-union workplaces provide disciplinary and grievance procedures. Non-union workplaces are also less likely to supply employees with family leave or to

Table B Impact of union status on employee relations

Non-union workplaces have:	Non-union (%)	Union (%)
Less supervisor training	10.3	22.3
Less selection/promotion procedures	39.9	57.4
More individual contracts	25.8	5.5
More individual performance pay	46.7	32.9
More bonus schemes	52.9	46.9
Less innovative work practices	31.0	47.0
Less joint consultation	14.4	43.1
Less disciplinary procedures	84.3	95.2
Less grievance procedures	48.7	76.1
Less family leave provision	23.0	41.4
Less equal employment opportunities policy	43.8	71.5
Less equal employment opportunities training	43.8	59.8
More individual philosophy	78.7	58.3
More dismissals (% of employees)	3.7	1.9
More labour turnover (% of employees)	27.5	17.6

Source: Adapted from Deery *et al.* 2001, tables 2 and 4, pp. 674 and 677

have a written policy on Equal Employment Opportunities/Affirmative Action (EEO/AA) or to train managers to deal with EEO/AA or sexual harassment complaints. Non-union workplaces are highly individualistic in their . . . approach to industrial relations and in the employee relations policies they pursue. They are significantly more likely to display a preference for dealing with employees directly rather than through a union, to place employees on individual contracts and to favour individual-based performance-related pay and bonus incentive schemes. On the other hand, both dismissal rates and turnover rates are significantly higher than in the unionised workplaces.

. . .

The evidence in this study suggests that non-union workplaces were neither bleak houses nor human resource innovators. Nevertheless, the practices that were identified [in Australia] had [much] in common with . . . non-union workplaces in Britain . . .

Overall in spite of the fact that non-union workplaces are very similar to union ones when it comes to training in general, communicating with employees, using meetings and the use of staff appraisals, they 'were far less committed to the provision of family leave and to policies designed to assist with gender equality'. Non-union workplaces 'were decidedly more individualistic in their contractual, remunerative and bargaining arrangements'.

The non-union workplace has become a more common feature of many labour markets. This case study alerts us to the fact that, in many respects, it is a different place in which to be employed than a unionised workplace.

UNIONS AND EQUALITY

In spite of falling trade union power, unions remain an important labour market institution that can impact on aspects of equality, namely earnings distribution, industrial injuries, equal opportunities and family friendly policies. Metcalf (2001) labels this the 'sword of justice' (p. 8) impact of unions.

We already know from Chapter 3 that the decline in union power since 1980 has been a contributory factor in the widening of pay inequality in the labour market. Between 1980 and 2000 union density in the UK has almost halved and the proportion of wages determined by collective bargaining fell from 70 per cent in 1980 to 35 per cent in 1998. According to empirical studies, for example Bell and Pitt (1998), this loss of union power has served to increase the distribution of earnings. Figure 7.18 illustrates a clear inverse relation between changes in union density and wage inequality in the aggregate economy over the period 1966–96.

As union density was rising up to the late 1970s, wage inequality, measured by the ratio of the 90th percentile to the 10th percentile in the wage distribution, was falling. In the 1980s and 1990s declining union density was accompanied by growing wage inequality. After examining US and British empirical studies of the link between changes in union power and wage inequality, Machin (1999) found that 'US estimates attribute between 12 per cent and 21 per cent of the rise in wage inequality to falling unionisation. The British results apportion around 17 per cent to 37 per cent' (p. 202). As we discovered in Chapter 3, rising wage inequality is due to more than union decline but the link does highlight the egalitarian role that unions play in the distribution of pay.

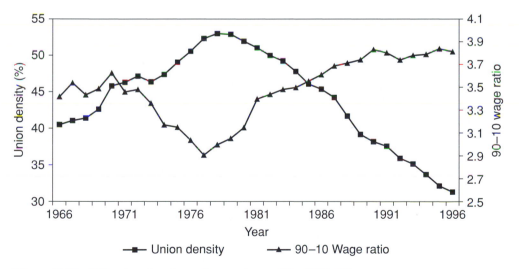

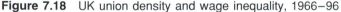

Figure 7.18   UK union density and wage inequality, 1966–96

Source: Machin 1999, figure 11.4, p. 202
Note: 90–10 wage ratio is the difference between what the person(s) in the 90th percentile of the wage distribution earns compared to the person(s) at the 10th percentile. The 90th will be a high earner (just in the top 10%); the 10th a low earner (just in the bottom 10%).

That wage inequality has increased within unionised and non-union establishments means that unions have been unable to prevent widening of pay even where they do have a presence. Unions' insistence that pay be related to the job rather than the individual job holder has helped to limit pay favouritism and discrimination. Traditionally unions have been against the introduction and spread of performance-related pay because of concerns over the subjective nature of management assessment of the contribution of individual workers. The introduction of performance-related pay has been an element of increasing labour market flexibility (see Chapter 8); this, along with the move away from collective bargaining over pay, has been intended to widen the distribution of wages. Heery (2000) maintained that performance-related pay was strongly associated with non-unionism and de-recognition of unions in establishments. Union pressure to have a standard rate of pay for a job was not only directed within single establishments but across establishments and firms. This served to limit pay dispersion within occupations and industries. This has been weakened by the shift away from collective bargaining and the move away from sector and industry wide agreements towards establishment level and individual worker pay deals. Metcalf et al. (2000) note that while about 25 per cent of private sector workers are covered by collective bargains only 10 per cent of these are national agreements.

Between the abolition of Wages Councils in 1992 and the introduction of the UK National Minimum Wage in 1999 trade unions provided the only effective institutional barrier to low pay. Unions have long played a role in truncating the bottom end of the earnings distribution by negotiating for their low paid members. In spite of the decline in union power, pay dispersion is much lower in the unionised sector than in the non-unionised sector. Rates of return to education and experience are lower for unionised workers reflecting the tighter distribution of pay.

Unions are important advocates of equal opportunities, family friendly policies and health and safety in the workplace. Metcalf (2001) states that 'non-union workplaces are 20 per cent less likely to have equal opportunities policy on gender than their unionised counterpart' (p. 12). When it comes to family-friendly policies, (parental leave, working from home, school term-time only contracts, full- to part-time switching, job sharing, nurseries, child care subsidies) designed to accommodate primarily female workers with child rearing responsibilities, 19 per cent of unionised workplaces had none of these in 1998, compared to 43 per cent of non-union workplaces having no family-friendly policies.

Although unions are more prevalent in more dangerous industries and establishments, union presence appears to lower average accident rates. In 1998 the mean accident at work rate in unionised workplaces was 1.6 per cent, whereas in non-union workplaces it was 2.1 per cent. This would appear to reflect union success in negotiating and supervising the implementation of health and safety provision. Litwin (2001) maintains that 'British trade unions lodge themselves in accident-prone workplaces and respond by reducing rates of injury . . . [they therefore] . . . serve as an effective institutional force for reducing injury rates' (pp. 10–11). Metcalf et al. (2000) calculate that the wage structure would be more widely distributed without the egalitarian

Table 7.9   UK pay gaps without unions and collective bargaining, 1998

	Wage inequality wider by (%) without	
	Trade unions	Collective bargaining
Male – Female	2.6	3.1
White – Black	1.4	3.3
Healthy – Sick	0.6	1.2
Non-manual – Manual	3.1	6.4

Source: Metcalf *et al.* 2000, p. 15

influence of trade unions. Table 7.9 contains estimates, derived from Labour Force Survey data for 1998, of what would happen to the gender pay gap, the ethnic pay gap, the comparative pay of healthy workers compared to those with health problems, and the difference in pay between non-manual and manual workers without the influence of unions and collective bargaining.

Quite clearly even in 1998 unions remained an egalitarian influence on the UK labour market helping to narrow the pay gap between men and women at work, between white and black workers, between non-manual staff and their manual colleagues and between healthy workers and those working while enduring health problems. To set these effects in context Metcalf (2001) reports that the introduction of the National Minimum Wage in 1999, which favoured low paid workers, predominantly female workers, 'narrowed the gender differential by a little under 1 per cent' (p. 11).

More generally Blau and Kahn (1996) reported that those OECD countries with decentralised bargaining frameworks had greater pay inequality than those with centralised wage bargaining.

TRADE UNIONS – SUMMARY

Union power varies across countries from the weakly unionised USA to strongly unionised Sweden. In the UK membership, density and strike measures of union power have

- increased markedly in the 1970s
- decreased throughout the 1980s and 1990s

However, the union wage mark-up does not follow such a clear pattern. There are two main economic models of trade union behaviour

- the right to manage model which in aggregate implies a Phillips curve relationship
- the efficient bargain model whose macroeconomic implications are much less precise

Both predict that unions raise wages above the non-union wage. A more recent theoretical innovation focuses attention on the wage bargaining framework. This suggests that

- the traditional view that uncoordinated bargaining by weak unions may correspond with low unemployment is borne out
- contrary to the traditional view centralised bargaining by strong unions may also be beneficial

The decline in union collective bargaining in the UK is creating a more fragmented and decentralised bargaining environment. Conventionally unions are held to adversely affect economic outcomes by

- reducing national output
- impairing productivity growth
- causing wage inflation
- disrupting production through strikes
- causing unemployment

Empirically the impact of unions appears

- inconsequential in the case of output
- ambiguous with regard to productivity
- clearly negative in the case of profits
- an unlikely cause of inflation, yet they may make inflation persist
- to show that estimates of the unemployment consequences of unions vary markedly. The wage mark-up and unemployment impact of UK unions does not appear to have been affected by the anti-union laws of the 1980s

Insider–outsider theory suggests reasons why the union mark-up persists as unemployment rises.

Trade unions are an important egalitarian force within the labour market. Unions are associated with equal opportunities and family friendly policies as well as with lower levels of industrial injury. Recent falls in union power have contributed to growing earnings inequality. Unions and collective bargaining continue to aid greater labour market equality in the areas of gender, race and health, and to assist manual workers.

TRADE UNIONS – QUESTIONS FOR DISCUSSION

1) What evidence is there to suggest that the union wage mark-up does not conform closely to other measures of trade union power?
2) Compare and contrast efficient bargain and right to manage models of trade union behaviour.

3) In what ways has the nature of bargaining between managers and workers in UK establishments changed in recent decades?
4) In what manner might the degree of coordination in wage bargaining make a difference to the impact of trade unions?
5) Do trade unions significantly impair the output and productivity performance of advanced industrialised economies?
6) Critically examine the argument that trade unions are the prime cause of inflation.
7) Explain the theoretical link between labour unionisation and unemployment. How significant is this link empirically?
8) What is insider–outsider theory? What does it tell us about union behaviour in the context of fluctuating unemployment?
9) In what ways and to what extent are unions associated with greater labour market equality?

SUGGESTED READING

Boeri, T., Brugiavini, A. and Calmfors, L. (eds) (2001) *The Role of Unions in the Twenty-First Century*, Oxford: Oxford University Press.
Booth, A. (1995) *The Economics of the Trade Union*, Cambridge: Cambridge University Press.

8

Labour market flexibility

INTRODUCTION

Between 1965 and 1975 civilian employment in the USA grew by 14.5 million whereas in the UK net employment declined by 0.04 million. The 1975–85 period saw US net employment grow by a further 15.6 million while the UK experienced a fall of 0.54 million.[1] The comparative inability of the UK economy to generate employment was explained in part by the greater rigidity of the UK labour market in particular and European labour markets in general. The UK since 1979 has witnessed substantial increases in and rapid fluctuations of unemployment, coupled with a concerted policy attempt to remove 'rigidities' from the labour market. This chapter seeks to define what is meant by the term 'flexibility' in the context of labour markets. It will then look at some of the policies that have been introduced to bring about greater flexibility. Flexible forms of employment and labour migration trends will be examined. We will assess the impact of UK Government policies, which have attempted to imitate what is believed to be greater labour market flexibility in the USA.

As an application of the topic of labour market flexibility we will examine European Monetary Union, which focuses attention on the importance of wage flexibility and labour migration for the success of the single currency, the Euro.

LABOUR MARKET FLEXIBILITY

Rosenberg (1989) identifies four types of labour market flexibility.

1 Wage flexibility, requiring that wage levels and wage differentials become more responsive to labour market conditions, and more specific to the firm as well as to the individual employee. Wages are to be more responsive to macroeconomic

factors such as unemployment, productivity and international competitiveness. Policies which might achieve greater wage flexibility include: abolishing minimum wages; weakening collective bargaining of across the board wage levels; reducing the welfare benefit floor for wages; and eliminating wage indexation.

2 Numerical flexibility, enhancing employers' ability to vary hours of work and the number of workers employed in response to changing product demand conditions. Policies that were aimed at greater numerical flexibility included: weakening employment protection legislation; reducing fixed-term employment contracts; and encouraging temporary and part-time working.

3 Functional flexibility, increasing firms' power to effectively utilise their workforce. This was supposedly to be achieved by: increasing worker mobility within the firm; multi-skilling; and reducing work demarcation.

4 Work time flexibility, giving firms more authority to set and change work schedules and the organisation of working time, including: hours of work; paid holidays; sick leave; overtime; out of normal hours working; and retirement.

With regard to wage and numerical flexibility (1 and 2),

> many neoclassical economists and policy makers . . . argue that the relatively high levels of unemployment and stagnating levels of employment in many European countries are due to high and inflexible real wages and the inability of employers to adjust their workforces . . . because of institutional rigidities in the labour market.
>
> (Rosenberg, 1989, p. 9)

At the microeconomic (firm or industry) level, lower real wages would in this argument reduce labour costs thereby increasing the demand for labour through factor substitution. Profits may also rise, leading to increased investment and a further rise in employment. Thus if real wages did not respond to adverse supply-side shocks (such as the OPEC oil price rises of 1973 and 1979) or adverse demand-side shocks (such as the monetary and fiscal policy tightening after 1979), then firms' profits would fall, deterring investment designed to expand capacity, as opposed to labour saving investment. Against this view, reducing real wages would adversely affect aggregate demand, output and employment, and might encourage a low-wage, low-productivity route for employers.

It may well be that post-Fordist production methods, that we encountered in Chapter 4 (flexible specialisation, the flexible firm and lean production), which require new management practices like total quality management (TQM), encourage wage rigidity. New management techniques place a premium on trust in the workplace. Trust can be reinforced by employment contracts along the lines of implicit contracts, where firms will offer workers fixed wage contracts that guarantee wages irrespective of product market and external labour market conditions, or efficiency wages, which use high and stable wages to guard against poor performance and increase workers' commitment to the firm.

Agnell (1999) points out that social norms with regard to fairness might be important in maintaining a certain degree of wage rigidity. Employers may be reluctant to cut wages because workers will see this as unfair and retaliate by reducing their effort at work.

On numerical flexibility specifically, employment protection legislation makes dismissing labour more difficult and more costly and this, it is claimed, may make the firm more wary of hiring labour, preferring to meet any increase in product demand from overtime working or by increasing the employment of capital relative to labour, i.e., investing in labour saving technology. Those in favour of reducing employment protection would claim that firms would not only reduce the size of their workforces more rapidly during a recession but would also take on more new employees during a boom. Functional flexibility (3) is claimed to permit the more efficient use of a firm's workforce, and hence to improve labour productivity, and to be a means of coping with uncertainty and volatility in product demand, which may have increased as the competitive and trading conditions facing firms became more open in the post-Second World War era. However, the existence of internal labour markets may mean that such functional flexibility can only be achieved if the firm provides some security of employment.

Working time flexibility (4) is likewise claimed to increase labour productivity per hour employed. In a dynamic setting productivity growth and employment growth are positively correlated. Productivity growth creates the scope to reduce unit costs and prices, enabling higher sales and thereby increasing output and employment. In a trading environment comparative productivity performance will impact upon the comparative advantage of nations and subsequent trade performance.

If flexibility is such a good thing in terms of employment growth, what institutional features of labour markets impede such flexibility? Trade unions, welfare benefits and Government employment protection legislation are seen as the main sources of labour market rigidity. The following are all aspects of worker security: labour market security – unemployment benefits and a state commitment to 'full employment'; income security – trade union wage bargaining and minimum wage legislation; employment security – employment protection legislation and raising the cost of redundancy to firms; job security and collective bargaining on working conditions and practices.

Thus policies that aim to increase labour market flexibility conflict with those which seek to enhance worker security. For those advocating greater flexibility, features of a labour market that guarantee worker security are seen as increasing the 'natural rate of unemployment' (see Chapter 10 for a critical examination of this concept). 'Excessive' unemployment benefits, minimum wage regulations, strong trade unions and employment protection legislation are all targets for policies that seek to increase labour market flexibility.

LABOUR MARKET POLICY

UK Government labour market policies after 1979 were clearly designed to imitate aspects of the US labour market, especially its greater flexibility. Table 8.1 summarises

Table 8.1 UK reforms with labour market impact

Reduce Union power

- Employment Act of 1980 abolishes statutory recognition procedures; extends grounds to refuse to join a union; limits picketing
- Employment Act of 1982 prohibits actions that force contracts with union employers; weakens the union closed shop; removes some union legal immunities
- Employment Act of 1984 further weakens union immunities, requires pre-strike ballots, strengthens employers' power to get injunctions against unions
- Employment Act of 1988 removes more union immunities; extends individual rights to work against a union
- Further restrictions on unions' power to take industrial action in 1993

Change Welfare State to increase work incentives

- Reductions in the replacement ratio for welfare benefits; eliminate benefits for young people
- Restart Programme introduced in 1986 required all the claimant unemployed to be interviewed about job search every six months
- Many administrative changes to make it more difficult to obtain benefits
- Maintain the real value of non-work benefits by linking them to consumer price inflation but lower their value relative to wages
- In 1995 unemployment benefit was replaced by the Jobseekers allowance
- 1998 New Deal programmes for young workers and long-term unemployed

Reduce Governmental role in markets

- Privatise pensions
- Abolished power of Wages Councils to set minimum wages in 1993
- Lower tax rates
- Reduce Government employment
- Privatisation
- Abolished Sunday trading restrictions in 1994

Enhance self-employment and skills

- Enterprise Allowance Scheme
- Training initiatives; Youth Training Scheme; Community Programme; Employment Training Programme; Training and Enterprise Councils; Modern Apprenticeships

Source: Adapted from Blanchflower and Freeman, 1993, table 2, p. 21

the main UK policy changes categorised by the goal of the reform. UK Governments during the 1980s and early 1990s pursued policies that were believed to make the labour market more flexible.

Part of the economic justification for privatisation was a deliberate change in the relative sizes of the public and private sectors of the economy. It was believed that the private sector would be more responsive to market conditions and be more efficient as a result of competitive market discipline. In terms of labour market flexibility there was a clear expectation that privatised firms would sweep away the rigidities built up while in the public sector.

In terms of engendering wage flexibility we have already questioned how effective the trade union reforms and reduction of union power in the UK were (see Chapter 7). Using Calmfors and Driffill's (1988) analysis, we were able to cast doubt on whether the drive towards decentralised wage bargaining in the UK during the 1980s was an appropriate labour market strategy. Furthermore in Figure 7.15 we saw that unit labour costs rose throughout the 1980s meaning that earnings growth outpaced productivity growth in every year since 1979.

In 1986 Wages Councils, which recommended minimum wages for young workers (under 21), were abolished; all Wages Councils except agriculture were removed by September 1993. These Councils never had any statutory power and their supposed employment disincentive effects rested solely on the presumption that they set wages above market clearing levels. In a study of the impact of minimum wages in agriculture, Dickens *et al.* (1994b) found that the Agricultural Wages Boards for England, Wales, Scotland and Northern Ireland did raise average wages and compress the earnings distribution among agricultural workers. The study concludes that there is 'no evidence that minimum wages have significantly lowered employment in any country', and indeed that they might even have preserved agricultural employment (p. 20).

The USA has statutory minimum wage rates yet these appear to have had very little effect on hampering employment growth or ratcheting up real wages; indeed rises in minimum wages have lagged behind increases in average earnings, a fact which suggests the growing irrelevance of minimum wage legislation for wage flexibility in the labour market.

The proportion of those unemployed who have been out of work for 12 months or more can be interpreted as an indication of labour market rigidity linked to welfare benefits. It also indicates the extent to which the unemployed fail to influence the labour market outcomes of those in work. When we come to examine long-term unemployment in more detail in Chapter 10 we will notice a clear distinction between the importance of long-term unemployment as a persistent labour market phenomenon in the EU countries and Australia on the one hand, and its comparative insignificance in the North American and Japanese labour markets on the other.

This distinction is not unrelated to the variety of benefit regimes and active labour market policies pursued in these counties. The UK has a range of benefits, which, although not particularly generous, are effectively indefinite. Grubb (1994) calculates that in 1990 the UK committed resources equivalent to 0.95 per cent of GDP in the form of unemployment benefit payments and 0.58 per cent to active labour market policy, such as training and job creation. This compares to Sweden whose generous benefits last for just over a year, yet cost resources equal to 0.81 per cent of GDP in 1990, and committed 0.95 per cent of national output to training and employment subsidies for the unemployed. At the other extreme US benefits last for six months costing 0.50 per cent of GDP in 1990, with a mere 0.21 per cent of GDP going on active labour market policies to help the unemployed. Jackman *et al.* (1996) draw together the comparative data reported in Table 8.2 on the generosity of state benefits (replacement rate), the duration of benefits and the commitment to active labour market policies (ALMP).

Active labour market measures should not be optional for the unemployed; there needs to be universal coverage in order to cut off the flow into long-term unemployment.

Table 8.2 Unemployment benefit regimes, 1989–94

	Replacement rate (percentage)	Benefit duration (yrs)	ALMP spend (percentage average output per worker)
Austria	50	4.0	8.3
Belgium	60	4.0	14.6
Denmark	90	2.5	10.3
Finland	63	2.0	16.4
France	57	3.0	8.8
Germany	63	4.0	25.7
Ireland	37	4.0	9.1
Italy	20	0.5	10.3
Netherlands	70	2.0	6.9
Norway	65	1.5	14.7
Portugal	65	0.8	18.8
Spain	70	3.5	4.7
Sweden	80	1.2	59.3
UK	38	4.0	6.4
Australia	36	4.0	3.2
Canada	59	1.0	5.9
New Zealand	30	4.0	6.8
USA	50	0.5	3.0

Source: Adapted from Jackman *et al.*, 1996, table 2, p. 35

On this basis Jackman *et al.* (1996) recommend the Swedish model where activity replaces benefits, which is also operated by Denmark yet with a longer 'passive' period. The recent deterioration in Sweden's unemployment experience can be attributed to macroeconomic mismanagement rather than to any failing of its labour market policies. Robinson's (1994) examination of the reasons for the fall in male labour force activity in the UK found that over three-quarters of the rise in labour force inactivity of males aged 25–54 between 1971 and 1991 was due to long-term sickness. For older men (aged 55–64) the rise in labour force inactivity since 1971 has been almost equally split between increases in early retirement and long-term sickness. An explanation for the rise in the incidence of long-term sickness proposed by Schmitt and Wadsworth (1994) rests on 'discouraged worker' effects, where unemployed males who find difficulty in gaining employment effectively withdraw from the labour market citing long-term sickness and claiming sickness benefit. Added to this could be the fact that changes in the operation of the benefit system during the 1980s made sickness benefit more attractive compared to unemployment benefit payments and provided incentives for staff administering the system to reduce the numbers claiming unemployment benefit.

The real value of welfare benefits in the UK has been significantly eroded since 1979. In 1982 earnings related benefit payments were abolished in favour of linking changes in benefit payments to retail price inflation. Given that earnings have risen faster than inflation since 1982 this has created a widening gap between income from work and that provided by welfare benefits. This has been reinforced by income tax rate reductions with the basic rate of direct tax falling from 33 per cent in 1979 to 25 per cent in 1988 and a combination of 20 per cent and 23 per cent in 1997. The rate for higher earners fell from 83 per cent in 1979 to 40 per cent in 1988. The net effect of these policies designed to increase wage flexibility has been to reverse a long-term trend towards income equality in favour of the increasing income inequality in the UK that we noted in Chapter 3. Gregg and Machin (1994) show that wage inequality in the UK is greater now than at any time in the past 100 years. In 1886 the lowest 10 per cent of wage earners earned 69 per cent of median wages, with the top 10 per cent earning 143 per cent of median wages. By 1990 the low wage earners earned only 64 per cent of median wages whereas high earners received 159 per cent of median wages. In a comparison of the UK with France, Germany, Italy, Japan, Sweden and the USA, Atkinson (1997) concludes that 'the United Kingdom stands out for the sharpness of the rise in recorded income inequality in the 1980s. This was unparalleled in the countries examined' (p. 301). Figure 3.10 contained the trends in US and UK Gini coefficients in the post-Second World War period.

While providing evidence of consistently greater income inequality in the USA, Figure 3.10 also showed that during the period 1979–93 the UK Gini coefficient was rising much more rapidly than measured income inequality in the USA. The rise in UK income inequality occurred at a time when individual workers experienced falling mobility across the income distribution. Dickens (1997) finds a high degree of immobility across decile boundaries within the British wage distribution in the early 1990s which appears to have followed a marked reduction in wage mobility in the late 1980s compared to the late 1970s, reflecting 'increasing permanent wage differences between individuals' (p. 27).

In terms of making wages more responsive to labour market conditions, empirical studies cast considerable doubt on the efficacy of policies designed to promote wage flexibility. Jackman and Savouri (1991) find that, apart from male manual workers, wages in the UK do not seem to be sensitive to local labour market conditions: 'Differences in non-manual wages across regions appear attributable largely to differences in the cost of living and house prices' (p. 32). Non-manual labour markets are more national in terms of vacancy advertising and the greater propensity of non-manual workers to migrate (Pissarides and Wadsworth 1989). Blanchflower and Freeman (1993) fail to find any significant change in the responsiveness of real wages to unemployment across the 1980s, with Beatson (1995) confirming that 'aggregate real wages in the UK appear to have been rigid by international standards' (p. 131). At the theoretical level efficiency wage models (Weiss, 1991), insider–outsider theory (Lindbeck and Snower, 1988), and implicit contract theory (Manning, 1990) all attempt to explain an observed lack of real wage flexibility. Numerical flexibility was the goal of policies designed to deregulate labour markets in the UK. Reductions in trade union power gave management more scope to alter the specification of employment contracts away from full-time permanent posts in favour of introducing temporary and part-time jobs. Employment protection legislation was weakened as in the case of workers' rights to claim unfair dismissal for which the qualifying period of employment was increased from six months to two years. Indirectly the reduction of the magnitude of public sector employment through privatisation and the contracting out of former state-provided goods and services reduced the employment security of labour after 1979. Bassett (1995) comments that 'British workers enjoy less job protection than employees in such OECD countries as Turkey and Greece, let alone Germany and Japan' (p. 30). Self-employment was encouraged by Government initiatives like the Enterprise Allowance Scheme which assisted the unemployed in trying to set up their own businesses. If these policies, which were conducive to numerical flexibility, were effective then we would expect to see a decline in the relative importance of full-time permanent employment across the 1980s as firms switched to using part-timers and workers on temporary contracts (atypical employment) and as labour suppliers turned increasingly to self-employment.

ATYPICAL AND SELF-EMPLOYMENT

British Labour Force Survey data in Table 8.3 confirm the decline in full-time employment from 1979 to 1995 and illustrate the growth of part-time working up until 2000, especially for females, along with an evident increase in self-employment in the 1980s, which was partially reversed in the 1990s. Although we appear to have strong circumstantial evidence of significant 1980s' employment trends that reflect aspects of numerical flexibility, more detailed analysis of changes in the British labour market suggests that all is not straightforward. Self-employment grows during the early 1980s' recession and the late 1980s' boom, then it falls during the early 1990s' recession and the late 1990s' boom.

Part-time employment has been growing in significance in the UK throughout the post-war period: however, the figures in Table 8.4 indicate a more rapid growth in the 1970s than in the 1980s, with the first half of the 1990s recording an almost static share for part-timers and the late 1990s witnessing a slight fall in the proportion of part-time employment.

Table 8.3 Forms of employment, Great Britain, 1979–2000 (thousands, not seasonally adjusted)

	Full-time		Part-time		Self-employment	
	male	*female*	*male*	*female*	*male*	*female*
1979	13,380	9,197	n.a.	n.a.	1,444	344
1985	11,136	5,017	437	4,040	2,029	685
1990	11,349	5,851	594	4,460	2,628	845
1995	10,539	5,802	803	4,530	2,470	798
2000	11,514	6,170	945	4,607	2,104	743

Sources: ONS, *Labour Force Survey Historical Supplement*, April 1993, July 1995, Spring 2000

Table 8.4 UK part-time employment (percentage of total employment)

1971	1981	1987	1989	1991	1995	2000
15.0	20.6	22.8	23.0	24.6	24.0	23.0

Source: Employment Department

Table 8.5 OECD part-time employment (percentage of total employment)

	1985	1990	1997	2000
Austria	7.0	n.a.	10.8	12.2
Belgium*	8.6	14.2	16.2	19.0
Denmark*	24.3	19.2	17.1	15.7
Finland	8.2	7.5	9.4	10.4
France	10.9	12.2	14.9	14.2
Germany	12.8	13.4	15.8	17.6
Greece	5.3	6.7	8.2	5.4
Ireland	6.5	9.8	15.2	18.4
Italy	5.3	8.8	11.3	12.2
Luxembourg	n.a.	7.6	11.1	13.0
Netherlands*	22.7	28.2	29.1	32.1
Portugal	6.0	6.8	10.2	9.2
Spain	5.8	4.6	7.9	7.8
Sweden*	25.4	14.5	14.2	14.0
UK	21.2	20.1	22.9	23.0
Australia	n.a.	22.6	26.0	26.2
Canada	n.a.	17.0	19.1	18.1
Japan	16.2	19.2	23.3	23.1
New Zealand	n.a.	19.6	22.4	22.6
Norway	n.a.	21.8	21.0	20.3
USA*	18.4	13.8	13.6	12.8

Source: OECD, *Employment Outlook* 2001
Note: * series change after 1985.

We already know from Table 1.10 that part-time working is a predominantly female phenomenon; the data in Table 8.5 shows part-time working grew between 1985 and 2000 in a range of OECD countries with the exception of Denmark, Norway, Sweden, Greece and the USA. Apart from the Netherlands, the UK stands out because of making greater use of part-time employment than other EU countries. This may well reflect the fact that until late 1994 part-time workers in the UK did not receive equal treatment in terms of holiday, sickness, termination and redundancy benefits. Lower wage rates and shorter average hours for females combine to produce the discrepancy between male and female earnings. Humphries and Rubery (1995) found that while full-time women workers gained in terms of relative pay during the 1980s, the 'terms and conditions of part-time employees . . . deteriorated significantly over the decade' (p. 246) to widen the gap between male and female part-time pay. In 2000 the Netherlands had the highest rate of part-time employment in the EU, with

Table 8.6 UK involuntary part-time working, 1984–99 (percentage of employees and self-employed working part-time)

	Total	Males		Females	
		Married	Single	Married	Single
1984	10	19	18	6	17
1987	9	23	20	6	14
1990	6	17	12	4	11
1991	8	19	13	5	12
1992	11	27	17	7	17
1993	17	33	25	8	18
1994	14	33	25	9	20
1999	11				

Source: ONS, *Labour Force Survey*, Spring various years
Note: For 1990 onwards married includes those 'living together'.

UK rates comparable to those of Norway, New Zealand and Japan and yet lower than those in Australia. Note the lower overall rates of part-time working in the Southern European countries (Greece, Portugal and Spain).

Recent Labour Force Survey data on the proportion of workers who feel forced to take a part-time job shows that involuntary part-time employment is clearly cyclical (i.e., falling in booms and rising in recessions) and is consistently greater amongst men, especially married men. The data in Table 8.6 shows that the incidence of working part-time because they could not find a full-time job is substantially greater for single women, whereas the vast majority of married women would appear to be content with working part-time.

Internationally the UK is not exceptional when it comes to involuntary part-time working. In 1991 for example when 1.8 per cent of UK employees were in part-time work against their will, this compared with a 14 country OECD average of 2.5 per cent, including 0.6 per cent in Germany, 2.2 per cent in the USA, and 4.1 per cent for Canada. This accords with Bentolila and Dolado's (1994) view that 'part-time jobs mostly play the role of matching the needs of employers and employees, rather than the flexibility-enhancing role' (p. 65).

As with part-timers, involuntary temporary working is evidently cyclical (falling during recessions, see Table 8.7) but with much higher rates of dissatisfaction among workers on temporary employment contracts.

Almost a quarter of British temporary workers are casual employees working mainly in distribution, hotels and public services. Most fixed contract workers are in the state sector, especially in education and the health service. Most male fixed contract workers are in construction, with most temporary female workers employed in clerical work, catering and cleaning. As Robinson (1994) maintains, 'there appears to be no obvious empirical backing for the growth of a core–periphery model in manufacturing firms' (p. 9), as the temporary employment pattern of the early 1990s is very 'traditional' in terms of the industries and occupations in which it is concentrated.

Table 8.7   UK involuntary temporary working, 1984–99
(percentage of employees working temporarily)

	Total	Males	Females
1984	35	44	28
1987	30	43	23
1990	24	30	21
1991	28	35	24
1992	36	43	31
1993	42	48	37
1994	42	48	37
1995	43	50	37
1996	41	47	36
1997	38	44	34
1998	36	42	31
1999	35	40	30

Source: ONS, *Labour Force Survey*, Spring various years

There is no firm evidence from the data in Table 8.8 that there has been any marked shift towards using temporary employment as a means of making the labour market more numerically flexible in the UK during the 1980s. From regular Labour Force Survey figures we know that temporary employment as a percentage of total employment is procyclical, rising during booms and falling in recessions. With the notable exception of Spain and to a lesser extent France, there has been no general trend towards increasing temporary employment elsewhere in the OECD during the 1980s (Table 8.8). UK employment protection legislation has never restricted the use of temporary employment contracts. Germany eased its restrictions on fixed-term employment in 1985 although this has had little discernible impact on the use of temporary contracts in German labour markets. In 1986 France eased constraints on fixed-term employment and extended the duration of such contracts to two years, which appears to have encouraged their use.

During the 1990s, however, the proportion of temporary employment increased in ten of the fifteen countries in Table 8.8. The percentage of temporary workers remained roughly constant in Japan and Spain and fell slightly in Denmark and Greece. As a point of comparison, 2.2 per cent of US employment was on fixed term contracts in 1996.

The rapid increase in the proportion of workers on fixed term contracts in the Netherlands, coupled with the rise in part-time employment we noted in Table 8.5, are elements of what has been referred to as the 'Dutch miracle'.

The rapidly increasing use of temporary employment in Spain reflects firms' increasing use of fixed-term contracts to evade the dismissals regulations that apply to full-time employees. Before 1984 the use of fixed-term contracts was limited to seasonal work; once this was relaxed there was a rapid growth in the use of fixed-term contracts for non-seasonal work especially in manufacturing. Since 1991 the percentage of total employment that was fixed term in Spain has remained around 30 per cent. Guell and

Table 8.8 Temporary employment, percentage of total dependent employment (excludes self-employed)

	1983	1987	1991	1998
Austria	n.a.	n.a.	n.a.	7.8
Belgium	5.4	5.6	5.1	7.8
Denmark*	12.3	11.2	11.9	10.1
Finland*	10.5	n.a.	12.0	17.7
France	3.3	7.1	10.2	13.9
Germany	10.0	11.6	9.5	12.3
Greece	16.3	16.6	14.7	13.0
Ireland (1996)	6.2	8.6	8.2	9.2
Italy	6.6	5.4	5.4	8.6
Japan (1996)	n.a.	10.5	10.5	10.4
Netherlands*	7.5	n.a.	7.6	12.7
Portugal	n.a.	17.0	16.5	17.3
Spain*	11.3	15.6	32.2	32.9
Sweden	n.a.	n.a.	10.0	12.9
UK	5.5	6.3	5.3	7.1

Source: OECD, Employment Outlook, July 1991, 1993, 1998
Note: * 1985.

Petrongolo (2000) find that Spanish employers seem to use one year fixed-term contracts as a probation device for new workers, especially for females and skilled workers. Firms are also willing to take on workers permanently after 3 years on fixed-term contracts as the only way to retain workers. Bentolila and Dolado (1994) compare the growth of temporary employment with employers' perceptions of labour market rigidity. Their results, illustrated in Figure 8.1, show the most rapid increases in the use of fixed-term contracts between 1985 and 1991 took place in those countries considered to have the most rigid labour markets. The UK records a low growth in temporary working and is considered the most flexible labour market in the EU.

De Grip et al. (1997) believe that in Europe the rise in part-time employment might help offset the increase in the unemployment rate, whereas temporary employment has no such effect and whose growth reflects the weaker labour market position of workers in times of high and rising unemployment.

Self-employment in the UK certainly grew more rapidly in the 1980s than previously. As the data in Table 8.9 shows, about 7 per cent of UK employees were self-employed in 1980, which amounted to 1.9 million persons. By 1993 there were 2.9 million self-employed, virtually 12 per cent of the workforce in employment in the UK. In September 1995 this figure had risen to 3.3 million or 13 per cent of total employment. Self-employment in the UK is a predominantly male phenomenon and is concentrated in the service sector. Some three-quarters of British self-employed workers are male. Campbell and Daly (1992) estimate that around 70 per cent of the growth in self-employment in the UK during the 1980s was in the construction industry, financial and other services. Self-employment actually fell by 11 per cent between

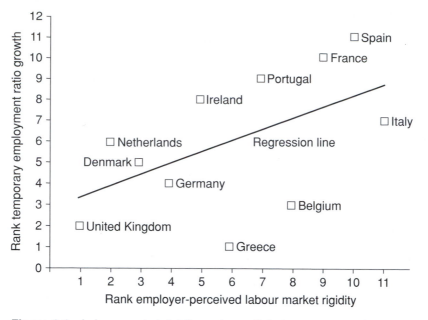
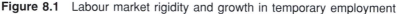

Figure 8.1 Labour market rigidity and growth in temporary employment

Source: Bentolila and Dolado, 1994, figure 1, p. 65
Note: 1 represents the least regulated market and lowest increase in temporary working;
11 the most rigid and greatest increase.

June 1990 and June 1993, with construction, hotels and distribution being particularly severely affected. This recent decline translates into male self-employment falling by 325,000 and female self-employment reduced by some 45,000. UK Government policy encouraged self-employment because of supposed links between the entrepreneurship, innovation and higher productivity of the self-employed. Self-employment was promoted as a means of increasing employment and as an escape route from unemployment. The Enterprise Allowance Scheme that channelled Government assistance to the self-employed during the 1980s was replaced in 1991 by the less generous Business Start Up Scheme; these policy initiatives may well have impacted on the fortunes of the self-employed. Crouchly *et al.*'s (1994) analysis does suggest a 'political' effect for male self-employment but not for female, with self-employment being insensitive to tax rates yet showing some susceptibility to interest rates.

The growth in numerical flexibility proxied by the growth in self-employment witnessed in the UK during the 1980s was not a widespread phenomenon. Table 8.9 shows that self-employment grew more rapidly in the UK in the 1980s than in any other advanced industrialised economy in Europe, apart from Finland, Ireland and Italy, which is an exceptional case with a tradition of reliance on self-employment. Austria, Denmark, France, Greece and the Netherlands all experienced reductions in the significance of self-employment during the 1980s. During the 1990s substantial increases in self-employment within Europe appear to have been confined to the

Table 8.9 Self-employment, 1970–2000, percentage of total employment (excludes agriculture)

	1970	1973	1980	1983	1990	1993	2000
Austria (1999)	12.7	11.7	8.8	8.1	6.6	6.3	7.4
Belgium (1998)	12.0	11.2	11.3	12.3	12.9	13.6	13.9
Czech Republic	n.a.	n.a.	n.a.	n.a.	n.a.	9.3	14.5
Denmark (1981)	10.5	9.3	8.3	8.5	7.2	7.0	6.6
Finland (1971)	6.7	6.5	6.0	7.0	9.3	9.9	9.7
France	12.5	11.4	10.7	10.0	9.3	8.8	8.1
Germany	10.3	9.1	7.0	7.4	8.5	8.2	9.2
Greece (1977)	n.a.	30.9	30.9	27.9	27.4	28.2	25.9
Ireland	10.8	10.1	10.3	10.7	13.1	14.0	12.9
Italy	24.5	23.1	19.2	20.7	22.2	22.3	23.2
Luxembourg (1999)	12.7	10.8	9.4	8.7	7.1	6.1	5.8
Netherlands (1975,1999)	n.a.	9.2	9.1	8.6	7.8	8.7	9.3
Norway	8.6	7.8	6.5	6.8	6.1	6.2	4.8
Poland (1998)	2.7	2.5	3.4	4.4	9.2	11.1	11.7
Portugal	13.1	12.7	14.9	17.0	16.7	18.1	16.8
Spain	16.1	16.3	16.3	17.0	17.1	18.6	16.0
Sweden*	5.6	4.8	4.5	4.8	7.3	8.7	8.9
UK	6.7	7.3	7.1	8.6	12.4	11.6	10.8
Australia	9.3	9.5	12.7	12.1	12.3	13.5	11.7
Canada	7.0	6.2	6.6	7.1	7.2	8.4	9.3
Japan	14.2	14.0	13.7	13.3	11.5	10.3	9.3
Korea (South)	n.a.	n.a.	27.1	27.1	21.8	23.1	24.8
New Zealand#	7.5	10.5	9.0	17.0	14.4	15.8	16.6
USA	6.9	6.7	7.3	7.8	7.5	7.6	6.6

Source: OECD, *Labour Force Statistics*, 1995, 2001
Note: * data series changes between 1983 and 1990, # 1971, 1976, 1986.

former Communist countries (Czech Republic, Poland) and Sweden. The pattern reflects high rates of self-employment in Southern Europe and Ireland with the rest of the EU having generally lower rates of self-employment. Overall there does not appear to have been any marked convergence between the countries of the EU since 1980 in terms of atypical (part-time and temporary) employment nor in self-employment. Of the other countries in Table 8.9 Canada and New Zealand witnessed increases in self-employment during both the 1980s and the 1990s; Australia and Japan recorded decreases in the proportion of self-employment. Between 1980 and 2000 self-employment fell in countries as diverse as South Korea and the USA.

Perhaps as a result of Government policies to enhance labour market flexibility, full-time workers in the UK work more hours per week than their European counterparts. The data in Table 8.10 shows this to have been the case in 1985, 1990 and 1995. Over this period average working hours per week have increased by one hour in the UK whereas full-time workers in Austria, Denmark, Germany, Greece, Netherlands, Ireland, and Italy have enjoyed shortening working weeks. By 1995 workers in the UK worked on average 2.7 hours per week longer than Portuguese workers and

Table 8.10 Employees' average total usual working hours per week (hours per week, full-time work)

	1985	1990	1995
Austria	40.7	40.1	39.3
Belgium	38.1	38.0	38.4
Denmark	40.6	39.0	39.0
France	39.5	39.6	39.9
Finland	n.a.	38.4	38.6
Germany	40.1	39.9	39.7
Greece	40.7	40.1	40.3
Netherlands	41.7	39.0	39.5
Ireland	40.4	40.4	40.2
Italy	38.8	38.6	38.4
Portugal	n.a.	41.9	41.2
Spain	n.a.	40.7	40.7
Sweden	n.a.	40.7	40.0
UK	42.9	43.7	43.9

Source: *Eurostat Yearbook*, 1997

over 4 hours per week longer than German workers. This situation may change following a ruling by the European Court of Justice in November 1996 which means that, in spite of the UK Government 'opt out' of the Social Contract of the Maastricht Treaty, the UK will have to implement an EU health and safety directive on working time, and the new Labour Government's April 1998 White Paper stated intention to adopt the Directive. The Directive imposes:

- a maximum 48 hour working week, including overtime;
- a minimum 3 weeks paid holiday per year, rising to 4 weeks in 1999;
- a maximum 8 hour shift in any 24 hour period for nightworkers;
- a minimum 11 hour daily rest;
- a minimum 24 hour rest period per week.

Perhaps the Directive's main impact will be on the 2.5 million UK workers who are believed to have had no paid annual leave in 1995 (IDS 1996).

LABOUR MARKET POLICY ASSESSED

Whether wage flexibility has increased over time is a difficult problem to solve. A study by Nickell *et al.* (2000) found that while the probability of continuously employed British male workers experiencing a 10 per cent or more reduction in real hourly pay had increased between the early 1980s and mid-1990s, a clear sign of greater wage insecurity, this was due to the fact that average rises in real pay were smaller in the 1990s than in the 1980s. This would shift the whole of the real wage change distribution to the left making negative pay rises more likely. Yet the study did find that real wage rate reduction probabilities had increased for older and more highly skilled workers between 1982 and 1996. In spite of this, real hourly pay reductions remained more likely for less skilled workers.

Pencavel (1994) reports that 'from 1960 to 1990 total employment increased by 10 per cent in the United Kingdom and by 77 per cent in the United States' (p. 622). Whereas American unemployment rates rose from 5.5 per cent in the early 1960s (1961–5) to 5.9 per cent in the late 1980s (1986–90), the corresponding figures for the UK were 1.6 per cent and 9.5 per cent respectively (Pencavel 1994, table 1, p. 623). The UK unemployment rate was 1.4 per cent in 1955, 2.2 per cent in 1960, 3.0 per cent in 1970, and 4.5 per cent in 1975. The years of the first Thatcher Government witnessed the unemployment rate rise from 5.0 per cent in 1979 to 12.5 per cent in 1983, with the subsequent economic recovery and Lawson boom still leaving the unemployment rate at 6.8 per cent in 1990. Unemployment then rose again to reach 10.4 per cent by the end of 1992. Unemployment began falling in February 1993 but still stood at 8 per cent at the end of 1996.[2] Although the comparative unemployment experience of the UK does not appear to have been markedly better than that of the USA during the 1980s and 1990s, Nickell *et al.* (2000) reported 'little or no evidence of any trend increase in the chances of men becoming unemployed over the last twenty years' (p. 11).

In general, policies designed to increase numerical flexibility appear not to have increased the mobility of UK labour. Blanchflower and Freeman (1993) calculate that for males the probability of making the transition from unemployment to working actually fell from 0.46 in 1979 to 0.32 in 1990. For females there was virtually no change with probabilities in both years at around 0.43 (their table 4, p. 22).

The increasing use of temporary contracts in Spain seems to have been a mixed blessing; Guell (2001) found that while total outflows from unemployment had increased it was mainly among those who had become unemployed because a temporary contract had come to an end – workers who were unemployed for any other reason tended to remain unemployed for longer after the introduction of temporary contracts (i.e., their unemployment duration dependence increased).

Summarising employment developments in the UK which should reflect numerical flexibility in the labour market, Robinson (1994) reminds us that the

> share of part-time employment is growing, but more slowly now than in past decades. The share of temporary employment is not growing at all. Whereas the share of self-employment did grow sharply after 1979, this growth went into reverse after 1990.
>
> (p. 10)

Rather than there being a simple link between one aspect of flexibility and performance, the relationship could be more complicated. Michie and Sheehan (1999) found that firms which used more modern human resource management methods and innovative work practices tended to engage in more research and development activity and more readily embrace technical change. This was not true of firms that sought more flexibility by relying on atypical employment.

Changes in labour law since 1979 could be regarded as conducive to increasing functional and work time flexibility by allowing management to introduce changes in working conditions. Indeed the lengthy newspaper industry disputes, which began in 1983, centred around the introduction of labour saving technology and the trade unions' involvement in setting and regulating workplace practices (Elgar and Simpson 1993). It is an example of what Deakin (1992) had in mind when he pointed out that Government trade union legislation in the 1980s increased the 'availability to firms of injunctions and related court interventions [providing] a powerful weapon which employers in some sectors used to limit union power' (p. 179). Yet extreme care must be taken over simply ascribing the decline in union power to Government-initiated changes in labour law, because, as we already know from Chapter 7, union density fell in a very wide range of OECD economies often without any legislative tightening. Furthermore, union density in the UK was in decline well before the most important piece of labour market legislation, the 1982 Employment Act, came into effect. Milner and Metcalf (1991) show that the UK strike record of the 1970s was not excessive compared to its previous experience and strike activity was falling towards an OECD average before the 1980s. Reductions in union density and strike activity may have had more to do with the rise in unemployment, the shift from manufacturing to services, falling public sector employment, and changes in the composition of the employed labour force (Towers, 1989; McConnell and Takla, 1990). However, it is undoubtedly the case that organised labour in the UK lost power in the 1980s. Data from the Workplace Industrial Relations Survey (WIRS) reveals that whereas in 1980 some two-thirds of workplaces were covered by a union negotiated collective agreement, by 1990 that proportion had fallen to just over half. Dismissals had increased from 9 per 1,000 workers in 1984 to 15 per 1,000 in 1990. A quarter of non-unionised workplaces had no proper disciplinary, grievance or health and safety procedures. Bargaining during the 1980s became increasingly decentralised, moving away from national agreements to focus on the workplace and, in the case of performance related pay, on the individual worker. However, in spite of a degree of 'individualisation of employment relationships', Deakin (1992) finds 'very little concrete evidence of systematic changes in recruitment strategies or in the arrangement of working time' (p. 186).

Increased functional flexibility and working time flexibility should, according to the deregulatory view, improve labour productivity. Table 8.11 shows that productivity growth accelerated in the UK in the 1980s compared to the 1970s. Labour productivity growth also improved compared to that recorded in other industrialised countries; as the UK moves from below average OECD performance in the 1960s and 1970s to record an above average growth rate for the 1980s.

Although both the extent of, and the reasons for this improved productivity performance are far from clear (see Chapter 2) it does not appear as though firms were fundamentally improving the quality of inputs through investment, research and development, (Haskel and Kay, 1990; and Buxton, 1994b) and education and training (see Chapter 5). In the context of labour market flexibility, Blanchflower and Freeman

Table 8.11 Labour productivity growth, 1960–99 (annual average percentage change)

	1960–73	1973–79	1980–90	1990–95	1995–99
Austria	5.8	3.2	1.9*	n.a.	2.9
Belgium (1970)	5.2	2.7	2.4	2.3	2.4
Denmark	4.3	2.6	1.7	1.9	1.6
Finland (1961)	4.9	3.2	2.8	3.0	2.8
France (1963)	5.4	3.0	2.7	1.8	1.6
Germany	4.5	3.1	2.3	2.2	1.8
Greece (1961)	8.8	3.3	1.3	0.9	2.0
Ireland (1961)	4.9	3.4	3.6	4.0	4.6
Italy	6.3	2.9	2.6	2.3	1.6
Luxembourg	n.a.	n.a.	n.a.	5.5	4.6
Netherlands (1970)	4.8	2.8	2.9	1.9	1.7
Portugal	7.5	0.5	1.7*	2.4	2.2
Spain (1964)	6.0	3.2	3.2	2.0	0.7
Sweden (1965)	3.7	1.5	1.2	1.8	1.6
UK (1962)	3.9	1.5	2.3	1.9	1.9
Australia	n.a.	n.a.	1.2	1.8	2.2
Canada (1966)	2.8	1.5	1.1	1.3	1.4
Japan (1962)	8.3	2.9	3.2	2.6	2.2
Korea	n.a.	n.a.	6.3	5.3	4.7
New Zealand	n.a.	n.a.	n.a.	0.5	0.9
Norway (1966)	3.7	−0.5	2.6	3.1	2.0
USA	2.2	0.0	1.3	1.3	2.0

Sources: OECD, *Economic Outlook*, 1994; Economics Department Working Paper 248, 2000
Notes: 1960–79 output per person employed; 1980–99 output per hour worked. Taking account of the hours worked will tend to reduce the measure of productivity compared to productivity per person employed.
* 1979–92.

(1993) point to 'a pattern of faster productivity growth in union than in non-union firms, suggesting that unions reduced restrictive work practices and took a more positive attitude toward productivity' (p. 6) during the 1980s. In spite of this, UK labour productivity growth slowed during the 1990s. Korea, Luxembourg and Ireland recorded the fastest labour productivity growth of the OECD countries during the 1990s. New Zealand and Spain both took steps to make their labour markets more flexible yet they recorded some of the slowest productivity growth rates in the 1990s.

When it comes to translating productivity growth into international competitiveness, Buxton (1994a) finds that between 1980 and 1990 the improvement in the UK's relative unit labour cost position (RULC), relative that is to our main trading competitors, primarily 'came about from the decline in the effective exchange rate' (p. 63). Figure 8.2 shows that after 1985 the growth of relative wage costs per person (RWCPP) outpaced the growth in relative labour productivity (RLP). Note how closely relative unit labour costs (RULC) track the effective exchange rate (EER) of sterling.

Given the link between the presence of trade unions and productivity improvements and the strong correlation of international labour cost competitiveness with

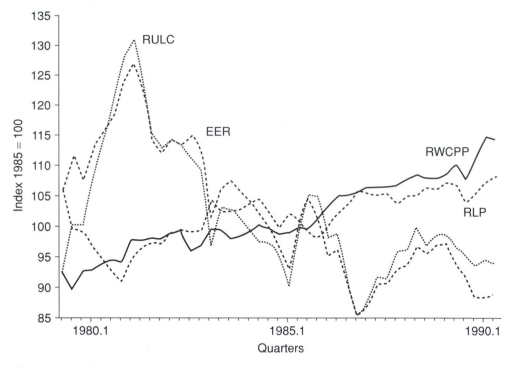

Figure 8.2 UK international competitiveness, 1979–90

Source: Buxton, 1994a, figure 4.4, p. 63

movements in the exchange rate, one must be cautious in assessing the contributions of labour market functional and working time flexibility.

Marsden (1995) maintains that 'in terms of internal flexibility within the enterprise, then, German firms would appear to be better placed than either their French or British counterparts' (p. 46). This seems to arise because German firms build strong internal labour markets on a foundation of technical competence that is the result of employer led initial vocational training. Given good employment security, high levels of trust through channels of management disclosure and occupational labour markets German workers have strong incentives to accept internal flexibility. Generally EU countries lie between Japan, where employment stability in large firms is higher but so is internal flexibility, and the USA, which may have lower internal flexibility but has much higher employment flexibility (laying off and hiring workers). According to Marsden (1995) EU countries have

> the worst of both worlds . . . [as a] . . . combination of employment stability and lack of internal flexibility could discourage employers from hiring new labour. First, it makes employment adjustments more difficult because it is harder to use redeployment of staff as an alternative. Secondly, if ILMs are fairly rigid, then it will make it harder for firms to use such practices as job rotation to enhance skills.
>
> (p. 47)

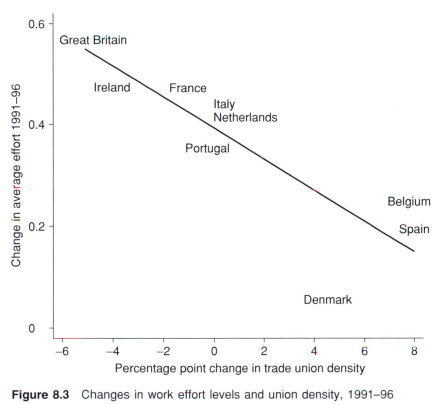

Figure 8.3 Changes in work effort levels and union density, 1991–96

Source: Green and McIntosh 2000, figure 3, p. 24

Dyer (1998) questions the whole concept of flexibility whether it arises from flexible specialisation, the flexible firm or lean production. She argues that 'rather than flexibility representing a fundamental shift in the way work is organised . . . it is more about intensifying the control of capital over labour by using new management techniques' (p. 232). Atypical employment and increasing work effort are symptoms of this greater control over labour. Green and McIntosh (2000) found that between 1991 and 1996 there had been an increase in work effort in the EU, especially in Britain. Work effort was defined in terms of speed of work and meeting tight deadlines. The change in effort levels in Britain was +0.56 (on a 1–7 scale) whereas in Denmark it was only +0.06. New technology and competition appeared to encourage greater effort. Employment protection legislation did not influence work effort but the decline in trade union power (density) was highly correlated with the rise in effort. The relationship between changes in trade union density and effort levels is illustrated in Figure 8.3.

Those countries where union density rose in the early 1990s, namely Denmark, Belgium and Spain, recorded the smallest increases in work effort. The greatest rise in work effort was experienced in those countries, Britain and Ireland, which had witnessed the greatest falls in trade union density. However, Green and McIntosh's

(2000) results leave plenty of scope for flexibility to account for some of the increase in work intensity, as they explain, 'we hypothesise that it is at least in part related to changing work procedures' (p. 14).

Nicoletti *et al.* (2001) point out that in order to obtain full advantage from increased labour flexibility, labour market reforms need to be accompanied by reducing barriers to trade and competition. Product market liberalisation in New Zealand and the UK (leading reform countries) is estimated to have increased employment rates by around 2.5 percentage points over the 1978–98 period; whereas more modest liberalisation in Greece, Italy and Spain added only approximately 0.4–1.0 percentage points to employment rates.

EUROPEAN MONETARY UNION AND LABOUR MARKET FLEXIBILITY

Eleven EU states embarked on the historic move to form a monetary union in January 1999. This resulted in the introduction of the Euro as a fully fledged working currency in January 2002. The likely success of this European Monetary Union (EMU) will depend upon a variety of political considerations such as national sovereignty and popular sentiment, as well as economic factors like synchronised growth cycles and convergent monetary and fiscal conditions. The political aspects have already kept Denmark, Sweden and the UK out of EMU, whereas a failure to meet the latter criteria barred Greece from entering the 'first wave' of the single currency project. Yet a key ingredient to the viability and likely impact of a single currency in Europe will be the nature and behaviour of labour markets across Europe. This section establishes the theoretical importance of labour market flexibility and labour mobility in a single currency area, before considering the nature and extent of such flexibility and mobility in the countries of the EU.

The conventional analysis of the role of labour under conditions of a common currency, such as those created by EMU, stems from the 'theory of optimum currency areas' developed by Mundell (1961) and McKinnon (1963). The most challenging scenario for countries in a single currency area is when they are subject to forces that have opposite effects on their economies, so called 'asymmetric shocks'. Take the example of a shift in EU consumer preferences away from UK goods towards German made products. The initial impact would be that

> output falls in the UK and
> output increases in Germany.

This would mean that

> unemployment would tend to rise in the UK and
> unemployment begin to fall in Germany.

Following the absorption approach which views the current account of the balance of payments as the relationship between domestic output minus domestic demand, the effect would be to move towards

UK current account deficit and
UK Government budget deficit.

This twin deficit problem arises (or in the case of existing deficits, worsens) because: UK output falls by more than UK domestic spending, due to the welfare benefit system automatically giving the unemployed spending power even though they do not contribute to output; UK income and corporation tax receipts fall and unemployment benefit payments rise during a recession. Conversely there is a move towards

German current account surplus and
upward pressure on the German price level.

The balance of payments improves as German consumer spending increases by less than the rise in the value of output because some of the rise in income is saved. Inflationary pressures increase because of the rise in demand for German output both at home and elsewhere in the EU.

Given that the UK and Germany are not in a single currency area, exchange rate adjustment which allows the German Mark to appreciate or the Pound to devalue, would reverse the original demand shifts as UK goods become more price competitive compared to German products. Such an exchange rate movement holds out the promise of solving the UK unemployment problem and the German inflation problem whilst moving the current account balances back towards equilibrium.

However, if the UK and Germany were joined in a monetary union such a simple exchange rate adjustment would no longer be an option. The situation could be brought back to equilibrium only by wage flexibility or labour mobility. Wage flexibility would require

- UK workers reducing their wages in the face of rising unemployment, while
- German workers increased their wages when faced with falling unemployment.

Such wage changes would push down the price of UK output making UK products more price competitive and push up the price of German products, thereby improving the UK current account and budget deficits as output and employment expand to meet rising demand.

Labour mobility would bring about a new equilibrium as unemployed workers migrate from the UK to Germany. Hence there would be no need for wages to fall in the UK or to rise in Germany as the UK's unemployment problem vanishes and inflationary pressures in Germany disappear.

Economic problems arising from an asymmetric shock would persist if wages in the UK were inflexible and if UK workers were immobile. Then all the burden of adjustment would rest on inflation in Germany leading to price rises, which would restore the price competitiveness of UK products. Yet the problem is compounded if Germany counters these inflationary pressures with tight monetary and fiscal policies preserving their own current account surplus, which means that the UK is stuck with unemployment and persistent deficits. Given that the European Central Bank is tasked with enforcing prudent monetary and fiscal policies to control inflation, this is a likely response to the increase in inflationary pressures. Hence the key conclusion to be reached is that monetary union between countries is only optimal as long as there is

> sufficient wage flexibility, and/or
> sufficient labour mobility.

Therefore the degree of labour flexibility and the extent of labour mobility within the EU are issues of crucial importance in the debate over monetary union.

An additional factor that could complicate monetary union is the existence of different labour market institutions (e.g., trade unions). Calmfors and Driffill (1988) suggested that there are differences in the degree of centralisation of wage bargaining between countries and that these could lead to different price, wage and employment outcomes. If countries in a monetary union have different labour market institutions, then when faced with the same economic shock, they may well react differently. For example the 1979–80 recession provided an adverse supply-side shock to all industrialised economies, yet in highly centralised Germany the reduction in aggregate supply was less marked than in the UK. More co-ordinated wage bargaining in Germany was able to deliver wage restraint whereas the more fragmented framework in the UK found it much more difficult to deliver wage moderation.

Given the importance of wage flexibility, which arises from optimum currency area theory and from consideration of labour market institutions we need to examine such flexibility within Europe.

WAGE FLEXIBILITY

It has become an aspect of conventional economic wisdom that the reason for the poorer unemployment performance of the EU in general and the UK in particular, compared to that of the USA, is because greater wage rigidity in Europe prevents the growth of employment. Figure 8.4 illustrates in a simple manner the fact that since 1970 the USA has recorded rapid employment growth combined with modest real wage increases; whereas in the UK rapid rises in the real wages of the already employed appear to have prevented the generation of net additional employment.

Between 1970 and 2000 employment in the USA grew by 72 per cent and real wages rose by almost 20 per cent, whereas in the UK employment expanded by 14 per cent as real wages increased by 70 per cent. Figure 8.4 does seem to support a standard labour supply and demand argument that greater responsiveness on the part of American labour suppliers moderating real wages to the recessionary circumstances of the mid-1970s, early 1980s and early 1990s, contributed to a better performance in subsequent employment generation. A number of studies confirm this impression of greater aggregate real wage flexibility in the USA yielding superior employment outcomes (e.g., Krugman 1990, Freeman 1995), with European labour markets frequently diagnosed as suffering from: higher trade union density; greater collective wage bargaining; and

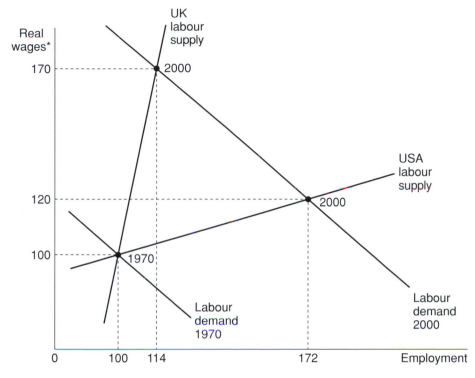

Figure 8.4

Source: USA Bureau of Labour Statistics 2001; UK Office of National Statistics 2001
Note: * using GDP deflator.

higher welfare benefit levels. However, the comparison between Europe and the USA is somewhat more complex than the conventional view suggests; union membership (density) is greater in most EU countries than the USA, yet American unions are more effective in terms of wage (mark-up) bargaining than European unions. While welfare benefits do not last long in the USA, they are more generous (replacement ratio) than those provided by a number of EU states including the UK. While studies by Layard *et al.* (1991) and Elmeskov and Pichelmann (1993) do find that the USA exhibits a higher degree of real wage flexibility than some European countries, the rankings in Table 8.12 show that the US labour market is not thought to be more wage flexible than all EU national labour markets. Although such a ranking may be susceptible to differences in model specification and different sample periods, it does serve to show that the US labour market is not simply more wage flexible than European labour markets. Smith (2000) found that over the 1991–6 period some 9 per cent of British employees who remain in the same job from one year to another have no nominal pay increase. However, Nickell and Quintini (2001) found that taking a two-year period this proportion fell to 1 per cent, with more than 10 per cent of workers having falling nominal hourly wage rates in the low inflation environment of the UK in the 1990s. Median real wage changes were positive.

Table 8.12 Real wage flexibility ranking, USA and EU countries

	Period 1 1956–85	Period 2 1970–91
Most flexible	Italy	Sweden
↑	Sweden	Austria
	Austria	Germany
	France	Finland
	Belgium	France
	USA	UK
	Netherlands	Netherlands
	Ireland	Spain
	Finland	Ireland, Italy
	Spain	USA
	Germany	Portugal
↓	UK	Belgium
Least flexible		Denmark

Sources: Period 1, Layard, Nickell and Jackman, 1991; period 2, Elmeskov and Pichelmann, 1993

Blanchflower and Oswald (1995) examine wage flexibility at the regional rather than the national level and find a very similar degree of responsiveness between local wages and local unemployment rates in both the USA and the EU.

The growth of income inequality in the USA and the UK (Atkinson, 1997), the European country which was most determined to attempt to emulate American labour markets through government policy during the 1980s, bears witness to an element of wage flexibility; the relative wages of the poorly qualified and low skilled have declined in both countries (Nickell and Bell 1995). Yet while this has been accompanied by overall employment expansion in the USA, this has not been the case in the UK. Such considerations lead Martin (1998) to observe that 'wage flexibility of itself, therefore, is unlikely to solve the European unemployment problem in general' (p. 37).

In spite of the fact that EU member states might exhibit levels of aggregate real wage flexibility comparable to those of the USA, European economic integration still faces a wage flexibility problem. The existence of a range of such flexibility in the EU does mean that European labour markets will generate different wage and employment responses even when confronted with symmetric shocks in a single currency environment; and that these differences will be delineated along national lines. Additionally, despite the fact that rates of job creation and job destruction are similar in Western Europe and the USA (Bertola and Rogerson 1997), Decressin and Fatas (1995) point to a far greater similarity in regional employment change in the USA (60 per cent) between 1966 and 1987 than in the EU (20 per cent); with Europe also exhibiting greater differences in the amplitude of year on year employment changes. Perhaps increasing international labour mobility within the EU will lessen the significance of differences in wage flexibility and employment volatility within Europe? As we shall discover in the next section, the main advantage that US labour markets have over European ones is greater labour mobility.

Table 8.13 Source relative to host country per capita income (GDP using PPP $), 1997

Host country	Source to host ratio (as percentage)
Australia	61
Belgium	78
Canada	44
Denmark	70
Finland	43
France	28
Germany	47
Italy	41
Japan	43
Netherlands	73
Norway	72
Sweden	90
Switzerland	76
UK	72
USA	22

Source: Coppel *et al.*, 2001, table 5, p. 13
Note: Based on 1995–8 immigration flows.

LABOUR MIGRATION

Labour mobility is influenced by a number of factors. Molle and Mourik (1988) group some of the more likely influences on labour migration into four categories:

- push – high unemployment, low wages and few job opportunities in the source country;
- pull – high wages, good social security and many job opportunities in the destination country;
- costs – transaction costs including housing, socio-cultural considerations, linguistic problems and assimilation difficulties;
- regulations – immigration restrictions which are illegal in the case of intra-EU migration of EU citizens.

OECD data, contained in Table 8.13, confirms the fact that in many cases relative incomes in host and source countries can be a powerful incentive to migrate. In seven of the sample of host countries, contained in Table 8.13, including Canada, Finland, Germany and Italy, source country income per capita was less than half that of the host country. This was not the case in the other Scandinavian countries or in Australia, Belgium, Netherlands and the UK. France and especially the USA stand out as countries whose immigration flows come from very low per capita income countries. In the case of France the two main source countries in 1997–8 were Algeria and Morocco; for the USA immigrants came mainly from Mexico and China. By contrast the two main source countries for Belgium immigration were France and the

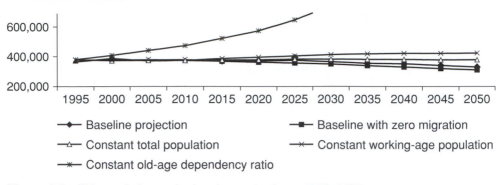

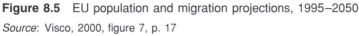

Figure 8.5   EU population and migration projections, 1995–2050

Source: Visco, 2000, figure 7, p. 17

Netherlands. French immigration patterns are dominated by historical (colonial) ties, whereas geographical proximity is dominating immigration to Belgium. The USA displays a mixture of geographical proximity in the case of Mexico, and the fact that Chinese migration is widely dispersed – they are the main immigration ethnic groups in Canada and Japan in 1997–8.

Studies of immigration into the USA, Freidberg and Hunt (1995) find no adverse effect on the unemployment rate. Gross (1999) did find that immigration raised unemployment in France in the short term but caused it to fall permanently in the long term. The contrast with the USA may reflect greater labour market rigidity in France slowing the speed of adjustment to immigration. Coppel *et al.* (2001) report 'no obvious relationship between immigration and unemployment' (p. 14, see also their figure 3, p. 15). The impact of immigration on lowering wages in the host country is generally found to be small. Freidberg and Hunt (1995) estimated that in order for native wages in the USA to fall by 1 per cent, the proportion of immigrants in the population would have to increase by a massive 10 per cent at least. In general the greatest wage impact falls on low skilled workers, with immigration often being found to increase the wages of high skilled host country workers. Visco (2000) contains some population and migration projections. Those for annual net immigration into the EU, reproduced in Figure 8.5, show that some increase in immigration would be required after 2010 in order to maintain a constant total population. A more rapid and larger increase in immigration would be needed during 2010–40 to keep the EU working age population constant. However, immigration levels of enormous magnitudes, 20 million per year during 2030–5, would be required to maintain 1995 old age dependency ratios. This is clearly not feasible given late 1990s net immigration levels in the EU of around 0.85 million per year. So even if EU migration policy were to be relaxed the proportion of old age citizens to those of working age will rise.

Immigration can have other positive effects as new migrant's consumption demands increase employment via derived demand for labour. Immigrants can also enhance labour market flexibility. Indeed the standard economic analysis of labour market integration with regard to labour mobility can be represented by the situation dis-

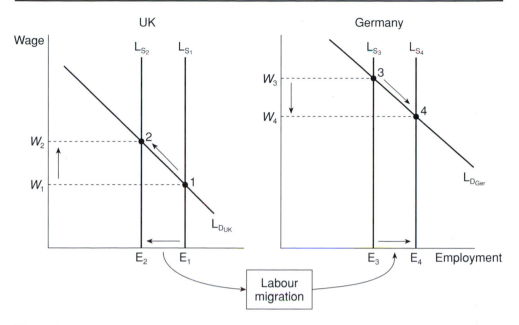

Figure 8.6

played in Figure 8.6. It shows that labour migration from the UK to Germany will narrow wage differentials. The implication of such labour mobility is that any unemployment in the UK or wage inflation pressures in Germany would be eased. If it continued labour migration would, at least in theory, bring about wage equality between the two countries once legitimate transactions costs associated with moving have been accounted for. However, a number of points need to be made about the limitations of this apparently straightforward approach to labour mobility:

- It is a static analysis with a fixed technology and accurate wage information which is freely available in both countries.
- It incorporates a degree of geographical mobility between countries and wage flexibility within countries that may not exist.
- It assumes that labour is homogeneous (and bilingual), in that it is not differentiated by skill and does not encounter problems such as UK qualifications and experience lacking recognition in Germany.
- It presumes that low labour mobility is caused by prohibition. Yet this may not be the case and simply allowing labour migration may not be enough to stimulate it.

Even at the theoretical level the conclusions from such an analysis of labour market integration are readily undermined. In the conventional model of international trade (Heckscher-Ohlin) the import and export of goods and services can substitute for factor flows including the cross border migration of labour. International trade is supposed to take account of different factor availability (endowments) between countries, and it is trade not factor mobility that should bring about factor price (in the case of labour that is wage) convergence. The large scale and rapid growth of intra-EU trade may well have reduced the importance of factor market integration within Europe. Empirical evidence on the relationship between labour mobility and trade within Europe is somewhat mixed. For example, Straubhaar (1988) calculated that the correlation between annual data on intra-EU migration and intra-EU trade from 1958 to 1973 was indeed consistent with the theoretical prediction of substitutability at −0.90. However, during the period 1973 to 1980 the data did not support the predicted substitution relationship with a correlation coefficient of +0.09. For the USA, Wong (1986) estimated a strong complementary relationship between movements of capital and labour and the volume of international trade over the period 1948–83. Rather than international labour migration and capital mobility supplanting trade or vice versa it appears to encourage international trade.

As factors of production, capital and labour can be viewed as substitutes for one another in the production process. In the EU it may well be that capital and labour flows are also substitutes. If it were capital that were immobile and labour that was mobile, then free trade among EU member states could lead to a geographical concentration of production (Amiti, 1997). The consequent agglomeration of the demand for skilled labour should result in higher productivity labour leaving weaker countries/ regions thereby accentuating national/regional labour market inequalities. Given that the most recent policy initiative likely to affect labour migration was the agreement to recognise professional qualifications awarded in other EU states, it may well be that it is the migration of qualified workers rather than unskilled workers that will be encouraged in the single currency area. Such an outcome will be reinforced by the widespread trend decline in the demand for unskilled workers in OECD countries (Nickell and Bell, 1995), which may be explained in terms of technological change (Berman et al., 1997) combined with the impact of increased competition in manufactured goods markets from producers outside the EU (Wood, 1994).

However, it is more likely that it is capital markets that are more highly integrated generating more fluid capital flows rather than labour migrations. Ghosh (1995) provides evidence for high levels of capital mobility for a sample of countries, including Germany and the UK, using data spanning the period 1960–88. International capital flows are not only high but appear to be 'excessive' in relation to the economic shocks experienced by countries during that period, most probably because of speculative short-term capital movements responding to changes in foreign exchange markets. The IMF (1998) attest to the extent of capital mobility when they state that 'by many measures national financial markets have become increasingly integrated into a single global financial system' (p. 188). The introduction of the Euro in the EU has boosted this process. Pelkmans (1997) uses a variant of Krugman's (1979) trade model with mobile capital and immobile labour widening differences between two regions. Figure 8.7 adapts this analysis to represent our own comparison between Germany and the UK. From a position of initial equality (at point B) let us suppose that a greater rate of technical innovation in Germany increases the rate of return on capital employed (shift of A–B line to D–E), which encourages capital flows to favour Germany (move

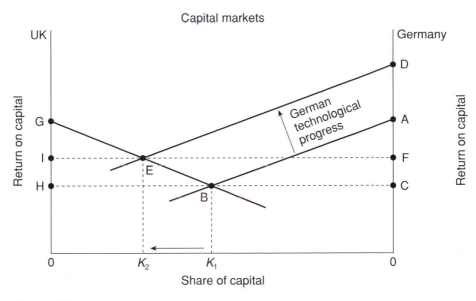

Figure 8.7

from K_1 to K_2). Not only does Germany become more capital rich than the UK but labour incomes increase in Germany (from area ABC to DEF) whilst they decrease in the UK (from area GBH to GEI). Because labour is immobile, migration from the UK to Germany is not permitted to undermine this increase in inequality. We would reasonably expect EMU to further increase cross-border capital flows within Europe, leaving different national rates of profit taxation as the only barrier to a truly common capital market.

In spite of the fact that the free movement of labour between member states was effected in 1968, actual labour migration in the EU is very low with only some 2 per cent of the EU-12 labour force in 1985 and 1990, that is around 1.9 million persons being migrant workers, including frontier dwellers. Over time the volume of migration within Europe has fallen since the large outflows of workers from Southern Europe and Ireland to Northern Europe in the 30 years following the end of the Second World War. For example, Eurostat (1994) data records annual average net emigration during the 1960s of: over 100,000 from Italy; about 60,000 from Spain; and around 40,000 from Greece. In 1960 Ireland experienced net emigration of some 42,000 persons, which by 1969 had fallen to only 7,500.

Teague and Grahl (1992) argue that the larger scale migrations of the 1950s and 1960s were not a byproduct of the creation of the EU since migration from outside the area exceeded that between member states. Straubhaar (1988) confirms this by reporting that during the period 1958–73 over 62 per cent of EU migration activity originated from outside the EU. In fact the pattern of migration in Europe has changed to such an extent that since the mid-1970s some Southern European countries have experienced net immigration (Begg, 1995).

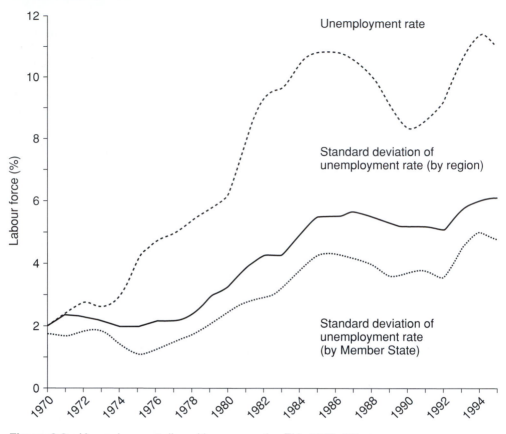

Figure 8.8 Unemployment disparities across the EU, 1970–95

Source: Martin, 1998, figure 1.6, p. 20

The lack of labour mobility in Europe is reflected in different national and regional unemployment rates that persist over time. Figure 8.8 shows that national and especially regional disparities in unemployment rates have indeed persisted within the EU and have widened since unemployment began to rise from the mid-1970s.

Within this general European trend, the UK is unusual in that its regional unemployment rates converged during the early 1990s as the recession hit at traditionally prosperous areas like South East England. Martin (1998) is unsure about whether this convergence in the UK is 'merely temporary or whether [it] represents more permanent features of the country's economic landscape' (p. 25). Indeed there was little evidence of regional convergence in the 1980s when Labour Force Survey data actually recorded some areas of high unemployment in Britain as having experienced net immigration by manual workers (Hughes and McCormick, 1994).

Jackman and Savouri (1991) demonstrate that labour's geographical mobility falls during recessions because of a reduction in the rate at which firms hire labour; hence the close correspondence between movements in vacancy rates and British regional

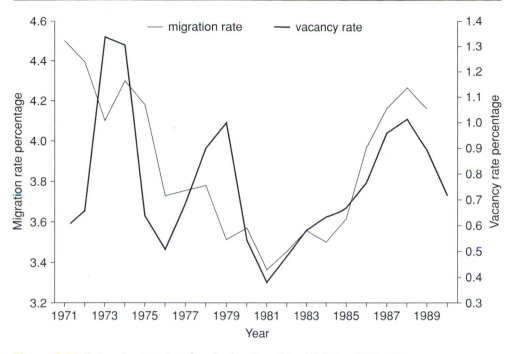

Figure 8.9 Determinants of regional migration, Great Britain, 1971–90

Source: Jackman and Savouri, 1991, figure 3c, p. 55

migration in Figure 8.9. Green *et al.* (1998) report that gross migration rates of the unemployed in Britain fell from just over 2.5 per cent in the mid-1970s to around 1 per cent in the mid-1990s.

Labour migration is much greater in the USA than in Europe. The OECD data presented in Table 8.14 shows that the USA possessed higher rates of internal labour mobility than the major EU countries in both 1975 and 1985. To the data in Table 8.14, there is no evidence that the regional migration differential between the USA and the EU countries has narrowed over time, indeed if anything it has widened.

Table 8.14 Comparative regional migration, 1975 and 1985 (persons changing residence region as percentage of total population)

	1975	*1985*
France	n.a.	1.2
Germany	1.3	1.0
Italy	0.8	0.6
UK	1.2	1.2
USA	3.0	3.0

Source: OECD, *Employment Outlook*, 1990

Table 8.15 Italy: South to North migration rates and unemployment rate differences, 1970–90

	Migration (percentage of population)	Unemployment differential (percentage point difference)
1970	14.5	2.5
1975	9.5	3.0
1980	8.0	5.5
1985	7.0	6.0
1990	6.5	13.0

Source: Faini *et al.*, 1997, figure 1, p. 573
Note: Figures are approximations extracted from a more detailed chart.

Eichengreen (1992) estimates an American inter-regional mobility elasticity with respect to unemployment differentials some 2 times higher than European rates. This may in part reflect the generally higher rates of unemployment across the EU than in the USA, thereby reducing Molle and van Mourik's (1988) 'pull' factor in Europe (see page 269 above). Yet in terms of 'push', Faini *et al.* (1997) show that migrations from Southern Italy to more prosperous Northern Italy have declined markedly in spite of a worsening unemployment differential between the two halves of the country (see Table 8.15). Prominent among their reasons for the decline of migration within Italy were an inefficient inter-regional job matching process, in which the state has a virtual monopoly, and the high cost of mobility caused by rent controls and high taxes on housing transactions.

Antolin and Bover (1997) find that regional migration within Spain is low and has also declined over time. They report net emigration from prosperous (low unemployment) areas and net immigration into higher unemployment areas. Spanish migration, unlike that in the USA, does not seem to be driven by high unemployment rates in general nor by personal experience of unemployment. A seemingly perverse migration pattern might well be the result of rational decisions taken by the unemployed and workers in Spain. Migration appears to be influenced by the unemployment benefit registering system, under which the unemployed need only search for jobs in their own province to secure benefits, and by the already employed moving to take advantage of lower house prices, improved quality of life and promotion opportunities in less prosperous regions.

Houseman and Abraham (1990) reported that identical shifts in regional employment produced much more migration in the USA than in Germany. Eichengreen (1992) found that migration in Britain and Italy was much less responsive to changes in regional wages and unemployment rates than was the case in the USA. Although Hughes and McCormick (1994) found that migration across Britain in the 1980s was influenced by wage differentials, neither the degree of wage flexibility nor the scale of migration were great enough to contribute much to narrowing regional unemployment differentials. Such a view is reinforced by the findings by Jackman and Savouri (1991) that wages in Britain were not particularly sensitive to local labour market conditions.

Regional unemployment disparities in Europe are more persistent than in the USA. Blanchard and Katz (1992) reported no significant relationship between regional unemployment differences that existed in 1975 and 1985 – indicating a much more fluid regional unemployment picture in the USA in which former high unemployment areas could in time become low unemployment areas, contrary to the general EU experience. They view such regional unemployment as an equilibrium phenomenon associated with adverse shocks to which, in the case of the USA, labour migration would appear to be the main adjustment mechanism for dealing with such shocks. Although relative nominal wages in the USA do fall in the face of an adverse shock they are not responsive enough to prevent a rise in unemployment. US labour mobility is therefore primarily a response to changes in unemployment rather than any wage variations.

CONCLUSIONS

The UK has experienced a number of important labour market trends since 1979: the decline in male labour force participation accompanied by a significant rise in long-term sickness and early retirement; the continued increase in female labour force participation; a growth in part-time, temporary and self-employment; two severe recessions which witnessed profound reductions in manufacturing employment; and a programme of Government policies to promote labour market flexibility. The decentralising and deregulating nature of UK labour market reforms, including trade union legislation, were influenced by the US example of a flexible labour market capable of job generation. The USA has relatively weak trade unions (see Chapter 7) and virtually no employment protection legislation, apart from a statutory minimum wage that is declining in real and relative terms (Rosenberg, 1989). However, the common perception that the USA is better able to create low skill, low pay jobs which the unemployed have to take because of the paucity of benefits is somewhat misleading. The evidence shows that the US economy is rather good at creating high skill, high pay jobs; in 'the last decade nearly half of all the jobs created in the American economy were in the professional and managerial occupations' (Robinson, 1994, p. 15). This casts doubt on such policies; meanwhile 'Britain's role as a relatively low-wage, low productivity economy appears to have been consolidated' (Nolan, 1994, p. 68). However, as we can tell from the data in endnote 1, employment in the UK did expand after reaching an historic post-war low in 1983 (22.88 million, an employment rate of just 67.6 per cent). Between 1985 and 1995 employment grew by 1.49 million with a further 1.78 million in employment by the year 2000 (an employment rate of 74.7 per cent).

Whether this expansion of employment was because Government policies succeeded in making the UK labour market more flexible is open to doubt. Union power and strike activity fell during the 1980s, all traces of minimum wage regulation were abolished, the benefit regime was tightened, marginal rates of income tax were reduced and enterprise in the form of self-employment was encouraged. While the closed shop was outlawed, unofficial strike action prohibited, and self-employment increased, there is no evidence that the UK was better prepared for the 1990–2 recession than the 1979–81 slump (Robinson, 1994). While Siebert (1997) comments favourably on an increase in UK labour market flexibility from 1980 into the early 1990s, he concludes that unemployment 'still remains high and possibly higher than one would have expected after all the institutional changes' (p. 43). This is because flexibility has not increased the transition from unemployment to employment (Blanchflower and Freeman, 1993). Nickell (1997) believes that cross-country comparisons yield clear lessons about which aspects of labour market flexibility impact on unemployment.

Benefits of indefinite duration, little active labour market policy, high unionisation combined with low co-ordination, high employment taxes and poor educational standards at the lower end of the labour market are associated with high unemployment; yet generous benefits, high unionisation that is combined with co-ordinated wage bargaining, and strong employment protection legislation are not. Any improvements in flexibility appear to have been at the cost of worker security and a marked increase in inequality that has very little to do with the proper functioning of labour markets. As Gregg and Machin (1994) conclude,

> it seems that the UK is experiencing big rises in inequality much like the USA but without the equalising impact of rapid transitions between employment states. . . . This does not appear to be very encouraging for the future health of the UK labour market.
>
> (p. 122)

Having established that in theory the nature of labour markets may well hold the key to the success of further economic integration in Europe, we were able to argue that in terms of real wage flexibility the EU might on average be comparable to that large single currency area, the USA. However, the very range of the degree of wage flexibility across EU member states may well pose problems for the single currency project. Additionally there is some doubt about whether a concerted policy attempt to 'Americanise' the UK labour market has succeeded in increasing aggregate wage flexibility and labour market performance (Beatson, 1995). When it comes to divergent labour market institutions generating different wage and employment outcomes, De Grauwe (1997) concedes that,

> institutional differences in the national labour markets will continue to exist for quite some time after the introduction of a common currency. This may lead to . . . severe adjustment problems when the exchange rate instrument has disappeared.
>
> (p. 27)

The success of the USA appears to rest heavily on a high degree of labour mobility, which, in spite of being permitted and encouraged, is absent in the EU. Intra-EU trade and capital mobility may well substitute for this lack of labour mobility, but whether this equalises or further divides the labour market experiences of European citizens is ambiguous in theory and as yet unknown in practice. What is more certain is that a lack of labour mobility will severely test the cohesion of EMU.

CASE STUDY – FLEXIBILITY AND NATIONAL CULTURE

We have looked at the concept of labour market flexibility, policies that enhance flexibility and the extent to which countries vary in the degree of flexibility they exhibit. Yet why is it that some countries have more flexible labour markets than others? Obviously flexibility may be path dependent, which means that history matters. But are there indicators of cultural differences that might both have influenced that history and helped determine current attitudes to flexibility? In an interesting paper, combining sociology with economics, Boyd Black (2001) 'Culturally Coded? The Enigma of Flexible Labour Markets', *Employee Relations*, 23 (4): 401–16, examines the link between employment flexibility and indicators of national culture.

The study focuses on employment flexibility, which we called numerical flexibility, at the microeconomic and the macroeconomic levels. Black (2001) is concerned with the aspects of flexibility on the right hand side of Figure A.

Microeconomic level

Pay bargaining structure Pay structure	Employment protection Part-time employment Self-employment Temporary employment Job tenure

Pay and benefits ———————————————————— **Employment/ working time**

Tax and benefit systems Aggregate real wage flexibility	Labour mobility Active labour market Programmes (ALMP) Aggregate employment Aggregate hours worked Aggregate unemployment

Macroeconomic level

Figure A Dimensions of labour market flexibility

Source: Adapted from Black, 2001, figure 1, p. 402

The purpose of this paper is to provide an . . . analysis of the cross-country variation in the dimensions of labour market [employment and working time] flexibility in which national culture is given a leading explanatory role. In effect, it is argued that the employment relationship is culturally embedded in a society. . . .

Culture is the collective programming of the mind that distinguishes one group . . . of people from another, with the word reserved for describing entire societies or nations. . . . In each society, there is a system of societal norms, consisting of the value systems (the mental programmes) shared by major groups of the population. These societal norms have led to the development and . . . maintenance of institutions in society with a particular structure and way of functioning. These institutions include family, legal, educational and political systems. . . . They will include labour market institutions and practices such as employment patterns, employment protection regulations, patterns of working time, and the patterns of job tenure which are linked to labour mobility. . . .

Societal norms affect behaviour and result in different labour market institutional outcomes. . . . Institutions in society, once they become facts, reinforce the societal norms . . . The institutions may be changed, but this will not necessarily affect societal norms. . . . This suggests it may be very difficult for policy makers to make national labour markets more . . . flexible as labour market institutions and practices are, to a considerable degree, held captive by their respective host cultures. These will resist changes that do not 'fit' the culture, . . . labour market flexibility is a product of cultural conditioning, and we would as a result expect to see variations in the indicators of flexibility across countries with different national cultures.

Black (2001) defines the cultures of different countries using four different categories:

(1) power distance (PD), defined as the degree of inequality among people that the population of a country considers as normal: from relatively equal (. . . small PD) to extremely unequal (large PD).
(2) individualism versus collectivism (IDV), defined as the degree to which people in a country prefer to act as individuals rather than as members of groups. . . .
(3) masculinity versus femininity (MAS), . . . is defined as the degree to which values like assertiveness, performance, success and competition, . . . prevail over values like the quality of life, maintaining warm personal friendships, service, care for the weak and solidarity . . .
(4) uncertainty avoidance (UA), defined as the degree to which people in a country prefer structured to unstructured situations. Structured situations are those in which there are clear rules as to how one should behave. These rules can be written down, but they can also be unwritten and imposed by tradition.

Countries are then rated according to these four cultural criteria using a scale from 0 which is low to around 110 which is high. The results of these ratings are shown in Table A.

The results in Table A display wide variations between national cultures. When combined with various aspects of employment flexibility the following conclusions about the links between culture and flexibility emerge:

Table A Cultural ratings

	PD	UA	IDV	MAS
Austria	11	70	55	79
Belgium	65	94	75	54
Denmark	18	23	74	16
Finland	33	59	63	26
France	68	86	71	43
Germany	35	65	67	66
Greece	60	112	35	57
Ireland	28	35	70	68
Italy	50	75	76	70
Netherlands	38	53	80	14
Norway	31	50	69	8
Portugal	63	104	27	31
Spain	57	86	51	42
Sweden	31	29	71	5
Switzerland	34	58	68	70
Turkey	66	85	37	45
UK	35	35	89	66
Australia	36	51	90	61
Canada	39	48	80	52
Israel	13	81	54	47
Japan	54	92	46	95
New Zealand	22	49	79	58
USA	40	46	91	62

Source: Adapted from Black, 2001, table 1, p. 407

(1) MAS is inversely related to the strength of employment protection regulation. 'Strong employment protection laws will be associated with a more feminine, caring culture (low MAS).' Countries, such as Denmark, Norway and Sweden, that have strong solidarity through employment protection, which is often associated with strong trade unions, have low MAS ratings.

(2) Employment protection is positively related to the UA index. 'High UA societies [Belgium, Greece and Portugal] like employment stability and are resistant to change.'

(3) '. . . the MAS variable is negatively associated with the share of part-time employment, the female activity rate and the female share of the labour force'. In general the more that women are involved in the labour force the more feminine the culture.

(4) The MAS variable was positively related to the '. . . employment to population ratio . . . The MAS index is also positively associated with the share of self-employment in the economy . . . Masculine societies live to work, while feminine societies work to live, . . . more masculine cultures with their greater emphasis on values such as assertiveness, success, challenge and advancement' encourage self-employment.

(5) '...low MAS countries, being more caring, would be expected to take more active measures to combat unemployment...' There is a statistically significant negative relationship between the MAS index and spending on Active Labour Market Programmes.

(6) Higher MAS countries tend to be lower unemployment rate countries. Black (2001) maintains that '...benefit duration is the key adjustable variable affecting the unemployment rate'.

(7) 'High IDV societies are less group oriented and there is less loyalty between the individual and the organisation. . . . The IDV index is positively associated with measures of labour mobility.'

(8) Low IDV, collectivist, societies tend to resort more to temporary employment contracts.

To summarise the key findings of this study,

> low MAS countries are associated with stricter employment protection. They are associated with a higher share of part-time employment, a higher female activity rate and a higher female share of the labour force, all conventional measures of labour market flexibility. However, at the same time they are associated with worse labour market outcomes. Low MAS countries have a lower overall labour supply, which suggests that in practice they have less employment flexibility. . . . In addition to exhibiting less flexibility, low MAS countries experience higher unemployment.
>
> The other key finding to emerge is that the IDV index is positively associated with labour mobility, as measured by job tenure. Labour mobility is lower and job tenure longer in more collectivist (low IDV) cultures, where there is more of a feeling of loyalty to a group.
>
> What has been demonstrated is evidence of statistical associations between culture and our employment and working time variables . . . the results are robust and statistically significant . . .

The main weakness of this study is that the data that was used to compile the cultural rankings in Table A is from the 1970s. While cultural norms will be fairly stable they are subject to change and the longer the period of time that elapses the more likely it is that those norms will change. The UK, for example, has become a more individualistic society since the 1970s and has been subject to an ongoing process of the feminisation of the workforce. Bearing these doubts about the precision of the rankings in mind, Black's (2001) study has a straightforward policy conclusion, *established culture patterns may well prove a source of resistance to moves in the direction of more flexibility* . . . If this is so then a variety of labour market institutional arrangements may well persist over time rather than a convergence towards a single, ever more flexible labour market model. In effect Black (2001) is setting down the cultural limits to labour market flexibility.

LABOUR MARKET FLEXIBILITY – SUMMARY

Labour market flexibility was defined in terms of

- wage flexibility
- numerical flexibility
- functional flexibility
- work-time flexibility

The potential advantage of flexible labour markets arose from the ability to respond more rapidly to changes in product market conditions and/or new technology. The downside of increased flexibility is that it undermines aspects of workers' job security. Comparison with the employment generating capacity of the more flexible US labour market has driven UK labour market policy since 1979. Policies designed to increase flexibility have included

- reducing trade union power
- reducing minimum wage regulation up until 1999
- privatisation
- reducing the generosity of welfare benefits
- encouraging atypical employment

The growth of part-time, fixed term and self-employment could be seen as an obvious sign of greater labour market flexibility. While there have been increases in predominantly female part-time employment throughout Europe, there have been no such trends for either, temporary or self-employment. Assessing the impact of other policies to enhance flexibility there is no unambiguous evidence of increased wage and employment flexibility. However, there is evidence that work effort has increased. There was also the suggestion that compared to other countries the UK may have an unfortunate combination of reasonable job security and a lack of flexibility at the firm level. Certainly the competitiveness of UK firms seems to have been dented by rising unit labour costs.

To emphasise the importance of labour market flexibility we examined European Monetary Union (EMU). The creation of a successful single currency in Europe relies, in theory, on the degree of wage flexibility and labour mobility. In both respects the actual degree of flexibility in the EU appears to be quite low. Compared to the USA

- regional wage flexibility in the EU appears to be on a par
- labour mobility in the EU is very low

The lack of labour mobility could place additional strain on EMU. It is the greater willingness of American workers to move from high to low unemployment areas that gives the US labour market a decisive flexibility advantage over Europe.

When we looked at labour migration in more detail we found that migration rates have fallen over time. This could be due to the fact that international trade and capital mobility are substitutes for migration. Immigration does not have adverse economic effects overall on the host nation. Increased immigration into the EU might maintain the size of the working population but the increasing age profile of the European population will place greater demands on the working population which immigration will not be able to prevent.

LABOUR MARKET FLEXIBILITY – QUESTIONS FOR DISCUSSION

1) Explain the four elements of labour market flexibility.
2) What sorts of policy should a government pursue in order to increase flexibility?
3) Using evidence from empirical studies, how successful have UK Government attempts to increase labour market flexibility been since 1980?
4) Referring to descriptive statistics, have there been any unambiguous trends in atypical employment in Europe in the 1980s and 1990s?
5) Explain why labour market flexibility is theoretically important in the context of international monetary integration.
6) In terms of labour market flexibility does the USA or the EU represent a better single currency area?
7) Examine the role that international labour migration can play in the flexibility of a host nation's labour markets.

SUGGESTED READING

Esping-Andersen, G. and Regini, M. (2000) *Why Deregulate Labour Markets?*, Oxford: Oxford University Press.
Felstead, A. and Jewson (eds) (1999) *Global Trends in Flexible Labour*, London: Macmillan.

9

Job search and vacancy analysis

INTRODUCTION

Burgess (1999) informs us that 'in the UK, some 8 million new hires are completed each year, relative to a workforce of around 25 million' (p. 1). This chapter contains two distinct but linked ideas. The first is the microeconomic analysis of the search for jobs. We will focus on the job search activity of unemployed workers. The second, which arose from search models, is the macroeconomic concept of the job matching function. This chapter will concentrate on a particular example of the matching function that sets out a relationship between unemployment and vacancies and generates a U–V or 'Beveridge' curve.

Pissarides (1985) identifies that as long ago as 1939 Hutt commented on individual labourers engaging in job search as a form of investment. Stigler (1962) analysed the labour market under conditions of incomplete information to derive an optimal search strategy. Hines (1971b) points out that job search by the unemployed was a part of the Clower/Leijonhufvud reappraisal of Keynes during the second half of the 1960s, which attempted to provide Keynesian macroeconomics with micro foundations. Yet in spite of these earlier interpretations, job search theory represents a relatively recent (circa 1970) development in the neoclassical explanation of unemployment.

Search theory is part of an explanation of equilibrium unemployment stemming from Friedman's (1968) analysis of the long-run Phillip's Curve relationship, which identified a 'natural rate' of unemployment. As such search theory was initially set the task of explaining voluntary frictional unemployment as a process whereby the unemployed accepted jobs offering higher nominal wage rates only to see their wages eroded by subsequently accelerating inflation, at which point they would quit work in order to engage in full-time search for an acceptable job (see Chapter 10 for a more detailed treatment of this analysis). Whether search theory provides an adequate explanation of such unemployment or whether it should be allocated a more modest role is the central concern of this chapter. We will also examine the role of welfare benefits as an application arising from job search.

The macroeconomic 'matching function' will be introduced and we will examine the relationship between unemployment and vacancies in some detail. Important insights into the operation of labour markets can be gained by examining the role of job vacancies in relation to unemployment. Although one could analyse vacancies by looking at employer search as the converse of microeconomic worker search, we shall concentrate on its macroeconomic aspects in the context of explaining aggregate unemployment. The key features of the macroeconomic analysis of vacancies are: to establish the theoretical relationship between vacancies and unemployment; to tell the empirical story of how this relationship has developed over time; and to suggest likely causes for changes in the unemployment–vacancy relationship.

SEARCH THEORY: A NUMERICAL EXAMPLE

Essentially search theory attempts to explain an aspect of behaviour in the labour market in which agents, both workers and firms, have incomplete information about market opportunities. Workers whether employed or unemployed, search for vacancies and wage offers, whilst employers search for workers whose productivity is varied, in a world where information is imperfect and costly to acquire. Because of our concern with unemployment let us concentrate on workers' search for jobs.

Workers are faced with many methods of searching. They can use jobcentres, newspapers, private recruitment agencies, direct enquiries and personal contacts. As an indication of the method of job search used by the unemployed in the USA, data for the year 2000 is contained in Table 9.1. Common to all methods of job search is an element of 'sampling' because of the impossibility of knowing all possible job offers

Table 9.1 Job search method used, 2000 (percentage of total jobseekers)*

Method	Percentage
Approach employer directly	64.5
Sent out CVs/Applications	47.7
Placed/Answered advertisements	13.1
Friends/Relatives	13.2
Public Employment Agency	17.4
Private Employment Agency	7.1
Other methods	10.1
Average Number of Methods Used	1.7

Source: US Bureau of Labour Statistics 2001
Note: * will sum to more than 100% because more than one search method can be used at any one time.

within any given time period. Given that search activity extends over more than one time period, the existence of search costs limit the amount of sampling, so that search can never be extensive enough to secure the highest paid vacancy (job offer) in all circumstances. Search costs can be direct in terms of stationary, postage, interview clothing, fares and so forth, or they can be indirect in terms of opportunities forgone. The opportunity cost of an extra week of job search for an unemployed worker is the post-tax wage, net of any state benefits, which could have been earned if the previous job offer had been accepted. Even employed job seekers engaged in on-the-job search suffer an opportunity cost in terms of leisure forgone when they search in their own time or take a day's leave to attend an interview. The object of job search is to set the benefits of search activity against the search costs and find and obtain an 'acceptable' job for the unemployed worker or a 'better' job for the employed job searcher. Search will also be affected by the searcher's attitude to risk and time preference reflected in the discount rate used to assess possible future income streams. In the light of the costs and possible benefits of job search the individual job searcher has to decide how extensive and how intensive their job search is to be.

To illustrate these features of job search let us look at the standard worker search model contained in Joll et al. (1983) and in McKenna (1990).[1] The assumptions of the model are as follows:

1) workers are homogeneous but face a variety of wage offers, given that non-wage job characteristics are known and are identical;
2) workers know the wage distribution but not which firm is offering which wage, this they can only discover through search;
3) workers prefer a higher to a lower wage as they seek to maximise their lifetime earnings;
4) each approach to a firm imposes a constant non-trivial search cost.

It becomes clear that each additional unit of sampling entails a marginal search cost with the benefit of additional search being the likelihood that a higher wage will be discovered. However, as knowledge of the likelihood of uncovering a higher wage is uncertain one is measuring the marginal benefit of search in terms of probability, that is the expected wage $E(W)$.

Take the numerical example set out in Table 9.2 of a worker searching amongst 155 firms with wage rates ranging from £120 to £160 per week. The job searcher is now able to calculate the expected wage from a single random selection across firms as

$$E(W) = \sum_{i=1}^{9}[(W_i \Pr(W = W_i)]$$
$$= (120 \times 0.0129) + \ldots + (160 \times 0.0194)$$
$$= 141.2225.$$

Note that $i = 1$–9 because there are nine wage intervals. $E(W) = 141.2225$ is simply the average wage, or mean value of the distribution. This implies that the worker

Table 9.2   Numerical example of job search

Wage rate, (W)	Number of firms	Probability of wage Pr(W)
£120	2	2/155 = 0.0129
£125	7	7/155 = 0.0452
£130	14	14/155 = 0.0903
£135	28	28/155 = 0.1806
£140	40	40/155 = 0.2581
£145	26	26/155 = 0.1677
£150	20	20/155 = 0.1290
£155	15	15/155 = 0.0968
£160	3	3/155 = 0.0194
	=155	= 1.0000

Source: Joll *et al.* 1983, table 4.2, p. 75

would expect to receive a first offer of £140 from sampling one firm but that this is by no means certain. But is this the optimal search intensity? Given that the worker is concerned with the maximum wage offer generated by search activity we need to investigate larger sample sizes. We can rewrite our previous single sample result as

$$E(\max W \mid n = 1) = E(W) = £141.2225$$

which is the expected maximum wage rate given samples of size n, in this case where $n = 1$. If we wish to explore samples of two firms ($n = 2$) we need to calculate the probabilities of all possible combinations of offers. There are eighty-one possible outcomes from samples of two firms ranging from £120, £120 through to £160, £160. Take for example the case of uncovering a combination of offers at wage rates of £120 and £125 per week. The probability of this outcome is

$$Pr(W = 120) \times Pr(W = 125) = 0.0129 \times 0.0452 = 0.00058308.$$

The maximum wage rate from this sample 125 multiplied by its probability 0.00058308 yields a figure of 0.0728850. Once all such products are calculated for all eighty-one combinations, they are summed to give the maximum expected wage from a sample size of two firms:

$$E(\max W \mid n = 2) = £146.04512$$

Obviously as the sample size increases the expected maximum wage increases albeit at a diminishing rate. As n approaches 155, so the expected maximum wage approaches £160. Yet we must not forget that this search process is constrained by the cost of searching. Using a fixed cost of £2 for each firm sampled enables us to calculate the expected return from search activity net of search costs – these are shown in Table 9.3. In this example the job searcher evidently maximises the expected net return to search activity, $R(n)$, with an optimal sample size of three firms ($n^* = 3$).

Table 9.3   Expected return from search activity

Sample size, n	E(max W| n)	Cost C(n)	Expected net return R(n) = E(max W| n) − Cn
1	141.2225	2	139.2225
2	146.0451	4	142.0451
3	148.4724	6	142.4724
4	150.0097	8	142.0097

This constitutes the so called 'Stigler decision rule' which maintains that the best an individual can expect from search activity is, in this case, achieved by sampling three firms per period.[2] Yet is it reasonable to suggest that individuals conduct job search on the basis of identifying the correct number of firms to approach and then take the best offer going? In circumstances where the distribution of wage offers is known, to the individual, the optimal sample size model is inferior to a sequential decision rule model. Introducing the concept of the reservation wage, defined as the minimum acceptable wage, the worker can approach each firm in turn (sequentially) and compare the wage on offer (W) with their reservation wage (r). When the worker uncovers an offer which at least matches their reservation wage they can stop searching and accept that job.

In the context of our numerical example we need to find the optimal reservation wage r^*, which will maximise the net return from job search activity. In a sequential decision rule search model there are only two possible outcomes: finding a wage offer where $W \geq r^*$; or obtaining a wage offer such that $W < r^*$. Thus,

$$\Pr(W < r) = 1 - \Pr(W \geq r).$$

Given that the individual is approaching each firm in turn, the expected return from searching a single firm sample is

$$R(r) = E(W \mid W \geq r)\Pr(W \geq r) + R(r)[1 - \Pr(W \geq r)] - C$$

which McKenna (1990) interprets as

> The expected return to searching once using a reservation wage, r, is the mean (expected) wage of all wages no less than r ... multiplied by the probability of finding such a wage, plus the expected return to searching once more multiplied by the probability that an unacceptable wage is found, less the cost of the first search.
>
> (pp. 44–45)

Solving the above equation for $R(r)$ we obtain the following expression:

$$R(r) = E(W \mid W \geq r) - C/\Pr(W \geq r).$$

The optimal reservation wage r^* is that which maximises this expression. Bearing in mind that

$$Pr(W \geqslant r) = \sum_{W \geq r} Pr(W)$$

and

$$E[W/W \geq r] = \frac{\sum_{w \geq r} W Pr(W)}{\sum_{w \geq r} Pr(W)}$$

we are in a position to calculate the mean expected wage of all wages no less than the reservation wage for each possible reservation wage value. Beginning with $r = £120$, where all wages are greater than or equal to £120, we get

$$\sum_{W \geq 120} Pr(W) = 1$$

and

$$E(W | W \geqslant 120) = \sum_{W \geq 120} W Pr(W) = E(W) = 141.2225.$$

If we take the case of a reservation wage of £125, then

$$\sum_{W \geq 125} Pr(W) = 0.9871$$

and

$$E(W | W \geqslant 125) = \frac{139.6745}{0.9871} = 141.4998.$$

Assuming search costs fixed at £2 per search one arrives at the expected return data contained in Table 9.4. Examination of the net return column of Table 9.4 shows the highest expected value is produced at a reservation wage of £145. Hence the optimum reservation wage for job searchers under these assumed conditions is $r^* = 145$. This can be shown diagrammatically using the marginal benefit (mb) and marginal costs

Table 9.4 Expected return from search costs fixed at £2 per search

Reservation wage, r	$E(W|W \geq r)$	$C/Pr[W \geq r]$	Expected return $R(r)$
120	141.2225	2.0000	139.2225
125	141.4998	2.0261	139.4737
130	142.2916	2.1234	140.1682
135	143.5950	2.3485	141.2465
140	145.9083	2.9806	142.9277
145	149.6016	4.8438	144.7678
150	152.7588	8.1566	144.5922
155	155.8003	17.2117	138.5886
160	160.0000	103.0928	56.9072

Source: Adapted from Joll *et al.*, 1983, table 4.5, p. 81

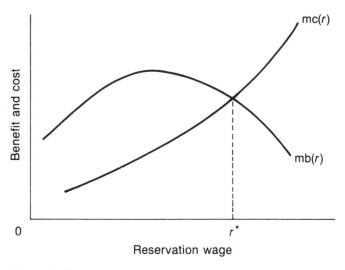

Figure 9.1

(mc) associated with each value the reservation wage could take.[3] The mb(r) curve in Figure 9.1 is essentially the expected wage given that it is greater than or equal to the reservation wage at each value that r could take. The mc(r) curve is the expected cost of search associated with varying amounts of sampling dependent upon the value taken by r. As Figure 9.1 shows, the optimal reservation wage r^* is located where the marginal cost and benefit functions equate.

The sequential rule model has dominated the analysis of job search mainly because it allows search to extend over time, which gives it an element of greater realism as a characterisation of how workers seek jobs. It also allows some interesting predictions about the duration of unemployment. For example we could investigate the likely effect of an increase in search costs for the unemployed through a reduction in welfare benefits. This is illustrated by the leftward shift in the mc(r) curve in Figure 9.2.

The impact of making search more costly in a sequential model framework would be to reduce the reservation wage from r^* to r^1, which by implication, reduces the duration of job search and of unemployment *ceteris paribus*.

Allowing changes in the distribution of real wage offers, leading to shifts in the mb(r) curve in Figure 9.3, will impact upon the optimum reservation wage and the duration of search and therefore upon the persistence of unemployment. In effect if wage rates increase, the mb(r) curve shifts up and to the right of its original position, thereby increasing the reservation wage to r^2. If on the other hand wage rates fall, the attraction of job search is lessened, the mb(r) curve shifts down and to the left, with the reservation wage falling to r^1.

By allowing the wage distribution to shift, search theory is attempting to cope with the cyclical element in economic activity. The distribution of real wages is supposed to shift downwards during a recession (something that requires flexible real wages); if job searchers realise this and adjust their reservation wages accordingly (to r^1 in

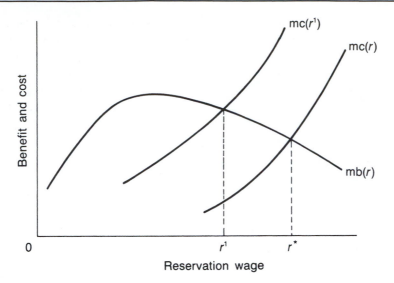

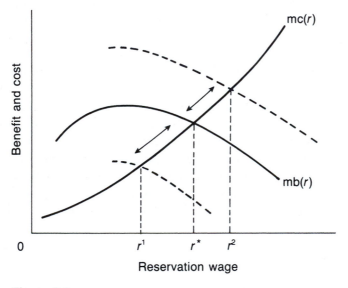

Figure 9.2

Figure 9.3

Figure 9.3), then they increase the probability of accepting a job offer and reduce unemployment duration.

Empirically it is far from clear whether or not real wages exhibit the pro-cyclical behaviour that Figure 9.3 and search theory requires. Brandolini (1993) provides a thorough survey of empirical studies into the movement of real wages over the cycle which highlights the fact that no consistent cyclical pattern emerges from studies of aggregate wage data. Some tentative evidence of the pro-cyclical movement of real wages is to be found amongst studies using microeconomic data. However, there is some doubt about whether such findings can be applied to the economy as a whole. Furthermore the results can differ from country to country and the pattern of real wages can change depending upon whether one uses output or employment as indicators of economic activity. Sumner and Silver (1989) show that real wages need not display a consistent pattern of behaviour over successive business cycles and have indeed switched between being pro and counter cyclical in the USA since 1900. This ambiguity serves to show that when it comes to the movement of real wages across business cycles, search theory when it suggests pro-cyclical fluctuations, is not appealing to an established fact.

Recognising that time itself is a scarce resource leads to a number of interesting implications. The age of the job searcher becomes an important consideration, because as a finite time horizon is approached, i.e., retirement, the earnings opportunities at every wage rate declines. Thus one would anticipate that reservation wages for older workers would be lower than those of prime age labour suppliers because the discounted return to any wage distribution will fall as the age of the job searcher increases. Yet a similar consideration should affect unemployed workers irrespective of their initial age (although the effect obviously increases with age), i.e., the longer they remain searching for work the lower the discounted return from the wage distribution (hence the mb(r) curve displays diminishing returns), thereby lowering the reservation wage and increasing the probability of leaving unemployment as time goes by. However, the persistence of long-term unemployment does not bear this out. The only way in which search theory can come to terms with this contradiction is to identify the welfare benefit system acting as a floor to prevent reservation wages (and thus unemployment) from falling. Indeed most of the theoretical and empirical work on the relationship between benefits and unemployment has focused on this search related aspect concerning the generosity of state benefits for the unemployed. This has introduced the concept of the 'replacement ratio' as the proportion of in work, post-tax income that the benefit system replaces when one becomes unemployed, as a measure of the generosity of benefits. As Joll *et al.* (1983) maintain, in the context of search theory

> state unemployment assistance can act as a subsidy to search. The higher is the benefit level the higher the reservation wage for unemployed searchers and therefore the more searchers there will be and the longer they will search.
>
> (p. 87)

The simple theory of job search views unemployment as merely an inability to find a job at a suitable wage. In such a scheme of things the level of the reservation wage determines the suitability of job offers. Hence factors that influence the reservation wage, namely welfare benefits and the wage distribution, are of crucial importance to the search theory approach to unemployment. In the next section we question the status of the relationship between welfare benefits and unemployment with regard to search theory.

BENEFITS, SEARCH AND UNEMPLOYMENT IN THEORY

The theoretical position in respect of welfare benefits, reservation wages and unemployment is clear in search theory. The flow diagram shows the hypothesised positive relationship between these variables under conditions of increasing state benefits.

↑ welfare → ↑ reservation → ↑ search → ↑ equilibrium
benefit   wages   duration   unemployment

But consider three (extreme?) cases; the first where the benefit system is so generous that the income from unemployment and other associated welfare entitlements exceeds the individual's reservation wage. In this case the unemployed worker ceases the search for job offers and lives off state benefits indefinitely. In a second scenario where benefits exactly equal the worker's reservation wage, the individual is indifferent between remaining unemployed and searching for an acceptable job offer. Yet if the income from benefits falls below the reservation wage to such an extent that all possible wage offers exceed the reservation wage, any job offer will be accepted.

At this point we encounter a difficult theoretical problem, because whilst any unemployment arising from our first two cases can be regarded as voluntary frictional unemployment, which is what search theory was established to explain, can unemployment under the final set of conditions be explained by search theory? Where all wage offers in the distribution exceed the benefit supported reservation wage can any unemployment be regarded as voluntary? As Hahn (1987) points out Keynes clearly deemed an individual to be involuntarily unemployed in such circumstances. Indeed there would be no incentive for rational agents to quit their existing job to engage in full-time search, any job search that did occur would be on-the-job search. If all search is on-the-job then search theory cannot explain frictional unemployment. If quitting is empirically insignificant as Pissarides (1985) maintains when he says that it 'accounts for a small fraction of the total flow into unemployment' (p. 171), this seriously undermines search theory's importance as an explanation of unemployment. Furthermore quitting a job voluntarily is penalised by the benefit system; in the UK it results in the loss of the first six months' benefit payments.

Such criticisms of search theory suggests that it is not wage offers but the existence of a vacancy that is of crucial importance, especially to the unemployed. A labour market with unemployment is characterised by excess supply, which obviously lowers the probability of a job offer. This in turn should, according to search theory, lower the optimum reservation wage such that search ends when a vacancy is discovered. In the search for vacancies, unemployment duration will depend upon search intensity as well as on net search costs. The probability of finding a vacancy, although not a feature of our numerical example, can be incorporated into a job search model. The probability of leaving unemployment is the product of the probability of finding a job offer, plus the probability of accepting that offer. In a labour market with high rates of unemployment compared to vacancies, this is an essential development of the basic job search model. Including the probability of finding a vacancy into job search affects

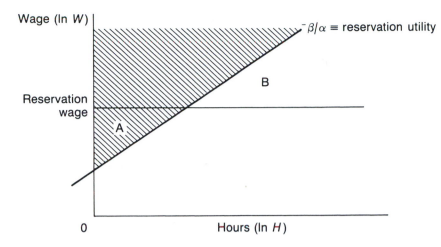

Figure 9.4

Source: Adapted from Blau 1991, figure 1, p. 192

the relationship between benefits and unemployment. The low likelihood of finding a vacancy during a period of comparatively high unemployment serves to lower reservation wages, resulting in a greater likelihood of accepting any offer which might be discovered.

| vacancy | → | reservation | → | search | → | equilibrium |
| probability | | wage | | duration | | unemployment |

As we shall see later in this chapter and then again in Chapter 10, data on the unemployed suggests that they rarely reject job offers.

However, before we move on to consider the empirical status of job search we need to address other theoretical problems. In an attempt to incorporate non-wage factors into the analysis of job search Blau (1991) proposed a model in which the utility of a job offer to an unemployed worker depends not only on the wage but also on the hours to be worked. The model takes a Cobb–Douglas form utility function,

$$U = W^\alpha H^\beta, \quad \text{with} \quad \alpha > 0$$

The optimal search strategy uses the reservation concept applied to utility rather than just to the wage offer. Within a finite search period, the individual seeks and accepts a job offer whose utility exceeds the reservation utility. Figure 9.4 illustrates the key conclusions of this model. The figure shows that offers above the reservation utility line $(-\beta/\alpha)$ will be accepted, i.e., those in the shaded area. Whereas a conventional reservation wage model in which hours are assumed not to matter at all, would predict offers in area A would have been rejected. The reservation utility model indicates they would be accepted because low wages are being compensated for by short hours. However, offers in area B are rejected in this model even though the wage exceeds the

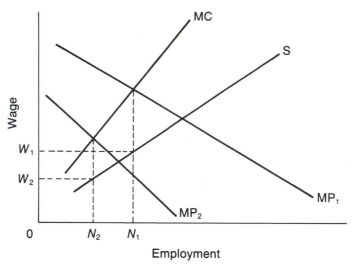

Figure 9.5

Source: Adapted from Fallon and Verry 1988, figure 7.4, p. 202

reservation wage because of the long hours associated with these job offers. The model is an important one because it serves to demonstrate the theoretical fragility of the link made by job search between benefits and unemployment via the reservation wage.

To further complicate matters we need to be aware that the generosity of the benefit system (measured by the replacement ratio) is only one aspect of the unemployment story. Another refers to the nature of the benefit regime, especially the effect of the duration of benefits. One may reasonably infer that a short period of benefit entitlement would yield more intensive search activity than a benefit regime within which the unemployed received state assistance indefinitely. This is an important consideration given the particular problems faced by the long-term unemployed in returning to work.

Fallon and Verry (1988) address the important assumption of search theory that there is a distribution of wage offers facing homogeneous searchers. What prevents there being a single wage for potential workers of a given productivity? Such a single market wage would undermine job search as a process to uncover an acceptable wage offer as there could only be one possible wage offer. Unemployment could still affect variable search intensity to uncover vacancies at that going wage, but what determines vacancies? Search theory usually relies on different firms offering different wages because of firm specific impacts from product demand shocks. But could it be that worker productivity varies across firms due to differences in the quantity and/or quality of capital employed, differences in training policies or in internal organisation? In Figure 9.5, productivity has a firm specific element, illustrated by the marginal productivity functions for firm 1 and 2 (MP_1 and MP_2) which enables wage rates in the two firms (W_1 and W_2) to diverge.

As a final theoretical complication Blau and Robins (1990) and Wadsworth (1991) raise the intriguing possibility that benefits may actually improve the effectiveness of job search by enabling the unemployed to finance job search activity. The argument is that benefits increase search extensiveness, thereby improving the quality of the resulting job matches. Indeed it does seem to be the case that benefit claimants do search more extensively than non-claimants and that this may lead to a faster rate of job offer arrival.

UNEMPLOYMENT FLOWS AND JOB SEARCH

It is important to recognise that measures of the level of unemployment, in terms of the number of thousand (or million) workers out of work, or the unemployment rate, as a proportion of the working population, are indicators of the stock of unemployment. The stock of unemployment is the result of the flows into and out of unemployment. The obvious implication is that changes in the unemployment stock, whether measured as a level or expressed as a rate, must equal the difference between the flow into unemployment and the flow out of unemployment. We are therefore looking at the flow of workers through unemployment.

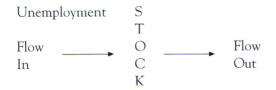

The flow into unemployment consists of a combination of labour market entrants, like school and college leavers, those voluntarily quitting their jobs, and those being made redundant by firms. The flow out of unemployment is being determined by retirement from the working population by the elderly unemployed and by successful job search by unemployed workers. Vacancies enter the picture because they represent the willingness of firms to employ, hence they are an important argument in the outflow rate. Therefore one could characterise rising unemployment rates during a recession as a consequence of increasing rates of inflow due to redundancies, combined with a fall in outflow as firms reduce vacancies. Conversely a boom could see inflow rates falling as firms ceased laying workers off, coupled with an increase in outflow rates as vacancies rose reflecting an increasing willingness on the part of firms to increase their workforces, thus reducing unemployment rates.

Figure 9.6 presents data on the unemployment flows of male workers for the UK between 1967 and 1998 (male unemployment is studied because there is likely to be less distortion due to female workers' restricted access to unemployment benefits). Its most striking feature is the decline in the outflow rate since the late 1960s up until 1980. By contrast, although the inflow rate is variable there is no discernable trend during the 1967–80 period. Pissarides (1986) makes the point that it is only during the 1979–83 period that an increasing inflow rate makes a non-trivial contribution to

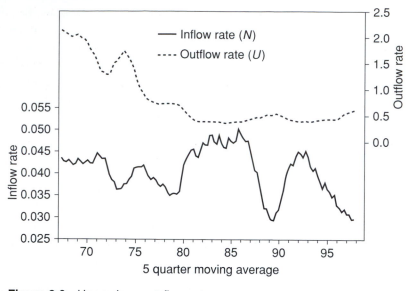

Figure 9.6 Unemployment flow rates

Source: Burgess and Turon 2000, figure 4, p. 36

the rise in unemployment. The increase in the rate of inflow to unemployment during 1979–83 is almost entirely due to the rise in redundancies. Yet it is the dramatic reduction in the outflow rate which dominates changes in the stock measure of the actual rate of unemployment during the late 1960s and 1970s. Actual male unemployment rates were: 1967 2.82 per cent; 1974 3.59 per cent; 1979 6.08 per cent. Since 1980 the outflow rate appears to have remained virtually constant with changes in the unemployment rate being due to variations in the rate of inflow into unemployment. In fact, due to the differences in the scales of these two flows, changes in outflow are about as variable as those of inflow after 1980.

Given the apparent dominance of the declining outflow rate in a period of rising unemployment, the crucial question that we need to address is why do the unemployed now not leave unemployment at the same rate as they did in the 1960s? Has search intensity fallen, with the unemployed not seeking and not accepting jobs as earnestly as they did before, or is it the case that the jobs are simply no longer available in sufficient numbers?

Having raised a number of theoretical issues surrounding the relationship between benefits, search and unemployment it is now time to assess the empirical standing of job search theory.

THE EMPIRICAL STATUS OF JOB SEARCH

We need to reiterate at the outset of any evaluation of the empirical aspects of search theory, the insignificance of voluntary quits to engage in full-time job search as a factor causing unemployment to fluctuate. As Sinclair (1987) observes for the UK

Labour-force turnover statistics reveal that about one in eight workers changes employer in any year, and of these, as many as 85 per cent are recruited directly from another job, with no intervening spell of unemployment.

(p. 184)

Indeed if quits were significant they would be a contributory factor to the flow into unemployment. Accordingly studies such as Pissarides (1986) consider quits as an inflow variable. He estimated that prior to 1979 more than half of the entry into unemployment was due to voluntary quits. However, during the 1967–79 period increases in unemployment are not the result of changes in the inflow rate. After 1979 it is the rise in redundancies that dominates the increase in the inflow rate. This is revealing because both Pissarides (1986) and Bean (1992) regard the increase in unemployment during the 1980s as being largely due to a reduction in the outflow rate, i.e., a fall in the probability of leaving unemployment. Pissarides (1986) commenting on the surge in UK unemployment during 1980–1 period notes that the

rise in the flow into unemployment, associated with a rise in redundancies, accounted for a rise in unemployment close to 3 percentage points [yet] the fall in the flow out of unemployment accounted for a rise . . . of about 5 percentage points.

(p. 502)

There are far higher outflow rates in North America than in EU countries, coupled with significant falls in the flow out of unemployment in a number of countries including the UK during the 1980s. Unemployment flows demonstrate that quits are not an important part of the unemployment story. However, job search intensity on the part of those already unemployed may well lie behind the declining outflow rates.

The key question now becomes, what factors identified from search theory might cause a decline in search intensity by unemployed job seekers? The prime suspect is, of course, welfare benefits through their impact on preventing the timely downward adjustment of reservation wages and the subsidy they provide to the search process.

It is difficult to estimate the effects of benefits on search intensity because of the problems associated with observing the search effort of the unemployed. Typically the number of search methods used has been the proxy for search effort. This reveals that the average number of search methods used declines as the duration of unemployment increases, and because of the way the benefit system is administered in the UK job search becomes increasingly concentrated on state run Jobcentres.

Schmitt and Wadsworth (1991) report the data in Table 9.5 which shows that the likelihood of unemployed workers using no search method in the previous week increases more than three fold from the first month to the period of long-term unemployment, i.e., over twelve months of unemployment. This provides some indicative evidence for the notion that as unemployment duration increases workers become discouraged job seekers and search effort falls. Discouraged job searchers will be a supply-side element in unemployment persistence and are part of the 'hysteresis' view that unemployment may breed unemployment, which is discussed more fully in

Table 9.5 Likelihood of unemployed using no search method

Unemployment duration (months)	Percentage of unemployed using no search method
< 1	6.8
1–3	12.7
3–6	10.5
6–12	16.2
≥ 12	22.9

Source: Adapted from Schmitt and Wadsworth 1991, table 1B, p. 29

Chapter 10. Yet one needs to be aware of the fact that there are also demand-side elements to take into consideration. They are: the 'deskilling' of the unemployed through lack of practice and technological change; and the adverse signal on an employment history that a spell of unemployment creates. Both effects will tend to reduce employers' demand for unemployed job seekers to fill vacancies. Indicative evidence of these effects comes from Gregory and Jukes (2001) who found that an unemployment episode reduced earnings upon re-employment by around 10 per cent. After a further two years of employment, earnings were only 3.7 per cent lower falling to 1.9 per cent thereafter. However, if a worker's spell of unemployment lasted for a year, then earnings on re-employment fell by a further 11 per cent giving an overall reduction of about 20 per cent. Even after two years of continuous employment, earnings for the previously long-term unemployed worker were still some 13 per cent below those of somebody who had never experienced unemployment. The wage impact of unemployment was more severe for older workers. Such discouragement would serve as a supply-side contribution to the further persistence of unemployment.

An empirical study that finds significant and substantial adverse effects of welfare benefits on unemployment in the UK is Minford (1983). He reports a positive elasticity of unemployment with respect to benefits of around 4.0, implying that if real benefits were to be reduced by 10 per cent, unemployment would fall by an incredible 40 per cent! This is way out of line with other estimates of the impact of benefits on unemployment and may reflect the fact that benefits and trade union density are the only trended variables to feature in the wage equation in the Liverpool model. In a study more representative of the consensus in the UK, Layard and Nickell (1985a) estimate an elasticity of unemployment to the replacement ratio of about 0.7.

Carling *et al.* (2001) report a link between benefit generosity and job search by the unemployed. When the Swedish government cut the unemployment benefit replacement ratio from 80 per cent to 75 per cent with effect from 1/1/1996, the rate of transition from unemployment to employment rose by 10 per cent. Job seekers appear to have reacted to the announcement of this policy change with more effective job search.

When it comes to estimating the impact of benefits on unemployment duration, Schmitt and Wadsworth (1991) state that in 'the United States . . . many estimates of benefit duration elasticities range around 0.4' (p. 1). Kiefer and Neumann (1989) in a survey of US unemployed male workers, report that although benefits have a significant impact on reservation wages the impact on unemployment duration is minimal. They state that if benefits were increased by 20 per cent this would raise the replacement ratio by '8.4 percentage points (from 42.1 per cent to 50.5 per cent) . . . and increase the duration of unemployment by about one-half week' (p. 174). Given that average unemployment duration in their sample was 39.1 weeks the benefit effect is inconsequential. In a study of male unemployment in the Netherlands during 1983–5, van den Berg (1990) estimated an average positive elasticity of unemployment duration with respect to changes in benefit levels of 0.03, implying that a 10 per cent fall in benefits would reduce unemployment duration by a mere 0.3 per cent. He also reports that unemployed Dutch males experience very low job offer arrival rates, of the order of a one per cent chance per week, coupled with high acceptance rates of the order of 97 per cent. This accords with a view that unemployed job searchers make a low number of regular applications, but that once they receive a job offer they do not reject it. The clear implication is that unemployment duration owes more to the lack of job offers rather than the rejection of such offers based upon an unfavourable comparison with a benefit induced reservation wage. But within a search framework benefits may affect search intensity, thereby impacting on the arrival rate of job offers. However, van den Berg (1990) also identifies factors other than benefits which affect the job search process. Unemployed graduates received job offers more than seven times as frequently as those with the lowest level of educational attainment. The poorly educated accept virtually every job that is offered to them, whereas university graduates are more choosy, exhibiting an 80 per cent chance of accepting the first job offered. More revealingly the least educated have an unemployment duration elasticity with respect to benefits of zero (0.10 for graduates). Very low elasticities are also reported for the young (18–23) and the old (46–64) unemployed of 0.01 and zero respectively, leading van den Berg (1990) to conclude that those 'who suffer most from long spells [of unemployment] are completely insensitive to the benefits policy instrument' (p. 855). Whilst this seems to be a final and well-founded assessment of the impact of benefit levels on unemployment, there is another aspect to consider – the nature of the benefit regime especially with regard to their duration. It may well be that the length of benefit entitlement affects the time horizon of the unemployed job searcher thereby influencing search intensity and unemployment persistence. Table 9.6 provides some descriptive statistics on benefit generosity and duration in the 1990s.

In a comparative study of unemployment in OECD countries Layard and Nickell (1992) attempt to evaluate the effect of both the benefit level (replacement ratio) and the length of entitlement to welfare benefits (benefit duration). Their study finds that the replacement ratio, a measure of the generosity of the benefit system, plays no role in explaining unemployment persistence (although it does influence wages and the equilibrium rate of unemployment). Benefit duration, on the other hand, was found to have an impact on unemployment persistence, largely because long periods of benefit entitlement, in some cases indefinite (e.g., as in the UK), enable the development of

Table 9.6   Unemployment and benefits

	Unemployment rate (%), 1999	Benefit duration (years), 1995	Replacement ratio (%) 1995	Active policy spend (% GDP) 1996–7
Austria	3.7	ind	71	0.35
Belgium	9.0	ind	60	1.25
Denmark	5.2	2.5	77	2.01
Finland	10.2	n.a.	87	1.67
France	11.3	3.8	79	1.28
Germany	8.7	ind	80	1.36
Greece (1998)	10.7	n.a.	27	0.68
Ireland	5.7	ind	64	1.64
Italy	11.4	0.5	47	0.94
Netherlands	3.2	ind	82	1.36
Portugal	4.5	n.a.	77	0.71
Spain	15.9	3.5	76	0.60
Sweden	7.2	1.2	85	2.97
United Kingdom	6.1	ind	67	0.58
United States	4.2	0.5	59	0.21
Japan	4.7	0.5	60	0.09

Source: OECD 1998, 2000
Note: ind. reflects the fact that the benefit system offers support that is effectively indefinite.

long-term (over 12 months) unemployment. Cockx and Ridder (2001) report that Belgium's social employment programme for those not covered by unemployment insurance (because of insufficient work experience or administrative delay) appears to increase welfare dependence. Machin and Manning (1999) maintain that long-lasting welfare benefits appear to explain the main difference in long-term unemployment between the EU and the USA. An obvious policy conclusion would be to limit benefit duration to help prevent the emergence of long-term unemployment. Yet as the last column of Table 9.6 reminds us, any restriction on benefit duration probably needs to be coupled with active labour market policies as in Sweden, which are not costless. Such policies would include the provision of quality education, relevant training and perhaps, in the end, employment subsidies or direct employment in the public sector. The primary importance of education comes across clearly from the studies of van den Berg (1990) and Schmitt and Wadsworth (1991). Indeed the latter's results seem to suggest that if Government wishes to increase the effectiveness of job search by the unemployed it should look to 'improve educational attainment, to limit the incidence of long-term unemployment, and to address the particular problems facing older workers' (p. 22). This advice concurs with that given by Sinclair (1987) when he warns against an over-reliance on search theory as a generator of policy. He counsels that one 'should be wary of thinking that government should . . . cut unemployment benefits in order to bring down unemployment'. This is not only because of the empirical doubts expressed about the magnitude of the improvement in unemployment that might result, but also because, 'longer search can bring an externality gain from an improved assignment of people to tasks' (p. 187).

AN EVALUATION OF SEARCH THEORY

Search theory is essentially a supply-side explanation of the phenomenon of unemployment in spite of attempts to extend it to consider employer search behaviour. The demand for labour and determination of wages that lie behind the distribution of wage offers are not adequately explained, thus search theory is not a complete analysis of unemployment. An indication of the importance of demand-side factors is contained in Manning (1999), which examined a small sample of low wage vacancies being offered by British hotels, supermarkets and restaurants. These vacancies attracted a small number of applications, just under 3 per vacancy, but were nearly all filled. When selecting for interview, employers demonstrated a clear dislike of applicants who were unemployed or lacked any relevant work experience.

Wages in search models are not determined by marginal productivity but include rents to compensate firms for unfilled vacancies and workers for spells of unemployment. The exact wage will be determined by the comparative bargaining power of firms and workers over the size of their rent element. Wages no longer reflect changes in productivity directly.

For Sinclair (1987) 'the fact that search is not the exclusive preserve of the unemployed detracts seriously from the appeal of the theory' (p. 184). The suggestion that workers voluntarily quit jobs in order to engage in full-time search does not appear to be a convincing one. Surely dissatisfied workers are best advised to engage in on-the-job search, or take the first job offered if already unemployed, and then continue to search for a better job from a position of strength, given discouraged worker and employment history effects. As we have seen the evidence relating to quits, on-the-job search, and offer acceptance rates among the unemployed indicate that this is indeed what happens.

Search theory attempts to deal with the cyclical component of unemployment by maintaining that during a recession, searchers do not realise that the wage distribution has shifted downwards. But one might question whether real wage rates are flexible even during a recession. Unless the unemployed revise their reservation wages down, they will reduce the probability of accepting a wage offer and therefore increase unemployment duration. But if firms reduce wages then they do not need to reduce vacancies, which vary in a pro-cyclical manner as we shall see in Figure 9.7. It could well be that any reservation wage effects would be swamped by the reduction in demand (i.e., fall in vacancies) during a recession. During a boom how can search theory explain the fact that the fall in unemployment lags by many years, the increase in demand indicated by a rise in vacancies? Searchers would need to have incorrect assessments of the wage distribution for a very long period of time indeed!

Gregg and Wadsworth (1996) point out that unemployed job searchers face the additional problem that the nature of labour market entry jobs has changed over time. Full-time employment has given way to part-time and temporary jobs and the wages of entry jobs have fallen relative to other sorts of jobs, with entry jobs having higher turnover. This means that there has been a shift away from entry jobs being suitable to the unemployed job seeker towards their being more appealing to those who come from households that already have at least one adult in work. This accounts for the rise of the all-work household and the no-work households since the early 1980s. It also helps explain the growing inequality in household income in the UK that we noted in Chapter 3.

In general a search equilibrium is an inefficient state of affairs because both firms and workers lose the costs they have incurred in searching once they meet and match.

A basic insight of job search is that increases in employment will not be instantaneous because it takes time to match up unemployed workers with advertised vacancies.

Search theory does not represent a convincing explanation for changes in the inflow to unemployment. It is probably best to regard it as an attempt to understand the behaviour of unemployed job searchers rather than as an explanation of how they came to be unemployed in the first place.

THE MATCHING FUNCTION

Partially as a response to the limitations of the original conception of search theory, economists have developed a macroeconomic form, the 'matching function'. This concentrates on the search activity of unemployed workers and employers with vacancies in seeking to make job matches. Pissarides (1992) is a good source as it emphasises the link between the matching function and search theory. He defines the matching function as giving 'the flow of jobs formed at any point in time in terms of a few aggregate variables' (p. 4). Thus at its simplest a matching function would take unemployment (U) and vacancies (V) into account, $M = m(U,V)$, where M is the number of jobs formed during a given time period. This enables the generation of unemployment within an equilibrium framework, where the flow into unemployment must equal the flow out of unemployment, because the matching function slows down the process of unemployed searchers getting jobs. Whilst the matching function allows one to discard aspects of search theory such as the reservation wage and the need for there to be a distribution of wages (although these can be incorporated into a matching model), matching models still suffer from the problem of identifying just what it is that causes the flow into unemployment.

Pissarides (1992) prefers not to use the term 'quits' and refers instead to 'job separations', which he sees as being 'private equilibrium outcomes: jobs break up because it is to the advantage of both the worker and the firm to terminate the employment relationship' (p. 15). This is an inadequate response to the criticisms levelled at search theory with regard to the insignificance of quits. One is bound to ask how common are such mutual agreements to 'terminate the employment relationship', especially during a recession? Once again the matching function like its search predecessor is at its weakest in explaining the flow into unemployment.

The Unemployment–Vacancy $(U–V)$ or 'Beveridge' curve that we will examine in detail later in this chapter, can be used to throw some light on the matching process. However, matching functions can be estimated directly. Petrongolo and Pissarides

(2000) survey a number of studies that estimate aggregate matching functions; generally the elasticity of the flow of hires with respect to unemployment lay in the 0.5–0.7 range. Incorporating job search from the already employed and new labour market entrants typically reduces the unemployment coefficient to 0.3–0.4, indicating that the unemployed are competing with other job searchers. The advantage of matching functions is that they can incorporate imperfect information, the varied nature of workers and slow mobility into the analysis of labour markets. Consider the example of imperfect information. Even if there were exactly the same number of vacancies as unemployed workers, there would still be unemployment unless firms and workers were fully informed about the state of the labour market. Without perfect information, firms would not know about the availability of workers, workers would not be fully aware of which firms had which vacancies and how many others had applied for a job. Some firms would have many applicants, others would have none. To this we could add that not all workers would be suitable for all jobs; applying at random would mean that some vacancies would remain unfilled and some workers will remain unemployed.

Coles and Smith (1998) do not rely on imperfect information or random applications. Job seekers will scan the vacancies on offer and only apply for ones that they find acceptable. They can apply for many jobs at once but if they were unemployed in the previous period the overall stock of vacancies does not interest them only the flow of new vacancies. Yet they must compete for the new vacancies not only with the already unemployed but also with workers who have just flowed into unemployment. The problem for job matching here is that not all jobs are the same nor are all workers.

Blanchard and Diamond (1994) suggest that if firms receive a number of applications for a job, they will rank them in order of preference before making a match with the most preferred applicant. This may disadvantage certain groups of workers such as the long-term unemployed.

Burgess and Profit (2001) use a matching function to see the effect that distance has on matching. They hypothesise that the greater the distance between a job seeker and a firm with a vacancy the greater the search costs. Their results from over three hundred travel-to-work areas in the UK suggest that there are externalities (spillover effects) between local labour markets. For example, high unemployment in neighbouring local labour markets increases the number of vacancies that are filled locally but reduces the flow out of unemployment. They also find a cyclical pattern: 'in a boom, the unemployed reduce their search radius and employers increase theirs; the situation is reversed in a recession' (p. 2).

By looking at a specific form of matching function, the U–V or Beveridge curve, we can appreciate the role that vacancies play in the labour market.

VACANCIES: SOME BASIC FACTS

A key element that is often ignored or merely assumed by search theory is the existence of job vacancies for the unemployed job seeker to find. Jackman *et al.* (1989)

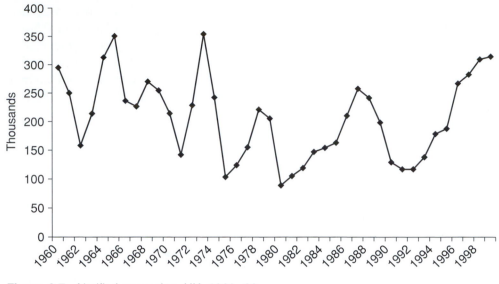

Figure 9.7 Notified vacancies, UK, 1960–99

Source: Compiled using ONS, statbase data

propose the adoption of an operational definition of a vacancy as 'a job which is currently vacant, available immediately and for which the firm has taken some specific recruiting action during the past four weeks' (p. 377). Thus a vacancy is not only an empty employment position but it is also part of an active hiring process on the part of the employer. One can distinguish two general types of vacancy:

a) replacement – which are current vacancies to replace workers who have already, or more speculatively, who are expected to quit or retire;
b) expansion – which are vacancies opened up by firms due to a desire to increase the workforce.

The first category does not represent any net increase in labour demand and consequently will not reduce unemployment. Replacement vacancies can fall and thereby increase unemployment through firms reducing the workforce by a process of 'natural wastage', i.e., not replacing workers who quit or retire. Expansion vacancies are a response to actual or anticipated changes in product demand or factor costs and will impact on unemployment. As many as 80 per cent of vacancies could be replacement ones, although this proportion is likely to exhibit a strong cyclical variation as expansion vacancies rise during a boom and fall during a recession.

Vacancies in general display a strong cyclical pattern, as the data in Figure 9.7, on changes in the stock of vacancies registered with the Government employment service (Jobcentres), clearly shows. There are marked declines in the UK stock of registered vacancies during the recessions of 1961–2, 1970–1, 1975–6, 1980–1 and 1990–1. During the booms of the 1980s and 1990s there were prolonged periods when

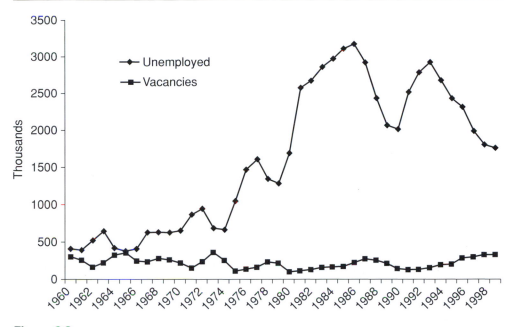

Figure 9.8

Source: As Figure 9.7

the stock of notified vacancies was rising. Figure 9.8 considers the number of regis-tered vacancies in relation to the number of registered unemployed job seekers.

On this scale it is difficult to see any clear relationship between unemployment and vacancies over time except the comparative inadequacy of job opportunities for the unemployed. However, there are a number of additional points to consider. The first is that not all available vacancies are registered with the Government-run Jobcentres. Probably the most influential estimate of the proportion of total vacancies notified to Jobcentres maintains that about one-third of all vacancies are notified. Roper (1989) points out that this notification rate time series is reliable if the duration of notified and non-notified vacancies (i.e., the length of time they remain unfilled) is on aver-age the same. Notified vacancy duration is increased by unsocial hours and the need for high skill levels, but low wages have an insignificant impact on duration. Layard (1989) presents data on vacancy duration broken down by occupational category which shows that in 1988, managerial and professional posts remained vacant for an average 2.2 months, falling to 0.6 months for unskilled manual jobs. Vacancy dura-tion depends upon the recruitment method adopted by firms to fill a vacancy. Infor-mal methods like personal contacts fill vacancies most quickly; of the formal methods the Jobcentre appears to be the fastest, with vacancies advertised in newspapers hav-ing the longest duration. The microeconomic analysis of vacancies suggests that firms may prefer to carry vacancies rather than offer a job to poorly matched workers. Continuing employer search for better matched workers will incur vacancy costs including lost output.

Considerations of data accuracy are important if the vacancy rate is to be used as a measure of unsatisfied labour demand. If we increase notified vacancy stocks by a factor of three to take account of the estimated notification rate, it is apparent from Figure 9.8 that vacancy numbers would still lie well below the level (stock) of unemployment from the mid-1970s to the end of the 1990s. This in itself may be viewed as a reasonable basis for the intuition that unemployment is largely a problem of deficient demand as proposed by the Keynesian model set out in the next chapter. Before we jump to any conclusions about the causes of unemployment based on casual empiricism, we need to examine the relationship between unemployment and vacancy rates, in order to appreciate what an analysis of vacancies can contribute to our understanding of unemployment.

UNEMPLOYMENT RATES AND VACANCY RATES

If we were to record the unemployment rate and the vacancy rate (suitably adjusted by the notification rate) for the UK labour market over time, we would observe that they appear to exhibit an inverse relationship. Figure 9.9 has done just that. During most of the 1960s corrected vacancy rates exceeded unemployment rates. In the 1970s a clear cyclical pattern emerges with vacancy rates falling during the recessions of 1970–1, 1974–5 and 1979–80, and with unemployment rates rising sharply during

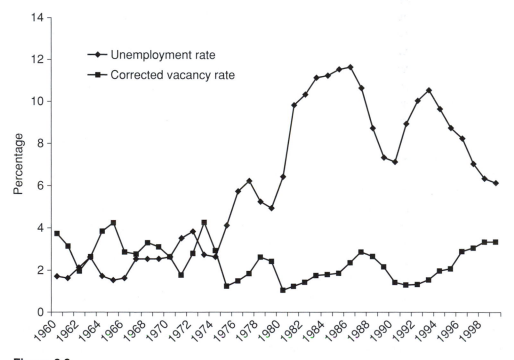

Figure 9.9

Source: As Figure 9.7

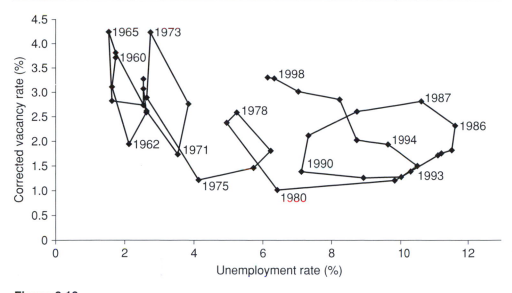

Figure 9.10

Source: As Figure 9.7

those years of recession. It is quite apparent from looking at the early 1990s recession that unemployment changes in a manner counter to the business cycle whereas vacancies change in a pro-cyclical manner.

According to Millard *et al.* (1999) changes in vacancies lead changes in unemployment, a fact that suggests that it is changes in the derived demand for labour proxied by vacancies rather than labour supply shocks that are the main element in cyclical unemployment.

If we now consider a plot of unemployment rates on one axis (the *x* axis) against vacancy rates on the other (the *y* axis) for the UK over time, we would expect the scatter diagram to show an inverse (i.e., downward sloping) relationship between unemployment and vacancies. As Figure 9.10 shows this is essentially what we have for the period 1960–99. This is the Unemployment–Vacancy, or U–V curve for short, which is also known as the Beveridge Curve.

A close examination of Figure 9.10 reveals a number of interesting features of the U–V curve relationship for the UK. The first thing to notice is the tendency of the U–V curve to move in anti-clockwise loops, e.g., 1960–5, 1970–5, 1976–80, and 1980–90. The next is to realise that the U–V relationship appears to have shifted to the right in each half decade from the early 1960s through to the mid-1980s. As Jackman *et al.* (1989) observe at around 2.5 per cent 'vacancy rates in the 1987 "recovery", the 1979 "boom" and the 1963 "slump" were the same' (p. 377).

Unemployment rates however, increased from approximately 2.5 per cent in 1963, to around 5 per cent in 1979, remaining in excess of 10 per cent in 1987. The 1980s appear to have witnessed an extremely severe shift in the U–V relationship. The experience of the early 1990s (1990–3) appears to follow the path of the early 1980s recession. However, since 1994 there has been a sustained fall in unemployment rates coupled with rising vacancy rates, which leads one to consider whether the underlying nature of the relationship, including the elasticity of the U–V curve, has altered fundamentally.

We need to examine these features of the U–V relationship at the theoretical level before we can comment on the implications of shifts in the observed U–V curve for our understanding of the phenomenon of unemployment.

THE THEORY OF THE BEVERIDGE (U–V) CURVE

This section follows and summarises the fine theoretical analysis of the U–V curve to be found in Bowden (1980). The problem is essentially one of explaining the simultaneous existence of unemployment and unfilled vacancies in the labour market. Figure 9.11 represents a labour market with not only the conventional demand and supply functions but with a range of employment levels, E, associated with a range of real wages.

Bowden (1980) suggests that E may be thought of 'as a clearing path, for it relates the actual quantity of employment to the forces of supply and demand' (p. 35). This view of the labour market proposes that unless real wages (W/P) immediately and instantaneously adjust labour demand and supply, then the market will be able to have disequilibrium wage levels such as W^1 and W^2. At W^1 low unemployment of a magnitude AB exists alongside substantial vacancies of AC. At W^2 there is mass unemployment of HJ, with a comparatively low level of vacancies of HI. Figure 9.11 suggests that even at what are equilibrium real wages W^*, vacancies and unemployment will coexist, with the equilibrium relationship between vacancies and unemployment

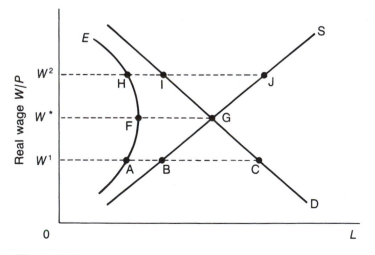

Figure 9.11

Source: Adapted from Bowden 1980, figure I(a), p. 36

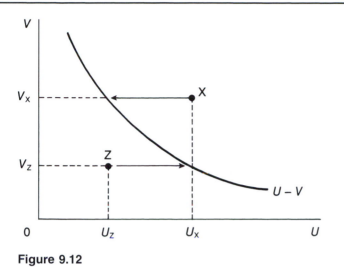

Figure 9.12

being $U = V$, both being of a magnitude FG. Hence there is an inverse relationship between vacancies and unemployment as real wages vary. Dividing the vacancy and unemployment levels contained in Figure 9.11 by supply (S) gives the plot of unemployment and vacancy rates in Figure 9.12.

Thus the U–V curve has been derived as the locus of combinations of unemployment and vacancy rates consistent with a conception of a labour market in which non-equilibrium wages can exist and in which the market clears on the short side (i.e., employment E does not equal B at W^1 nor G at W^* or I at W^2). There are two explanations advanced in support of the notion that the market clears on the short side. The first stems from a realistic conception of time which allows frictions in labour market adjustment to permit that even if $S = D$, labour turnover activity means that some firms will be in the process of hiring workers while other firms will be losing some of their workers. Unless this labour turnover activity is perfectly coordinated, then less than perfect coordination i.e., friction, enables unemployment and unfilled vacancies to coexist. Another justification rests upon the argument that to eradicate an inverse relationship between unemployment and vacancies at the aggregate level all individual sub-markets of a labour market need a 'coincident pattern of supply and demand'. Failing that, as the number of sub-markets increases, an aggregate U–V curve approaches the smooth continuous form shown in Figure 9.12.

The U–V curve might be regarded as a series of combinations of vacancies at various unemployment rates, which are equilibrium combinations in the sense of being compatible with market clearing in the labour market, albeit on the short side. At a point above the U–V curve, like X in Figure 9.12, vacancies V_x are greater than they should be at the unemployment rate U_x, outflows should therefore exceed inflows and unemployment should fall. Conversely, at points below the U–V curve such as Z, vacancy rates V_z are inadequate to sustain a rate of unemployment of U_z, hence inflow exceeds outflow and unemployment rises.

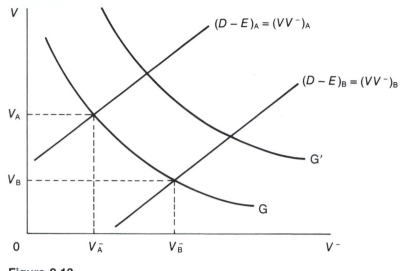

Figure 9.13

Source: Adapted from Bowden 1980, figure 2, p. 39

However, such arguments do not mean that the aggregate U–V curve derived from a modified conventional market analysis need be a stable, invariant relationship. Indeed, our prior observations about actual U–V curves suggest that this is not the case; we need to explain anti-clockwise dynamics and identify possible causes of shifts in the U–V relationship.

Following Bowden (1980) we introduce the notion of redundancy or lay-offs as negative hiring. Thus firms may recruit workers through positive vacancies V or reduce their workforce through negative vacancies (V^-). Therefore the difference between aggregate labour demand D, which will be influenced by real wages and product demand, and existing employment E is related to our vacancy concepts thus,

$$V - V^- = D - E,$$

where net vacancies equal the incremental demand for labour.

One would anticipate the relationship between V and V^- to be an inverse one, with a high V associated with a low V^-. This is reflected in the G curve in Figure 9.13, which locates pairs of V and V^-. If some firms are hiring workers while others are making them redundant, positive and negative vacancies will be unevenly distributed among firms. The greater the dispersion of these labour demand states between firms the further from the origin the G curve will be, G' for example.[4]

Any level of incremental labour demand ($D - E$) is associated with a combination of positive and negative vacancies ($V - V^-$). Hence in Figure 9.13 a high level of incremental demand such as $(D - E)_A$ is associated with high positive vacancies V_A and relatively low negative vacancies $V_{\bar{A}}$. For a lower level of labour demand

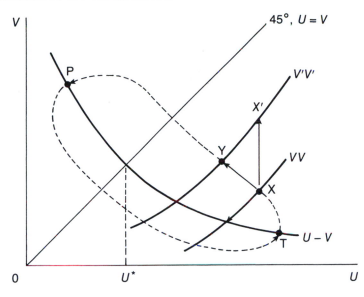

Figure 9.14

Source: Adapted from Bowden 1980, figure 3, p. 42

such as $(D - E)_B$ vacancies are low V_B and negative vacancies are comparatively high (V_B^-).

Returning to the U–V curve but taking with us the notion that incremental demand will be positively sloped in the V^-,V and the U,V planes, consider Figure 9.14. Taking a position off the U–V curve such as X, if labour demand is fixed as is shown by a fixed VV curve, then the movement from X is along VV towards the U–V curve. This is essentially what was proposed in Figure 9.12.

Allowing labour demand D to increase either because product demand has risen or real wages have fallen, has the effect of shifting the VV curve upwards, that is to V'V'. Now there are two forces acting upon a point such as X. One to move it along the VV curve to a location on the U–V curve, the other to shift it to a position like X' on the V'V' curve. The net result of this combination of forces is to move the labour market from position X in the direction of Y. If we let P stand for the peak of an economic cycle and T the trough of a recession, the labour market follows an anti-clockwise loop in the unemployment–vacancy plane (i.e., the broken line in Figure 9.14).

Thus for Bowden (1980) the U–V curve is a 'locus of temporary equilibria, each point of which corresponds to a given demand for labour' (p. 43).

Observed U–V points will move in an anticlockwise direction around that 'locus of temporary equilibria' because of the continual changes to which the demand for labour is subjected in the real world. If the underlying U–V curve is shifted outwards then the constellation of observed U–V points will spiral outwards as well.

What factors would cause the underlying U–V relationship to shift further away from the origin? In Bowden's model a number of interesting shift factors are present.

Taking the 45° line along which unemployment rates equal vacancy rates, the intersection of the U–V curve with this line yields a rate of unemployment U^*, at which $U = V$. This as we noted earlier can be regarded as an equilibrium condition for the simultaneous existence of unemployment and vacancies in the labour market. If this entails no real wage disequilibrium (i.e., if it corresponds to W^* in Figure 9.11) then one could interpret U^* as the 'natural rate of unemployment'. Hence any factors including increasing benefits or declining productivity, which increase the 'natural rate' (or NAIRU) could shift the U–V curve outwards.

The speed of labour market clearing also influences the location of the U–V curve. Any decrease in the speed of market clearing, which is an aspect of market efficiency, will serve to shift the U–V curve outwards. Employment protection legislation may have slowed down labour market clearing by making employers more choosy in their hiring of new workers. If benefits do make the unemployed more choosy in their job search, or if discouraged worker and adverse employment history effects are significant then the U–V curve would tend to shift outwards.

Another interesting feature of this model is that a more uneven distribution of labour demand states among firms or between industries will shift the U–V locus further from the origin, in much the same way that it shifted the G curve out in Figure 9.13. This is interesting because it implies that divergence in the employment structure of economies, such as the shift away from manufacturing to service sector employment, which in the UK was particularly marked during the 1980s, might show up as outward shifts in the U–V locus. With one sector of the economy in decline (in employment terms) and another expanding we would witness an increase in negative and positive vacancies at the same time, i.e., a shift out of the G curve in Figure 9.13. Bowden (1980) states that 'any form of dispersion in the demand for labour, whether by skills or by industries, can be expected to lead to an outward shift in the observed U–V diagram' (p. 47). Having set out a theoretical case for the existence of the U–V curve and considered an explanation for its dynamic path and shifts over time, we now turn to empirical studies of the U–V curve.

EMPIRICAL STUDIES OF THE BEVERIDGE (U–V) CURVE

After establishing that unemployment is primarily the consequence of a declining outflow rate (see Figure 9.6 above), Pissarides (1986) uses the U–V theoretical framework to analyse the rise in British male unemployment between 1967 and 1983. He treats the inflow rate as exogenous and constant. He estimates an equation for outflow as a function of vacancies, the U–V curve representing combinations of unemployment and vacancy rates where estimated outflow equals exogenously given inflow. The location of an economy along the U–V curve is determined by a 'vacancy supply' curve (VS) which takes the role of labour demand or Bowden's (1980) VV curve in Figure 9.14. Vacancy supply is brought about by the activity of job creation.

The story of the changes in unemployment in relation to vacancies can be characterised as one of shifts in the U–V and VS curves across the period 1967–83,

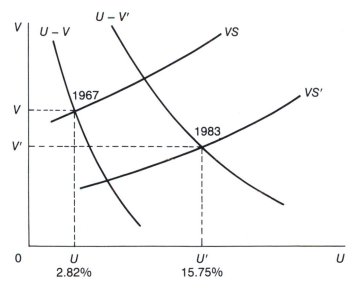

Figure 9.15

Table 9.7 Unemployment rate changes (percentage points)

	1967–74	1974–9	1979–83
Actual change	0.77	2.49	9.67
Estimated change consisting of	0.75	2.28	10.05
total *VS* shift	−0.50	1.47	2.75
total *U–V* shift	1.25	0.81	7.30

Source: Adapted from Pissarides 1986, table 3, p. 554

shown in Figure 9.15. Pissarides' (1986) study then seeks to account for increases in unemployment rates in terms of factors which may have caused the shifts in the U–V and VS functions. Table 9.7 summarises the overall results for three sub-periods and identifies the composition of the estimated changes in unemployment which are fairly close approximations to the actual changes in male unemployment rates.

As we can see from the results in Table 9.7 the U–V curve appears to have shifted to the right in all three periods, although much more so during 1979–83 than previously. In 1967–74 the expansion of the demand for labour is reflected in the leftward shift of the VS curve which partially offset the rise in the unemployment rate. Between 1974 and 1979 rising unemployment is being largely attributed to a fall in demand, shifting the VS curve to the right. This continues into the final sub-period but rising unemployment rates are dominated by the adverse shift in the U–V curve during 1979–83.

Table 9.8 Unemployment rate changes (percentage points), causal factors

	1967–74	1974–9	1979–83
Total *VS* shift	−0.50	1.47	2.75
of which			
profit/interest rates	−0.12	0.73	0.04
competitiveness	−0.13	0.00	0.58
fiscal deficit	−0.13	0.86	0.53
trade union mark-up	0.37	0.30	0.95
unexplained	−0.49	−0.42	0.65
Total *U–V* shift	1.25	0.81	7.30
consisting of			
inflow rate	−0.19	−1.30	3.80
outflow rate	1.44	2.11	3.50
of which			
mismatch	0.00	0.05	−0.17
benefits	−0.06	−0.04	0.90
time trend	1.50	2.10	2.77

Source: Adapted from Pissarides 1986, table 3, p. 554

Disaggregating these estimated shifts in the U–V and VS curves allows us to focus on specific causal factors. Table 9.8 presents a limited breakdown of the components of the total U–V and VS induced changes in unemployment rates. Beginning with the VS shifts, the results suggest that on the demand-side profitability, competitiveness and the Government's tightening fiscal stance all moved in a direction unfavourable to employment prospects after 1974. Somewhat surprisingly the impact of the trade union mark-up, a supply-side variable, increased during the early 1980s after having an almost constant adverse effect on unemployment during the 1970s. This indicates that unions may be effective in resisting wage reduction pressure from employers but are less effective at preventing job losses during a recession.

Turning to the U–V shifts, Table 9.8 shows that reductions in the inflow rate helped to restrain the rise in unemployment between 1967 and 1979. Unemployment rates rose during the late 1960s and throughout the 1970s because of the marked reductions in the outflow rate. However, an interesting feature of these results is that neither industrial mismatch nor unemployment benefits (the replacement ratio) appear to contribute towards increasing unemployment before the early 1980s. Thereafter the impact of benefits increases but its contribution is a modest 0.9 of a percentage point rise in the male unemployment rate. Mismatch appears to be an insignificant factor which plays a distinctly perverse role in this unemployment story.[5] The sharp rise in the inflow rate during 1979–83, is dominated by the increase in redundancies that took place over this period, particularly in the manufacturing sector.[6]

The time trend is an admission of the fact that Pissarides cannot identify what exactly is causing the reduction in the outflow rate over the entire 1967–83 period. This leaves the major reason for shifts in the U–V curve increasing unemployment up

Table 9.9 Unemployment exit probability by duration (annual average)

Duration (months)	1979	1980	1981	1982	1983	1984	1985
0–3	0.57	0.47	0.39	0.40	0.41	0.41	0.44
3–6	0.23	0.18	0.18	0.20	0.19	0.17	0.16

Source: Adapted from Budd *et al.* 1988, table 3, p. 1077

to 1979 unaccounted for. It also fails to explain a significant and substantial cause of the U–V shift and consequent unemployment increase for 1979–83. Layard (1986) suggests that the role of the long-term unemployed has been overlooked. Discouraged worker and employment history effects will impact on outflows through a reduction in search intensity and greater caution on the part of firms when hiring workers especially in conditions of strong employment protection legislation.[7]

The proportion of long-term unemployed in total unemployment in the UK increased from a low of 10 per cent at the beginning of 1967 to 30 per cent by 1979, rising to 43 per cent by 1988 (see Table 10.4). A study by Budd *et al.* (1988) takes up the issue of the long-term unemployed and examines their impact within a U–V framework. By calculating the exit (i.e., outflow) probabilities of those who have been unemployed for up to three months and contrasting these with the probability of those unemployed for up to six months the study reveals a marked difference between the outflow prospects of the unemployed by duration.

The data in Table 9.9 shows a marked fall in the exit probability as the duration of unemployment increases, and this occurs well before long-term unemployment of twelve months or more is reached. It also shows that these probabilities declined during the first half of the 1980s.

By developing a model to explain changes in the proportion of long-term unemployment in terms of variations in exit probabilities, Budd *et al.* (1988) hope to be able to account for the outward shift of the U–V curve. Their approach depends upon the validity of identifying the proportion of long-term unemployed as a proxy measure for the search intensity of the unemployed and their suitability to employers (employment history). Their preferred estimate of the U–V curve is

$$\log U_t = 0.5332 - 0.1987 \log V_t + 1.2057 \log U_{t-1} - 0.4964 \log U_{t-2} \\ + 0.0854 \log R_{t-1} - 0.0059T + 0.0001T^2$$

where U is unemployment, V is vacancies, R is the ratio of long-term to total unemployment and T is time. From this Budd *et al.* (1988) conclude that 'only the long-term unemployment ratio and the time trends have a robust, stable effect on the position of the U–V curve' (p. 1085). Considering the U–V shift from 1975 to 1984 they believe that some 43 per cent of the movement in the curve is accounted for by the growth in the proportion of long-term unemployment, the rest being due to the time trend. The lower search intensity and lower suitability of the long-term unemployed represent what

Budd *et al.* (1988) call a 'significant structural change in the labour market' (p. 1085). Once again this study was unable to find any role for the benefit system via the replacement ratio in explaining the increase in unemployment. Neither did an index of industrial mismatch appear to play any part in shifting the U–V curve.

Jackman *et al.* (1989) take a slightly different approach to the U–V relationship by estimating the link between the duration of unemployment and the duration of vacancies in months. As one would expect there is a similar inverse relationship between these durations to that observed between unemployment and vacancy rates. There has been a substantial increase in the length of unemployment duration at any given level of vacancy duration, indicating that declining search intensity might have a role in the U–V duration story. Duration data for 1967 and 1987 reveals that vacancy duration was virtually identical in these two years at 1.02 and 1.06 months respectively. Unemployment duration on the other hand increased from 1.52 months in 1967 to 7.70 months in 1987.

The outcome of this empirical study points to a decline in the effectiveness of the matching process between firms with vacancies and unemployed job searchers over time. As Jackman *et al.* (1989) conclude, shifts in the U–V relationship appear to hinge on two factors 'workers become more choosy about taking jobs [and] firms become more choosy about hiring workers' (p. 393). Yet again there was no support for either the replacement ratio or mismatch as variables capable of explaining observed U–V shifts, although the proportion of long-term unemployed was found to be a significant factor in some versions of their model.

Empirical studies of the U–V curve, which point to the comparative unimportance of mismatch as a causal factor in the increase in unemployment, provide an interesting applied topic for the analysis of vacancies. Gregg and Petrongolo (1997) suggest that it may not be the overall effectiveness of matching that is shifting the U–V curve by declining from the late 1960s to the late 1980s before improving in the 1990s, but the competition that unemployed job seekers face from other groups of workers, new entrants and those returning to the labour market, filling vacancies. Indeed the fact that the U–V curve shifts means that there are variables other than unemployment and vacancies that are affecting the relationship.

Nickell *et al.* (2001) point out that the UK shares a pattern an improving U–V tradeoff (leftward shift) since the mid-1980s with Canada, Denmark, the Netherlands and the USA. There is some evidence of more minor improvements in Australia, Austria, New Zealand and Portugal but there were more rightward shifts in Belgium, Finland, France, Germany, Japan, Norway, Spain and Sweden after the mid-1980s. Nickel *et al.* (2001) identify longer unemployment benefit duration, increased unionisation and geographical immobility (house ownership) as causes of rightward U–V shifts but somewhat surprisingly increased employment protection legislation shifts the Beveridge curve to the left as it improves the efficiency of human resource management in firms. These causal factors are key ingredients in job searching and matching efficiency.

Although the studies referred to are instructive, Petrongolo and Pissarides (2000) maintain that 'no single [variable] or combination of variables can account for the deterioration of the matching rate since the mid-1970s' (p. 21).

CASE STUDY – FORMAL AND INFORMAL JOB SEARCH IN CHICAGO

The method of job search by which workers uncover vacancies and are then matched varies according to a number of factors. David Reingold (1999) 'Social Networks and the Employment Problem of the Urban Poor', *Urban Studies*, 36 (11): 1907–32, examined a sample of adult residents from Chicago's poor inner city areas to discover whether they used formal methods of job search or whether they relied upon word-of-mouth from friends and relatives to find out about employment opportunities.

High rates of unemployment among the urban poor are of concern to academics and policy makers alike. In theory we would expect high unemployment in a local labour market to severely limit the employment opportunities of low skilled workers. This combined with large numbers of such job seekers might mean that firms would seek to fill vacancies using low cost methods. Informal word-of-mouth is a no cost method of filling a vacancy. Given the lack of alternative employment opportunities available locally, workers are more likely to resort to these informal methods of job search.

Although Reingold's (1999) sample was drawn from poor inner city areas of Chicago they are not from the most deprived parts of the city; the study looked at adults from areas with rates of poverty between 20 and 39 per cent. The sample '[was] sorted into one of three categories: those who found their current job through word-of-mouth; those who found their job through other methods, such as advertisements and employment agencies; and those who are not working'. The results of this sorting by race and gender are contained in Table A.

> The general pattern is that men are more likely than women to have found their current job through a friend or relative, and Mexicans of both sexes are more likely than either blacks, whites or Puerto Ricans to have found their current job through a personal contact. . . .
>
> In general, those individuals who found their job through a personal contact are, on average, less educated than those who found their job through other methods.

However, this was not the case for white men and women, nor for Mexican men and Puerto Rican women in Chicago.

When the study looks at the composition of the social networks of job seekers

Table A   Method of Job Acquisition (% distribution)

	Not working	Personal contacts	Other (formal) methods
Males			
White	8.1	25.8	66.1
Black	31.6	28.2	40.1
Mexican	6.7	55.8	37.4
Puerto Rican	20.9	42.6	36.5
Females			
White	52.4	13.6	34.0
Black	49.3	14.8	35.9
Mexican	49.5	31.6	18.9
Puerto Rican	64.0	13.1	22.9

Source: Adapted from Reingold 1999, table 3, p. 1914

one of the more surprising results is that black women who found their job through a friend or relative have networks with much higher rates of welfare receipt and of unemployment. They also have lower rates of educational attainment than do black women who found their job through some other method. There is also a difference in the percentage of a respondent's network that is on public aid between black men who found their job through word-of-mouth and those who did not. Perhaps these differences reflect the tendency of employers to recruit through informal referrals for unskilled jobs which are more likely to be filled by people who have lower levels of education, and who are embedded in networks composed of less-educated welfare recipients who are not working. It is also possible that welfare recipients and other non-workers pass on to friends and relatives job information acquired through unemployment offices and welfare agencies.

. . .

In general, those . . . who are not working tend to be younger, are less likely to be married and have fewer years of education than either those who found their job through personal contacts or those who used some other methods.

. . . non-working females tend to have more constricted social networks, except for Mexican women; however, non-working male respondents are situated in social networks similar to those in which working male respondents are situated. Not surprisingly, unemployed respondents have social networks with less human capital, i.e., their networks have less education, lower rates of employment and are more likely to be on public aid.

Unfortunately, the study cannot tell us which came first; do these low quality social networks cause people to withdraw from the labour market, or is it the fact that they are unemployed that causes the poor quality of their social network?

In conclusion, although

it does not appear that any particular group is excluded from employment opportunities that are largely filled through word-of-mouth, there are ethnic differences in the rate of finding a job through word-of-mouth, as well as ethnic . . . differences in the way that social networks operate in the labour market. . . . Employed black men seem to be more dependent on finding jobs through informal methods than are employed men in any other group. This may reflect difficulties some black men experience finding jobs through formal means, either because of discrimination or the perception among black men that they are at a disadvantage when using formal job-search methods. The greater dependence of black men on personal contacts to broker job-seekers and job vacancies may explain why there is a perception that black economic progress depends more on who you know than what you know.

Nevertheless, higher levels of education actually decrease informal job-finding for blacks, as well as for Puerto Ricans. . . . Another important finding is the higher rate of word-of-mouth job-finding among Puerto Ricans and Mexicans. This is likely to reflect the lower average rate of educational attainment of both Spanish-speaking groups, making them more likely to compete for unskilled positions that employers largely fill through word-of-mouth.

Certainly the limited English language ability of recent immigrants in some of the ethnic communities in Chicago reduces 'their ability to use more formal job-search methods, while increasing their dependence on personal contacts for job-finding'.

There is a caveat concerning the extent to which we can extrapolate the findings of this study. Reingold (1999) mentions 'Chicago's notorious reputation as one of America's most racially segregated cities, if not the most segregated . . .' This fact may have had an influence particularly on the ethnically homogeneous nature of workers' social networks. 'Perhaps in other cities with less segregation there is more interaction between ethnic and racial groups.'

Overall, this case study shows that there are differences between workers who resort to formal and informal methods of job search. Although the general state of the labour market does exert an important influence, in poor urban areas the social networks of residents help organise labour markets in terms of matching job seekers with vacancies. Successful job search seems to be a combination of what you know and who you know.

JOB SEARCH AND VACANCIES- SUMMARY

This chapter covered both job search and the role of vacancies in the analysis of unemployment. Our microeconomic analysis of worker job search highlighted:

- the variety of search methods
- the importance of search costs set against the expected benefit of finding an acceptable job
- the concept of the reservation wage
- the role of welfare benefits in subsidising job search by unemployed workers

A simple policy prescription based on this analysis asserted that:

- reducing welfare benefits would
- make search more costly, thereby
- reducing the reservation wage
- increasing the intensity of job search, and
- shortening unemployment duration

If real wages change in a pro-cyclical manner (i.e., rise in booms and fall in recessions) then the benefit of job search would behave accordingly thereby:

- increasing the reservation wage and job search during a boom
- reducing the reservation wage and shortening search during a recession

Although the theoretical position is clear, the empirical situation:

- casts doubt about the movement of real wages during business cycles
- casts considerable doubt on the magnitude of the relationship between welfare benefits and unemployment duration
- questions the scope for reducing unemployment using the benefit policy instrument
- identifies educational attainment as a key variable influencing the fortunes of unemployed job searchers

Search theory is not a general theory of unemployment because it is unable to account for the flow into unemployment. At best it is a supply-side attempt to analyse the job seeking behaviour of the already unemployed.

We were able to identify a number of features about vacancies which informed our understanding of unemployment:

- that vacancies vary in a cyclical manner
- that vacancy and unemployment rates exhibit an inverse relationship over time
- that this $U–V$ curve relationship has a firm theoretical basis

- that the $U–V$ relationship has shifted over time particularly in the EU countries

For the UK our main conclusions were:

- up to around the end of 1966 there appeared to be a fairly stable $U–V$ relationship
- which subsequently shifted outwards, and
- the most marked shift occurred during the first half of the 1980s

Upon investigation:

- demand-side factors coupled with a decrease in the effectiveness of job matching emerged as important causal factors, and
- worker search intensity and job suitability are also important, particularly with regard to the long-term unemployed

JOB SEARCH AND VACANCIES – QUESTIONS FOR DISCUSSION

1) Recalculate the third and fourth columns of Table 9.4 using costs of £6 *per search*. What happens to the value of the optimum reservation wage? (Remember that the Pr(W) data is in Table 9.2.)
2) Outline the theory of job search in order to establish the relationship between welfare benefits, job search and unemployment.
3) What empirical evidence is there to support the link between welfare benefits and unemployment suggested by search theory?
4) Based on an understanding of search theory, should labour market policy makers reduce the generosity of the welfare benefit system in order to reduce unemployment?
5) Why is job search theory not a general theory of unemployment?
6) Explain what unemployment flows are and how they have varied over time and between countries.
7) What factors might account for the fact that the UK vacancy rate in 1987 was the same as it was in 1963 yet the unemployment rate had increased fivefold?
8) Is the $U–V$ curve a stable feature of an economy or is it a 'locus of temporary equilibria'?
9) What does incorporating vacancies into an analysis of unemployment tell us about the importance of the long-term unemployed?
10) Explain the link between the $U–V$ relationship and mismatch in the labour market.

SUGGESTED READING

Mortensen, D. and Pissarides, C. (1999) 'New Developments in Models of Search in the Labour Market', in O. Ashenfelter and D. Card (eds) *Handbook of Labour Economics*, Volume 3, Amsterdam: Elsevier Science.

Nickell, S., Nunziata, L., Ochel, W. and Quintini, G. (2001) 'The Beveridge Curve, Unemployment and Wages in the OECD from the 1960s to the 1990s', London School of Economics Centre For Economic Performance, Discussion Paper 502.

10

Unemployment

INTRODUCTION

The explanation of persistent, mass unemployment was the central challenge that Keynes (1936) addressed in the General Theory. The descriptive statistics in the next section clearly show that, for the industrialised world, unemployment re-emerged as a significant empirical problem during the 1970s, became particularly severe in the first half of both the 1980s and the 1990s, and is rising once again at the end of 2001. As students of labour economics we need to be aware of the time path and general composition of unemployment as background knowledge for our theoretical understanding of why the labour market does not appear to clear at anything like a full employment equilibrium.

A condensed history of economic thought regarding unemployment would begin with a pre-Keynesian neoclassical labour market in which real wages were too high to bring about full employment. Keynesian explanations of unemployment, stressing the importance of deficient aggregate demand, came to dominate the economics discipline and serve as a guide for economic policy making for much of the post-1945 period. However, doubts, both theoretical and empirical, about the Keynesian approach to unemployment began to gather strength from around the mid-1960s. Initially this took the form of the Monetarism most closely associated with Friedman (1968), but by the mid-1970s New Classical macroeconomics incorporating rational expectations, of which Lucas (1978) is a good example, emerged as an influential explanation of unemployment. Yet this was not the last word in the study of unemployment. Throughout the 1980s a number of theoretical developments have sought to explain the phenomena associated with recent trends in mass unemployment – particularly its persistence. These developments have included the implicit contract and insider–outsider approaches, as well as job search models to which we have already referred.

But we need to look more closely at other explanations of what has come to be known as 'hysteresis' before we can recommend policies to reduce unemployment with any degree of confidence.

THE STATISTICAL PICTURE

To begin with a few cautionary words about unemployment data collection. In the UK, unemployment figures are based upon information generated by the Government's Employment Department through its role as administrator of the unemployment benefit system. Before 1982 the number of people counted as unemployed during any month was based upon those who had registered as unemployed with an Employment Office. In 1982, who was to be counted as unemployed was redefined as those claiming unemployment benefit. The advantage of measuring unemployment in this way is its simplicity. The obvious weaknesses of the claimant measure are that it may include benefit recipients who are not actively seeking work and exclude the unemployed who are not entitled to receive state unemployment benefits.

An alternative way of measuring unemployment is to use monthly surveys of a representative sample of households to determine those who do not have a paid job, but who have actively sought work in the preceding four weeks or are waiting to start work. This is the approach used by international agencies such as the International Labour Organisation (ILO) and OECD, and in a number of countries including the USA, Canada, Japan and Sweden. Since 1984 the UK has conducted a twice a year Labour Force Survey that provides an alternative measure of unemployment.

Figure 10.1 compares the claimant rate measure with the ILO survey based unemployment rate for the UK since 1984. As to which is the more accurate measure of unemployment it was widely believed that the UK claimant count introduced a downward bias into its unemployment count particularly because it excluded married women who were out of work. In Figure 10.1 the claimant unemployment rate is consistently below the ILO rate. The claimant rate is certainly very susceptible to administrative changes in the benefit system of which there have been more than twenty since 1979.

Through the UK Labour Force Survey, the more widespread ILO survey method has been available as a check on the claimant measure of unemployment. In 1986 there was a 69,000 discrepancy between the benefit claimant count of 3.07 million unemployed and the ILO compatible survey total of 3.14 million. The discrepancy between the two measures appears to grow as unemployment falls and narrows as unemployment rises. The differences between the two measures was

    69,000 in 1986
   357,000 in 1990
   120,000 in 1993
   579,000 in 2000.

Whilst recognising the shortfalls in any system of data collection we shall tell the unemployment story with the statistics at our disposal.

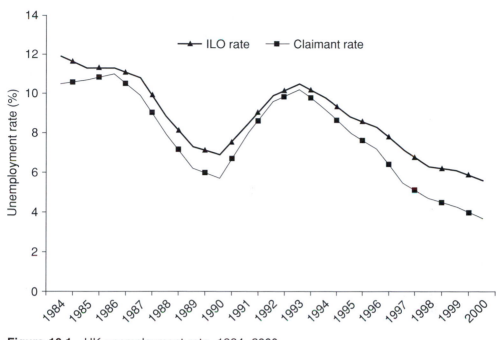

Figure 10.1 UK unemployment rate, 1984–2000

Source: Compiled using ONS, *Labour Market Trends*, various years

Taking the long historical view of unemployment in the UK contained in Figure 10.2 we can make a number of initial observations. The first thing to note is the volatility of the unemployment rate in the period before the 1914–18 War.[1] Unemployment falls as a consequence of that war but is soon followed by a severe recession during the 1920s only to be superseded by even higher unemployment rates in the 1930s, with unemployment peaking at a rate of 17.6 per cent in 1932. The Second World War has an evident impact on reducing unemployment. The remarkable feature of the post-1945 unemployment landscape is the low and relatively stable unemployment experienced up until the mid-1970s. Thereafter it climbs rapidly, particularly in the early 1980s.

However, it is clear from Figure 10.2 that unemployment is on a rising trend from the mid-1950s. OECD data reveals that the UK unemployment rate was at 1.4 per cent in 1955, by 1960 it had risen to 2.2 per cent yet as late as 1970 the rate was only 3.0 per cent. However, by 1975 it was at 4.5 per cent. The years of the first Thatcher Government witnessed unemployment rise from 5.0 per cent in 1979 to 12.5 per cent in 1983. A prolonged period of economic growth during the rest of the 1980s, which ended in the re-emergence of inflation, left unemployment at 6.9 per cent in 1990. Unemployment then rose again to reach 10.5 per cent in 1993. A period of sustained economic growth reduced the unemployment rate to 5.6 per cent in 2000.

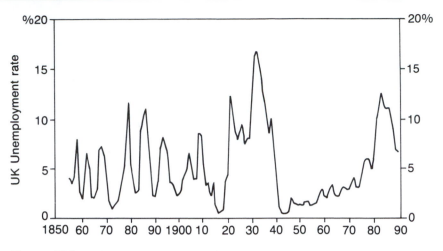

Figure 10.2

Source: Layard *et al.* 1991, figure 2a, p. 3

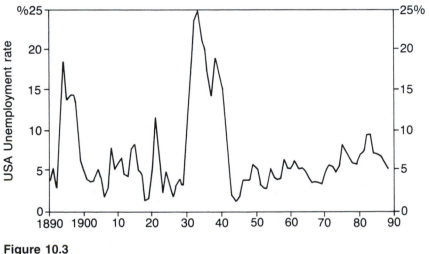

Figure 10.3

Source: Layard *et al.* 1991, figure 2b, p. 3

Figure 10.3 shows a historical time series for US unemployment rates. This begins by clearly showing that the 1890s recession in the USA where unemployment averaged 10.4 per cent was much more severe than that in the UK with average unemployment of 4.1 per cent. However, mean unemployment rates in the early part of the twentieth century, 1900–13, were very similar in the USA and UK (4.7 per cent and 4.4 per cent respectively). US unemployment falls during the First World War, but after a brief post-war recession, the 1920s were a period of relative prosperity in the USA. This prosperity was brought to an abrupt end in the recession that followed the Wall Street Crash of 1929, which saw unemployment peak at 24.9 per cent in 1932. Once again

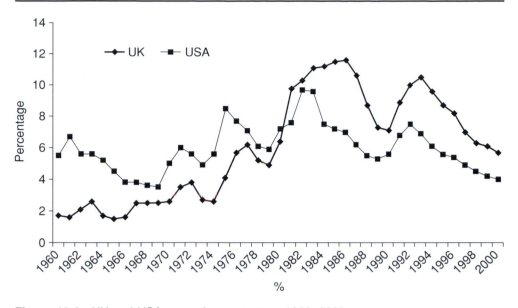

Figure 10.4   UK and USA unemployment rates, 1960–2000

Source: OECD, various years

it was the Second World War which signalled the end of the 1930s depression.[2] Although relatively stable and modest by its own historical standards, US unemployment rates were generally higher than those of the UK in the post-1945 period. However, this pattern was convincingly reversed by the early 1980s recession and subsequent economic history. OECD data shows that US unemployment rose from 4.3 per cent in 1955 to 5.5 per cent in 1960. It was 5.0 per cent in 1970 and rose rapidly to 8.5 per cent in 1975, falling back to 5.9 per cent by 1979. The early 1980s' recession in the USA saw unemployment peak at 9.7 per cent in 1982 before falling to 5.6 per cent in 1990. The early 1990s' recession saw the US unemployment rate rise to 7.5 per cent in 1992 before the sustained growth of the remainder of the 1990s reduced the unemployment rate to 4.2 per cent in 2000.

The changing pattern of the comparative unemployment experience of the USA and the UK in the 1960–2000 period is shown in Figure 10.4. After UK unemployment rates rose above those of the USA in 1981 they remained higher for the remainder of the 1980s and throughout 1990s. That the rise in unemployment in the post-Second World War period was widespread throughout the industrialised world is brought out by the comparative data contained in Table 10.1. This underlines both the particular severity of the early 1980s recession and the significant disparity in unemployment rates among OECD countries. Of the European Union (EU) countries in 2000 Spain stands out as being a high unemployment economy. Unemployment rates are also high in Finland, France and Italy. Ireland used to suffer from high unemployment, yet rapid economic growth particularly during the 1990s has reduced

Table 10.1   Unemployment rates, 1960–2000 (annual average percentage)

	1960–74	1975–79	1980–84	1985–89	1990–94	1995–99	2000
Australia	2.2	5.5	7.5	7.5	9.0	8.1	6.3
Austria	1.4	1.6	2.8	3.5	4.7	4.2	3.7
Belgium	2.4	7.0	11.3	10.3	7.9	9.5	7.0
Canada	5.1	7.5	9.8	8.8	10.3	8.8	6.8
Denmark	1.8	6.1	9.3	8.5	8.7	6.0	4.7
Finland	n.a.	n.a.	6.0	5.0	10.9	12.8	9.7
France	2.1	4.9	7.9	10.1	10.6	11.9	9.5
Germany	0.8	3.5	5.7	6.3	6.0	9.0	7.9
Greece	n.a.	n.a.	7.2	6.7	7.8	9.8	11.4
Ireland	5.2	8.1	11.6	16.9	14.7	9.4	4.2
Italy	3.9	4.7	6.3	7.6	9.6	11.7	10.5
Japan	1.3	2.0	2.4	2.6	2.4	3.7	4.7
Netherlands	1.6	5.3	9.9	9.5	6.3	5.3	2.9
New Zealand	0.2	1.0	4.0	4.8	9.4	6.7	6.0
Norway	1.9	1.9	2.5	3.0	5.5	4.1	3.5
Portugal	n.a.	n.a.	8.2	6.9	5.1	6.2	4.1
Spain	2.5	5.8	15.6	19.7	19.6	20.1	14.1
Sweden	1.5	1.5	2.4	1.9	5.8	8.8	5.9
UK	2.9	5.4	10.3	9.5	9.2	7.3	5.5
USA	4.8	6.9	8.2	6.1	6.6	4.9	4.0

Sources: OECD, *Economic Outlook*, December 1990; OECD, *Main Economic Indicators*, October 1993; OECD and Eurostat 2001

the unemployment rate to the level of Austria and Germany. Recorded unemployment in Germany rose after unification in 1990. The UK is clearly amongst a middle rank of nations including Denmark and Portugal. The comparatively low unemployment rates that Sweden enjoyed have been undermined during the 1990s. Japanese unemployment rates are at a lower level than the other countries in this sample, yet have increased to historically high levels during the depression of the 1990s reaching a rate of 5.3 per cent in September 2001. Australian and Canadian unemployment rates reflect the severity of the 1980s recession, closely mirroring UK and US experience. New Zealand's agriculturally-based economy appears to have experienced a marked drift away from the low unemployment rates it enjoyed during the 1960s and 1970s.[3]

Thus far we have been dealing with average annual unemployment rates. In the extreme an average annual unemployment rate of 10 per cent could mean either that 10 per cent of the labour force (LF) had been unemployed for a whole year, or that every worker had been unemployed for 36.5 days during that year. Obviously for any given unemployment rate, the more widely distributed the experience of unemployment the shorter is the duration of that unemployment. In our fictitious example of 10 per cent unemployment the first extreme interpretation yields an unemployment duration of 12 months, whereas in the latter case it is approximately 1.2 months. As we saw in Chapter 9, the unemployment rate (U/LF) can be thought of as a stock measure which is the outcome of two unemployment flows; the unemployment inflow

S; and the outflow H from unemployment. When $S = H$ unemployment is in a 'steady state', in that the unemployment rate is constant although there has been some change in who is actually unemployed. If $S < H$ unemployment falls and when $S > H$ it rises. Following Layard *et al.* (1991, pp. 217–25) one can estimate the average duration of unemployment from the unemployment rate and the inflow rate. Assuming a steady state,

$$U/LF \equiv (S/LF)(U/S)$$

where S/LF is the inflow rate, and U/S is the average time that those who flow into unemployment remain unemployed, i.e., the average duration. Hence we can easily calculate the average duration of unemployment (U/S) as the unemployment rate (U/LF) divided by the inflow rate (S/LF),

$$U/S \equiv (U/LF)/(S/LF).$$

In the EU, Spain is the outstanding example of a low inflow but high unemployment duration labour market although these are features of many other EU states including the UK. North American labour markets have high rates of inflow but short average durations of unemployment. Traditionally countries as diverse as Japan and Sweden appear to have had the best of both worlds, in that they combined low inflow rates with short durations which obviously yielded low unemployment rates. However, the unemployment experience of first Sweden and then Japan deteriorated markedly during the 1990s.

These important cross country differences need to be supplemented with an understanding of how unemployment flows and durations have changed over time. In Figure 9.6 we tracked the movement of unemployment flows in the UK since the late 1960s. An important feature of the path taken by British unemployment over this period was the remarkable consistency of the inflow rate (see Figure 9.6). Apart from increases in inflow during the 1973–75 period and again between 1979 and 1980, the rising trend in unemployment appears to be a consequence of the increase in unemployment duration. The periods 1974–8 and 1980–4 witnessed significant rises in the average completed spells of unemployment. The rapid fall in unemployment rates in the second half of the 1980s appears to have been 'caused' by reductions in both the inflow rate and the duration of unemployment. In the USA rising unemployment rates appear to have been the consequence of a more evenly balanced growth in both inflow and duration between the late 1960s and early 1980s. Similarly the reduction in unemployment rates since 1983 has been 'caused' by falling inflows and durations.

Boheim and Taylor (2000) provide some interesting details on unemployment duration in Britain during the 1990s; they found that average (median) unemployment duration was longer for men at 4.70 months than for women, 3.19 months. This appeared to be due to the greater likelihood that unemployed women would enter part-time employment or else leave the labour force to become economically inactive.

A phenomenon closely allied to the issue of unemployment duration is the growth in the significance of the long-term unemployed. Table 10.2 presents some data that

Table 10.2 Long-term unemployment, 1979, 1988, 1995 and 2000 (percentage of unemployed with duration longer than 12 months)

	1979	1988	1995	2000
Australia	18	28	31	29
Austria	n.a.	13	17	32
Belgium	62	78	62	61
Canada	4	7	14	12
Denmark (1983)	33	29	28	21
Finland	n.a.	2	32	30
France	30	45	46	40
Germany	29	47	48	52
Greece	n.a.	50	51	55
Ireland	38	66	63	57
Italy	51	69	63	61
Japan	n.a.	21	18	22
Luxembourg	n.a.	40	22	32
Netherlands	36	50	43	44
New Zealand	n.a.	21	23	21
Norway	4	6	27	7
Portugal (1985)	56	41	49	41
Spain	28	62	57	51
Sweden	7	8	16	30
UK	30	43	44	28
USA	4	7	10	7

Source: OECD, *Employment Outlook*, 1990, 2001

highlights the increase in the proportion of those unemployed who have been out of work for 12 months or more. Long-term unemployment grew in significance in all of these countries during the 1980s. During the 1990s the proportion of long-term unemployed stabilised and then fell due to a combination of prolonged economic growth (from 1992 in the UK) and policies targeted at the unemployed (the New Deal in the UK). However, even in 2000 a clear distinction can still be made between the importance of long-term unemployment as a persistent labour market phenomenon in the EU countries and Australia, and its comparative insignificance in the North American labour markets. Denmark stand out as an EU country with a comparatively low proportion of long-term unemployment, whereas in Belgium and Italy more than 60 per cent of the unemployed have been out of work for 12 months or more. As we shall see later on in this chapter, this distinction is not unrelated to the variety of benefit regimes and active labour market policies pursued in these countries.

The implication of the rise in long-term unemployment is that unemployment rates have risen as unemployment outflow rates have fallen increasing the duration of unemployment. Burgess and Turon (2000) question this by pointing out that changes in unemployment outflow lag behind changes in inflow by about a year and that inflow shocks are more immediate and more important than outflow shocks when affecting unemployment. Hence the main driving force behind changes in unemployment are

Table 10.3   Age-related unemployment rates, UK 2000

Age	Male	Female	Total
16–24	16.4	12.7	14.7
25–34	5.5	4.6	5.1
35–44	4.4	4.1	4.3
45–59	4.4	2.9	3.7
60–64	5.5	–	5.5
16–59/64	6.5	5.3	6.0

Source: ONS, *Labour Force Survey*, 2000

inflow (labour-demand) shocks with outflow being partly determined by unemployment itself.

Turning away from the nature of unemployment for the moment, let us consider some of the features which appear to characterise the unemployed. It is a well established fact that unemployment differs markedly according to a worker's age and gender. Table 10.3 presents UK age-related unemployment rates for both male and female workers. It is clearly the case that young workers are much more likely to be unemployed than their older more experienced counterparts. Those aged 16–24 had the highest unemployment rates in 2000, 45–59 year olds had the lowest rates. From a human capital perspective an additional benefit of work experience appears to be the decreased likelihood of unemployment. However, unemployment rates rise for men aged 60–64 indicating the problems associated with getting work when an unemployed person is close to retirement. Note that in the UK female unemployment rates are below those of male workers in all age categories; this is not a feature of other countries in the EU but is a characteristic the UK shares with the USA and Japan.

Within the EU the only country that does not have higher unemployment rates for younger workers is Germany. Eurostat data from 1999 records unemployment rates of 8.9 per cent for both workers aged 15–24 and for workers aged 25 and over. Table 10.4 shows that in most cases the discrepancy between age-related unemployment rates is substantial, with the exceptions of Austria and Ireland.

Unemployment rates differ according to the marital status of workers, with married men and women enjoying lower unemployment rates than their unmarried counterparts. The data in Table 10.5 shows that in 2000 in the USA unemployment rates were lowest for both married men and women, rising for those who were widowed, divorced or separated, and higher still for those who had never married. Note that although the overall female unemployment rate is higher than the male rate in the USA, the female rates are lower for divorced and single women than for males.

Unemployment data also reveals noteworthy differences in the experience of unemployment for groups of workers categorised by education, occupation and ethnic origin. In a human capital context the reduced incidence of unemployment as educational attainment increases represents a benefit that enhances the rate of return to education as an investment. Table 10.6 confirms that it is clearly the case in both Britain and the USA that unemployment falls as the level of formal education completed

Table 10.4   EU unemployment rates by age, 1999

	15–24 years	25 plus years
Italy	32.9	9.0
Greece	31.7	8.9
Spain	29.5	13.2
Finland	28.6	8.7
France	26.5	10.5
Belgium	22.6	7.2
Sweden	16.3	6.7
UK	12.3	4.9
Denmark	10.0	4.3
Portugal	9.1	3.8
Germany	8.9	8.9
Ireland	8.4	5.0
Netherlands	7.4	2.9
Luxembourg	6.8	2.0
Austria	5.9	4.5
EU-15	18.3	8.2

Source: Eurostat, *Labour Force Surveys*, 1999

Table 10.5   Unemployment rate (%) by marital status, USA, 2000

	Male	Female
Married	2.0	2.7
Widowed, divorced, separated	4.4	4.2
Single	7.6	6.9
Total	3.9	4.1

Source: US Bureau of Labour Statistics

Table 10.6   Unemployment rate (%) by education

	Male	Female	All
Great Britain (1998)			
No qualifications	15.6	8.4	12.2
Lower intermediate	8.3	5.9	7.1
Higher intermediate	4.5	3.8	4.2
University degree	3.0	2.9	3.0
USA (2000)*			
No qualifications	5.5	7.8	6.4
High School graduate	3.4	3.5	3.5
Below Bachelors degree	2.6	2.8	2.7
University graduate	1.5	1.8	1.7

Sources: Labour Force Survey, Spring 1998; US Bureau of Labour Statistics, 2001
Note: * Adult workers aged 25 plus.

Table 10.7 US occupational unemployment rates (%), 2000

Managerial and professional	1.7
Technical, sales and administration	3.6
Service occupations	5.3
Precision production and craft	3.6
Operators and labourers	6.3
Farming, forestry and fishing	6.0
Total of all occupations	4.0

Source: US Bureau of Labour Statistics 2001

increases. According to Pryor and Schaffer (1999) unemployment in the USA is also linked to lower functional literacy, which can be rectified through the education system. There is a similar inverse relationship between occupational classification and unemployment where the higher the occupational (skill) category the lower the incidence of unemployment. Table 10.7 shows that in the USA less skilled workers lower down the occupational ladder endure higher unemployment rates. The spectre of labour market discrimination casts a shadow over unemployment. There are significant and enduring differences in unemployment rates between ethnic minority workers and majority population workers in the USA and Britain. This provides circumstantial evidence that available jobs are unequally distributed among workers on the basis of ethnic characteristics rather than upon genuine productivity criteria. Around 5 per cent of the total British labour force are classified as being from an ethnic minority background. Table 10.8 reflects the fact that unemployment rates increase almost four-fold between white majority workers and those from the Pakistani and Bangladeshi ethnic minority groups which suffer the highest rate of unemployment in Great Britain.

For the USA, Table 10.9 confirms that ethnic minority workers are more likely to be unemployed than their white majority counterparts. This shows that in the USA in 2000, black workers suffered the highest rates of unemployment, and that this is so for both males and females. Amongst Hispanic workers those of Puerto Rican origin experience the highest rate of unemployment.

Unemployment has an important regional aspect. The Department of Labour provides data to show state unemployment rates in the USA varying from 1.7 per cent in North Dakota in September 2001 to the 6.6 per cent recorded in the District of

Table 10.8 Great Britain unemployment rates (%), 1998

	Male	*Female*	*All*
White	6.3	4.9	5.7
Indian	9.1	9.0	9.1
Black	15.4	13.7	14.6
Pakistani/Bangladeshi	19.7	22.3	20.4
Mixed/Other	14.8	10.1	12.7

Source: ONS, *Labour Force Survey*, 1998

Table 10.9   US unemployment rates (%), 2000*

	Male	Female	All
White	2.5	2.8	2.6
Black	5.6	5.2	5.4
Hispanic	–	–	4.4
Total	2.8	3.2	3.0

Source: US Bureau of Labour Statistics, 2001
Note: * Adult workers aged 25 plus. Note that the
Hispanic category is composed of workers of Mexican,
Puerto Rican and Cuban origin.

Table 10.10   Great Britain regional unemployment rates (%), 1965–2000

	1965	1970	1975	1980	1985	1990	2000
England							
South East	0.9	1.6	4.0	4.2	8.7	4.0	3.3
East Anglia	1.3	2.2	4.7	5.3	8.8	3.7	3.6
South West	1.5	2.9	6.0	6.4	10.2	4.4	4.1
W. Midlands	0.9	2.3	5.5	7.3	13.7	6.0	6.2
E. Midlands	0.9	2.3	4.5	6.1	11.7	5.1	5.1
Yorks/Humber	1.1	2.9	5.2	7.3	13.1	6.8	6.0
North West	1.6	2.7	6.6	8.5	14.9	7.7	5.3
North East	2.6	4.8	6.9	10.4	16.6	8.9	9.1
Wales	2.6	3.9	7.0	9.4	14.3	6.6	6.1
Scotland	3.0	4.3	6.5	9.1	14.2	8.0	7.6
N. Ireland*	–	–	9.0	13.0	17.6	13.3	7.0

Sources: *Employment Gazette*, various years; ONS, *Labour Force Survey*, Spring 2000
Note: * Series changes between 1980 and 1985.

Columbia. Unemployment rates within the EU in April 2000 ranged from 1.7 per
cent in Aland (Finland) to 33.1 per cent in Reunion (France). For the UK
Table 10.10 gives a regional breakdown of unemployment statistics since 1965. Traditionally Northern Ireland had by far the highest rate of unemployment with more
than 1 in 6 of the labour force being out of work in the mid-1980s; however, sustained
growth during most of the 1990s virtually halved the unemployment rate by the year
2000. Areas traditionally associated with high unemployment, such as Scotland, Wales
and the North East of England, still experience unemployment rates well above the
UK average. However, the once prosperous West Midlands, which was at the heart of
British manufacturing industry during the 1960s, now records rates of unemployment
substantially higher than the national average. With the exception of 1990, the South
East of England has maintained the lowest unemployment rates throughout this period.
Yet even within the comparatively benign unemployment climate of the South East,
there are wide variations in unemployment rates. The population of London experience
an overall unemployment rate greater than the regional rate. For example, in 2000 the
unemployment rate in London was 7 per cent the same as that of Northern Ireland.

More generally, throughout the EU, Overman and Puga (1999) found that, between 1986 and 1996, high unemployment regions tended to remain high unemployment areas, whereas those regions with intermediate unemployment in 1986 had moved towards the extremes of either high or low unemployment. This polarisation of regional unemployment within the EU appears to be due to firms locating in or relocating to low unemployment areas. Changes in regional employment are leading to changes in regional unemployment in the EU. The process of economic integration in Europe is leading to the increased agglomeration (geographical concentration) of productive activity.

This completes our statistical outline of unemployment. Obviously there is much more to be said about the human aspects of the experience of unemployment. This can be approached by examining the possible relationships between unemployment and such factors as illness and crime. For our more limited purpose of understanding the main economic analyses of unemployment we need to move on and summarise the major theories concerning unemployment. But as we do so remember the following passage from Routh (1986).

> Those in employment each play a part in [the] complex system by which humanity is preserved and renewed . . . Those who are unemployed are bystanders . . . Alienation and anomie accompany loss of a job and the inability to find one. The routine of the working day establishes a gauge by which other activities can be measured. It gives meaning to rest and recreation and constant reassurance to the worker of his/her social importance and orientation.
>
> (p. 2)

THEORIES OF UNEMPLOYMENT

The important phases of economic theorising about unemployment in the twentieth century can be identified as follows.

1 Classical theory, which is pre-Keynesian and which rests squarely on the microeconomic analysis of the labour market forces of supply and demand that we encountered in Chapters 1 and 2. Essentially this approach views unemployment as the consequence of real wages being and remaining too high to allow the labour market to clear. Government wage regulation and especially powerful trade unions (see Chapter 7) are identified as significant causal factors. In many respects, this approach reaches its culmination in Pigou (1933), before being forcefully revived by the New Classical school of macroeconomists.

2 Keynesian unemployment theories stem from Keynes (1936) and came to dominate the analysis of unemployment until about the mid-1960s. Two general strands of thought are contained within this approach: a) that unemployment is associated with wage rigidity; and b) that unemployment is essentially a consequence of deficient product demand. The Keynesian view of unemployment was encapsulated in the conventional Phillips (1958) curve relationship.

3 Concern over inflation and the empirical breakdown of any stable Phillips curve relationship provided a sympathetic environment for the intellectual challenge to the Keynesian approach to unemployment. Initially this challenge came in the form of the Monetarism associated with Friedman (1968). Yet by the early 1970s a more forceful critique in the form of New Classical macroeconomics came to prominence, which emphasised the centrality of the natural rate of unemployment and the importance of rational expectations in making labour supply and demand decisions. This approach came to deny any scope for macroeconomic policy to adjust output and employment, emphasising instead supply-side policies influencing welfare benefits and union behaviour (see Lucas 1978, and Minford 1984).

4 The 1980s saw the development of a number of theoretical innovations which extend the analysis of unemployment in the Keynesian mode. These are: a) the temporary equilibrium models of Malinvaud (1977) and the empirical work of Coen and Hickman (1987); b) the attempts by Blanchard and Summers (1986) and Lindbeck and Snower (1988) to explain unemployment hysteresis using insider–outsider models; and c) the hysteresis–NAIRU model detailed in Layard *et al.* (1991).

We summarise each of the main theoretical approaches to unemployment in turn, beginning with the classical theory of unemployment.[4]

CLASSICAL THEORY

The essential feature of the classical theory of unemployment is that the labour market forces of supply and demand respond to changes in real wages. Thus as we saw in Chapter 1, labour supply increases as real wages rise and decreases as they fall (see Figure 1.13). In Chapter 2 we suggested that labour demand was directly related to the marginal productivity of labour (*ceteris paribus*) as an input in the process of production. Diminishing marginal productivity ensured that the short-run demand for labour curve had the conventional negative slope (see Figure 2.5). Bringing these market forces together, the classical theory of the labour market overtly stated that real wages (W/P) should and would in the absence of impediments, adjust to bring about market clearing. Thus in an equilibrium, such as represented by ABCD in Figure 10.5, both the labour market and the product market would clear. Market clearing in a pre-Keynesian world would obviously be at a 'full-employment' equilibrium. Any unemployment that was associated with point C would be merely frictional and would be purely microeconomic in character. For general and enduring unemployment to arise, market imperfections had to move the labour market from point C and keep it from returning to point C. To understand this train of reasoning, from a position of an initial general equilibrium, let us allow powerful trade unions and/or Government wage regulation to increase money wages. This has the effect of shifting out the money wage function in Figure 10.6 from W^* to W^1 and is reflected in the move from D to E. In effect real wages W/P have risen because money wages W have increased whilst prices P remain unchanged. This is because in the pre-Keynesian

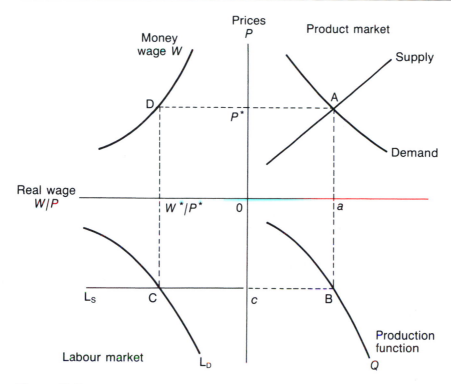

Figure 10.5

Source: Adapted from Sinclair 1987, figure 3.6, p. 65

scheme of things, prices are determined not by costs of production, but by the quantity of money in the economy. According to the 'quantity theory of money', unless the quantity of money (M) in the economy changes, there is no reason for the general level of prices to change.[5] Firms respond to these higher real wages by reducing their demand for labour, as the marginal productivity based factor demand theory suggests, from C to G in Figure 10.6. The impact on the production function is shown by the movement along it from B to J. This reflects the fact that, in the product market, firms are responding to increasing marginal costs (i.e., higher wages) by reducing supply as shown by the leftward shift in the product supply curve from S^* to S^1, bringing about a move from point A to R in Figure 10.6.

Classical unemployment U has emerged because real wages are too high, represented by the rectangle RJGE. Households are constrained in the labour market, in the sense that at a real wage of W^1/P^* they would like to supply an amount of labour c, but are restricted to g. They are also constrained in the product market. Households would like to buy an amount of goods a but they face a supply of only r. Thus there is excess demand in the product market combined with excess supply (unemployment) in the labour market.

Now if the labour market were a competitive one, a position like G would be an untenable one, because unemployed workers could compete with those already

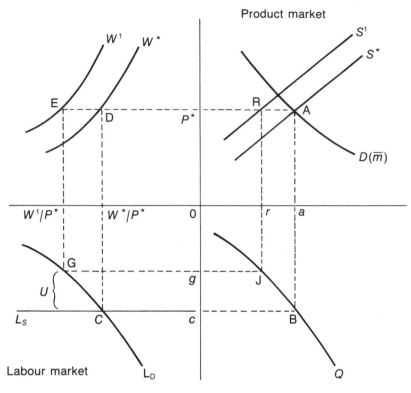

Figure 10.6

employed by offering themselves for work at lower real wage rates, thereby moving the labour market back towards equilibrium at point C. In the classical system unemployment should not endure and the remedy for unemployment is crystal clear, real wages must fall. The fact that they did not and that unemployment did appear to endure could only be explained, within the classical system, by powerful trade unions acting as a monopolistic element by artificially restricting labour supply. This interference with competitive labour supply prevented real wages falling and re-establishing equilibrium at its full-employment level. Thus unemployment in the classical system relies upon markets not clearing. Figure 10.7 shows how union interference with labour supply can create and maintain classical unemployment.

A strong trade union will push up the real wage from W^* to W^1 reducing labour demand from C to G. However, it will also prevent the reduction of that real wage. The firm is effectively faced with the union imposed labour supply function L_{Stu}, which ensures that measured unemployment of FG endures.

The policy prescription following from a classical analysis of unemployment is clear: reduce Government regulation; and reduce trade union power – to make the labour market more competitive. Any expansionary Government policy that increases the money stock above M may initially entice an increase in the planned demand for goods, but the product market already suffers from excess demand. There will be no

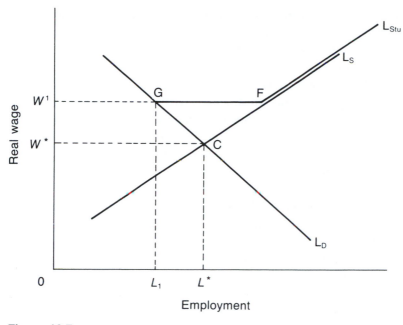

Figure 10.7

Source: Adapted from Trevithick 1992, figure 5.1, p. 93

change in employment because an expansionary monetary policy will feed through to inflation leaving the real wage unaffected, and at W^1/P^* the real wage already equals the marginal revenue productivity of labour.

KEYNESIAN THEORY

Trevithick (1992) emphasises that the 'really pivotal assumption in the [classical] account – the assumption to which Keynes was to take grave exception – was that the real wage rate is a variable capable of direct adjustment by the process of bargaining between employers and workers' (p. 17). It is Keynes's rejection of this 'pivotal assumption' about the disequilibrium adjustment of the classical system that marks the point of departure for Keynesian analysis of the labour market.

Whilst Keynes accepted the marginal productivity based theory of labour demand (set out in Chapter 2), he claimed that in a money using economy, as opposed to a direct or real barter economy, workers and firms only negotiate about money wages.[6] Price expectations may form an input into the bargaining process, but the general level of prices is beyond the control of the firm and the union, thus the real wage cannot be directly negotiated. In Trevithick's view the 'impotence of the two parties to the wage bargain to bring about a reduction in the real wage rate is what makes Keynesian unemployment involuntary' (p. 96). Two theories emerged from Keynes's (1936) work: 1) The labour market fails to clear because of money wage rigidity. Yet because of the comparative flexibility of prices, the product market clears. As in the classical analysis, unemployment is associated with excessive real wages: 2) Both the labour market and the product market are characterised by excess supply. This is the more obviously Keynesian unemployment in that it is associated with deficient product demand and not with excessive real wages.

Take the first case where there is excess supply in the labour market at the current real wage, Keynesians would maintain that even without unions or other institutional obstacles to wage reduction (e.g., custom) a reduction in money wages through bargaining would not eradicate unemployment. This is so because, if one accepts the orthodox microeconomic principle of setting price equal to marginal cost, lower money wages reduce the marginal cost of production resulting in lower prices. As labour costs dominate short-run production costs, lower money wages lead to a more or less equiproportionate fall in the general level of prices. Hence price deflation breaks the link between money wage reductions and the reductions in the real wage which appear necessary to reduce unemployment.[7] In spite of the similarity of this unemployment with classical unemployment, the classical policy prescription does not apply. Unemployment can be reduced by expansionary fiscal or monetary policy which raises output, increases prices by a greater proportion than money wages rise, thereby reducing the real wage and, through the marginal productivity theory of labour demand, increasing employment.

For the second Keynesian case examine Figure 10.8. This shows the more familiar Keynesian unemployment exhibiting excess supply in both the product and labour markets. Although we have considered this case before (see Figure 3.3), it is worthwhile comparing the Keynesian outcome with the Walrasian market clearing outcome. Beginning from a situation of general equilibrium ABCD let us raise the general level of prices from P^* to P^2. This has in effect reduced real wages. Firms react to these higher prices and lower real wages by seeking to expand output to T and increase employment to N. Both of these notional points arising from the planned expansion of output are unsustainable because there is deficient demand at F in the goods market. Firms register this excess supply in the form of a build up of unsold stocks. This has come about because households' real money balances (the money wage divided by the price level) have fallen from M/P^* to M/P^2 as the price level has risen. Thus actual demand in the product market has fallen from A to F. Firms are forced to accept that product demand has in fact fallen, so although they would have liked to have increased output they are compelled to reduce production from B to J. Hence their effective demand for labour falls from C to K. Thus FJKH becomes the Keynesian unemployment equilibrium. The firm is quantity constrained in the goods market and the household is quantity constrained in the labour market. Both firms and households have been forced to operate away from their supply curves with the result that excess supply characterises both markets.

Expansionary macroeconomic policies which encourage an increase in the demand for goods will increase the demand for labour, in the manner described by the Keynesian multiplier, and thereby reduce unemployment. For example, an expansion of the money stock above M would shift product demand out to the right, increasing employment and reducing unemployment, although this effect may be partially (wholly for

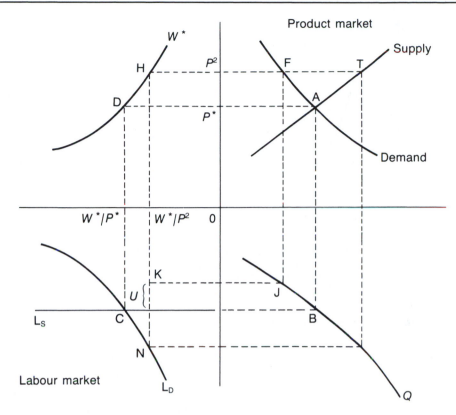

Figure 10.8

Source: Adapted from Sinclair 1987, figure 3.8, p. 68

Monetarist and New Classical economists) offset by inflation increasing the general price level. The classical policy prescription of reducing the real wage in the presence of Keynesian unemployment would only exacerbate the problem by reducing product demand and therefore labour demand still further.

THE PHILLIPS CURVE

Phillips (1958) appeared to provide conclusive evidence of a stable inverse relationship between money wage inflation and unemployment for the UK between 1861 and 1957. Figure 10.9 represents his original fitted convex curve bounded by 0.8 per cent unemployment and 1.0 per cent wage deflation, which crossed the horizontal axis at around 5.5 per cent unemployment. Although the original Phillips curve related money wage inflation to unemployment, it was quickly adapted to relate the increase in prices in general, i.e., inflation, to unemployment. Initially further investigations appeared to bear out the validity of the Phillips curve as a robust empirical phenomenon. Figure 10.10 for example presents inflation and unemployment data for the USA during the 1960s which is compatible with the Phillips curve.

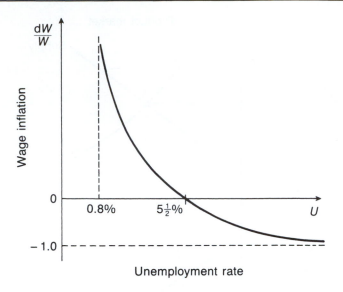

Figure 10.9

Source: Trevithic 1992, figure 6.1, p. 122

The Phillips curve, although it began as an empirical phenomenon, appeared to be consistent with the Keynesian income–expenditure model of economic activity. Lipsey (1960) justified the Phillips curve in terms of microeconomic wage determination and provided a theoretical link between unemployment and inflation by proposing that changes in money wages responded to the state of the labour market: excess demand for labour increased money wage rate changes; excess labour supply decreased money wage rate changes. Whether the labour market was in a state of excess demand or supply could be assessed by comparing unemployment with unfilled vacancies (see Chapter 9). Essentially if, $U > V$ if there was excess supply in the labour market; and $U < V$ if there was excess labour demand.

The suggested tradeoff between unemployment and inflation gave the Phillips curve significance as a guide to macroeconomic demand management policy. It appeared that policy makers could choose either a combination of high unemployment and low inflation, which characterised the USA in the early 1960s (see Figure 10.10), or they could opt for lower unemployment and higher inflation, which the USA experienced in the late 1960s.

However, we need to be clear about what the Phillips curve is actually showing. Is it presenting us with a one-off stable tradeoff between inflation (price or wage) and unemployment? If Lipsey (1960) is right to associate excess demand in the labour market with money wage growth in excess of productivity growth, then the Phillips curve is, as Trevithick maintains, 'a disequilibrium adjustment mechanism' (p. 129). As such, policy makers cannot (nor could they ever) just choose points along the Phillips curve, as Figures 10.9 and 10.10 implied, because money wage changes and unemployment rates are always moving to eliminate excess demand or supply in the labour market.

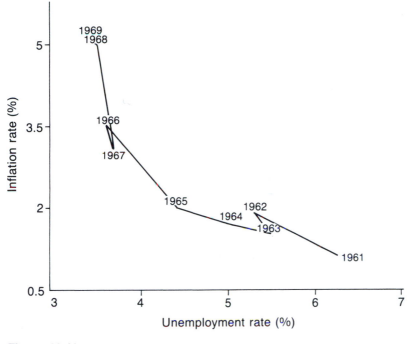

Figure 10.10

Source: OECD, *Economic Outlook*, various issues

The empirical breakdown of the Phillips curve relationship, as a stable tradeoff between inflation (wage or price) and unemployment, was brought about by the events of the 1970s and 1980s. Figures 10.11 and 10.12 bear witness to the actual behaviour of inflation and unemployment, in the USA and the UK, which was entirely inconsistent with the simple Phillips curve story.

In the USA, as Figure 10.11 shows, the data for 1970 indicates a break with the conventional Phillips curve. For the UK, as Figure 10.12 shows, there is clearly something amiss with the Phillips curve as an empirical regularity as early as 1968. Note that in both countries empirical problems for the Phillips curve are evident well before the first OPEC oil price crisis of late 1973 which boosted inflation in 1974. Changes in inflation and unemployment rates following 1992 in the USA and after 1993 in the UK have brought the Phillips curves back towards their 1960s positions.

More recently the relationship between wages and unemployment has been investigated in terms of 'wage curves', see Blanchflower and Oswald (1994). For example, Bell *et al.* (2000) estimated the elasticity for wages with respect to unemployment for UK male workers to be −0.04 in the short term and −0.09 in the long term. Yet the most important element in the breakdown of the Phillips curve was the theoretical assault upon both it and the Keynesian theory with which it was associated. This attack came from Monetarist and later from New Classical economics, both of which

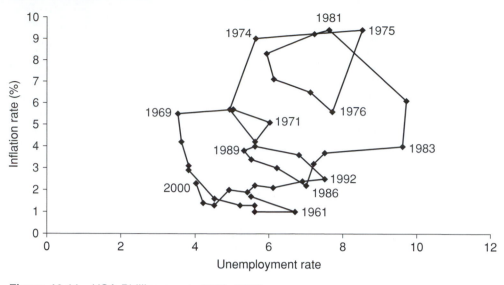

Figure 10.11   USA Phillips curve, 1960–2000

Source: OECD, *Economic Outlook*, various issues

provided alternative explanations about the nature of the relationship between inflation and unemployment which seemed better equipped to account for the empirical
turbulence of the 1970s and 1980s.

MONETARISM AND UNEMPLOYMENT

The Monetarist critique of the Phillips curve rests upon the Classical insistence on
the importance of real wages in the labour market and two innovations; the formal
consideration of the role of expectations; and the introduction of the concept of a
'natural rate of unemployment'.

The Monetarist critique begins by re-establishing the importance of real as opposed
to money wages in the labour market. It maintains that Phillips (1958) and Lipsey
(1960) theoretically mis-specified the relationship in terms of the rate of change
of money wages instead of the expected rate of change of real wages. Thus in Figure 10.13 all points on the conventional Phillips curve to the left of U* show the
unemployment rate falling because workers take jobs at higher money wages, in the
belief that real wages have risen.

U* represents the 'natural rate of unemployment', defined as that rate of unemployment which is consistent with price level stability or with a constant rate of inflation.
Yet the natural rate concept also possesses another characteristic; it is that rate of
voluntary or frictional unemployment consistent with long-run equilibrium in the
labour market. This market clearing aspect of the natural rate is shown in Figure
10.14, where L_F represents the labour force or notional labour supply as opposed to the
effective labour supply L_S. That is not to say that the 'natural rate' is necessarily fixed;

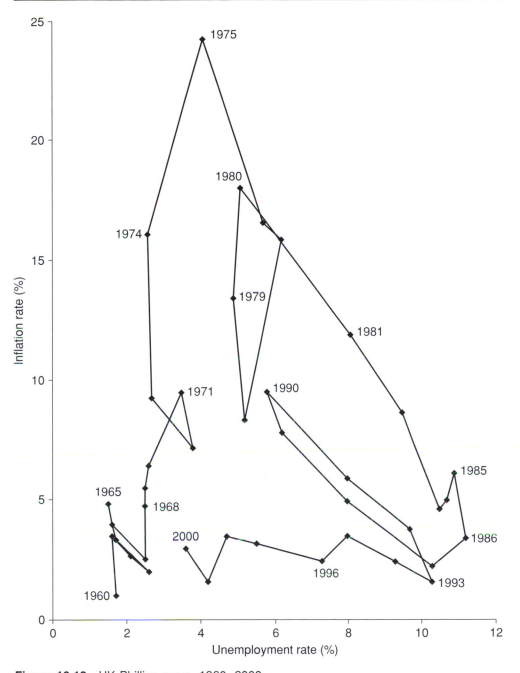

Figure 10.12 UK Phillips curve, 1960–2000

Source: ONS, *Economic Trends*, annual supplement, various years

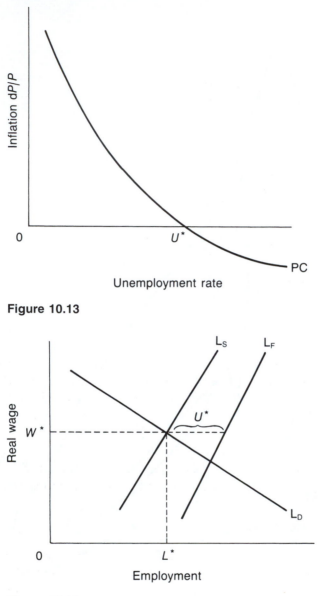

Figure 10.13

Figure 10.14

anything that increases labour market friction e.g., factors which increase job search duration or increase labour market mismatch, will increase the natural rate.

The simple Phillips curve implicitly assumed that inflation expectations equalled zero. It was Phelps (1967) who first proposed that the Phillips curve tradeoff should be viewed as a relationship between unexpected inflation and the rate of unemployment, a position that was developed by Friedman's (1968) influential work.[8] Friedman (1968) suggested that actual inflation in a particular time period $(dP/P)_t$, had two main

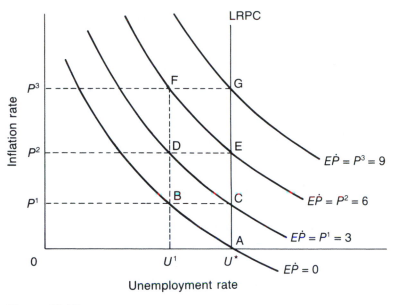

Figure 10.15

components – inflation expectations, $E(dP/P)_t$, and an aggregate demand element reflecting unemployment. We shall focus on changes in Government policy reflected in changes in money supply $(dMS/MS)_t$. Friedman (1968) formally modelled inflation expectations as adaptive. He assumed that they were formed by past experience of inflation, $(dP/P)_{t-1}$, and would adapt to any change in the experience of inflation. He also allowed for the possibility of errors made in predicting inflation. Those errors had a random element e_t and a systematic element related to aggregate demand and reflected in the unemployment rate (U_t). Thus errors in predicting inflation could be represented by

$$(dP/P)_t - E(dP/P)_t = \emptyset\, f(U_t) + e_t.$$

Whilst the random element could be assumed to be normally distributed with a zero mean, the systematic element is present as long as unemployment deviates from its natural rate (U^*). Thus as long as Government pursues expansionary macroeconomic policies, thereby expanding money supply growth, in order to try and hold unemployment down to U^1 in Figure 10.15, inflation will accelerate and agents will make persistent, systematic errors in predicting inflation.

To understand the importance of building expectations of inflation into the analysis, which had the effect of shifting the conventional Phillips curve outwards, consider the series of events illustrated by Figure 10.15. The Monetarist view of accelerating inflation would allow a pattern of activity that moves the economy from point A to point G. Starting at A the Government decides that unemployment at U^* is too high and should be reduced to U^1. Aggregate demand is expanded accordingly, possibly along Keynesian lines, with money supply (MS) increasing by say 3 per cent as a consequence. Firms, aware of the higher prices they will be able to charge in conditions of greater demand, offer money wage rises of 3 per cent. Unemployed workers interpret this as an increase in real wages because they expect inflation to remain at its former rate, i.e., 0 per cent. Hence they take job offers and unemployment falls to U^1 as the economy moves along the conventional Phillips curve from A to point B. However, by the beginning of the next period, prices have risen by 3 per cent and so have expectations of future inflation. To reflect this change in inflation expectations, from 0 per cent to 3 per cent, the short-run Phillips curve shifts upwards. Thus real wages have not risen at all. Now we have reached a crucial stage of the Monetarist account of unemployment. Those marginal, formerly unemployed workers, now realise that they have not enjoyed higher real wages, they therefore quit employment and increase unemployment back to its natural rate. The economy is said to tend to move from B to C. Only money wage increases above 3 per cent will now keep unemployment in the short run below U^*. If the Government wishes to hold unemployment down to U^1 and avoid the move to point C, further monetary expansion, and therefore higher inflation, shift the economy from B to D. Yet again the economy tends towards the natural rate of unemployment as it seeks to move to point E. Only continuous monetary expansion and accelerating inflation will keep marginal workers in employment. Hence for Friedman there is no long-run tradeoff between unemployment and inflation. The long-run, expectations augmented Phillips curve (LRPC) is vertical from its anchor at the natural rate of unemployment (U^*). As long as Government is prepared to accept that unemployment associated with point E, inflation will stabilise at a constant rate of 6 per cent per annum in this case. Friedman's (1968) expectations augmented Phillips curve analysis proposed a series of short-run curves, associated with different expectations of inflation, anchored by the natural rate of unemployment (U^*). The policy recommendations accompanying this analysis were straightforward: the unemployment rate was immune to aggregate demand management in the long run; there might be some short-run Phillips curve effects but the natural rate would reassert itself; the cost of trying to hold onto any short-run reduction in unemployment below the natural rate was accelerating inflation; inflation could be reduced but at the cost of increasing unemployment above the natural rate in the short run; unemployment could only be effectively reduced by microeconomic measures which increased the flexibility (lessened the frictions) of the labour market. Thus the prudent Monetarist would advise directing macroeconomic policy to control inflation, whilst using microeconomic policies, such as reducing the adverse impact of trade unions and welfare benefits, to reduce the long-run 'natural rate' of unemployment.

Monetarism provided a severe theoretical challenge to the Keynesian view of unemployment from the late 1960s. Its shifting short-run Phillips curves also seemed more capable of telling the stagflation story of the 1970s. Yet a more virulent strain of market clearing theory was about to seize the theoretical initiative in the 1970s, New Classical economics.

NEW CLASSICAL ECONOMICS AND UNEMPLOYMENT

New Classical economists, such as Lucas (1972,1978) and Minford (1983), go beyond the monetarism of Friedman (1968) and Phelps (1967) when they maintain that not only is the long-run Phillips curve vertical about the 'natural rate' but so is the relationship between inflation and unemployment in the short run. This provides the basis for the New Classical assertion that macroeconomic policy is utterly ineffective when used to influence unemployment. These features of the New Classical analysis appear to arise from the incorporation of 'rational expectations' into New Classical models.

Rational expectations questions whether economic agents make persistent, systematic errors in forming predictions.[9] In the case of unemployment it replaces Friedman's adaptive expectations through undermining the systematic element he included in inflation forecasting errors (see p. 349 above). Expectations can contain errors but rationality requires that they be truly random, distributed around a mean value of zero, and contain no systematic component. Somewhat more controversially the hypothesis requires that in order to form rational expectations agents must behave as if they know the correct underlying model, correct that is for the purposes of prediction. Whilst they need not know the correct model, which presumably differs for Keynesians, Monetarists, and New Classicals, they must behave as if they did. As Trevithick (1992) wryly observes, '[h]ow agents perform this prodigious feat of mimicry without actually using some form of the correct model remains decidedly mysterious' (p. 154). Nevertheless, rational expectations are held to fulfil, over time and on average, the outcome predicted by the correct model. So if the Government announces a monetary expansion directed at reducing unemployment, workers anticipate price rises to match any money wage increases, marginal workers are not tempted into employment and unemployment stubbornly remains at the natural rate. Rational expectations deny workers the money illusion that Friedman gave them to produce the short-run Phillips curve tradeoff.

For New Classical macroeconomics (see Lucas, 1978) any deviations of the actual unemployment rate from the natural rate should be random, with such deviations arising from errors in predicting the price level, caused only by unanticipated and unannounced changes in policy by the monetary authorities. Even such deviations will only be temporary, as agents learn about the change in policy and change their inflation predictions and consequent behaviour accordingly.

The policy implication of a New Classical analysis of unemployment is that there is no role for macroeconomic demand management. The only policies likely to have any effect are microeconomic, supply-side ones which increase the willingness and ability to work and the willingness and ability to employ. Such policy recommendations include: reducing the replacement ratio; cutting income and profit taxes; curbing union power; improving labour productivity; lowering employment taxes (e.g., UK employers' national insurance contributions); removing employment protection legislation, including minimum wages; seeking to reduce labour market mismatches. These are held to be policies that act upon the real supply-side forces in the economy rather than on monetary demand-side forces. As such they can affect the underlying natural rate of unemployment.

Lest it be thought that the New Classical analysis of unemployment represents the pinnacle of intellectual activity within the sub discipline of labour economics, we now present a short critique of it.

A CRITIQUE OF THE NEW CLASSICAL VIEW

There has been a great deal of criticism directed at the rational expectations hypothesis itself (see Routh 1986 for example) but whilst the hypothesis does place some demands on our credulity it is not the fundamental weakness of the New Classical model. Sinclair (1987, pp. 215–21) provides some examples of where rational expectations do not undermine the case for effective macroeconomic policy. He states that there is

> a widespread but erroneous belief that rational expectations deprive the authorities of the power to stabilise output and unemployment. This is not true. . . . Everything depends upon the assumptions of the model into which rational expectations are inserted.

> (p. 218)

Trevithick (1992, pp. 174–7) provides an example of a Keynesian model incorporating rational expectations. What gives New Classical economics its distinctive features is the insistence on continuous market clearing. The crucial question to ask is, what justifies the full employment/market clearing assumption in New Classical macroeconomics?

New Classical economics suggests that there is no scope for macroeconomic policy to adjust output and employment. Although the thrust of Keynesian theory has been to construct a general model incorporating both unemployment and full employment, Trevithick (1992) reminds us that 'it is axiomatic to the new classical macroeconomics that market economies are characterised by states of more or less continuous full employment' (p. 160). To understand the implications of this assumption of full employment take the case illustrated in Figure 10.16 of an increase in the stock of money, an increase in aggregate demand from AD_0 to AD_1.

Full-employment national income, output and employment is at Y^*, which corresponds with the natural rate of unemployment U^* in previous figures. If the economy were to expand to Y_1, the unemployment rate would fall to U^1. Assuming the economy is at point A with full employment of Y^*, the increase in aggregate demand will, according to Keynesians, move the economy from A to C. So will it for the New Classicals, but if and only if the increase in money stock is anticipated by agents. Yet if it is unanticipated and agents are caught unawares by the monetary authorities, New Classical economics suggests a short-run movement to B until price expectations are fully adjusted.

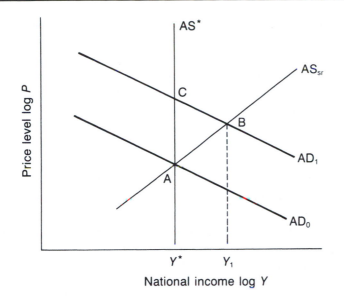

Figure 10.16

It is quite clear from this example that the ineffectiveness of macroeconomic policy to influence unemployment derives not from the rational expectations hypothesis, but from the New Classical insistence on continuous market clearing, allied to the natural rate hypothesis, which located the economy at Y^* in the first place.[10] When it comes to interpreting the short-run aggregate supply curve AS_{sr}, how can New Classical economics maintain that suppliers, including labour suppliers, increase output above Y^* in response to increases in the absolute price level? The New Classical response is that each firm and labour supplier sees rising demand as an increase for their particular product/labour relative to all others. Hence they increase output and labour supply only to find out later that the rise in demand is general, at which point they reduce output and withdraw from employment moving the economy from Y_1 to Y^*. This answer itself raises the problem of how some information about increases in demand and prices disseminates rapidly but that agents remain unaware of the general situation. Would firms really expand output if they knew that factor input prices had risen? It is reasonable to suggest that initially workers might mistakenly see an increase in money wages as an increase in real wages, but firms need to observe a fall in real wages before they expand output and employment. New Classical economics appears to have firms responding to product price changes but not to changing production costs. In which case, how can trade unions have an adverse effect on employment?

The New Classical view of the business cycle, caused by changes in monetary policy (Lucas 1978), suggests that observed unemployment does not fluctuate around its natural rate, but that changes in actual unemployment are due to fluctuations of the natural rate. Of crucial importance is the need for workers to distinguish the 'temporary' from the 'permanent' components of any change in real wages. Then we need to accept that workers respond more to 'temporary' real wage movements through variations in their labour supply. 'Hence, even though unemployment may be fluctuating markedly over time, workers are never 'off' their notional labour supply curve' (Trevithick 1992, p. 169).

The extreme assumption of continuous market clearing can be seen at work in this account of fluctuating unemployment. The problems are obvious; how are workers to know if real wages have 'temporarily' deviated from a long-run (permanent) trend rate of growth? And once they know such things are they going to voluntarily alter their labour supply on the basis of such a temporary–permanent comparison? The implication of the New Classical approach is that a reduction in the money stock (or more realistically a reduction in the rate of growth of money supply), will result in workers perceiving a 'temporary' reduction in real wages, which reduces the supply of labour as workers voluntarily withdraw from the workforce, thereby increasing the natural rate of unemployment and actual measured unemployment as they opt for more leisure, whilst awaiting the return of real wages to their 'permanent' level.

This is a bizarre account of fluctuations in unemployment which is both profoundly counter-intuitive and counter-factual. Just consider how firms respond to the same circumstances, if workers think real wages have fallen will not firms seek to employ more workers? Conversely if real wages are regarded as having risen, will unemployment really fall just because workers are willing to supply more labour? No, because firms will see the same rise in real wages and reduce their demand for labour. The problem with Lucas's (1978) almost exclusively supply-side account of unemployment is that, not only does it present workers as strange inter-temporal speculators, substituting between employment and leisure, but it also has employers apparently misreading market signals in the opposite direction to which workers read them.[11] In such a world redundancies come about presumably because firms obligingly dismiss workers so that they can enjoy more leisure as real wages fall!

New Classical economics suggests the following flow of causation in its account of unemployment.

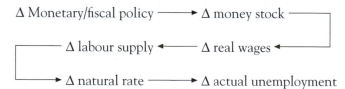

As we shall see in the next section the hypothesised relationship between the natural rate and actual unemployment generates additional problems for the New Classical analysis of the labour market.

THE NATURAL RATE OF UNEMPLOYMENT

Friedman's (1968) original formulation of the natural rate of unemployment suggested that it was the rate at which price expectations were fulfilled and actual inflation was neither rising nor falling, and the rate was corresponding to full employment.

Table 10.11 Unemployment rates (annual average %), 1955–98

	1955–66	1969–73	1974–81	1981–86	1986–90	1991–97	1994–98
UK NAIRU	2.0	3.8	7.5	9.5	9.6	9.1	7.3
Actual rate	2.0	3.4	5.8	11.3	8.9	9.0	8.0

Source: Nickell, 1999, table 1.6, p. 21

This conception of the natural rate incorporating labour market clearing was taken up by New Classical economics, indeed Lucas (1972) attempts to provide a theoretical justification for the natural rate proposition. More recently the natural rate hypothesis has been stripped of its labour market clearing element as part of a renewal of analysis consistent with the Keynesian, non-market clearing, tradition.[12] The 'non-accelerating inflation rate of unemployment' (NAIRU) is therefore the more generally applicable natural rate concept.

Concerns about the natural rate of unemployment fall into four categories: theoretical doubts about the existence of a unique natural rate; the difficulties in empirically estimating the natural rate; doubts about the interpretation of natural rate estimates; and concern over the co-movement of natural rate and actual unemployment.

Sinclair (1987, pp. 235–6) provides examples of quantity rationed models, which under conditions of both Classical and Keynesian unemployment can generate multiple unemployment equilibria. The importance of such multiple equilibria is that the equilibrium or natural rate of unemployment is no longer unique to any given set of economic circumstances.

Estimates of the NAIRU for the UK are contained in Table 10.11. An important point to bear in mind is that such NAIRU estimates are not derived from the real forces that are meant to determine the natural rate (labour market mismatch, productivity, union power, taxation, welfare benefits, etc.) but from the equalisation of current and expected inflation, from which an implied natural rate is forthcoming. During the period 1955–66, inflation in the UK was essentially stable, hence expected inflation basically equalled actual inflation and the actual unemployment rate can be taken to be the estimated natural rate. From 1967 through to 1981 the UK experienced accelerating inflation; therefore the estimated natural rate is significantly greater than the actual rate. A similar set of circumstances prevailed in the USA. As inflation falls in the UK during the early 1980s the estimated NAIRU must be below the actual rate of unemployment. In the second half of the 1980s inflation begins to rise again so actual unemployment must be below its estimated natural rate. As inflation falls and remains fairly subdued for most of the 1990s actual unemployment is below the estimated NAIRU.

The peculiar feature of such estimates is that, by definition, for inflation to accelerate, the natural rate of unemployment (NAIRU) must be greater than the actual rate. In terms of Figure 10.15, U^* must be greater than U^1. Indeed the variation in inflation is what determines the estimate of the natural rate. But in theory it is stated that it is

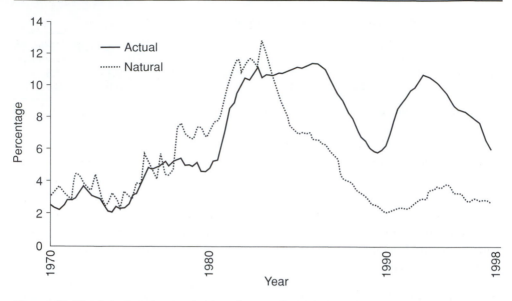

Figure 10.17   Actual and natural rates of unemployment

Source: Minford 1998, figure 5.5, p. 125

the actual rate being less than the natural rate which causes inflation to accelerate. The problem being that whilst in theory it is the relationship of actual to natural unemployment that determines movements in inflation, empirically it is the fluctuation of inflation that determines the estimated NAIRU and actual rate of unemployment relationship. An interesting feature of the estimates contained in Table 10.11 is that the natural rate moves in the same direction as actual unemployment over time. This co-movement of natural and actual unemployment can be given two very different interpretations. The first would be from supporters of the natural rate hypothesis, such as New Classical economists, that movements in the natural rate largely determined the path taken by the actual rate. Indeed this is the view underlying the relationship between the actual and equilibrium rate of unemployment produced by Minford (1998) and reproduced in Figure 10.17. He is clearly suggesting that the supply side of the labour market deteriorated during the late 1970s causing the increase in equilibrium unemployment (the broken line). After a lag this impacted on actual unemployment (the bold line). Because actual unemployment was usually below its equilibrium rate from 1970 to 1984, this would result in accelerating inflation. To reflect the fact that inflation falls during the 1980s, equilibrium unemployment falls below actual unemployment. Why does equilibrium unemployment fall? Because of the supply-side policy programme of the 1980s comprising: income and profit tax reduction; restrictive trade union legislation; a reduction in the replacement ratio; privatisation; and the improvement in productivity.

If this is the case, why does the actual unemployment rate increase during 1990 to exceed 11 per cent by the end of 1992? There is no prior increase in equilibrium unemployment being predicted in Figure 10.17, which could be rationalised in terms of a marked supply-side deterioration during the late 1980s. After 1990 it appears as though movements in the natural rate are lagging those of the actual rate rather than preceding them. Layard *et al.* (1991) along with Blanchard and Katz (1997) and Mortensen and Pissarides (1999) see unemployment as an untrended cyclical variable in the USA and Japan, whereas the rise in average unemployment across cycles in the EU was put down to increases in natural rate unemployment.

A much more likely explanation of the co-movement of actual and natural (equilibrium) unemployment over time is that the actual rate itself determines what the natural rate will be. This is the essence of the concept of unemployment hysteresis, that there is no unique natural rate of unemployment but a different set of equilibrium rates for each different time path that actual unemployment might take. Our consideration of hysteresis will lead to the most promising recent analysis of unemployment from within the Keynesian tradition.

UNEMPLOYMENT HYSTERESIS

Hysteresis in a labour market context refers to the high degree of dependence of current unemployment upon past unemployment. Pure hysteresis would demand that current unemployment be explained in terms of unemployment in previous time periods with coefficients summing to one. For the purpose of explaining the persistent nature of unemployment we do not need such absolute determinacy to be able to use hysteresis as a meaningful concept. Simple linear auto-regressions of unemployment, conducted by Blanchard and Summers (1986), for the UK and USA over the period 1890–1985 produced the following results:

UK $\quad u = 0.93u_{(-1)} + e$

USA $\quad u = 0.90u_{(-1)} + e$.

This encourages them to state that 'unemployment exhibits a very high degree of persistence over the past century' (p. 21).

Unemployment is not the only labour market variable to exhibit persistence, Figure 10.18 shows that in the UK vacancies also contain important permanent shocks but unlike unemployment these begin to decline after about 10 quarters. Shocks to unemployment have an impact that shows no sign of returning to the previous equilibrium even after 30 quarters (7.5 years). Employment also displays strong permanent shocks feeding into total hours worked. Average hours worked and average earnings display persistence even after 30 quarters but at a far lower level than the other UK labour market variables. The key question is what factors could explain the marked persistence of unemployment? Blanchard and Summers (1986) summarise and reject the most obvious suspects: aggregate demand shocks; unemployment benefits; mismatch; and the productivity slowdown. They do so in the following terms. Adverse aggregate demand shocks such as: the OPEC oil price rises; tight

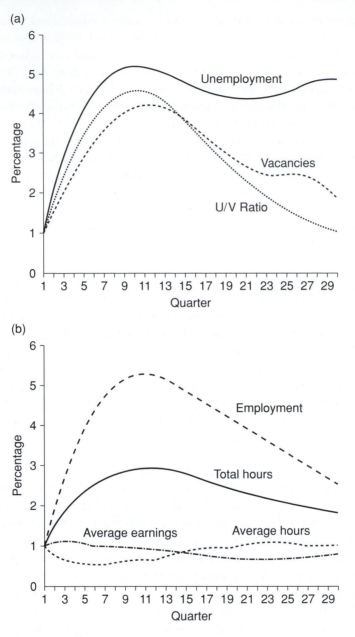

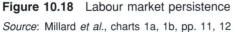

Figure 10.18 Labour market persistence

Source: Millard *et al.*, charts 1a, 1b, pp. 11, 12

monetary policies; and recessionary fiscal policies will all increase unemployment but, without some other factors, they cannot explain the persistence of higher unemployment. In terms of the Phillips curve aggregate demand shocks alone cannot explain the increase in the unemployment rate consistent with steady state inflation.

Unemployment benefits may increase unemployment through a reduction in job search intensity.

However, there is no clear evidence that the replacement ratio for the UK increased significantly after 1967. When it comes to using mismatch to explain the persistence of the rise in unemployment, that may have been brought about by a combination of structural change and real wage rigidity, we find that regional and occupational mismatch show no unambiguous increases. Industrial mismatch increased markedly in the UK during the sharp recession of 1979–81, after generally declining since 1967. In Chapter 2 we outlined the productivity performance of a number of OECD countries. It was obvious that there was a productivity growth slowdown associated with the 1970s oil price shocks. But the UK and USA both experienced productivity improvements during the past century which have not been associated with any marked reduction in unemployment. The exceptional but temporary period of poor productivity performance of the 1970s cannot explain protracted unemployment.

Having dismissed these conventional explanations of unemployment persistence, we are left with the phenomenon of hysteresis and the question: what could possibly cause hysteresis? Some suggested mechanisms by which a sustained rise in actual unemployment above the natural rate could in effect raise the natural rate itself are: insider–outsider effects; the long-term unemployed; and capital stock/utilisation considerations.

Blanchard and Summers (1986) use an insider–outsider model to try and capture unemployment hysteresis. Such an approach suffers from two important sets of problems. The first is the lack of empirical support for insider–outsider models referred to in Chapter 7. The second centres around theoretical weaknesses. In order to generate persistence in unemployment, Blanchard and Summers (1986) have to make specific assumptions about the membership of the insider (employed) group, their variable m. At the extreme where membership of the insider group equals those currently employed ($m = 1$), an adverse demand shock will leave real wages unaffected with employment bearing all the downward adjustment, and a favourable shock will feed through to higher wages leaving employment (and thereby unemployment as well) completely unaffected. The wage bargaining framework in their model is an unusual one in the sense that insiders, possibly through a trade union, set the wage unilaterally (see Chapter 7 for other models of wage bargaining). In which case the degree of unemployment persistence appears to depend upon the extent to which the firm can influence the wage setting behaviour of insiders. An obvious implication of insider–outsider analysis is that insider effects on unemployment persistence are likely to be strongest when and where the insider group is strongest. It is reasonable to identify insiders with the unions which exist to represent their collective interests. This raises the empirical problem of accounting for unemployment persistence in the 1980s and early 1990s in countries like the UK which have witnessed an erosion of union power and influence since 1979. It also raises the problem of accounting for lower unemployment persistence in the more heavily unionised Scandinavian economies. Given this problem it may well be that one needs to look at another aspect of wage bargaining, namely the degree of decentralistion in the bargaining process (see Chapter 7).

The argument that unemployment deteriorates the human capital of the unemployed is a persuasive one. This deterioration, unless it is acted upon through training or work experience programmes, is likely to be most marked in the long-term unemployed. The specific impact of the long-term unemployed on unemployment hysteresis works through human capital deterioration by making long-term unemployed workers less desirable to firms. Yet it can also work through the job search process by making unemployed workers less effective job seekers as they become discouraged by past job search failures. Hughes and Hutchinson (1988) suggest that because long-term unemployment reduces the probability of being re-employed, 'the numbers unemployed are likely to build up at times of low labour demand in a way that is irreversible' (p. 35). In other words as actual unemployment rises so does the irreversible long-term component. This growth in irreversible unemployment appears as an increase in the natural rate. Jenkinson (1987) concludes his study with the view that 'unemployment causes the NRU ... the NRU does not cause unemployment ... Such evidence as there is for the UK certainly seems to throw considerable doubt upon the relevance of the NRU as a structural parameter of the economy' (p. 52). The clear implication of this argument being that the natural rate is not determined by real supply-side forces and underlies the actual rate, but that demand-side factors largely determine, in the short term, actual unemployment, and actual unemployment determines, after a lag, natural rate unemployment.

The capital shrinkage argument rests upon the relationship between actual ouput (Y), output produced by full capacity utilisation of the existing capital stock (Y_c) and full employment ouput (Y_f). The usual Classical and Keynesian models assume full utilisation of the existing capital, $Y_f = Y_c$. Keynesian unemployment generally implies that, $Y < Y_f \leq Y_c$. Yet unemployment could also be brought about by the economy encountering a capacity constraint arising from a capital stock that was inadequate for full employment, i.e., $Y = Y_c < Y_f$. In this manner unemployment would persist. Consider the following sequence of events: unemployment rises in response to an adverse aggregate demand shock; this may lead to a reduction in investment thereby shrinking the capital stock Y_c; subsequent expansion of aggregate demand may be curtailed by the supply-side constraint of capital shortage; provoking inflation or balance of payments deficit in the capital goods sector. Blanchard and Summers (1986) are not convinced by the capital shortage explanation of unemployment hysteresis. At the theoretical level, pure hysteresis would imply no substitution of labour for capital. Historically they argue that

> substantial disinvestment during the 1930s did not preclude the rapid recovery of employment associated with rearmament in a number of ... countries. Nor did the very substantial reduction in the size of the civilian capital stock that occurred during the war prevent the attainment of full employment after the war in many countries.

(p. 27)

The essential point being that, whilst any capital shortage effects will obviously slow down the supply response to any increase in demand and therefore put an upward pressure on prices, they are not, nor empirically have they been, the primary cause of unemployment hysteresis.

Having rejected capital shortage and insider–outsider effects as independent explanations of unemployment hysteresis and drawn attention to the important phenomenon of long-term unemployment, we now turn our attention to structural unemployment.

STRUCTURAL UNEMPLOYMENT AND MISMATCH

Conventionally unemployment is classified by economists according to the categories: classical (excessive real wage, probably union induced) unemployment; demand deficient (Keynesian) unemployment; frictional (search) unemployment; and structural (including mismatch) unemployment.

Roper (1989) contains a concise survey of attempts to identify the unemployed by type. Dow and Dicks-Mireaux (1958) attempted to split unemployment into a Keynesian 'demand deficient' component and what amounts to a mismatch component. Mismatch in this case is being viewed as the unemployment remaining when unemployment equals vacancies in the labour market. As Roper (1989) remarks, mismatch is regarded as 'that level of unemployment that would exist if an equal number of vacancies existed given the current U–V curve' (p. 65). The clear implication is that any unemployment that is not due to mismatch is caused by deficient aggregate demand. Such a deficiency can be inferred in conditions where $U > V$. Indeed Armstrong and Taylor (1981) categorise any aggregate unemployment in excess of aggregate vacancies as demand deficient, which obviously assumes that labour market equilibrium is where $U = V$. Frictional unemployment is equal to that which comes from summing the minimum unemployment and vacancies in each sector of the economy. Structural unemployment, which has occupational, industrial and geographical dimensions, is identified with mismatch, which Jackman and Roper (1987) define as 'a situation in which the characteristics of unemployed workers, particularly in terms of skill, work experience or location, differ from those of the jobs that are available' (p. 10). Familiar policy implications of such a definition are that structural unemployment could be reduced by: moving unemployed workers between occupational and industrial sectors through education and training; encouraging geographical mobility through subsidising workers moving to take up a job; redistributing the geographical dispersion of vacancies through regional policy.

Jackman and Roper (1987) give a clear theoretical account of structural unemployment in a U–V context. Consider Figure 10.19 which shows an aggregate U–V curve with two combinations of unemployment and vacancy rates (A and B) in the two sectors of the economy (1 and 2). Point D shows the economy-wide position which is a weighted average of A and B. Structural unemployment is measured by the distance 1/2BC which is 'the number of people who will have to move as a proportion of the labour force in order that the share of unemployment in each sector should equal its share of vacancies' (p. 12). If this were to happen aggregate unemployment would fall from D to E.

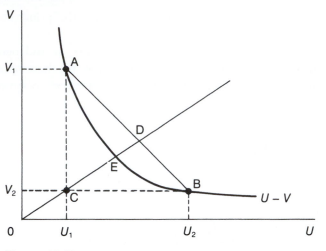

Figure 10.19

Source: Adapted from Jackman and Roper 1987, figure 1, p. 13

Given the rapid and substantial shift in the structural composition of employment in the UK since 1979 (see Chapter 2), one would have expected mismatch to have increased and for rising structural unemployment to be a significant feature of the current labour market. It is therefore somewhat of a challenge that empirical studies which include an analysis of vacancies find mismatch to be an insignificant cause of increasing unemployment.

Layard and Nickell (1987) represents an influential example of what is perhaps the dominant view within labour economics of the role of mismatch in the unemployment story. Figure 10.20 reproduces their indices of the three dimensions of mismatch for the UK, regional, occupational and industrial mismatch.

Regional mismatch is measured by comparing unemployment and vacancies in each geographical region and then examining regional differences in the unemployment to vacancy ratios. The idea is that a lack of regional mismatch would yield identical U–V ratios in each region. Upon this measure Figure 10.20 clearly shows a reduction in regional mismatch in the UK over the 1964–85 period, coupled with a pro-cyclical pattern of regional mismatch falling during downturns in economic activity. Thus regional mismatch has not been responsible for the increase in unemployment.

The index of occupational mismatch does not exhibit any clear trend over time except to follow a counter-cyclical pattern of rising during recessions. The index of industrial mismatch contained in Figure 10.20 does show a marked increase in the 1979–81 recession. This probably reflects the changes in the structure of employment that took place at this time rather than being a cause of the increase in unemployment at this time. Layard and Nickell (1987) conclude that 'increases in mismatch are not an important reason for the outward shift of the U–V curve' (p. 154).

Jackman and Roper (1987) provide estimates of regional, occupational and industrial mismatch for the UK which display an almost identical pattern to those

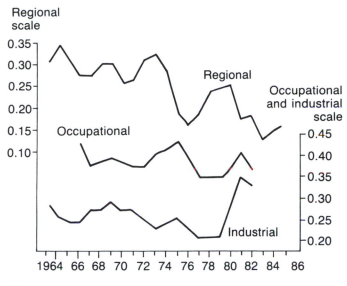

Figure 10.20

Source: Layard and Nickell 1987, figure 5.14, p. 153

in Figure 10.20. However, when it comes to international comparisons, data from a number of OECD countries shows that the reduction in regional mismatch over time is a common phenomenon except in the Netherlands. The essentially constant trend in UK occupational mismatch in Figure 10.20 contrasts with declines in most other countries, especially France and Germany, and increases in Norway and Sweden. Sweden also appears to have suffered an increase in industrial mismatch similar to the UK's during 1979–82, whereas France and Germany in particular did not have unprecedented levels of industrial mismatch in 1982. Yet in spite of the sharp increase in industrial mismatch in the UK, due to the increasing 'imbalance between manufacturing and services' (p. 32), Jackman and Roper (1987) conclude that there has been 'no systematic tendency for structural imbalances to increase in recent years in the UK or, . . . in the main industrialised economies of Western Europe' (p. 33). This confirms our view that increasing mismatch was not a cause of the increase in unemployment which got underway in the late 1960s and which accelerated sharply in the early 1980s. This does not mean that mismatch and the structural unemployment with which it is associated is unimportant; although increased mismatch has not caused higher unemployment, it remains an important element of unemployment. For Britain, Layard *et al.* (1991) calculate that in the mid-1980s 'mismatch could easily account for one-third of total unemployment' (p. 310). Nickell and Bell (1995) estimate that the decline in the relative demand for unskilled workers in Britain could have accounted for some 20 per cent of the long-term rise in unemployment. We are now in a position to understand the influential NAIRU–hysteresis theory contained in Layard *et al.* (1991).

AN ECLECTIC THEORY OF UNEMPLOYMENT

The theory of unemployment presented in Layard *et al.* (1991) encompasses an impressive array of different elements: demand shocks; insider effects; union bargaining; unemployment benefits; inflation; and the NAIRU. Although the authors correctly maintain that there are both Classical and Keynesian elements to their theory (hence my use of the term eclectic) it is firmly based in the non-market clearing tradition. The eclectic nature of the theory is a strength rather than a weakness; after all why should unemployment have a single cause or possess an unambiguous set of characteristics? Coen and Hickman (1987) tried to grapple with the multi-causality of unemployment using a model combining both Classical and Keynesian elements.

Figure 10.21 contains the essence of the Coen and Hickman (1987) model. L_F represents the labour force, which determines the maximum available labour. L_D is the notional demand for labour with no constraints and $L_D(Y_0)$ is the effective labour demand with deficient aggregate demand based upon sales quantity constraints. These concepts allow us to identify a number of important features of the labour market. L^* is a natural level of employment consistent with overall market clearing. $D - A$ is total unemployment, $D - C$ is natural or equilibrium unemployment, $C - B$ is Keynesian unemployment, with $B - A$ representing Classical unemployment.

Coen and Hickman (1987) attempt to empirically estimate each component of unemployment by trying to calculate: a natural rate without reference to inflation (to try and avoid the actual–NAIRU co-movements); the wage gap $W_1 - W^*$; and the

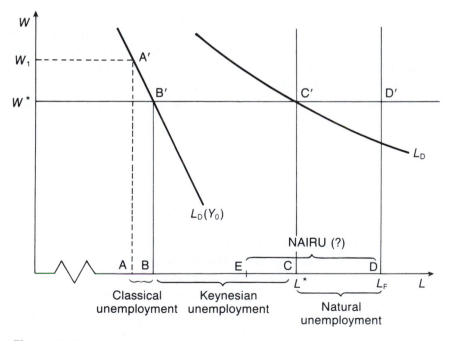

Figure 10.21

Source: Trevithick 1992, figure 8.8, p. 194

elasticity of constrained labour demand $L_D(Y_0)$. This will enable the calculation of Classical unemployment leaving Keynesian unemployment as a residual. Their main findings are low natural unemployment rates for the USA, UK and Germany, with Keynesian unemployment largely dominating the rise in total unemployment from the early 1970s. Although the categorisation and estimation method they employ have been criticised, the main weakness of their approach is that it cannot account for unemployment persistence. Any explanation of unemployment must also take inflation into account; therefore what is needed is a theory embodying both the NAIRU and hysteresis.

Layard *et al.* (1991) offer such a theory. At the microeconomic level they use a 'right to manage' model of trade union bargaining to help generate an upward pressure on wages. The unions' power in this context is best measured by the wage mark-up over the outside alternative wage. This power is influenced by the following factors: increased by raising benefits increasing the replacement ratio; increased by decreasing product market competition; increased by decentralised wage bargaining between unions and employers; and increased when unemployment is falling through the increased job security felt by insiders, i.e., employed union members. This last consideration produces what Layard *et al.* (1991) identify as 'the basic insider mechanism of hysteresis' (p. 143). Because if unemployment in the last period was high relative to this period, inflationary wage pressure increases, which leads to a high level of non-inflationary unemployment.

However, satisfying the utility of the median union member is not the only aspect of wage determination, firms are also held to have an interest in setting wages above the market clearing level. This is the 'efficiency wage' argument that we came across in Chapter 4. Worker effort is influenced by wages in the firm relative to elsewhere, but unemployment also has an impact. If unemployment is high, the relative wage difference need not be so great as when it is low to generate a given level of effort. Firms may also wish to influence the flow of applicants for any vacancy through the offered wage. Essentially the higher the offered wage, the better the average quality of applicant. Efficiency wages do not clear the labour market but produce queues of applicants for jobs. If labour markets do not clear then unemployment will arise.

Wages are only one-half of the microeconomics in the model presented by Layard *et al.* (1991); the price setting behaviour of firms is a key ingredient in their unemployment story. In essence prices are influenced positively by demand, especially in the short run, and demand is inversely related to unemployment. Hence, unemployment can be linked to the price setting behaviour of firms, and hysteresis need not be restricted solely to the determination of wages. Firms are deemed to be in a monopolistic, rather than a perfectly competitive market environment, and to practice marginal cost-plus pricing. They take marginal costs of production (including wages) into account but, through a profit mark-up, set prices above marginal cost. Given these competitive and pricing conditions, the impact of demand fluctuations on prices is limited. However, it is reasonable to suggest that as demand rises so might prices, because firms may increase the mark-up and because as capacity utilisation rises so will marginal costs as older, less efficient machinery is brought into use and as night or weekend shift

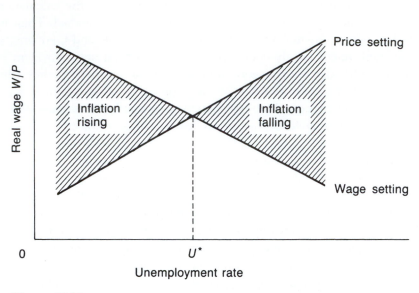

Figure 10.22

working is resorted to. These are reasons why prices may fluctuate with demand in the short run; in the long run the responsiveness of prices to demand is likely to be lessened.

Bringing wage and price determination together, Layard et al. (1991) maintain that inflation will only be stable in the short run when the real wages (W/P) sought by wage setters (unions and firms) and by price setters (firms) are equal. The variable which ensures consistency between wage and price setting behaviour is unemployment. The relationship between wage and price setting, determining equilibrium real wages and unemployment in the short run, is illustrated in Figure 10.22.

Figure 10.23 presents the long-run relationship. The feasible real wage (FRW) is equivalent to the price setting function in Figure 10.22 and can be defined as that real wage, for a given productivity, which price setters are willing to allow. It is horizontal to reflect the ambiguity that surrounds the relationship between prices and economic activity. It is debateable whether, in the long run, the price mark-up over wage costs rises as economic activity increases, thereby reducing the real wage, or not. The target real wage (TRW) is determined by the wage setting activity of unions and firms. U^* still defines the NAIRU but, whereas in Figure 10.22 a short-run NAIRU was being determined, Figure 10.23 shows a long-run NAIRU. An increase in wage pressure increases the target real wage to TRW_1 and the NAIRU to U_1. Increased wage pressure could be brought about by; a rise in union power; more fragmented bargaining; an increase in benefits; a rise in long-term unemployment; or less competitive product markets. Note that similar wage pressure in the case of a positively sloped FRW (price setting) function, as in Figure 10.22, would generate both a short run increase in the NAIRU and in real wages, i.e., stagflation.[13]

The implication of the Layard et al.'s (1991) approach is that positive demand shocks increase inflation and reduce unemployment temporarily, but that adverse supply shocks

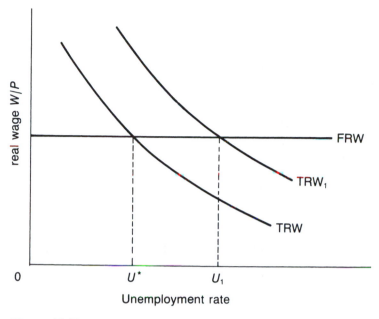

Figure 10.23

raise the NAIRU and increase unemployment. The unfortunate aspect of the early 1980s recession was that an adverse supply shock, the second OPEC oil price rise of 1979, was combined with significant demand deflation directed towards reducing inflation. Both served to increase unemployment. Because of persistence, the favourable commodity price and demand conditions of the mid-1980s had left EU countries with inflation and unemployment at high levels at the end of the 1980s. This persistence, which was not a feature of the US and non-EU European economies, is essentially due to the duration of benefits (rather than their simple generosity), the decentralised nature of wage bargaining, and the lack of intensive labour market policies to prevent the rise of the long-term unemployed. These institutional variables although they only make a partial contribution to explaining the unemployment rate individually, combine to make a major contribution in a cross sectional estimation of 20 countries for the 1983–8 period. Layard *et al.* (1991, p. 55) report the following results.

$$
\begin{aligned}
\text{Unemployment rate (percentage)} = \ &0.24 + 0.92 \text{ benefit duration (years)} \\
&+ 0.17 \text{ replacement ratio (\%)} \\
&- 0.13 \text{ active policy spend (\%)} \\
&+ 2.45 \text{ collective bargaining (1–3)} \\
&- 1.42 \text{ union co-ordination (1–3)} \\
&- 4.28 \text{ employer co-ordination (1–3)} \\
&- 0.35 \text{ change in inflation (\% point)}
\end{aligned}
$$

$R^2 = 0.91$.

The strengths of this eclectic approach to unemployment lie in its theoretical breadth, the impressive empirical performance of the model, and in the clear policy prescriptions that flow from it. In theoretical terms, introducing hysteresis has produced a theory that is no longer a natural rate of unemployment hypothesis. Equilibrium unemployment and structural aspects of labour and product markets can be shifted by both supply-side and demand-side shocks. According to Cross (1995) 'the natural rate hypothesis is not consistent with hysteresis' (p. 198). In policy terms changes in aggregate demand can be used to shift the hysteresis enhanced natural rate of unemployment. We will now consider policies to cut unemployment in more detail.

POLICIES TO CUT UNEMPLOYMENT

The policy prescription of the Classical model of unemployment, that real wages needed to be lowered, were inadequate to the task of explaining the persistent mass unemployment of the 1930s. The Keynesian model identified a role for deficient aggregate demand as a cause of unemployment and focused attention on the role of Government in stimulating aggregate demand to reduce unemployment. The Phillips curve relationship suggested that there would be a cost in the form of an increase in the rate of inflation to pay for such demand management to cut unemployment. Monetarism emphasised the danger that such aggregate demand stimulation would lead not to a one-off increase in the price level but to a process of ever accelerating inflation, without there being any long-term benefit in the form of lower unemployment. New Classical economics denied any role for aggregate demand management in influencing unemployment even in the short term, placing all the emphasis on policies designed to improve the supply side of the labour market.

The early Keynesian analysis of unemployment undoubtedly placed too much reliance on stimulating aggregate demand in order to reduce unemployment. This ignored the complexity of the unemployment problem, which was illustrated in the work of Coen and Hickman (1987) and Layard *et al.* (1991). However, the reaction of policy makers, especially in the UK, to the perceived inadequacy of the Keynesian analysis has left an unfortunate legacy. A confused mixture of Monetarist and New Classical pronouncements have misled UK policy makers into believing: that unemployment was not influenced by Government demand-side measures; recessionary anti-inflation policies would temporarily increase unemployment but it would revert to its natural rate; and that the natural rate could itself be lowered by supply-side policies. However, it appears, from even the most cursory of glances at Figure 10.12, as though low relatively stable inflation is coupled with much higher rates of unemployment in the early 1990s than was the case in previous decades, in spite of the vigorously pursued supply-side improvements enacted since 1979. In addition to those supply-side improvements it has taken sustained increases in aggregate demand, stimulated by interest rate reductions, to bring down unemployment during the 1990s.

What is needed is a battery of policies which reflect the multi-faceted nature of the unemployment problem. Policies are needed to prevent the emergence of long-term unemployment. In this respect the New Classical concern with the generosity of unemployment benefits (the replacement ratio) is not the issue. It is the duration of benefits that matter most; they should be limited to a finite period of one year for the able bodied unemployed. The receipt of unemployment benefit must also be conditional on evidence of energetic job search. In the UK the Restart programme, introduced in 1987, involved compulsory interviews backed up by the threat to suspend unemployment benefits. This tightening of the benefit regime was targeted at the long-term unemployed. It was a deliberate attempt to increase the search intensity of the unemployed and reduce their unemployment duration. Dolton and O'Neill (1996) found that the Restart interview after 6 months' unemployment did increase the probability of unemployment outflow to a job. Outflows to training were small but the interview did challenge claimants' eligibility for benefits leading to a surge in the number signing off, thereby reducing recorded unemployment. Richardson (1997) advocates wages subsidies targeted at the long-term unemployed as a means of reducing unemployment with little adverse effects on other workers.

Jackman *et al.* (1996) stress the need to prevent the emergence of long-term unemployment. Great effort needs to be made to ensure that this is not a passive year of unemployment. Given that reducing employment taxes, encouraging work-sharing and early retirement have no long-term effect on unemployment, benefits must be combined with good quality training, employment subsidies, and in the final resort temporary employment in the state sector.

The need for training is not controversial, it will make good the deterioration in human capital that unemployment brings and it will help to overcome occupational and skill mismatches. Employment subsidies are designed to increase the demand for unemployed labour by subsidising the cost of taking on an unemployed worker. Such a policy is open to the charge that active intervention in the labour market will create a number of harmful distortions. It may be that a subsidy is being paid for workers who would have been employed in any case. Yet the more clearly the subsidy is targeted at those whose probability of recruitment is low, i.e., the long-term unemployed, the less the deadweight loss involved in such a policy spend. However, even a targeted employment subsidy is open to the charge that it might cause displacement, that is that the long-term unemployed will be recruited at the expense of the short-term unemployed. Yet such a displacement can be supported on the grounds that the short-term unemployed have a greater influence on the behaviour of insiders, and on equity grounds that long-term unemployment is more demoralising and financially destructive than a short spell of unemployment. The subsidy would be for a limited period after hiring and be regulated to encourage genuine recruitment rather than displacing existing employees. Richardson (1998) examined the impact of the Australian Special Youth Employment Training Program (SYETP), which was an employment subsidy scheme that operated from 1976 to 1985 before being superseded by the Jobstart program. The study found little evidence that subsidised jobs ended once the subsidy expired. It also found that the experience of subsidised employment had 'a large and significant positive effect on subsequent employment prospects' (p. 13). If subsidised workers are not only being removed from unemployment by the subsidised job but also are less likely to return to unemployment in future then concentrating on young

Table 10.12 Spending on active labour market policies (percentage of GDP), 1990 and 1997

	1990	1997
Austria	0.3	0.4
Belgium	1.2	1.3
Denmark	1.1	1.8
Finland	1.0	1.6
France	0.8	1.4
Germany	1.0	1.2
Greece	0.4	0.4
Ireland	1.4	1.7
Italy	1.4	1.1
Luxembourg	0.3	0.3
Netherlands	1.3	1.7
Portugal	0.6	0.9
Spain	0.9	0.6
Sweden	1.7	2.1
UK	0.6	0.4
EU	0.9	1.1
Australia	0.3	0.5
Canada	0.5	0.5
Japan	0.1	0.1
New Zealand	0.9	0.7
Norway	0.9	1.0
USA	0.2	0.2
Total OECD	0.7	0.8

Source: Adapted from Martin 2000, table 1, p. 85

workers like SYETP did, and the UK's New Deal did initially, makes sense because of greater lifetime gains.

Whether providing employment subsidies specifically for unskilled workers would reduce their unemployment is doubted by Nickell and Bell (1995), especially given the decline in demand for unskilled workers in OECD economies. Cutting employment taxes on unskilled workers would also be limited by demand in the face of skill biased technological change, the wage insensitive nature of labour demand and the constraint of the minimum wage.

Job creation, usually in the public sector, should be used as a last resort for those unemployed reaching the end of the benefit period who have not been placed upon a training scheme or recruited into the private sector via the subsidy scheme.

There are international differences in the pursuit of such active labour market policies towards the unemployed. The data in Table 10.12 shows measures of spending on active policies ranging from 0.1 per cent of GDP in Japan to 2.1 per cent in Sweden in 1997. There is little evidence in Table 10.12 of any switch towards active policies in the OECD away from passive policies such as paying unemployment benefits and early retirement pensions. According to Martin (2000) 'Italy, Norway,

Table 10.13 Lessons from the policy evaluation literature

Active policy	Helps	Does not help	General observations
Formal classroom training	Women re-entrants	Prime-age males, older workers with low level education	Courses need to signal relevance and high quality. Small scale programmes are best
On-the-job training	Women re-entrants, single mothers	Prime-age men	Must directly meet labour market needs. Requires strong links with employers
Job-search assistance	Most unemployed especially sole parents, women		Combine with increased job search monitoring and work tests
Special youth measures		Disadvantaged youths	Need to combine education, work skills, work-based learning. Focus on attitudes to work, adult mentors
Employment subsidies	Long-term unemployed. Women re-entrant		Needs careful targeting
Business Start-up	Men 30–40 better educated		Only works for a small section of the unemployed
Direct job creation	Severely disadvantaged	Most adult unemployed	Few long-term advantages. Low marginal product jobs.

Source: Adapted from Martin 2000, table 4, p. 92

Portugal and Sweden were the only OECD countries where spending on active measures was equal to or exceeded spending on passive measures in 1997' (p. 88). When it comes to identifying which sort of active policies succeed, Martin (2000) draws the lessons from a number of policy evaluation studies published between 1993 and 1999 that are reproduced in Table 10.13.

Training programmes appeared to increase employment opportunities, especially for women. Helping the unemployed with job search, e.g., through job clubs, is the least costly type of policy and the one that yields consistently positive results. Special programmes for the young unemployed have a disappointing track record with the general observations in Table 10.13 being drawn from the few successful JOBSTART sites in the USA. The New Deal for Young People that was introduced throughout Great Britain in April 1998 aimed to provide those aged 18–24 with various options after 6 months unemployment. Around 72 per cent of those entering the programme were men. After a period of intensive supervised job search, the remaining unemployed had to choose between subsidised employment, education and training or environmental and voluntary work. Dorsett (2001) found that in terms of young men obtaining sustained work, subsidised jobs appeared to offer the best route followed by extended supervised intensive job search. Education and training for the disadvantaged youths on the New Deal had a disappointing record. Perhaps the pay-off to full-time education may be longer term and might show up in enhanced earnings rather than short-term employment success.

In spite of the apparent success of subsidised employment in the British New Deal, employment subsidies carry the risk that subsidised jobs would have been created anyway (deadweight) and subsidised workers may replace non-subsidised employees (substitution). Policies that subsidise private sector employment appear to suffer from substantial deadweight and substitution effects. Martin's (2000) evaluation of wage subsidy programmes in Australia, Belgium, Ireland and the Netherlands implies 'that for every 100 jobs subsidised by these schemes only 10 were net gains in employment' (p. 97). Aiding the unemployed to start their own businesses by becoming self-employed seems to help mainly men in their 30s. Direct job creation in the public sector appears to do very little to help the unemployed get proper jobs in the open labour market.

In June 1998 a New Deal programme for the long-term unemployed aged 25 and over was introduced in Britain. Initially this focused on those who had been unemployed for 2 years, but this was extended in April 2001 to those who had been out of work for 18 months. In excess of 80 per cent of those entering the New Deal for the long-term unemployed were men. The structure was similar to the New Deal for young people, a period of intensive supervised job-search which if unsuccessful was followed by either subsidised employment or full-time education and training for up to one year. By the end of May 2001 almost half (48 per cent) of the participants in this programme had returned to claiming unemployment benefits, with less than one-quarter (23 per cent) entering employment. Of the 72,160 people moving into employment 12,550 had jobs that lasted less than 13 weeks. Of the 59,610 having more enduring employment, 13,010 were in subsidised jobs.

Active labour market policies like the New Deal are not costless. The lessons from Table 10.13 point towards programmes that are carefully framed and closely monitored. No one scheme is going to help all sections of the unemployed at the same time or to the same extent. A broad strategy would aim to shift the burden of expenditure away from benefit payments towards providing a good employment service and quality training. An extreme non-interventionist model would be that of the USA. The latter has, in general, had lower rates of unemployment than the UK, but it is not regarded as a politically viable alternative model of welfare provision for the UK.

Sweden is at the other extreme, yet Swedish unemployment in the 1990s rose quite markedly (Table 10.1). In the face of altered macroeconomic policy during the recession of the early 1990s the Swedish model with its heavy emphasis on supply-side active labour market policy proved incapable of dealing with the problem. Asset prices fell, domestic demand and output contracted, fiscal policy was tight, monetary policy tightened as orthodox anti-inflation policy was followed and devaluation of the krona was ruled out until November 1992. According to Robinson (1995), by 1993/94 Sweden was spending around 2 per cent of GDP on active labour market policies and 2.5 per cent on passive unemployment benefits. For Britain at the time the proportions were 0.5 per cent and 1.25 per cent respectively. In such circumstances it is doubtful whether Swedish style active labour market policies do pay for themselves.

Wage bargaining in the UK appears to be a mixture of the worst features of both the US and Swedish models. It has a fairly high union coverage but decentralised, uncoordinated bargaining. The USA has decentralised bargaining but union coverage in the USA is very low and in what appears to be continual decline. In Sweden union coverage is very high but so is union and employer coordination. UK policy makers are faced with a stark choice to continue the 1980s policy of reducing union power through legislation which did little to erode the union wage mark-up (see Chapter 7), or to establish a highly centralised wage bargaining framework which is based upon a high degree of employer coordination. A mechanism through which to achieve some degree of coordination in bargaining to reduce wage pressure is the tax based incomes policy suggested by Layard *et al.* (1991, pp. 485–90). This envisages a set norm for nominal wage growth agreed by representatives of employers, workers and Government; firms and unions may agree bargains above that norm but they will then be taxed upon excessive wages. Either the firm or the workers may be taxed for exceeding the norm, but the tax must be sharply progressive to act as a disincentive to excessive bargains. An acknowledged distortion is that it penalises productivity based wage bargains which might reduce worker effort. Layard *et al.* (1991, p. 489) accept this as inevitable but believe that it is a cost worth paying to reduce unemployment and not generating wage pressure. The more important drawback of this proposed reform of the wage bargaining framework is that it requires a strong social cohesion between unions, employers and Government who need to be aware of the damaging effects of wage pressure and who are willing to take the employment consequences of a bargain into account.

The suggested reforms including cutting benefit duration are not intended to be cheap alternatives for a Government seeking to reduce public expenditure. Quality education and training, employment subsidies and public sector employment will be costly in the short term. However, the redirection of public expenditure on labour market programmes away from benefit payment into more active and effective measures is likely to be self-financing in the longer term. All these policy recommendations are designed to improve the supply side of the labour market and come into effect once unemployment has arisen. However, there is still a role for demand management to avoid exacerbating unemployment. For Robinson (1995) the main lesson from the experience of Swedish unemployment is that both 'demand management and supply-side policies are necessary ingredients of an employment strategy' (p. 39). In the UK the severity of the policy-inspired demand contraction of the early 1980s clearly aggravated the rise of unemployment and the subsequent problem of unemployment persistence. Of the early 1990s recession in the UK, Trevithick (1992) writes, the plummeting levels of employment and, to a lesser extent, of output are, quite simply, the result of the decline in both consumption, and investment expenditure which, in turn, were brought about . . . through the punishing impact of high interest rates over a long period of time. It is hard to imagine a recession which is more Keynesian in origin!

(pp. 227–8)

Nickell *et al.* (2001) estimate that about 55 per cent of the increase in unemployment in Europe, from the 1960s to the first half of the 1990s, was due to adverse labour market institutions (unemployment benefit duration, lack of geographical mobility and trade union density) with much of the remainder being due to the lack of aggregate demand during recessions. The main lesson to be learned from our investigation of unemployment is that it may have some demand-side and supply-side causes which require a combination of demand-side and supply-side cures.

CASE STUDY – EMU AND UNEMPLOYMENT

In general, unemployment rates in Europe fell during the 1990s. Will this continue after the single European currency, the Euro, became fully operational in 2002? While it is too early to give a definitive answer to this question we know from Chapter 8 that in theory flexible labour markets should be more important after European Monetary Union (EMU). In this case study, Andre Van Poeck and Alain Borghijs (2001) 'EMU and Labour Market Reform: Needs, Incentives and Realisations', *World Economy*, 1327–52, examine whether the introduction of the single currency has stimulated or hindered the sorts of labour market reform that appear to be needed to deal with persistent and high unemployment.

Van Poeck and Borghijs (2001) begin by looking at the difference between EMU and non-EMU countries in terms of estimated rates of equilibrium unemployment, the NAIRU. We have dealt with, at some length, the shortcomings of estimating NAIRUs and will bear these in mind as we follow the train of the argument of this case study. Table A compares the equilibrium unemployment rates of EMU and non-EMU countries.

Average equilibrium unemployment was higher in EMU countries than in non-EMU countries at the end of the 1990s.

It is now generally accepted that a high degree of real wage rigidity is one of the main causes of high equilibrium unemployment rates. Real wage rigidity is often supported by labour market institutions giving incentives for real wage hikes or preventing a real wage decline in the wake of an adverse supply shock to the labour market. Labour market institutions that are assumed to support real wage hikes and downward real wage rigidity are the degree of centralisation, co-operation and co-ordination in the wage

Table A   Equilibrium unemployment rates (%)

EMU countries	1990	1999	Non-EMU countries	1990	1999
Increasing NAIRU					
Finland	5.6	9.0	Japan	2.2	4.0
Germany	5.3	6.9	Sweden	3.8	5.8
Italy	9.1	10.4			
Stable NAIRU					
Austria	4.6	4.9	Australia	6.5	6.8
Belgium	8.4	8.2	New Zealand	7.0	6.1
France	9.3	9.5	Norway	4.6	3.7
Greece	8.4	9.5			
Decreasing NAIRU					
Ireland	14.1	7.1	Canada	9.0	7.7
Netherlands	7.5	4.7	Denmark	6.9	6.3
Portugal	4.8	3.9	Switzerland	3.0	2.4
Spain	17.4	15.1	UK	8.6	7.0
			US	5.4	5.2
Average NAIRU	8.6	8.1	Average	5.7	5.5

Source: Adapted from Van Poeck and Borghijs 2001, table 1, p. 1328

bargaining process, employment protection legislation, the level and duration of unemployment benefits and the share of active labour market policy.

. . .

Given the persistent unemployment problem in most of the EMU countries and the apparent link between labour market performance and labour
market institutions, it is clear that there is a need for reforming these
institutions in a way that increases real wage flexibility and reduces the
pressure for real wage hikes.

From Chapter 8 we know that when countries are hit by negative demand
shocks they can devalue their currency and/or lower domestic interest rates.
These policy responses are not available to individual EMU member states.

The only option for an EMU member to restore demand is to go through
an adjustment process in the labour market, . . . labour market reform in
EMU is needed to bring down equilibrium unemployment and to ease the
adjustment process in the wake of negative shocks.

Although labour market reform might be needed it is far from clear whether
EMU has increased the incentives for member states to implement flexibility
enhancing reforms that are often unpopular. Bear in mind that 'reform in a
single member state only brings equilibrium unemployment in the union down
by a small amount, the benefits of a reduced inflation . . . are only marginal'. The
narrow anti-inflation remit of the European Central Bank (ECB) means that
there is no possibility that labour market reform could be sweetened by any

temporary monetary expansion. The requirement to control fiscal deficits in EMU, which could have stimulated flexibility enhancing reforms, might well be relaxed. Overall there is no unambiguous evidence that EMU has provided any greater incentives for national governments to undertake labour market reform. But did the prospect of joining EMU in the 1990s stimulate more reform in European countries?

According to Van Poeck and Borghijs (2001) the prospect of joining EMU did not function

> well as an incentive to step up institutional reform in the 1990s. . . . Changes in unemployment benefits, taxes and active labour market policy were lower in EMU countries. Progress in wage formation is virtually identical, while EMU countries score better [than non-EMU countries] with respect to employment protection legislation.

While initially high unemployment non-EMU countries like Australia, New Zealand and the UK engaged in a lot of labour market reform during the 1990s this was not the case among high unemployment EMU countries. It may be that

> formal labour market reform has been substituted in EMU by a consensus . . . to moderate wages. . . . The empirical finding that wage bargaining co-ordination in EMU countries has increased may support this argument. . . . Wage moderation has proved successful in a macroeconomic environment with good growth performance and without any major shocks [the 1990s]. It may become apparent that more structural reform is needed once the macroeconomic environment becomes more unfavourable.

This case study has shown that in spite of a greater theoretical need for labour market reform EMU countries undertook less reform than non-EMU countries during the 1990s. It is not clear whether EMU itself provides powerful incentives to undertake such reform. While labour market reforms might reduce equilibrium unemployment, they are likely to prove politically unpopular in EMU countries. The unemployment outlook for EMU countries improved during the 1990s mainly because of wage moderation on the part of unions in co-ordinated bargaining with employers. EMU may yet face sterner tests if the generally benign macroeconomic environment of the 1990s is not repeated.

UNEMPLOYMENT – SUMMARY

From descriptive statistics we noted a number of features about unemployment:

- the volatility of UK and US unemployment rates prior to the Second World War
- relatively low and stable unemployment rates in the post-war period until the mid-1970s

- the significant rises in unemployment of the early 1980s
- the widespread rise in unemployment rates during the early 1990s
- falling unemployment during the remainder of the 1990s
- countries differ in their unemployment flow characteristics
- young workers have a higher incidence of unemployment than more experienced workers
- married workers have a lower incidence of unemployment than the unmarried
- unemployment rates fall as the level of educational attainment increases
- unemployment rates are higher for ethnic minority workers than for their white colleagues in the UK and USA
- there exist significant regional differences in unemployment

At the theoretical level we summarised:

- Classical unemployment with its emphasis on excessively high real wages
- Keynesian theory pointing to the significance of money wages and stressing the importance of deficient aggregate demand
- the Phillips curve which initially suggested a fairly stable inverse relationship between unemployment and inflation
- the Monetarist critique which re-established the primacy of real wages, incorporated adaptive expectations, and introduced the concept of a natural rate of unemployment into the analysis
- New Classical economics included the natural rate concept in models containing the rational expectations hypothesis
- the notion of unemployment hysteresis underlined the persistent nature of much unemployment

Our main conclusion at this stage was that no single theoretical approach seemed capable of capturing the complexity of unemployment in OECD economies, particularly with regard to its persistence.

The simple generosity of welfare benefits (replacement ratio) and structural mismatch do not feature as significant elements in the shift of the U–V curve and its associated rise in unemployment.

We considered Layard *et al.*'s (1991) promising eclectic model which encompasses:

- a right to manage model of union wage bargaining
- insider–outsider effects
- the degree of bargaining coordination
- welfare benefit generosity and duration
- firms' cost plus pricing in an imperfectly competitive market environment
- a natural rate concept, the NAIRU

This model appeared to be capable of dealing with demand- and supply-side shocks and the variety of unemployment experiences of the OECD economies.

It also yielded some definite policy proposals:

- reduce the duration of benefits
- provide high quality education and training for the unemployed
- target employment subsidies
- give temporary state sector employment
- coordinate wage bargaining possibly using a tax based incomes policy

We stressed the need to combine supply-side active labour market policies with demand management in order to tackle unemployment.

UNEMPLOYMENT – QUESTIONS FOR DISCUSSION

1) Summarise the Classical view of unemployment.
2) What reasons did Keynesians advance for the fact that labour markets in major industrialised economies do not appear to clear at anything like a full employment equilibrium?
3) Explain what is meant by the 'natural rate of unemployment'. What implications does such a concept have for labour market policy?
4) What justification is there for viewing New Classical theory as providing 'a bizarre account of fluctuations in unemployment which is both profoundly counter-intuitive and counter-factual'?
5) Define unemployment hysteresis and suggest what may account for such a phenomenon.
6) Explain what determines the NAIRU in the Layard *et al.* (1991) eclectic model of unemployment.
7) Critically examine the unemployment policy prescriptions arising from Classical, Keynesian and New Classical models and contrast these with those that arise from the Layard *et al.* (1991) model.

SUGGESTED READING

Landesmann, M. and Pichelmann, K. (eds) (2000) *Unemployment in Europe*, Basingstoke: Macmillan Press.

Nickell, S. and Layard, R. (1999) 'Labour Market Institutions and Economic Performance', in O. Ashenfelter and D. Card (eds) (1999) *Handbook of Labour Economics*, Volume 3, Amsterdam: Elsevier Science.

Trevithick, J.A. (1992) *Involuntary Unemployment: Macroeconomics from a Keynesian Perspective*, Hemel Hempstead: Harvester Wheatsheaf.

11

Trade, globalisation and labour markets

INTRODUCTION

In this chapter we will investigate the link between international trade and labour markets. After setting the scene with some general observations about trade trends and patterns, we will explain what globalisation is and briefly set out how it has emerged before pointing to some of the implications more integrated international economic activity have for labour markets. We shall examine the relative shift in employment and therefore, by implication, in labour demand in terms of the deindustrialisation thesis. This allows us to set the 'shake out' of manufacturing industry, that is the rapid decline in employment after 1979 against the longer-term reduction in the importance of manufacturing in industrialised countries.

TRADE FLOWS

Throughout the post-Second World War era international trade has grown rapidly. A glance at Figure 11.1 shows that during the period 1950–97 world trade increased more rapidly than world output. At a very aggregate level this is indicative evidence of the continuing integration of the world economy. For any representative country, foreign goods and services have become increasingly important in the consumption package of economic agents (consumers, firms, governments) since 1950.

The more rapid growth of trade than output was not a feature of the international economy before the Second World War. The period 1913–37 witnessed a growth in international trade (1.3 per cent annual growth) below the rate of growth of world output (1.8 per cent). Obviously the First World War (1914–18) severely dislocated international trade. It seems as though the trade system was slow to recover, because

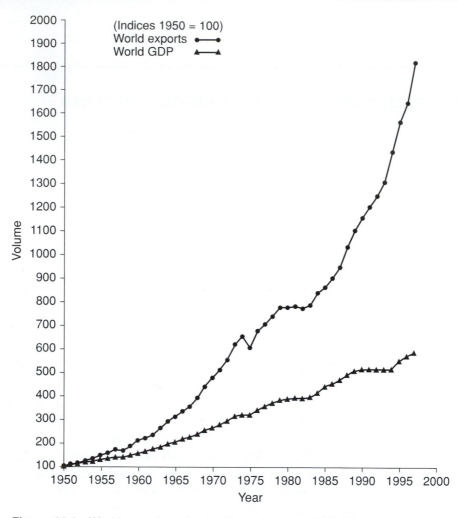

Figure 11.1   World exports and output in real terms, 1950–97

Source: Husted and Melvin 2000, figure 1.1, p. 11

even by 1924 the volume of world trade was only 7 per cent higher than it had been in 1913 (Kitson and Michie 1995, p. 9). Although the 1920s was a period of recession in the UK other economies were faring somewhat better (e.g., the USA). Overall world output grew by an annual average 3.7 per cent during 1924–9 with trade recording a 5.7 per cent growth rate (Kitson and Michie 1995, table 1.2, p. 8). During the Great Depression of the 1930s the volume of world exports actually fell. The worst years of the inter-war depression were 1929–32. During these three years world output declined at an annual average rate of 6.2 per cent whilst trade collapsed at a rate of 9.9 per cent per year. Although a patchy recovery set in after 1932, by 1937 world trade had still not reached its 1929 level. With the onset of the Second World War (1939–45) international trade was about to receive its most serious shock.

A number of features of the post-Second World War era distinguish it from the 1920s and 1930s and may help account for that record of faster growth. Consider:

1 the relative stability of the international monetary order under the Bretton Woods system (1950–71), compared to the instability of flawed attempts to return to the Gold Standard and the competitive devaluations which characterised the inter-war period;
2 note slower rates of both trade and output growth which accompanied increased exchange rate volatility following the breakdown of Bretton Woods in the early 1970s;
3 the increasingly free trade regime promoted by the General Agreement on Tariffs and Trade (GATT) and its successor the World Trade Organisation (WTO) reductions in tariffs, after they had escalated during the protectionist 1920s and peaked in the early 1930s;
4 the creation and expansion of regional free trade areas such as the EU (1957), EFTA (1958) and NAFTA (1995);
5 the move towards deeper economic integration particularly in the EU during the 1980s;
6 the globalisation of production and finance through the growth of multinational companies and the development of global capital markets;
7 the ideological and policy shifts from protectionism to liberalisation and deregulation, beginning in the 1970s.

The bulk of goods traded across national boundaries are manufactured products, and the fastest rate of growth since 1950 took place in the trade of those manufactured goods. These facts, taken together, mean that industrialised countries play the most significant role in international trade, and that international economic integration may well have gone furthest in those industrialised countries. In 1997 the percentage shares of total exports accounted for by the various regions of the world were,

EU	38
Asia	28
USA and Canada	16
Latin America	5
Middle East	4
Africa	2
Rest of world	7

Asian exports are dominated by those of Japan, the Newly Industrialised Countries of South East Asia (especially Hong Kong, Malaysia, South Korea, Taiwan) and increasingly China.

The Industrial Revolution not only established the UK as the first industrial nation but lead to it becoming the premier trading nation as well. In spite of Britain's attempt to reimpose its dominance on the international trade system, by 1929 the USA had overtaken the UK as the world's leading trading nation. After the Second

Table 11.1 Trade (exports) in relation to the
economy, 1980 and 1998 (percentage of GNP)

	1980	1998
USA	10	12
Austria	36	42
Belgium	57	73
Denmark	33	34
Finland	33	40
France	22	24
Germany	n.a.	27
Greece	16	15
Ireland	48	76
Italy	22	27
Netherlands	51	56
Portugal	25	31
Spain	16	26
Sweden	29	44
UK	27	29
Australia	19	21
Canada	28	41
Japan	14	9
New Zealand	30	29
China	6	22
Hong Kong	90	125
Malaysia	58	118
Singapore	215	187
South Korea	34	38

Source: World Bank 1999

World War, the overwhelming strength of the US economy was reflected in a dominant share of international trade activity up until the early 1970s. Britain became a
less significant trading power as Germany and Japan emerged as important trading
nations. By 1989 a rank order of shares of industrial exports (Jepma *et al.* 1996, table
1.1, p. 17) put the UK (with 4.9 per cent) in fifth place behind the USA (11.8 per
cent), Germany (11.0 per cent), Japan (8.9 per cent), and France (5.8 per cent). The
UK was only just ahead of Italy (4.6 per cent), Canada (3.9 per cent) and the
Netherlands (3.5 per cent).

As well as countries differing in terms of their significance to international trade,
the economic importance of international trade differs between countries. Table 11.1
contains evidence of a slightly surprising fact that whilst the USA is the single most
important player in international trade, trade is not a particularly important part
of aggregate economic activity in the USA. Trade is much more important in relation
to the rest of the economy in the Netherlands, Germany and the UK than in either
the USA or Japan. Less surprising might be the fact that international trade is exceptionally important to city states like Hong Kong (now united with China) and

Table 11.2 Intra and inter regional trade (percentage of region's total trade), 1958 and 1989

	1958	1989	Percentage change
Intra – North America	28	35	+25
North America – EU	11	18	+64
North America – Asia	10	29	+190
Intra – EU	30	58	+93
EU – North America	12	9	–25
EU – Asia	3	7	+133
Intra – Asia	34	42	+24
Asia – North America	19	30	+58
Asia – EU	10	15	+50

Source: IMF, *Direction of Trade*
Note: North America = USA, Canada, and Mexico. EU6 in 1958, EU12 in 1989. Asia = India, ASEAN, Japan, and Northeast Asia.

Singapore. With a few exceptions the importance of trade for the economies of the world, an indicator of international economic integration, increased between 1980 and 1998.

One way to conceptualise recent developments in the pattern of international trade is to view it as an increasingly tri-polar system based upon the EU, North America and Asia. Busch and Milner (1994) produce IMF data that shows intra-regional trade increased in all three main economic regions, North America, EU Europe, and Asia, between 1958 and 1989. Table 11.2 records increases of about one-quarter in intra-regional trade within both North America and Asia over the 1960s, 1970s and 1980s.

In Europe trade among the EU states almost doubled, to account for well over half (58 per cent) of all EU trading activity in 1989. The largest percentage increases over the period were recorded in North American and EU trade with Asia. In the EU, intra-regional trade dominates that conducted with the other two trading areas. In spite of modest increases in intra-regional trade in North America and Asia, it is evident that they have maintained and developed their trading links with other regions to a much greater extent than Europe has. The three main economic regions combined accounted for some 82 per cent of world exports in 1997. Asia's share shows a fairly steady growth throughout the period since 1960. North America's share is fairly constant, increasing markedly in the early 1980s, with Europe returning to long-term trend in the late 1980s. Whilst this is not conclusive evidence of an increase in regionalism, trade does appear to be dominated by three regional blocs. Busch and Milner (1994) see the pressure for regional free trade arrangements like the EU and NAFTA as coming from international firms. They cite three main factors driving international firms: 'the growing export dependence of firms; the greater degree of firm multinationality; and the shift in the composition of trade . . . from inter- to intra-industry trade' (p. 268). All three are aspects of globalisation.

GLOBALISATION

According to Mishra (1999) 'globalisation is an economic phenomenon driven by politics and ideology' (p. 1). There are a number of features of the international economic order which any form of analysis needs to recognise. These are that:

- market economies are becoming more internationally integrated, through lowered national boundaries, through multi-lateral agreements like GATT, the WTO and regional free trade areas like the EU and NAFTA;
- technological advance has supported international integration by making rapid communication and transfer both feasible and less costly;
- multinational company activity in both production and finance has increased international integration;
- it is now more difficult for individual nation states to direct and control economic activity (both productive and financial) within their national boundaries; and
- free market ideology has provided the intellectual foundation for globalisation.

There are a number of different perspectives concerning globalisation (see Held *et al.* (1999)), yet any definition of the concept of a global economy must refer to the system generated by globalising production (usually associated with the rise of multinational firms) and global finance. Global production is characterised by: multinationals; desire for cost minimisation; reduction of tax liability; desire to avoid regulation; need to control labour; search for political stability; search for state subsidies. Global finance is characterised by: being virtually unregulated; having a 24-hour network; being electronically integrated; being based on city markets e.g., New York, Tokyo, Hong Kong, Singapore, Frankfurt, Paris, London. There is the potential for contradiction between the two components of the global economy. Production requires stability in politics and finance in order to expand through investment and trade. This results in a dislike of volatile financial markets, variable, especially accelerating inflation and rapidly fluctuating exchange rates. Producers have increasingly turned to financing expansion through debt rather than by equity investment. This gives finance a degree of control and power over production because of its credit creation ability. However, global finance can be volatile and is itself in a potentially fragile position being subject to corporate failure and Government debt default.

For Underhill (1994) the globalisation of economic structures and markets has 'reduced the economic space controlled by the state and intensified the competition its domestic economic constituency has to bear' (p. 36). The EU single market is a good example where politically influential multinational producer and financial firms have pressed for structural changes in intergovernmental negotiations that have freed up goods and factor markets in Europe. This has been to the general detriment of labour in the EU (aspects of EU social legislation ameliorates this loss to labour). Yet the single market has fed back onto domestic politics and has increased the competitive pressures on firms.

Inter-governmental bodies such as the IMF, World Bank and the European Central Bank were the result of deliberate attempts to make states accountable to an international monetary order. (GATT and the WTO could be viewed in a similar manner with regard to trade.) Global financial markets, however, were not an integral part of the Bretton Woods set up. Therefore we need to explain how they emerged.

THE EMERGENCE OF GLOBAL FINANCIAL MARKETS

The list of reasons behind the globalisation of international finance includes:

- improving telecommunications technologies which reduced the cost and difficulty of transferring funds;
- financial market confidence recovered from the 1930s' crisis in the stable environment of the late 1950s and early 1960s;
- the expansion of demand for international financial services which accompanied the post-war growth of trade and multinational firms;
- the enormous surplus funds deposited on international financial markets by OPEC states after 1973;
- the incentive provided by floating exchange rates during the 1970s for agents to diversify their assets internationally in the face of volatile currency fluctuations; and
- conservative financial companies and cartels changed during the late 1970s and throughout the 1980s in response to increased domestic competitive pressures (including financial deregulation and liberalisation).

These are all contributory factors to the globalisation of finance. Yet one should resist seeing globalisation as an inevitable market driven phenomenon, backed by technological feasibility, over which nation states had little control. Remember that the Bretton Woods system incorporated capital controls and tight exchange controls that were used to screen international financial transactions. As Bretton Woods collapsed in the early 1970s Japan and Europe pressed for a more ordered financial system, including Bretton Woods type cooperative controls. However, from a political economy perspective, the key to financial globalisation lays in the attitude of the USA. The USA opposed moves to reintroduce capital and exchange controls in the early 1970s. Indeed early in 1974 it abolished its remaining capital controls and was content to allow the dollar to float. There are a number of reasons why the USA adopted this deregulatory and liberalising stance:

- international transactions are less important to the US economy than they are to the likes of Japan and Western Europe, hence any exchange rate fluctuation will impact less on the US economy than on the UK economy because a greater proportion of UK GDP is accounted for by international activity;
- the USA believed it had a distinct advantage over other financial markets, in terms of size and the lack of regulation, which would attract investment to the US and to the dollar, thereby funding current account and budget deficits;
- the increasing influence of neoliberal ideology in the USA (e.g., Friedman, Hayek) which argued for floating exchange rates and the more efficient global allocation of capital promised by 'free' international financial markets;

- floating exchange rates promised more latitude in domestic economic policy making and Government disinterest in 'speculative' financial flows; and
- 'free' financial markets would impose monetary discipline on Governments which Keynesian policies were believed to have eroded in the post-war era.

These types of consideration found support in the USA among: private financial interests; conservative finance officials; some intellectuals; and multinational firms. Yet the neoliberal influence extended beyond the USA. Tight exchange controls were considered by the Labour Government in the UK (1976) and by the Socialist Government in France (1983). However, both rejected it as a strategy and accepted the discipline of financial markets, which were becoming increasingly internationalised and global. In both Governments policy makers were disillusioned with Keynesianism and becoming interested in the neoliberal ideas of monetary discipline and free markets, including, as we saw in Chapter 8, labour markets. Private financial interests and multinational firms were against reimposing controls. Such a policy move would also have put Britain and France at odds with other EU states and the USA.

The role of the state is evident in the story of the triumph of financial market liberalisation. In the 1960s Britain had supported the growth of the 'Eurodollar' market in London. This was a relatively and comparatively regulation-free environment, trading assets denominated in foreign currencies, mainly dollars. The British Government supported this market by giving it a physical base as it sought to maintain London as an international financial centre. The US Government tacitly supported the Eurodollar market because of the leading role being played by US banks and corporations in the market. It also helped to increase the attractiveness of the dollar at a time when the dollar-based Bretton Woods system was coming under pressure because of an expanding dollar supply.

In 1979 the UK followed the US move of 1974 in abolishing capital controls. This was both a manifestation of the new Thatcher Government's neoliberal ideology, and an attempt to increase the attractiveness of London as an international financial centre vis-à-vis New York. In 1986 the London Stock Exchange was deregulated ('big bang') to match the 1975 liberalisation of the New York Stock Exchange.

The USA and Britain had led a flurry of financial liberalisation. In 1984–5 both Australia and New Zealand abolished capital controls. By 1988 the EU had committed itself to the complete abolition of internal capital controls within two years. In 1989–90 Sweden, Finland and Norway removed what had been the most rigid controls in the advanced industrialised world. During the 1980s even Japan gradually eased its restrictive capital controls. This flurry of activity can be seen as a process of competitive deregulation, designed to secure a share of a growing global financial market from New York and London.

THE IMPACT OF GLOBALISATION ON LABOUR MARKETS

The logic of globalisation highlights features which impede competitiveness. Attention has focused on labour market rigidities. Concern over the changes brought about by globalisation may well lie behind firms' drive, accommodated by Government policy, to increase the share of atypical employment, reducing workers' sense of job security. We saw in Chapter 8 that the debate over labour market flexibility was based upon a presumption that unionised, regulated labour markets did not function as well as less impeded ones, in terms of generating employment and responding to shocks and technological change. The object of labour market flexibility was to increase the supply-side responsiveness of the labour market, i.e., increase the elasticity of labour supply. However, the rigidities identified in European labour markets are elements of social protection that were built up in the post-War period. Getting rid of labour market rigidities means dismantling part of the state-provided social protection (generous, long lasting welfare benefits, support for unions, pensions and healthcare, employment protection legislation). For employers the greater competitiveness brought about by globalisation may bring about reductions in the generosity of firm provided healthcare and pensions, as firms seek to reduce non-wage costs.

The triumph of free market ideology, especially in the USA and the UK, appears to have been accompanied by increased inequality in the labour market (see Chapter 3). Could globalisation be responsible for the increased polarity of income and employment? In a study of the relationship between wages and unemployment in the UK, Bell *et al.* (2000) found that the impact of current unemployment on wages had increased over time indicating increased product and labour market competition. One possibility was that UK firms were in a more competitive environment with overseas producers; however, Bell *et al.* (2000) were 'unable to detect any interaction between the unemployment effect and import penetration' (p. 15). Import penetration even in the UK manufacturing sector had no impact on wages or the elasticity of wages with respect to unemployment between 1977 and 1997.

Research into the impact of globalisation on labour by Haskel and Slaughter[1] has found that the elasticity of demand for labour in manufacturing industries in the USA and the UK increased between 1978 and 1992. Figure 11.2 shows that in the UK the magnitude of the elasticity of labour demand was greater for unskilled workers (the lower line) and that the increase in elasticity (the fall in the lines plotted in Figure 11.2) during the 1980s appears to have been more marked for the unskilled. Note that the elasticities for both types of manufacturing workers are negative indicating downward sloping demand curves.

The evidence from Figure 11.2 coupled with the fact that demand elasticities for unskilled workers in multinational firms have increased more rapidly than those working in domestic companies, are seen by Haskel as instances of the impact of globalisation operating through changing prices and increased capital mobility. Globalisation has not only shifted the demand curve for unskilled workers in US and UK manufacturing to the left but it has also changed the slope of that demand curve making it more elastic.

However, the simultaneous deterioration of the relative labour market position of unskilled workers concentrated in basic manufacturing in the advanced industrialised economies of the North and the improvement in the relative wages and employment

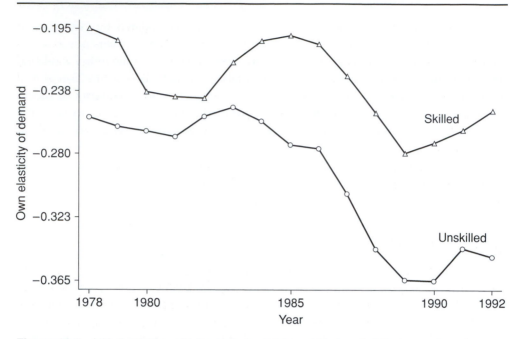

Figure 11.2   UK elasticities of labour demand for unskilled and skilled manufacturing workers (smoothed 3 year moving average), 1978–92

Source: Haskel (2002, see endnote 1)

Table 11.3   Labour market and production changes (percentage per annum), 1970 to 1990

	North	*South*
Unskilled/skilled		
Wages	−0.9	+2.3
Employment	−4.2	+1.3
Shares of GDP		
Manufacturing	−0.22	+0.10
Services	+0.20	+0.14
Primary	−0.08	−0.55
Non-traded	+0.10	+0.36
Standard of living	+2.2	+1.1

Source: Minford 1998, table 7.1, p. 155

of unskilled workers in the developing countries of the South provides circumstantial evidence of the impact of globalisation (both trade and financial) on labour markets. The data in Table 11.3 shows that during the 1970s and 1980s whilst the ratio of unskilled to skilled wages and employment fell in Northern economies, they rose in the developing economies of the South.

The economies of the North (OECD countries) have seen the share of manufacturing in their GDP shrink while industrialisation in the South has taken place as unskilled workers increasingly find employment in basic manufacturing usually at the expense of agriculture (primary sector). Both parts of the World expanded their traded services. The growth rate of per capita GDP (standard of living) was twice as fast in the richer North as in the poorer Southern economies over this period. For Minford (1998) 'globalisation . . . increases both sorts of countries' productivity in the sorts of goods they are best at producing' (p. 172).

The link between international trade and the deteriorating position of unskilled workers, especially in basic manufacturing in advanced industrialised countries, finds expression in the deindustrialisation hypothesis.

DEINDUSTRIALISATION

Thirlwall and Gibson (1992) maintain that 'over the last three decades, the UK has been experiencing a severe process of deindustrialisation' (p. 366). Both the early 1980s and the early 1990s recessions in the UK impacted heavily on manufacturing employment, which along with the emergence of manufacturing trade deficits in the 1980s lends support to the view that Britain underwent accelerated deindustrialisation after 1979 (Wells 1989). Labour productivity improved but whether this can be sustained is debatable. Manufacturing employment has declined since the 1950s in the UK and a number of other industrialised economies, including Belgium, France, Germany and the Netherlands. However, this is not a universal phenomenon among developed countries; manufacturing employment has actually increased in Canada, Italy, Japan, Norway and the USA. Table 11.4 provides some detail of the changes in manufacturing employment levels between 1960 and 2000.

Group One countries, of which the UK is the most outstanding example, experienced a loss of manufacturing employment during the period 1960–79 which accelerated during the 1980s and 1990s. Germany recorded falling manufacturing employment throughout the entire 1960–2000 period, but the rate of employment decline slowed after 1980. Group Three nations experienced a growth in industrial employment during the 1960s and 1970s which the severe recession of the first half of the 1980s and 1990s reversed. The Netherlands, after suffering manufacturing job losses, managed to increase manufacturing employment after 1979 to more than compensate for earlier losses. Group Five countries, including the USA, recorded a gain in manufacturing employment for the whole period in spite of job losses after 1980; in the case of Japan, declines in manufacturing employment did not occur until well into the 1990s. Group Six countries recorded job gains for the entire 1960–2000 period, although the rate of increase in manufacturing employment has slowed markedly during the 1980s and 1990s. We would not be surprised to see declining employment in manufacturing in Denmark and Ireland during the first two decades of the 21st Century.

Table 11.4 Manufacturing employment (percentage change), 1960 to 2000

	1960–1979	1980–2000
Group one		
Austria#	−1.0	−15.9
Belgium*	−14.9	−26.8
France#	−16.3	−26.8
UK	−19.3	−33.1
Group two		
Germany*	−11.3	−4.4
Group three		
Australia	+5.9	−7.7
Norway	+11.8	−24.0
Sweden	+9.3	−26.2
Group four		
Netherlands#	−4.2	+4.6
Group five		
Canada*	+45.6	−1.9
Finland*	+35.0	−28.7
Greece (1997)	+66.2	−17.9
Italy	+26.3	−9.6
Japan	+38.5	−3.4
Spain#	+36.5	−10.6
USA	+25.3	−9.1
Group six		
Denmark	+7.0	+1.0
Ireland	+35.7	+2.0
Portugal	+51.5	+5.4

Source: OECD, *Labour Force Statistics*, 1985, 2001
Note: * 1998; # 1999.

WEAK EXPLANATIONS OF DEINDUSTRIALISATION

There are a number of alternative explanations of deindustrialisation. A common fallacy is what Thirlwall and Gibson (1992) call the 'technical change hypothesis' (p. 372). This maintains that technological progress destroys employment in manufacturing through a saturation of demand for industrial products and/or through the application of labour saving technology or mechanisation. However, this view does not stand up to scrutiny. As we can see from Figures 11.3 and 11.4 below, there has been no lack of demand for manufactured products in the UK since the early 1950s. Indeed, technological progress opens up the possibility of new product development thereby creating new demands for industrial products, remember the car, TV and personal computer. Furthermore as Broadberry (1994) identifies, the UK possessed technological leadership for much of the 19th Century, when UK manufacturing employment was growing rapidly. The USA had a technological advantage until the 1970s again accompanied by increases in manufacturing employment. Japan assumed technological leadership in the 1970s and 1980s without any loss of manufacturing employment. A contrary view of the link between technology and employment growth, with a stronger empirical foundation, would see the problem as not one of technological progress but the lack of such progress adversely affecting manufacturing employment growth.

Bacon and Eltis's (1976) 'crowding out hypothesis' has been used to argue that the expansion of the public sector that accompanied the growth of Government expenditure and the expansion of the welfare state in the post-war period, starved UK private sector manufacturing of productive resources which caused its decline. Such an argument would be difficult to apply to those countries that witnessed the simultaneous increase in both the public sector and manufacturing employment after 1960. For the UK there is little evidence that manufacturing has been starved of labour as a factor of production. Figure 2.18 showed clearly that employment in manufacturing fell during periods of rising unemployment, labour surplus rather than labour shortage, because output growth fell below productivity growth.

The problem for the UK lies in the slow growth of demand for UK manufactured products, both at home and abroad, reflected in the slow growth of output rather than any resource starvation due to public sector expansion. Remember that the dein-dustrialisation of the 1980s took place against a background of reductions in Government budget deficits and lower public sector employment as privatisation reduced the size of the public sector. Note that, in general, reductions in employment in manufacturing have been mainly male full-time, whereas the growth of employment during the 1980s and 1990s has been female with a substantial part-time component.

DEINDUSTRIALISATION AND TRADE SPECIALISATION

Following Rowthorn and Wells (1987) and Wells (1989) we shall set out the decline in UK manufacturing in terms of output and employment before presenting the deindustrialisation argument in the context of foreign trade. During the 1980s UK manufacturing output experienced a severe slump in which output collapsed by some 19.6 per cent from a peak in June 1979 to its January 1981 trough. Thereafter output grows by 27.1 per cent between 1982 and 1988. When we examine the longer-term output growth trends we discover, as Figure 11.3 shows, that until the early 1970s the growth rate of manufacturing output, in constant prices, was generally faster than that of GDP whilst the service sector grew at a somewhat slower rate.

The severe 1979–81 slump evidently reverses the growth relationship between manufacturing, services and national output. Yet it is also apparent that the slump in manufacturing output in the mid-1970s was far less severe and less enduring than that experienced in the early 1980s. Although manufacturing output recovers after the early 1980s slump, the same cannot be said of employment in manufacturing (see Figure 11.3). The problem before us is to explain that collapse in manufacturing employment. It certainly did not come about because of any lack of expenditure on manufactured products in the UK.

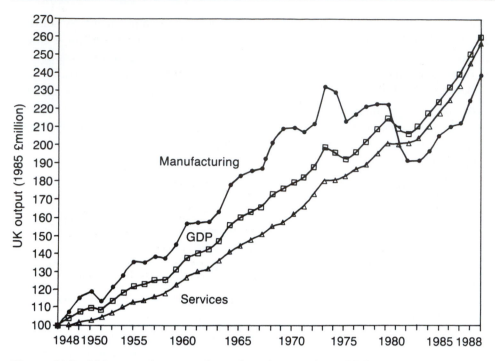

Figure 11.3 UK output, by sector (manufacturing, services, GDP), 1948–88, at constant 1985 £million, reference base 1948 = 100

Source: Wells 1989, figure 2.5, p. 29

Until recently, domestic expenditure patterns have not unduly favoured the service sector. Figure 11.4 shows that the 1980s boom in service sector spending only served to place it back to its early 1950s share following the consumer durables boom which witnessed washing machines replace laundries and TV take the place of theatre and cinema going. Whereas the proportion of expenditure devoted to manufactured goods almost doubled, the share accounted for by food consumption virtually halved between 1952 and 1988. Manufacturing and service sector expenditures, both of which are income elastic, benefited from the recent rapid growth in consumer spending. Between 1979 and 1988 manufacturing sector expenditure grew by some 51 per cent, whilst that of the service sector rose by nearly 58 per cent in real terms (constant 1985 £). The importance of this finding is to show that the severe recession in UK manufacturing output and employment was not due to any profound shift in the pattern or strength of consumer spending. This disparity between expenditure and output/employment trends shows up in the marked trend deterioration of the manufacturing trade balance. Figure 11.5 illustrates the varying fortunes of UK manufacturing in expenditure and output trends.

The declining trade performance of manufacturing has important balance of payments implications. Table 11.5 illustrates the balance of payments position associated with the trade in manufactured goods. The data shows the progressive decline of substantial surpluses generated by manufactured trade from a 1950s peak to their

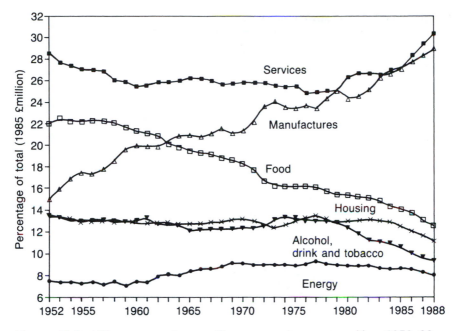

Figure 11.4 UK consumers' expenditure, percentage composition, 1952–88, at constant 1985 £million

Source: Wells 1989, figure 2.15, p. 42

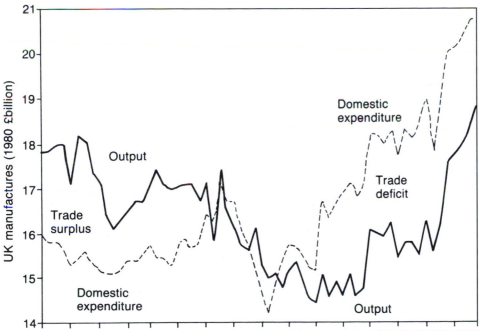

Figure 11.5 UK manufactures, domestic expenditure and output, 1973–88, at constant 1980 £billion

Source: Wells 1989, figure 2.19, p. 47

Table 11.5 UK balance of payments in manufactured goods
(percentage of GDP, current prices)

1951–1960	+8.4	1985	−1.1	1993	−1.2
1961–1965	+6.4	1986	−1.6	1994	−1.1
1966–1970	+4.9	1987	−2.0	1995	−1.1
1971–1975	+3.5	1988	−3.3	1996	−1.1
1976–1980	+3.2	1989	−3.4	1997	−0.9
1981–1982	+1.6	1990	−2.1	1998	−1.7
1983	−0.9	1991	−0.6	1999	−2.3
1984	−1.4	1992	−1.2	2000	−2.7

Source: ONS, *UK National Accounts, UK Balance of Payments*,
various years
Note: + = surplus, − = deficit.

complete disappearance in 1983. During the remainder of the 1980s and throughout the 1990s the UK continued to import a greater value of manufactured products than it managed to export.

The balance of payments constraint on the UK economy could conceivably be tighter as a result of the rapid decline in manufacturing. If the shift from manufacturing to service sector employment entails a shift away from activities which produce a high proportion of exportables to activities which generate very low proportions of exportable services, then the UK would experience balance of payments problems at lower rates of growth in the 1990s than would have been the case in the 1950s.

The UK's ability to fund deficits on trade in manufactured goods is highly questionable. Initial surpluses in non-manufactured trade, particularly in food, raw materials and fuel, coupled with a weak growth in the service sector trade balance have proved to be transitory features of the 1980s. An improvement in commodity trade was reversed by the mid-1980s, as was the fuel trade position, which having improved, primarily because of North Sea oil, deteriorated after production peaked in the mid-1980s. The picture emerging from the trade in non-factor services (tourism, consultancy, civil aviation, shipping, financial services and the like) and UK earnings from overseas investments is not an encouraging one. While both show a growth after the 1979–82 recession the strength and endurance of that improvement is very doubtful. Overall the UK's ability to fund the deficit on manufacturing with surpluses arising from other aspects of its trading activities was undermined during the course of the 1980s. Consequently record current account deficits have been experienced (1989 in particular) which have had to be funded by inflows of foreign funds.

The early 1980s recession witnessed a sharp acceleration of the process of deindustrialisation. Post 1983 the UK is evidently suffering shortfalls in the domestic supply of manufactured products, which takes the form of a deteriorating sectoral balance of payments position. As Wells (1989) observes,

> the rump of UK manufacturing production which remains . . . may well . . . have a higher level of labour productivity and be more profitable than before – but it is totally inadequate in terms of the volume of its internationally competitive

capacity and, hence, the scale of its output to meet the requirements which UK society places upon it.

(p. 58)

The deindustrialisation experienced in the UK can be of two general types, either positive or negative. Positive deindustrialisation is the result of sustained growth in a fully employed, highly developed economy, where rapid productivity growth in manufacturing yields increased output at lower levels of employment. Those displaced manufacturing workers are not unemployed because they are absorbed into the growing service sector. Negative deindustrialisation questions whether displaced workers will be fully employed by the service sector. It suggests that structural unemployment will increase over time. Declining rates of economic growth up to 1983 indicate a greater likelihood that deindustrialisation has been negative in nature. Between 1960 and 1973 the average annual increase in non-oil GDP was 2.8 per cent. This fell to 0.3 per cent during the period 1973–83.

Rowthorn and Wells consider three possible explanations for the deindustrialisation of the UK economy. A 'maturity thesis' links the UK's experience with a general theory of economic development and structural change. Economic development entails the persistent decline of agriculture as economies industrialise. As they further mature the relative importance of manufacturing inevitably falls as non-domestic service employment rises.

Support for the maturity thesis comes from the international nature of the decline in manufacturing employment. The approximate peaks for manufacturing employment as a proportion of the labour force among major industrialised economies were

1955	USA and the UK
1966	France and Switzerland
1973	West Germany and Japan.

A second approach is to explain the decline in manufacturing employment with regard to the changing structure of foreign trade. This 'specialisation thesis' views the UK of the 1950s as a highly specialised 'workshop economy', importing raw materials, food and oil while exporting manufactured products. To support this view of the UK economy, between 1950 and 1953 the balance of payments recorded a

10.5 per cent GDP surplus on manufactured trade and
13.3 per cent GDP deficit on non-manufactured trade.

These figures were unprecedented and they have never been equalled. Since the 1950s the structure of UK trade has changed markedly, such that by 1983 there was a

0.5 per cent GDP deficit on manufactured trade and
1.0 per cent GDP surplus on non-manufactured trade.

Rowthorn and Wells point to a number of factors which could account for this change in the pattern of the UK's trade. Food and raw material imports became much cheaper in real terms between the 1950s and the 1980s. Domestic food production increased as did service industry exports. North Sea oil production substantially reduced the UK's demand for non-manufactured imports. Finally, there is the effect associated with the 'failure thesis'. Poor economic growth, low growth of manufacturing output, poor productivity and profit performance combined with a lack of investment all contribute to a failure of UK manufacturing to compete internationally or produce at an output level sufficient for full employment. Thus the result is deindustrialisation and increasing unemployment.

Rowthorn and Wells summarise the cause of the fall in the demand for labour in British manufacturing since 1945 as 'an example of negative deindustrialisation resulting from poor industrial performance, compounded by the effects of changes in trade specialisation'.

CASE STUDY – GLOBALISATION, UNEMPLOYMENT AND CHINA

Globalisation has occurred and it appears as though on balance its impact has been positive. Yet are there features of the globalisation phenomenon that threaten the well being of workers? Raphael Kaplinsky (2001) 'Is Globalisation All It is Cracked Up to Be?', *Review of International Political Economy*, 8 (1): 45–65, believes that there are. This case study focuses on the likely labour market impact of the entry of China and India into world markets.

> Many of the world's population . . . have gained as openness has grown. However, there is compelling evidence that the benefits of globalisation have not been evenly spread . . . [Kaplinsky (2001) argues that] . . . increasing globalisation of factor and financial markets leads to growing inequality and poverty, both in developing and industrialised countries. . . . As China increases its participation in the global economy and as India and other low wage developing economies follow the same path, it is likely that there will be a further squeeze on the incomes of many, not just of the unskilled, but also increasingly of semi-skilled and skilled labour.

Globalisation, as measured by trade openness, has grown at a rapid rate since 1970 (see Table A) especially in the two most populous countries China and India.

Table A   Trade (imports and exports) as % GDP

	1970	1980	1990	1995
East Asia and Pacific	18.6	31.9	44.4	58.3
Latin America and Caribbean	23.4	32.5	31.1	35.6
Sub-Saharan Africa	44.3	59.5	53.2	56.1
China	5.2	12.9	26.9	40.4
India	8.2	16.6	18.3	27.7
World	27.1	38.7	37.9	42.5

Source: Adapted from Kaplinsky 2001, table 1, p. 47

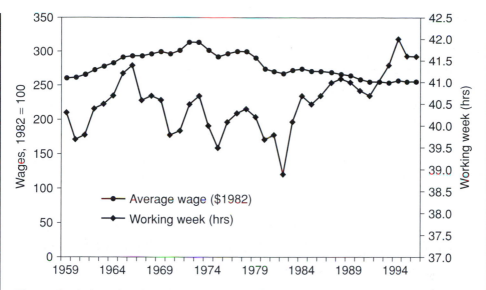

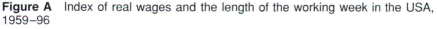

Figure A   Index of real wages and the length of the working week in the USA, 1959–96

Source: Calculated from *United States 1997*: table B-45

Greater globalisation has not brought about faster rates of economic growth or increased standards of living across the globe. Instead across vast swathes of the developing world real incomes have fallen.

> This prevalence of falling real incomes is not confined to developing countries. Real wages in the Netherlands fell between 1979 and 1997. in the USA, real wages were lower in the mid-1990s than they were in the late 1960s, and family incomes have only held up as a consequence of longer working hours (see Figure A) and more working members of the family.

> [The] . . . rapid growth of China and India in recent years . . . which have seen a significant rise in average per capita incomes . . . produces an equalising trend [in inter-country income distribution. Yet,] . . . although average income in China may have risen, worsening income inequality means that very large numbers of the Chinese population have either been excluded from the gains from growth, or may even be worse off.

Nor was the growth of inequality confined to China; we have already seen in Chapter 3 how income inequality increased in the UK during the 1980s and 1990s.

Kaplinsky (2001) maintains that increasing globalisation has made labour an abundant factor thereby putting its income under pressure. Over the past couple of decades the world has experienced 'immiserizing growth – that is, an expansion of economic activity which coincides with a decline in real incomes.'

Table B

	USA %		EU* %		Global %	
Share of merchandise imports from China	1990	3.1	1989	2.7	1990	0.8
	1997	6.0	1997	7.6	1997	4.0

Source: Adapted from Kaplinsky 2001, table 7, p. 57
Note: * manufactured goods.

Now while notions of immiserizing growth can be traced back to Malthus and Marx, what might make the current situation unique is that globalisation may have brought workers in developing countries into more direct competition with workers in industrialised countries.

> This is because, increasingly, workers in the developing world possess both the skills and the industrial experience to compete with rich country labour forces even in the industrial sector which was formerly the specialized preserve of the rich economies in global trade.

This means that the incomes of skilled workers in industrialised countries are likely to come under increasing pressure.

The importance of China is that it accounted for 23 per cent of the global labour force in 1995 (India 20 per cent). The data in Table B shows that imports from China grew rapidly in the 1990s. Not all of these products are low technology goods produced by unskilled workers.

> By 1996, . . . there were more than 6 million university graduates. More than 3 million students entered technical schools, and a growing number have begun studying abroad.
>
> . . .
>
> In itself, none of this need lead to a decline in global wages if there is full employment in China. However, even after a period of significant growth, . . . China faces rapidly rising open unemployment.

Nor are the unemployed in China all unskilled; 'the average education level of the officially registered unemployed is above the average level for the workforce as a whole. . . .' This may not bode well for skilled workers in industrialised countries.

In conclusion there are benefits that flow from globalisation, 'there are undoubted efficiency gains arising from international specialisation. In a competitive world, these efficiency gains will be reflected in a reduction in product costs and an improvement in product availability and quality.' The main labour market threat from globalisation is unemployment, which opens up the possibility of

- falling real incomes
- growing income inequality
- increased pressure for protectionism.

Increasing protectionism has already taken the guise of concern over labour and environmental standards. The continued expansion of the supply of skilled labour in developing countries (China in this case study), coupled with unemployment among skilled workers in those countries, opens up the possibility of declining real incomes and employment of skilled workers in industrialised countries. We have already argued, in Chapters 3 and 5, that, to a great extent, skilled labour has benefited from skill-biased technological change and increased income inequality in industrialised countries. However, globalisation has increased the demand elasticity of labour (Chapter 11) while increased flexibility has increased its supply elasticity (Chapter 8). If Kaplinsky (2001) is right about globalisation increasing the competitiveness of skilled labour markets globally, then we, as both students of labour economics and skilled workers, could be in for some interesting times.

DEINDUSTRIALISATION, TRADE AND EMPLOYMENT

Singh (1989) presents an alternative explanation of the role of trade in deindustrialisation that introduces the concepts of an 'efficient manufacturing sector' and 'long-term structural disequilibrium'. The implication is that an advanced industrialised economy could experience severe deindustrialisation through trade if it had an inefficient manufacturing sector or if it were in long-term disequilibrium. The UK would be in long-term structural disequilibrium if manufacturing import and export propensities do not allow current account balance at a given desired level of employment and a desired rate of real wage growth. Hence manufacturing trade performance is held to be crucial to achieving current account balance and long-term growth potential. Singh's (1989) empirical study of the 1970s found that, for the UK, with an 'inefficient manufacturing sector', trade did lead to a net loss of jobs. However, the study concluded that 'it was not manufacturing trade with the Third World but rather with other advanced countries which was the main cause of the disequilibrium' (Singh and Zammit 1995, p. 104). Wood (1994) disputes this by suggesting that manufactured exports from the South (Third World) to the North (First World) are an important element in deindustrialisation.

The data in Table 11.6 confirms that manufactured exports dominate the North's exports to the South. However, it also shows that by 1989 more than half of the

Table 11.6 Manufactured exports as percentage of total exports, 1955–89

	1955	1970	1980	1989
North to South	73.2	78.1	78.6	79.4
South to North	5.0	15.6	15.2	53.3
South to North fuel	20.4	33.1	66.4	24.8

Source: Wood 1994, table 1.1, p. 2

South's exports to the North consisted of manufactured goods. Closer inspection of the data clearly indicates that the temporary increase in the dominance of oil exports masked the rise in Southern manufacturing exports during the 1970s. Northern and Southern manufactured exports are not identical. Those from the North are characterised by a high skilled labour intensity, those from the South by high unskilled labour intensive manufacturing. Wood (1994) adopts the view that, for the South, export-oriented industrialisation is a good development strategy. South Korea and Taiwan are examples of countries that initially developed and prospered due to the expansion of unskilled labour intensive manufactured exports. For the North the changing pattern of trade may be beneficial, imports from the South could substitute for domestic production in low skill, low productivity areas like toys, clothing and leather goods. Foreign exchange and prosperity earned by the South's exports expand the market for the North's exports of high skill, high productivity manufacturing and services, thereby expanding Northern employment. The shift away from unskilled to skilled employment may have led to structural unemployment and widening skill based wage differentials in the North (see Chapter 3). Wood's approach is consistent with conventional trade theory (Heckscher-Ohlin). It ignores capital, arguing that financial and physical capital is internationally mobile but that labour is immobile. This means that differences in labour skill availability (endowment) are the basis for international trade. Skill endowments are fixed in the short term yet can change due to migration, education and training. Wood (1994) simplifies matters by assuming no North–South migration and significant obstacles to skill formation (imperfect capital markets, ability, background, increasing returns to skill formation, education and training infrastructure externalities). Better quality and lower cost (in real terms) transport and communications, coupled with reductions in barriers to trade (GATT and the WTO) have increased the importance of enduring differences in skill endowments for manufactured trade patterns and performance.

The main problem with this analysis concerns the magnitude of North–South trade effects. Previous studies like Singh (1989) found the effects to have been very small. Indeed if Wood (1994) had used the conventional factor content of trade (fct) approach, assuming balanced North–South trade in manufactures, the impact on the North would be to reduce manufacturing employment by less than 1 per cent (Wood 1994, table 3.8, p. 98). Yet the fct approach may underestimate the effects by ignoring the fact that the North and South are producing and different manufactured products using different technologies. The data in Table 11.7 summarises Wood's (1994) main estimates for the various labour markets.

It is evident that Wood's (1994) approach yields higher estimates of the impact of trade both on job creation in developing countries in the South and job destruction in the North than the more conventional fct approach commonly used in earlier studies. Furthermore, it points to a marked difference in the experience of skilled and unskilled manufacturing labour, especially in the Northern economies. However, these estimates should be treated with caution because they are subject to quite a wide margin of error,

Table 11.7 Impact of North–South trade on manufacturing employment (millions of person years, cumulative to 1990)

	North			South		
	Export	Import	Net	Export	Import	Net
Conventional (fct) approach						
Total labour	4.4	−5.5	−1.1	19.9	−15.3	4.6
Wood (1994)						
Total labour	3.9	−12.9	−9.0	25.5	−2.6	22.9
of which						
Skilled	2.0	−1.8	0.1	3.4	−1.3	2.1
Unskilled	2.0	−11.1	−9.2	22.1	−1.3	20.8

Source: Wood 1994, table 4.9, p. 149

> North −9.0 million . . . +/− 3 million
> South +22.9 million . . . +/− 5 million.

Sachs and Shatz (1996) supports Wood's (1994) claim that rising unemployment and falling relative wages of the unskilled in Northern economies is linked to the growth of manufactures from low labour cost developing countries. However, Berman *et al.* (1997) in their study of skill biased technological change (see Chapter 5) find that less than 9 per cent of the displacement of unskilled workers from manufacturing industries in 10 OECD countries was due to trade with developing countries. Minford (1998) calculates that some 40 per cent of the collapse in employment of unskilled workers in Northern economies is due to globalisation (with almost 60 per cent of this due to skill biased technological change and just over 40 per cent due to trade). Unskilled workers may have been able to find some respite from the threat of a more internationally competitive environment brought about by globalisation in the growing non-traded sector (see Table 11.3). Rowthorn and Ramaswamy (1997) maintain that globalisation via increased trade only accounts for between 10 and 20 per cent of the changes in wages and income distribution in advanced (Northern) economies. SBTC has been a more important influence on the labour market. The increased capital mobility brought about by globalisation and immigration from developing countries appears to have had only modest effects on the labour markets of the North. Yet as it progresses, globalisation can only further increase the sensitivity of Northern workers to external shocks.

CONCLUDING REMARKS

International trade is composed mainly of manufactured products. Trading activity in these products is concentrated in the industrialised countries of the capitalist world. The importance of individual countries in this trade network has changed over time. The importance of international trade to the overall economic well being of nations varies. The current trade pattern may reasonably be represented as a tri-polar system in which intra-regional trade plays a substantial part, especially in Europe.

If the links between international financial markets and domestic financial markets are strong, and if the link between financial markets and real economic activity is strong, then globalisation of finance leaves national governments very little scope for divergent national economic policies. Hence competition between nations takes place in areas like labour standards. Yet if these links are complicated and weak there is more scope for divergent economic and social policies. If endogenous growth theory is correct then restructuring a national financial system to encourage R and D investment (or education and training) could prove significant and sustainable, even if international financial markets constrain interest rate policy.

The obvious implication of deindustrialisation in a trading context for the UK is that there is now a tighter balance of payments constraint on growth than hitherto. Figure 11.6 clearly shows that external balance was only likely to be achieved in the 1990s at far higher rates of unemployment than was the case in the 1960s.

It is reasonable to suggest from a Keynesian absorption approach to the balance of payments (see Caves *et al.* 1999, p. 333), that the relationship between the external balance and unemployment should be a positive one. As Aggregate Demand increases, unemployment should fall but, depending on the inclination of the economy to import as income rises (marginal propensity to absorb), the balance of payments will tend to deteriorate. However, it becomes clear that the UK economy has not been moving up and down a stable curve; the relationship has shifted during the 1970s and particularly during the 1980s, a fact that is consistent with the deindustrialisation thesis. Past deindustrialisation in the UK has been accompanied by increases in structural unemployment (it has been negative in nature). The changing structure of UK trade, particularly the shift from being a net exporter in manufactured products to being a net importer, has contributed to deindustrialisation, which has impacted more heavily on unskilled workers. The role of North–South manufactured trade in deindustrialisation for Northern economies like the UK, may have been greater than was conventionally thought, yet it still appears to have played a minor role in the declining fortunes of unskilled workers in Europe and North America. According to Ghosh (2000) increases in manufactured trade with some developing countries has had

> adverse effects on employment and wages of low-skilled workers in the industrialised countries, but such effects have been quite small . . . both skilled and unskilled workers in the developing countries . . . have derived significant benefits from trade-induced growth of employment and wages. The global net effects are certainly positive and substantial.
>
> (p. 304)

An important effect of globalisation in the UK has been to increase the demand elasticity for workers, particularly the unskilled. When combined with increases in the elasticity of labour supply, sought by policies designed to increase flexibility, this means that the UK labour market is a much more fluid, possibly more volatile and potentially less secure place (especially for the unskilled) than it was in 1980.

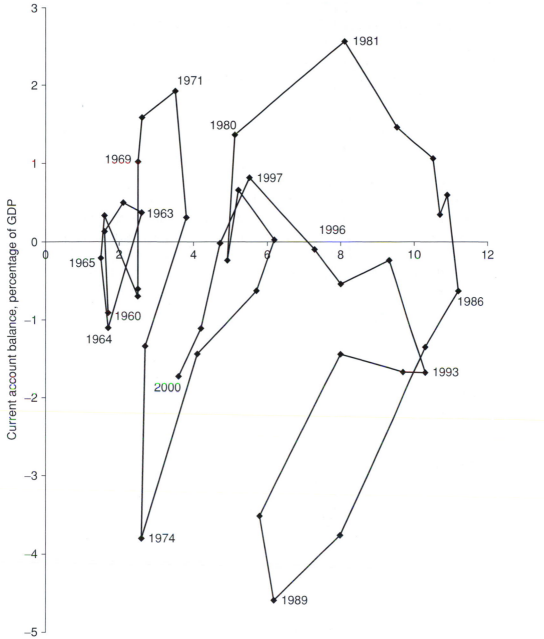

Figure 11.6   UK unemployment and balance of payments, 1960–2000

Source: ONS, Economic Trends, annual supplement, various years

TRADE, GLOBALISATION AND LABOUR MARKETS – SUMMARY

International trade has grown more rapidly than output since the end of the Second World War. International capital markets have become more integrated, particularly since the early 1970s. These are two important elements of economic globalisation. The labour market consequences of globalisation that we discussed focused on

- removing labour market rigidities
- increasing wage polarisation in advanced industrialised countries (North)
- increasing labour demand elasticities
- undermining the position of unskilled workers in the North

We have already examined the issue of labour market rigidities in Chapter 8, where we noted the widespread if somewhat uneven trend towards greater labour flexibility in the North. In Chapter 3 we discovered that wage differentials according to skill have grown over time especially in the UK. The contribution of globalisation to these two trends is by no means clear. However, they have taken place against a background of greater integration creating a more competitive international environment. We addressed the issue of the undermining of unskilled workers in the North in this chapter by looking at the deindustrialisation hypothesis.

We discovered that deindustrialisation is a widespread phenomenon in the mature economies of the North, but that it has been especially rapid in the UK during the 1980s and to a lesser extent the 1990s. The main points to emerge from our analysis of deindustrialisation were that

- deindustrialisation in the UK was not due to any lack of expenditure on manufactured products
- estimates of the impact of deindustrialisation on the wages and employment of unskilled manufacturing workers vary but that the most reliable lie in the 10–20 per cent range
- skill-biased technological change was a more important factor than deindustrialisation in undermining the position of unskilled workers in the North
- there was a marked deterioration in the balance of payments position of UK manufacturing during the 1980s
- this has apparently tightened the balance of payments constraint on the UK economy's ability to grow and reduce unemployment through a stimulation of aggregate demand alone

In general, the impact of globalisation on labour markets has been beneficial because of the gains made by workers in developing countries. Yet globalisation and the drive for greater flexibility (Chapter 8) have made the labour market forces of demand and supply more responsive.

QUESTIONS FOR DISCUSSION

1) In what ways might the increase in international trade and capital mobility associated with globalisation undermine the position of workers in advanced industrialised economies?

2) Using the following diagram illustrate how globalisation may have impacted on the demand for unskilled workers in UK manufacturing plants between 1978 and 1992.

3) Explain what is meant by deindustrialisation.

4) If the substantial and rapid reduction in UK manufacturing employment during the 1980s and 1990s did not come about because of any lack of expenditure on manufactured products, why in your opinion did it come about?

5) Examine the link between international trade and the changing situation of unskilled workers in the North.

6) Explain what is being depicted in Figure 11.6 and comment on its likely significance for the prospects of reducing unemployment in the UK.

SUGGESTED READING

Rowthorn, R. and Ramaswamy, R. (1997) 'Deindustrialisation: Causes and Implications', Washington, DC: *IMF Working Paper 97/42*.

Standing, G. (1999) *Global Labour Flexibility: Seeking Distributive Justice*, Basingstoke: Macmillan.

Notes

1 LABOUR SUPPLY

1 The imposed maximum number of hours (H_m) is capable of a number of interpretations. It may be a statutory maximum as in the case of long distance lorry drivers. Or it could refer to the total number of hours available to the individual of which work is only one component, such that

$$H_m = T = H + L$$

where T is the time available, H is the hours of work and L is leisure. More complicated models of the allocation of time (e.g., Becker 1965) would distinguish between paid market work and domestic work in the home, such that

$$T = H_D + H_p + L$$

with H_D being domestic work and H_p being market work.

2 The notion that an individual might derive some positive utility from the activity of working could be incorporated into the analysis. We shall do so implicitly by suggesting that it is incorporated into the positioning of the indifference map. The greater the satisfaction derived from work the stronger the tendency towards working longer hours, therefore the further to the right would the indifference map be located.

Indifference map I in Figure 1 (see p. 407) represents individuals with a low intrinsic utility from work. Map II reflects a greater degree of satisfaction derived from work. Thus at an initial wage rate of OR_1 type II individuals would be prepared to work longer hours than those in category I. This might still be the case even if type II were offered a lower wage rate OR_0.

3 An anonymous referee suggested the following model which is not limited by the unidirectionality of influence from the husband's to the wife's work pattern that the diagrammatic exposition implies. The model employs a Cobb-Douglas household utility function containing a combination of income and leisure,

$$U = Y L_h^a L_w^b$$

where Y is household income and L_h and L_w are the hours of leisure consumed by the husband and wife respectively. Utility is to be maximised subject to the constraint,

$$Y = W_h(T - L_h) + W_w(T - L_w)$$

where T represents the number of hours per period, and W_h and W_w are the hourly rates of pay for the husband and wife respectively. The maximisation problem can be solved using the Lagrangian multiplier method with the solution being given by the following equations:

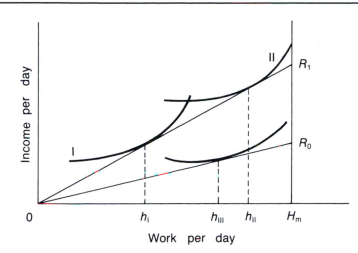

Figure 1

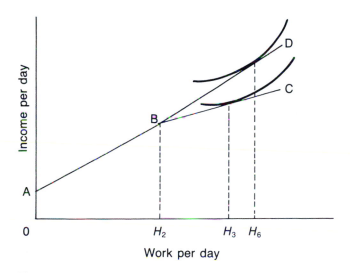

Figure 2

$$L_h = aT(W_h + W_w)[1 - b/(1 - b)]/W_h(1 + a)[1 - ab/(1 + a)(1 + b)]$$
$$L_w = b[T(W_h + W_w) - W_hL_h]/W_w(1 + b).$$

As an example suppose $a = 0.4$, $b = 0.2$, $W_h = 5$, $W_w = 3$ with $T = 168$. Under these conditions $L_h = 67.0$ and $L_w = 33.6$. If we now raise the wife's wages such that $W_w = 4$ then the leisure time enjoyed by both the husband and the wife increases. $L_h = 75.4$ and $L_w = 47.3$. The important feature of this outcome being that the wife's wage affects both her labour supply and that of her husband as well.

4 To demonstrate the fact that increasing female pay rates relative to those of males would tend towards increasing female labour supply take the case of Figure 1.10(b). Yet this time let us increase female wage rates from BC to BD (Figure 2).

   For the same indifference mapping this move towards more equal wage rates for women results in an increase in female labour supply from H_3 to H_6.

5 There is an assumption here that the household derives positive utility from the domestic activities undertaken. Whilst you may not like washing up you are said to appreciate clean crockery.

Obviously there is a role for technological change embodied in domestic appliances to have an impact on household labour supply in such allocation of time models. Household utility is given by

$$U = f(x, L_H, L_w, D)$$

where X is the consumption set, L is the hours of leisure of the husband (H) and wife (W) and D is the collective domestic activity. D embodies the notion of household production that goods and services can be combined with time at home to produce domestically e.g., cook a meal.

6   A neoclassical microeconomist might be tempted to seek to explain such an unequal division of labour within the household by suggesting that the household seeks the most efficient means of completing domestic tasks. Given that the man commands on average a higher wage rate than the woman, the woman is more likely to be engaged in domestic activity. Such an argument tends towards acceptance of an inequitable status quo. It becomes even more obvious if it is suggested that there are significant differences between men and women in the comparative advantage each possesses re market activity and domestic chores. Becker (1965) maintains that the focus of attention should be the opportunities available to household members rather than seeking intellectual justifications for the outcome of past and current inequalities of opportunities 'the allocation of the time of any member is greatly influenced by the opportunities open to other members'.

7   Forcing people to seek and obtain jobs they otherwise would not take on the grounds of unsuitability may not be an optimal policy from an allocative efficiency point of view. It could be that subsidised job search is beneficial if it reduces such misallocation and subsequent labour turnover rates which impose costs to be borne by the firm.

2 LABOUR DEMAND AND PRODUCTIVITY

1   The demand elasticites were presented by Johnathan Haskel of Queen Mary and Westfield College, University of London at a research seminar at the University of North London on 4/2/2002. They should form part of a forthcoming paper jointly written by J. Haskel and M. Slaughter.

2   Whilst we do not address the issue directly it is clear that factor services other than labour have their own adjustment costs. Capital equipment obviously has installation and running-in costs. There is also likely to be a relationship between the timing of capital investment and that of the hiring and firing of labour. A firm may cease recruiting (and investing) if it anticipates a recession. A rise in the cost of labour leads to an earlier halt on hiring which is then resumed later than it would have been if labour costs were lower.

3   Recognising the importance of labour demand adjustment costs is consistent with Oi's (1962) conception of labour as a quasi-fixed factor in which hiring and firing costs drive a wedge between wages and the marginal revenue productivity of labour.

4   Nickell (1986) provides the detailed specification of the dynamic model which produced the outcome in Figure 2.10. He also considers the case of convex symmetrical adjustment costs which yield the employment path shown in Figure 3. In this case employment is always being adjusted but actual employment never closely tracks the equilibrium time path. Adjustment costs moderate employment changes such that labour is hoarded, i.e., not fully shed during slumps in the expectation that business will once again pick up.

5   Introducing voluntary quits into the analysis affects the pattern of labour demand because during a slump it reduces the amount of downward adjustment (firing) the firm has to make compulsorily. During the boom phase of the cycle it increases the amount of hiring required as not only must the increase in output be achieved but workers who quit must be replaced. It is the case that voluntary quitting generally increases during booms, as alternative employment opportunities expand, and diminish during recessions, the opposite of what the firm would wish. On the assumption that quitters represent a constant proportion of the labour force, Nickell (1978) suggests that the relationship between output and labour demand would change from that shown in Figure 2.11 to something like Figure 4.

6   Cost plus pricing is the practice of determining prices by calculating average costs of production and then adding a profit mark up. This has long been recognised as being a popular method for setting prices, see Hall and Hitch (1939). Approximately two-thirds of UK manufacturers' production costs are labour costs. This proportion may well be higher in the more labour intensive

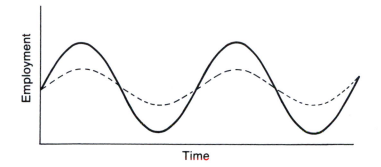

Figure 3 ——, equilibrium employment, no adjustment costs; -----, actual employment, convex adjustment costs

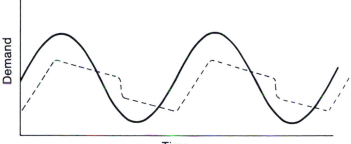

Figure 4 ——, output demand; -----, labour demand

service sector. Layard and Nickell (1985a) model prices P, which strictly speaking is the GDP deflator, in terms of the mark up on wages P/W. This depends upon aggregate demand (@), the impact of technical progress on efficiency (A) and the capital to labour ratio K/L:

price equation $P/W = f(@,K/L,A)$

with the price mark up negatively related to the capital/labour ratio.

7 The data in Table 1 demonstrates international differences in the prevalence of self-employment in Europe. The importance of self-employment in Italy is somewhat exceptional among industrialised nations, with rates more in common with the lesser developed economies of Ireland, Portugal and Spain. Self-employment is very prevalent in Greece. Rates in the UK appear higher than the group of low self-employment countries including Austria, Denmark, Germany and Luxembourg.

8 The relative wage variables in this study reflect labour shares in net output, the relationship between nominal wage rates and the nominal rate of return on capital employed, the capital–labour ratio, and the proportion of white-collar employees in the workforce. Oulton(1990) reports that the inclusion of the relative wage variables increases the R^2 statistic from 0.63 to 0.76.

3 WAGE DETERMINATION AND INEQUALITY

1 Wealth in the UK is more unequally distributed than income as the Lorenz curve shown in Figure 5 illustrates.

The curve suggests that the top 10 per cent of the UK population owned almost 50 per cent of the nation's wealth and around 30 per cent of its income. The top 25 per cent owned 72 per cent of marketable wealth with the top 50 per cent accounting for 93 per cent of wealth in the UK.

Table 1 Self-employment rates (%), 1995

	Male	Female
Austria	12.4	8.8
Belgium	18.4	11.0
Denmark	11.9	4.0
Finland	18.7	9.6
France	15.3	6.9
Germany	11.9	5.9
Greece	42.2	18.7
Ireland	28.5	7.9
Italy	28.9	16.6
Luxembourg	11.6	7.1
Netherlands	13.2	8.8
Portugal	28.1	22.9
Spain	24.2	17.0
Sweden	16.3	5.9
Switzerland	17.9	14.1
UK	17.7	7.0

Source: OECD, *Labour Force Statistics*

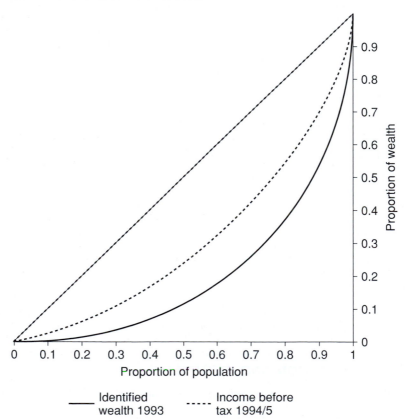

| ——— | Identified wealth 1993 | - - - - | Income before tax 1994/5 |

Figure 5 Wealth and income in the UK, Lorenz curves

Source: Board of Inland Revenue, Inland Revenue Statistics, 1996, tables 3.3, 13.3, pp. 35, 131, 132

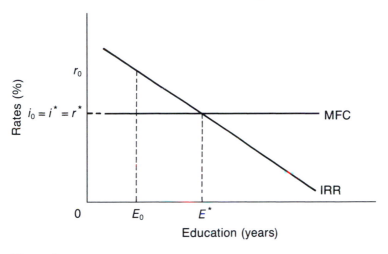

Figure 6

2 If firms offer a variety of wage rates, the employment impact of a minimum wage depends on the firm's wages in relation to the minimum wage. Firms that pay in excess of the minimum wage need not be affected. Low pay firms that find it profitable to do so will expand employment (they were labour supply constrained), firms that do not find it profitable will reduce employment (they are demand constrained). Dickens *et al.* (1994a) adopt this approach using imperfectly competitive firms with a degree of monopsony power.

5 HUMAN CAPITAL

1 There are a couple of points of clarification that need to be made in connection with this exposition. The first is to note that the internal rate of return to education schedule is analogous to that of the marginal efficiency of capital. The second is that the positive slope of the MFC schedule incorporates capital market imperfection. In a perfect world Figure 5.2 would have a horizontal MFC schedule to reflect the perfectly elastic supply of finance at the market rate of interest $i*$ (Figure 6).

2 The assumption that both young and old face the same capital market conditions is somewhat difficult to justify. As age increases so should personal wealth, hence human capital investment costs can be met from lower cost sources of finance such as savings. Given capital market imperfection, loans can be secured with other assets such as one's home thereby reducing a financial institution's assessment of the risk involved and the rate of interest charged. Therefore Figure 5.3 should contain two MFC schedules, one for the young and a lower one for the older human capital investor (Figure 7).

3 A caveat to this general statement must be made concerning the expected tenure of young and older employees. A firm contemplating productivity and earnings enhancing training will have to assess the turnover of young and older labour. Young workers may have a lower expected tenure than their older counterparts who will therefore be viewed more favourably as recipients of training. A similar consideration may result in an asymmetry in the access of male and female workers to training opportunities.

4 The situation is not quite as clear cut as this suggests because given that $A_H > A_L$ and $W_H > W_L$ for identical levels of human capital, the high ability individual faces higher costs in forgone earnings at identical levels of human capital, which may deter additional investment. The implicit assumption being made in the text is that lower human capital acquisition costs for A_H individuals are at least neutralising this effect. Ashenfelter and Rouse (1998) contains empirical evidence from the USA that greater ability lowers costs, leading to more education.

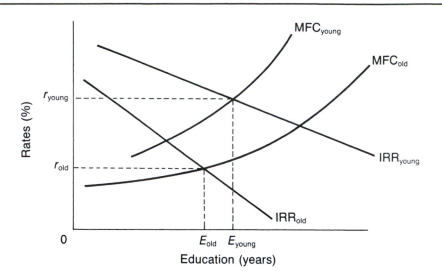

Figure 7

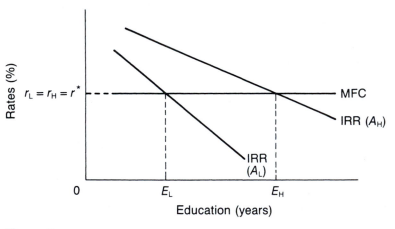

Figure 8

5 This is still the case even if we assume no capital market imperfections (Figure 8). In spite of the fact that the rates of return for individuals of different ability have been set equal, those of high ability A_H invest in and attain higher levels of human capital than those of lesser ability A_L.

6 More accurately the y term represents the difference between observed actual earnings and potential earnings. Potential earnings is a concept of earnings with no return to experience or subsequent on-the-job training so that the return to education alone can be isolated. Psacharopoulos (1987) explains the relationship between observed and potential earnings as shown in Figure 9. Assume an individual completes a given level of education, say a university degree at time 0. BF is the actual earnings profile but this contains a return to experience and on-the-job training as well. If these elements were absent from this occupation AY would have been observed and is thus the flat equivalent age–earnings profile. The implied sacrifice of AB in the first year of work increases the subsequent potential earnings of the graduate, the broken line AF. Time j_0 is the overtaking year of experience, a concept used by Mincer (1974) with CD a measure of earnings forgone in order to pursue on-the-job training during that year.

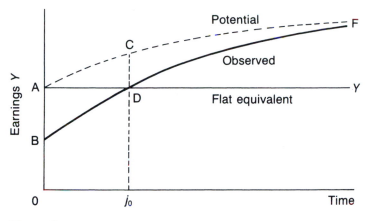

Figure 9

Source: Adapted from Psacharopoulos 1987, figure 2, p. 221

7 This list of criticisms is by no means an exhaustive one. It consciously ignores dual labour market theories which emphasise institutional demand effects using the concept of the internal labour market, i.e., the labour market within the firm itself. Dual labour market theorists distinguish a primary (secure, full-time, well paid) from a secondary (temporary, part-time, poorly paid) market whose barrier is not constructed from human capital investments. We give this view a fuller treatment in Chapter 6, when we consider labour market discrimination.

Nor is the Marxist view of education included. Contrary to agency theory this 'radical' perspective sees education as instilling attitudes and characteristics into workers consistent with capitalist firms' objectives. Education is also seen as reinforcing class differences, maintaining and justifying the existing social order. For a fuller treatment of these perspectives with respect to education, readers are directed in the first instance to McNabb (1987).

8 Ger[a]   Germany
Che   Switzerland
Aut   Austria
Aus   Australia
Ita   Italy
USA   United States of America
Prt   Portugal
Fin   Finland
Fra   France
UK   United Kingdom
Swe   Sweden
Irl   Ireland
Esp   Spain
Can   Canada
Nld   Netherlands
Nzl   New Zealand
Dnk   Denmark
Bel   Belgium
Nor   Norway

6 LABOUR MARKET DISCRIMINATION

1 For a detailed derivation of Figure 6.3 upon the basis of an employer tastes model encompassing utility maximisation see Joll *et al.* (1983), pp. 131–40.

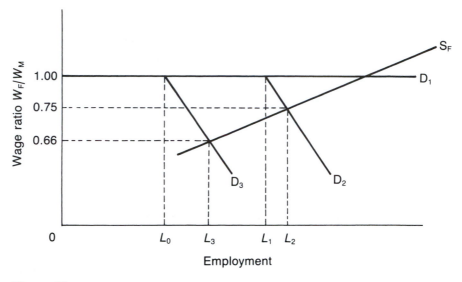

Figure 10

2 Note that similar results can be obtained by adjusting the proportion of employers who discriminate, i.e., the location of L_0 rather than the slope of the D_F function. In this case the proportion of firms who are prepared not to discriminate increases, as shown by the move from L_0 to L_1 in Figure 10. This of itself shifts the demand for female labour from D_3 to D_2 reducing the earnings differential from 0.66 to 0.75 whilst also increasing female employment to L_2.

3 Remember that a monopsonist is a sole buyer, as opposed to a monopolist – a sole seller, of in this case labour services. Rothschild (1954) provides an early exposition of monopsony applied to the labour market and contrasted with the perfectly competitive situation.

4 An alternative to the residual approach to the empirical estimation of discrimination is suggested and employed by Kamalich and Polachek (1982). The idea of what they termed 'reverse regression' is that holding wages W constant, to identify differences in the education S, work experience X and job tenure T of groups of workers categorised by sex and race using a dummy variable Z. Thus,

$$S = \alpha_0 + \alpha_1 W + \alpha_2 X + \alpha_3 T + \alpha_4 Z$$

$$X = \alpha_0 + \alpha_1 W + \alpha_2 S + \alpha_3 T + \alpha_4 Z$$

$$T = \alpha_0 + \alpha_1 W + \alpha_2 S + \alpha_3 X + \alpha_4 Z$$

Using 1976 data the study obtained estimates of sex and race discrimination using the conventional 'residual' approach. After adjusting for schooling, experience and tenure they find that women earned 35.1 per cent less than men, with blacks earning 13.3 per cent less than whites. However, when the 'reverse regression' approach is used on the same data there was no clear cut evidence of discrimination. If there were discrimination, the above equations would show this as statistically significant positive values of the α coefficients, implying that in order to obtain the same wage as men, women would need more education, experience and tenure. Similarly blacks would need more by way of education, experience and tenure to earn the same as whites if discrimination were present. There were differences between women and men and between blacks and whites, but these appear to compensate for each other. Women had more education but less experience and shorter tenure than male workers. Black workers had less education than whites but had more work experience and greater tenure. Kamalich and Polachek state that their results 'indicate that for the economy as a whole clear-cut discrimination does not exist . . . they cast a shadow of doubt on many previous studies of discrimination' (1982, p. 461). Sloane (1985) suggests that 'residual and reverse regression approaches should be used together to provide upper and lower-bound estimates of discrimination' (p. 125).

5 These figures are based on the data in Table 2.

Table 2   UK female economic activity (%), 2000

With children under 5 years old	Single	Married/cohabiting
Working full-time	11	21
Working part-time	21	39
Unemployed	8	3
Economic inactivity	60	37

Source: ONS, *Labour Force Survey*, Spring 2000

7 TRADE UNIONS AND LABOUR MARKETS

1   Union density can be measured either by taking union membership as a percentage of the entire labour force, employed and unemployed, or as a percentage of employees only. Table 7.3 provides calculations of union density as a proportion of employees which gives a higher percentage than a calculation based upon the whole labour force.
2   Gomez *et al.* (2001) make the interesting suggestion that the difference between Canadian and US union densities reflects the fact that the demand for union membership in the USA is being suppressed by a combination of a more restrictive legal environment and greater employer resistance to unions organising. If these were removed and the effective demand for unions was satisfied, then the USA would have union densities as high as those of Canada.
3   A more detailed interpretation of the vertical contract curve C_2 would make the point that this reflects a neutral union attitude to risk (see Ulph and Ulph (1990)). One could also describe the attempt to maximise the $W_u - W_a$ mark-up as the union seeking to maximise its economic rent, see Laidler and Estrin (1989) pp. 370–1. In such a case the wage rate is a means of distributing economic rent between firms and unions, what Layard and Nickell (1986) call the 'battle of the mark-ups'.
4   The significance of the union's attitude to the risk of job losses is that it will be incorporated into its utility function (U) and will be reflected in the location of the union indifference mapping. If unions are extremely risk averse and are unwilling to countenance any threat to jobs, then an indifference mapping such as R in Figure 11, will result in the wage equalling the non-union

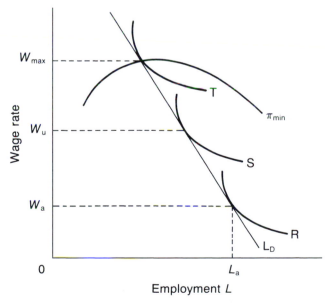

Figure 11

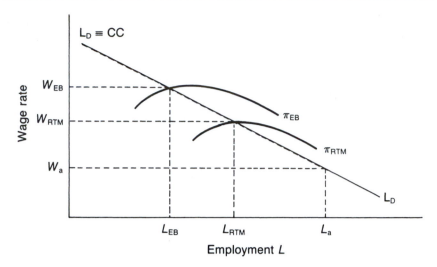

Figure 12

alternative W_a. The more prepared the union is to run the risk of job losses the more it tends towards a higher wage bargain such as W_u. If the union is indifferent to job losses (i.e., risk neutrality) and has sufficient bargaining power, the maximum wage (W_{max}) is feasible. Such an attitude is implied by indifference mapping T.

5 In a related example Manning (1992) is able to undermine the conventional outcome of the two microeconomic models of union behaviour. If unions are not concerned about employment (risk neutral) the contract curve and the labour demand curve become identical, thereby yielding an identical wage/employment outcome for both the efficient bargain and right to manage models. Yet if the right to manage (RTM) employer is able to change the pre- and post-agreement revenue functions via control of investment, this could increase profits and affect the wage and employment outcome in a way not open to the efficient bargain (EB) firm. Figure 12 shows the variation in the ex post-revenue functions resulting in a divergence in profits with $\pi_{RTM} > \pi_{EB}$. This brings about a divergence in the wage and employment outcomes facing the different types of firm with the unconventional result that $L_{RTM} > L_{EB}$.

6 Figure 7.10
Aus   Australia
Nor   Norway
Swe   Sweden
Ger   Germany
Ne   Netherlands
Fr   France
UK   United Kingdom
It   Italy
Jap   Japan
USA   United States of Ameria
Swi   Switzerland

7 Figure 7.11
E   Spain
F   France
P   Portugal
I   Italy
NL   Netherlands
D   Germany
CH   Switzerland

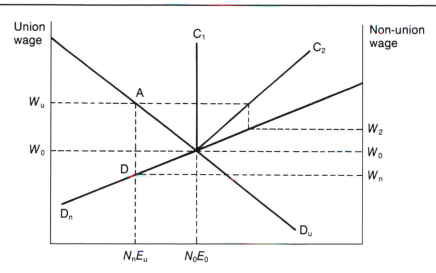

Figure 13

UK   United Kingdom
EIR   Republic of Ireland
B   Belgium
N   Norway
A   Austria
DK   Denmark
SF   Finland
S   Sweden

8 Mayhew and Turnbull (1989) question the theoretical basis of estimating output losses due to allocative inefficiency as a consequence of union activity. If one uses an efficient bargain model the prediction of the outcome following a union won wage increase becomes more problematic. Simplifying the example they provide on pp. 122–3, we can represent a labour market seeking general equilibrium between its unionised and non-unionised components as shown in Figure 13. From an initial equilibrium of W_0 for both union (u) and non-union (n) workers, suppose the union pushes wages for its members up to W_u. In a right to manage model this would result in an outcome identical to that in Figure 7.12. But what if under conditions of efficient bargaining the market faced a vertical contract curve like C_1? This would raise union workers' share of the surplus at the expense of firms' profits but the employment in both labour markets is unaffected. If the contract curve had a positive slope like C_2 this would imply expanding unionised employment and raising non-union wages to W_2. The existence of any output losses becomes extremely unlikely.

9 Neumann and Rissman (1984) using a similar model found empirical support for the view that the state through welfare assistance and employment protection legislation can substitute for unions and that this accounts for their long-term trend decline in the USA.

10 A comparison between unit labour cost growth in the UK and Sweden is illustrated in Figure 14. Over the 1980–2000 period as a whole unit labour costs grew more rapidly in the UK than in the much more heavily unionised Sweden. Between 1995 and 2000 unit labour costs have remained almost constant in Sweden while over the same period they rose by just over 17 per cent in the UK.

8 LABOUR MARKET FLEXIBILITY

1 The figures for the UK are from working age population in employment data used to produce Figure 15. For 1959–71, the working age population is defined as women aged 15–59, men aged 15–

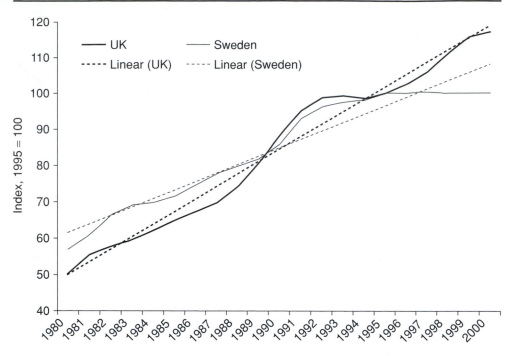

Figure 14

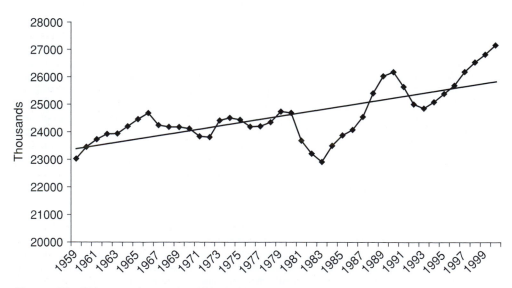

Figure 15   UK unemployment, 1959–2000

Source: Compiled using ONS, Labour Market Trends, various years

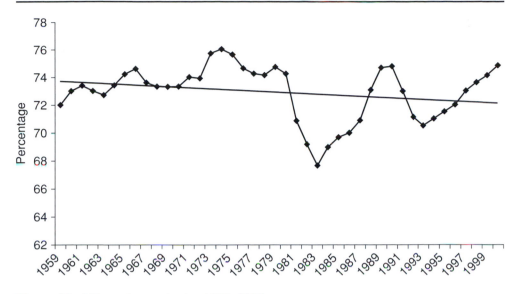

Figure 16 UK employment rate, 1959–2000

Source: As Figure 15

Table 3 Sectoral changes in British employment, thousands (percentage changes in brackets)

	June 1980–83		June 1990–93	
	Men	*Women*	*Men*	*Women*
Agriculture	−18 (−7)	−4 (−4)	−15 (−7)	−8(−10)
Energy/Transport	−186(−10)	−29 (−8)	−169(−12)	−29 (−7)
Manufacturing	−943(−20)	−440(−22)	−590(−17)	−267(−18)
Construction	−198(−18)	+8 (+7)	−252(−27)	−3 (−2)
Hotel/Distribution	−63 (−3)	−139 (−6)	−110 (−5)	−158 (−6)
Finance/Business service	+78 (+9)	+101(+13)	−74 (−6)	−48 (−4)
Other services	−17 (−1)	−34 (−1)	+16 (+1)	+175 (+4)
Total	−1347(−10)	−537 (−6)	−1194(−10)	−338 (−3)

Source: Robinson, 1994, table 11, p. 40

64. From 1972 onwards, 16–59 and 16–64. The overall trend of the number in employment is rising in Figure 15. The employment rate in Figure 16 is the proportion of the population who are in employment. Peak employment years are 1966, 1974, 1979, 1990 and 2000. Trough years are 1972, 1976, 1983 and 1993. The overall trend of the employment rate in Figure 16 shows a slight decline.
2 Robinson (1994) provides detailed employment data reproduced in Table 3 showing that although the recession of 1980–3 was proportionately more severe in the manufacturing sector than the 1990–3 recession, both impacted severely on manufacturing employment, particularly for females who are more heavily concentrated in the industries vulnerable to international competition such as textiles, clothing and footwear. Construction was badly affected by the 1990–3 recession. Financial and business services which managed to expand employment in the early 1980s suffered a downturn in the early 1990s. The only sector to expand through the 1990–3 recession was other services, where women gained the largest share of employment.

9 JOB SEARCH AND VACANCY ANALYSIS

1 More detailed and more advanced models are to be found in the survey by Mortensen (1986) and in the various empirical applications of job search contained in Kiefer and Neumann (1989).

2 The reference to Stigler comes from Stigler (1962). The effect of increasing the cost of search from £2 to £3 per firm can be shown using this numerical example. Table 9.3 would then show:

Sample size (n)	E(max W|n)	Cost C(n)	Expected net return R(n) = E(max W|n) – Cn
1	141.2225	3	138.2225
2	146.0451	6	140.0451
3	148.4724	9	139.4724
4	150.0097	12	138.0097

The optimal sample size (n*) is reduced from 3 to 2 firms. Increasing the cost of search reduces search activity. An adverse i.e., down-ward shift in the wage distribution would also reduce job search.

3 The fact that Figure 9.1 contains smooth, continuous curves to represent the mb(r) and mc(r) functions implies an infinite and continuous series of wage offers and reservation wages within the £120–£160 range.

4 If all firms were identical $VV^- = 0$ and the G curve becomes the axis VOV^-.

5 Mismatch is equivalent to what Dow and Dicks-Mireaux (1958) term unemployment due to 'maladjustment', what would today be seen as unemployment arising from matching inefficiency.

6 If workers quit voluntarily they show up in the unemployment inflow, when made redundant they also show up in the inflow, yet if a firm reduces its demand for labour through 'natural wastage', i.e., not replacing retiring/quitting workers, this reduces outflow. Redundancy legislation may have resulted in firms' increasing use of natural wastage in order to avoid costly lay-offs, thereby depressing outflow rates. In this context the main employment protection laws in the UK were: 1965 Redundancy Payments Act; 1971 Industrial Relations Act; 1975 Employment Protection Act. During rapid or severe downturns in economic activity, firms have to resort to redundancies thereby increasing the inflow rate. There was a roughly constant redundancy rate between 1977 and 1979, followed by a sharp rise in lay-offs from the third quarter of 1979 to the second quarter of 1981.

7 Pissarides (1986) does not include wage inflation in his model which may lead him to understate the role of supply-side variables. The initial work on vacancies was concerned with investigating the relationship between unemployment and wage inflation. Hence there is a link between the U–V and the Phillips curves, such that if the U–V function experiences an outward shift then the tradeoff between unemployment and inflation becomes less advantageous.

10 UNEMPLOYMENT

1 Sinclair (1987, pp. 6–12) informs us that the first UK unemployment data was collected by trade unions as early as 1851, a consequence of providing unemployment insurance to their members. Thus the coverage of the early statistics is minimal, although it increases as one approaches the First World War. After that war coverage becomes almost universal, for male workers, because of the operation of the 'national insurance' benefit system.

2 Exceptional unemployment rates in the 1930s were not confined to the UK and the USA. Australia experienced unemployment of 29 per cent in 1932. Canadian unemployment reached 22.3 per cent in 1933, falling sharply to 13.2 per cent in 1936. Japan witnessed 'high' unemployment of 6.8 per cent in 1932. The highest reported unemployment rate of 36.3 per cent was recorded in the Netherlands in 1935. See Sinclair (1987, pp. 7–16) for more detailed pre-1940 statistics.

Table 4 Unemployment rates (%), 1999

	Male	Female
Argentina (1998)	11.9	14.3
Armenia (1998)	4.9	15.0
Azerbaijan	1.0	1.4
Bahamas	5.9	9.6
Barbados	8.4	16.4
Brazil (1996)	7.2	11.6
Chile (1998)	7.0	7.6
Columbia	17.2	23.3
Costa Rica	4.9	8.2
Croatia	12.8	14.5
Cyprus (1998)	2.8	4.2
Czech Republic	7.3	10.5
Egypt (1998)	5.1	19.9
Gaza Strip	15.1	17.4
Georgia	15.3	12.2
Hong Kong (1998)	5.1	4.0
Hungary	7.5	6.3
Israel (2000)	8.5	8.1
Jamaica (1996)	9.9	23.0
Latvia	15.5	13.3
Lebanon (1997)	9.0	7.2
Lithuania	15.6	12.6
Malta	6.3	2.6
Mexico	1.8	2.6
Morocco	20.3	27.6
Nicaragua (1998)	8.8	14.5
Pakistan (2000)	4.2	14.9
Peru	7.5	8.6
Philippines	9.5	9.2
Poland (2000)	15.2	18.5
Puerto Rica	13.2	9.6
Russia	13.6	13.1
Singapore	4.5	4.6
Slovenia (2000)	7.5	7.4
South Africa	21.0	30.5
South Korea	7.1	5.1
Sri Lanka (1998)	7.1	16.2
St Lucia	16.0	20.3
Trinidad/Tobago	11.3	18.9
Ukraine	12.2	11.5
Uruguay	8.7	14.6
Zambia (1996)	15.0	16.0
UK	6.7	5.1
USA	4.1	4.3

Source: ILO, *World Employment Report*, 2001

3 The International Labour Office (ILO) provides unemployment data for a wide selection of countries. Among the countries not reported in Table 10.1 the ILO reports the figures for 1999 contained in Table 4.

4 The best single source for the theory of unemployment is Trevithick (1992). Its treatment of the Classical, Keynesian and New Classical theories is excellent, the critique of New Classical theory is expressive and telling. Students are advised to read Trevithick (1992) before turning to Sinclair (1987) which covers a variety of formal models of unemployment. Lindbeck and Snower (1988) is an essential reference for insider–outsider models and Layard et al. (1991) must be consulted in order to understand the influential hysteresis–NAIRU model.

5 Given that the stock of money determines prices, along the lines suggested by the quantity theory, unemployment can be seen as a maladjustment between money wages and money stock. If money stock falls so does the price level, therefore money wages must fall sufficiently to fully offset that fall in the absolute price level. If they do not, then real wages have effectively risen, thereby increasing unemployment.

6 Whether Keynes accepted that labour supply moved in response to real wages or only to money wages is less clear. Conventionally it has been interpreted that Keynes saw changes in labour supply as due to changes in money wages. This relies on 'money illusion' misleading workers to alter their labour supply. Trevithick (1992) takes the view that 'Keynes's labour supply function is in almost all respects identical to its neoclassical counterpart, [comparing] various real wage rates with the marginal disutility of employment' (p. 116).

7 This ignores the possible expansionary tendency of deflation to reduce the rate of interest and stimulate investment if the liquidity trap can be avoided and if the bankruptcies associated with unemployment and deflation do not deter would be investors (the Keynes effect). It also ignores the 'real balance effect' where because some assets would remain fixed in nominal terms, deflation will increase private sector wealth holdings in real terms (real net worth) thus stimulating additional consumption.

8 Phelps (1967) suggested a long-run Phillips curve with a negative slope but that this would be much steeper than the conventional short-run curves. For Friedman (1968) the long-run Phillips curve was to be vertical. Thus Phelps initially held out some role for the effectiveness of aggregate demand management which Friedman denied for the long-run outcome.

9 Readers interested in the rational expectations hypothesis and its range of applications are directed to the surveys by Begg (1982), Shaw (1984) and Sheffrin (1983).

10 Trevithick (1992) rightly points out that the use of this AD–AS analysis in Figure 10.16 hides some alarming assumptions. AD's negative and shallow slope implies that price deflation stimulates the growth of output and employment (via an increase in Y) in a responsive manner. The 'Keynes effect' and the 'real balance effect' are included, but they were considered to be relatively insignificant in the Keynesian scheme of things. The other factor is a simple quantity theory of money effect, of an inverse relationship between the price level and income. Take the Cambridge form of the quantity theory; $m = k + p + y$. If money supply (m) does not change and k is a constant, then if the price level (p) falls, income (y) must rise. Aggregate Demand (AD) is in effect,

$$AD = m' - k' - p$$

where m' is log m and k' is log k. For Trevithick (1992)

> the AD function is simply a collapsed form of the familiar IS–LM diagram where the price level is not taken as constant . . . [it] is a shorthand depiction in (p,y) space of what is happening to the IS and LM curves . . . as a result of falling money wages and prices.
>
> (p. 164)

The 'Keynes effect' shifts the LM function and the 'real balance' effect shifts IS (Figure 17). As prices fall from P_1 to P_2 this raises the real money stock from M_1/P_1 to M_2/P_2, which leads to the interest rate r falling, which in turn increases investment and real income Y.

11 Friedman (1968) avoided this problem by assuming that only workers suffered from short-run money illusion.

12 See Lindbeck and Snower (1988, pp. 15–60) for a concise categorisation of explanations of unemployment according to whether they assume market clearing or not.

13 An increase in long-term unemployment raises the NAIRU because it does not exert any dampening influence on collective bargaining, thus the TRW effectively shifts upwards (Figure 18).

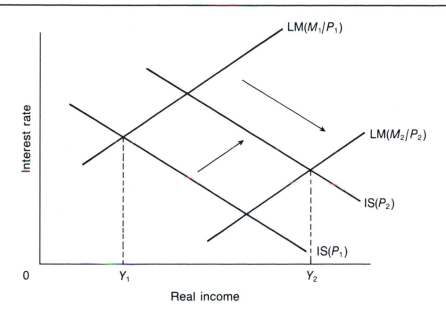

Figure 17

Source: Adapted from Trevithick 1992, figure 5.4, p. 102

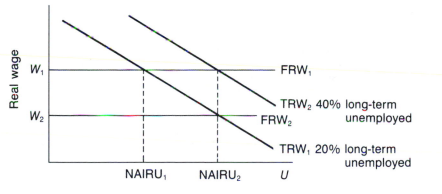

Figure 18

Capital shrinkage could be represented as an adverse, i.e., downward shift of the FRW, thereby increasing the value of the NAIRU across a recession.

11 TRADE, GLOBALISATION AND LABOUR MARKETS

1 Figure 11.2 was presented by Jonathan Haskel of Queen Mary and Westfield College, University of London at a Norman Stang Research Seminar at the University of North London on 4/2/2002. The joint research with M. Slaughter will form part of a forthcoming paper.

Bibliography

Abowd, J. and Ashenfelter, O. (1981) 'Anticipated Unemployment, Temporary Layoffs and Compensating Wage Differentials', in S. Rosen (ed.) *Studies in Labour Markets*, Chicago, IL: University of Chicago Press.

Acemoglu, D. (1997) 'Training and Innovation in an Imperfect Labour Market', *Review of Economic Studies*, 64: 445–64.

Acemoglu, D. and Angrist, J. (1999) 'How Large are the Social Returns to Education? Evidence from Compulsory Schooling Laws', *NBER Working Paper* 7444.

Acemoglu, D. and Angrist, J. (2001) 'Consequences of Employment Protection? The Case of the Americans with Disabilities Act', *Journal of Political Economy*, 109 (5): 915–57.

Acemoglu, D. and Pischke, J. (1999) 'Beyond Becker: Training in Imperfect Labour Markets', *Economic Journal*, 109: F112–F142.

Addison, J. and Blackburn, M. (1999) 'Minimum Wages and Poverty', *Industrial and Labour Relations Review*, 52 (3): 393–409.

Agnell, J. (1999) 'On the Benefits from Rigid Labour Markets: Norms, Market Failures and Social Insurance', *Economic Journal*, 109: F143–F164.

Aldrich, M. and Buchele, R. (1986) *The Economics of Comparable Worth*, Cambridge MA: Ballinger.

Alogoskoufis, G.S. and Manning, A. (1988) 'On the Persistence of Unemployment', *Economic Policy*, 7: 428–69.

Altonji, J. and Blank, R. (1999) 'Race and Gender in the Labour Market', in Ashenfelter, O. and Card, D. (eds) (1999) *Handbook of Labour Economics*, Volume 3, Amsterdam: Elsevier Science.

Amin, A. (1991) 'Flexible Specialisation and Small Firms in Italy: Myths and Realities', in A. Pollert (ed.) *Farewell to Flexibility?*, Oxford: Basil Blackwell.

Amiti, M. (1997) 'Specialisation Patterns in Europe', London School of Economics Centre for Economic Performance, Discussion Paper 363.

Anderton, B. and Mayhew, K. (1994) 'A Comparative Analysis of the UK Labour Market', in R. Barrell (ed.) *The UK Labour Market: Comparative Aspects and Institutional Developments*, Cambridge: Cambridge University Press.

Antolin, P. and Bover, O. (1997) 'Regional Migration in Spain: The Effect of Personal Characteristics and of Unemployment, Wage and House Price Differentials Using Pooled Cross-Sections', *Oxford Bulletin of Economics and Statistics*, 59 (2): 215–35.

Armstrong, H. and Taylor, J. (1981) 'The Measurement of Different Types of Unemployment', in J. Creedy (ed.) *The Economics of Unemployment in Britain*, London: Butterworth.

Arnal, E., Wooseok, O. and Torres, R. (2001) 'Knowledge, Work Organisation and Economic Growth', OECD Labour Market and Social Policy Occasional Paper 50.

Arrow, K.J. (1973) 'Higher Education as a Filter', *Journal of Public Economics*, 2 (3): 193–216.

Ashenfelter, O. and Card, D. (eds) (1999) *Handbook of Labour Economics*, Volume 3, Amsterdam: Elsevier Science.

Ashenfelter, O. and Hannan, T. (1986) 'Sex Discrimination and Product Market Competition', *Quarterly Journal of Economics*, C1 (1): 149–73.

Ashenfelter, O. and Layard, R. (eds) (1986) *Handbook of Labour Economics*, Amsterdam: North Holland.

Ashenfelter, O. and Pencavel, J. (1969) 'American Trade Union Growth: 1900–1960', *Quarterly Journal of Economics*, 83: 434–48.

Ashenfelter, O. and Rouse, C. (1998) 'Income, Schooling and Ability: Evidence From a New Sample of Identical Twins', *Quarterly Journal of Economics*, 113 (1): 253–84.

Ashworth, J. and Ulph, D. (1981) 'Household Models', in C. Brown (ed.) *Taxation and Labour Supply*, London: George Allen and Unwin.

Atkinson, A. (1997) 'Bringing Income Distribution in From the Cold', *Economic Journal*, 107 (441): 297–321.

Atkinson, J. (1984) 'Manpower Strategies for Flexible Organisations', *Personnel Management*, (August): 28–9.

Autor, D., Katz, L. and Krueger, A. (1998) 'Computing Inequality: Have Computers Changed the Labour Market?', *Quarterly Journal of Economics*, 113 (4): 1269–314.

Bacon, F. and Eltis, W. (1976) *Britain's Economic Problem: Too Few Producers*, London: Macmillan.

Baily, M. and Solow, R. (2001) 'International Productivity Comparisons Built From the Firm Level', *Journal of Economic Perspectives*, 15 (3): 151–72.

Bain, G. and Elsheikh, F. (1976) *Union Growth and the Business Cycle*, Oxford: Basil Blackwell.

von Bardeleben, R., Beicht, U. and Kalman, F. (1995) *Betriebliche Kosten und Nutzen der Ausbildung: Reprasentative Ergebnisse aus Industrie, Handel und Handwerk*, Bielefeld: Bertelsmann.

Barro, R. (1997) *Determinants of Economic Growth: A Cross-country empirical study*, Cambridge, MA: MIT Press.

Barro, R. and Sala-I-Martin, X. (1995) *Economic Growth*, New York: McGraw-Hill.

Barron, J., Berger, M. and Black, D. (1997) *On The Job Training*, Upjohn Institute for Employment Research.

Bassanini, A., Scarpetta, S. and Visco, I. (2000) 'Knowledge, Technology and Economic Growth: Recent Evidence From OECD Countries', OECD Economics Department Working Paper 32/2000.

Bassett, P. (1995) 'Job Regulation Rules UK', London: *The Times* (2/1/1995): 30.

Battu, H., Belfield, C. and Sloane, P. (1999) 'Overeducation Among Graduates: A Chort View', *Education Economics*, 7 (1): 21–38.

Bayoumi, T., Coe, D. and Helpman, E. (1999) 'R and D Spillovers and Global Growth' *Journal of International Economics*, 47: 399–428.

Bazan, S. and Martin, J. (1991) 'The Impact of the Minimum Wage on Earnings and Employment in France', *OECD Economic Studies*, 16: 199–221.

Bean, C. (1992a) 'Identifying the Causes of British Unemployment', London School of Economics Centre for Economic Performance, Seminar Paper, 23/10/1992.

Bean, C. and Symons, J. (1989) 'Ten Years of Mrs T', London School of Economics Centre for Labour Economics, Discussion Paper 370.

Beatson, M. (1995) *Labour Market Flexibility*, Sheffield: Employment Department, Research Series no. 48.

Beck, R.M. (1980) 'Discrimination and White Economic Loss', *Social Forces*, 59: 148–68.

Becker, G.S. (1957) *The Economics of Discrimination*, Chicago, IL: University of Chicago Press.

—— (1964) *Human Capital: A Theoretical and Empirical Analysis, with Special Reference to Education*, New York: Columbia University Press.

—— (1965) 'A Theory of the Allocation of Time', Economic Journal, 75: 493–517.

Begg, D. (1982) *The Rational Expectations Revolution in Macroeconomics*, Oxford: Philip Allan.

Begg, D., Fischer, S. and Dornbusch, R. (2000) *Economics*, sixth Edition, London: McGraw-Hill.

Begg, I. (1995) 'Factor Mobility and Regional Disparities in the European Union', *Oxford Review of Economic Policy*, 11 (2): 96–113.

Belfield, C. (2000) *Economic Principles for Education: Theory and Evidence*, Cheltenham: Edward Elgar.

Bell, B. (1997) 'The Performance of Immigrants in the United Kingdom: Evidence From the GHS', *Economic Journal*, 107: 333–44.

Bell, B., Nickell, S. and Quintini, G. (2000) 'Wage Equations, Wage Curves and All That', London School of Economics Centre for Economic Performance, Discussion Paper 472.

Bell, B. and Pitt, M. (1998) 'Trade Union Decline and the Distribution of Wages in the UK: Evidence from Kernal Density Estimation', *Oxford Bulletin of Economics and Statistics*, 60 (4): 509–28.

Benabou, R. (1996) 'Inequality and Growth', *NBER Macroeconomics Annual*.

Bentolila, S. and Dolado, J.J. (1994) 'Labour Flexibility and Wages: Lessons From Spain', *Economic Policy*, 18: 55–99.

Berman, E., Bound, J. and Machin, S. (1997) 'Implications of Skill-Biased Technological Change: International Evidence', London School of Economics Centre for Economic Performance, Discussion Paper 376.

Berndt, E. and Wood, D. (1986) 'Energy Price Shocks and Productivity Growth in US and UK Manufacturing', *Oxford Review of Economic Policy*, 2 (3): 1–31.

Bertola, G. and Rogerson, R. (1997) 'Institutions and Labour Reallocation', *European Economic Review*, 41 (6): 1147–71.

Black, B. (2001) 'Culturally Coded? The Enigma of Flexible Labour Markets', *Employee Relations*, 23 (4): 401–16.

Blackaby, D. and Hunt, L. (1989) 'The Manufacturing Productivity "Miracle": A Sectoral Analysis', in F. Green (ed.) *The Resructuring of the British Economy*, Brighton: Harvester Wheatsheaf.

Blanchard, O.J. and Diamond, P.A. (1994) 'Ranking, Unemployment Duration and Wages', *The Review of Economic Studies*, 61: 417–34.

Blanchard, O.J. and Katz, L.W. (1992) 'Regional Evolutions', *Brookings Papers on Economic Activity*, 1: 1–75.

—— (1997) 'What We Know and Do Not Know About the Natural Rate', *Economic Perspectives*, 11: 51–72.

Blanchard, O.J. and Summers, L.H. (1986) 'Hysteresis and the European Unemployment Problem', *National Bureau of Economic Research, Macroeconomics Annual*, 15–78.

Blanchflower, D. and Freeman, R. (1993) 'Did the Thatcher Reforms Change British Labour Market Performance?', London School of Economics Centre for Labour Economics, Discussion Paper 168.

Blanchflower, D. and Oswald, A. (1990) 'Working Internationally', London School of Economics Centre for Labour Economics, Discussion Paper 371.

—— (1994) 'Estimating a Wage Curve for Britain 1973–90', *Economic Journal*, 104: 1025–43.

—— (1995) 'An Introduction to the Wage Curve', *Journal of Economic Perspectives*, 9 (3): 153–67.

Blau, D. (1991) 'Search for Non-wage Job Characteristics: A Test of the Reservation Wage Hypothesis', *Journal of Labour Economics*, 9 (2): 186–205.

Blau, D. and Robins, P. (1990) 'Job Search Outcomes for the Employed and Unemployed', *Journal of Political Economy*, 98: 637–55.

Blau, F. (1998) 'Trends in the Well-Being of American Women, 1970–1995', *Journal of Economic Literature*, 36 (1): 112–65.

Blau, F. and Kahn, L. (1996) 'International Differences in Male Wage Inequality: Institutions versus Market Forces', *Journal of Political Economy*, 104 (4): 791–837.

—— (2000) 'Gender Differences in Pay', *Journal of Economic Perspectives*, 14 (4): 75–99.

Blaug, M. (1976) 'The Empirical Status of Human Capital Theory: A Slightly Jaundiced Survey', *Journal of Economic Literature*, 14 (3): 827–55.

Blundell, R., Dearden, L., Goodman, A. and Reed, H. (2000) 'The Returns to Higher Education in Britain: Evidence from a British Cohort', *Economic Journal*, 110: F82–F99.

Blundell, R. and MaCurdy, T. (1999) 'Labour Supply: A Review of Alternative Approaches', in O. Ashenfelter and D. Card (eds) *Handbook of Labour Economics*, Volume 3, Amsterdam: Elsevier Science.

Boeri, T., Brugiavini, A. and Calmfors, L. (eds) (2001) *The Role of Unions in the Twenty-First Century*, Oxford: Oxford University Press.

Boheim, R. and Taylor, M. (2000) 'Unemployment Duration and Exit States in Britain', *Institute for Social and Economic Research*, Colchester, UK: University of Essex.

Booth, A. (1991) 'Job-Related Formal Training', *Oxford Bulletin of Economics and Statistics*, 53: 281–94.

—— (1995) *The Economics of the Trade Union*, Cambridge: Cambridge University Press.

Booth, A. and Frank, J. (1999) 'Earnings, Productivity and Performance-Related Pay', *Journal of Labour Economics*, 17 (3): 447–63.

Booth, A. and Snower, D. (1996) *Acquiring Skills, Market Failures, Their Symptoms and Policy Responses*, Cambridge: Cambridge University Press.

Borjas, G. (1990) 'Immigration and Self Selection', in J. Abowd and R. Freeman (eds) *Immigration, Trade and the Labour Market*, Chicago, IL: Chicago University Press.

—— (1998) 'The Economic Progress of Immigrants', NBER Working Paper 6506.

Bowden, R.J. (1980) 'On the Existence and Secular Stability of U–V Loci', *Economica*, 47: 35–50.

Bowden, S. and Turner, P. (1991) 'Productivity and Long-Term Growth Potential in the UK Economy, 1924–1968', *Applied Economics*, 23: 1425–32.

Bowles, S. and Gintis, H. (1975) 'The Problem with Human Capital Theory: A Marxian Critique', *American Economic Review*, 65 (2): 74–82.

Bragg, B. (1986) 'Power in the Union', *Talking with the Taxman about Poetry*, Line Records.

Brandolini, A. (1993) 'In Search of a Stylised Fact: Do Real Wages Exhibit a Consistent Pattern of Cyclical Variability?', London School of Economics, Centre for Economic Performance, Discussion Paper 112.

Bresnahan, T. (1999) 'Computerisation and Wage Dispersion: An Analytical Reinterpretation', *Economic Journal*, 109: F390–F415.

Broadberry, S.N. (1994) 'Technological Leadership and Productivity Leadership in Manufacturing Since the Industrial Revolution: Implications for the Convergence Debate', *Economic Journal*, 104 (423): 291–302.

Brown, C. (1988) 'The 1988 Tax Cuts, Work Incentives and Revenue', *Fiscal Studies*.

—— (1999) 'Minimum Wages, Employment and the Distribution of Income', in O. Ashenfelter and D. Card (eds) *Handbook of Labour Economics*, Volume 3, Amsterdam: Elsevier Science.

Brown, C. and Medoff, J.L. (1978) 'Trade Unions in the Production Process', *Journal of Political Economy*, 86: 355–79.

Brown, C. and Sandford, C. (1991) 'Taxes and Incentives: The Effects of the 1988 Cuts', Institute for Public Policy Research.

Brown, D., Ingram, P. and Wadsworth, J. (1997) 'Free to Choose', London School of Economics, Centre for Economic Performance, Centre Piece 2 (1): 2–5.

Brown, J.N. and Ashenfelter, O. (1986) 'Testing the Efficiency of Employment Contracts', *Journal of Political Economy*, 94, 3, (2): S40–S87.

Brown, W. and Wadhwani, S. (1990) 'The Economic Effects of Industrial Relations Legislation Since 1979', London School of Economics Centre for Labour Economics, Discussion Paper 376.

Bryson, A. (2001) 'Union Effects on Managerial and Employee Perceptions of Employee Relations in Britain', London School of Economics Centre for Economic Performance, Discussion Paper 494.

Budd, A., Levine, P. and Smith, P. (1988) 'Unemployment, Vacancies and the Long-Term Unemployed', *Economic Journal*, 98: 1071–91.

Budd, J. and Na, I. (2000) 'The Union Membership Wage Premium for Employees Covered by Collective Bargaining Agreements', *Journal of Labour Economics*, 18 (4): 783–807.

Bulow, J. and Summers, L. (1986) 'A Theory of Dual Labour Markets with Application to Industrial Policy, Discrimination and Keynesian Unemployment', *Journal of Labour Economics*, 4: 376–414.

Burgess, S. (1999) 'The Reallocation of Labour: An International Comparison Using Job Tenure Data', London School of Economics Centre for Economic Performance, Discussion Paper 416.

Burgess, S. and Profit, S. (2001) 'Externalities in the Matching of Workers and Firms in Britain', London School of Economics Centre for Economic Performance, Discussion Paper 490.

Burgess, S. and Turon, H. (2000) 'Unemployment Dynamics, Duration and Equilibrium: Evidence from Britain', London School of Economics Centre for Economic Performance, Discussion Paper 474.

Burkhauser, R., Couch, K. and Wittenburg, D. (1996) 'Who Gets What From Minimum Wage Hikes: A Re-Estimation of Card and Kreuger's Distributional Analysis in *"Myth and Measurement: The New Economics of the Minimum Wage"'*, *Industrial and Labour Relations Review*, 49 (3): 547–52.

—— (2000) 'A Reassessment of the New Economics of the Minimum Wage Literature With Monthly Data From the Current Population Survey', *Journal of Labour Economics*, 18 (4): 653–80.

Busch, M. and Milner, H. (1994) 'The Future of the International Trading System: International Firms, Regionalism and Domestic Politics', in R. Stubbs and G. Underhill (eds), *Political Economy and the Changing Global Order*, London: Macmillan.

Buxton, T. (1994a) 'The Competitiveness of UK Manufactured Exports', in T. Buxton, P. Chapman and P. Temple, *Britain's Economic Performance*, London: Routledge.

—— (1994b) 'Overview: The Foundations of Competitiveness: Investment and Innovation', in T. Buxton, P. Chapman and P. Temple, *Britain's Economic Performance*, London: Routledge.

Cain, G. (1986) 'The Economic Analysis of Labour Market Discrimination: A Survey', in O. Ashenfelter and R. Layard (eds), *Handbook of Labour Economics*, Volume 1, Amsterdam: North Holland.

Calmfors, L. and Driffell, J. (1988) 'Centralisation of Wage Bargaining', *Economic Policy*, April.

Campbell, M. and Daly, M. (1992) 'Self-Employment into the 1990s', *Employment Gazette*, (June): 269–92.

Canziani, P. (1997) 'Firing Costs and Stigma: An Empirical Analysis', London School of Economics Centre for Economic Performance, Discussion Paper 358.

Card, D. (1992) 'Do Minimum Wages Reduce Employment?: A Case Study of California', *Industrial Labour Relations Review*, 46 (1): 38–54.

—— (1999) 'Education and Earnings', in Ashenfelter, O. and Card, D. (eds) (1999) *Handbook of Labour Economics*, Volume 3, Amsterdam: Elsevier Science.

Card, D. and Krueger, A. (1995) *Myth and Measurement: The New Economics of the Minimum Wage*, Princeton, NJ: Princeton University Press.

Carline, D. (1985) 'Trade Unions and Wages', in D. Carline (*et al.*) *Labour Economics*, Harlow: Longmans.

Carline, D., Pissaridies, C., Siebert, W.S. and Sloane, P. (1985) *Labour Economics*, Harlow: Longmans.

Carling, K., Holmlund, B. and Vejsiu, A. (2001) 'Do Benefit Cuts Boost Job Finding? Swedish Evidence From the 1990s', *Economic Journal*, 111 (474): 766–90.

Carruth, A., Disney, R. (1988) 'Where Have Two Million Trade Union Members Gone?', *Economica*, 55: 1–19.

Caves, R., Frankel, J. and Jones, R. (1999) *World Trade and Payments: An Introduction*, New York: Addison Wesley Longman.

Champernowne, D. and Cowell, F. (1998) *Economic Inequality and Income Distribution*, Cambridge: Cambridge University Press.

Charlwood, A. (2001) 'Why Do Non-Union Employees Want to Unionise? Evidence From Britain', London School of Economics Centre for Economic Performance, Discussion Paper 498.

Chevalier, A. (2000) 'Graduate Overeducation in the UK', London School of Economics Centre for the Economics of Education, mimeo.

Chiswick, B. (1984) 'Review of the Economics and Politics of Race by T. Sowell', *Journal of Economic Literature*, 22: 1158–60.

Clark, A. (1990) 'Efficient Bargains and the McDonald–Solow Conjecture', *Journal of Labour Economics*, 8: 502–28.

Clark, K.B. and Summers, L.H. (1988) 'Labour Force Participation: Timing and Persistence', in R. Cross (ed.) *Unemployment, Hysteresis and the Natural Rate Hypothesis*, Oxford: Basil Blackwell.

Cockx, B. and Ridder, G. (2001) 'Social Employment of Welfare Recipients in Belgium: An Evaluation', *Economic Journal*, 111 (470): 322–52.

Coen, R.M. and Hickman, B.J. (1987) 'Keynesian and Classical Unemployment in Four Countries', *Brookings Papers on Economic Activity*, 1, 123.

Coles, M. and Smith, E. (1998) 'Marketplaces and Matching', *International Economic Review*, 39: 239–54.

Coppel, J., Dumont, J. and Visco, I. (2001) 'Trends in Immigration and Economic Consequences', OECD Economics Department Working Paper 284.

Coulombe, S. and Tremblay, J-F. (2001) 'Human Capital and Regional Convergence in Canada', *Journal of Economic Studies*, 28 (3): 154–80.

Cross, R. (ed.) (1988) *Unemployment, Hysteresis and the Natural Rate Hypothesis*, Oxford: Basil Blackwell.

—— (1995) *The Natural Rate of Unemployment: Reflections on 25 Years of the Hypothesis*, Cambridge: Cambridge University Press.

Crouch, C. (1993) *Industrial Relations and European State Traditions*, Oxford: Clarendon Press.

Crouchly, R., Abell, P. and Smeaton, D. (1994) 'An Aggregate Time Series of Non-Agricultural Self-Employment in the UK', London School of Economics Centre for Economic Performance, Discussion Paper 209.

Darity, W. and Williams, R. (1985) 'Peddlers Forever?: Culture, Competition and Discrimination', *American Economic Review*, 72 (2): 256–61.

Davies, J. (2000) 'International Comparisons of Labour Disputes in 1998', ONS *Labour Market Trends*, 108 (4): 147–52.

Davies, R.J. (1979) 'Economic Activity, Incomes Policy and Strikes: A Quantitative Analysis', *British Journal of Industrial Relations*, 17: 205–23.

Deakin, S. (1992) 'Labour Law and Industrial Relation', in J. Michie (ed.) *The Economic Legacy 1979–1992*, London: Academic Press.

Decressin, J. and Fatas, A. (1995) 'Regional Labour Market Dynamics in Europe', *European Economic Review*, 39 (9): 1627–65.

Decry, S., Walsh, J. and Knox, A. (2001) 'The Non-Union Workplace in Australia: Black House or Human Resource Innovator?', *International Journal of Human Resource Management*, 12 (4): 669–83.

Decry, S., Walsh, J. and Knox, A. (2001) 'The Non-Union Workplace in Australia: Bleak House or Human Resource Innovator?', *International Journal of Human Resource Management*, 12 (14): 669–83.

DeFina, R. (1983) 'Unions, Relative Wages and Economic Efficiency', *Journal of Labour Economics*, 1: 408–29.

DeGrauwe, P. (1997) *The Economics of Monetary Integration*, Oxford: Oxford University Press.

DeGrip, A., Hoevenberg, J. and Willems, E. (1997) 'Atypical Employment in the European Union', *International Labour Review*, 136 (1): 49–72.

Denison, E.F. (1979) *Accounting for Slower Economic Growth: The United States in the 1970s*, Washington, DC: Brookings Institution.

—— (1980) 'The Contribution of Capital to Economic Growth', *American Economic Review*, 70 (2): 220–4.

Denny, K. and Nickell, S.J. (1992) 'Unions and Investment in British Industry', *Economic Journal*, 102 (413): 874–87.

Desai, T., Gregg, P., Steer, J. and Wadsworth, J. (1999) 'Gender and the Labour Market', in P. Gregg and J. Wadsworth (eds), *The State of Working Britain*, Manchester: Manchester University Press.

Dex, S. and Shaw, L.B. (1986) *British and American Women at Work: Do Equal Employment Opportunities Matter?*, London: Macmillan.

Dex, S. and Sloane, P. (1989) 'The Economics of Discrimination: How Far Have We Come?', in R. Drago and R. Perlman (eds) *Microeconomic Issues in Labour Economics*, Hemel Hempstead: Harvester Wheatsheaf.

DFEE (2000) 'Skills for All: Research report from the National Skills Task Force', London: Department for Education and Employment.

Dickens, R. (1997) 'Caught in a Trap? Wage Mobility in Great Britain', London School of Economics Centre for Economic Performance, Discussion Paper 183.

Dickens, R., Machin, S., and Manning, A. (1994a) 'The Effect of Minimum Wages on Employment: Theory and Evidence from Britain', London School of Economics Centre for Economic Performance, Discussion Paper 183.

Dickens, R., Machin, S., Manning, A., Metcalf, D., Wadsworth, J. and Woodland, S. (1994b) 'The Effect of Minimum Wages on UK Agriculture', London School of Economics Centre for Economic Performance, Discussion Paper 204.

Dickens, W. and Lang, K. (1993) 'Labour Market Segmentation Theory: Reconsidering the Evidence', in W. Darity (ed.) *Labour Economics: Problems in Analysing Labour Markets*, Boston, MA: Kluwer Academic Publishers.

DiLiberto, A. and Symons, J. (2001) 'Education and Italian Regional Development', London School of Economics Centre for Economic Performance, Discussion Paper 496.

Disney, R. (1990) 'Explanations of the Decline in Trade Union Density in Britain: An Appraisal', *British Journal of Industrial Relations*, 28 (2): 165–77.

Disney, R., Haskel, J. and Heden, Y. (2000) 'Restructuring and Productivity Growth in the UK Establishment', University of London, Queen Mary and Westfield College, mimeo.

Doeringer, P. and Piore, M. (1971) *Internal Labour Markets and Manpower Analysis*, Lexington, MA: Lexington Books.

Dolton, P. and O'Neill, D. (1996) 'Unemployment Duration and the Restart Effect: Some Experimental Evidence', *Economic Journal*, 106: 387–400.

Dolton, P. and Vignoles, A. (2000) 'The Incidence and Effects of Overeducation in the Graduate Labour Market', *Economics of Education Review*.

Dorsett, R. (2001) 'The New Deal for Young People: Relative Effectiveness of the Options in Reducing Male Unemployment', London: Policy Studies Institute Research Discussion Paper, 7.

Dow, J. and Dicks-Mireaux, L. (1958) 'The Excess Demand for Labour: A Study of Conditions in Great Britain, 1946–56', *Oxford Economic Papers*, 10: 1–33.

Drago, R. and Garvey, G. (1998) 'Incentives for Helping on the Job: Theory and Evidence', *Journal of Labour Economics*, 16 (1): 1–25.

Duncan, G. and Stafford, F. (1980) 'Do Union Members Receive Compensating Wage Differentials?', *American Economic Review*, 70: 355–71.

Duranton, G. and Monastiriotis, V. (2000) 'Mind the Gaps: The Evolution of Regional Inequalities in the UK 1982–1997', London School of Economics, Centre for Economic Performance, Discussion Paper 485.

Dyer, S. (1998) 'Flexibility Models: A Critical Analysis', *International Journal of Manpower*, 19 (4): 223–33.

Edgeworth, F.Y. (1922) 'Equal Pay to Men and Women for Equal Work', Economic Journal, 32: 431–457.

Edwards, R. (1979) *Contested Terrain: The Transformation of the Workplace in the Twentieth Century*, New York: Basic Books.

Eichengreen, B. (1992) 'Labour Markets and European Monetary Unification', in P. Masson and M. Taylor (eds) *Policy Issues in the Operation of Currency Unions*, Cambridge: Cambridge University Press.

Eissa, N. (1995) 'Taxation and Labour Supply of Married Women: The Tax Reform Act of 1986 as a Natural Experiment', NBER Working Paper, 5023.

Elgar, J. and Simpson, R. (1993) 'The Impact of the Law on Industrial Disputes in the 1980s', in D. Metcalf and S. Milner (eds) *New Perspectives on Industrial Disputes*, London: Routledge.

Elliott, R.F. (1976) 'The National Wage Round in the United Kingdom: A Sceptical View', *Bulletin of the Oxford University Institute of Economics and Statistics*, 38: 179–201.

Elmeskov, J. and Pichelmann, K. (1993) 'Interpreting Unemployment: The Role of Labour Force Participation', *OECD Economic Studies*, 21: 137–58.

Esping-Andersen, G. and Regini, M. (2000) *Why Deregulate Labour Markets?*, Oxford: Oxford University Press.

Esteve-Volart, B. (2000) 'Sex Discrimination and Growth', New York: *IMF Working Paper* 00/84.

Faini, R., Giampaolo, G., Gennar, P. and Rossi, F. (1997) 'An Empirical Puzzle: Falling Migration and Growing Unemployment Differentials Among Italian Regions', *European Economic Review*, 41: 571–9.

Fallon, P. and Verry, D. (1988) *The Economics of Labour Markets*, Oxford: Philip Allan.

Fawcett, M. (1918) 'Equal Pay for Equal Work', *Economic Journal*, 28: 1–6.

Feinstein, C. (1990) 'British Economic Growth', *Economic Review*, 7 (5): 19–23.

Felstead, A. and Jewson, N. (eds) (1999) *Global Trends in Flexible Labour*, London: Macmillan.

Fernie, S. and Metcalf, D. (1999) '(Not) Hanging on the Telephone: Payments Systems in the New Sweatshops', *Advances in Industrial and Labour Relations*, 9: 23–67.

Forster, M. (2000) 'Trends and Driving Factors in Income Distribution and Poverty in the OECD Area', OECD Labour Market and Social Policy Occasional Paper, 42.

Forth, J. and Millward, N. (2000) 'The Determinants of Pay Levels and Fringe Benefit Provision in Britain', London: National Institute of Economic and Social Research, Discussion Paper 171.

Freeman, R.B. (1977) 'The Decline in Ecomonic Rewards to College Education', *Review of Economics and Statistics*, 59 (1): 18–29.

—— (1986) 'The Demand for Education', in O. Ashenfelter and R. Layard (eds) *Handbook of Labour Economics*, Amsterdam: North Holland.

—— (1995) 'Are Your Wages Set in Beijing?', *Journal of Economic Perspectives*, 9 (3): 15–32.

Freeman, R.B. and Kleiner, M. (1999) 'Do Unions Make Enterprises Insolvent?', *Industrial and Labour Relations Review*, 52 (4): 510–27.

Freeman, R.B. and Medoff, J. (1984) *What Do Unions Do?*, New York: Basic Books.

Freidberg, R. and Hunt, J. (1995) 'The Impact of Immigration on Host Country Wages, Employment and Growth', *Journal of Economic Perspectives*, 9 (2): 23–44.

Friedman, M. (1968) 'The Role of Monetary Policy', *American Economic Review*, 58: 1–17.

Garen, J. (1988) 'Compensating Wage Differentials and the Endogeneity of Job Riskiness', *Review of Economics and Statistics*, 70: 9–16.

Gemmell, N. (1996) 'Evaluating the Impacts of Human Capital Stocks and Accumulation on Economic Growth: Some New Evidence', *Oxford Bulletin of Economics and Statistics*, 58 (1): 9–28.

Ghosh, A. (1995) 'International Capital Mobility Amongst the Major Industrialised Countries: Too Little or Too Much?', *Economic Journal*, 105 (428): 107–28.

—— (2000) 'Trade Liberalisation, Employment and Global Inequality', *International Labour Review*, 139 (3): 281–305.

Godfrey, L. (1971) 'The Phillips Curve: Incomes Policy and Trade Union Effects', in H.G. Johnson and A.R. Nobay (eds) *The Current Inflation*, London: Macmillan.

Goldin, C. (1990) *Understanding the Gender Gap: An Economic History of American Women*, Oxford: Oxford University Press.

Gomez, G., Martin Lipset, S. and Meltz, N. (2001) 'Frustrated Demand for Unionisation: the Case of the United States and Canada Revisited', London School of Economics Centre for Economic Performance, Discussion Paper 492.

Gospel, H. (1997) 'The Revival of Apprenticeship Training in Britain?', London School of Economics Centre for Economic Performance, Discussion Paper 372.

Gospel, H., Lockwood, G. and Willman, P. (2000) 'The Right to Know: Disclosure of Information for Collective Bargaining and Joint Consultation', London School of Economics Centre for Economic Performance, Discussion Paper 453.

Green, A., Gregg, P. and Wadsworth, J. (1998) 'Regional Unemployment Changes in Britain', in P. Lawless, R. Martin and S. Hardy (eds) *Unemployment and Social Exclusion: Landscapes of Labour Market Inequality*, London: Jessica Kingsley.

Green, D. (1993) 'The Impact of Trade Union Membership on Training in Britain', *Applied Economics*, 25: 1033–43.

—— (1999) 'Immigrant Occupational Attainment: Assimilation and Mobility Over Time', *Journal of Labour Economics*, 17 (1): 49–79.

Green, F., Felstead, A. and Gallie, D. (2000) 'Computers Are Even More Important Than You Thought: An Analysis of the Changing Skill-Intensity of Jobs', London School of Economics Centre for Economic Performance, Discussion Paper 439.

Green, F. and McIntosh, S. (2000) 'Working on the Chain Gang? An Examination of Rising Effort Levels in Europe in the 1990s', London School of Economics Centre for Economic Performance, Discussion Paper 465.

Green, F. and McIntosh, S. and Vignoles, A. (1999) 'Overeducation and Skills: Clarifying the Concepts', London School of Economics Centre for Economic Performance, Discussion Paper 435.

Greenhalgh, C. (1980) 'Male–Female Wage Differentials in Great Britain: is Marriage an Equal Opportunity?', *Economic Journal*, 90: 651–775.

Gregg, P. and Machin, S. (1994) 'Is the UK Rise in Inequality Different?', in R. Barrell (ed.) *The UK Labour Market: Comparative Aspects and Institutional Developments*, Cambridge: Cambridge University Press.

Gregg, P., Machin, S. and Metcalf, D. (1991) 'Signals and Cycles, Productivity Growth and Changes in Union Status in British Companies, 1984–1989', London School of Economics Centre for Economic Performance, Discussion Paper 49.

Gregg, P. and Petrongolo, B. (1997) 'Random or Non-Random Matching? Implications for the Use of the *U–V* Curve as a Measure of Matching Effectiveness', London School of Economics Centre for Economic Performance, Discussion Paper 348.

Gregg, P. and Wadsworth, J. (1996) 'Mind the Gap, Please? The Changing Nature of Entry Jobs in Britain', London School of Economics Centre for Economic Performance, Discussion Paper 303.

Gregory, M. and Jukes, R. (2001) 'Unemployment and Subsequent Earnings: Estimating Scarring Among British Men 1984–94', *Economic Journal*, 111 (475): F607–F625.

Gregory, M. and Sandoval, V. (1994) 'Low Pay and Minimum Wage Protection in Britain and the EC', in R. Barrell (ed.) *The UK Labour Market: Comparative Aspects and Institutional Developments*, Cambridge: Cambridge University Press.

Griliches, Z. (1997) 'Education, Human Capital and Growth: A Personal Perspective', *Journal of Labour Economics*, 15 (1): S330–S342.

Grimshaw, D. and Rubery, J. (2001) 'The Gender Pay Gap: A Research Review', Manchester: Equal Opportunities Commission Research Discussion Series.

Groot, W. (1996) 'The Incidence of and Returns to Overeducation in the UK', *Applied Economics*, 28: 1345–50.

—— (1998) 'Empirical Estimates of the Rate of Depreciation of Education', *Applied Economic Letters* 5: 535–8.

Gross, D.M. (1999) 'Three Million Foreigners, Three Million Unemployed? Immigration and the French Labour Market', IMF Working Paper, WP/99/124.

Grubb, D. (1994) 'Direct and Indirect Effects of Active Labour Market Policies in OECD Countries', in R. Barrell (ed.) *The UK Labour Market: Comparative Aspects and Institutional Developments*, Cambridge: Cambridge University Press.

Guell, M. (2001) 'Fixed-Term Contracts and the Duration Distribution of Unemployment', London School of Economics Centre for Economic Performance, Discussion Paper 505.

Guell, M. and Petrongolo, B. (2000) '"Workers" Transitions from Temporary to Permanent Employment: The Spanish Case', London School of Economics Centre for Economic Performance, Discussion Paper 438.

Hahn, F.H. (1987) 'On Involuntary Unemployment', *Economic Journal*, 97 (2): 1–16.

Hall, R. and Hitch, C. (1939) 'Price Theory and Business Behaviour', Oxford Economic Papers, 2.

Hamermesh, D. (1986) 'The Demand for Labour in the Long Run', in O. Ashenfelter and R. Layard (eds) *Handbook of Labour Economics*, Volume 1, Amsterdam: North Holland.

—— (1993) *Labour Demand*, Princeton, NJ: Princeton University Press.

Hamermesh, D. and Wolfe, J. (1990) 'Compensating Wage Differentials and the Duration of Wage Loss', *Journal of Labour Economics*, 8: S175–S197.

Harmon, C. and Walker, I. (2001) 'The Returns to Education: A Review of Evidence, Issues and Deficiencies in the Literature', UK DfEE Research Report 254.

Harmon, C., Walker, I. and Westergaard-Nielsen, N. (2001) *Education and Earnings in Europe: A Cross Country Analysis of the Returns to Education*, Cheltenham: Edward Elgar.

Haskel, J. (1999) 'Small Firms, Contracting-Out, Computers and Wage Inequality: Evidence from UK Manufacturing'. *Economica*, 66 (261): 1–22.

Haskel, J. and Kay, J. (1990) 'Productivity in British Industry Under Mrs Thatcher', in T. Congdon (*et al.*) *The State of the Economy*, London: Institute of Economic Affairs.

Haskel, J. and Heden, Y. (1999) 'Computers and the Demand for Skilled Labour: Industry and Establishment-Level Panel Evidence for the UK', *Economic Journal*, 109 (454): C68–C79.

Hassel, A. (1999) 'The Erosion of the German System of Industrial Relations', *British Journal of Industrial Relations*, 37 (3): 483–505.

Heckman, J. (1993) 'What Has Been Learned About Labour Supply in the Last Twenty Years', *American Economic Review*, 83: 116–21.

Heery, E. (2000) 'Trade Unions and the Management of Reward', in G. White and J. Drucker (eds) *Reward Management: Critical Perspectives*, London: Routledge.

Held, D., McGrew, A., Goldblatt, D. and Perraton, J. (1999) *Global Transformations*, Cambridge: Polity Press.

Hellerstein, J., Neumark, D. and Troske, K. (1999) 'Wages, Productivity and Worker Characteristics: Evidence From Plant-Level Production Functions and Wage Equations', *Journal of Labour Economics*, 17 (3): 409–46.

Hines, A.G. (1964) 'Trade Unions and Wage Inflation in the United Kingdom, 1893–1961', *Review of Economic Studies*, 31: 221–52.

—— (1971a) 'The Determinants of the Rate of Change of Money Wage Rates and the Effectiveness of Incomes Policy', in H.G. Johnson and A.R. Nobay (eds) *The Current Inflation*, London: Macmillan.

—— (1971b) *On the Reappraisal of Keynesian Economics*, London: Martin Robertson.

Hirsch, B. (1991) *Labour Unions and the Economic Performance of Firms*, Kalamazoo, MI: W.E. Upjohn Institute.

Hocquet, L. (1999) 'Vocational Training as a Force for Equality?: Training Opportunities and Outcomes in France and Britain', *International Journal of Manpower*, 20 (3/4): 231–53.

Hodson, R. and England, P. (1986) 'Industrial Structure and Sex Differences in Earnings', *Industrial Relations*, 25: 16–32.

Houseman, S. and Abraham, K. (1990) 'Regional Labour Market Responses to Demand Shocks: A Comparison of the United States and West Germany', Paper for the Association of Public Policy and Management, San Francisco, CA (October).

Hughes, G. and McCormick, B. (1994) 'Did Migration in the 1980s Narrow the North–South Divide?', *Economica*, 61: 509–27.

Hughes, P. and Hutchinson, G. (1988) 'Is Unemployment Irreversible?', *Applied Economics*, 20: 31–42.

Humphries, J. and Rubery, J. (eds) (1995) *The Economics of Equal Opportunities*, Manchester: Equal Opportunities Commission.

Husted, S. and Melvin, M. (2001) *International Economics*, Fifth Edition, New York: Addison Wesley Longman.

IDS (1996) 'Report 726', Income Data Services.

IMF (1998) 'International Capital Markets', *World Economic and Financial Surveys*, Washington, DC: International Monetary Fund.

Jackman, R., Layard, R. and Nickell, S. (1996) 'Combating Unemployment: Is Flexibility Enough?', London School of Economics Centre for Economic Performance, Discussion Paper 293.

Jackman, R., Layard, R. and Pissarides, C. (1989) 'On Vacancies', *Oxford Bulletin of Economics and Statistics*, 51 (4): 377–94.

Jackman, R. and Roper, S. (1987) 'Structural Unemployment', *Oxford Bulletin of Economics and Statistics*, 49 (1): 9–36.

Jackman, R. and Savouri, S. (1991) 'Regional Wage Determination in Great Britain', London School of Economics Centre for Economic Performance, Discussion Paper 47.

Jenkinson, T. (1987) 'The Natural Rate of Unemployment: Does it Exist?', *Oxford Review of Economic Policy*, 3 (3): 20–6.

Jepma, C., Jager, H. and Kamphuis, E. (1996) *Introduction to International Economics*, Harlow: Longman.

Johnson, H.G. and Meiszkowski, P. (1970) 'The Effect of Unionisation on the Distribution of Income: A General Equilibrium Approach', *Quarterly Journal of Economics*, 84: 539–61.

Joll, C., McKenna, C., McNabb, R. and Shorey, J. (1983) *Developments in Labour Market Analysis*, London: Allen and Unwin.

Jones, D. and Makepeace, G. (1996) 'Equal Worth, Equal Opportunities: Pay and Promotion in an Internal Labour Market', *Economic Journal*, 106: 401–9.

Kamalich, R.E. and Polachek, S.W. (1982) 'Discrimination: Fact or Fiction? An Examination Using an Alternative Approach', *Southern Economic Journal*, 49: 450–61.

Kaplinsky, R. (2001) 'Is Globalisation All It is Cracked Up to Be?', *Review of International Political Economy*, 8 (1): 45–65.

Katz, L. and Autor, D. (1999) 'Changes in the Wage Structure and Earnings Inequality', in Ashenfelter, O. and Card, D. (eds) (1999) *Handbook of Labour Economics*, Volume 3, Amsterdam: Elsevier Science.

Keil, M., Robertson, D. and Symons, J. (2001) 'Minimum Wages and Employment', London School of Economics, Centre for Economic Performance, Discussion Paper 493.

Kennan, J. (1995) 'The Elusive Effects of Minimum Wages', *Journal of Economic Literature*, 33 (4): 1950–65.

Keynes, J.M. (1936) *The General Theory of Employment, Interest and Money*, London: Macmillan.

Kidd, Sloan, P. and Ferko, I. (2000) 'Disability and the Labour Market: An Analysis of British Males', *Journal of Health Economics*, 19: 961–81.

Kiefer, N. and Neumann, G. (1989) *Search Models and Applied Labour Economics*, Cambridge: Cambridge University Press.

Kiley, M. (1999) 'The Supply of Skilled Labour and Skill-Biased Technological Progress', *Economic Journal*, 109 (458): 708–24.

Killingsworth, M.R. (1983) *Labour Supply*, Cambridge: Cambridge University Press.

Kim, D. (1999) 'The Effects of Rising Female Labour Supply on Male Wages', *Journal of Labour Economics*, 17 (1): 23–48.

Kitson, M. and Michie, J. (1995) 'Trade and Growth: An Historical Perspective', in J. Michie and J. Grieve-Smith (eds), *Managing the Global Economy*, Oxford: Oxford University Press.

Korenman, S. and Neumark, D. (1991) 'Does Marriage Really Make Men More Productive?', Journal of Human Resources, 26 (2): 282–307.

Korotov, R. and Hsu, E. (2002) 'A Road-Map for Creating Efficient Corporate Internal Labour Markets', *Career Development International*, 7 (1): 37–46.

Kramarz, F. and Roux, S. (1999) 'Within-Firm Seniority Structure and Firm Performance', London School of Economics Centre for Labour Economics, Discussion Paper 420.

Krueger, A. (2000) *Education Matters: Selected Essays by Alan B. Krueger*, Cheltenham: Edward Elgar.

Krugman, P. (1979) 'Increasing Returns, Monopolistic Competition and International Trade', *Journal of International Economics*, 9 (4): 469–79.

—— (1990) *The Age of Diminished Expectations*, Cambridge, MA: MIT Press.

Labour Research Department, (1986) 'Women's Pay: Claiming Equal Value', London.

Laidler, D. and Estrin, S. (1989) *Introduction to Microeconomics*, Hemel Hempstead: Philip Allan.

Landesmann, M. and Pichelmann, K. (eds) (2000) *Unemployment in Europe*, Basingstoke: Macmillan Press.

Layard, R. (1986) 'Discussion', *Economic Policy*, October: 541–3.

—— (1989) 'European Unemployment: Cause and Cure', London School of Economics Centre for Labour Economics, Discussion Paper 368.

Layard, R. and Nickell, S. (1985a) 'The Causes of British Unemployment', *National Institute Economic Review*, 111: 62–85.

—— (1985b) 'Unemployment, Real Wages and Aggregate Demand in Europe, Japan and the US', London School of Economics, Centre for Labour Economics, Discussion Paper 214.

—— (1986) 'Unemployment in Britain', *Economica*, 53: S121–S170.

—— (1987) 'The Labour Market', in R. Dornbusch and R. Layard (eds) *The Performance of the British Economy*, Oxford: Clarendon Press.

—— (1992) 'Unemployment in the OECD Countries', London School of Economics Centre for Economic Performance, Discussion Paper 81.

—— (1999) 'Labour Market Institutions and Economic Performance', in O. Ashenfelter and D. Card (eds) (1999) *Handbook of Labour Economics*, Volume 3, Amsterdam: Elsevier Science.

Layard, R., Nickell, S. and Jackman, R. (1991) *Unemployment: Macroeconomic Performance and the Labour Market*, Oxford: Oxford University Press.

Layard, R. and Psacharopoulos, G. (1974) 'The Screening Hypothesis and the Returns to Education', *Journal of Political Economy*, 82: 985–98.

Lazear, E. (1996) 'Performance Pay and Productivity', NBER Working Paper 5672.

—— (1998) *Personnel Economics For Managers*, New York: J Wiley and Sons.

—— (1999) 'Personnel Economics: Past Lessons and Future Directions', *Journal of Labour Economics*, 17 (2): 199–236.

Lazear, E. and Rosen, S. (1981) 'Rank-Order Tournaments as Optimum Labour Contracts', *Journal of Political Economy*, 89: 841–64.

Leahy, D. and Montagna, C. (2000) 'Unionisation and Foreign Direct Investment: Challenging Conventional Wisdom', *Economic Journal*, 110 (462): C80–C92.

Leslie, D. (1982) 'Labour Supply in the UK: A Review', in M. Artis (*et al.*) *Demand Management, Supply Constraints and Inflation*, Manchester: Manchester University Press.

Leslie, D. and Wise, J. (1980) 'The Productivity of Hours in UK Manufacturing and Production Industries', *Economic Journal*, 90: 74–84.

Leuthold, J. (1968) 'An Empirical Study of Formula Income Transfers and the Work Decision of the Poor', *Journal of Human Resources*, 3: 312–23.

Lewis, H.G. (1986) 'Union Relative Wage Effects', in O. Ashenfelter and R. Layard (eds) *Handbook of Labour Economics*, Amsterdam: North Holland.

Li, E. (1986) 'Compensating Differentials and Cyclical and Non-Cyclical Unemployment', *Journal of Labour Economics*, 4: 277–300.

Lillard, L. and Tan, H. (1992) 'Private Sector Training: Who Gets It and What Are Its Effects?', *Research in Labour Economics*, 13: 1–62.

Lindbeck, A. and Snower, D.J. (1988) *The Insider–Outsider Theory of Employment and Unemployment*, Cambridge, MA: MIT Press.

Lipsey, R.G. (1960) 'The Relationship Between Unemployment and the Rate of Change of Money Wage Rates in the UK: A Further Analysis', *Economica*, 27: 1–31.

Lissenburgh, S. (2000) 'Gender Discrimination in the Labour Market: Evidence From the BHPS and EiB Surveys', London: Policy Studies Institute Research, Discussion Paper 3.

Litwin, A.S. (2001) 'Trade Unions and Industrial Injury in Great Britain', London School of Economics, Centre for Economic Performance, Discussion Paper 493.

Loewenstein, M. and Spletzer, J. (1999) 'General and Specific Training: Evidence and Implications', *Journal of Human Resources*, 34 (4): 710–33.

Lucas, R.E. (1972) 'Expectations and the Neutrality of Money', *Journal of Economic Theory*, 4: 103–24.

—— (1978) 'Unemployment Policy', *American Economic Review*, 68: 353.

—— (1988) 'On the Mechanics of Economic Development', *Journal of Monetary Economics*, 22: 3–42.

—— (1993) 'Making a Miracle', *Econometrica*, 61 (2): 251–72.

Lynch, L. (1992) 'Private Sector Training and the Earnings of Young Workers', *American Economic Review*, 82 (1): 299–312.

Lynch, L. and Black, S. (1998) 'Beyond the Incidence of Employer-Provided Training', *Industrial and Labour Relations Review*, 52 (1): 64–81.

Machin, S. (1999) 'Wage Inequality in the 1970s, 1980s and 1990s', in P. Gregg and J. Wadsworth (eds) *The State of Working Britain*, Manchester: Manchester University Press.

—— (2000) 'Union Decline in Britain', London School of Economics Centre for Economic Performance, Discussion Paper 455.

Machin, S. and Manning, A. (1996) 'Employment and the Introduction of a Minimum Wage in Britain', *Economic Journal*, 106 (436): 667–76.

—— (1999) 'Long-Term Unemployment in Europe', in O. Ashenfelter and D. Card (eds) (1999) *Handbook of Labour Economics*, Volume 3, Amsterdam: Elsevier Science.

Machin, S. and van Reenen, J. (1998) 'Technology and Changes in Skill Structure: Evidence from Seven OECD Countries', *Quarterly Journal of Economics*, 113: 1215–44.

MaCurdy, T.E. and Pencavel, J.H. (1986) 'Testing Between Competing Models of Wage and Employment Determination in Unionised Markets', *Journal of Political Economy*, 94 (2): S3–S39.

McConnell, C.R. and Brue, S.L. (1995) *Contemporary Labour Economics*, Fourth Edition, New York: McGraw Hill.

McConnell, S. and Takla, L. (1990) 'Mrs Thatcher's Trade Union Legislation: Has it Reduced Strikes?', London School of Economics Centre for Economic Performance, Discussion Paper 374.

McDonald, I.M. and Solow, R.M. (1981) 'Wage Bargaining and Employment', *American Economic Review*, 71 (4): 896–908.

McGregor, D. (1960) *The Human Side of Enterprise*, New York, McGraw-Hill.

McIntosh, S. (1999) 'A Cross-Country Comparison of the Determinants of Vocational Training', London School of Economics Centre for Economic Performance, Discussion Paper 432.

McKenna, C.J. (1990) 'The Theory of Search in Labour Markets', in D. Sapsford and Z. Tzannatos (eds) *Current Issues in Labour Economics*, London: Macmillan.

McKinnon, R. (1963) 'Optimal Currency Areas', *American Economic Review*, 53: 717–25.

McNabb, R. (1987) 'Labour Market Theories and Education', in G. Psacharopoulos (ed.) *Economics of Education: Research and Studies*, Oxford: Pergamon Press.

—— (1989) 'Compensating Wage Differentials: Some Evidence for Britain', *Oxford Economic Papers*, 41: 327–38.

McNabb, R. and Psacharopoulos, G. (1981) 'Racial Earnings Differentials in the UK', *Oxford Economic Papers*, 33: 413–25.

McNabb, R. and Ryan, P. (1990) 'Segmented Labour Markets', in D. Sapsford and Z. Tzannatos (eds) *Current Issues in Labour Economics*, London: Macmillan.

Malinvaud, E. (1977) *The Theory of Unemployment Reconsidered*, Oxford: Basil Blackwell.

Manning, A. (1987) 'An Integration of Trade Union Models in a Sequential Bargaining Framework', *Economic Journal*, 97: 121–39.

—— (1990) 'Implicit Contract Theory', in D. Sapsford and Z. Tzannatos (eds) *Current Issues in Labour Economics*, London: Macmillan.

—— (1992) 'How Robust is the Microeconomic Theory of the Trade Union?', London School of Economics Centre for Economic Performance, Discussion Paper 65.

—— (1996) 'The Equal Pay Act as an Experiment to Test Theories of the Labour Market', *Economica*, 63 (250): 191–212.

—— (1999) 'Pretty Vacant: Recruitment in Low-Wage Labour Markets', London School of Economics Centre for Economic Performance, Discussion Paper 418.

Manning, A. and Robinson, H. (1998) 'Something in the Way She Moves: A Fresh Look at an Old Gap', London School of Economics Centre for Economic Performance, Discussion Paper 389.

Manning, A. and Thomas, J. (1997) 'A Simple Test of the Shirking Model', London School of Economics Centre for Economic Performance, Discussion Paper 374.

Marsden, D. (1995) 'Management Practices and Unemployment', London School of Economics Centre for Economic Performance, Discussion Paper 241.

Marsden, D., French, S. and Kubo, K. (2000) 'Why Does Performance Pay De-Motivate? Financial Incentives versus Performance Appraisal', London School of Economics Centre for Economic Performance, Discussion Paper 476.

Martin, J. (2000) 'What Works Among Active Labour Market Policies: Evidence From OECD Countries' Experiences', OECD Economic Studies, 30.

Martin, R. (1998) 'Regional Dimensions of Europe's Unemployment Crisis', in P. Lawless, R. Martin and S. Hardy (eds) *Unemployment and Social Exclusion: Landscapes of Labour Market Inequality*, London: Jessica Kingsley.

Mason, G. (1996) 'Graduate Utilisation and the Quality of Higher Education in the UK', National Institute for Economic and Social Research, Discussion Paper 158.

Mauro, M.J. (1982) 'Strikes as a Result of Imperfect Information', *Industrial and Labour Relations Review*, 35 (4): 522–38.

Mayhew, K. and Rosewell, B. (1979) 'Labour Market Segmentation in Britain', *Oxford Bulletin of Economics and Statistics*, 41: 81–115.

Mayhew, K. and Turnbull, P. (1989) 'Models of Union Behaviour: A Critique of Recent Literature', in R. Drago and R. Perlman (eds) *Microeconomic Issues in Labour Economics*, Hemel Hempstead: Harvester Wheatsheaf.

Metcalf, D. (1999a) 'The Low Pay Commission and the National Minimum Wage', *Economic Journal*, 109: F46–F66.

—— (1999b) 'The British National Minimum Wage', London School of Economics, Centre for Economic Performance, Discussion Paper 419.

—— (2001) 'British Unions: Dissolution or Resurgence Revisited', London School of Economics, Centre for Economic Performance, Discussion Paper 493.

Metcalf, D., Hansen, K. and Charlwood, A. (2000) Unions and the Sword of Justice: Unions and Pay Systems, Pay Inequality, Pay Discrimination and Low Pay', London School of Economics, Centre for Economic Performance, Discussion Paper 452.

Metcalf, D., Wadsworth, J. and Ingram, P. (1992) 'Do Strikes Pay?', London School of Economics, Centre for Economic Performance, Discussion Paper 92.

Michie, J. and Grieve-Smith, J. (1995) *Managing the Global Economy*, Oxford: Oxford University Press.

Michie, J. and Sheehan, M. (1999) 'HRM Practices, R and D Expenditure and Innovative Investment: Evidence from the UK's 1990 Workplace Industrial Relations Survey', *Industrial and Corporate Change*, 8 (2): 211–34.

Mill, John Stuart (1885) *Principles of Political Economy*.

Millard, S., Scott, A. and Sensier, M. (1999) 'Business Cycles and the Labour Market: Can Theory Fit the Facts?', Bank of England Working Paper.

Milner, S. and Metcalf, D. (1991) 'A Century of UK Strike Activity: An Alternative Perspective', London School of Economics, Centre for Economic Performance, Discussion Paper 22.

Mincer, J. (1962) 'On-the-job Training: Costs, Returns and Some Implications', *Journal of Political Economy*, 70 (5): part 2.

—— (1974) Schooling, Experience and Earnings, New York: National Bureau of Economic Research.

—— (1985) 'Intercountry Comparisons of Labour Force Trends and Related Developments: An Overview', *Journal of Labour Economics*, 3: S1–S33.

Minford, P. (1982) 'Trade Unions Destroy a Million Jobs', *Journal of Economic Affairs*, London: Institute of Economic Affairs.

—— (1983) 'Labour Market Equilibrium in an Open Economy', *Oxford Economic Papers*, 35: 207–44.

—— (1984) *Unemployment Cause and Cure*, Oxford: Martin Robertson.

—— (1990) 'The Labour Market', in T. Congdon (*et al.*) *The State of the Economy*, London: Institute of Economic Affairs.

—— (1998) *Markets Not Stakes: The Triumph of Capitalism and the Stakeholder Fallacy*, London: Orion Business Books.

Mishra, R. (1999) *Globalisation and the Welfare State*, Cheltenham: Edward Elgar.

Molle, W. and van Mourik, A. (1988) 'International Movements of Labour Under Conditions of Economic Integration: the Case of Western Europe', *Journal of Common Market Studies*, 26 (3): 317–42.

Montgomery, E. (1989) 'Employment and Unemployment Effects of Unions', *Journal of Labour Economics*, 7 (2): 170–90.

Mortensen, D. (1986) 'Job Search and Labour Market Analysis', in O. Ashenfelter and R. Layard (eds), *Handbook of Labour Economics*, Volume 2, Amsterdam: North Holland.

Mortensen, D. and Pissarides, C. (1999) 'Job Reallocation, Employment Fluctuations and Unemployment', London School of Economics Centre for Economic Performance, Discussion Paper 421.

Mortensen, D. and Pissarides, C. (1999) 'New Developments in Models of Search in the Labour Market', in O. Ashenfelter and D. Card (eds) *Handbook of Labour Economics*, Volume 3, Amsterdam: Elsevier Science.

Muellbauer, J. (1986) 'Productivity and Competitiveness in British Manufacturing', *Oxford Review of Economic Policy*, 2 (3): i–xxv.

Mundell, R. (1961) 'A Theory of Optimal Currency Areas', *American Economic Review*, 51: 717–25.

Murphy, K. (1999) 'Executive Compensation', in O. Ashenfelter and D. Card (eds) *Handbook of Labour Economics*, Volume 3, Amsterdam: Elsevier Science.

Neumann, G.R. and Rissman, E.R. (1984) 'Where Have All the Union Members Gone?', *Journal of Labour Economics*, 2: 175–92.

Neumark, D. and Wascher, W. (1998) 'Minimum Wages and Training Revisited', NBER Working Paper, 6651.

Nickell, S. (1978) 'Fixed Costs, Employment and Labour Demand Over the Cycle', *Economica*, 45: 329–45.

—— (1986) 'Dynamic Models of Labour Demand', in O. Ashenfelter and R. Layard (eds) *Handbook of Labour Economics*, Amsterdam: North Holland.

—— (1990) 'Unemployment: A Survey', *Economic Journal*, 100: 391–439.

—— (1997) 'Unemployment and Labour Market Rigidities: Europe versus North America', *Journal of Economic Perspectives*, 11 (3): 54–74.

—— (1999) 'Unemployment: Questions and Some Answers', *Economic Journal*, 108: 802–816.

Nickell, S. and Bell, B. (1995) 'The Collapse in Demand for the Unskilled and Unemployment across the OECD', *Oxford Review of Economic Policy*, 11 (1): 40–62.

Nickell, S., Jones, T. and Quintini, G. (2000) 'A Picture of Job Insecurity Facing British Men', London School of Economics, Centre for Economic Performance, Discussion Paper 479.

Nickell, S. and Layard, R. (1999) 'Labour Market Institutions and Economic Performance', in O. Ashenfelter and D. Card (eds) (1999) *Handbook of Labour Economics*, Volume 3, Amsterdam: Elsevier Science.

Nickell, S., Nunziata, L., Ochel, W. and Quintini, G. (2001) 'The Beveridge Curve, Unemployment and Wages in the OECD from the 1960s to the 1990s', London School of Economics Centre For Economic Performance, Discussion Paper 502.

Nickell, S. and Quintini, G. (2001) 'Nominal Wage Rigidity and the Rate of Inflation', London School of Economics, Centre for Economic Performance, Discussion Paper 489.

Nickell, S. and Quintini, G. (2002) 'The Consequences of the Decline in Public Sector Pay in Britain: A Little Bit of Evidence', *Economic Journal*, 112 (477): F107–F118.

Nickell, S. and van Reenen, J. (2000) 'Technological Innovation and Economic Performance in the UK', London School of Economics, Centre for Economic Performance, Discussion Paper 488.

Nickell, S., Vainiomanski, J. and Wadhwani, S. (1992) 'Wages, Unions, Insiders and Product Market Power', London School of Economics, Centre for Economic Performance, Discussion Paper 77.

Nickell, S., Wadhwani, S. and Wall, S. (1991) 'Productivity Growth in UK Companies 1975–1986', London School of Economics Centre for Economic Performance, Discussion Paper 26.

Nicoletti, G., Bassanini, A., Ernst, E., Jean, S., Santiago, P. and Swaim, P. (2001) 'Product and Labour Market Interactions in OECD Countries', OECD Economics Department Working Paper 312.

Nolan, P. (1994) 'Labour Market Institutions, Industrial Restructuring and Unemployment in Europe', in J. Michie and J. Grieve-Smith (eds) *Unemployment in Europe*, London: Academic Press.

Office for National Statistics (ONS) (various years), *Labour Force Survey*.

OECD (1998) *Employment Lookout*, Paris: Organisation for Economic Cooperation and Development.

Oi, W. (1962) 'Labour as a Quasi-Fixed Factor', *Journal of Political Economy*, 70 (6): 538–55.

O'Mahony, M. (1999) *Britain's Productivity Performance 1959–1996: An International Perspective*, London: National Institute of Economic and Social Research.

—— (2000) Revised edition of O'Mahony, M. (1999).

Oulton, N. (1990) 'Labour Productivity in UK Manufacturing in the 1970s and in the 1980s', *National Institute Economic Review*, May, 71–91.

Overman, H. and Puga, D. (1999) 'Unemployment Clusters Across European Regions and Countries', London School of Economics Centre for Economic Performance, Discussion Paper 434.

Pelkmans, J. (1997) *European Integration: Methods and Economic Analysis*, Harlow: Longmans.

Pencavel, J.H. (1977) 'The Distributional and Efficiency Effects of Trade Unions in Britain', *British Journal of Industrial Relations*, 15 (2): 137–56.

—— (1986) 'Labour Supply of Men: A Survey', in O. Ashenfelter and R. Layard (eds) *Handbook of Labour Economics*, Amsterdam: North Holland.

—— (1994) 'British Unemployment: Letter from America', *Economic Journal*, 104 (424): 621–32.

—— (1998) 'The Market Work Behaviour and Wages of Women, 1975–94', *Journal of Human Resources*, 33 (4): 771–804.

Petrongolo, B. and Pissarides, C. (2000) 'Looking into the Black Box: A Survey of the Matching Function', London School of Economics Centre for Economic Performance, Discussion Paper 470.

Phelps, E.S. (1967) 'Phillips curves, Expectations of Inflation and Optimal Unemployment Over Time', *Economica*, 34: 254–81.

Phillips, A.W. (1958) 'The Relation between Unemployment and the Rate of Change of Money Wage Rates in the United Kingdom, 1861–1957', *Economica*, 25: 283–99.

Pigou, A.C. (1933) *The Theory of Unemployment*, London: Macmillan.

Pike, M. (1984) 'Female Discrimination in the Labour Market', *Economic Review*, 7 (5): 3–7.

Piore, M. and Sabel, C. (1984) *The Second Industrial Divide*, New York: Basic Books.

Pissarides, C. (1985) 'Job Search and the Functioning of Labour Markets', in D. Carline *et al.* *Labour Economics*, Harlow: Longmans.

—— (1986) 'Unemployment and Vacancies in Britain', *Economic Policy*, October: 503–59.

—— (1992) 'Search Theory at Twenty-One', London School of Economics Centre for Economic Performance, Discussion Paper 90.

Pissarides, C. and Wadsworth, J. (1989) 'Unemployment and the Inter-Regional Mobility of Labour', *Economic Journal*, 99: 739–55.

Polachek, S.W. and Siebert, W.S. (1993) *The Economics of Earnings*, Cambridge: Cambridge University Press.

Polivka, A. (1996) 'Contingent and Alternative Work Arrangements Defined', *Monthly Labour Review*, October: 3–9.

Pryke, R. (1981) *The Nationalised Industries: Policies and Performance Since 1968*, Oxford: Martin Robinson.

Pryor, F. and Schaffer, D. (1999) *Who's Not Working and Why: Employment, Cognitive Skills, Wages and the Changing US Labour Market*, Cambridge: Cambridge University Press.

Psacharopoulos, G. (1981) 'Returns to Education: An Updated International Comparison', *Comparative Education*, 17: 321–341.

—— (1985) 'Returns to Education', *Journal of Human Resources*, 14 (4): 584–604.

—— (ed.) (1987) *Economics of Education: Research and Studies*, Oxford: Pergamon Press.

—— (1994) 'Returns to Investment in Education: A Global Update', *World Development*, 22 (9): 1325–43.

Psacharopoulos, G. and Layard, R. (1979) 'Human Capital and Earnings: British Evidence and a Critique', *Review of Economic Studies*, 46: 485–503.

Purdy, D. and Zis, G. (1974) 'On the Concept and Measurement of Union Militancy', in D. Laidler and D. Purdy (eds) *Inflation and Labour Markets*, Manchester: Manchester University Press.

Raff, D. and Summers, L. (1987) 'Did Henry Ford Pay Efficiency Wage Rates?', *Journal of Labour Economics*, 5 (2): S57–S86.

Rasmussen, D.W. and Kim, I. (1992) 'The Growth of US Labour Productivity, 1950–1989', *Applied Economics*, 24: 285–9.

Rebitzer, J.M. (1989) 'Efficiency Wages and Implicit Contracts: An Institutional Evaluation', in R. Drago and R. Perlman (eds) *Microeconomic Issues in Labour Economics*, Hemel Hempstead: Harvester Wheatsheaf.

—— (1993) 'Radical Political Economy and the Economics of Labour Markets', *Journal of Economic Literature*, 31 (3): 1394–434.

Rees, A. (1963) 'The Effects of Unions on Resource Allocation', *Journal of Law and Economics*, 6: 69–78.

Reich, M. (1981) *Racial Inequality*, Princeton, NJ: Princeton University Press.

Reingold, D. (1999) 'Social Networks and the Employment Problem of the Urban Port', *Urban Studies*, 36 (11): 1907–32.

Reynolds, L., Masters, S. and Moser, C. (1998) *Labour Economics and Labour Relations*, Eleventh Edition, Englewood Cliffs, NJ: Prentice Hall.

Richardson, J. (1997) 'Wage Subsidies for the Long-Term Unemployed: A Search Theoretic Analysis', London School of Economics Centre for Economic Performance, Discussion Paper 347.

—— (1998) 'Do Wage Subsidies Enhance Employability? Evidence from Australian Youth', London School of Economics Centre for Economic Performance, Discussion Paper 387.

Riedesel, P.L. (1979) 'Racial Discrimination and White Economic Benefits', *Social Science Quarterly*, June: 120–9.

Riley, J. (1974) 'Competitive Signalling', *Journal of Economic Theory*, 10: 175–86.

—— (1976) 'Information Screening and Human Capital', *American Economic Review, Papers and Proceedings*, 66.

Robinson, J. (1933) *The Economics of Imperfect Competition*, London: Macmillan.

Robinson, P. (1994) 'The British Labour Market in Historical Perspective: Change in the Structure of Employment and Unemployment', London School of Economics Centre for Economic Performance, Discussion Paper 202.

—— (1995) 'The Decline of the Swedish Model and the Limits to Active Labour Market Policy', London School of Economics Centre for Economic Performance, Discussion Paper 259.

—— (1997) 'The Myth of Parity of Esteem: Earnings and Qualifications', London School of Economics Centre for Economic Performance, Discussion Paper 354.

Robinson, P. and Mannacorda, M. (1997) 'Qualifications and the Labour Market in Britain 1984–94: Skill Biased Change in Demand for Labour or Credentialism?', London School of Economics Centre for Economic Performance, Discussion Paper 330.

Rodrik, D. (1994) 'King Kong Meets Godzilla: The World Bank and the East Asian Miracle', in A. Fishlow (ed.) *Miracle or Design?: Lessons From the East Asian Miracle*, Washington: Overseas Development Council.

Romer, P.M. (1986) 'Increasing Returns and Long Run Growth', *Journal of Political Economy*, 94 (5): 1002–37.

—— (1990) 'Endogenous Technological Change', *Journal of Political Economy*, 98 (5): 2.

Roper, S. (1989) 'The Economics of Job Vacancies', *British Review of Economic Issues*, 11 (24): 49–73.

Rosenberg, S. (1980) 'Male Occupational Standing and the Dual Labour Market', *Industrial Relations*, 19: 34–49.

—— (ed.) (1989) *The State and the Labour Market*, New York: Plenum Press.

Rothschild, K.W. (1954) *The Theory of Wages*, Second Edition, London: Routledge and Kegan Paul.

Routh, G. (1986) *Unemployment: Economic Perspectives*, London: Macmillan.

Rowthorn, R. and Ramaswamy, R. (1997) 'Deindustrialisation: Causes and Implications', Washington, DC: IMF Working Paper 97/42.

Rowthorn, R. and Wells, J. (1987) *Deindustrialisation and Foreign Trade*, Cambridge: Cambridge University Press.

Sachs, J. and Shatz, H. (1996) 'US Trade With Developing Countries and Wage Inequality', *American Economic Review*, 86 (2): 234–9.

Sako, M. (1997) 'Wage Bargaining in Japan: Why Employers and Unions Value Industry-Level Coordination', London School of Economics, Centre for Economic Performance, Discussion Paper 334.

Sanderson, M. (1999) *Education and Economic Decline in Britain, 1870 to the 1990s*, Cambridge: Cambridge University Press.

Schmitt, J. and Wadsworth, J. (1991) 'A Test of the Effect of Benefits on Search Activity in a Model of Endogenous Job Offer Arrivals', London School of Economics Centre for Economic Performance, Discussion Paper 38.

—— (1994) 'Why Are Two Million Men Inactive? The Decline in Male Labour Force Participation in Britain', London School of Economics Centre for Economic Performance, Discussion Paper 336.

Schultz, T.W. (1961) 'Investment in Human Capital', *American Economic Review*, 51: 1–17.

Shaw, G.K. (1984) *Rational Expectations: An Elementary Exposition*, Brighton: Harvester Wheatsheaf.

Sheffrin, S.M. (1983) *Rational Expectations*, Cambridge: Cambridge University Press.

Shorey, J. (1984) 'Employment Discrimination and the Employer Tastes Model', *Scottish Journal of Political Economy*, 31: 157–75.

Siebert, H. (1997) 'Labour Market Rigidities: At the Root of Unemployment in Europe', *Journal of Economic Perspectives*, 11 (3): 37–53.

—— (1998) 'Labour Productivities and Labour Costs in Euroland', Kiel Working Paper No. 886, Kiel: Institute of World Economics.

Siebert, W.S. (1985) 'Developments in the Economics of Human Capital', in D. Carline (*et al.*) *Labour Economics*, Harlow: Longmans.

—— (1997) 'Overview of European Labour Markets', in J. Addison and W. Siebert (eds) *Labour Markets in Europe: Issues of Harmonisation and Regulation*, London: Dryden Press.

Sims, C. (1974) 'Output and Labour Input in Manufacturing', *Brookings Papers on Economic Activity*, 3: 695–735.

Sinclair, P. (1987) *Unemployment: Economic Theory and Evidence*, Oxford: Basil Blackwell.

Singh, A. (1989) 'Third World Competition and Deindustrialisation in Advanced Countries', *Cambridge Journal of Economics*, 13 (1): 103–20.

Singh, A. and Zammit, A. (1995) 'Employment and Unemployment, North and South', in J. Michie and J. Grieve-Smith (eds) *Managing the Global Economy*, Oxford: Oxford University Press.

Sloane, P.J. (1985) 'Discrimination in the Labour Market', in D. Carline (*et al.*) *Labour Economics*, Harlow: Longmans.

Sloane, P.J. and Siebert, W.S. (1980) 'Low Pay Amongst Women – the Facts', in P.J. Sloane (ed.) *Women and Low Pay*, London: Macmillan.

Smith, A. (1776) *The Wealth of Nations*, A.S. Skinner (ed.), London: Harmondsworth Penguin, 1974.

Smith, J.C. (2000) 'Nominal Wage Rigidity in the United Kingdom', *Economic Journal* (Conference Papers), 110: C176–C195.

Smith, S.W. (1998) 'Labour Markets', in B. Atkinson, F. Livesey and B. Milward (eds) *Applied Economics*, Basingstoke: Macmillan.

Smith, S.W., Grahl, J. and Michie, J. (2003) *European Labour Markets*, London: Routledge.

Solow, R.M. (1956) 'A Contribution to the Theory of Economic Growth', *Quarterly Journal of Economics*, 70: 65–94.

Sorensen, E. (1990) 'The Crowding Hypothesis and Comparable Worth', *Journal of Human Resources*, 25 (1): 55–89.

Soskice, D. (1990) 'Wage Determination: The Changing Role of Institutions in Advanced Industrial Economies', *Oxford Review of Economic Policy*, 6 (4): 36–61.

Spence, M.A. (1974) *Market Signalling: Informational Transfer in Hiring and Related Screening Processes*, Cambridge MA: Harvard University Press.

Standing, G. (1999) *Global Labour Flexibility: Seeking Distributive Justice*, Basingstoke: Macmillan.

Steedman, H. (1999) 'Looking Into the Qualifications "Black Box": What Can International Surveys Tell Us About Basic Competence?', London School of Economics Centre for Economic Performance, Discussion Paper 431.

Stevens, M. (1994) 'A Theoretical Model of On-The-Job Training With Imperfect Competition', *Oxford Economic Papers*, 46 (4): 537–62.

—— (1999) 'Human Capital Theory and UK Vocational Training Policy', *Oxford Review of Economic Policy*, 15 (1): 16–32.

Stewart, M. (1990) 'Union Wage Differentials, Product Market Influences and the Division of Rents', *Economic Journal*, 100: 1122–37.

Stewart, M. and Greenhalgh, C. (1984) 'Work History Patterns and Occupational Attainment of Women', *Economic Journal*, 94: 493–519.

Stigler, G. (1962) 'Information in the Labour Market', *Journal of Political Economy*, 70: 94–105.

Straubhaar, T. (1988) 'International Labour Migration Within a Common Market: Some Aspects of EC Experience', *Journal of Common Market Studies*, 27 (1): 45–62.

Sumner, S. and Silver, S. (1989) 'Real Wages, Employment and the Phillips Curve', *Journal of Political Economy*, 97: 706–20.

Symons, J. and Layard, R. (1984) 'Neoclassical Demand for Labour Functions for Six Major Economies', *Economic Journal*, 94: 788–99.

Szymanski, A. (1976) 'Racial Discrimination and White Gain', *American Sociological Review*, 41: 403–14.

—— (1978) 'White Workers' Loss from Racial Discrimination: Reply to Villemez', *American Sociological Review*, 43: 776–82.

Teague, P. and Grahl, J. (1992) *Industrial Relations and European Integration*, London: Lawrence and Wishart.

Thirlwall, A. and Gibson, H. (1992) *Balance of Payments Theory and the UK Experience*, London: Macmillan.

Thurow, L. (1976) *Generating Inequality*, New York: Basic Books.

Topel, R. (1999) 'Labour Markets and Economic Growth', in O. Ashenfelter, and D. Card, (eds) (1999) *Handbook of Labour Economics*, Volume 3, Amsterdam: Elsevier Science.

Towers, B. (1989) 'Running the Gauntlet: British Trade Unions Under Thatcher, 1979–1988', *Industrial and Labour Relations Review*, 42 (2): 163–88.

Towers Perrin (2000) World-wide Total Remuneration, www.towers.com.

Traxler, F., Blaschke, S. and Kittel, B. (2001) *National Labour Relations in Internationalised Markets: A Comparative Study*, Oxford: Oxford University Press.

Trevithick, J.A. (1992) *Involuntary Unemployment: Macroeconomics from a Keynesian Perspective*, Hemel Hempstead: Harvester Wheatsheaf.

Tzannatos, Z. (1990) 'The Economics of Discrimination: Theory and British Evidence', in D. Sapsford and Z. Tzannatos (eds) *Current Issues in Labour Economics*, London: Macmillan.

Ulph, A. and Ulph, D. (1990) 'Union Bargaining: A Survey of Recent Work', in D. Sapsford and Z. Tzannatos (eds) *Current Issues in Labour Economics*, London: Macmillan.

Underhill, G. (1994) 'Conceptualising the Changing Global Order', in R. Stubbs and G. Underhill (eds) *Political Economy and the Changing Global Order*, Basingstoke: Macmillan.

van den Berg, G. (1990) 'Search Behaviour Transitions to Non-Participation and the Duration of Unemployment', *Economic Journal*, 100: 842–65.

Van Poeck, A. and Borghijs, A. (2001) 'EMU and Labour Market Reform: Needs, Incentives and Realisations', *World Economy*, 1327–52.

Villemez, W.J. (1978) 'Black Subordination and White Economic Wellbeing', *American Sociological Review*, 43: 772–5.

Visco, I. (2000) 'Migration, Development and the Labour Market', OECD Conference Paper.

Viscusi, W. (1993) 'The Value of Risks to Life and Health', *Journal of Economic Literature*, 31 (4): 1912–46.

Viscusi, W. and O'Connor, C. (1984) 'Responses to Chemical Labelling: Are Workers Bayesian Decision-Makers?', *American Economic Review*, 74: 942–56.

Visser, J. (1990) *In Search of Inclusive Unionism*, Boston, MA: Kluwer Press.

—— (1996) *Unionisation Trends Revisted*, University of Amsterdam, mimeo.

Voos, P. and Mishel, L. (1986) 'The Union Impact on Profits: Evidence from Industry Price-Cost Margin Data', *Journal of Labour Economics*, 4 (1): 105–33.

Wadsworth, J. (1991) 'Unemployment Benefits and Search Effort in the UK Labour Market', *Economica*, 58: 17–34.

Waldfogel, J. (1998) 'Understanding the "Family Gap" in Pay for Women With Children', *Journal of Economic Perspectives*, 12 (1): 137–56.

Ward, R. and Zis, G. (1974) 'Trade Union Militancy as an Explanation of Inflation: An International Comparison', *Manchester School*, 42: 46–65.

Wasmer, E. (1999) 'Labour Supply Dynamics, Unemployment and Human Capital Investments', London School of Economics Centre for Economic Performance, Discussion Paper 411.

Weinberg, B. (2000) 'Computer Use and the Demand for Female Workers', *Industrial and Labour Relations Review* 53 (2): 290–308.

Weiss, A. (1991) *Efficiency Wages: Models of Unemployment, Layoffs, and Wage Dispersion*, Oxford: Clarendon Press.

—— (1995) 'Human Capital vs. Signalling Explanations of Wages', *Journal of Economic Perspectives*, 9 (4): 133–54.

Welch, F. (1997) 'Wages and Participation', *Journal of Labour Economics*, 15 (1): S77–S103.

Wells, J. (1989) 'Uneven Development and Deindustrialisation in the UK Since 1979', in F. Green (ed.) *The Restructuring of the British Economy*, Brighton: Harvester Wheatsheaf.

West, M., Patterson, M., Dawson, J. and Nickell, S. (1999) 'The Effectiveness of Top Management Groups in Manufacturing Organisations', London School of Economics Centre for Economic Performance, Discussion Paper 436.

Willis, R.J. (1986) 'Wage Determinants: A Survey and Reinterpretation of Human Capital Earnings Functions', in O. Ashenfelter and R. Layard (eds) *Handbook of Labour Economics*, Amsterdam: North Holland.

Wong, K. (1986) 'Are International Trade and Factor Mobility Substitutes?', *Journal of International Economics*, 21: 25–43.

Wood, A. (1994) *North–South Trade, Employment and Inequality*, Oxford: Clarendon Press.

—— (1998) 'Globalisation and the Rise of Labour Market Inequalities', *Economic Journal*, 108: 1463–82.

Woodbury, S. and Bettinger, D. (1991) 'Culture, Human Capital and the Earnings of West Indian Blacks', manuscript, Lansing, MI: Michigan State University Department of Economics.

Woodhall, M. (1987) 'Earnings and Education', in G. Psacharopoulos (ed.) *Economics of Education: Research and Studies*, Oxford: Pergamon Press.

World Bank (1993) *The East Asian Miracle*, Oxford: Oxford University Press.

—— (1999) *World Development Report 1999/2000*, Oxford: Oxford University Press.

Zabalza, A. and Arrufat, J.L. (1985) 'The Extent of Sex Discrimination in Britain' in A. Zabalza and Z. Tzannatos (eds) *Women and Equal Pay: the Effects of Legislation on Female Employment and Wages*, Cambridge: Cambridge University Press.

Zis, G. (1977) 'On the Role of Strike Variables in UK Wage Equations', *Scottish Journal of Political Economy*, 24 (1): 43–53.

Index